W9-BRR-054

SOURCES

In the interest of relevance and readability, the editors have slightly adapted the selections for this book. For the complete texts, please refer to the original sources.

Chapter One: Bill George. *Authentic Leadership.* San Francisco: Jossey-Bass, 2003.

Chapter Two: James M. Kouzes and Barry Z. Posner. *The Leadership Challenge.* (3rd ed.) San Francisco: Jossey-Bass, 2002.

Chapter Three: Warren Bennis and Burt Nanus. *Leaders.* (2nd ed.) New York: HarperCollins, 2003.

Chapter Four: Henry Mintzberg. "Rounding Out the Manager's Job." *Sloan Management Review,* Fall 1994, 11–26.

Chapter Five: Rosabeth Moss Kanter. *Rosabeth Moss Kanter on the Frontiers of Management.* Boston: Harvard Business School Press, 1997.

Chapter Six: Joan Magretta (ed.). *Managing in the New Economy.* Boston: Harvard Business School Press, 1999.

Chapter Seven: Jeffrey Pfeffer. *The Human Equation.* Boston: Harvard Business School Press, 1998.

Chapter Eight: Edward E. Lawler III. *Treat People Right!* San Francisco: Jossey-Bass, 2003.

Chapter Nine: Richaurd Camp, Mary E. Vielhaber, and Jack L. Simonetti. *Strategic Interviewing.* San Francisco: Jossey-Bass, 2001.

Chapter Ten: Dana M. Muir. *A Manager's Guide to Employment Law.* San Francisco: Jossey-Bass, 2003.

Chapter Eleven: Douglas K. Smith. *Make Success Measurable!* Hoboken, N.J.: Wiley, 1999.

Chapter Twelve: Rosabeth Moss Kanter, Barry A. Stein, and Todd D. Jick. *The Challenge of Organizational Change.* New York: Free Press, 1992.

Chapter Thirteen: David A. Nadler, with Mark B. Nadler. *Champions of Change.* San Francisco: Jossey-Bass, 1998.

Chapter Fourteen: Lee G. Bolman and Terrence E. Deal. *Reframing Organizations.* (3rd ed.) San Francisco: Jossey-Bass, 2003.

Chapter Fifteen: Steven B. Sample. *The Contrarian's Guide to Leadership.* San Francisco: Jossey-Bass, 2002.

Chapter Sixteen: Terry Pearce. *Leading Out Loud.* (2nd ed.) San Francisco: Jossey-Bass, 2003.

Chapter Seventeen: David R. Caruso and Peter Salovey. *The Emotionally Intelligent Manager.* San Francisco: Jossey-Bass, 2004.

Chapter Eighteen: James M. Kouzes and Barry Z. Posner. *Encouraging the Heart.* San Francisco: Jossey-Bass, 1999.

Chapter Nineteen: Edward E. Lawler III. *Rewarding Excellence.* San Francisco: Jossey-Bass, 2000.

Chapter Twenty: Harvey Robbins and Michael Finley. *The Accidental Leader.* San Francisco: Jossey-Bass, 2004.

Chapter Twenty-One: Cynthia D. McCauley and Ellen Van Velsor (eds.). *The Center for Creative Leadership Handbook on Leadership Development.* (2nd ed.) San Francisco: Jossey-Bass, 2004.

Chapter Twenty-Two: Clinton O. Longenecker and Jack L. Simonetti. *Getting Results.* San Francisco: Jossey-Bass, 2001.

Chapter Twenty-Three: J. Davidson Frame. *Managing Projects in Organizations.* San Francisco: Jossey-Bass, 2003.

Chapter Twenty-Four: Patrick Lencioni. *Death by Meeting.* San Francisco: Jossey-Bass, 2004.

Chapter Twenty-Five: Kathleen Kelley Reardon. *The Secret Handshake.* New York: Doubleday, 2001.

Chapter Twenty-Six: Patrick J. McKenna and David H. Maister. *First Among Equals.* New York: Free Press, 2002.

Chapter Twenty-Seven: Marick F. Masters and Robert R. Albright. *The Complete Guide to Conflict Resolution in the Workplace.* New York: Amacom, 2002.

Chapter Twenty-Eight: Patrick Lencioni. *The Five Dysfunctions of a Team.* San Francisco: Jossey-Bass, 2002.

Chapter Twenty-Nine: Deborah L. Duarte and Nancy Tennant Snyder. *Mastering Virtual Teams.* (2nd ed.) San Francisco: Jossey-Bass, 2001.

Chapter Thirty: Robert I. Sutton. *Weird Ideas That Work.* New York: Free Press, 2002.

Chapter Thirty-One: Parker J. Palmer. *Let Your Life Speak.* San Francisco: Jossey-Bass, 2000.

Chapter Thirty-Two: Robert E. Quinn. *Building the Bridge As You Walk On It.* San Francisco: Jossey-Bass, 2004.

Chapter Thirty-Three: David B. Batstone. *Saving the Corporate Soul and (Who Knows?) Maybe Your Own.* San Francisco: Jossey-Bass, 2003.

Chapter Thirty-Four: Bill George. *Authentic Leadership.* San Francisco: Jossey-Bass, 2003.

Management Skills

A Jossey-Bass Reader

JOSSEY-BASS BUSINESS & MANAGEMENT SERIES

JOSSEY-BASS
A Wiley Imprint
www.josseybass.com

Published by Jossey-Bass
A Wiley Imprint
989 Market Street, San Francisco, CA 94103-1741   www.josseybass.com

Jossey-Bass books and products are available through most bookstores. To contact Jossey-Bass directly call our Customer Care Department within the U.S. at 800-956-7739, outside the U.S. at 317-572-3986 or fax 317-572-4002.

Jossey-Bass also publishes its books in a variety of electronic formats. Some content that appears in print may not be available in electronic books.

Credits appear on page 799.

Library of Congress Cataloging-in-Publication Data

Management skills : a Jossey-Bass reader.—1st ed.
    p. cm. — (Jossey-Bass business & management series)
  Includes bibliographical references and index.
  ISBN 0-7879-7341-6 (alk. paper)
  1. Executive ability. 2. Management. 3. Leadership. I. Series.
  HD38.2.M358 2005
  658.4'09-dc22
                                    2004014544

Printed in the United States of America
FIRST EDITION
PB Printing   10 9 8 7 6 5 4 3 2 1

The Jossey-Bass
Business & Management Series

Contents

On-line instructor's guide available at www.wiley.com/college/jbreaders

Preface

Management is a vast topic area. There are countless definitions of the word and countless books employing those definitions. Management can be as straightforward as balancing a budget or as complex as leading organizational change. Our task in compiling this book has been to discern the most important and timeless aspects of management and to select the best writing on those aspects by the leading thinkers in the field.

The chapters in this book focus on the management of people. No task is more crucial for managers than to maximize the potential of the people they manage, whose collective energy and talent can provide far greater competitive advantage to an organization than any other resource. The authors in this book agree that at its core, management is a relationship. To be truly successful, managers must be able to lead, inspire, and champion their followers. Although some reserve the term *leader* for those who hold the most senior offices, many of the authors featured in this book believe everyone has the opportunity, and possibly the duty, to be a leader. In Chapter Three, Warren Bennis and Burt Nanus contend that "managers are people who do things right and leaders are people who do the right thing." In the best case, a manager does both.

We leave it to other management books to explain how to handle the minute details. The authors in this book, while providing practical ideas on a wide variety of topics, always have the big picture in mind. These chapters will do more than provide advice on handling today's crisis; they will help in building and sustaining success over the course of a career. Inevitably, the business landscape will change again and again in the coming decades, but the skills for effective management presented in this book will always remain relevant.

Part One, "What Makes a Great Manager?" begins with inspiration and the importance of being honest and true to self. The manager's job is complex; the later chapters in this part aid managers in seeing the many facets of their job and how they are shifting. Leadership begins and ends with authenticity, Bill George explains in Chapter One; managers need to develop their own leadership style consistent with their personality and character. James M. Kouzes and Barry Z. Posner have found that people willingly follow someone whom they believe is honest, forward looking, competent, and inspiring. In Chapter Two, they explore these characteristics and stress that leadership is a relationship of service to a purpose and to people. In Chapter Three, Warren Bennis and Burt Nanus insist that everyone has leadership potential and that leadership is not so much the exercise of power as it is the empowerment of others. Henry Mintzberg models the manager's job from the inside out in Chapter Four, displaying all of the components of managerial work. Organizations are transforming and in the process are dramatically altering the realities of managerial work, Rosabeth Moss Kanter explains in Chapter Five; managers must learn new ways to manage, confronting changes in their own bases of power and recognizing the need for new ways to motivate people. Peter Drucker concludes in an interview with T George Harris in Chapter Six that information is replacing authority.

The chapters in Part Two, "Creating and Shaping the Work Environment," will help managers create the best work environment possible by providing models, assessments, and benchmarks to make the best personnel decisions and prepare for successful change. In Chapter Seven, Jeffrey Pfeffer explores seven practices, some of which appear to fly in the face of conventional wisdom, that characterize many successful organizations. Edward E. Lawler III lays out hiring strategies for determining how well a candidate will fit the current and future needs of an organization in Chapter Eight. In Chapter Nine, Richaurd Camp, Mary E. Vielhaber, and Jack L. Simonetti provide assessments to help maximize the interview process and explain the goals, skills, and perspectives necessary for the task. Dana M. Muir presents a road map in Chapter Ten for navigating through the legal implications of almost any employment-related decision a manager might make. Finding and using performance metrics that make sense and have universally recognized measurements are key to achieving performance goals, explains Douglas K. Smith in Chapter Eleven. In Chapter Twelve, Rosabeth Moss Kanter, Barry A. Stein, and Todd D. Jick stress that change implementers must be concerned not only with what to change to; they must also be concerned with what they are changing from. They describe five events that often spark change and point out strategies for preparing for a change process. In Chapter Thirteen, David A. Nadler, with Mark B. Nadler, believes that managers must commit to fully understanding every aspect of the change they lead and must buy into it on both an intellectual and emotional level.

Part Three, "Communicating, Leading, and Motivating People," deals with some of the so-called soft skills that are essential to the success of any manager. A skilled manager can turn people into an organization's most important asset. As the chapters in this part show, these skills can be learned; no one has to be born with charisma or be a "natural leader" to get the most out of employees. In Chapter Fourteen, Lee G. Bolman and Terrence E. Deal describe how the politically astute manager can build and maintain relationships with others strategically and ethically, both inside and outside the organization. Steven B. Sample emphasizes in Chapter Fifteen the value of effective listening in making decisions and advocates the use of a circle of advisers. Terry Pearce addresses the other side of the coin; in Chapter Sixteen, he explains that in order to communicate and motivate effectively, managers must first earn the trust of their listeners. The ability to identify and understand the emotions of others is a great help in communication, as illustrated by David R. Caruso and Peter Salovey in Chapter Seventeen. In Chapter Eighteen, James M. Kouzes and Barry Z. Posner present a set of motivational practices with which managers can lead and inspire their employees to reach the highest level of performance. Edward E. Lawler III explores in Chapter Nineteen the more practical side of motivation and employee satisfaction: reward systems, including pay and other benefits. Another important type of communication is feedback; Harvey Robbins and Michael Finley list in Chapter Twenty effective (and not-so-effective) ways to let employees know how they are doing and how to adapt assessments for different personality types. Part Three ends with a discussion of developmental relationships by Cynthia D. McCauley and Christina A. Douglas; they show that mentoring and other on-the-job learning experiences both motivate employees and improve their effectiveness.

Part Four, "Getting the Work Done," examines the ever popular topic of execution. These chapters consider how great managers roll up their sleeves and make things happen. In Chapter Twenty-Two, Clinton O. Longenecker and Jack L. Simonetti list five keys to getting results, one of the most important tasks for managers. J. Davidson Frame acknowledges in Chapter Twenty-Three that managers do not always have the resources they would like in order to accomplish their goals; he offers ideas for getting the necessary support for projects. In Chapter Twenty-Four, Patrick Lencioni provides a model for managing meetings in order to make them not only more useful but also more enjoyable. Kathleen Kelley Reardon investigates in Chapter Twenty-Five how to negotiate to get what you need. Patrick J. McKenna and David H. Maister explain in Chapter Twenty-Six how to calmly keep things running during a crisis situation.

Part Five, "Leading Complex Organizational Processes," examines several of the most difficult issues facing managers: handling conflict, leading teams, working with virtual employees, and leading innovation. In Chapter Twenty-Seven, Marick F. Masters and Robert R. Albright lay out action steps for collaborative conflict resolution and describe the skills needed to make it work. Patrick Lencioni dissects the common flaws of teams and presents methods for overcoming these obstacles to successful teamwork in Chapter Twenty-Eight. Deborah L. Duarte and Nancy Tennant Snyder reveal in Chapter Twenty-Nine best practices for working with virtual teams and provide an audit to determine one's virtual management skill needs. Robert I. Sutton demonstrates in Chapter Thirty how to encourage innovation and creativity in employees with a focus on the bottom line.

Part Six, "Sustaining the Great Manager," contains final inspiring words to guide managers through their life's work. In Chapter Thirty-One, Parker J. Palmer explains that good leadership comes from people who have penetrated their own inner darkness and found the strength for authentic leadership in their hearts. In Chapter Thirty-Two, Robert E. Quinn identifies the need to move from constant action to an appreciation of the power of reflection, and then to integrate the two. David Batstone encourages people inside a company to ask themselves again and again, "What are we in business for?" in Chapter Thirty-Three. Chapter Thirty-Four concludes with Bill George urging managers not to wait until they have the top job to become leaders.

Acknowledgments

Special thanks to our great reviewers, whose expertise helped guide the organization of this book: Joan Gallos, Paul Cohen, Peter Cohan, Alan Shrader, and Susan Call. Thanks also to Sheri Gilbert and Judy Rivelli for their valuable contributions. And of course, we couldn't have done it without our excellent team: Kathe Sweeney, Jeff Wyneken, Carolyn Miller, Akemi Yamaguchi, Paula Goldstein, and Michael Cook.

San Francisco   TAMARA KELLER
September 2004   ROB BRANDT

Management Skills

Part One

What Makes a Great Manager?

Chapter One

Leadership Is Authenticity, Not Style

Bill George

Something ignited in my soul,
Fever or unremembered wings,
And I went my own way,
Deciphering that burning fire.
Pablo Neruda

Not long ago I was meeting with a group of high-talent young executives at Medtronic. We were discussing career development when the leader of the group asked me to list the most important characteristics one has to have to be a leader in Medtronic. I said, "I can summarize it in a single word: authenticity."

After years of studying leaders and their traits, I believe that leadership begins and ends with authenticity. It's being yourself; being the person you were created to be. This is not what most of the literature on leadership says, nor is it what the experts in corporate America teach. Instead, they develop lists of leadership characteristics one is supposed to emulate. They describe the styles of leaders and suggest that you adopt them.

This is the opposite of authenticity. It is about developing the image or persona of a leader. Unfortunately, the media, the business press, and even the movies glorify leaders with high-ego personalities. They focus on the style of leaders, not their character. In large measure, making heroes out of celebrity CEOs is at the heart of the crisis in corporate leadership.

The Authentic Leader

Authentic leaders genuinely desire to serve others through their leadership. They are more interested in empowering the people they lead to make a difference than they are in power, money, or prestige for themselves. They are as guided by qualities of the heart, by passion and compassion, as they are by qualities of the mind.

Authentic leaders are not born that way. Many people have natural leadership gifts, but they have to develop them fully to become outstanding leaders. Authentic leaders use their natural abilities, but they also recognize their shortcomings and work hard to overcome them. They lead with purpose, meaning, and values. They build enduring relationships with people. Others follow them because they know where they stand. They are consistent and self-disciplined. When their principles are tested, they refuse to compromise. Authentic leaders are dedicated to developing themselves because they know that becoming a leader takes a lifetime of personal growth.

Being Your Own Person

Leaders are all very different people. Any prospective leader who buys into the necessity of attempting to emulate all the characteristics of a leader is doomed to fail. I know because I tried it early in my career. It simply doesn't work.

The one essential quality a leader must have is to be your own person, authentic in every regard. The best leaders are autonomous and highly independent. Those who are too responsive to the desires of others are likely to be whipsawed by competing interests, too quick to deviate from their course, or unwilling to make difficult decisions for fear of offending. My advice to the people I mentor is simply to be themselves.

Being your own person is most challenging when it feels like everyone is pressuring you to take one course and you are standing alone. In the first semester of business school we watched *The Loneliness of the Long Distance Runner.* Initially I did not relate to the film's message, as I had always surrounded myself with people to avoid being lonely. Learning to cope with the loneliness at the top is crucial so that you are not swayed by the pressure. Being able to stand alone against the majority is essential to being your own person.

Shortly after I joined Medtronic as president, I walked into a meeting where it quickly became evident that a group of my new colleagues had prearranged a strategy to settle a major patent dispute against Siemens on the basis of a royalty-free cross-license as a show of good faith. Intuitively, I knew the strategy was doomed to fail, so I stood alone against the entire group, refusing to go along. My position may not have made me popular with my new teammates, but it was the right thing to do. We later negotiated a settlement with Siemens for more than $400 million, at the time the second-largest patent settlement ever.

DEVELOPING YOUR UNIQUE LEADERSHIP STYLE

To become authentic, each of us has to develop our own leadership style, consistent with our personality and character. Unfortunately, the pressures of an organization push us to adhere to its normative style. But if we conform to a style that is not consistent with who we are, we will never become authentic leaders.

Contrary to what much of the literature says, your type of leadership style is not what matters. Great world leaders— George Washington, Abraham Lincoln, Winston Churchill, Franklin Roosevelt, Margaret Thatcher, Martin Luther King, Mother Teresa, John F. Kennedy—all had very different styles. Yet each of them was an entirely authentic human being. There is no way you could ever attempt to emulate any of them without looking foolish.

The same is true for business leaders. Compare the last three CEOs of General Electric: the statesmanship of Reginald Jones, the dynamism of Jack Welch, and the empowering style of Jeff Immelt. All of them are highly successful leaders with entirely different leadership styles. Yet the GE organization has rallied around each of them, adapted to their styles, and flourished as a result. What counts is the authenticity of the leader, not the style.

Having said that, it is important that you develop a leadership style that works well for you and is consistent with your character and your personality. Over time you will have to hone your style to be effective in leading different types of people and to work in different types of environments. This is integral to your development as a leader.

To be effective in today's fast-moving, highly competitive environment, leaders also have to adapt their style to fit the immediate situation. There are times to be inspiring and motivating, and times to be tough about people decisions or financial decisions. There are times to delegate, and times to be deeply immersed in the details. There are times to communicate public messages, and times to have private conversations. The use of adaptive styles is not inauthentic, and is very different from playing a succession of roles rather than being yourself. Good leaders are able to nuance their styles to the demands of the situation and to know when and how to deploy different styles.

Let me share a personal example to illustrate this point. When I first joined Medtronic, I spent a lot of time learning the business and listening to customers. I also focused on inspiring employees to fulfill the Medtronic mission of restoring people to full health. At the same time, I saw many ways in which we needed to be more disciplined about decisions and spending, so I was very challenging in budget sessions and put strict controls on head count additions. At first some people found this confusing. Eventually, they understood my reasons for adapting my style to the situation and that I had to do so to be effective as their leader.

BEING AWARE OF YOUR WEAKNESSES

Being true to the person you were created to be means accepting your faults as well as using your strengths. Accepting your shadow side is an essential part of being authentic. The problem comes when people are so eager to win the approval of others that they try to cover their shortcomings and sacrifice their authenticity to gain the respect and admiration of their associates.

I too have struggled in getting comfortable with my weaknesses—my tendency to intimidate others with an overly challenging style, my impatience, and my occasional lack of tact. Only recently have I realized that my strengths and weaknesses are two sides of the same coin. By challenging others in business meetings, I am able to get quickly to the heart of the issues, but my approach unnerves and intimidates less confident people. My desire to get things done fast leads to superior results, but it exposes my impatience with people who move more slowly. Being direct with others gets the message across clearly but often lacks tact. Over time I have moderated my style and adapted my approach to make sure that people are engaged and empowered and that their voices are fully heard.

I have always been open to critical feedback, but also quite sensitive to it. For years I felt I had to be perfect, or at least appear that I was on top of everything. I tried to hide my weaknesses from others, fearing they would reject me if they knew who I really was. Eventually, I realized that they could see my weaknesses more clearly than I could. In attempting to cover things up, I was only fooling myself.

The poem "Love after Love," by Nobel Prize–winning poet Derek Walcott, speaks to the benefits of being in touch with your disowned aspects and welcoming them into your life. As I have been able to do so in recent years, I have become more comfortable with myself and more authentic in my interactions with others.

> *The time will come when with elation you will greet yourself,*
> *Arriving at your own door, in your own mirror,*

And each will smile at the other's welcome;
  Saying, sit here. Eat.
You will love again the stranger who was yourself.
Give wine, give bread, give back your heart
To the stranger who has loved all your life,
Whom you abandoned for another, who knows you
  by heart.
Take down the love letters from the bookshelf, the
  photographs, the desperate notes.
Sit. Feast on your life.

THE TEMPTATIONS OF LEADERSHIP

Congressman Amory Houghton, one of the most thoughtful members of the U.S. Congress, tells the story of his predecessor's advice as he was taking over as CEO of Corning Glass. "Think of your decisions being based on two concentric circles. In the outer circle are all the laws, regulations, and ethical standards with which the company must comply. In the inner circle are your core values. Just be darn sure that your decisions as CEO stay within your inner circle."

We are all painfully aware of corporate leaders who pushed beyond the outer circle and got caught, either by the law or by the financial failure of their companies. More worrisome are the leaders of companies who moved outside their inner circles and engaged in marginal practices, albeit legal ones. Examples include cutting back on long-term investments just to make the short-term numbers, bending compensation rules to pay executives in spite of marginal performance, using accounting tricks to meet the quarterly expectations of security analysts, shipping products of marginal quality, compromising security analysts by giving them a cut on investment banking deals, and booking revenues before the products are shipped in an effort to pump up revenue growth. The list goes on and on.

All of us who sit in the leader's chair feel the pressure to perform. As CEO, I felt it every day as problems mounted or sales lagged. I knew that the livelihood of tens of thousands of employees, the health of millions of patients, and the financial fortunes of millions of investors rested on my shoulders and those of our executive team. At the same time I was well aware of the penalties for not performing, even for a single quarter. No CEO wants to appear on CNBC to explain why his company missed the earnings projections, even by a penny.

Little by little, step by step, the pressures to succeed can pull us away from our core values, just as we are reinforced by our "success" in the market. Some people refer to this as "CEO-itis." The irony is that the more successful we are, the more tempted we are to take shortcuts to keep it going. And the rewards—compensation increases, stock option gains, the myriads of executive perquisites, positive stories in the media, admiring comments from our peers—all reinforce our actions and drive us to keep it going.

In a recent interview with *Fortune* magazine, Novartis CEO Daniel Vasella talked about these pressures:

> Once you get under the domination of making the quarter—even unwittingly—you start to compromise in the gray areas of your business, that cut across the wide swath of terrain between the top and the bottom. Perhaps you'll begin to sacrifice things that are important and may be vital for your company over the long term. . . . The culprit that drives this cycle isn't the fear of failure so much as it is the craving for success. For the tyranny of quarterly earnings is a tyranny that is imposed from within. . . . For many of us the idea of being a successful manager is an intoxicating one. It is a pattern of celebration leading to belief, leading to distortion. When you achieve good results, you are typically celebrated, and you begin to believe that the figure at the center of all that champagne toasting is yourself. You are idealized by the outside world, and there is a natural tendency to believe that what is written is true.

Like Vasella, who is one of the finest and most authentic leaders I know, all leaders have to resist these pressures while continuing to perform, especially when things aren't going well. The test I used with our team at Medtronic is whether we would feel comfortable having the entire story appear on the front page of the *New York Times*. If we didn't, we went back to the drawing boards and reexamined our decision.

DIMENSIONS OF AUTHENTIC LEADERS

Let's examine the essential dimensions of all authentic leaders, the qualities that true leaders must develop. I have determined through many experiences in leading others that authentic leaders demonstrate these five qualities:

- Understanding their purpose
- Practicing solid values
- Leading with heart
- Establishing connected relationships
- Demonstrating self-discipline

Acquiring the five dimensions of an authentic leader is not a sequential process; rather, leaders are developing them continuously throughout their lives. I think of them as five sections of a circle that blend together to form the authentic leader, as shown in Figure 1.1.

Understanding Your Purpose

In Wonderland, Alice comes to a fork in the road where she sees a cat in a tree. Alice asks the cat, "Which road should I take?" "Do you know where you want to go?" inquires the cat. "No," says Alice. To which the cat replies, "Then any road will get you there."

FIGURE 1.1. **Dimensions of Authentic Leadership**

To become a leader, it is essential that you first answer the question, "Leadership for what purpose?" If you lack purpose and direction in leading, why would anyone want to follow you?

Many people want to become leaders without giving much thought to their purpose. They are attracted to the power and prestige of leading an organization and the financial rewards that go with it. But without a real sense of purpose, leaders are at the mercy of their egos and are vulnerable to narcissistic impulses. There is no way you can adopt someone else's purpose and still be an authentic leader. You can study the purposes others pursue and you can work with them in common purposes, but in the end the purpose for your leadership must be uniquely yours.

To find your purpose, you must first understand yourself, your passions, and your underlying motivations. Then you must seek an environment that offers a fit between the organization's purpose and your own. Your search may take experiences in several organizations before you can find the one that is right for you.

The late Robert Greenleaf, a former AT&T executive, is well known for his concept of leaders as servants of the people. In *Servant Leadership*, he advocates service to others as the leader's primary purpose. If people feel you are genuinely interested in serving others, then they will be prepared not just to follow you but to dedicate themselves to the common cause.

One of the best examples of a leader with purpose was the late David Packard, cofounder of Hewlett-Packard. I met him in early 1969 when he was the new deputy secretary of defense and I was the special assistant to the secretary of navy. Packard had taken a leave from H-P to serve his country. A big, powerful, yet modest man, he immediately impressed me with his openness, his sincerity, and his commitment to make a difference through his work.

He returned to H-P a few years later to build it into one of the great companies of its time through his dedication to the company's mission, known as "The H-P Way," and to excellence in R&D and customer service. He inspired H-P's employees to incredible levels of commitment. At his death he was one of the wealthiest people in the world, yet no one would ever have known it by his personal spending. Most of his money went into funding philanthropic projects. Dave Packard was a truly authentic leader, a role model for me and for many in my generation.

Then there's John Bogle, who for fifty years has been a man with a mission to transform the management of investors' funds. Bogle created the first no-load mutual fund in 1974 and founded Vanguard, the nation's leading purveyor of index funds.

Bogle has not only been a pioneer in financial services, he has been the leading advocate of financial funds as stewards of their investors' money. His values and his integrity stand in stark relief with those in the financial community who seek to use investment funds for their personal gain.

Practicing Solid Values

Leaders are defined by their values and their character. The values of the authentic leader are shaped by personal beliefs, developed through study, introspection, and consultation with others—and a lifetime of experience. These values define their holder's moral compass. Such leaders know the "true north" of their compass, the deep sense of the right thing to do. Without a moral compass, any leader can wind up like the executives who are facing possible prison sentences today because they lacked a sense of right and wrong.

While the development of fundamental values is crucial, integrity is the one value that is required in every authentic leader. Integrity is not just the absence of lying, but telling the whole truth, as painful as it may be. If you don't exercise complete integrity in your interactions, no one can trust you. If they cannot trust you, why would they ever follow you?

I once had a colleague who would never lie to me, but often he shared only positive parts of the story, sheltering me from the ugly side. Finally, I told him that real integrity meant giving me the whole story so that together we could make sound decisions. Rather than thinking less of him if he did so, I assured him I would have a higher opinion of his courage and integrity.

Most business schools and academic institutions do not teach values as part of leadership development. Some offer ethics courses, often in a theoretical context, but shy away from discussing values. Others assume erroneously their students already have well-solidified values. What they fail to realize is the importance of solidifying your values through study and dialogue, and the impact that your environment has in shaping your values.

As Enron was collapsing in the fall of 2001, the *Boston Globe* published an article by a Harvard classmate of Enron CEO Jeff Skilling. The author described how Skilling would argue in class that the role of the business leader was to take advantage of loopholes in regulations and push beyond the laws wherever he could to make money. As Skilling saw the world, it was the job of the regulators to try and catch him. Sound familiar? Twenty-five years later, Skilling's philosophy caught up with him, as he led his company into bankruptcy.

One of my role models of values-centered leadership is Max DePree, the former CEO of furniture maker Herman Miller. DePree is a modest man guided by a deep concern for serving others; he is true to his values in every aspect of his life. His humanity and values can be seen through the exemplary way in which his company conducts itself. DePree describes his philosophy of values-centered leadership in his classic book, *Leadership Is an Art*. DePree also subscribes to Greenleaf's ideas on servant leadership, and expands them by offering his own advice, "The leader's first job is to define reality. The last is to say thank you. In between the leader must become a servant and a debtor."

DePree believes that a corporation should be "a community of people," all of whom have value and share in the fruits of their collective labor. DePree practices what he preaches. While he was CEO, his salary was capped at twenty times that of an hourly worker. In his view tying the CEO's salary to that of the workers helps cement trust in leadership. Contrast that with today's CEOs, who are earning—on average—five hundred times their hourly workers' wage. As DePree said recently, "When leaders indulge themselves with lavish perks and the trappings of power, they are damaging their standing as leaders."

Leading with Heart

Over the last several decades, businesses have evolved from maximizing the physical output of their workers to engaging the minds of their employees. To excel in the twenty-first century, great companies will go one step further by engaging the hearts of their employees through a sense of purpose. When employees believe their work has a deeper purpose, their results will vastly exceed those who use only their minds and their bodies. This will become the company's competitive advantage.

Sometimes we refer to people as being big-hearted. What we really mean is that they are open and willing to share themselves fully with us, and are genuinely interested in us. Leaders who do that, like Sam Walton, founder of Wal-Mart, and Earl Bakken, founder of Medtronic, have the ability to ignite the souls of their employees to achieve greatness far beyond what anyone imagined possible.

One of the most big-hearted leaders I know is Marilyn Nelson, chair and CEO of the Carlson Companies, the privately held hospitality and travel services giant. When she became CEO several years ago, she inherited a hard-nosed organization that was driven for growth but not known for empathy for its employees. Shortly after joining the company, Nelson had what she refers to as her "epiphany." She was meeting with the group of M.B.A. students who had been studying the company's culture. When she asked the students for feedback, Nelson got a stony silence from the group. Finally, a young woman raised her hand and said, "We hear from employees that Carlson is a sweatshop that doesn't care."

That incident sent Nelson into high gear. She created a motivational program called "Carlson Cares." As the company was preparing for its launch, Nelson's staff told her they needed more time to change the culture before introducing the program. Nelson decided that she could not wait and decided to become the company's role model for caring and empathy. She immediately set out to change the environment, using her passion, motivational skills, and sincere interest in her employees and her customers. She took the lead on customer sales calls and interacted every day with employees in Carlson operations. Her positive energy has transformed the company's culture, built its customer relationships, accelerated its growth, and strengthened its bottom line.

Establishing Enduring Relationships

As Krishnamurti says, "Relationship is the mirror in which we see ourselves as we are."

The capacity to develop close and enduring relationships is one mark of a leader. Unfortunately, many leaders of major companies believe their job is to create the strategy, organization structure, and organizational processes. Then they just delegate the work to be done, remaining aloof from the people doing the work.

The detached style of leadership will not be successful in the twenty-first century. Today's employees demand more personal relationships with their leaders before they will give themselves fully to their jobs. They insist on having access to their leaders, knowing that it is in the openness and the depth of the relationship with the leader that trust and commitment are built. Bill Gates, Michael Dell, and Jack Welch are so successful because they connect directly with their employees and realize from them a deeper commitment to their work and greater loyalty to the company. Welch, in particular, is an interesting case because he was so challenging and hard on people. Yet it was those very challenges that let people know that he was interested in their success and concerned about their careers.

In *Eyewitness to Power*, David Gergen writes, "At the heart of leadership is the leader's relationship with followers. People will entrust their hopes and dreams to another person only if they think the other is a reliable vessel." Authentic leaders establish trusting relationships with people throughout the organization as well as in their personal lives. The rewards of these relationships, both tangible and intangible, are long lasting.

I always tried to establish close relationships with my colleagues, looking to them as a closely knit team whose collective knowledge and wisdom about the business vastly exceeds my own. Many corporate leaders fear these kinds of relationships. As another CEO said to me, "Bill, I don't want to get too close to my subordinates because someday I may have to terminate them." Actually, the real reason goes much deeper than that. Many leaders—men in particular—fear having their weaknesses and vulnerabilities exposed. So they create distance from employees and a sense of aloofness. Instead of being authentic, they are creating a persona for themselves.

Demonstrating Self-Discipline

Self-discipline is an essential quality of an authentic leader. Without it, you cannot gain the respect of your followers. It is easy to say that someone has good values but lacks the discipline to convert those values into consistent actions. This is a hollow excuse. None of us is perfect, of course, but authentic leaders must have the self-discipline to do everything they can to demonstrate their values through their actions. When we fall short, it is equally important to admit our mistakes.

Leaders are highly competitive people. They are driven to succeed in whatever they take on. Authentic leaders know that competing requires a consistently high level of self-discipline to be successful. Being very competitive is not a bad thing; in fact, it is an essential quality of successful leaders, but it needs to be channeled through purpose and discipline. Sometimes we mistake competitive people who generate near-term results by improving operational effectiveness for genuine leaders. Achieving operational effectiveness is an essential result for any leader, but it alone does not ensure authenticity or long-term success.

The most consistent leader I know is Art Collins, my successor as CEO of Medtronic. His self-discipline is evident every day and in every interaction. His subordinates never have to worry about what kind of mood Art is in, or where he stands on an important issue. Nor does he deviate in his behavior or vacillate in his decisions. He never lets his ego or his emotions get in the way of taking the appropriate action. These qualities make working with Art easy and predictable, enabling Medtronic employees to do their jobs effectively.

Mother Teresa is a compelling example of an authentic leader. Many think of her as simply a nun who reached out to the poor, yet by 1990 she had created an organization of four thousand missionaries operating in a hundred countries. Her organization, Missionaries of Charity, began in Calcutta and spread to 450 centers around the world. Its mission was "to reach out to the destitute on the streets, offering wholehearted service to the poorest of the poor." Not only did she have a purpose, clear values, and a heart filled with compassion, she also created intimate relationships with people and exercised self-discipline, all the dimensions of an authentic leader. I doubt that any of us will ever be like Mother Teresa, but her life is indeed an inspiration.

○   ○   ○

Bill George was the CEO and chairman of the board of Medtronic. He is an executive-in-residence at Yale University School of Management and professor of leadership and governance at IMD in Lausanne, Switzerland.

Chapter Two

Credibility Is the Foundation of Leadership

James M. Kouzes
Barry Z. Posner

Without credibility, you can't lead.
Brian Carroll, Challenge Bank, Australia

You can't follow someone who isn't credible,
who doesn't truly believe in what they're doing—
and how they're doing it.
Gayle Hamilton, Pacific Gas and Electric

Model the way, inspire a shared vision, challenge the process, enable others to act, and encourage the heart: these are the leadership practices that emerge from personal-best cases. But they paint only a partial picture. The portrayal can be complete and vivid only when we add in what constituents expect from their leaders. What leaders say they do is one thing; what constituents say they want and how well leaders meet these expectations is another. Leadership is a reciprocal process between those who aspire to lead and those who choose to follow. Any discussion of leadership must attend to the dynamics of this relationship. Strategies, tactics, skills, and practices are empty without an understanding of the fundamental human aspirations that connect leaders and constituents.

To balance our understanding of leadership, we investigated the expectations that constituents have of leaders. We asked constituents to tell us what they look for and admire in a leader. Their responses affirm and enrich the picture that emerged from our studies of personal bests. Clearly, those who aspire to lead must embrace their constituents' expectations.

What People Look for and Admire in Their Leaders

We began our research on what constituents expected of leaders more than two decades ago by surveying thousands of business and government executives. We asked the following open-ended question: "What values (personal traits or characteristics) do you look for and admire in your leader?"[1] In response to that question, respondents identified more than 225 different values, traits, and characteristics. Subsequent content analysis by several independent judges, followed by further analyses, reduced these items to a list of twenty characteristics, each with a few synonyms for clarification.

We've administered this questionnaire to over seventy-five thousand people around the globe, and we update the findings continuously. We distribute the checklist and ask respondents to select the seven qualities that they "most look for and admire in a leader, someone whose direction they would willingly follow." We tell them that the key word in this question is *willingly*. What do they expect from a leader they would follow not because they *have to*, but because they *want to?* We often ask respondents to imagine they are electing a leadership council of seven members and that there are twenty candidates in the running; these candidates are ideal qualities, not specific individuals.

The results of these surveys have been striking in their regularity over the years. It appears that a person must pass several essential tests before others are willing to grant the title leader. In Table 2.1, we present three sets of data gathered over the past two decades.

Although all characteristics receive some votes, and therefore each is important to some people, what is most striking and most evident is that, consistently over time and across continents, only four have continuously received over 50 percent of the votes. (For data on how these top four rank in different countries, see Table 2.2.) Some of the other qualities have flirted with consensus, but what people most look for and admire in a leader has been constant. As the data clearly show, for people to follow someone willingly, the majority of constituents must believe the leader is

- Honest
- Competent
- Forward looking
- Inspiring

To understand the constituent's perspective even more fully, we expanded our work to include written case studies of the behaviors of admired leaders. People responded to questions about leaders with whom they had personal experience and for

TABLE 2.1. **Characteristics of Admired Leaders**

Characteristic	Percentage of Respondents Selecting That Characteristic		
	2002 Edition	1995 Edition	1987 Edition
Honest	88	88	83
Forward Looking	71	75	62
Competent	66	63	67
Inspiring	65	68	58
Intelligent	47	40	43
Fair-minded	42	49	40
Broad-minded	40	40	37
Supportive	35	41	32
Straightforward	34	33	34
Dependable	33	32	33
Cooperative	28	28	25
Determined	24	17	17
Imaginative	23	28	34
Ambitious	21	13	21
Courageous	20	29	27
Caring	20	23	26
Mature	17	13	23
Loyal	14	11	11
Self-controlled	8	5	13
Independent	6	5	10

Note: These percentages represent respondents from six continents: Africa, North America, South America, Asia, Europe, and Australia. The majority are from the United States. Since we asked people to select seven characteristics, the total adds up to 500 percent.
Source: J. M. Kouzes and B. Z. Posner, *The Leadership Challenge.* Copyright © 2000.

whom they had great admiration and respect. From these case studies (now numbering over a thousand) we collected specific examples of actions of respected leaders, information on the

TABLE 2.2. **Some Cross-Cultural Comparisons of the Characteristics of Admired Leaders**

| Country | *Percentage of Respondents Selecting Each Characteristic* | | | |
	Honest	*Forward Looking*	*Competent*	*Inspiring*
Australia	93	83	59	73
Canada	88	88	60	73
Japan	67	83	61	51
Korea	74	82	62	55
Malaysia	95	78	62	60
Mexico	85	82	62	71
New Zealand	86	86	68	71
Scandinavia	84	86	53	90
Singapore	65	78	78	94
United States	88	71	69	63

affective nature of admired leader-constituent relationships, and details about the types of projects or programs involved. These data came from sources in North America, Mexico, Western Europe, Asia, and Australia. Focus groups conducted subsequent to the collection of early cases further enabled us to determine the behaviors of admired leaders. Additionally, we conducted in-depth interviews with more than forty respected leaders and asked them to comment as constituents on the actions they believed exemplified quality leadership. Through a series of quantitative studies, we gained further insight into the leadership actions that influence people's assessments of credibility.[2]

These investigations of admired leader attributes reveal consistent and clear relationships with the stories we heard people tell us about their personal-best leadership experiences. The

Five Practices of Exemplary Leadership and the characteristics of admired leaders are complementary perspectives on the same subject. When they're performing at their peak, leaders are doing more than just getting results. They're also responding to the expectations of their constituents, underscoring the point that leadership is a relationship and that the relationship is one of service to a purpose and service to people. Here's a closer look at each of the four attributes that have been selected by the majority of respondents over the last two decades.

Honest

In almost every survey we've conducted, honesty has been selected more often than any other leadership characteristic; overall, it emerges as the single most important ingredient in the leader-constituent relationship. The percentages vary, but the final ranking does not. Since the very first time we conducted our studies in the early 1980s, honesty has been at the top of the list.

It's clear that if people anywhere are to willingly follow someone—whether it be into battle or into the boardroom, the front office or the front lines—they first want to assure themselves that the person is worthy of their trust. They want to know that the person is truthful, ethical, and principled. When people talk to us about the qualities they admire in leaders, they often use "integrity" and "character" as synonymous with honesty. No matter what the setting, everyone wants to be fully confident in their leaders, and to be fully confident they have to believe that their leaders are people of strong character and solid integrity. That nearly 90 percent of constituents want their leaders to be honest above all else is a message that all leaders must take to heart.[3]

We—all of us—don't want to be lied to or deceived. We want to be told the truth. We want a leader who knows right from wrong. Yes, we want our team to win, but we don't want to be led—or misled?—by someone who cheats in the process of attaining victory. We want our leaders to be honest because their honesty is a reflection on our own honesty. Of all the qualities that people look for and admire in a leader, honesty is by far the most personal. More than likely this is also why it consistently ranks number one. It's the quality that can most enhance or most damage our own personal reputations. If we follow someone who's universally viewed as being of impeccable character and strong integrity, then we're likely to be viewed the same. But if we willingly follow someone who's considered dishonest, our own images are tarnished. And there's perhaps another, more subtle, reason why honesty is at the top. When we follow someone we believe to be dishonest, we come to realize that we've compromised our own integrity. Over time, we not only lose respect for the leader, we lose respect for ourselves.

Just how do constituents measure a characteristic as subjective as honesty? In our discussions with respondents, we learned that the leader's behavior provided the evidence. Regardless of what leaders say about their own integrity, people wait to be shown; they observe the behavior. Consistency between word and deed is how people judge someone to be honest.

Honesty is strongly tied to values and ethics. We appreciate people who take a stand on important principles. We resolutely refuse to follow those who lack confidence in their own beliefs. Confusion over where the leader stands creates stress; not knowing the leader's beliefs contributes to conflict, indecision, and political rivalry. We simply don't trust people who can't or won't tell us their values, ethics, and standards.

Forward Looking

More than 70 percent of our most recent respondents selected the ability to look ahead as one of their most sought-after leadership traits. People expect leaders to have a sense of direction and a concern for the future of the organization. This expectation directly corresponds to the ability to envision the future that leaders described in their personal-best cases. But whether we call that ability vision, a dream, a calling, a goal, or a personal agenda, the message is clear: leaders must know where they're going if they expect others to willingly join them on the journey.

Two other surveys that we conducted with top executives reinforce the importance of clarity of purpose and direction. In one study, nearly three hundred senior executives rated "developing a strategic planning and forecasting capability" as their most critical concern. When asked to select the most important characteristics in a CEO, these same senior managers ranked "a leadership style of honesty and integrity" first and "a long-term vision and direction for the company" second.[4]

By the ability to be forward looking, people don't mean the magical power of a prescient visionary. The reality is far more down-to-earth: it's the ability to set or select a desirable destination toward which the company, agency, congregation, or community should head. Vision reveals the beckoning summit that provides others with the capacity to chart their course toward the future. As constituents, we ask that a leader have a well-defined orientation toward the future. We want to know what the organization will look like, feel like, be like when it arrives at its destination in six quarters or six years. We want to have it described to us in rich detail so that we'll know when we've arrived and so that we can select the proper route for getting there.

There is one significant finding about the quality of being forward looking that's important to note. When we survey individuals at the most senior levels in organizations, the percentage of people who select forward looking as a desired leader characteristic is around 95 percent. When we administer our checklist to people in front-line supervisory roles, the percentage of people selecting forward looking is around 60 percent. This wide gap indicates an important difference in expectation that's clearly tied to the breadth, scope, and time horizon of the job. More senior people see the need for a longer-term view of the future than do those at the front lines of operations. This also suggests a major developmental need for individuals as they move into roles that are more strategic in nature.

Competent

To enlist in another's cause, we must believe that the person is competent to guide us where we're headed. We must see the leader as capable and effective. If we doubt the leader's abilities, we're unlikely to enlist in the crusade.

Leadership competence refers to the leader's track record and ability to get things done. It's the kind of competence that inspires confidence that the leader will be able to guide the entire organization, large or small, in the direction in which it needs to go. It doesn't refer specifically to the leader's abilities in the core technology of the operation. In fact, the type of competence demanded seems to vary more with the leader's position and the condition of the organization. While we demand a base level of understanding of the fundamentals of the industry, market, or professional service environment, we also know that leaders can't be expected to be the most technically competent in their fields. Organizations are too complex and multifunctional for that ever to be the case. This is particularly true as people reach the more senior levels. For example, those who hold officer positions are definitely expected to demonstrate abilities in strategic planning and policymaking. If a company desperately needs to clarify its core competence and market position, a CEO with savvy in competitive marketing may be perceived as a fine leader. But in the line function, where people expect guidance in technical areas, these same strategic marketing abilities will be insufficient. A leader on the line or at the point of customer or client contact will typically have to be more technically competent than someone less engaged in providing services or making products. Yet it's not necessary that even the front-line leader have superior technical competence compared to the constituents. Much more significant is that the leader takes the time to learn the business and to know the current operation.

Relevant experience is a dimension of competence and one that is different from technical expertise. Experience is about active participation in situational, functional, and industry events and activities and the accumulation of knowledge derived from participation. Experience correlates with success, and the broader your experience, the more likely you are to be successful across organizations and industries. An effective leader in a high-technology company, for example, may not need to be a master programmer, but must understand the business implications of electronic data interchange, networking, and the World Wide Web. A health care administrator with experience only in the insurance industry is more than likely doomed; the job needs extensive experience in the delivery of human services. There may be notable exceptions, but it is highly unlikely that a leader can succeed without both relevant experience and, most important, exceptionally good people skills.

A leader must have the ability to bring out the best in others—to enable others to act. In fact, new research is revealing that the ability to enable others to act has become the critical differentiator between success and failure in the executive ranks. We think it applies equally at all organizational levels, as well as to leaders in all settings. The most important competency a leader brings to the role is the ability to work well with others. Leadership is a relationship, and relationship skills are what shape success.

Inspiring

We also expect our leaders to be enthusiastic, energetic, and positive about the future. We expect them to be inspiring—a bit of the cheerleader, as a matter of fact. It's not enough for a leader to have a dream about the future. A leader must be able to communicate the vision in ways that encourage us to sign on for the duration. We all long to find some greater sense of purpose and worth in our day-to-day working lives. Although the enthusiasm, energy, and positive attitude of a good leader may not change the content of work, they certainly can make the context more meaningful. Whatever the circumstances, when leaders breathe life into our dreams and aspirations, we're much more willing to enlist in the movement.

Inspiring leadership speaks to our need to have meaning and purpose in our lives. Furthermore, being upbeat, positive, and optimistic about the future offers people hope. This is crucial at any time, but in times of great uncertainty, leading with positive emotions is absolutely essential to moving people upward and forward.[5] When people are worried, discouraged, frightened, and uncertain about the future, the last thing needed is a leader who feeds those negative emotions. Instead, we need leaders who communicate in words, demeanor, and actions that they believe we will overcome. Emotions are contagious, and positive emotions resonate throughout an organization and into relationships with other constituents. To get extraordinary things done in extraordinary times, leaders must inspire optimal performance—and that can only be fueled with positive emotions.

Some react with discomfort to the idea that being inspiring is an essential leadership quality. Some have even told us, "I don't trust people who are inspiring." No doubt this is a response to the crusaders who have led people to death or destruction. Others told us they were skeptical of their own ability to inspire others. Such lack of faith in others and in yourself is a terrible mistake. In the final analysis, leaders must uplift their constituents' spirits and give them hope if they're to voluntarily engage in challenging pursuits. Enthusiasm and excitement are essential, and they signal the leader's personal commitment to pursuing a dream. If a leader displays no passion for a cause, why should anyone else?

Putting It All Together: Credibility Is the Foundation

Honest, forward-looking, competent, and inspiring: these are the characteristics that have remained constant during two decades of growth and recession, the surge in new technology enterprises, the birth of the World Wide Web, the further globalization of the economy, the ever-changing political environment, and the expansion and bursting of the Internet bubble. The relative importance of the most desired qualities has varied over time, but there has been no change in the fact that these are the four qualities people want most in their leaders. Whether we believe our leaders are true to these values is another matter, but what we would like from them has remained constant.

This list of four consistent findings is useful in and of itself—and there's a more profound implication revealed by our research. These key characteristics make up what communications experts refer to as "source credibility." In assessing the believability of sources of communication—whether newscasters, salespeople, physicians, or priests; whether business managers, military officers, politicians, or civic leaders—researchers typically evaluate people on three criteria: their perceived trustworthiness, their expertise, and their dynamism. Those who are rated more highly on these dimensions are considered to be more credible sources of information.

Notice how strikingly similar these three characteristics are to the admired leader qualities of honest, competent, and inspiring—three of the top four items selected in our survey. What we found in our investigation of admired leadership qualities is that more than anything, people want leaders who are credible. Credibility is the foundation of leadership.

Above all else, we must be able to believe in our leaders. We must believe that their word can be trusted, that they'll do what they say, that they're personally excited and enthusiastic about the direction in which we're headed, and that they have the knowledge and skill to lead.

Because this finding has been so pervasive and so consistent, we've come to refer to it as The First Law of Leadership: If you don't believe in the messenger, you won't believe the message.

Credibility Makes a Difference

At this point, cynics might well say, "So what? I know people who are in positions of power and who are enormously wealthy, yet people don't find them credible. Does credibility really matter? Does it make a difference?"

It's a legitimate question, and we feel compelled to address it. But rather than ask about "top management" or "elected officials," we asked questions about people closer to home. We asked people to rate their immediate manager. As part of our quantitative research, using a behavioral measure of credibility, we asked organization members to think about the extent to which their immediate manager exhibited credibility-enhancing behaviors. We found that when people perceive their immediate manager to have high credibility, they're significantly more likely to:

- Be proud to tell others they're part of the organization.
- Feel a strong sense of team spirit.
- See their own personal values as consistent with those of the organization.
- Feel attached and committed to the organization.
- Have a sense of ownership of the organization.

When people perceive their manager to have low credibility, on the other hand, they're significantly more likely to:

- Produce only if they're watched carefully.
- Be motivated primarily by money.
- Say good things about the organization publicly but criticize it privately.
- Consider looking for another job if the organization experiences problems.
- Feel unsupported and unappreciated.

This evidence of the significant impact of leadership credibility on employee attitudes and behavior certainly provides clear dictates for organizational leaders. Credibility makes a difference, and leaders must take it personally. Loyalty, commitment, energy, and productivity depend on it.

Credibility goes far beyond employee attitudes. It influences customer and investor loyalty as well as employee loyalty. In an extensive study of the economic value of business loyalty, Frederick Reichheld and his Bain & Company colleagues found that businesses concentrating on customer, employee, and investor loyalty generate superior results compared to those engendering disloyalty. They found further that disloyalty can dampen performance by a stunning 25 to 50 percent.[6] Loyalty is clearly responsible for extraordinary value creation. So what accounts for business loyalty? When they investigated this question, the researchers found that "the center of gravity for business loyalty—whether it be the loyalty of customers, employees, investors, suppliers, or dealers—is the personal integrity of the senior leadership team and its ability to put its principles into practice."[7] And what's true for bricks-and-mortar companies is just as true for Web companies. "In fact, when Web shoppers were asked to name the attributes of e-tailers that were most important in earning their business, the number one answer was 'a Web site I know and trust.' All other attributes, including lowest cost and broadest selection, lagged far behind. Price does not rule the Web; trust does."[8]

The Requirement and the Predicament of Being Forward Looking

As much as we demand that leaders be credible before we will willingly follow them, credibility alone doesn't satisfy us; we demand something more from our leaders. We expect leaders to have a sense of direction, a vision for the future: we expect them to be forward looking. Although we expect credible newscasters, for example, to be independent when reporting what's happening today, we expect leaders to have a point of view on today's events and to be firm about the destination of our national, organizational, or civic journey. We may want newscasters to be cool, reasoned, and objective, but we want leaders to articulate the exciting possibilities. Leaders don't just report the news; they make the news.

The dilemma is that leaders who are forward looking are also biased—biased about the future. They aspire to change the way things are and guide us to a better tomorrow. But this very admirable and desirable leadership quality means that leaders often become the target of those who propose an alternative future. Thus, when a leader takes a position on issues—when that leader has a clear point of view and a partisan sense of where the country, community, or company ought to be headed—that individual will be seen as less believable than someone who takes no stand. Consequently—ironic as it might seem—by the very nature of the role they play, leaders will always have their credibility questioned by those who oppose them.[9]

What does this mean for aspiring leaders? First, society places leaders in an awkward situation. We demand that they be credible, but we also contribute to undermining their credibility by expecting them to focus on a clear direction for the future. Leaders must learn how to balance their personal desire to achieve important ends with the constituents' need to believe that the leader has others' best interests at heart.

Second, because of this dilemma, leaders must be ever diligent in guarding their credibility. Their ability to take strong stands—to challenge the status quo, to point us in new directions—depends on their being perceived as highly credible. Credibility matters as much to leaders as it does to other sources of information, if not more. If leaders ask others to follow them to some uncertain future—a future that may not be realized in their lifetime—and if the journey is going to require sacrifice, isn't it reasonable that constituents should believe in them? To believe in the exciting future possibilities leaders present, constituents must first believe in their leaders' trustworthiness, expertise, and dynamism.

This is not to suggest for one second that leadership is a popularity contest. It's totally unrealistic for any leader to expect 100 percent of potential constituents to willingly enlist.[10] Leaders have to learn to thrive on the tensions between their own calling and the voice of the people.

Opinions about those in leadership positions also tend to rise and fall with events. Americans generally have less confidence in many institutions now than they did in the 1970s when Gallup first began testing them. When times are good, people exhibit more confidence in their leaders; when times are bad, they show less. The more severe the events and the more compressed the time frame, the more cynical people are likely to become. And cynics have significantly less trust in their management than those who are upbeat. Nearly half of cynics doubt the truth of what management tells them, and only a third believe management has integrity. Three-quarters believe that top executives do pretty much what they want to no matter what people think.[11] And while most individuals believe that big government is low on the trust scale, many would be surprised to learn that only about 30 percent of the people on average have had confidence in big business over the past thirty years. With only a couple of exceptions, confidence in all institutions has tended downward since the 1970s.[12]

So it's understandable that in a period of drastic restructuring, with attendant layoffs and shrinking family incomes, the credibility of business, labor, church, and government leaders declines. A natural suspicion of power and the confluence of events—such as the financial and political scandals of the 1980s and 1990s, or the bursting of the Internet bubble, the drastic drop in stock portfolio values in mid-2001, and the Enron scandal in 2002—certainly explain a great deal about why leaders have lost credibility. Bad timing, bad times, and bad behavior can often tarnish trust.

Credibility problems aren't simply a function of the economic cycles, however. Even in the toughest of times, some leaders are held in extremely high regard, while others just fall out of respect. Some leaders stay true to their principles whatever the situation, and some are simply too weak, too amoral, too corrupt, or too mercenary to stand firm against the sirens of temptation or the gales of uncertainty. They have no strong bonds of belief that hold them firmly in place when they're lured by wealth, fame, or power, or are tossed about by turmoil, chaos, and disruptive change.

It would be absolutely reckless for leaders to attribute the majority of credibility gains or losses to the situation. Leaders must never take credibility for granted, regardless of the times or their positions. In any circumstance, credibility is one of the hardest attributes to earn and to sustain. It's personal—and the most fragile of human qualities. It's earned minute by minute, hour by hour, month by month, year by year. But it can be lost in very short order if not attended to. By and large people are willing to forgive a few minor transgressions, a slip of the tongue, a misspoken word, a careless act. But there comes a time when enough is enough. And when leaders have used up all of their credibility, it's nearly impossible to earn it back.

What Is Credibility Behaviorally?

Credibility is the foundation of leadership. Our data confirm this assertion time and time again. But what is credibility behaviorally? How do you know it when you see it?

We've asked this question of tens of thousands of people over nearly twenty years, and the response we get is always the same. Here are some of the common phrases people have used to describe how they know credibility when they see it:

"Leaders practice what they preach."

"They walk the talk."

"Their actions are consistent with their words."

"They put their money where their mouth is."

"They follow through on their promises."

"They do what they say they will do."

That last is the most frequent response. When it comes to deciding whether a leader is believable, people first listen to the words, then they watch the actions. They listen to the talk, and then they watch the walk. They listen to the promises of resources to support change initiatives, and then they wait to see if the money and materials follow. They hear the promises to deliver, and then they look for evidence that the commitments are met. A judgment of "credible" is handed down when words and deeds are consonant. If people don't see consistency, they conclude that the leader is, at best, not really serious, or, at worst, an outright hypocrite. If leaders espouse one set of values but personally practice another, we find them to be duplicitous.

If leaders practice what they preach, we're more willing to entrust them with our career, our security, and sometimes even our life.

This realization leads to a straightforward prescription for leaders on how to establish credibility. It is: DWYSYWD: Do What You Say You Will Do.

This commonsense definition of credibility corresponds directly to one of the Five Practices of Exemplary Leadership identified in the personal best cases. DWYSYWD has two essential elements: say and do. To be credible in action, leaders must be clear about their beliefs; they must know what they stand for. That's the "say" part. Then they must put what they say into practice: they must act on their beliefs and "do." The practice of Modeling the Way links directly to these two dimensions of people's behavioral definition of credibility. This practice includes the clarification of a set of values and being an example of those values to others. This consistent living out of values is a behavioral way of demonstrating honesty and trustworthiness. We trust leaders when their deeds and words match.

o   o   o

James M. Kouzes is chairman emeritus of the Tom Peters Company, executive fellow in the Center for Innovation and Entrepreneurship at the Leavey School of Business, Santa Clara University, and a leadership speaker.

Barry Z. Posner is dean and professor at the Leavey School of Business, Santa Clara University. He is also a speaker and executive development program leader.

Chapter Three

Management vs. Leadership

Warren Bennis
Burt Nanus

The problem with many organizations, and especially the ones that are failing, is that they tend to be overmanaged and underled (see Exhibit 3.1). They may excel in the ability to handle the daily routine, yet never question whether the routine should be done at all. There is a profound difference between management and leadership, and both are important. "To manage" means "to bring about, to accomplish, to have charge of or responsibility for, to conduct." "Leading" is "influencing, guiding in direction, course, action, opinion." The distinction is crucial. *Managers are people who do things right, and leaders are people who do the right thing.* The difference may be summarized as activities of vision and judgment—*effectiveness*—versus activities of mastering routines—*efficiency*.

EXHIBIT 3.1. **Let's Get Rid of Management**

People
don't want
to be
managed.
They want
to be led.
Whoever heard
of a world
manager?
World leader,
yes.
Educational leader.
Political leader.
Religious leader.
Scout leader.
Community leader.
Labor leader.
Business leader.
They lead.
They don't manage.
The carrot
always wins
over the stick.
Ask your horse.
You can *lead* your
horse to water,
but you can't
manage him
to drink.
If you want to
manage somebody,
manage yourself.
Do that well
and you'll
be ready to
stop managing.
And start
leading.

Source: A message as published in the *Wall Street Journal* by United Technologies Corporation, Hartford, Connecticut 06101.

o   o   o

But hard it is to learn the mind of any mortal, or the heart,
till he be tried in chief authority. Power shows the man.
Sophocles, *Antigone*

Leaders have a significant role in creating the state of
mind that is the society. They can serve as symbols of the
moral unity of the society. They can express the values that
hold the society together. Most important, they can conceive
and articulate goals that lift people out of their petty
preoccupations, carry them above the conflicts that tear a
society apart, and unite them in the pursuit of objectives
worthy of their best efforts.
John W. Gardner[1]

"The employees were willing to take a chance because they felt
a part of something magic and they *wanted* to work that extra
hour or make that extra call, or stay on that extra Saturday.
Maybe if we had a different management that did exactly the
same thing, except to instill that—yes, *magic*—we would not
have made it." That was Jerry Neely talking about his company,
Smith International, the world's second largest manufacturer of
oil drilling and rigging equipment.

Werner Erhard, the founder of est, didn't use the word
magic, but he seemed to be talking about something parallel:

There is this place in people, where they are aligned, where they
don't need to be told what to do; they more or less sort out for
themselves what needs to be done and where they can work in
harmony with other people, not as a function of a bunch of

agreements or contracts, but out of a sense of harmony. . . . It's something akin to what you see on a sailboat in a crew working together when one of the lines breaks. Very few, if any, orders are given and nobody waits for the other guy and nobody gets in the other guy's way—there's something about sailors in which there is an alignment, a kind of coming from the whole and nobody needs to give orders.

What these two leaders refer to as either "magic" or "alignment" is the epiphany of effective leadership: leaders as catalysts, leaders capable of deploying their ideas and themselves into some consonance and thereby committing themselves to a greater risk—the exposure and intimacy that most of us emotionally yearn for, rhetorically defend, but in practice shun. At their best, these leaders—a fairly disparate group in many superficial ways—commit themselves to a common enterprise and are resilient enough to absorb the conflicts; brave enough, now and then, to be transformed by its accompanying energies; and capable of sustaining a vision that encompasses the whole organization. The organization finds its greatest expression in the consciousness of a common social responsibility, and that is to translate that vision into a living reality.

This is "transformative leadership,"[2] the province of John Gardner and those he alludes to: leaders who can shape and elevate the motives and goals of followers. Transformative leadership achieves significant change that reflects the community of interests of both leaders and followers; indeed, it frees up and pools the collective energies in pursuit of a common goal.

Now we can make some sweeping generalizations about transformative leadership: it is collective, there is a symbiotic relationship between leaders and followers, and what makes it collective is the subtle interplay between the followers' needs and wants and the leader's capacity to understand, one way or another, these collective aspirations. Leadership is "causative," meaning that leadership can invent and create institutions that can empower employees to satisfy their needs. Leadership is morally purposeful and elevating, which means, if nothing else, that leaders can, through deploying their talents, choose purposes and visions that are based on the key values of the workforce and create the social architecture that supports them. Finally, leadership can move followers to higher degrees of consciousness, such as liberty, freedom, justice, and self-actualization.

But as we've made plain, most organizations are managed, not led. Management typically consists of a set of contractual exchanges, "you do this job for that reward," or, as Erhard said, "a bunch of agreements or contracts." What gets exchanged is not trivial: jobs, security, money. The result, at best, is compliance; at worst, you get a spiteful obedience. The end result of the leadership we have advanced is completely different: it is empowerment. Not just higher profits and wages, which usually accompany empowerment, but an organizational culture that helps employees generate a sense of meaning in their work and a desire to challenge themselves to experience success. Leadership stands in the same relationship to empowerment that management does to compliance. The former encourages a "culture of pride," while the latter suffers from the "I only work here" syndrome. Our hope for our readers is to extricate the reality of transformative leadership from that which is either accidental or mystical to something that is masterable, knowable, and graspable and can be made available to all future and present leaders, which inevitably leads us to the topic of management education.

MANAGEMENT EDUCATION

"Management education" is, unfortunately, the appropriate description for that which goes on in most formal educational and training programs, both within and outside universities. Management education relies heavily, if not exclusively, on mechanistic, pseudo-rational "theories" of management and produces tens of thousands of new M.B.A.s each year. The gap between management education and the reality of leadership in the workplace is disturbing, to say the least, and probably explains why the public seems to hold such a distorted (and negative) image of American business life.

But the image problem, though serious, is hardly the major problem. The major problem is that what management education does do moderately well is to train good journeymen/women managers; that is, the graduates acquire technical skills for solving problems. They are highly skilled problem solvers and staff experts. Problem solving, while not a trivial exercise, is far removed from the creative and deeply human processes required of leadership. What's needed is not *management* education but *leadership* education.

The typical course that passes for management education starts with a number of dubious assumptions such as, "If you don't know what your objectives are, try to identify them." Or, "If you don't know what your alternatives are, search until you find them." Or, "If you don't know what to do, then undertake research [or hire consultants] to establish the cause-and-effect connections in your activities."

Such recommendations are not altogether stupid. There's some experience we can cite where efforts to establish goals can be positive, but it's rarely of long-run help. The idea of establishing goals first and then taking action relies on a rationalistic fiction that has obvious limitations, such as: How does one go about searching for alternatives? What are the techniques of search? How do you go about finding alternatives that have not been invented? And how do you avoid the creation of pseudo-alternatives as ways of making a preferred alternative look good?

The world is far more fascinatingly complex than the straight linear thinking that dominates so much of what passes for management education: the nature of the problem itself is often in question, the information (and its reliability) is problematical, there are multiple and conflicting interpretations and different value orientations, the goals are unclear and conflicting, and we could go on and on. The point is that most management education makes certain assumptions that are dangerously misleading—namely, that the goals are clear, alternatives known, technology and its consequences certain, and perfect information available. It sounds terrifyingly similar to the courses in microeconomics on which, unfortunately, so much of management education is based.

What makes matters even worse is that much of the human element is either avoided or shortchanged in most curricula. And when the "human side" is touched on here or there—as it is in the elite schools of management—it is often accompanied by embarrassed sighs or academic pejoratives such as "soft" or "poetic" or "impressionistic"—attitudes and words that discredit the ideas before they're even understood.

DISPELLING MYTHS

It might be useful now to turn to some recurring myths that, in our view, both diminish much of what passes for management education and, at the same time, tend to discourage potential leaders from "taking charge" of their organizations. These myths include the following:

○ *Myth 1: Leadership is a rare skill.* Nothing can be further from the truth. While *great* leaders may be as rare as great runners, great actors, or great painters, everyone has leadership potential, just as everyone has some ability at running, acting, and painting. While there seems to be a dearth of great leaders today, particularly in high political offices, there are literally millions of leadership roles throughout the country and they are all filled, many of them more than adequately.

More important, people may be leaders in one organization and have quite ordinary roles in another. We know of a college professor who is a general in the U.S. Army Reserves and a clerk at JCPenney who is a powerful leader of a church group. A taxi driver we know is the director of an amateur theater group, and a retired beer salesman is the mayor of a decent-sized town.

The truth is that leadership opportunities are plentiful and within the reach of most people

○ *Myth 2: Leaders are born, not made.* Biographies of great leaders sometimes read as if they had entered the world with an extraordinary genetic endowment, that somehow their future leadership role was preordained. Don't believe it. The truth is that major capacities and competencies of leadership can be learned, and we are all educable, at least if the basic desire to learn is there and we do not suffer from serious learning disorders. Furthermore, whatever natural endowments we bring to the role of leadership, they *can* be enhanced; nurture is far more important than nature in determining who becomes a successful leader.

This is not to suggest that it is easy to learn to be a leader. There is no simple formula, no rigorous science, no cookbook that leads inexorably to successful leadership. Instead, it is a deeply human process, full of trial and error, victories and defeats, timing and happenstance, intuition and insight. Learning to be a leader is somewhat like learning to be a parent or a lover; your childhood and adolescence provide you with basic values and role models. Books can help you understand what's going on, but for those who are ready, most of the learning takes place during the experience itself. As one of our leaders put it concerning his own leadership development, "It's not easy, you know, learning how to lead; it's sort of like learning how to play the violin in public."

o *Myth 3: Leaders are charismatic.* Some are, most aren't. Among the ninety, there were a few—but damned few—who probably correspond to our fantasies of some "divine inspiration," that "grace under stress" we associated with JFK or the beguiling capacity to spellbind for which we remember a Churchill. Our leaders were all "too human"; they were short and tall, articulate and inarticulate, dressed for success and dressed for failure, and there was virtually nothing in terms of physical appearance, personality, or style that set them apart from their followers. Our guess is that it operates in the other direction; that is, charisma is the result of effective leadership, not the other way around, and that those who are good at it are granted a certain amount of respect and even awe by their followers, which increases the bond of attraction between them.

o *Myth 4: Leadership exists only at the top of an organization.* We may have played into this myth unintentionally by focusing exclusively on top leadership. But it's obviously false. In fact, the larger the organization, the more leadership roles it is likely to have. General Motors has thousands of leadership roles available to its employees. In fact, now many large corporations are moving in the direction of creating more leadership roles through "entrepreneurship," the creation of small entrepreneurial units within the organization with the freedom and flexibility to operate virtually as small, independent businesses. William Kieschnick, former CEO of ARCO, told us that one of the biggest problems he faced was to inspire the entire multibillion-dollar corporation "with an entrepreneurial spirit . . . which means that we need leadership at every single unit, at every level—and I think this is happening." As organizations learn more about this, there will almost certainly be a multiplication of the leadership roles available to employees.

○ *Myth 5: The leader controls, directs, prods, manipulates.* This is perhaps the most damaging myth of all. As we have stressed with monotonous regularity, leadership is not so much the exercise of power itself as the empowerment of others. Leaders are able to translate intentions into reality by aligning the energies of the organization behind an attractive goal. It is Carlo Maria Giulini, formerly the conductor of the Los Angeles Philharmonic, who claims that "what matters most is human contact, that the great mystery of music making requires real friendship among those who work together." It is Irwin Federman, past president of Monolithic Memories, who believes that "the essence of leadership is the capacity to build and develop the self-esteem of the workers." It is William Hewitt, who took over John Deere and Company in the mid-fifties when it was a sleepy, old-line farm-implements firm and made it into a world leader because, as one employee put it, "Hewitt made us learn how good we were."

These leaders lead by pulling rather than by pushing; by inspiring rather than by ordering; by creating achievable, though challenging, expectations and rewarding progress toward them rather than by manipulating; by enabling people to use their own initiative and experiences rather than by deny-ing or constraining their experiences and actions.

  ◦ *Myth 6: The leader's sole job is to increase shareholder value.* Most executives, economists, and investors applaud this state-ment. In our view, it is not so much wrong as misleading and too limited. Exclusive attention to shareholder value often leads to decisions that slight other important stakeholders at great cost to the long-term viability of the organization. For exam-ple, consider the typical downsizing scenario. A CEO slashes today's payroll to improve next year's bottom line for share-holders. Investors celebrate, but in the process, worker morale and productivity often sink, customer service declines, and product quality is jeopardized. We find that a pretty strange measure of effective leadership! At the very least, the statement needs to be revised to read, "An important part of the leader's job is to increase *long-term* shareholder value," but even that falls somewhat short.

Leaders expect managers to *operate* the organization, pay-ing attention almost exclusively to bottom-line performance. Though hardly uninterested in current performance, leaders see themselves as having a different responsibility. Their pri-mary concern is in *building* the organization to ensure its long-term viability and success. The leader is the major instrument an organization has for articulating its dreams, pointing the way toward their achievement, and helping people work together effectively to create brighter futures. For real leaders, then, making profit is a *requirement*, not a vision or goal; nor does it animate or empower the workforce. The excessive and exclu-sive obsession with the enshrined bottom line will only lead to destructive "short-termism" along with a tremendous cost to the long-term viability of the organization. Thus, a broader and, in our view, far more satisfactory statement of the leader's main role would be as follows: "The leader's primary responsibility is to serve as trustee and architect of the organization's future, building the foundations for its continued success."

Once these myths are cleared away, the question becomes not one of how to become a leader but rather how to improve one's effectiveness at leadership—how to take charge of the leadership in an organization. It is equally important for organizations to modify their social architecture to encourage and develop the style of transformative leadership we have been advocating.

o o o

Warren Bennis is University Professor and Distinguished Professor of Business Administration at the University of Southern California and the founding chairman of USC's Leadership Institute.

Burt Nanus is professor emeritus of management at the University of Southern California and a well-known expert on leadership.

Chapter Four

Rounding Out the Manager's Job

Henry Mintzberg

Tom Peters tells us that good managers are doers. (Wall Street says they "do deals.") Michael Porter suggests that they are thinkers. Not so, argue Abraham Zaleznik and Warren Bennis: good managers are really leaders. Yet for the better part of this century, the classical writers—Henri Fayol and Lyndell Urwick, among others—kept telling us that good managers are essentially controllers.

It is a curiosity of the management literature that its best-known writers all seem to emphasize one particular part of the manager's job to the exclusion of the others. Together, perhaps they cover all the parts, but even that does not describe the whole job of managing.

If you turn to the more formalized literature, you will find all kinds of lists—of tasks or roles or "competencies." But a list is not a model (even if presented in the form of a circle. Meaning the ends have been joined), and so the integrated work of managing still gets lost in the process of describing it. And without such a model, we can neither understand the job properly nor deal with its many important needs—for design, selection, training, and support.

To play with a metaphor, if the toughest nut to crack in our knowledge of management has been the manager's job itself, then that may well be because we have done just that. We have been so intent on breaking the job into pieces that we never came to grips with the whole thing. It is time, therefore, to consider the integrated job of managing.

That is what I set out to do several years ago, after becoming discouraged with all those lists and circles (including one from my own initial study of managerial work, first published in 1973).[1] I did not feel the need to go find out what managers do. We knew that already, I believed, based on a considerable body of research and publication over the past decades. Our need was for a framework to put all this together, a model of managing, if you like. People had to be able to "see" the job in one place, in order to deal with its component parts comprehensively and interactively. In fact, as my ideas developed, the metaphor of the nut came alive, for the model has taken the form of an interacting set of concentric circles.

Using this model, I began to spend time with managers at work, both to check out and to flesh out the model, especially as it applies to different managerial jobs and styles. I have been spending a day with each of a number of managers—observation reinforced by interviewing—not to draw any definitive conclusions so much as to get a flavor of as wide a variety of managerial jobs and styles as possible. So far they number twenty-three, ranging from the head of one of Europe's largest state health care systems to the "front country" manager of a Canadian mountain park. (Examples used throughout this chapter will give a sense of the variety of managers I have studied so far.)

This chapter presents the model, building the image of the manager's job from the inside out, beginning at the center with the person and his or her frame and working out from there, layer by layer. Once this description is complete, I shall discuss briefly the jobs and styles of some of the managers I have observed to give a sense of how readers might use the model to better appreciate their own jobs or those of the managers around them. I shall also comment on the effective practice of managerial work, concluding, as you may have already guessed, that this is one job that has to be "well rounded"!

The Person in the Job

We begin at the center, with the person who comes to the job. People are not neutral when they take on a new managerial job, mere putty to be molded into the required shape. Indeed, greater appreciation of this fact would allow us to be more careful in how we select managers in the first place—or else more flexible in how we let them mold their jobs to themselves in the second.

Figure 4.1 shows that an individual comes to a managerial job with a set of values, by this stage in life probably rather firmly set—for example, that the radio station he manages should provide intelligent fare. He or she also brings a body of experience that, on one hand, has forged a set of skills or competences, perhaps honed by training, and, on the other, has provided a base of knowledge that comes, for example, from spending thirty-five years on a major police force before becoming its commissioner. That knowledge is, of course, used directly, but it is also converted into a set of mental models, key means by which managers interpret the world around them—for example, how the head nurse on a hospital ward perceives the behavior of the surgeons with whom she must work. Together, all these characteristics greatly determine how any manager approaches a given job—his or her style of managing. Style will come to life as we begin to see how a manager carries out what his or her job requires.

THE FRAME OF THE JOB

Embed the person depicted in a given managerial job and you get managerial work. At the core of it is some kind of frame for the job, the mental set the incumbent assumes to carry it out. Frame is strategy, to be sure, possibly even vision, but it is more than that. We can show it as three increasingly specific components, emanating from the person concentrically in Figure 4.2.

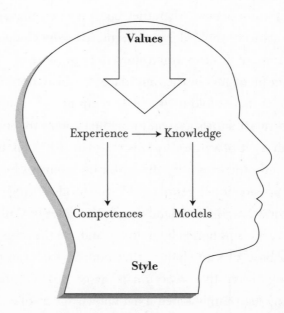

FIGURE 4.1. **The Person in the Job**

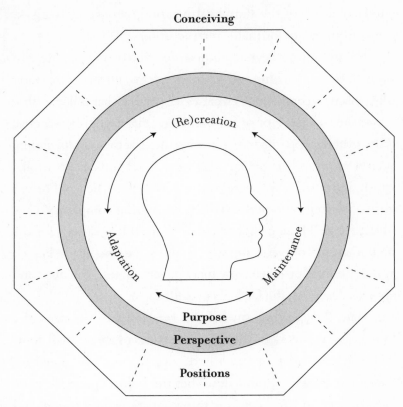

FIGURE 4.2. **The Frame of the Job**

First is purpose, namely, what the manager is seeking to do fundamentally with the unit he or she is supposed to manage—for example, to increase the state funding for a hospital or to open more stores in a retail chain. As depicted around the circle, a manager may create a unit, maintain the effective functioning of a unit already created, adapt the unit to some new condition, or recreate in some more ambitious way a unit previously created. To use a metaphor, a manager may build the track in the first place, keep the unit on track (or put it back on track), improve or shift the track, or else rebuild the track. The head nurse seeks to keep her unit running smoothly; the chief executive of the state health care system accepts a government mandate for major restructuring.

The two circles beyond purpose describe two further dimensions of frame, encompassing both strategy and structure. First is perspective, equivalent to what Peter Drucker has called a "theory of the business" (or of any unit being managed).[2] Perspective is the overall approach to the management of the unit, including such notions as "vision" and "culture." Second are positions, which, in contrast, are more concrete, closer to Michael Porter's view of strategy and perhaps many consulting companies' view of structure. These positions consider specific locations for the unit in its environment, and specific ways of doing its work, such as the products produced, the markets served, the structures and systems designed, the facilities provided.[3]

Alain Noël, who studied the relationship between the frames and the work of the chief executives of three small companies, has said that managers have "occupations" and they have "preoccupations."[4] Frame describes the preoccupations, while roles (discussed later) describe the occupations. But frame does give rise to a first role in this model as well, which I call *conceiving*, namely, thinking through the purpose, perspective, and positions of a particular unit to be managed over a particular period of time.

Different managers conceive their frames in different ways. In other words, the style of performing this first role can vary significantly. First, the frame can be imposed by some outside person or force, or else it can be developed by the manager himself or herself. And second, that frame may range from being rather sharp to rather vague, for example, from "cutting costs by 10 percent before year end" to "getting this place in order." The frame of any managerial job, as suggested by its placement in the center of the rounding model, is a kind of magnet for the behaviors that surround it. So long as the frame is rather sharp, it holds those behaviors together tightly. But when the frame is vague, the different issues considered and the different activities performed risk flying off in all directions. That is presumably why there has been so much demand in recent years for clearer "vision" in strategic thinking.

As shown in Figure 4.3, these two sets of dimensions produce four broad styles of conceiving the frame. A frame that is self-selected but vague allows the manager wide latitude to a maneuver but offers little real sense of direction. Managerial style is likely to become opportunistic, as in the case of a health care manager who uses any possible means to bring his unit under control, but having a vague frame imposed on the manager (such as "empower your people") may provide little real help and risks evoking a passive style of management (unless, of course, the manager sharpens it). A sharp frame that the

Selection of Frame		Clarity of Frame	
		Vague	Sharp
	Imposed	Passive style	Driven style
	Invented	Opportunistic style	Determined style

FIGURE 4.3. **Four Styles of Conceiving the Frame**

manager selects would tend to lead to a determined, sometimes "visionary," style of management. For example, the head of a fashion museum sees her role as the preservation of a national heritage. A sharp frame that is, in contrast, imposed could well lead to a driven style of management, as in the example of that chief executive of the state medical system who tries to honor the government's intentions.

THE AGENDA OF THE WORK

Given a person in a particular managerial job with a particular frame, the question arises as to how this is manifested in the form of specific activities. That happens through the agenda to carry out the work, and the associated role of scheduling, which has received considerable attention in the literature of management, for example, in the empirical work of John Kotter.[5] Agenda is considered in two respects here, again shown as concentric circles (in Figure 4.4), the inner one more general, the outer one more specific.

First, the frame gets manifested as a set of current issues, in effect, whatever is of concern to the manager, broken down into manageable units—what Tom Peters likes to call "chunks." Ask any manager about his or her work, and the almost inevitable first reply will be about the "issues" of central concern, those things "on the plate," as the saying goes—promoting public exhibitions at the museum and developing a state-of-the-art storage facility for its clothing, for example. Or take a look at the agendas of meetings, and you will likewise see a list of issues (rather than decisions). These, in effect, operationalize the frame (as well as change it, of course, by feeding in new concerns).

As already noted, the sharper the frame, the more integrated the issues. The more realizable they may be as well, since it is a vague frame that gives rise to that all-too-common

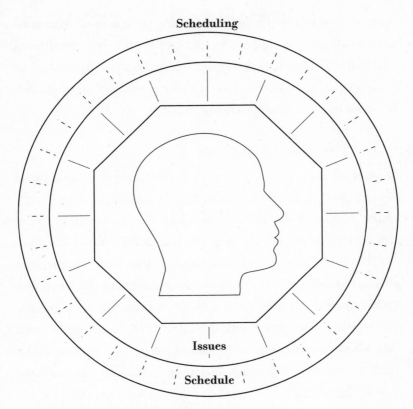

FIGURE 4.4. **The Agenda of the Work**

phenomenon of the unattainable "wish list" in an organization. Sometimes a frame can be so sharp, and the issues therefore so tightly integrated, that they all reduce to what Noël has called one "a magnificent obsession."[6] In effect, all the concerns of the manager revolve around one central issue, for example, imposing those changes on the state health care system or expanding that retail chain.

Second, the frame and the issues get manifested in the more tangible schedule, the specific allocations of managerial time on a day-by-day basis. Also included here, however implicitly, is the setting of priorities among the issues. The scheduling of time and the prioritization of issues are obviously of great concern to all managers, and, in fact, are themselves significant consumers of managerial time. Accordingly, a great deal of attention has been devoted to these concerns, including numerous courses on "time management."

THE CORE IN CONTEXT

If we label the person in the job with a frame manifested by an agenda (that is, all the circles so far discussed), the central core of the manager's job, then we turn next to the context in which this core is embedded, the milieu in which the work is practiced.

The context of the job is depicted in Figure 4.5 by the lines that surround the core. I have so far been using the word *unit* rather freely. Let me be more specific. A manager, by definition, has formal authority over an organizational unit, whether that be a whole organization in the case of a chief executive or a division, department, or branch, and so on, in the case of a manager within the hierarchy. Context can thus be split into three areas, labeled "inside," "within," and "outside" on Figure 4.5.

Inside refers to the unit being managed, shown below the manager to represent his or her formal authority over its people and activities—the hospital ward in the case of the head nurse, for example. *Within*, shown to the right refers to the rest of the organization, other members and other units with which the manager must work but over which he or she has no formal authority—the doctors, the kitchen, the physiotherapists in the rest of the hospital, to continue with the same example. (Of course, in the case of the chief executive, there is no inside separate from within: that person has authority over the entire organization.) And *outside* refers to the rest of the context not formally part of the organization with which the manager must work—in this example, patients' relatives, long-term-care

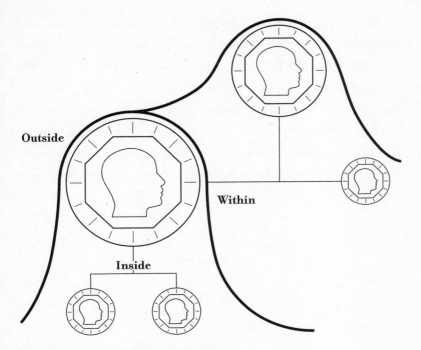

FIGURE 4.5. **The Core in Context**

institutions to which some of the unit's patients are discharged, nursing associations, and so on. The importance of this distinction (for convenience, we shall mostly refer to inside versus outside) is that much of managerial work is clearly directed either to the unit itself, for which the manager has official responsibility, or at its various boundary contexts, through which the manager must act without that responsibility.

Managing on Three Levels

We are now ready to address the actual behaviors that managers engage in to do their jobs. In other words, we turn now from the largely cerebral roles of conceiving and scheduling at the core to the more tangible roles of getting things done. The essence of the model, designed to enable us to "see" managerial work comprehensively, is that these roles are carried out on three successive levels, each inside and outside the unit. Again, this is depicted by concentric circles of increasing specificity, shown in Figure 4.6.

From the outside (or most tangible level) in, managers can manage action directly, they can manage people to encourage them to take the necessary actions, and they can manage information to influence the people in turn to take their necessary

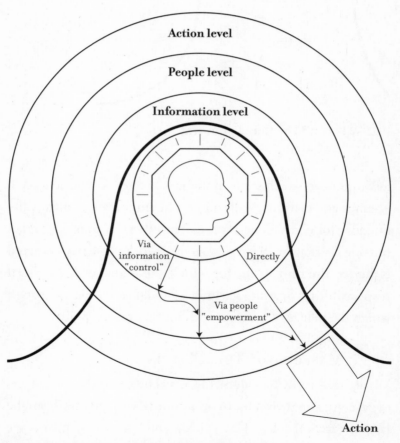

FIGURE 4.6. **Three Levels of Evoking Action**

actions. In other words, the ultimate objective of managerial work, and of the functioning of any organizational unit, the taking of action, can be managed directly, indirectly through people, or even more indirectly by information through people. The manager can thus choose to intervene at any of the three levels, but once done, he or she must work through the remaining ones. Later we shall see that the level a given manager favors becomes an important determinant of his or her managerial style, especially distinguishing so-called doers, who prefer direct action; leaders, who prefer working through people; and administrators, who prefer to work by information.

The discussion that follows describes managerial behavior in terms of roles, each pertaining to a given level and directed either inside or outside the unit (or both). We shall begin with the innermost circle, of information, containing the most conceptual roles, and work out to the more tangible or specific ones.

In presenting these roles, it should be emphasized that all managers perform all of them as the essence of their work. Styles of managers do vary, to be sure, but not in whether these roles are performed so much as in which of them is favored and how they are performed. This model of roles on levels directed inside and outside the unit thus provides the basis for understanding different styles of managing as well as different contexts in which that managing takes place.

Managing by Information

To manage by information is to sit two steps removed from the purpose of managerial work. The manager processes information to drive other people who, in turn, are supposed to ensure that necessary actions are taken. In other words, here the managers' own activities focus neither on people nor on actions per se, but rather on information as an indirect way to make things happen. Ironically, while this was the classic perception of managerial work for the first half of this century (as I discuss later), in recent years, it has also become a newly popular, in some quarters almost obsessional, view epitomized by the so-called bottom-line approach to management.

The manager's various informational behaviors may be grouped into two broad roles, here labeled communicating and controlling, shown in Figure 4.7.

Communicating refers to the collection and dissemination of information. In Figure 4.7, communicating is shown by double

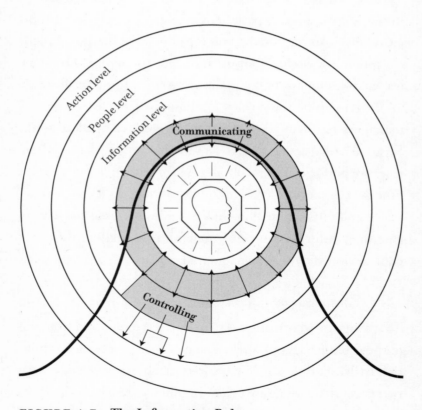

FIGURE 4.7. **The Information Roles**

arrows to indicate that managers devote a great deal of effort to the two-way flow of information with the people all around them—employees inside their own units, others in the rest of the organization, and, especially, as the empirical evidence makes abundantly clear, a great number of outsiders with whom they maintain regular contact. Thus, the head of the one regional division of the national police force spent a good part of his day passing information back and forth between the central headquarters and the people on his staff.

Managers scan their environments, they monitor their own units, and they share with and disseminate to others considerable amounts of the information they pick up. A point worth emphasizing, and one emphasized in almost every serious study of managerial work, is that the formal information—in other words, information capable of being processed in a computer—does not play a particularly dominant role here. Oral information—much of it too early or too soft to formalize, such as gossip and hearsay—and even nonverbal information, namely, what is seen and "felt" but not heard, forms a critical part of every serious managerial job (or, at least, every managerial job performed seriously).

In my initial study, I described managers as nerve centers of their units, who use their status of office to gain access to a wide variety of informational sources. Inside the unit, everyone else is a specialist who generally knows more about his or her specialty than the manager. But because the manager is connected to all those specialists, he or she should have the broadest base of knowledge about the unit in general. This should apply to the head of an 800,000-person health care system, with regard to broad policy issues, no less than to the clinical director of one of its hospital units, with regard to the service rendered there. And externally, by virtue of their status, managers have access to other managers who are themselves nerve centers of their own units. And so they tend to be exposed to powerful sources of external information and thus emerge as external nerve centers as well. The health care chief executive can thus talk to people running health care systems in other countries and so gain access to an array of information perhaps inaccessible even to his most influential reports.

The result of all this is that a considerable amount of the manager's information turns out to be privileged, especially when we consider how much of it is oral and nonverbal. Accordingly, to function effectively with the people around them, managers have to spend considerable time sharing their information, both with outsiders (in a kind of spokesperson role) and with insiders (in a kind of disseminator role).

I found in my initial study of chief executives that perhaps 40 percent of their time was devoted almost exclusively to the communicating role—just to gaining and sharing information—leaving aside the information processing aspects of all the other roles. In other words, the job of managing is fundamentally one of processing information, notably by talking and, especially, listening. Thus, Figure 4.7 shows the inner core (the person in the job, conceiving and scheduling) connected to the outer rings (the more tangible roles of managing people and action) through what can be called the membrane of information processing all around the job.

What can be called the controlling role describes the managers' efforts not just to gain and share information, but to use it in a directive way inside their units to evoke or provoke general action by the people who report to them. They do this in three broad ways: they develop systems, they design structures, and they impose directives. Each of these seeks to control how other people work, especially with regard to the allocation of resources, and so what actions they are inclined to take.

First, developing systems is the most general of these three, and the closest to conceiving. It uses information to control people's behaviors. Managers often take charge of establishing and even running such systems in their units, including those of planning and performance control (such as budgeting). The head nurse, for example, dispensed with one of the hospital's key control systems and instead developed her own. Robert Simons has noted how chief executives tend to select one such system and make it key to their exercise of control, in a manner he calls "interactive."[7]

Second, managers exercise control through designing the structures of their units. By establishing responsibilities and defining hierarchical authority, they again exercise control rather passively, through the processing of information. People are informed of their duties, which in turn is expected to drive them to carry out the appropriate actions. Thus, a day spent with the head of an international environmental organization involved considerable attention to reorganization.

Third is imposing directives, which is the most direct of the three, closest to the people and action, although still informational in nature. Managers pronounce: they make specific choices and give specific orders, usually in the process of "delegating" particular responsibilities and "authorizing" particular requests. In effect, managers manage by transmitting information to people so that they can act. Thus, a deputy minister in the Canadian government met with a number of his policy analysis people to provide rather specific comments about his wishes on drafts of reports they had submitted to him.

If a full decision-making process can be considered in the three stages of diagnosing, designing, and deciding—in other words, identifying issues, working out possible solutions, and selecting one[8]—then here we are dealing with a restricted view of decision making. *Delegating* means mostly diagnosing ("Would you please handle this problem in this context"), while *authorizing* means mostly deciding ("Okay, you can proceed"). Either way, the richest part of the process, the stage of designing possible solutions, resides with the person being controlled rather than with the manager himself or herself, whose own behavior remains rather passive. Thus, the manager as controller seems less an actor with sleeves rolled up, digging in, than a reviewer who sits back in the office and passes judgment. That is why this role is characterized as informational; I will describe a richer approach to decision making in the section on action roles.

The controlling role is shown in Figure 4.7 propelling down into the manager's own unit, since that is where formal authority is exercised. The single-headed arrows represent the imposed directives, while the pitchfork shape symbolizes both the design of structure and the development of systems. The proximity of the controlling role in Figure 4.7 to the manager's agenda reflects the fact that informational control is the most direct way to operationalize the agenda, for example, by using budgets to impose priorities or delegation to assign responsibilities.

The controlling role is, of course, what people have in mind when they refer to the "administrative" aspect of managerial work. Interestingly, it encompasses almost the entire set of activities described by the classical writers. In the 1930s, for example, Gulick and Urwick popularized the acronym POSD-CORB (planning, organizing, staffing, directing, coordinating, reporting, and budgeting).[9] Planning, organizing, directing, and budgeting are all clearly focused here, while reporting, coordinating, and staffing have important, although not exclusive, controlling aspects (staffing in the sense of deciding). Thus, it must be concluded that the long, popular description of managerial work was not so much wrong as narrow, focusing almost exclusively on one restricted aspect of the job: informational control of the unit through the exercise of formal authority.

Managing Through People

To manage through people, instead of by information, is to move one step closer to action but still to remain removed from it. That is because here the focus of managerial attention becomes affect instead of effect. Other people become the means to get things done, not the manager himself or herself, or even the substance of the manager's thoughts.

After several decades of POSDCORB thinking and Taylorist technique, the Hawthorne experiments of the 1930s demonstrated with dramatic impact that management has to do with more than just the passive informational control of subordinates.[10] People entered the scene, or at least they entered the textbooks, as entities to be "motivated" and later "empowered." Influencing began to replace informing, and commitment began to vie with calculation for the attention for the manager. Indeed, in the 1960s and 1970s especially, the management of people, quite independent of content—of the strategies to be realized, the information to be processed, even the actions to be taken—became a virtual obsession of the literature, whether by the label of "human relation," "Theory Y," or "participative management" (and later "quality of work life," to be replaced by "total quality management").

For a long time, however, these people remained subordinates in more ways than one. "Participation" kept them subordinate, for this was always considered to be granted at the behest of the managers still fully in control (compared with the more constitutional involvement of certain professionals, such as doctors in hospitals, or even of certain European workers who, under "codetermination," gained legal representation on boards of directors). So does the currently popular term *empowerment*, which implies that power is being granted, thanks to the managers. (Hospital directors do not "empower" physicians!) People also remained subordinates because the whole focus was on those inside the unit, not outside it. Not until serious research on managerial work began did it become evident how important to managers were contacts with individuals outside their units (who, for example, go entirely without mention in POSDCORB!). Virtually every single study of how all kinds of managers spent their time has indicated that outsiders, of an enormously wide variety, generally take as much of managers' attention as so-called subordinates. We shall thus describe two people roles here, shown in Figure 4.8, one internal, called leading, and one external, called linking.

The *leading* role has probably received more attention in the literature of management than all the other roles combined. And so we need not dwell on it here. But neither can we ignore it: managers certainly do much more than lead people in their own units, and leading certainly infuses much else of what managers do (as, in fact, do all the roles, as we have already noted about communicating). But their work just as certainly cannot be understood without this dimension.[11] We can describe the role of leading on three levels, as indicated in Figure 4.8.

First, managers lead on the individual level, "one on one," as the expression goes. They encourage and drive the people of

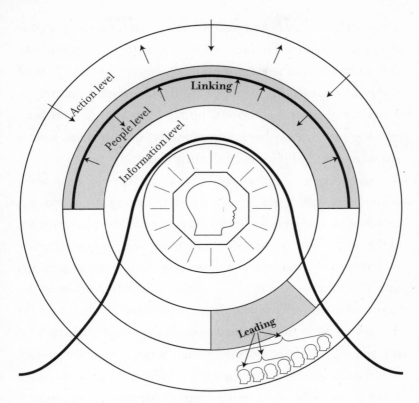

FIGURE 4.8. **The People Roles**

their units—motivate them, inspire them, coach them, nurture
them, push them, mentor them, and so on. All managers,
from the chief executive of the major police force to the front-
country manager in the mountain park, stop to chat with their
people informally during the day to encourage them in
their work. Second, managers lead on the group level, especially
by building and managing teams, an effort that has received
considerable attention in recent years. Again, team meetings,
including team building, figured in many of my observations,
for example, the head of a London film company who brought
film-making teams together for both effective and affective purposes. And third, they lead on the unit level, especially with

regard to the creation and maintenance of culture, another subject of increasing attention in recent years (thanks especially to the Japanese). Managers, for example, engage in many acts of a symbolic nature ("figurehead" duties) to sustain culture, as when the head of the national police force visited its officer training institute (as he does frequently) to imbue the force's norms and attitudes in its graduating class.

All managers seem to spend time on all three levels of leadership, although, again, styles do vary according to context and personality. If the communicating role describes the manager as the nerve center of the unit, then the leading role must characterize him or her as its "energy center," a concept perhaps best captured in Maeterlinck's wonderful description of the "spirit of the hive."[12] Given the right managerial chemistry (in the case of Maeterlinck's queen bee, quite literally!), it may be the manager's mere presence that somehow draws things together. By exuding that mystical substance, the leader unites his or her people, galvanizing them into action to accomplish the unit's mission and adapt it to a changing world.

The excess attention to the role of leading has probably been matched by the inadequate attention to the role of linking. For, as already noted, in their sheer allocation of time, managers have been shown to be external linkers as much as they are internal leaders. In 1964, Leonard Sayles emphasized this in his path-breaking book, and I repeated it in 1973, as did John Kotter in 1982.[13] Yet, still the point seems hardly appreciated. Indeed, now more than ever before, it must be understood, given the great growth of joint ventures and other collaborating and networking relationships between organizations, as well as the gradual reconception of the "captive" employee as an autonomous "agent" who supplies labor.

Figure 4.8 suggests a small model of the linking role. The arrows go in and out to indicate that the manager is both an advocate of its influence outside the unit and, in turn, a recipient of much of the influence exerted on it from the outside. In the middle are two parallel lines to represent the buffering aspect of this role—that managers must regulate the receipt of external influence to protect their units. To use a popular term, they are the gatekeepers of influence. Or, to add a metaphor, the manager acts as a kind of valve between the unit and its environment. Nowhere was this clearer than in my observation of three levels of management in a national park system: a regional director, the head of one mountain park, and the front-country manager of that park. They sit in an immensely complex array of forces—developers who want to enhance their business opportunities, environmentalists who want to preserve the natural habitat, tourists who want to enjoy the beauty, truckers who want to drive through the park unimpeded, politicians who want to avoid negative publicity, and so forth. It is a delicate balancing, or buffering, act indeed!

All managers, as emphasized in other research and my studies cited earlier, appear to spend a great deal of time networking—building vast arrays of contacts and intricate coalitions of supporters beyond their own units, whether within the rest of the organization or outside, in the world at large. To all these contacts, the manager represents the unit externally, promotes its needs, and lobbies for its causes. In response, these people are expected to provide a steady inflow of information to the unit as well as various means of support and specific favors for it. This networking was most evident in the case of the film company managing director, who even in one day exhibited an impressive network of contacts in order to negotiate her complex contracts with various media in different countries.

In turn, people intent on influencing the behavior of an organization or one of its subunits will often exercise pressure directly on its manager, expecting that person to transmit the influence inside, as was most pointedly clear in the work of the park managers. Here, then, the managerial job becomes one of delicate balance, a tricky act of mediation. Those managers who let external influence pass inside too freely—who act like sieves—are likely to drive their people crazy. (Of course, those who act like sponges and absorb all the influence personally are likely to drive themselves crazy!) And those who block out all influence—who act like lead to X-rays—are likely to detach their units from reality (and so dry up the sources of external support). Thus, what influence to pass on how, bearing in mind the quid pro quo that influence exerted out is likely to be mirrored by influence coming back in, becomes another key aspect of managerial style, worthy of greatly increased attention in both the study of the job and the training of its occupants.

Managing Action

If managers manage passively by information and affectively through people, then they also manage actively and instrumentally by their own direct involvement in action. Indeed, this has been a long-established view of managerial work, although the excess attention in this century, first to controlling and then to leading, and more recently to conceiving (of planned strategy), has obscured its importance. Leonard Sayles, however, has long and steadily insisted on this, beginning with his 1964 book and culminating in *The Working Leader* (published in 1993), in which he makes his strongest statement yet, insisting that managers must be the focal points for action in and by their units.[14] Their direct involvement must, in his view, take precedence over the pulling force of leadership and the pushing force of controllership.

I shall refer to this involvement as the *doing* role. But, in using this label—a popular one in the managerial vernacular ("Mary Ann's a doer!")—it is necessary to point out that managers, in fact, hardly ever "do" anything. Many barely even dial their own telephones! As already noted, watch a manager and you will see someone whose work consists almost exclusively of talking and listening, alongside, of course, watching and "feeling." (That, incidentally, is why I show the manager at the core of the model as a head and not a full body!)

What "doing" presumably means, therefore, is getting closer to the action, ultimately being just one step removed from it. Managers as doers manage the carrying out of action directly, instead of indirectly through managing people or by processing information. In effect, a "doer" is really someone who gets it done (or, as the French put it with their expression *faire faire*, to make something get made). And the managerial vernacular is, in fact, full of expressions that reflect just this: "doing deals," "championing change," "fighting fires," "juggling projects." In the terms of decision making introduced earlier, here the manager diagnoses and designs as well as decides: he or she gets deeply and fully involved in the management of particular activities. Thus, in the day I spent with the head of the small retail chain, I saw a steady stream of all sorts of people coming and going, most involved with some aspect of store development or store operations, and there to get specific instructions on how to proceed next. He was not delegating or authorizing, but very clearly managing specific developmental projects step by step.

Just as they communicate all around the circle, so too do managers "do" all around it, as shown in Figure 4.9. They manage projects and solve problems, or put out fires, inside their units, and they "do deals" and negotiate agreements with outsiders. Let us consider each in turn.

Doing inside involves projects and problems. This does not imply that projects are independent of problems or that either are exclusively internal. Rather, it means that much "doing" has to do with changing the unit itself, both proactively and reactively. Managers champion change to exploit opportunities for

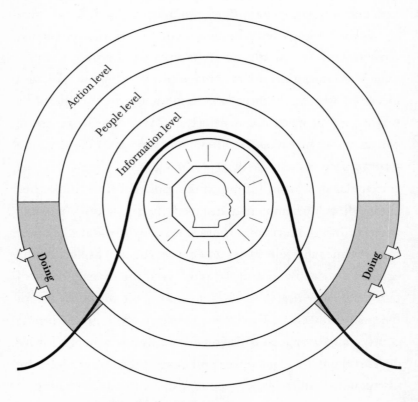

FIGURE 4.9. **The Action Roles**

their units, and they handle its problems and resolve its crises, often with hands-on involvement. Indeed, the president of a large French systems company spent part of his day in a meeting on a very specific customer contract. Asked why he attended, he said it was a leading-edge project that could well change his company. He was being informed, to be sure, but also "doing" (more than controlling): he was an active member of the team.

The difference between deciding in the controlling role and acting in the doing role is the difference, in effect, between sitting in a managerial office and passing judgment on the issues floating by—"Roberta, please handle this," "No, Joe, you can't do that"—and getting out of the office and actively engaging an issue from its initial identification to its final resolution. Here the manager becomes a true designer (or, in the example above, a partner in the design), not of abstract strategies or of generalized structures, but of tangible projects of change. And the evidence, in fact, is that managers at all levels typically juggle many such projects concurrently, perhaps several dozen in the case of chief executives. Hence the popularity of the term *project management*.

Managers "do" inside in two other respects as well. For one thing, they substitute, sometimes doing the routine work of their units in place of other people. (The front-country manager nearly spent part of the day cruising a river for the body of a person who had a few days earlier gone over a waterfall in a boat!) Of course, when managers are replacing absent employees, this may be considered another aspect of handling problems. Second, some managers continue to do regular work after they have become managers. For example, the head nurse saw a patient (just as the pope leads prayers or a dean might teach a class). Done for its own sake, this might be considered separate from managerial work. But such things are often done for very managerial reasons as well. This may be an effective way of keeping in touch with the unit's work and finding out about its problems, in which case it falls under the role of communicating. Or it may be done to demonstrate involvement and commitment with others in the unit, in which case it falls under the role of culture building in the role of leading.

Doing outside takes place in terms of deals and negotiations. Again, these are two sides of the same coin, in that managers negotiate in order to "do deals," and also negotiate once the deal is done. And, again as well, there is no shortage of evidence on the importance of negotiating as well as dealing in managerial work. Most evident in my observations was the managing director of the film company, who was working on one intricate deal after another that day. This was a small company, and making deals was a key part of her job. In larger organizations, senior managers may have all kinds of specialized negotiators supporting them (for example, lawyers for contracts and labor relations specialists for union bargaining). Yet that does not release them from having to spend considerable time on negotiations themselves, especially when critical moments arise. After all, they are the ones who have the authority to commit the resources of their unit, and it is they who are the nerve centers of its information as well as the energy centers of its activity, not to mention the conceptual centers of its strategy. All around the circles, therefore, action connects to people who connect to information, which connects to the frame.

The Well-Rounded Job of Managing

I opened this chapter by noting that the best-known writers of management all seem to emphasize one aspect of the job—in the terms we now have, "doing" for Tom Peters, "conceiving" for Michael Porter, "leading" for Abraham Zaleznik and Warren Bennis, "controlling" for the classical writers, and so on. Now it can be appreciated why all may well be wrong: heeding the advice of any one of them must lead to the lopsided practice of managerial work. Like an unbalanced wheel at resonant frequency, the job risks flying out of control. That is why it is important to show all of the components of managerial work on a single integrated diagram, as in Figure 4.10, to remind people, at a glance, that these components form one job and cannot be separated.

Acceptance of Tom Peters's urgings—" 'Don't think, do' is the phrase I favor"[15]—could lead to the centrifugal explosion

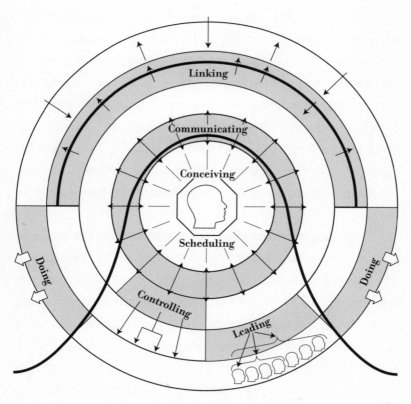

FIGURE 4.10. **Managerial Work Rounded Out**

of the job, as it flies off in all directions, free of a strong frame anchoring it at the core. But acceptance of the spirit of Michael Porter's opposite writings—that what matters most is conception of the frame, especially of strategic positions—could produce a result no better: centripetal implosion, as the job closes in on itself cerebrally, free of the tangible connection to its outer actions. Thinking is heavy and can wear down the incumbent, while acting is light and cannot keep him or her in place. Only together do they provide the balance that seems so characteristic of effective management.

Too much leading produces a job free of content—aimless, frameless, and actionless—while too much linking produces a job detached from its internal roots—public relations instead of public service. The manager who only communicates or only conceives never gets anything done, while the manager who only "does" ends up doing it all alone. And, of course, we all know what happens to managers who believe their job is merely to control (or, these days, to their organizations, as the detached managers escape in their golden parachutes). If I combine the more cerebral roles, we end up with a "think-link-lead-do" model. Or, as someone who read this description remarked, "Well, then, management is a form of thinking and leading by doing."

A bad pun may thus make for good practice: the manager must practice a well-rounded job. Or, if you prefer, anyone who wants to hold this job must swallow the whole pill (which may not, in fact, be a bad metaphor, since the outer coating of doing provides the immediate effect, while each successive layer in this time-release capsule provides deeper, less accessible, but more long-term effects). The different roles are somewhat substitutable, to be sure—for example, pushing employees through controlling by systems instead of pulling them through leading by culture. But, more important, they are complementary.

In fact, while we may be able to separate the components of this job conceptually, I maintain that they cannot be separated behaviorally. In other words, it may be useful, even necessary, to delineate the parts for purposes of design, selection, training, and support. But this job cannot be practiced as a set of independent parts. As noted, the core is a kind of magnet that holds the rest together, while the communication ring acts as a membrane that allows the flow of information between inner thinking and outer behaviors, which themselves tie people to action.

Indeed, the most interesting aspects of this job may well fall on the edges, between the component parts. For example, Andrew Grove, president of Intel, likes to describe what he does as "nudging," a perfect blend of controlling, leading, and doing.[16] This can mean pushing people, tangibly but not aggressively, as might happen with pure doing, and not coldly, as with pure controlling, but with a sense of leading. There are similar edges between the inside and the outside, thinking and behaving, and communicating and controlling, as we shall see.

Managers who try to "do" outside without "doing" inside inevitably get themselves into trouble. Just consider all those chief executives who "did the deal," acquired the company or whatever, and then dropped it into the laps of others for execution. Likewise, it makes no more sense to conceive and then fail to lead and do (as has been the tendency in so-called strategic planning, where controlling has often been considered sufficient for "implementation") than it makes sense to do or to lead without thinking through the frame in which to embed these activities. A single managerial job may be carried out by a small team, but only if its members are so tightly knitted together—especially by that ring of communication—that they act as a single entity.

Earlier I mentioned how leading, while identifiable as some activities, tends to infuse almost all managerial work. But the same is true of communicating, as noted, and of conceiving (which cannot be saved for some ethereal mountain retreat), and of scheduling. Likewise, just as the core role of conceiving cannot be separated from the surface role of doing, so too can the inside roles of controlling, leading, and doing not be separated from the outside ones of linking and doing. In fact, at the limit, they blend into one another. Leading and controlling have been described here as inside roles, linking as an outside role. But a manager with considerable influence over an outsider—say, a captive supplier—can exercise leadership as well as direct control, while one whose own employees begin to act as free agents may have to relate to them as a linker more than a leader (as the chief of any clinical service in a hospital can tell you).

MANAGING IN STYLE

To describe the various components that make up the job of managing as integrated, infused, and well rounded is not to imply that all managers do all of them with equal emphasis. Managerial work does vary, according to the needs of a particular job and the approach of its particular incumbent. Different managers end up emphasizing different things in different ways. Paradoxically, however, this may best be understood through a systematic framework of what they all do in common. Accordingly, I use the model in Figure 4.10 to consider briefly some questions of managerial style (including the effect of context). Style is considered to have an impact on managerial work in three ways: which roles a particular manager favors, how he or she performs these roles, and what kind of relationship exists among these roles.

First, and most obviously, managers in different contexts have to emphasize different roles. For example, as noted above, the managers of autonomous professionals, as in hospitals or universities, tend to favor linking over leading (let alone controlling), since professionals tend to come to their work naturally empowered. In other words, they need little encouragement or supervision, although they do require considerable external support. However, when experts must work in teams, as in some research laboratories or in professional sports, leadership becomes rather critical, particularly at the group level. Entrepreneurs, in contrast, who run their own business, tend to emphasize doing (alongside conceiving), as they involve themselves deeply in specific issues. Interestingly, the same thing tends to be true of first-line managers, even in conventional big businesses, for example, foremen in factories who must resolve steady streams of operating problems. Senior executives of large diversified firms, on the other hand, give greater attention to controlling, particularly through their systems of performance control and their decisions to authorize major capital expenditures.

Of course, regardless of the context, individual managers are often personally predisposed to favor particular roles or aspects of the job. Considering this from the inside out, we can, for example, distinguish a conceptual style of management, which focuses on the development of the frame, an administrative style, which concerns itself primarily with controlling, an interpersonal style, which favors leading on the inside or linking on the outside, and an action style, which is concerned mainly with tangible doing. And as we move out in this order, the overall style of managing can be described as less opaque, more visible.

Even in how they respond to requests, managers can exhibit subtle yet significant variations in style. Asked for advice by an employee, for example, a manager may respond as a communicator ("Payroll has some data on this"), a controller ("Don't do it"), or a leader ("How do *you* feel about it?"). Of course, the doer may say, "Just leave it with me"! All kinds of opportunities arise in managing to substitute, combine, and give nuance to the different roles.

Second, regardless of which roles or aspects of the job a particular manager emphasizes, his or her personal style is manifested particularly in how these are performed. We have already seen this, for example, in different approaches to linking at the extremes (the sieve, the lead, the sponge), and the different approaches to conceiving the frame (passive, driven, opportunistic, and determined styles). Similarly, we saw different predispositions to leading (favoring the individual, group, or unit level). Other obvious variations in style can be delineated according to how each of the remaining components of the model might be carried out.

A final aspect of managerial style has to do with the interrelationships among the various components of managerial work. For example, an important distinction can be made between deductive and inductive approaches to managerial work. The former proceeds from the core out, as the conceived frame is implemented through scheduling that uses information to drive people to get action done. We can call this a cerebral style of managing—highly deliberate—noting that it has been popular from the early POSDCORB writers to the current proponents of strategic planning and bottom-line thinking. But there is an alternate, emergent view of the management process as well, which proceeds inductively, from the outer surface to the inner core. We might label it an *insightful* style. As Karl Weick puts it, managers act in order to think. They try things to gain experience, retain what works, and then, by interpreting the results, gradually evolve their frames.[17]

Of course, the preferred approach may well vary with context as well as personal inclination. When a situation is well understood, the cerebral style seems logical, while, under conditions of ambiguity, the insightful style may make more sense. Part of our problem in recent years, in educating managers as well as in their own practice, has been a predisposition toward the cerebral style in situations of increasing ambiguity that require inductive insight. Even "doing" is one step removed from the action. How then is a manager who relies on controlling—three steps removed—to come to serious grips with any real problem in an organization?

Clearly, there is an infinity of possible contexts within which management can be practiced. But just as clearly, perhaps, a model such as the one presented here can help to order them and so come to grips with the difficult requirements of designing managerial jobs, selecting the right people to fill them, and training people accordingly. It is in these areas that we are in greatest need of rich theory, and this kind of description may be one step toward the development of it. In particular, the model may help in the hitherto intractable problem of delineating a useful list of competences that underlie the effective performance of managerial work.

To give some idea of the flesh that might be put on the skeleton of this model, let me describe briefly a few of the managers I have observed. This gives a sense of how context and personal predisposition interact with the various components of the job to define reality:

○ Ann was director of nursing services for a hospital near London; Peter was the manager of a district in the National Health Service of England. The difference in their work was marked. Ann can be described as "managing down," Peter as "managing up."

Ann was intimately connected to the delivery of health care on a daily basis, knowledgeable about every imaginable detail of her hospital's operations. It is people like her who keep the system running. She conceived and she managed outside, to be sure, and her relationships with the autonomous doctors are best described as linking. But mostly she seemed to maintain the internal operations by a certain amount of "doing" combined with a good deal of leading as well as some controlling, all infused with that "spirit of the hive."

Peter, in contrast, managed largely up, being more concerned with the administrative intricacies of the hierarchy under which he sat than the district over which he ostensibly had authority. District management is necessarily detached from the daily delivery of health care, and so managing inside seemed to be restricted largely to formalized controlling, particularly with regard to systems of resource allocation. I found less "doing" here and not a great deal of leading. Outside linking seemed to be the focus, to maintain good ties with the upper echelons of the hierarchy. As a result, buffering came naturally to this job. If Ann's style could be described as involved and insightful, then Peter's was cerebral and deductive.

○ Carol ran a film company in London, producing quality films mostly for television. She could afford to manage neither exclusively up nor exclusively down, although she had to use a different style for each. Trying to capture both the what and the how, I described her work as "hard dealing and soft leading." Carol seemed to be a doer above all, specifically on the outside, using a vast array of contracts to "do the deals" of film contracts. But once the deal was done, a team had to be assembled, and its work, by competent professionals, had to be not so much controlled as monitored, to ensure that it remained responsive to the client's needs. Thus, Carol's outside work was focused and intense—"doing" in detail and with a vengeance—while her inside work seemed to be gentler and somewhat more indirect—leading rather than doing. And her overall orientation had to be rather opportunistic, for this is a highly fashionable business. But there was a frame here too, not crystal clear perhaps, but sharp enough to help select the projects and maintain a sense of unity in the company. Carol's own style would appear to be more insightful than cerebral and more inductive than deductive.

○ Norman ran a large Canadian national police force, where he had spent his career. Linking was important: this is a highly sensitive job in which informing and buffering are critical. And so, in his words, he arranged for "no surprises," especially for the politicians. But above all, he protected and strengthened the culture of the force, which is legendary. This served as his frame, in a way, on which he laid his own liberal stamp. Controlling is obviously not absent from the job of police commissioner, but this one tilted especially toward the collective level of leading.

○ Fabienne was the head nurse of a surgical ward in a Canadian hospital. The contrast between her job and Norman's is marked, except in its essence: the importance placed on the leading role. There was much less formality in her job and much less movement: she managed on her feet mostly in the nursing station, around which all revolved. If Norman was "on top" of things hierarchically and colloquially, then Fabienne was in the middle of them. This allowed her to solve problems quickly and informally. Linking was relatively less important here; indeed, Fabienne was "not crazy about the whole PR thing," as she put it. Instead, she could be described as "doing" to lead (in contrast to Norman's and Carol's linking to lead), blending her different activities into a central frame that she described as a "caring" style of management: she believed in serving her nurses much as she once served her patients. Management as "blended care" would seem to be most effective, especially in contrast to the all-too-common style of management as interventionist cure![18]

These are but a few of the managers in context, but their brief profiles may give a sense of the richness with which the work and the style of managing can be described. We have a long way to go in understanding this most important of jobs. I can only hope that closing this initial circle may be one helpful way to proceed.

o   o   o

Henry Mintzberg is professor of management studies at McGill University in Montreal. He specializes in managerial work, strategy formation, and forms of organizing.

Chapter Five

The New Managerial Work

Rosabeth Moss Kanter

Managerial work is undergoing such enormous and rapid change that many managers are reinventing their profession as they go. With little precedent to guide them, they are watching hierarchy fade away and the clear distinctions of title, task, department, even corporation, blur. Faced with extraordinary levels of complexity and interdependency, they watch traditional sources of power erode and the old motivational tools lose their magic.

The cause stems from the new environment facing organizations. Competitive pressures are forcing corporations to adopt new flexible strategies and structures. Many of these are familiar: acquisitions and divestitures aimed at more focused combinations of business activities, reductions in management staff and levels of hierarchy, increased use of performance-based rewards. Other strategies are less common but have an even more profound effect. In a growing number of companies, for example, horizontal ties between peers are replacing vertical ties as channels of activity and communication. Companies are asking corporate staffs and functional departments to play a more strategic role with greater cross-departmental collaboration. Some organizations are turning themselves nearly inside out—buying formerly internal services from outside suppliers, forming strategic alliances and supplier-customer partnerships that bring external relationships inside where they can influence company policy and practice. These emerging practices involve the application of entrepreneurial creativity and flexibility to established businesses, and they help organizations become change-adept.

Such practices come highly recommended by the experts who urge organizations to become leaner, less bureaucratic, more entrepreneurial. But so far, theorists have given scant attention to the dramatically altered realities of managerial work in these transforming corporations. We don't even have good words to describe the new relationships. "Superiors" and "subordinates" hardly seem accurate, and even "bosses" and "their people" imply more control and ownership than managers today actually possess. "Associates" is the term of preference in many companies instead of "employees," but then, what do we call their managers? On top of it all, career paths are no longer straightforward and predictable but have become idiosyncratic and confusing.

Some managers experience the new managerial work as a loss of power because much of their authority used to come from hierarchical position. Now that everything seems negotiable by everyone, they are confused about how to mobilize and motivate staff. For other managers, the shift in roles and tasks offers greater personal power. The following case histories illustrate the responses of three managers in three different industries to the opportunities and dilemmas of structural change:

○ Hank was vice president and chief engineer for a leading heavy equipment manufacturer that was moving aggressively against foreign competition. One of the company's top priorities was to increase the speed, quality, and cost-effectiveness of product development. So Hank worked with consultants to improve collaboration between manufacturing and other functions and to create closer alliances between the company and its outside suppliers. Gradually, a highly segmented operation became an integrated process involving project teams drawn from component divisions, functional departments, and external suppliers. But along the way, there were several unusual side effects. Different areas of responsibility overlapped. Some technical and manufacturing people were co-located. Liaisons from functional areas joined the larger development teams. Most unusual of all, project teams had a lot of direct contact with higher levels of the company.

Many of the managers reporting to Hank felt these changes as a loss of power. They didn't always know what their people were doing, but they still believed they ought to know. They no longer had sole input into performance appraisals; other people from other functions had a voice as well, and some of them knew more about employees' project performance. New career paths made it less important to please direct superiors in order to move up the functional line.

Moreover, employees often bypassed Hank's managers and interacted directly with decision makers inside and outside the company. Some of these so-called subordinates had contact with division executives and senior corporate staff, and sometimes they sat in on high-level strategy meetings to which their managers were not invited.

At first Hank thought his managers' resistance to the new process was just the normal noise associated with any change.

Then he began to realize that something more profound was going on. The reorganization was challenging traditional notions about the role and power of managers and shaking traditional hierarchy to its roots. And no one could see what was taking its place.

o When George became head of a major corporate department in a large bank holding company, he thought he had arrived. His title and rank were unmistakable, and his department was responsible for determining product-line policy for hundreds of bank branches and the virtual clerks—in George's eyes—who managed them. George staffed his department with M.B.A.s and promised them rapid promotion.

Then the sand seemed to shift beneath him. Losing market position for the first time in recent memory, the bank decided to emphasize direct customer service at the branches. The people George considered clerks began to depart from George's standard policies and to tailor their services to local market conditions. In many cases, they actually demanded services and responses from George's staff, and the results of their requests began to figure in performance reviews of George's department. George's people were spending more and more time in the field with branch managers, and the corporate personnel department was even trying to assign some of George's M.B.A.s to branch and regional posts

To complicate matters, the bank's strategy included a growing role for technology. George felt that because he had no direct control over the information systems department, he should not be held fully accountable for every facet of product design and implementation. But fully accountable he was. He had to deploy people to learn the new technology and figure out how to work with it. Furthermore, the bank was asking product departments like George's to find ways to link existing products or develop new ones that crossed traditional categories. So George's people were often away on cross-departmental teams just when he wanted them for some internal assignment.

Instead of presiding over a tidy empire the way his predecessor had, George encountered what looked to him like chaos. The bank said senior executives should be "leaders, not managers," but George didn't know what that meant, especially since he seemed to have lost control over his subordinates' assignments, activities, rewards, and careers. He resented his perceived loss of status.

The CEO tried to show him that good results achieved the new way would bring great monetary rewards, thanks to a performance-based bonus program that was gradually replacing more modest yearly raises. But the pressures on George were also greater, unlike anything he'd ever experienced.

○ For Sally, purchasing manager at an innovative computer company, a new organizational strategy was a gain rather than a loss, although it changed her relationship with the people reporting to her. Less than ten years out of college, she was hired as an analyst—a semiprofessional, semiclerical job—then promoted to a purchasing manager's job in a sleepy staff department. She didn't expect to go much further in what was then a well-established hierarchy. But after a shocking downturn, top management encouraged employees to rethink traditional ways of doing things. Sally's boss, the head of purchasing, suggested that "partnerships" with key suppliers might improve quality, speed innovation, and reduce costs.

Soon Sally's backwater was at the center of policymaking, and Sally began to help shape strategy. She organized meetings between her company's senior executives and supplier CEOs. She sent her staff to contribute supplier intelligence at company seminars on technical innovation, and she spent more of her own time with product designers and manufacturing planners. She led senior executives on a tour of supplier facilities, traveling with them in the corporate jet.

Because some suppliers were also important customers, Sally's staff began meeting frequently with marketing managers to share information and address joint problems. Sally and her group were now also acting as internal advocates for major suppliers. Furthermore, many of these external companies now contributed performance appraisals of Sally and her team, and their opinions weighed almost as heavily as those of her superiors.

As a result of the company's new direction, Sally felt more personal power and influence, and her ties to peers in other areas and to top management were stronger. But she no longer felt like a manager directing subordinates. Her staff had become a pool of resources deployed by many others besides Sally. She was exhilarated by her personal opportunities but not quite sure the people she managed should have the same freedom to choose their own assignments. After all, wasn't that a manager's prerogative?

Hank's, George's, and Sally's very different stories say much about the changing nature of managerial work. However hard it is for managers at the very top to remake strategy and structure, they themselves will probably retain their identity, status, and control. For the managers below them, structural change is often much harder. As work units become more participative and team oriented, and as professionals and knowledge workers become more prominent, the distinction between manager and nonmanager begins to erode.

The New Managerial Quandaries

○ At American Express, the CEO instituted a program called "One Enterprise" to encourage collaboration between different lines of business. One Enterprise has led to a range of projects where peers from different divisions work together on such synergistic ventures as cross-marketing, joint purchasing, and cooperative product and market innovation. Employees' rewards are tied to their One Enterprise efforts. Executives set goals and can earn bonuses for their contributions to results in other divisions.

But how do department managers control their people when they're working on cross-departmental teams? And who determines the size of the rewards when the interests of more than one area are involved?

○ At Security Pacific National Bank, internal departments became forces in the external marketplace. For example, the bank developed a joint venture with local auto dealers to sell fast financing for car purchases, involving the information technology department in work with outside partners. The department is now a profit center selling its services inside and outside the bank.

But what is the role of bank managers accountable for the success of such entrepreneurial ventures? And how do they shift their orientation from the role of boss in a chain of command to the role of the customer?

○ At Digital Equipment Corporation, emphasis on supplier partnerships to improve quality and innovation multiplied the need for cross-functional as well as cross-company collaboration. Key suppliers were included on product planning teams with engineering, manufacturing, and purchasing staff. Digital used its human resource staff to train and do performance appraisals of its suppliers, as if they were part of the company. In cases where suppliers were also customers, purchasing and marketing departments had to start exchanging information and working collaboratively.

But how do managers learn enough about other functions to be credible, let alone influential, members of such teams? How do they maintain adequate communication externally while staying on top of what their own departments are doing? And how do they handle the extra work of responding to projects initiated by other areas?

○ At Banc One, a growing reliance on project teams spanning more than seventy affiliated banks led the CEO to propose eliminating officer titles because of the lack of correlation between status as measured by title and status within the collaborative team.

But then what do rank and hierarchy mean anymore, especially for people whose careers consist of a sequence of projects rather than a sequence of promotions? What does *career* mean? Does it have a shape? Is there a ladder?

○ At Alcan, the search for new uses and applications for its core product, aluminum, led to an experiment with a new venture process. Managers and professionals from line divisions formed screening teams to consider and refine new venture proposals coming from inside and outside the company. A venture manager, chosen from the screening team, took charge of concepts that pass muster, drawing on Alcan's worldwide resources to build the new business. In one case of global synergy, Alcan created a new product for the Japanese market using Swedish American technology and Canadian manufacturing capacity.

But why should senior managers release staff to serve on screening and project teams for new businesses when their own businesses are making do with fewer and fewer people? How do functionally oriented managers learn enough about worldwide developments to know when they might have something of value to offer someplace else? And how do the managers of these new ventures ever go back to the conventional line organization as middle managers once their venture has been folded into an established division?

 o At IBM, an emphasis on customer partnerships to rebuild market share led to practices that reversed tradition. IBM formed joint development teams with customers, where engineers from both companies share proprietary data. The company moved from merely selling equipment to actually managing a customer's management information system. Eastman Kodak handed its U.S. data center operations to IBM to consolidate and manage, which meant lower fixed costs for Kodak and greater ability to focus on its core businesses rather than on ancillary services. Some three hundred former Kodak people switched to filling Kodak's needs as IBM employees, while committees of IBM and Kodak managers oversaw the partnership.

But who exactly do the people in such arrangements work for? Who is in charge? And how do traditional notions of managerial authority square with such a complicated set of relationships?

To understand what managers must do to achieve results in the change-adept corporation, we need to look at the changing picture of how such companies operate. The picture has five elements:

1. There are a greater number and variety of channels for taking action and exerting influence.

2. Relationships of influence are shifting from the vertical to the horizontal, from chain of command to peer networks.

3. The distinction between managers and those managed is diminishing, especially in terms of information, control over assignments, and access to external relationships.

4. External relationships are increasingly important as sources of internal power and influence, even of career development.

5. As a result of the first four changes, career development has become less intelligible but also less circumscribed. There are fewer assured routes to success, which produces anxiety. At the same time, career paths are more open to innovation, which produces opportunity.

To help companies implement their competitive organizational strategies, managers must learn new ways to manage, confronting changes in their own bases of power and recognizing the need for new ways to motivate people.

THE BASIS OF POWER

The changes I've described can be scary for people like George and the managers reporting to Hank, who were trained to know their place, to follow orders, to let the company take care of their careers, to do things by the book. Now the book is gone. In the new corporation, managers have only themselves to count on for success. They must learn to operate without the crutch of hierarchy. Position, title, and authority are no longer adequate tools, not in a world where subordinates are encouraged to think for themselves and where managers have to work synergistically with other departments and even other companies. Success depends increasingly on tapping into sources of good ideas, on figuring out whose collaboration is needed to act on those ideas, on working with both to produce results. In short, the new managerial work implies very different ways of obtaining and using power.

The emerging, more entrepreneurial corporation is not only leaner and flatter; it also has many more channels for action. Cross-functional projects, business-unit joint ventures, labor-management forums, innovation funds that spawn activities outside mainstream budgets and reporting lines, strategic partnerships with suppliers or customers—these are all overlays on the traditional organization chart, strategic pathways that ignore the chain of command.

Their existence has several important implications. For one thing, they create more potential centers of power. As the ways to combine resources increase, the ability to command diminishes. Alternative paths of communication, resource access, and execution erode the authority of those in the nominal chain of command. In other words, the opportunity for greater speed and flexibility undermines hierarchy. As more and more strategic action takes place in these channels, the jobs that focus inward on particular departments decline in power.

As a result, the ability of managers to get things done depends more on the number of networks in which they're centrally involved than on their height in a hierarchy. Of course, power in any organization always has a network component, but rank and formal structure used to be more limiting. For example, access to information and the ability to get informal backing were often confined to the few officially sanctioned contact points between departments or between the company and its vendors or customers. Today these official barriers are disappearing, while so-called informal networks are growing in importance.

In the change-adept organization, managers add value by deal making, by brokering at interfaces, rather than by presiding over their individual empires. It was traditionally the job of the top executives or specialists to scan the business environment for new ideas, opportunities, and resources. This kind of environmental scanning is now an important part of a manager's job at every level and in every function. And the environment to be scanned includes various company divisions, many potential outside partners, and large parts of the world. At the same time, people are encouraged to think about what they know that might have value elsewhere. An engineer designing windshield wipers, for example, might discover properties of rubber adhesion to glass that could be useful in other manufacturing areas.

Every manager must think cross-functionally because every department has to play a strategic role, understanding and contributing to other facets of the business. In Hank's company, the technical managers and staff working on design engineering used to concentrate only on their own areas of expertise. Under the new system, they have to keep in mind what manufacturing does and how it does it. They need to visit plants and build relationships so they can ask informed questions.

One multinational corporation, eager to extend the uses of its core product, put its R&D staff and laboratory personnel in direct contact with marketing experts to discuss lines of research. Similarly, the superior economic track record of Raytheon's New Products Center—dozens of new products and patents yielding profits many times their development costs—derived from the connections it builds between its inventors and the engineering and marketing staffs on the business units it serves.

This strategic and collaborative role is particularly important for the managers and professionals on corporate staffs. They need to serve as integrators and facilitators, not as watchdogs and interventionists. They need to sell their services, justify themselves to the business units they serve, literally compete with outside suppliers. Some large companies have put overhead charges for corporate staff services on a pay-as-you-use basis. Formerly, these charges were either assigned uniformly to users and nonusers alike, or the services were mandatory. Product managers sometimes had to work through as many as eight layers of management and corporate staff to get business plans approved. Now these staffs must prove to the satisfaction of their internal customers that their services add value.

By contrast, some banks still have corporate training departments that do very little except get in the way. They do no actual training, for example, yet they still exercise veto power over urgent divisional training decisions and consultant contracts. Such roadblock departments are the first targeted for extinction, as traditional banking evolves into a highly competitive information-technology-rich financial services industry requiring business units to act fast and find whatever resources and services they need quickly inside or outside the company.

As managers and professionals spend more time working across boundaries with peers and partners over whom they have no direct control, their negotiating skills become essential assets. Alliances and partnerships transform impersonal, arm's-length contracts into relationships involving joint planning and joint decision making. Internal competitors and adversaries become allies on whom managers depend for their own success. At the same time, more managers at more levels are active in the kind of external diplomacy that only the CEO or selected staffs used to conduct.

In the collaborative forums that result, managers are more personally exposed. It is trust that makes partnerships work. Since collaborative ventures often bring together groups with different methods, cultures, symbols, even languages, good deal making depends on empathy—the ability to step into other people's shoes and appreciate their goals. This applies not only to intricate global joint ventures but also to the efforts of engineering and manufacturing to work together more effectively. Effective communication in a cooperative effort rests on more than a simple exchange of information; people must be adept at anticipating the responses of other groups. "Before I get too excited about our department's design ideas," an engineering manager told me, "I'm learning to ask myself, 'What's the marketing position on this? What will manufacturing say?' That sometimes forces me to make changes before I even talk to them."

An increase in the number of channels for strategic contact within the change-adept organization means more opportunities for people with ideas or information to trigger action: salespeople encouraging account managers to build strategic partnerships with customers, for example, or technicians searching for ways to tap new-venture funds to develop software. Moreover, top executives who have to spend more time on cross-boundary relationships are forced to delegate more responsibility to lower-level managers. Delegation is one more blow to hierarchy, of course, since subordinates with greater responsibility are bolder about speaking up, challenging authority, and charting their own course.

For example, it is common for new-venture teams to complain publicly about corporate support departments and to reject their use in favor of external service providers, often to the consternation of more orthodox superiors. A more startling example occurred in a health care company where members of a task force charged with finding synergies among three lines of business shocked corporate executives by criticizing upper management behavior in their report. Service on the task force had created collective awareness of a shared problem and had given people the courage to confront it.

The search for internal synergies, the development of strategic alliances, and the push for new ventures all emphasize the political side of a leader's work. Executives must be able to juggle a set of constituencies rather than control a set of subordinates. They have to bargain, negotiate, and sell instead of making unilateral decisions and issuing commands. The leader's task, as Chester Barnard recognized long ago, is to develop a network of cooperative relationships among all the people, groups, and organizations that have something to contribute to an economic enterprise. More entrepreneurial change-oriented strategies magnify the complexity of this task. After leading Teknowledge, a producer of expert systems software, through development alliances with six corporations including General Motors and Procter & Gamble, company chairman Lee Hecht, said he felt like the mayor of a small city. "I have a constituency that won't quit. It takes a hell of a lot of balancing." The kind of power achieved through a network of stakeholders is very different from the kind of power managers wield in a traditional bureaucracy. The new way gets more done, but it also takes more time. And it creates an illusion about freedom and security.

The absence of day-to-day constraints, the admonition to assume responsibility, the pretense of equality, the elimination of visible status markers, the prevalence of candid dialogues across hierarchical levels—these can give employees a false sense that all hierarchy is a thing of the past. Yet at the same time, employees still count on hierarchy to shield them when things go wrong. This combination would create the perfect marriage of freedom and support—freedom when people want to take risks, support when the risks don't work out.

In reality, less benevolent combinations are also possible, combinations not of freedom and support but of insecurity and loss of control. There is often a pretense in change-oriented companies that status differences have nothing to do with power, that the deference paid to top executives derives from their superior qualifications rather than from the power they have over the fates of others. But the people at the top of the organization chart still wield power—and sometimes in ways that managers below them experience as arbitrary. Unprecedented individual freedom also applies to top managers, who are now free to make previously unimaginable deals, order unimaginable cuts, or launch unimaginable takeovers. The reorganizations that companies undertake in their search for new synergies can uncover the potential unpredictability and capriciousness of corporate careers. A man whose company was undergoing drastic restructuring told me, "For all of my ownership share and strategic centrality and voice in decisions, I can still be faced with a shift in direction not of my own making. I can still be reorganized into a corner. I can still be relocated into oblivion. I can still be reviewed out of my special project budget."

These realities of power, change, and job security are important because they affect the way people view their leaders. When the illusion of simultaneous freedom and protection fades, the result can be a loss of motivation.

SOURCES OF MOTIVATION

One of the essential, unchanging tasks of leaders is to motivate and guide performance. But motivational tools are changing fast. More and more businesses are doing away with the old bureaucratic incentives and using entrepreneurial opportunity to attract the best talent. Managers must exercise more leadership even as they watch their bureaucratic power slip away. Leadership, in short, is more difficult yet more critical than ever before.

Because of the unpredictability of even the most benign restructuring, managers are less able to guarantee a particular job—or any job at all—no matter what a subordinate's performance level. The reduction in hierarchical levels curtails a manager's ability to promise promotion. New compensation systems that make bonuses and raises dependent on objective performance measures and on team appraisals deprive managers of their role as the sole arbiter of higher pay. Cross-functional and cross-company teams can rob managers of their right to direct or even understand the work their so-called subordinates do. In any case, the shift from routine work, which was amenable to oversight, to "knowledge" work, which often is not, erodes a manager's claim to superior expertise. And partnerships and ventures that put lower-level people in direct contact with each other across departmental and company boundaries cut heavily into the managerial monopoly on information. At a consumer packaged-goods manufacturer that replaced several levels of hierarchy with teams, plant team members in direct contact with the sales force often had data on product-ordering trends before the higher-level brand managers who set product policy.

As if the loss of carrots and sticks was not enough, many managers can no longer even give their people clear job standards and easily mastered procedural rules. Change-adept corporations seek problem-solving, initiative-taking employees who will go the unexpected extra mile for the customer. To complicate the situation further still, the complexities of work in the new organization—projects and relationships clamoring for attention in every direction—exacerbate the feeling of overload.

With the old motivational tool kit depleted, leaders need new and more effective incentives to encourage high performance and build commitment. There are five new tools:

○ *Mission.* Helping people believe in the importance of their work is essential, especially when other forms of certainty and security have disappeared. Good leaders can inspire others with the power and excitement of their vision and give people a sense of purpose and pride in their work. Pride is often a better source of motivation than the traditional corporate career ladder and the promotion-based reward system. Technical professionals, for example, are often motivated most effectively by the desire to see their work contribute to an excellent final product.

○ *Agenda control.* As career paths lose their certainty and companies' futures grow less predictable, people can at least be in charge of their own professional lives. More and more professionals are passing up jobs with glamour and prestige in favor of jobs that give them greater control over their own activities and direction. Leaders give their subordinates this opportunity when they give them release time to work on pet projects, when they emphasize results instead of procedures, and when they delegate work and the decisions about how to do it. Choice of their next project is a potent reward for people who perform well.

○ *Share of value creation.* Entrepreneurial incentives that give teams a piece of the action are highly appropriate in collaborative companies. Because extra rewards are based only on measurable results, this approach also conserves resources. Innovative companies are experimenting with incentives like phantom stock for development of new ventures and other strategic achievements, equity participation in project returns, and bonuses pegged to key performance targets. Given the cross-functional nature of many projects today, rewards of this kind must sometimes be systemwide, but individual managers can also ask for a bonus pool for their own areas, contingent, of course, on meeting performance goals. And everyone can share the kinds of rewards that are abundant and free—awards and recognition.

○ *Learning.* The chance to learn new skills or apply them in new arenas is an important motivator in a turbulent environment because it's oriented toward securing the future. "The learning organization" has become a business buzzword as companies seek to learn more systematically from their experience and to encourage continuous learning for their people. In the world of high technology, where people understand uncertainty, the attractiveness of any company often lies in its capacity to provide learning and experience. By this calculus, access to training, mentors, and challenging projects is more important than pay or benefits. Some prominent companies—General Electric, for example—have always been able to attract top talent, even when they could not promise upward mobility, because people see them as a training ground, a good place to learn, and a valuable addition to a résumé.

○ *Reputation.* Reputation is a key resource in professional careers, and the chance to enhance it can be an outstanding motivator. The professional's reliance on reputation stands in marked contrast to the bureaucrat's anonymity. Professionals have to make a name for themselves, while traditional corporate managers and employees stayed behind the scenes. Indeed, the accumulation of reputational capital provides not only an immediate ego boost but also the kind of publicity that can bring other rewards, even other job offers. Managers can enhance reputation—and improve motivation—by creating stars, by providing abundant public recognition and visible awards, by crediting the authors of innovation, by publicizing people outside their own departments, and by plugging people into organizational and professional networks.

The change-adept organization is predicated on a logic of flexible work assignments, not of fixed job responsibilities. To promote innovation and responsiveness, two of today's competitive imperatives, managers need to see this new organization as a cluster of activity sets, not as a rigid structure. The work of leadership in this new corporation will be to organize both sequential and synchronous projects of varying length and breadth, through which varying combinations of people will move, depending on the tasks, challenges, and opportunities facing the area and its partners at any given moment.

Leaders need to carve out projects with tangible accomplishments, milestones, and completion dates and then delegate responsibility for these projects to the other people who flesh them out. Clearly delimited projects can counter overload by focusing effort and can provide short-term motivation when the fate of the long-term mission is uncertain. Project responsibility leads to ownership of the results and sometimes substitutes for other forms of reward. In companies where product development teams define and run their own projects, members commonly say that the greatest compensation they get is seeing the advertisements for the products. "Hey, that's mine! I did that!" one engineer told me he trumpeted to his family the first time he saw a commercial for his group's innovation.

This sense of ownership, along with a definite time frame, can spur higher levels of effort. Whenever people are engaged in creative or problem-solving projects that will have tangible results by deadline dates, they tend to come in at all hours, to think about the project in their spare time, to invest in it vast sums of physical and emotional energy. Knowing that the project will end and that completion will be an occasion for reward and recognition makes it possible to work much harder.

Leaders in the new organization do not lack motivational tools, but the tools are different from those of traditional corporate bureaucrats. The new rewards are based not on status but on contribution, and they consist not of regular promotion and automatic pay raises but of excitement about mission and a share of the glory and the gains of success. The new security is not employment security (a guaranteed job no matter what) but employability security—increased value in the internal and external labor markets. Commitment to the organization still matters, but today managers build commitment by offering project opportunities. The new loyalty is not to the boss or to the company but to projects that actualize a mission and offer challenge, growth, and credit for results.

The old bases of managerial authority are eroding, and new tools of leadership are taking their place. Managers whose power derived from hierarchy and who were accustomed to a limited area of personal control are learning to shift their perspectives and widen their horizons. The new managerial work consists of looking outside a defined area of responsibility to sense opportunities and of forming project teams drawn from any relevant sphere to address them. It involves communication and collaboration across functions, across divisions, and across companies whose activities and resources overlap. Thus, rank, title, or official charter will be less important factors in success at the new managerial work than having the knowledge, skills, and sensitivity to mobilize people and motivate them to do their best.

o   o   o

Rosabeth Moss Kanter is professor of business administration at Harvard Business School. She is former editor of the *Harvard Business Review* and a consultant to major corporations around the world.

Chapter Six

The Postcapitalist
Executive

An Interview with
Peter F. Drucker

T George Harris

For half a century, Peter F. Drucker has been teacher and adviser to senior managers in business, human service organizations, and government. Sometimes called the godfather of modern management, he combines an acute understanding of socioeconomic forces with practical insights into how leaders can turn turbulence into opportunity. With a rare gift for synthesis, Drucker nourishes his insatiable mind on a full range of intellectual disciplines, from Japanese art to network theory in higher mathematics. Yet he learns most from in-depth conversations with clients and students: a global network of men and women who draw their ideas from action and act on ideas.

Since 1946, when his book, *Concept of the Corporation*, redefined employees as a resource rather than a cost, Drucker's works have become an ever-growing resource for leaders in every major culture, particularly among Japan's top decision makers in the critical stages of their rise to world business leadership. A goodly share of productive organizations worldwide are led by men and women who consider Drucker their intellectual guide, if not their personal mentor.

Drucker's most productive insights have often appeared first in the *Harvard Business Review*. He has written thirty *Harvard Business Review* articles, more than any other contributor. In the September–October 1992 issue, he published core concepts from his major new work, *Postcapitalist Society* (HarperCollins, 1993). *Harvard Business Review* editors sent T George Harris, a Drucker collaborator for twenty-four years, to the Drucker Management Center at the Claremont Graduate School in California for two days of intensive conversation about the book's practical implication for today's executives:

> *Peter, you always bring ideas down to the gut level where people work and live. Now we need to know how managers can operate in the postcapitalist society.*

You have to learn to manage in situations where you don't have command authority, where you are neither controlled nor controlling. That is the fundamental change. Management textbooks still talk mainly about managing subordinates. But you no longer evaluate an executive in terms of how many people report to him or her. That standard doesn't mean as much as the complexity of the job, the information it uses and generates, and the different kinds of relationships needed to do the work.

Similarly, business news still refers to managing subsidiaries. But this is the control approach of the 1950s or 1960s. The reality is that the multinational corporation is rapidly becoming an endangered species. Businesses used to grow in one of two ways: from grassroots up or by acquisition. In both cases, the manager had control. Today businesses grow through alliances, all kinds of dangerous liaisons and joint ventures, which, by the way, very few people understand. This new type of growth upsets the traditional manager who believes he or she must own or control sources and markets.

How will the manager operate in a work environment free of the old hierarchies?

Would you believe that you're going to work permanently with people who work for you but are not your employees? Increasingly, for instance, you outsource when possible. It is predictable, then, that ten years from now a company will outsource all work that does not have a career ladder up to senior management. To get productivity, you have to outsource activities that have their own senior management. Believe me, the trend toward outsourcing has very little to do with economizing and a great deal to do with quality.

Can you give an example?

Take a hospital. Everybody there knows how important cleanliness is, but doctors and nurses are never going to be very concerned with how you sweep in corners. That's not part of their value system. They need a hospital maintenance company. One company I got to know in southern California had a cleaning woman who came in as an illiterate Latino immigrant. She is brilliant. She figured out how to split a bed sheet so that the bed of a very sick patient, no matter how heavy, could be changed. Using her method, you have to move the patient about only six inches, and she cut the bed-making time from twelve minutes to two. Now she's in charge of the cleaning operations, but she is not an employee of the hospital. The hospital can't give her one single order. It can only say, "We don't like this; we'll work it out."

The point is, managers still talk about the people who "report" to them, but that word should be stricken from management vocabulary. Information is replacing authority. A company treasurer with outsourced information technology, IT, may have only two assistants and a receptionist, but his decisions in foreign exchange can lose—or make—more money in a day than the rest of the company makes all year. A scientist decides which research *not* to do in a big company lab. He doesn't even have a secretary or a title, but his track record means that he is not likely to be overruled. He may have more effect than the CEO. In the military, a lieutenant colonel used to command a battalion, but today he may have only a receptionist and be in charge of liaisons with a major foreign country.

Amid these new circumstances, everybody is trying to build the ideal organization, generally flat with few layers of bosses and driven directly by consumer satisfaction. But how do managers gear up their lives for this new world?

More than anything else, the individual has to take more responsibility for himself or herself, rather than depend on the company. In this country, and beginning in Europe and even Japan, you can't expect that if you've worked for a company for five years you'll be there when you retire forty years from now. Nor can you expect that you will be able to do what you want to do at the company in forty years time. In fact, if you make a wager on any big company, the chances of it being split within the next ten years are better than the chances of it remaining the way it is.

This is a new trend. Big corporations became stable factors before World War I and in the 1920s were almost frozen.

Many survived the Depression without change. Then there were thirty or forty years when additional stories were built onto skyscrapers or more wings added onto corporate centers. But now they're not going to build corporate skyscrapers. In fact, within the past ten years, the proportion of the workforce employed by Fortune 500 companies has fallen from 30 percent to 13 percent.

Corporations once built to last like pyramids are now more like tents. Tomorrow they're gone or in turmoil. And this is true not only of companies in the headlines like Sears or GM or IBM. Technology is changing very quickly, as are markets and structures. You can't design your life around a temporary organization.

Let me give you a simple example of the way assumptions are changing. Most men and women in the executive program I teach are about forty-five years old and just below senior management in a big organization or running a midsize one. When we began fifteen or twenty years ago, people at this stage were asking, "How can we prepare ourselves for the next promotion?" Now they say, "What do I need to learn so that I can decide where to go next?"

If a young man in a gray flannel suit represented the lifelong corporate type, what's today's image?

Taking individual responsibility and not depending on any particular company. Equally important is managing your own career. The stepladder is gone, and there's not even the implied structure of an industry's rope ladder. It's more like vines, and you bring your own machete. You don't know what you'll be doing next, or whether you'll work in a private office or one big amphitheater or even out of your home. You have to take responsibility for knowing yourself, so you can find the right jobs as you develop and as your family becomes a factor in your values and choices.

*That's a significant departure from what managers could
expect in the past.*

Well, the changes in the manager's work are appearing
everywhere, though on different timetables. For instance, I
see more career confusion among the many Japanese students
I've had over the years. They're totally bewildered. Though
they are more structured than we ever were, suddenly the
Japanese are halfway between being totally managed and having to take responsibility for themselves. What frightens them
is that titles don't mean what they used to mean. Whether you
were in India or France, if you were an assistant director of
market research, everybody used to know what you were doing.
That's not true any more, as we found in one multinational. A
woman who had just completed a management course told me
not long ago that in five years, she would be an assistant vice
president of her bank. I'm afraid I had to tell her that she might
indeed get the title, but it would no longer have the meaning
she thought it did.

Another rung in the ladder?

Yes. The big-company mentality. Most people expect
the personnel department to be Papa—or Ma Bell. When the
AT&T personnel department was at its high point thirty years
ago, it was the power behind the scenes. With all their testing
and career planning, they'd know that a particular twenty-
seven-year-old would be, by age forty-five, an assistant operating manager and no more. They didn't know whether he'd be
in Nebraska or Florida. But unless he did something quite
extraordinary, his career path until retirement was set.

Times have certainly changed. And, in fact, the Bell people
have done better than most, because they could see that change
coming in the antitrust decision. They couldn't ignore it. But

most people still have a big-company mentality buried in their assumptions. If they lose a job with Sears, they hunt for one with Kmart, unaware that small companies create most of the new jobs and are about as secure as big companies.

Even today, remarkably few Americans are prepared to select jobs for themselves. When you ask, "Do you know what you are good at? Do you know your limitations?" they look at you with a blank stare. Or they often respond in terms of subject knowledge, which is the wrong answer. When they prepare their résumés, they still try to list positions like steps up a ladder. It is time to give up thinking of jobs or career paths as we once did and think in terms of taking on assignments one after the other.

How does one prepare for this new kind of managerial career?

Being an educated person is no longer adequate, not even educated in management. One hears that the government is doing research on new job descriptions based on subject knowledge. But I think that we probably have to leap right over the search for objective criteria and get into the subjective, what I call *competencies*. Do you really like pressure? Can you be steady when things are rough and confused? Do you absorb information better by reading, talking, or looking at graphs and numbers? I asked one executive the other day, "When you sit down with a person, a subordinate, do you know what to say?" Empathy is a practical competence. I have been urging this kind of self-knowledge for years, but now it is essential for survival.

People, especially the young, think that they want all the freedom they can get, but it is very demanding, very difficult to think through who you are and what you do best. In helping people learn how to be responsible, our educational system is more and more counterproductive. The longer you stay in school, the fewer decisions you have to make. For instance, the decision whether to take French II or art history is really based on whether one likes to get up early in the morning. And graduate school is much worse.

Do you know why most people start with big companies? Because most graduates have not figured out where to place themselves, and companies send in the recruiters. But as soon as the recruits get through training and into a job, they have to start making decisions about the future. Nobody's going to do it for them.

And once they start making decisions, many of the best move to midsize companies in three to five years, because there they can break through to top management. With less emphasis on seniority, a person can go upstairs and say, "I've been in accounting for three years, and I'm ready to go into marketing." Each year I phone a list of my old students to see what's happening with them. The second job used to be with another big company, often because people were beginning to have families and wanted security. But with two-career families, a different problem emerges. At a small organization, you can often work out arrangements for both the man and the woman to move to new jobs in the same city.

Some of the psychological tests being developed now are getting better at helping people figure out the competencies. But if the world economy is shifting from a command model to a knowledge model, why shouldn't education determine who gets each job?

Because of the enormous danger that we would not value the person in terms of performance but in terms of credentials. Strange as it may seem, a knowledge economy's greatest pitfall is in becoming a Mandarin meritocracy. You see creeping cre-dentialism all around. Why should people find it necessary to tell me so-and-so is really a good researcher even though he or she doesn't have a Ph.D.? It's easy to fall into the trap because degrees are black-and-white. But it takes judgment to weigh a person's contribution.

The problem is becoming more serious in information-based organizations. As Michael Hammer pointed out three years ago in the *Harvard Business Review*, when an organization reengineers itself around information, the majority of manage-ment layers becomes redundant. Most turn out to have been just information relays. Now, each layer has much more infor-mation responsibility. Most large companies have cut the num-ber of layers by 50 percent, even in Japan. Toyota came down from 20-odd to 11. GM has streamlined from 28 to maybe 19, and even that number is decreasing rapidly. Organizations will become flatter and flatter.

As a result, there's real panic in Japan, because it's a vertical society based on subtle layers of status. Everybody wants to become a *kachō*, a supervisor or section manager. Still, the United States doesn't have the answer either. We don't know how to use rewards and recognition to move the competent people into the management positions that remain. I don't care for the popular theory that a generation of entrepreneurs can solve our problems. Entrepreneurs are monomaniacs. Managers are synthesizers who bring resources together and have that ability to "smell" oppor-tunity and timing. Today perception is more important than analysis. In the new society of organizations, you need to be able to recognize patterns to see what is there rather than what you expect to see. You need the invaluable listener who says, "I hear us all trying to kill the new product to protect the old one."

How do you find these people?

One way is to use small companies as farm clubs, as in baseball. One of my ablest friends is buying minority stakes in small companies within his industry. When I said it didn't make sense, he said, "I'm buying farm teams. I'm putting my bright young people in these companies so they have their own commands. They have to do everything a CEO does in a big company."

And do you know the biggest thing these young executives have to learn in their new positions? My friend continued, "We have more Ph.D.s in biology and chemistry than we have janitors, and they have to learn that their customers aren't Ph.D.'s, and the people who do the work aren't." In other words, they must learn to speak English instead of putting formulas on the blackboard. They must learn to listen to somebody who does not know what a regression analysis is. Basically, they have to learn the meaning and importance of respect.

A difficult thing to learn, let alone teach.

You have to focus on a person's performance. The individual must shoulder the burden of defining what his or her contribution will be. We have to demand—and *demand* is the word, nothing permissive—that people think through what constitutes the greatest contribution that they can make to the company in the next eighteen months or two years. Then they have to make sure that contribution is accepted and understood by the people they work with and for.

Most people don't ask themselves this question, however obvious and essential it seems. When I ask people what they contribute to an organization, they blossom and love to answer. And when I follow with, "Have you told other people about it?" the answer is often, "No, that would be silly because they know." But of course "they" don't. We are a hundred years past the simple economy in which most people knew what others did at work. Farmers knew what most farmers did, and industrial workers knew what other factory workers did. Domestic servants understood each other's work, as did the fourth major group in that economy: small tradesmen. No one needed to explain. But now nobody knows what others do, even within the same organization. Everybody you work with needs to know your priorities. If you don't ask and don't tell, your peers and subordinates will guess incorrectly.

What's the result of this lack of communication?

When you don't communicate, you don't get to do the things you are good at. Let me give you an example. The engineers in my class, without exception, say they spend more than half their time editing and polishing reports—in other words, what they are least qualified to do. They don't even know that you have to write and rewrite and rewrite again. But there are any number of English majors around for that assignment. People seldom pay attention to their strengths. For example, after thinking for a long time, an engineer told me he's really good at the first design, at the basic idea, but not at filling in the details for the final product. Until then, he'd never told anybody, not even himself.

You're not advocating self-analysis alone, are you?

No. You not only have to understand your own competencies, but you also have to learn the strengths of the men and women to whom you assign duties, as well as those of your peers and boss. Too many managers still go by averages. They still talk about "our engineers." And I say, "Brother, you don't have engineers. You have Joe and Mary and Jim and Bob, and each is different." You can no longer manage a workforce. You manage individuals. You have to know them so well you can go and say, "Mary, you think you ought to move up to this next job. Well, then you have to learn not to have that chip on your shoulder. Forget you are a woman; you are an engineer. And you have to be a little considerate. Do not come in at ten minutes to five on Friday afternoon to tell people they have to work overtime when you knew it at 9 A.M."

The key to the productivity of knowledge workers is to make them concentrate on the real assignment. Do you know why most promotions now fail? One-third are outright disaster, in my experience, while another third are a nagging backache. Not more than one in three works out. No fit. The standard case, of course, is the star salesman promoted to sales manager. That job can be any one of four things—a manager of salespeople, a market manager, a brand manager, or a super-salesman who opens up an entire new area. But nobody figures out what it is, so the man or woman who got the promotion just tries to do more of whatever led to the promotion. That's the surest way to be wrong.

Expand on your idea of information responsibility and how it fits into postcapitalist society.

Far too many managers think computer specialists know what information they need to do their job and what information they owe to whom. Computer information tends to focus too much on inside information, not the outside sources and customers that count. In today's organization, you have to take responsibility for information because it is your main tool. But most don't know how to use it. Few are information literate. They can play "Mary Had a Little Lamb" but not Beethoven.

I heard today about a brand manager in a major over-the-counter drug company who tried to get the scientific papers on the product he markets. But the corporate librarian complained to his superior. Under her rules, she gives hard science only to the company's scientists and lawyers. He had to get a consultant to go outside and use a computer database to pull up about twenty journal articles on his product so he'd know how to develop honest advertising copy. The point of the story is that this brand manager is way ahead of the parade: ninety-nine out of a hundred brand managers don't know they need that kind of information for today's consumers and haven't a clue how to get it. The first step is to say, "I need it."

And many people don't recognize the importance of this step. I work with an information manager at a large financial institution that has invested $1.5 billion in information. He and I talked all morning with his department's eight women and ten men. Very intelligent, but not one began to think seriously about what information they need to serve their customers. When I pointed this out, they said, "Isn't the boss going to tell us?" We finally had to agree to meet a month later so that they could go through the hard work of figuring out what information they need and—more important—what they do not need.

So a manager begins the road to information responsibility first by identifying gaps in knowledge.

Exactly. To be information literate, you begin with learning what it is you need to know. Too much talk focuses on the technology, even worse on the speed of the gadget, always faster, faster. This kind of "techie" fixation causes us to lose track of the fundamental nature of information in today's organization. To organize the way work is done, you have to begin with the specific job, then the information input, and finally the human relationships needed to get the job done.

The current emphasis on reengineering essentially means changing an organization from the flow of things to the flow of information. The computer is merely a tool in the process. If you go to the hardware store to buy a hammer, you do not ask if you should do upholstery or fix the door. To put it in editorial terms, knowing how a typewriter works does not make you a writer. Now that knowledge is taking the place of capital as the driving force in organizations worldwide, it is all too easy to confuse data with knowledge and information technology with information.

What's the worst problem in managing knowledge specialists?

One of the most degenerative tendencies of the past forty years is the belief that if you are understandable, you are vulgar. When I was growing up, it was taken for granted that economists, physicists, psychologists—leaders in any discipline—would make themselves understood. Einstein spent years with three different collaborators to make his theory of relativity accessible to the layman. Even John Maynard Keynes tried hard to make his economics accessible. But just the other day, I heard a senior scholar seriously reject a younger colleague's work because more than five people could understand what he's doing. Literally.

We cannot afford such arrogance. Knowledge is power, which is why people who had it in the past often tried to make a secret of it. In postcapitalism, power comes from transmitting information to make it productive, not from hiding it.

That means you have to be intolerant of intellectual arrogance. And I mean intolerant. At whatever level, knowledge people must make themselves understood, and whatever field the manager comes from, he or she must be eager to understand others. This may be the main job of the manager of technical people. He or she must not only be an interpreter but also work out a balance between specialization and exposure.

Exposure is an important technique. For an exotic example, look at weather forecasting, where meteorologists and mathematicians and other specialists now work with teams of experts on satellite data. Europeans, on the one hand, have tried to connect these different disciplines entirely through information managers. On the other hand, Americans rotate people at an early stage. Suppose you put a Ph.D. in meteorology on a team that is to work on the new mathematical model of hurricanes for three years. He isn't a mathematician, but he gets exposed to what mathematicians assume, what they eliminate, what their limitations are. With the combination of exposure and translation, the American approach yields forecasts that are about three times more accurate than the European, I'm told. And the exposure concept is useful in managing any group of specialists.

Is the fact that some teams provide exposure as well as interpreters a reason that the team has become such a hot topic?

There's a lot of nonsense in team talk, as if teams were something new. We have always worked in teams, and while sports give us hundreds of team styles, there are only a few basic models to choose from. The critical decision is to select the right kind for the job. You can't mix soccer and doubles tennis. It's predictable that in a few years, the most traditional team will come back in fashion, the one that does research first, then passes the idea to engineering to develop, and then on to manufacturing to make. It's like a baseball team, and you may know I have done a little work with baseball team management.

The great strength of baseball teams is that you can concentrate. You take Joe, who is a batter, and you work on batting. There is almost no interaction, nothing at all like the soccer team or the jazz combo, the implicit model of many teams today. The soccer team moves in unison, but everyone holds the same relative position. The jazz combo has incredible flexibility because everyone knows each other so well that they all sense when the trumpet is about to solo. The combo model takes great discipline and may eventually fall out of favor, especially in Japanese car manufacturing, because we do not need to create new models as fast as we have been.

I know several German companies that follow the baseball team model, whether they know it or not. Their strength is clear: they are fantastic at exploiting and developing old knowledge, and Germany's midsize companies may be better than their big ones simply because they concentrate better. On the other hand, when it comes to the new, from electronics to biotech, German scientists may do fine work, but their famous apprenticeship system discourages innovation.

So, beyond all the hype, teams can help the executive navigate a postcapitalist society?

Thinking about teams helps us highlight the more general problem of how to manage knowledge. In the production of fundamental new knowledge, the British groups I run into are way ahead of anybody. But they never have done much with their expertise, in part because many British companies don't value the technically oriented person enough. I don't know of a single engineer in top management there. My Japanese friends are just the opposite. While they still do not specialize in scientific advances, they take knowledge and make it productive very fast. In this country, on the other hand, we have not improved that much in existing industries. The automobile business, until recently, was perfectly satisfied doing what it did in 1939. But as we are discovering in computers and in biotech, we may be at our very best when it comes to groundbreaking technology.

Where is the lesson in all this for the manager?

The lesson is that the productivity of knowledge has both a qualitative and a quantitative dimension. Though we know very little about it, we do realize executives must be both managers of specialists and synthesizers of different fields of knowledge—really of knowledges, plural. This situation is as threatening to the traditional manager, who worries about high-falutin' highbrows, as it is to the intellectual, who worries about being too commercial to earn respect in his or her discipline. But in the postcapitalist world, the highbrow and the lowbrow have to play on the same team.

That sounds pretty democratic. Does a postcapitalist society based more on knowledge than capital become egalitarian?

No. Both of these worlds miss the point. Democratic bespeaks a narrow political and legal organization. Nor do I use the buzzword *participative*. Worse yet is the empowerment concept. It is not a great step forward to take power out at the top and put it in at the bottom. It's still power. To build achieving organizations, you must replace power with responsibility.

And while we're on the subject of words, I'm not comfortable with the word *manager* anymore, because it implies subordinates. I find myself using *executive* more, because it implies responsibility for an area, not necessarily dominion over people. The word *boss*, which emerged in World War II, is helpful in that it can be used to suggest a mentor's role, someone who can back you up on a decision. The new organizations need to go beyond senior-junior polarities to a blend with sponsor and mentor relations. In the traditional organization—the organization of the last hundred years—the skeleton, or internal structure, was a combination of rank and power. In the emerging organization, it has to be mutual understanding and responsibility.

° ° °

T George Harris has launched many magazines and edited the *Harvard Business Review*. He consults with Procter & Gamble on media strategy.

Peter F. Drucker is a writer, teacher, and consultant specializing in strategy and policy for businesses and social sector organizations. He has been hailed in the United States and abroad as the seminal thinker, writer, and lecturer on the contemporary organization.

Part Two

Creating and Shaping the Work Environment

Chapter Seven

Seven Practices of Successful Organizations

Jeffrey Pfeffer

In this chapter, I extract from the various studies, related literature, and personal observation and experience a set of seven dimensions that seem to characterize most, if not all, of the systems producing profits through people:[1]

1. Employment security
2. Selective hiring of new personnel
3. Self-managed teams and decentralization of decision making as the basic principles of organizational design
4. Comparatively high compensation contingent on organizational performance
5. Extensive training
6. Reduced status distinctions and barriers, including dress, language, office arrangements, and wage differences across levels

7. Extensive sharing of financial and performance information throughout the organization

This list focuses on basic dimensions, some of which, such as compensation and reduction of status differences, have multiple components. It is, however, still the case that several of the dimensions of high-performance work arrangements listed, for instance, employment security and high pay, appear to fly in the face of conventional wisdom. This chapter outlines these practices, provides examples to illustrate both their implementation and their impact, and explains their underlying logic.

EMPLOYMENT SECURITY

In an era of downsizing and rightsizing—or, as Donald Hastings, CEO of Lincoln Electric, called it in a speech to the Academy of Management in 1996, "dumbsizing"—how can I write about employment security as a critical element of high-performance work arrangements? First, because it is simply empirically the case that most research on the effects of high-performance management systems have incorporated employment security as one important dimension in their description of these systems. That is because "one of the most widely accepted propositions . . . is that innovations in work practices or other forms of worker management cooperation or productivity improvement are not likely to be sustained over time when workers fear that by increasing productivity they will work themselves out of their jobs."[2]

This was recognized long ago by Lincoln Electric, the successful arc welding and electric motor manufacturer that has dominated its markets for decades. Years ago, it began offering guaranteed employment to workers after two (and now three) years on the job. It has not had a layoff since 1948. Nor is it the case that this is just because the company has never faced hard times. In the early 1980s, a recession and high interest rates caused Lincoln's domestic sales to fall about 40 percent over an eighteen-month period. Nevertheless, it did not resort to lay-offs. One thing the company did to avoid laying off people was to redeploy them. Factory workers who had made Lincoln's products were put in the field with the task of selling them, in the process actually increasing Lincoln's market share on penetration. Over the years, Lincoln has enjoyed gains in productivity that are far above those for manufacturing as a whole, and its managers believe that the assurance workers have that innovations in methods will not cost them or their colleagues their jobs has significantly contributed to these excellent results. Similarly, when General Motors wanted to implement new work arrangements in its innovative Saturn plant in the 1990s, it guaranteed its people job security except in the most extreme circumstances. When New United Motors was formed to operate the Fremont automobile assembly plant, it offered its people job security. How else could it ask for flexibility and cooperation in becoming more efficient and productive?

Many additional benefits follow from employment assurances besides workers' free contribution of knowledge and their efforts to enhance productivity. One advantage to firms is the decreased likelihood that they will lay off employees during downturns. How is this a benefit to the firm? In the absence of some way of building commitment to retaining the workforce—either through pledges about employment security or through employment obligations contractually negotiated with a union—firms may lay off employees too quickly and too readily at the first sign of financial difficulty. This constitutes a cost for firms that have done a good job selecting, training, and developing their workforce. Layoffs put important strategic assets on the street for the competition to employ. When a colleague and I interviewed the vice president for people at Southwest Airlines, she noted that the company had never had a layoff or furlough in an industry where such events were common. When we asked why, she replied, "Why would we want to put our best assets, our people, in the arms of the competition?" Seeing its people as strategic assets rather than as costs, Southwest has pursued a careful growth strategy that avoided overexpansion and subsequent cuts in personnel.

Employment security policies will also lead to more careful and leaner hiring, because the firm knows it cannot simply let people go quickly if it has overestimated its labor demand. Leaner staffing can actually make the workforce more productive, with fewer people doing more work. The people are often happy to be more productive because they know they are helping to ensure a result that benefits them—having a long-term job and a career. Furthermore, employment security maintained over time helps to build trust between people and their employer, which can lead to more cooperation, forbearance in pressing for wage increases, and better spirit in the company. Herb Kelleher, the CEO of Southwest, has written:

> Our most important tools for building employee partnership are job security and a stimulating work environment. Certainly there were times when we could have made substantially more profits in the short term if we had furloughed people, but we didn't. We were looking at our employees' and our company's longer-term interests. . . . As it turns out, providing job security imposes additional discipline, because if your goal is to avoid layoff, then you hire very sparingly. So our commitment to job security has actually helped us keep our labor force smaller and more productive than our competitors'.[3]

For organizations without the strategic discipline or vision of Southwest, a guarantee of employment security can help the firm avoid making a costly decision to lay people off that has short-term benefits and long-term costs

If you want to see just how costly such layoff decisions can be, consider Silicon Valley. Executives from the semiconductor and electronics industries often write newspaper and magazine articles and testify before Congress in favor of permitting immigration of skilled workers. These executives favor immigration because they manage companies that are frequently short of necessary talent. The executives complain about their difficulty in recruiting qualified personnel in their expanding industry.

What you won't see in their articles or testimony, but what you will find if you look at newspapers from a few years ago, is that many of these very same firms laid off engineers, technicians, and other skilled workers in some instances just two or three years—or even less—before subsequently complaining about labor scarcity. Think about it. My friends in the valley have perfected the art of buying high and selling low. When times are tough in the industry, common sense suggests that that is exactly the time to recruit and build your workforce. Competition for talented staff will obviously be less, and salaries need not be bid up in attempts to lure people from their existing jobs. By hiring when times are poor and developing a set of policies, including assurance that people will be retained, a firm can become an employer of choice, and the organization will not have to enter the labor market at its very peak to acquire the necessary workforce. Instead, many firms do exactly the opposite. They lay people off in cyclical downturns and then, when the entire industry is booming and staff is scarce, they engage in often-fruitless bidding contests to rehire the skills that they not long ago sent packing.

Employment security can confer yet another benefit, in that it encourages people to take a longer-term perspective on their jobs and organizational performance. In a study of the financial performance of 192 banks, John Delery and Harold Doty observed a significant relationship between employment security and the bank's return on assets, an important measure of financial performance: "The greater the employment security given to loan officer, the greater the returns to banks."[4] Why might this be? In a bank that hires and lays off loan officers quickly to match economic fluctuations, the typical loan officer will worry only about booking loans—just what they have typically been rewarded for doing. With employment security and a longer-term perspective on the job, the bank officer may be more inclined to worry as well about the repayment prospects of the loan and about building customer relationships by providing high levels of service. Although a specific loan officer's career may prosper by being a big loan producer and moving quickly from one bank to another, the bank's profitability and performance are undoubtedly enhanced by having people who take both a longer-term and a more comprehensive view of their jobs and of the bank's financial performance. This is likely to occur, however, only with the prospect of long-term continuity in the employment relationship.

The idea of employment security does not mean that the organization retains people who don't perform or work effectively with others—that is, performance does matter. Lincoln Electric has very high turnover for employees in their first few months on the job, as those who don't fit the Lincoln culture and work environment leave. Southwest will fire people who don't provide the level of customer service the firm is well known for delivering and don't want to improve. Employment security means that employees are not quickly put on the street for things, such as economic downturns or the strategic mistakes of senior management, over which they have no control. The policy focuses on maintaining total employment, not on protecting individuals from the consequences of their individual behavior on the job.

The idea of providing employment security in today's competitive world seems somehow anachronistic or impossible and very much at variance with what most firms seem to be doing. But employment security is fundamental to the implementation of most other high-performance management practices, such as selective hiring, extensive training, information sharing, and delegation. Companies are unlikely to invest the resources in the careful screening and training of new people if those people are not expected to be with the firm long enough for it to recoup these investments. Similarly, delegation of operating authority and the sharing of sensitive performance and strategic information require trust, and that trust is much more likely to emerge in a system of mutual, long-term commitments.

Selective Hiring

Organizations serious about obtaining profits through people will expend the effort needed to ensure that they recruit the right people in the first place. This requires several things. First, the organization needs to have a large applicant pool from which to select. In 1993, for example, Southwest Airlines received about 98,000 job applications, interviewed 16,000 people, and hired 2,700. In 1994, applications increased to more than 125,000 for 4,000 hires. Some organizations see processing this many job inquiries as an unnecessary expense. Southwest sees it as the first step toward ensuring that it has a large applicant pool from which to select its people. Similarly, Singapore Airlines, frequently listed as one of Asia's most admired companies, one of the most profitable airlines in the world, and consistently ranked quite high in ratings of service quality, is extremely careful and selective in its recruiting practices. Flight attendants are an important point of contact with the customer and one way in which Singapore Airlines differentiates its service. Consequently, senior management becomes personally involved in flight attendant selection. Prospective generalist staff, from which the ranks of managers will come, must pass a series of tests and clear two rounds of interviews, including interviews with a panel of senior management. "From an initial pool of candidates, about 10 percent are shortlisted and only 2 percent [one out of fifty] are selected."[5]

Second, the organization needs to be clear about what are the most critical skills and attributes needed in its applicant pool. The notion of trying to find "good employees" is not very helpful—organizations need to be as specific as possible about the precise attributes they are seeking. At Southwest Airlines, applicants for flight attendant positions are evaluated on the basis of initiative, judgment, adaptability, and their ability to learn. These attributes are assessed in part from interviews employing questions evoking specific instances of these attributes. For instance, to assess adaptability, interviewers ask, "Give an example of working with a difficult coworker. How did you handle it?"[6] To measure initiative, one question asks, "Describe a time when a coworker failed to pull their weight and what you did about it."

Third, the skills and abilities hired need to be carefully considered and consistent with the particular job requirements and the organization's approach to its market. Simply hiring the "best and the brightest" may not make sense in all circumstances. Enterprise Rent-A-Car is today the largest car rental company in the United States, with revenues in 1996 of $3 billion, and it has expanded at a rate of between 25 and 30 percent a year for the past eleven years. It has grown by pursuing a high customer service strategy and emphasizing sales of rental car services to repair garage customers. In a low-wage, often unionized, and seemingly low-employee-skill industry, virtually all of Enterprise's people are college graduates. But these people are hired primarily for their sales skills and personality and for their willingness to provide good service, not for their academic performance. Dennis Ross, the chief operating officer, commented, "We hire from the half of the college class that makes the upper half possible. . . . We want athletes, fraternity types, people people." Brian O'Reilly interpolates Enterprise's reasoning: "The social directors make good sales people, able to chap up service managers and calm down someone who has just been in a car wreck. . . . The Enterprise employees hired from the caboose end of the class have something else going for them . . . a chilling realization of how unforgiving the job market can be."[7]

Fourth, organizations should screen primarily on important attributes that are difficult to change through training and should emphasize qualities that actually differentiate among those in the applicant pool. An important insight on the selection process comes from those organizations that tend to hire more on the basis of basic ability and attitude than on applicants' specific technical skills, which are much more easily acquired. This has been the practice of Japanese organizations for some time. "Japanese recruitment seeks to find the individual with the proper character whom it can train. . . . Instead of searching for applicants with necessary skills for the job, the focus is on social background, temperament, and character references."[8]

Sophisticated managers know that it is much more cost-effective to select on those important attributes that are difficult or impossible to change and to train people in those behaviors or skills that are more readily learned. At Southwest Airlines, a top pilot working for another airline who actually did stunt work for movie studios was rejected because he was rude to a receptionist. Southwest believes that technical skills are easier to acquire than a teamwork and service attitude. Ironically, many firms select for specific, job-relevant skills that, while important, are easily acquired. Meanwhile, they fail to find people with the right attitudes, values, and cultural fit—attributes that are harder to train or change and that are quite predictive of turnover and performance. To avoid having to retrain or resocialize people who have acquired bad habits at their previous employers, companies like Southwest prefer to hire individuals without previous industry experience. Many also prefer to hire at the entry level, obtaining individuals who are eager to prove themselves and who don't know what can't be done.

It is tempting to hire on the basis of ability or intelligence rather than fit with the organization—so tempting that one occasionally observes firms trying to differentiate among a set of individuals who are basically similar in intelligence or ability while failing to try to distinguish those who will be well suited to the organization from those who will not. One of my favorite examples of this is recruitment at Stanford Business School. Stanford has a class of about 370 M.B.A.s, selected from an initial applicant pool that in recent years has exceeded six thousand. These are obviously talented, motivated, and very intelligent individuals. Distinguishing among them on those criteria would be difficult, if not impossible. But many firms seek to do the impossible—they try to get around the school's policy of not releasing grades in an effort to figure out who are the smartest students and to assess differences in ability among a set of applicants through interviewing techniques such as giving them problems or cases to solve. Meanwhile, although many job recruits will leave their first job within the first two years, and such turnover and the requirement to refill those positions are exceedingly expensive, few firms focus primarily on determining fit—something that does vary dramatically.

Two firms that take a more sensible and pragmatic approach to hiring are Hewlett-Packard and PeopleSoft, a producer of human resource management software. For instance, one M.B.A. job applicant reported that in interviews with PeopleSoft, the company asked very little about personal or academic background, except about learning experiences from school and work. Rather, the interviews focused mostly on whether the person saw herself as team oriented or as an individual achiever; what she liked to do outside school and work; and her philosophy on life. The specific question was, "Do you have a personal mission statement? If you don't, what would it be if you were to write it today?" Moreover, the people interviewing the applicant presented a consistent picture of PeopleSoft as a company and of the values that were shared among employees. Such a selection process is more likely to produce cultural fit. A great deal of research evidence shows that the degree of cultural fit and value congruence between job applicants and their organizations significantly predicts both subsequent turnover and job performance.[9]

Firms serious about selection put applicants through several rounds of interviews and a rigorous selection procedure. At Subaru-Isuzu's U.S. manufacturing plant, getting hired involved going through multiple screening procedures including written tests and assessment center exercises and could take as long as six months or more. The fastest hire took nine weeks.[10] Such a lengthy selection process has several outcomes. First, it ensures that those who survive it have been carefully scrutinized. Second, it ensures that those eventually hired into the firm develop commitment. Applicants selected become committed as a consequence for having gone through such a lengthy and rigorous process—if they didn't really want the job, why would they go through it? At Subaru-Isuzu, the selection process "demanded perseverance," ensured that those who were hired had "the greatest desire and determination," and, since it required some degree of sacrifice on the part of the people, encouraged self-elimination and built commitment among those who survived.[11] Third, this type of process promotes the feeling on the part of those who are finally selected that they are part of an elite and special group, a feeling that causes them to enter the organization with a high level of motivation and spirit. Laurie Graham's participant observation study of Subaru-Isuzu concluded that "the fact that so much money, time, and effort went into the selection of employees reinforced the belief that the company was willing to go to great lengths to select the best."[12]

Rigorous selection requires a method, refined and developed over time through feedback and learning, to ensure that the firm can identify the skills it is seeking from the applicant pool. At Southwest Airlines, the company tracks who has interviewed job applicants. When someone does especially well or poorly, the organization can actually try to assess what the interviewers saw or missed, and why. It is puzzling that organizations will ensure the quality of their manufacturing or service delivery processes by closing the loop on that process through feedback, while almost no organizations attempt to do the same thing with their recruiting process. Sources of applicants, scores on tests, or interview ratings, and other selection mechanisms must be validated against the subsequent performance of the people selected if there is to be any hope of improving the effectiveness of the process over time.

The following list summarizes the main points about how to go about selective hiring to build a high-performance organization:

- Have a large number of applicants per opening.

- Screen for cultural fit and attitude—not for skills that can be readily trained.

- Be clear about what are the most critical skills, behaviors, or attitudes crucial for success; isolate just a small number of such qualities, and be as specific as possible. Simply seeking "the best and brightest" frequently doesn't make sense.

- Use several rounds of screening to build commitment and to signal that hiring is taken very seriously.

- To the extent possible, involve senior people as a signal of the importance of the hiring activity.

- Close the loop by assessing the results and performance of the recruiting process.

SELF-MANAGED TEAMS AND DECENTRALIZATION AS BASIC ELEMENTS OF ORGANIZATIONAL DESIGN

Organizing people into self-managed teams is a critical component of virtually all high-performance management systems. Numerous articles and case examples as well as rigorous, systematic studies attest to the effectiveness of teams as a principle of organization design. One researcher concluded that "two decades of research in organizational behavior provides considerable evidence that workers in self-managed teams enjoy greater autonomy and discretion, and this effect translates into intrinsic rewards and job satisfaction; teams also outperform traditionally supervised groups in the majority of . . . empirical studies."[13]

In a manufacturing plant that implemented high-performance work teams, for example, a 38 percent reduction in the defect rate and a 20 percent increase in productivity followed the introduction of teams.[14] Honeywell's defense avionics plant credits improved on-time delivery—reaching 99 percent in the first quarter of 1996 as compared to below 40 percent in the late 1980s—to the implementation of teams.[15] A study of the implementation of teams in one regional Bell telephone operating company found that "self-directed groups in customer services reported higher customer service quality and had 15.4% higher monthly sales revenues."[16] In the case of network technicians, the implementation of self-directed work teams saved "an average of $52,000 in indirect labor costs for each self-directed team initiated."[17] Moreover, membership in self-directed work teams positively affected employee job satisfaction, with other factors that might also affect satisfaction statistically controlled. "More than 75% of surveyed workers who are currently in traditional work groups say they would volunteer for teams if given the opportunity. By contrast, less than 10% who are now in teams say they would like to return to traditional supervision."[18]

Teams offer several advantages. First, teams substitute peer-based for hierarchical control of work. "Instead of management devoting time and energy to controlling the workforce directly, workers control themselves."[19] Peer control is frequently more effective than hierarchical supervision. Someone

Seven Practices of Successful Organizations | 147

may disappoint his or her supervisor, but the individual is much less likely to let down his or her workmates. At New United Motor Manufacturing (NUMMI), the work process is organized on a team basis with virtually no buffers of either in-process inventories or employees. As a consequence, "all the difficulties of one person's absence fall on those in daily contact with the absentee—the co-workers and immediate supervisor— producing enormous peer pressure against absenteeism."[20] Team-based organizations also are largely successful in having all of the people in the firm feel accountable and responsible for the operation and success of the enterprise, not just a few people in senior management positions. This increased sense of responsibility stimulates more initiative and effort on the part of everyone involved.

The tremendously successful natural foods grocery store chain, Whole Foods Markets, organized on the basis of teams, attributes much of its success to that arrangement. Between 1991 and 1996, the company enjoyed sales growth of 864 percent and net income growth of 438 percent as it expanded, in part through acquisitions as well as internal growth, from ten to sixty-eight stores. In its 1995 annual report, the company's team-oriented philosophy is clearly stated.

> Our growing Information Systems capability is fully aligned with our goal of creating a more intelligent organization—one which is less bureaucratic, elitist, hierarchical, and authoritarian and more communicative, participatory, and empowered. The ultimate goal is to have all team Members contributing their full intelligence, creativity, and skills to continuously improve the company. . . .
>
> Everyone who works at Whole Foods Market is a Team Member. This reflects our philosophy that we are all partners in the shared mission of giving our customers the very best in products and services. We invest in and believe in the collective

wisdom of our Team members. The stores are organized into self-managing work teams that are responsible and accountable for their own performance.[21]

Each store is a profit center and has about ten self-managed teams in it, with team leaders and clear performance targets. Moreover, "the team leaders in each store are a team, store leaders in each region are a team, and the company's six regional presidents are a team."[22] Although store leaders recommend new hires, teams must approve hires for full-time jobs, and it takes a two-thirds vote of the team members to do so, normally after a thirty-day trial period. Through an elaborate system of peer store reviews, Whole Foods encourages people to learn from each other. By sharing performance information widely, the company encourages peer competition. "At Whole foods, pressure for performance comes from peers rather than from headquarters, and it comes in the form of internal competition."[23]

Second, teams permit employees to pool their ideas to come up with better and more creative solutions to problems. The idea, similar to brainstorming or group problem solving, involves pooling ideas and expertise to increase the likelihood that at least one member of the group will come up with a way of addressing the problem. In the group setting, each participant can build on the others' ideas, particularly if the members are trained in effective group process and problem solving. Teams at Saturn and at the Chrysler Corporation's Jefferson North plant "provide a framework in which workers more readily help one another and more freely share their production knowledge—the innumerable 'tricks of the trade' that are vital in any manufacturing process."[24]

Third, and perhaps most important, by substituting peer for hierarchical control, teams permit removal of layers of hierarchy and absorption of administrative tasks previously performed by specialists, avoiding the enormous costs of having people whose sole job it is to watch people watch people who watch other people do the work. Administrative overhead is costly because management is typically well paid. Eliminating layers of management by instituting self-managing teams saves money. Self-managed teams can also take on tasks previously done by specialized staff, thus eliminating excess personnel and, just as important, putting critical decisions in the hands of individuals who may be closer to the relevant information.

The AES Corporation is an immensely successful global developer and operator of electric power and steam plants, with sales of more than $835 million and six thousand employees in 1996. A 1982 investment in the company of $10,000 would be worth more than $10 million in 1996. The company "has never formed corporate departments or assigned officers to oversee project finance, operations, purchasing, human resources, or public relations. Instead, such functions are handled at the plant level, where plant managers assign them to volunteer teams."[25] Front-line people develop expertise in these various task domains, including finance, and receive responsibility and authority for carrying them out. They do so effectively. Of course, mistakes get made, but learning follows. The AES structure saves on the costs of management—the organization has only five levels—and it economizes on specialized staff. The company developed a $400 million plant in Cumberland, Maryland, with a team of just ten people who obtained more than thirty-six separate permit approvals and negotiated the complex financing, including tax-exempt bonds and ten lenders. Normally, projects of this size require "hundreds of workers, each with small specific tasks to perform within large corporations."[26] The savings and increased speed and flexibility of the AES team-based approach are clear and constitute an important source of the firm's competitive advantage.

At Vancom Zuid-Limburg, a joint venture in the Netherlands that operates a public bus company, the organization has enjoyed very rapid growth in ridership and has been able to win transport concession by offering more services at the same price as its competitors. The key to this success lies in its use of self-managed teams and the consequent savings in management overhead:

> Vancom is able to [win transport contracts] mainly because of its very low overhead costs. . . . One manager supervises around forty bus drivers. . . . This management-driver ratio of 1 in 40 substantially differs from the norm in this sector. At best, competitors achieve a ratio of 1 in 8. Most of this difference can be attributed to the self-managed teams. Vancom . . . has two teams of around twenty drivers. Each team has its own bus lines and budgeting responsibilities. . . . Vancom also expects each individual driver to assume more responsibilities when on the road. This includes customer service (e.g., helping elderly persons board the bus); identifying problems (e.g., reporting damage to a bus stop), and active contributions (e.g., making suggestions for improvement of the services).[27]

How can moving to self-managed teams, possibly eliminating layers of administration and even specialized staff, be consistent with the earlier discussion of employment security? Eliminating positions need not entail the elimination of the people doing these jobs—those individuals can be redeployed to other tasks that add more value to the organization. In the case of Lincoln Electric, recall that, at least temporarily, factory workers became salespeople, something that Mazda Motors also did when it faced a production employee surplus because of low sales in the 1980s. At SAS Airlines, staff that formerly did market research and planning were moved to positions where they had a more direct effect on customer service and operations. At

Solectron, a contract manufacturer of electronics, institution of self-managed teams meant that managers, who typically had engineering degrees, could spend more time rethinking the overall production system and worrying about the technology strategy of the company—activities that added a lot more value than directly supervising $7 per hour direct labor. Often many tasks, such as the development of new products and new markets and the evaluation and introduction of new production technologies, require the time and strategic talents of managers, and these activities and decisions add much more value to the organization by using the knowledge and capabilities of the people. Consequently, a move to self-managed teams is consistent with maintaining employment when other, often more important, things are found for supervisors and specialized staff to do.

Even organizations for which working in formal teams is not sensible or feasible can benefit from one of the sources of team success: decentralization of decision making to front-line people, who have the knowledge and ability to take effective action. The Ritz-Carlton Hotel chain, winner of the Malcolm Baldrige National Quality Award in 1992, provides each of its people with discretion to spend up to $2,500, without any approval, in order to respond to guest complaints. Hampton Inn Hotel, a low-prices hotel chain, instituted a 100 percent satisfaction guarantee policy for its guests and permitted employees to do whatever was required to make the guests happy:

> A few years ago while working as a guest services representative at a Hampton Inn Hotel, I overheard a guest at our complimentary continental breakfast complaining quite loudly that his favorite cereal was not available. Rather than dismiss the person as just another disgruntled guest, I looked at the situation and saw an opportunity to make this guest happy. I gave him his money back—not for the continental breakfast, but for the cost

of one night's stay at our hotel. And I did it on the spot, without checking with my supervisor or the general manager of the hotel.[28]

These policies may seem wasteful, but they're not. Ritz-Carlton managers will tell you that a satisfied customer will talk to ten people and an unhappy customer to one hundred. Spending money to keep clients satisfied is a small price to pay for good advertising and encouraging guests to return. Similarly, at the Hampton Inn, "company research suggests that the guarantee strongly influences customer satisfaction and loyalty to Hampton Inn, and that guests who have experienced the guarantee are more likely to stay with Hampton Inn again in the future."[29] It is important to realize that successful implementation of guest satisfaction programs or, for that matter, programs to use the ideas and knowledge of the workforce requires decentralizing decision making and permitting people at all levels to exercise substantial influence over organizational decisions and processes. All of this requires trust, a commodity in short supply in many organizations that have become accustomed to operating with an emphasis on hierarchical control.

HIGH COMPENSATION CONTINGENT ON ORGANIZATIONAL PERFORMANCE

Although labor markets are far from perfectly efficient, it is nonetheless the case that some relationship exists between what a firm pays and the quality of the workforce it attracts. It is amusing to see firms announce simultaneously that first, they compete on the basis of their people and that their goal is to have the very best workforce in their industry, and second, that they intend to pay at (or sometimes slightly below) the median wage for comparable people in the industry. The level of salaries sends a message to the firm's workforce—they are truly valued or they are not. After all, talk is cheap, and many organizations can and do claim that people are their most important asset even as they behave differently.

I sometimes hear the statement that high compensation is a consequence of organizational success, rather than its progenitor, and a related comment that high compensation (compared to the average) is possible only in certain industries that either face less competition or have particularly highly educated employees. But neither of these statements is correct. Obviously, successful firms can afford to pay more and frequently do so, but high pay can also produce economic success.

When John Whitney assumed the leadership of Pathmark, a large grocery store chain in the eastern United States in 1972, the company had about ninety days to live according to its banks and was in desperate financial shape. Whitney looked at the situation and discovered that 120 store managers in the chain were paid terribly. Many of them made less than the butchers, who were unionized. He decided that the store managers were vital to the chain's success and its ability to accomplish a turnaround. Consequently, one of the first things he did was to give the store managers a substantial raise—about 40 to 50 percent. The subsequent success of the chain was, according to Whitney, because the store managers could now focus on improving performance instead of worrying and complaining about their pay. Furthermore, in a difficult financial situation, the substantial raise ensured that talent would not be leaving for better jobs elsewhere, thereby making a turnaround more difficult. Whitney has consistently tried to pay a 15 percent wage premium in the many turnaround situations he has managed, and he argues that this wage premium and the resulting reduced turnover facilitates the organization's performance.

The idea that only certain jobs or industries can or should pay high wages is belied by the example of many firms including Home Depot, the largest home improvement and building supply company in the United States, with about 8 percent of the market and approximately 100,000 employees. The company has been successful and profitable, and its stock price has shown exceptional returns. Even though the chain emphasizes everyday low pricing as an important part of its business strategy and operates in a highly competitive environment, it pays its staff comparatively well for the retail industry, hires more experienced people with building industry experience, and expects its sales associates to provide a higher level of individual customer service:

> At Home Depot, clients can expect to get detailed instruction and advice concerning their building, renovation, and hardware needs. This requires a higher level of knowledge than is typical of retail sales worker. Management considers the sales associates in each department as a team, with wide discretion over department operations. Associates also receive above average pay for this retail segment.[30]

Contingent compensation also figures importantly in most high-performance work systems. Such compensation can take a number of different forms, including gain sharing, profit sharing, stock ownership, pay for skill, or various forms of individual or team incentives. Wal-Mart, AES Corporation, Southwest Airlines, Whole Foods Markets, Microsoft, and many other successful organizations encourage share ownership. When employees are owners, they act and think like owners. Moreover, conflict between capital and labor can be reduced by linking them through employee ownership. Since

1989, PepsiCo has offered a broad-based stock option plan available to 100,000 people, virtually its entire full-time labor force. Publix, a supermarket chain with 478 stores in the southeastern United States, earned 2.75 percent on net sales in 1995 in an industry where the average is 1 percent. The company has enjoyed rapid expansion. It is important to note that the sixty-four-year-old company "has always been owned entirely by its employees and management, and the family of its late founder. . . . Employees become eligible for stock after working one year and one thousand hours. . . . Employees . . . wear name badges proclaiming that each is a stockholder."[31] Home Depot, the number-one-rated Fortune 500 service company for profit growth, makes sure its managers own stock in the company. At Starbucks, the rapidly growing coffee outlet chain, 100 percent of the employees, even those working part time, receive stock options in the company.[32] But such widespread encouragement of stock ownership remains quite rare. Hewitt Associates, a compensation consulting firm, estimated that in 1993, "only 30 large companies now have stock option plans available to a broad range of employees. Instead, most companies simply give stock options to employees once they reach a certain level in the corporation. Many workers then exercise the options and sell the stock in a single transaction. . . . They do not acquire a stake in the company."[33]

As various schemes for encouraging employee stock ownership have become increasingly trendy, in part because they frequently have tax advantages and, more important, are relatively straightforward to implement, it is critical to keep two things in mind. First, little evidence suggests that employee ownership by itself affects organizational performance. Rather, employee ownership works best as part of a broader philosophy or culture that incorporates other practices as well:

> An employee ownership culture is . . . a high-performance work-place in which each employee becomes an owner who is afforded certain rights in exchange for assuming new responsibilities. Such a culture is achieved by following the "working for yourself" thrust of employee ownership in conjunction with a battery of practices intended to create a non-bureaucratic, less hierarchical organization focused on performance.[34]

Merely putting in ownership schemes without providing training, information sharing, and delegation of responsibility will have little effect on performance because even if people are more motivated by their share ownership, they don't necessarily have the skills, information, or power to do anything with that motivation.

Second, many organizations treat stock options and share ownership as psychologically equivalent, but they are not. An option is just that—the potential or option to acquire shares at some subsequent point in time, at a given price. If the stock price falls below the option price, the option has no value. As Bill Gurley, one of Wall Street's premier technology analysts, has argued, "The main problem with stock options is that they do not represent true ownership." Gurley goes on to describe the two potential negative effects that follow from the option holder's being given the upside but protected from the downside:

> There is a huge incentive for option holders to take undue risk [and] there is an incentive for [people] to roam around. Try your luck at one job, and if it doesn't pan out, move on to the next one. . . . An aggressive stock-option program has many of the same characteristics as leverage. When times are good, they are doubly good . . . when times turn bad, the effects of stock option compensation can be quite devastating.[35]

If, by contrast, someone purchases stock, even at a slightly discounted price, that person has made a behavioral commitment with much more powerful psychological consequences. The person remains an owner, with psychological investment in the company, even when the stock price falls. Consequently, share ownership builds much more powerful commitments and psychologically binds people to their organizations more than do options, even when the economic consequences of the two schemes are largely similar.

One worry I sometimes hear voiced about share ownership concerns inevitable declines in stock price. When I asked AES people working at the power plant in Thames, Connecticut, specifically about this issue, I was told that people do watch the stock price, but when it goes down, most employees want to buy more. One person stated, "We feel we're part of the entrepreneurs. The fluctuations in stock price reinforce the fact that we're responsible. If there were only upside, we're taking a free ride. The fact that the stock price fluctuates and that people gain and lose accordingly makes people feel like they are more of an owner of the company."

A number of organizations use profit sharing to great effect, particularly when it extends throughout the organization. At Southwest Airlines, profit sharing causes its people to focus on costs and profits because they receive a percentage of those profits. At Hewlett-Packard, quarterly profit-sharing payments are greeted with anticipation and excitement. The enthusiasm of vice presidents and secretaries alike, the excited talk pervading the organization, makes it clear that when profit sharing covers all employees, the social pressure to continue producing good results becomes both powerful and widespread.

Profit sharing also makes compensation more variable, permitting adjustments in the labor bill without layoffs. At Lincoln Electric, profit sharing averages around 70 percent of individual employee salaries. When business falls, profit-sharing payments fall and labor expenses decrease—without having to break the firm's commitment to employment security. This variable component of wage costs, achieved through profit sharing, has permitted Lincoln to ride out a substantial sales decrease without laying off anyone covered by its guaranteed employment policy.

Paying for skill acquisition encourages people to learn different jobs and thereby to become more flexible. Gain sharing differs from profit sharing in that it is based on incremental improvements in the performance of a specific unit. Levi Strauss, for instance, has used gain sharing in its U.S. manufacturing plants. If a plant becomes more efficient in its use of labor and materials, the people share in the economic gains thereby achieved. They share in these gains even if profits in the firm as a whole are down. Why should employees in a plant in which they have achieved efficiency gains be penalized for problems in the general economy that have adversely affected sales or, for that matter, by the performance of other parts of the organization over which they have no control?

For a number of reasons, contingent compensation is important. First, simply, it is a matter of equity and fairness. If an organization produces greater returns by unharnessing the power of its people, justice suggests that some proportion of those gains should accrue to those who have produced the results as opposed to going solely to the shareholders or management. If people expend more effort and ingenuity, observe better results as a consequence of that effort, but then receive nothing, they are likely to become cynical and disillusioned and to stop trying.

Second, contingent compensation helps to motivate effort, because people know they will share in the results of their work.

At Whole Foods, a gain-sharing program "ties bonuses directly to team performance—specifically, sales per hour, the most important productivity measurement."[36] Teams, stores, and regions compete on the basis of quality, service, and profitability, with the results translating into bonuses. At Solectron, the implementation of self-managed teams positively affected quality and productivity. But when bonuses based on team performance were instituted, productivity and quality improved yet again.

Managers sometimes ask how to prevent employment security from turning into something resembling the civil service, with people just marking time. The answer is by coupling employment security with some form of group-based incentive, such as profit or gain sharing or share ownership. The organization thus unleashes the power of the team, whose economic interests are aligned with high levels of economic performance. Explaining Whole Foods's exceptional performance record, CEO John Mackey stated the following: "Whole Foods is a social system. . . . It's not a hierarchy. We don't have lots of rules handed down from headquarters in Austin. We have lots of self examination going on. Peer pressure substitutes for bureaucracy. Peer pressure enlists loyalty in ways that bureaucracy doesn't."[37] Peer pressure is stimulated by profit sharing and stock ownership that encourages team members to identify with the organization and to work hard on its behalf.

TRAINING

Virtually all descriptions of high-performance management practices emphasize training, and the amount of training provided by commitment as opposed to control-oriented management systems is substantial. Training in steel minimills, for example, was almost 75 percent higher in mills relying on commitment as opposed to those relying on control. The previously cited study of automobile assembly plants showed that training was substantially higher in flexible or lean compared to mass production systems. Training is an essential component of high-performance work systems because these systems rely on front-line employee skill and initiative to identify and resolve problems, to initiate changes in work methods, and to take responsibility for quality. All of this requires a skilled and motivated workforce that has the knowledge and capability to perform the requisite tasks:

> Having a work force that is multiskilled, adaptable to rapidly changing circumstances, and with broad conceptual knowledge about the production system is critical to the operation of a flexible production system. The learning process that generates these human capabilities is an integral part of how the production system functions, not a separate training activity.[38]

Training is often seen as a frill in many U.S. organizations, something to be reduced to make profit goals in times of economic stringency. Data from the worldwide automobile assembly plant study, in this instance, from fifty-seven plants, are particularly instructive in illustrating the extent to which U.S. firms, at least in this industry, underinvest in training compared to competitors based in other countries. Table 7.1 presents information on the amount of training provided in automobile assembly plants operating in various countries and with different ownership.

The data in the table are startling. In terms of the amount of training provided to newly hired production workers, U.S. firms operating in either the United States or Europe provide by far the least. Japanese plants in North America provide about 700 percent more training, and plants in newly industrialized

TABLE 7.1. **Amount of Training for Production Workers in Automobile Assembly Plants**

Ownership/ Location	Hours of Training in the First Six Months for New Workers	Hours per Year for Those with Less Than One Year Experience
Japanese/Japan	364	76
Japanese/North America	225	52
United States/North America	42	31
United States/Europe	43	34
European/Europe	178	52
Newly industrialized countries	260	46
Australia	40	15

Source: J. P. MacDuffie and T. A. Kochan, "Do U.S. Firms Invest Less in Human Resources? Training in the World Auto Industry," *Industrial Relations* 34 (1955): 156.

countries such as Korea, Taiwan, and Brazil provided more than 750 percent more training than do U.S. plants. Only the amount of training provided in Australia compares with the U.S. level. Similar, although not as dramatic, differences exist in the training provided for experienced production workers. Once again, the United States and Australia lag, with Japanese firms operating in Japan providing more than twice as much training to experienced workers. It is, of course, possible that U.S. firms' training is so much better and so much more efficient that it accomplishes just as much with a small fraction of the effort. This explanation cannot be definitively ruled out because the study did not measure (which would be almost impossible in any event) the consequences or the effectiveness of training. Although this explanation for the differences is possible, it is not very plausible. Rather, the differences in training reflect the different views of people held by the different firms and their corresponding production systems. "The Japanese-owned plants appear to train a lot because they rely heavily on flexible production, while the U.S.-owner plants in Europe and the Australian plants appear to train very little because they follow traditional mass production practices and philosophies."[39] U.S. automobile plants serious about pursuing profits through people show substantially larger training expenditures. Workers coming to Saturn initially "receive between 300 and 600 hours of training and then at least 5 percent of their annual work time (92 hours)" goes to training.[40]

The differences in training levels also reflect differences in time horizon—the Japanese firms and Saturn, with their policies of employment security, intend to keep their people longer, so it makes more sense for them to invest more in developing them. This illustrates a more general point—that the returns from any single high-performance management practice depend importantly on the entire set of practices that have been implemented. A firm that invests a lot in training but considers its people to be expendable costs to be quickly shed in times of economic difficulty will probably see little return from its training investment.

Studies of firms in the United States and the United Kingdom consistently provide evidence of inadequate levels of training and training focused on the wrong things: specialist skills rather than generalist competence and organizational culture. For instance, a case study of eight large organizations operating in the United Kingdom found one, W. H. Smith, a retailing and distribution organization, in which fewer than half of the people received any training at all in the past year. Furthermore, in only two of the organizations "did more than half the respondents indicate that they thought they received the training they needed to do their jobs well,"[41] and fewer than half of the organizations had a majority of employees who felt they were encouraged to develop new skills. What training is provided frequently focuses narrowly on specific job skills. "One Lloyds Bank senior manager said, 'People's perceptions of development would be that it is inadequate. But of course they are looking at being developed as generalists and I want them to be specialists more and more.'"[42] And all of this is occurring in a world in which we are constantly told that knowledge and intellectual capital are critical for success. Knowledge and skill *are* critical—and too few organizations act on this insight.

Training can be a source of competitive advantage in numerous industries for firms with the wisdom to use it. Consider, for instance, the Men's Wearhouse, an off-price specialty retailer of men's tailored business attire and accessories. Because four of the ten occupations expected to generate the most job growth through 2005 are in the retail trade sector, and in 1994, 17.9 percent of all American workers were employed in retail trade, this industry has some importance to the U.S. economy.[43] Yet the management of people in retailing is frequently abysmal. Turnover is typically high, as is the use of part-time employees, many of whom work part time involuntarily. Employees are often treated poorly and subjected to arbitrary discipline and dismissals. Wages in retailing are comparatively low and are falling compared to other industries, and skill and career development and training are rare. The industry is characterized by both intense and increasing competition, with numerous bankruptcies of major retailing chains occurring in the past decade.

The Men's Wearhouse went public in 1991 and in its 1995 annual report noted that since that time, it had achieved compounded annual growth rates in revenues and net earnings of 32 and 41 percent, respectively. The value of its stock increased by approximately 400 percent over this period. In 1995, the company operated 278 stores with a total revenue of $406 million. The key to its success has been how it treats its people and particularly the emphasis it has placed on training, an approach that separates it from many of its competitors. The company built a 35,000-square-foot training center in Fremont, California, its headquarters. In 1994, some six hundred "clothing consultants" went through Suits University, and that year the company added "Suits High and Selling Accessories U to complement our core program."[44] "New employees spend about four days in one of about thirty sessions held every year, at a cost to the company of about $1 million."[45] During the winter, experienced store personnel come back to headquarters in groups of about thirty for a three- or four-day retraining program.

The Men's Wearhouse has invested far more heavily in training than have most of its competitors, but it has prospered by doing so:

> Our shrink is 0.6 percent, only about a third of the industry average. And we spend zero on monitors in our stores. We have no electronic tagging and we spend nothing on security. . . . We feel that if you create a culture and an environment that is supportive of employees, you don't have to spend money on security devices. . . . My sense is that our rate of turnover is significantly lower than elsewhere.[46]

Not only does the typical U.S. firm not train as much, but because training budgets often fluctuate with company economic fortunes, a perverse, procyclical training schedule typically develops: training funds are most plentiful when the firm is doing well. But when the firm is doing well, its people are the busiest and have the most to do and consequently can least afford to be away for training. By contrast, when the firm is less busy, individuals have more time to develop their skills and undertake training activities. But that is exactly when training is least likely to be made available.

Training is an investment in the organization's staff, and in the current business milieu, it virtually begs for some sort of return-on-investment calculations. But such analyses are difficult, if not impossible, to carry out. Successful firms that emphasize training do so almost as a matter of faith and because of their belief in the connection between people and profits. Taco Inc., for instance, a privately owned manufacturer of pumps and valves, with annual sales of under $100 million, offers its 450 employees "astonishing educational opportunities—more than six dozen courses in all,"[47] in an on-site learning center. It cost the company $250,000 to build the center, and annual direct expenses and lost production cost about $300,000. Asked to put a monetary value on the return from operating the center, however, the company's chief executive, John Hazen White, said, "It comes back in the form of attitude. People feel they're playing in the game, not being kicked around in it. You step to the plate and improve your work skills; we'll provide the tools to do that."[48]

Even Motorola does a poor job of measuring its return on training. Although the company has been mentioned as reporting a three dollar return for every one dollar invested in training, an official from Motorola's training group said that she did not know where these numbers came from and that the company is notoriously poor at evaluating its $170 million investment in training. The firm mandates forty hours of training per employee per year and believes that the effects of training are both difficult to measure and expensive to evaluate. Training is part and parcel of an overall management process and is evaluated in that light.

REDUCTION OF STATUS DIFFERENCES

The fundamental premise of high-performance management systems is that organizations perform at a higher level when they are able to tap the ideas, skill, and effort of all of their people. One way in which they do this is by organizing people in work teams, a topic already briefly covered in this chapter. But neither individuals nor teams will feel comfortable or encouraged to contribute their minds as well as their physical energy to the organization if it has sent signals that they are not both valuable and valued. In order to help make all organizational members feel important and committed to enhancing organizational operations, therefore, most high-commitment management systems attempt to reduce the status distinctions that separate individuals and groups and cause some to feel less valued.

This is accomplished in two principal ways—symbolically, through the use of language and labels, physical space, and dress, and substantively, in the reduction of the organization's degree of wage inequality, particularly across levels. At Subaru-Isuzu, everyone from the company president on down was called an associate. The company's literature stated, "SIA is not hiring workers. It is hiring Associates . . . who work as a team to accomplish a task."[49] It is easy to downplay the importance of titles and language in affecting how people relate to their organization—but it is a mistake to do so:

> The title "secretary" seems subservient, Wilson [a consultant at Miss Paige Personnel agency in Sherman Oaks, California] said, "whereas administrative assistant sounds more career-oriented, and they like that." . . . Paul Flores . . . said employees at the Prudential Insurance Co. of America treat him better because of his new title. . . . When he moved to the supply unit, he became a SIMS (supply inventory management system) technician. . . . Instead of people saying, "I want it now," they say, "Get it to me when you can."[50]

At NUMMI, everyone wears the same colored smock; executive dining rooms and reserved parking don't exist. Lincoln Electric also eschews special dining rooms—management eats with the employees—as well as reserved parking and other fancy perquisites. Anyone who has worked in a manufacturing plant has probably heard the expression, "The suits are coming." Differences in dress distinguish groups from each other and, consequently, help to inhibit communication across internal organizational boundaries. At Kingston Technology, a private firm manufacturing add-on memory modules for personal computers, with 1994 sales of $2.7 million per each of its three hundred people (a higher level of revenue per employee than Exxon, Intel, or Microsoft), the two cofounders sit in open cubicles and do not have private secretaries.[51] Solectron, too, has no special dining rooms and the chief executive, Ko Nishimura, does not have a private office or a reserved parking space. Parking has become quite tight as the company has expanded, and shuttle buses ferry employees in from more distant parking lots. Ko Nishimura rides these same shuttles and has said that he learns more riding in with the employees than from almost anything else he does. The reduction of status differences encourages open communication, necessary in an organization in which learning and adaptation are encouraged.

Status differences are reduced and a sense of common fate developed by limiting the difference in compensation between senior management and other employees. Whole Foods Markets, whose sales in 1996 were over $800 million and which has enjoyed substantial growth and stock price appreciation, has a policy limiting executive compensation. "The Company's publicly stated policy is to limit annual compensation paid to any executive officer to eight times the average full-time salary of all Team Members."[52] In 1995, the CEO, John Mackey, earned $130,000 in salary and a bonus of $20,000. Nor does Whole Foods circumvent this restriction on executives shares in the company. In 1995, Mr. Mackey received options at the market price on four thousand shares of stock.

Herb Kelleher, the CEO of Southwest Airlines who has been on the cover of *Fortune* magazine with the text, "Is he America's best CEO?" earns about $500,000 per year including base and bonus. Moreover, when in 1995 Southwest negotiated a five-year wage freeze with its pilots in exchange for stock options and occasional profitability bonuses, Kelleher agreed to freeze his base salary at $395,000 for four years.

> Southwest's compensation committee said the freeze, which leaves Mr. Kelleher's salary unchanged from his 1992 contract, "is pursuant to a voluntary commitment made by Mr. Kelleher to the Southwest Airlines Pilots' Association." . . . The . . . compensation committee said the number of options granted Mr. Kelleher, at his recommendation, was "significantly below" the number recommended by an independent consultant as necessary to make Mr. Kelleher's contract competitive with pay packages for rival airline chief executives.[53]

Sam Walton, the founder and chairman of Wal-Mart, was typically on Graef Crystal's list of one of the most underpaid CEOs. These individuals are, of course, not poor. Each of them owns stock in the companies they manage. But stock ownership is encouraged for employees in these companies. Having an executive's fortune rise and fall together with those of the other employees differs dramatically from providing them large bonuses and substantial salaries even as the stock price languishes and people are being laid off.

Clearly, practices that reduce status differences are consistent with rewards contingent on performance—as long as these contingent rewards are applied on a group or organizational level so that the benefits of the performance of the many are not awarded to the few. Reducing status differences by reducing wage inequality does limit the organization's ability to use individual incentives to the extent that the application of individual rewards increases the dispersion of wages. This is not necessarily a bad thing. Many managers and human resource executives mistakenly believe that placing individual pay at risk increases overall motivation and performance, when it is actually the contingency of the reward itself, not the level at which it is applied (individual, group, or organizational), that has the impact.

SHARING INFORMATION

Information sharing is an essential component of high-performance work systems for two reasons. First, the sharing of information on things such as financial performance, strategy, and operational measures conveys to the organization's people that they are trusted. John Mackey, the chief executive of Whole Foods Markets, has stated, "If you're trying to create a high-trust organization, . . . an organization where people are all-for-one and one-for-all, you can't have secrets."[54] Whole Foods shares detailed financial and performance information with every employee—things such as sales by team, sales results for the same day last year, sales by store, operating profits by store, and even information from its annual employee morale survey—so much information, in fact, that "the SEC has designated all 6,500 employees 'insider' for stock-trading purposes."[55] AES Corporation also shares detailed operational and financial information with its employees to the extent that they are all insiders for purposes of securities regulation. But Whole

Foods goes even further, sharing individual salary information with every employee who is interested:

> The first prerequisite of effective teamwork is trust. . . . How better to promote trust (both among team members and between members and leaders) than to eliminate a major source of distrust—misinformed conjecture about who makes what? So every Whole Foods store has a book that lists the previous year's salary and bonus for all 6,500 employees—by name.[56]

This idea may at first seem strange. But think about your organization. If it is anything like mine, where salaries are secret, when it's time for raises, people spend time and effort attempting to figure out what others got and how their raise (and salary) stacks up. This subtle attempt to find out where you stand takes time away from useful activities. Moreover, individuals frequently assume the worst—that they are doing worse than they actually are—and in any event, they don't have enough information to trust the salary system or, for that matter, the management that administers it. John Mackey of Whole Foods instituted the open salary disclosure process to signal that at least this company had nothing to hide, nothing that couldn't be seen—and questioned—by any team member.

Contrast that organization with *Fortune* magazine, where a now-retired senior editor told me that after the Time-Warner merger when the company was saddled with debt, senior personnel were called together and told to "cut expenses by 10 percent." When the editor asked to see the expense budget and how it was allocated, he was told he could not. He resigned soon after. What message does an organization send if it says, "Cut expenses, but, by the way, I don't trust you (even at senior levels) enough to share expense information with you"?

A second reason for sharing information is this: even motivated and trained people cannot contribute to enhancing organizational performance if they don't have information on important dimensions of performance and, in addition, training on how to use and interpret that information. The now famous case of Springfield ReManufacturing beautifully illustrates this point. On February 1, 1983, Springfield ReManufacturing Corporation (SRC) was created when the plant's management and employees purchased an old International Harvester plant in a financial transaction that consisted of about $100,000 equity and $8.9 million debt, an 89-to-1 debt-to-equity ratio that has to make this one of the most leveraged of all leveraged buy-outs. Jack Stack, the former plant manager and now chief executive, knew that if the plant was to succeed, everyone had to do their best and to share all of her or his wisdom and ideas for enhancing the plant's performance. Stack came up with a system called "open-book management" that has since become a quite popular object of study—so popular that SRC now makes money by running seminars on it. Although the method may be popular as a seminar topic, fewer organizations are actually willing to implement it.

The system has a straightforward underlying philosophy, articulated by Stack:

> Don't use information to intimidate, control or manipulate people. Use it to teach people how to work together to achieve common goals and thereby gain control over their lives. . . . Cost control happens (or doesn't happen) on the level of the individual. You don't become the least-cost producer by issuing edicts from an office. . . . The best way to control costs is to enlist everyone in the effort. That means providing people with the tools that allow them to make the right decisions.[57]

Implementing the system involved first making sure that all of the company's people generated daily numbers reflecting their work performance and production costs. Second, it involved sharing this information, aggregated once a week, with all of the company's people, everyone from secretaries to top management. Third, it involved extensive training in how to use and interpret the numbers—how to understand balance sheets and cash flow and income statements. "Understanding the financials came to be part of everyone's job."[58]

Springfield ReManufacturing has enjoyed tremendous financial success. In 1983, its first year of operation, sales were about $13 million. By 1992, sales had increased to $70 million, the number of employees had grown from 119 at the time of the buy-out to 700, and the original equity investment of $100,000 was worth more than $23 million by 1993.[59] No one who knows the company, and certainly not Jack Stack or other managers, believes this economic performance could have been achieved without a set of practices that enlisted the cooperation and ingenuity of all of the firm's people. The system and philosophy of open-book management took a failing International Harvester plant and transformed it into a highly successful, growing business. Similarly impressive results have been reported in case studies of Manco, a Cleveland-based distributor of duct tape, weather stripping, and mailing materials; Phelps County Bank, located in Rolls, Missouri; Mid-States Technical Staffing Services, located in Iowa; Chesapeake Manufacturing Company, a packaging materials manufacturer; Allstate Insurance; Macromedia, a software company; and Pace Industries, a manufacturer of die cast metal parts.[60]

If sharing information makes simple, common sense, you might wonder why sharing information about operations and financial performance is not more widespread. One reason is that information is power, and sharing information diffuses that power. At an International Harvester plant, "the plant manager's whole theory of management was 'Numbers are power, and the numbers are mine.'"[61] If holding performance information is the critical source of the power of a firm's leaders, however, let me suggest that the organization badly needs to find some different leaders.

Another rationale for not sharing information more widely with the workforce is managers' fears that the information will leak out to competitors, creating a disadvantage for the organization. When Bob Beck, now running human resources at Gateway 2000, manufacturer of personal computers sold largely by mail order, was the executive vice president of human resources at the Bank of America in the early 1980s, he told his colleagues that the organization could never improve customer service or retention until it shared its basic business strategy, plans, and measures of performance with its entire workforce. When his colleagues on the executive committee noted that this information would almost certainly leak out to the competition, Beck demonstrated to them what ought to be common knowledge—in most instances, the competition already knows.

When organizations keep secrets, they keep secrets from their own people. I find it almost ludicrous that many companies in the electronics industry in Silicon Valley go to enormous lengths to try to keep secrets internally, when all you have to do to penetrate them is to go to one of the popular bars or restaurants in the area and listen in as people from different companies talk quite openly with each other. When people don't know what is going on and don't understand the basic principles and theory of the business, they cannot be expected to positively affect performance. Sharing information and providing training in understanding and using it to make better business decisions works.

CONCLUSION

Firms often attempt to implement organizational innovations such as those described in this chapter piecemeal. This tendency is understandable—after all, it is difficult enough to change some aspect of the compensation system without also having to be concerned about training, recruitment and selection, and how work is organized. Implementing practices in isolation may not have much effect, however, and under some circumstances, it could actually be counterproductive. For instance, increasing the firm's commitment to training activities won't accomplish much unless changes in work organization permit these more skilled people to actually implement their knowledge. If wages are comparatively low and incentives are lacking that recognize enhanced economic success, the better-trained people may simply depart for the competition. Employment security, too, can be counterproductive unless the firm hires people who will fit the culture and unless incentives reward outstanding performance. Implementing work teams will probably not by itself accomplish as much as if the teams received training in both specific technical skills and team processes, and it will have less effect still if the teams aren't given financial and operating performance goals and information. "Whatever the bundles or configurations of practices implemented in a particular firm, the individual practices must be aligned with one another and be consistent with the [organizational] architecture if they are ultimately to have an effect on firm performance."[62] It is important to have some overall philosophy or strategic vision of achieving profits through people, because an overall framework increases the likelihood of taking a systematic as contrasted with a piecemeal approach to implementing high-commitment organizational arrangements.

Clearly, it requires time to implement and see results from many of these practices. For instance, it takes time to train and upgrade the skills of an existing workforce and even more time to see the economic benefits of this training in reduced turnover and enhanced performance. It takes time not only to share operating and financial information with people but also to be sure that they know how to understand and use it in decision making; even more time is needed before the suggestions and insights implemented can provide business results. It certainly requires time for employees to believe in employment security and for that belief to generate the trust that then produces higher levels of innovation and effort. Consequently, taking a long-term view of a company's development and growth becomes at least useful, if not absolutely essential, to implementation of high-performance organizational arrangements. One way of thinking about various institutional and organizational barriers and aids to implementing high-performance management practices is therefore to consider each in terms of its effects on the time horizon that characterizes organizational decision.

Although the management practices described in this chapter come directly from a number of systematic studies that have examined the effects of the management of the employment relationship on economic performance, are supported by numerous case examples, and seem to be logical and based on straightforward common sense, in fact a number of them are at some substantial variance from both dominant practice and conventional wisdom. Employment security is out of fashion;

compensation systems are returning, in some instances, to the piecework characteristic of Frederick Taylor and scientific management; training is talked about more often than done; and arguments have been offered that executive compensation and associated status differences are too low, particularly in countries other than the United States.

o   o   o

Jeffrey Pfeffer is professor of organizational behavior in the Graduate School of Business at Stanford University, where he has taught since 1979.

Chapter Eight

Hire the Right People

Edward E. Lawler III

People can rarely be forced to fit into an organization after they are hired. This makes hiring the right employees absolutely essential. As much as humanly possible, you need to select applicants who will fit into your culture and perform effectively—and who will ultimately contribute to your organization's virtuous spiral.

What Leads to Good Hiring Decisions

Hiring requires a disciplined process and clear practices that thoroughly assess the competencies, skills, knowledge, personality, and needs of the people you consider hiring. Through the hiring process, you need to be able to determine how well a candidate will fit the current and future needs of your organization. Fit can be quite complex and difficult to determine, so you need to use specific and objective criteria that are based on the kinds of work your organization offers and the kinds of skills, knowledge, competencies, and personality that people need to possess to perform that work effectively.

The hiring process represents the first critical point in the relationship between an organization and its employees. But keep in mind that this is often not the last time you will be making job placement decisions concerning your employees.

Today, as organizations continuously seek to fill newly created jobs and eliminate old ones, many current employees will seek out new opportunities, and you will need to decide whether to move them up or laterally to a new job. As time goes on, further changes in the skill needs of your organization are also likely to create situations where you will have to decide which employees to retain and which to terminate.

Effective decisions about whom to retain and whom to terminate are critical in upgrading the quality of your workforce and being sure that it has the skills to execute the core competencies and capabilities your organization needs.

The selection process is particularly important because it is a clear decision point. As such, it is very important that you test the major principles and practices that your organization uses to guide its selection and placement decisions against the ones that are recommended in this chapter.

Convey the Importance of Hiring

All too often organizations use a hiring process that solely emphasizes selecting the best individual. But the hiring process needs to be more than just an effort to hire the best people. It needs to introduce them to your organization in a way that gives them a realistic expectation of what work will be like and places them in an environment that helps them make a good decision as to whether the organization represents a good fit for them.

A careful selection process can be critical to giving individuals the view that they are valued by the organization, that the organization is a desirable place to work, and that it cares about its human capital. It can help give new hires the impression that they are fortunate to be working for the organization. People tend to value membership in organizations that have high entrance standards and carefully assess all potential members. This is an important phenomenon and one that organizations need to put front and center as they design their selection processes.

Southwest Airlines interviews twenty-five applicants for every one they hire. They can do this because they have a clearly established, attractive brand as an employer. It allows the company to hire people who are potentially a great fit and helps convince new hires that they are truly special and fortunate to get a job with Southwest.

Microsoft puts every new employee through an intensive multiple-day interview process. Job candidates talk to people from different parts of the organization and are asked very difficult interview questions. No one who survives the process has any doubt that Microsoft takes hiring seriously.

Use Objective Data

In my view, organizations need to increasingly use objective data in the hiring process. Many available assessment tools can be brought into play here, from personality tests to knowledge exams to realistic job previews and work samples.

There is no magic formula concerning how much and what kind of data you need from people to determine whether they

will be a good fit with your organization. But a useful general-
ization is that you need to determine if the applicant has all of
the following:

- The skills and knowledge you require
- The competencies required to learn new skills and adjust
  to new tasks
- The interpersonal skills to deal with coworkers and
  customers
- The motivation to perform well

In my view, data about these issues are best obtained from
multiple sources. Interviews are not enough, nor are tests or
background checks; instead, you need to use all of them, as well
as any other sources of data on how job candidates have performed in the past.

Don't Neglect Background and Ethics

A good rule of thumb in hiring decisions is that past behavior
is the best predictor of future behavior. For this reason, don't
neglect checking on an individual's past history, through both
reference checks and résumé validation.

As surprising as it may seem, nearly 35 percent of all job
applicants put false data on their résumés and job applications.
This is true for even high-profile individuals, so don't assume
that integrity can be questionable only up to a certain level of
executive.

For example, Al Dunlop, who became known as "Chainsaw
Al" because of his downsizing of Scott Paper and his destruction of Sunbeam Corporation, circulated a falsified résumé for
years. To make his background look better, he modified his
employment history so that it excluded a stint he had as a CEO
of a small company that ended up in bankruptcy. Surprisingly,

this omission was discovered only after his failure at Sunbeam Corporation.

A stranger example of résumé falsification is the case of Al Martin, a major league baseball player who played for the Seattle Mariners and several other major league teams. He included in his biography the claim that he played college football for the University of Southern California. He even talked to his teammates about plays that he made during his football career. It all sounded good, but Martin never played football at USC; in fact, he never attended USC at all. Then there is the case of the Pulitzer Prize–winning professor who claimed to have been active in the Vietnam War. He even lectured in his class about his exploits. The problem was that during his military career, he never went overseas. When the truth came out, his university suspended him.

The moral is, be diligent in checking an applicant's background. You don't want to end up in the situation of hiring someone, only later to discover evidence of ethical lapses or poor judgment in the past.

Involve the People Who Will Work with the New Hire

In most cases, it is beneficial to involve the people who will be working with the new hire in the selection process. There are at least two reasons for this. First, they are familiar with the work situation, so they can ask and answer relevant questions and bring an informed perspective to the hiring process. Second, their commitment to helping the individual be successful once in the organization is partly determined by whether they have endorsed the hire.

This second point is often overlooked but is an important factor to consider. People will often make an extra effort to see that someone is successful when they have been asked for their opinion on whether to hire the applicant. This is particularly true in group and team situations. When team members have an active role in interviewing and hiring, they will work hard to ensure the success of the individual who is hired.

However, if you involve people in the selection process, be sure that they are fully trained in the legal and organizational issues involved. Managers and others who are going to be involved in recruitment and selection need to know about testing, interviewing, behavior-based selection interview processes, and what questions cannot be asked.

Failure to train interviewers and managers involved in selection and placement processes can lead to disaster. It can result not only in bad hiring decisions but also in significant legal liabilities caused by behaviors that violate regulations with respect to discrimination and the rights of applicants. It can also result in new hires having unrealistic expectations.

Validate Your Selection Results

It is very important that your organization validate its selection process on a regular basis. I am not talking about simply tracking the success rate of individuals who are hired. Validation efforts need to determine the accuracy of the different parts of your organization's selection process in predicting the performance of individuals once they have joined the organization.

There are literally thousands of studies on the selection practices used in companies. These studies consistently show that many widely used practices, such as simple personality tests and unstructured interviews, are not valid predictors of how effective an employee will be. Some of these practices may be fine in serving another purpose, such as contributing to a realistic job preview or increasing the commitment of employees to helping the individual succeed, but they are not valid predictors of whether someone will actually be successful.

Every selection process must have at least some tests or processes that have been validated, and these need to be the major factors in determining who is hired. Ignoring this point can open you to numerous legal and ethical problems. You owe it to yourself and the applicants to use validated selection processes. To do otherwise is to invite trouble. Hiring the wrong individual has high organizational and social costs because it typically leads to poor performance, premature turnover, and weakened organizations.

Apply the Same Selection Process to Career Moves

I recommend that the same principles I have enumerated to guide the selection of new hires be used in the placement of current employees in new positions. They need to be given a realistic preview of the nature of the job and what the work will be like. They need to be assessed in terms of whether they can do the work. And the individuals with whom they will work need to have input into whether they are given the job.

Often the placement processes in organizations are relatively informal, relying on networking to choose candidates. As a result, placement decisions are often seen as unfair and arbitrary. In most cases, the systems are in fact dysfunctional because they do not create a culture that continuously emphasizes the importance of managing human capital well.

Although it is more time-consuming and in some ways more bureaucratic, it is typically far better to go through a public process in order to fill a vacant position. This is true even though the intention is to fill it with someone who already works for the organization. You should make a public announcement that the opening exists, that there is an opportunity for individuals to apply, and that there will be a formal process to select the best-qualified individual.

It is only by conducting a thorough, formal process that the best placement decisions can be made and that people can feel that they have opportunities within the organization to develop and advance their careers. This practice can also help organizations better understand the career aspirations of their employees and help them assess the knowledge, skills, and competencies of their workforce.

Provide Continuous Feedback

To support treating people right, creating a good fit between individuals and organizations needs to be a continuous process. It must start with a selection process that is well developed and carefully done and must continue throughout the employee's entire history with an organization. Rather than being an event-driven process, it needs to be an ongoing process. By this, I mean rather than being something that occurs only when a job opening occurs and individuals are screened for that opening, it needs to be an ongoing process in which individuals are given the opportunity to take on new tasks, assignments, and work roles.

The process should involve making public the opportunities that exist internally, notifying people of their opportunities, and giving them feedback on how they are progressing in their skill and knowledge development. GE, Honeywell, and a number of other companies have taken steps to formalize career development feedback to individuals. They do an annual talent review that looks at the development of all their key employees. In the case of GE, the CEO looks at the top two thousand managers in the corporation. The outcome of this review is a decision to develop some employees and to terminate those whose skills are not developing or do not suit the direction in which the corporation is heading.

Eliminating individuals who no longer fit the strategic direction of the business is a realistic part of maintaining a virtuous spiral in an organization. It is, perhaps, the most important step an organization can take to indicate that the continued employment of its employees depends on their performance and skills. To prevent the implementation of this policy from being dysfunctional, decision making has to be handled extremely well. It needs to involve a valid assessment of the person's performance and skills, feedback to the individual, and an opportunity to improve their skills and performance when there is a problem.

Best Practices in Hiring and Placement

In my research, I have found a variety of selection and placement practices that support a good fit between individuals and organizations. This is an area where rapid change is occurring in what organizations actually do. The increasing importance of human capital is motivating organizations to try new approaches and to make sure that they are using the best possible practices. I will highlight some of the most powerful practices organizations are using and analyze the implications of their use in terms of treating people right.

Realistic Job Previews

The goal of a realistic job preview is to make sure the applicant knows precisely what the job entails, what is expected, and what rewards are offered. But realistic job previews can be much more than that. They can be an opportunity to verify that the applicant can perform the job in the way that you want.

In fact, one of the best practices in conducting realistic previews is to have applicants actually do the work or produce a work sample.

One company I worked with in the customer service sector simulates for applicants some typical customer service encounters that occur. They use real customers with the applicants, and then ask the customers whether they would like to be served by the job applicant in the future.

Southwest Airlines bases its hiring decisions on a realistic preview. It has job applicants tell jokes and make announcements in front of a group of employees. This is intended to simulate the kinds of situations found aboard airplanes and as such serves the needs of both the company and the applicants. It gives the organization considerable information about how the applicants will perform while giving them a good sense of the type of work that they will be expected to handle.

Some companies ask that applicants do an internship—a very effective way to give them a chance to experience the work while giving the organization a chance to assess the candidate. Particularly if the internship lasts several months, both the individual and the organization can get a good feeling for how well the person fits into the culture.

Other companies hire applicants as temporary employees to ensure that they have firsthand experience on the job before agreeing to hire them. One manufacturing firm I studied had a significant turnover problem in one of its plants. Although the facility was clean and safe, the work was very repetitive, and a large number of new employees, having an unrealistic idea of what their jobs would be like, were disappointed once they started and soon left. To implement a realistic job preview, the company opted to hire all applicants only as temporary workers for at least four weeks. After this trial period, those who were good performers were given the opportunity to become full-time employees, and the others were released. The people who stayed usually turned out to be excellent long-term employees.

Another application of realistic job previews is to begin to socialize and educate people into your organization's culture. This can be accomplished in many ways. One simple technique is to have job applicants interview with most or all of the people they will work with. Comprehensive interviews can provide applicants with a good sense of the social and cultural atmosphere they will encounter.

To provide a preview, some organizations such as Ford Motor Company and Cummins Engines show applicants a video that presents views of people doing the actual work. Let me interject a small caution about this, though. Your video can be as forthright as you want it to be, but you may want to use some discretion. Years ago, Ford produced a video called *Don't Color It Like Disneyland* that portrayed their jobs so honestly that no applicant could doubt the boring nature of Ford's assembly line work. The cold directness of the video helped reduce turnover, because people knew from the start what to do expect, but Ford decided to cease using it because it left such a negative image of the company.

Realistic job previews should also be used for job changes that involve your current employees. Although these employees already work for you, the same benefits can be gained by asking them to go through a realistic job preview.

For example, FedEx uses a realistic preview situation to select first-level supervisors from its employees. When employees say they are interested in being promoted to this level, they are asked to come to a workshop, designed to have candidates participate in a number of simulations of the kind of interpersonal situations that first-line supervisors face. FedEx offers this workshop only on weekends, specifically to emphasize to the candidates that being a supervisor involves a significant time commitment over and above being a nonmanagement employee. Demanding a weekend of time is thus a way to initially screen applicants with respect to their commitment to being successful as a first-line supervisor.

Realistic job previews cannot always be done because in some cases people need training or certification before they can do the work required. But when they can be done, they are clearly a win-win proposition. They help avoid wrong hires, and they provide applicants with enough information to decide if the work situation will meet their needs. In my view, they also are extremely important from the point of view of treating people right, in that they support informed choice and help people become more thoughtful decision makers in managing their careers.

Matching the Interview Process with the Job

Unstructured interviews that are simply general discussions rarely provide data that improve selection decisions. However, interviews with targeted questions can provide valid data and can help facilitate the selection decision, especially if the interview process focuses on the behaviors you need the person to excel in.

For example, if you are looking for someone to fulfill an entrepreneurial role in your organization, you want to know whether the applicant has demonstrated entrepreneurial behavior in the past. You can find this out only by asking specific questions in interviews about past experiences, entrepreneurial efforts, and so on. The same is true if you are looking to hire someone who can work effectively in teams. Questions concerning the roles applicants have played in teams in the past, examples of successful teams they have been on, and the like can be critical in determining whether candidates have shown propensity in the past to work effectively in a team environment.

General Electric is a good example of a company that uses carefully structured interviews to select managers. Interviewers ask key questions about applicants' past behavior in order to determine whether they have a history of demonstrating leadership. For example, candidates for a managerial job are asked what positions they have had in the past that required them to be leaders. Follow-up questions then focus on how they got things done, what their leadership style was, and what results were produced.

Microsoft adds an interesting twist to the interviewing process: it has at least one "outsider," a person who will not work with the applicant, meet and assess the applicant. Microsoft does this to avoid too much of a "groupthink" phenomenon in the hiring process and to obtain a broader perspective on who gets hired. Part of the rationale is to avoid developing pockets of divergent cultures because different parts of the organization engage in their own hiring and selection activities.

Testing

In today's world, organizations must constantly meet the challenge of jobs that have a changing portfolio of tasks and assignments, and they must constantly make decisions about fitting employees to tasks and tasks to employees. This means that it is increasingly important to hire people with an eye toward how well they fit the organization's need for change, particularly in regard to their ability and willingness to learn new skills.

This is where psychological testing is a best practice worthy of adoption in most organizations. Testing can indicate, for example, the underlying competencies and personalities of people and thus be a good predictor of someone's ability to learn specific knowledge and skills. Where people are being hired for their potential, it makes a great deal of sense to assess their ability to learn.

It also makes sense, in many situations, to use tests to assess an individual's personality, which is relatively fixed by the time a person enters the workforce. A test that assesses personality can be a predictor of how the person will react to changes in the work environment and to learning opportunities.

Although they can be useful, personality tests have an important limitation. Some people do not provide accurate data when completing tests. They often provide the answers they think the company wants to hear. That is why it is very important to compare any data that come from tests with data from interviews and other assessments of personality that might be available. For example, test data can be compared to interview reports about how people have made their career choices, as well as the kinds of activities they prefer.

Tailoring the Selection Process to the Employment Contract

When organizations have the need for different types of employees—for example, contrast those who are needed for immediately applicable technical skills and knowledge with those who are hired with development in mind—it becomes important to tailor the selection process to the hiring situation.

The selection process for those who are hired for their particular technical expertise and operational excellence will usually need to focus on their present skills and their motivation to apply those skills to a specific project. You especially want to assess whether it is possible to develop commitment among these employees, by which I do not mean loyalty to the organization but rather commitment to performing well on an already identified task, under existing working conditions.

As for long-term developmental hires, obviously your selection process needs to be extensive, rigorous, and in depth. What matters most in selecting them is an evaluation not so much of a set of specific skills as of their underlying competencies, working style, personality, willingness to learn, long-term career aspirations, and preferences with respect to rewards. It is also particularly important to look at their fit with the culture of your organization.

Web-Based Tracking Systems

In recent years, technology has come to the rescue to improve many aspects of the hiring process. One excellent innovation is Internet-based systems that track job applicants during the selection process. As people go from interview to interview, the interviewers can access the system to record their impressions, as well as to raise additional questions that future interviewers should follow up on as the candidate circulates.

Microsoft has an excellent Web-enabled interviewing process. As part of a carefully structured interview, interviewers ask a number of questions to test an applicant's ability to think. After each interview, the interviewer enters key issues on the appropriate Web site, suggesting follow-up questions that should be asked by the next interviewer. This creates a dynamic process that is both structured and cumulative, since it is informed by previous answers. The result is a selection experience that Microsoft feels is very effective at both hiring the right people and giving applicants an honest sense of what working at Microsoft is like.

Evaluating Your Selection and Placement System

Consistently evaluating the effectiveness of your selection and placement system is a best practice that I highly recommend. I am referring to actions that go beyond validating its predictive accuracy. This is important, but more needs to be done. You need to collect survey data regarding the satisfaction of employees with the hiring process on a regular and systematic basis. Dow Chemical, for example, does this in assessing its internal job-posting system. Employees are regularly asked about whether they feel the system is meeting their needs.

It can also be useful to look at how outside job candidates view the entire hiring process of the organization. Find out what impression they get about your company and whether they feel they were treated fairly in the process. Gather this information from people who joined the company as well as those who did not.

Overall, the selection and placement systems of your organization are so important to your human capital management that you cannot afford not to continually assess and improve them.

Managing Layoffs and Downsizing

Reductions in staff are high-risk actions for organizations. When carelessly and indiscriminately managed, layoffs and downsizings can ruin your brand, damage your culture in ways that make the people who remain less productive, result in the loss of significant knowledge and social capital, and be major triggers of death spirals. In many ways, how you handle layoffs can be even more crucial to your reputation for treating people right than initial hiring decisions.

The truth is, many companies simply overreact to downturns in their business. A growing body of evidence says that organizations tend to eliminate too many people in times of economic distress, incurring long-term costs that are often far greater than the short-term savings. These costs include losing people who are not easily rehired when the economic downturn is over; losing people who carry some of your organizational capabilities and core competencies; losing your social capital, which is found in the relationships and implicit knowledge that former employees have; and causing existing employees to lose faith in your company and its management, resulting in turnover among the remaining employees when the labor market improves.

Clearly, it would be foolish to argue against all staff reductions. Sometimes layoffs and downsizings are necessary for a variety of good reasons: your strategy changes, a restructuring is needed to bring in different skills, or an economic downturn forces the need for cost reductions. Sometimes building a new core competency can be accomplished only by recruiting new employees.

But there are significant advantages to not downsizing or doing only a little of it. For example, in an economic downturn, you may be able to grab market share or even gain a dominant position over competitors who overreduce their staff. This is particularly true if your competitors lose their ability to service their customers well or if they are in a poor position to recover when the downturn is over. You can also use a period of downturn to develop new products or to improve your employees' skills and knowledge, either of which can boost you over competitors and launch or support a virtuous spiral.

In my view, staff reductions should be used only as a last resort, after weighing the many other less disruptive options you may have to reduce labor costs, including these:

- Voluntary leaves/terminations
- Shorter working hours
- Pay reductions
- Delayed start dates for new hires
- Cutting back on the use of temporary employees
- Shortened workweeks
- Reduced bonus and variable pay amounts
- Reduced benefits and extras

If involuntary reductions in staff are necessary, I also believe it is critical that senior management make a strong case for them as the only practical alternative under the business conditions. It is important that management and employees have a good understanding of the nature of the business, the economic condition of the industry, and the status of the organization so that everyone comprehends why the reductions are needed. When the business case is compelling, reductions may slow down your virtuous spiral, but they don't have to end it.

Downsizing must be handled in ways that fully support your value proposition and your brand. For example, in deciding whom to lay off, many companies follow the traditional method of basing layoffs on seniority, but this does not really fit the demands of today's business environment. It often means that some of your best employees will be lost, and as a result, your organization's ability to perform will be diminished.

Reductions in staff are nearly always more effective when based on performance and ability, assuming you have good performance measures on which to decide. This means that you need to be sure to have done your homework to obtain high-quality data on the performance of your people through regular performance appraisals. Making performance-based staff reductions on the basis of poor or inadequate performance data is perhaps the worst step you can take; it damages your credibility and fosters mistrust among the remaining employees. It can also result in the wrong individuals being laid off; it may even lead to lawsuits.

In addition, once you decide to lay off an employee, be sure to assess whether the person is someone you may want to ask to rejoin the organization at a later date. Particularly in the case of a business cycle downturn, you can benefit by rerecruiting laid-off employees, so it is important to make sure that good performers leave the organization with positive feelings. You can foster goodwill in a number of ways, including a good severance package, offering placement services, and career counseling.

Some of the best practices I have seen in managing layoffs occurred in technology firms during the 2001 technology downturn. For example, Cisco paid employees part of their salaries if they went to work for volunteer organizations or contributed their time to public service. Other organizations paid tuition for laid-off employees so that they could improve their knowledge and be ready to reenter the organization at a later date with better skills and a positive attitude toward the company. Charles Schwab offered a $7,500 "hire-back" bonus to anyone rehired within eighteen months. And at Microsoft and a host of other technology companies, the best employees were offered incentives to stay.

It is hardly surprising that these companies created these practices, given the importance of human capital to them and the difficulties they had recruiting and retaining it in the 1990s.

Their response to the downturn is perhaps an indicator that more organizations in the future will be centered on human capital and will deal with future economic downturns in the spirit of treating people right.

Not all firms dealt effectively with the downturn. Some firms overreacted to it and reduced their labor force too extensively. Many even showed less concern for their employees than they had in the past, perhaps reflecting the death of the loyalty contract in their firms. Because they overreacted, they lost credibility as employers and as a result will likely have difficulty in responding when the markets for their businesses turn around.

IMPLICATIONS FOR INDIVIDUALS

The recommendations in this chapter for how organizations need to approach their selection and placement process have powerful implications for all individuals. The more that organizations adopt these hiring procedures and best practices, the more you can benefit by finding satisfying and rewarding jobs.

But in order to benefit, you must be an effective manager of your job search and career. The overarching message to learn here is that as valuable human capital, you have increased importance to organizations.

However, to capitalize on your capital, as it were, you must develop a strong sense of your knowledge and skills and of what you find rewarding about work. The first step of this process is to fashion your own value proposition.

Your ability to gather data on yourself is an increasingly important element in successful career management. One way to do this is to not be shy about applying for jobs, both internal and external; and to use the selection process to learn something about the options that are available to you, as well as about your personal strengths, interests, and competencies. If the opportunity presents itself, negotiate with prospective employers for complete feedback on the results of any tests they ask you to take. This includes psychological tests, assessment center processes, or any other experiences they have where data have been gathered about you that can give you insight into your own needs, desires, and competencies. In fact, it makes sense for you to target positions that are likely to give you direct feedback about your abilities.

As an active manager of your own career, check employment postings on your company's Web site on a regular basis. In addition, look outside your organization to see what is available. It is impossible to be a good self-manager without actively gathering information about the various opportunities that exist for you.

Learn to exercise discipline in accepting jobs. Avoid putting yourself in situations that do not have a high likelihood of meeting your needs or in which you risk performing less than successfully. This can happen if you present an image of yourself that is not realistic. For the selection and placement process to work well, you need to be candid in your self-description and accurate in the information you give organizations.

An organization's selection process usually yields important information about its culture and concern for its human capital. Be especially cautious of any organization that doesn't take the selection process seriously and fails to gather good data from job applicants. That reflects a serious lack of attention to the importance of human capital to the organization, a lack that might come back to haunt you should you decide to work there.

A long hiring process—which can be frustrating at times—may actually be a good sign. That often means the company values its people and wants to take its time—à la Microsoft—in choosing new hires. Microsoft takes several weeks and requires intensive time commitments from potential applicants, but its process is well designed and results in selecting good employees, who then are sure they want to work there.

Of course, the process can become too long and too bureaucratic, and you want to avoid organizations that keep you on hold indefinitely. For example, some government agencies, such as the Los Angeles Police Department, are infamous for taking six months to a year to process a job applicant. This is clearly the type of situation to flee from.

If you are applying for a position and are offered an employment contract or are in a position to ask for one, don't hesitate to pay a great deal of attention to the contract's termination clause. In the past, the idea of an applicant discussing a termination agreement was considered counterproductive, if not insulting. Many executives interpreted this to mean that an applicant lacked confidence and was not committed to staying with the organization a long time.

Today, however, senior executives almost always have employment contracts that include termination clauses. Indeed, they often get extremely generous payments when they leave the organization (ten of millions of dollars in the case of key executives who have left Disney and Mattel, to mention just two examples), even if they leave because of poor performance. Obviously, most employees cannot realistically expect to get a generous severance package if they are let go as a result of performance or downsizing.

But if you are in high demand, you may well be able to at least get an employment contract that calls for weeks or months of pay as part of the severance package. You may also be able to negotiate for the immediate vesting of your stock options and a continuation of your benefits.

At the very least, you should ask about specific policies regarding severance benefits when you join an organization. (You should also research as much as possible the history of how reductions in staff have been handled, particularly with respect to severance pay and unvested options.) In short, the day has come when you absolutely must pay serious attention to your exit strategy and take it into consideration when deciding which job to choose and the kind of deal you can make.

Finally, it is now time to recognize that your "job" is likely to be a regularly changing set of duties and responsibilities rather than a fixed set of tasks. Historically, many companies have had job descriptions that adequately captured what people were expected to do for a considerable period of time. But with today's rapid pace of change in business strategies, organizational design, and technology, it is unrealistic to continue thinking that today's jobs can be set in stone.

Instead, you should think of your job as likely having opportunities to take on new tasks and assignments on a regular basis. Each change represents a chance to learn a new skill and perhaps something about yourself. Rather than resisting new assignments and change, I suggest that you embrace them, eagerly agreeing to participate in new activities and to learn new areas of expertise.

The fact is, there is little security in today's business environment. It is critical that you clearly realize that the only security you have in this chaotic business world consists of your skills, your knowledge, and your track record. So take full advantage of all the learning and growing opportunities any new environment offers you. As I tell my M.B.A. students, take the best job you are offered, learn everything you can, work hard while you are there—and be prepared to leave.

o   o   o

Edward E. Lawler III is a professor and director of the Center for Effective Organizations at the University of Southern California's Marshall School of Business. He is also a consultant.

Chapter Nine

Managing the Interview Process

Richaurd Camp
Mary E. Vielhaber
Jack L. Simonetti

W hat does it take to be a good interviewer? The answer depends on the goals you are trying to achieve through the interview process. People who think of an interview as simply a conversation rarely identify specific goals for their interviews. In this chapter, we will demonstrate that good interviewers develop realistic goals and manage the interview process. Good interviewers also need a range of skills and the ability to shift among a variety of perspectives to achieve their interviewing goals.

This chapter begins with the potential goals that interviewers have in mind when they interview an applicant for a job. An assessment is provided to help you evaluate the goals you set for your interviews and determine if they are realistic.

We will also discuss the problems that occur when interviewers try to accomplish too much in a single interview or are not clear about what they need to achieve. Finally, we will present specific strategies for developing realistic goals and managing the interview process.

POTENTIAL GOALS OF INTERVIEWING

Most interviewers focus on some combination of three interviewing goals. First, interviewers attempt to accurately measure whether the candidate has what it takes to do the job. Second, they try to influence the candidate's job decision by selling the positive features of the job and the organization. Third, they assist the candidate in making an appropriate job choice by providing a balanced view of the challenges and rewards of the job. At first glance, the three goals may seem to be contradictory. In this chapter, we will argue that if you manage the interview process, you will decrease the possibility that you are focusing on contradictory goals. As you read about each of these goals, think about what you are trying to achieve in your interviews.

Accurately Measuring Whether the Candidate Can Do the Job

An interview is a test for the interviewer. It is also a test for the interviewee. Most people don't think of it that way, but it is really a test that measures whether someone has what the interviewer is looking for. You pass the test if you are hired; you fail if the interviewer determines you lack what is needed for the job.

Most interviewers would probably agree that they want the interview to be a test of whether the candidate can effectively perform the job. To measure whether the candidate can do the job requires that interviewers try to measure candidates on a variety of factors. For example, you probably would want to know if the candidate had the technical abilities to perform the job effectively, and if the person would fit into the culture and get along with the other workers and the boss.

Often the interview is an inaccurate measurement of the candidate's ability to perform the job. Instead of focusing on how the candidate is likely to behave on the job, many interviewers rely on impressions—what they like and what they don't like about the candidate.

Certainly not every job requires the interviewer to make an accurate measurement of the applicant's ability to do the job. In some jobs, particularly low-skill jobs, there is not much difference between good and minimally acceptable or even bad employees. The strategic interviewing approach focuses on jobs where you can differentiate performance among employees. We suggest that accurate measurement is unlikely to occur unless interviewers realize that their interview goals should focus not on their likes and dislikes but on what is needed to be a good employee.

Influencing the Candidate's Job Choice

Convincing the applicant to accept the job if it is offered is another potential interviewing goal. To achieve this goal, interviewers sell the organization and the job to the candidate by painting a positive picture. Interviewers emphasize positive information such as the work the person will be doing, the comfortable working conditions, and the advantages of the company's location. They may also discuss future job opportunities within the company or the company's vision and future prospects. Because of its overwhelmingly positive nature, this information is often called public relations, or simply PR. Human resource professionals and managers who attend our interviewing seminars at the University of Michigan say that they provide PR to persuade the candidate that their organization is a better place to work than other organizations that the candidate may be considering.

Accurately measuring whether the candidate can do the job is logically consistent with influencing a candidate to accept a job if it is offered. If the candidate can do the job, certainly the interviewer would want to recruit this person who is likely to be a good employee. However, interviewers need different strategies to attain these separate goals. Accurate measurement requires an objective, unbiased individual who will focus on the correct information—evidence of job-related skills. Influencing requires the interviewer to be an advocate and salesperson. Research indicates that interviewers act differently based on their objective. Interviewers who were focused on influence talked 50 percent more, volunteered twice as much information, and asked half as many questions as interviewers who were more focused on measurement.[1] Although many interviewers can focus on both goals, interviewers must recognize the strategy differences and make sure that their actions are consistent with their goals.

Assisting the Candidate in Making an Appropriate Job Choice

Most interviewers also try to provide realistic job information to candidates to help them make the decision about joining the organization. Typically, this information describes the specific job and situation that the applicant will face if hired. Many interviewers characterize this information as their attempt to give the applicant a balanced view of the job. The interviewers give a preview of the positives associated with the position along with the negatives (euphemized as the "challenges"). Negatives might include difficult working conditions, extensive travel on the job, or a history of conflict between departments. This type of balanced positive and negative job information is called a realistic job preview, or RJP.[2]

Why would an interviewer provide the RJP instead of selling the candidate solely on the advantages of the position? If the goal is to get the candidate interested and on-board, why jeopardize success? Why provide applicants with impartial information that may lead to their rejecting the position? The reason to be honest about the negatives on the job is that you are interested not only in recruiting candidates but in retaining the ones you hire. More important, if people assume positions with a clear picture of what they will face, they will be more likely to manage the challenges.

The logic of realistic job previews is that if someone is going to quit, it is always best if they "quit" before they are hired. If an applicant withdraws from consideration after you have provided an RJP, you have helped him or her determine that the job is not a good match.

Alan G. Frost, director of management development for Home Depot, partially credits videos that give applicants a clear picture of the demands on the job with the retailer's 11.4 percent decline in employee turnover. According to Frost, store managers who are eager to hire may understate the stress of a job in order to fill the position. Although the candidate may temporarily solve the manager's need for employees, rapid turnover actually has many more costs besides the vacancy in the position.[3] Overall, the research on RJPs has shown mixed results in terms of impact on turnover. RJPs tend to work best for more intelligent, more committed, and more experienced applicants.[4]

Providing RJPs to assist the candidate in making an appropriate job choice requires strategies that are different from those for the two previous goals. In a sense, the interviewer becomes an advocate for the candidate, providing accurate information for making a good decision. Again, while it is possible to focus on this goal as well as the others in the same interview, interviewers must make sure that they use appropriate strategies for each goal. Interviewers need to be careful, however, not to become so much of an advocate for the candidate that they diminish the goal of accurate measurement.

Assessing the Time Spent on Achieving Your Interview Goals

Most interviewers do not take the time to think about their goals for an interview. They simply do it. Take a minute and use the assessment in Exhibit 9.1 to roughly estimate how much time you devote to the PR and RJP parts of your interviews. Column 1 lists some activities that occur in the interview, along with a brief description. In column 2, record an estimate of how much time you would devote to each activity in a sixty-minute interview. If you manage other interviewers, use the assessment to audit how your interviewers typically use their time in interviews. Keep in mind that times may vary depending on the candidate and level of the job, but try to give typical numbers.

If you are like most other interviewers, you estimated five to ten minutes for each activity. This means you probably spend between twenty-five and fifty minutes on activities other than measuring whether the candidate can do the job. As a result, in

EXHIBIT 9.1. **Assessment: How Do You Spend Your Time in an Interview?**

Activity	Time You Typically Devote to This Activity or Goal
The beginning of the interview—making small talk and introducing the process for the interview.	
The end of the interview—closing it effectively.	
Providing an opportunity for the interviewee to ask questions.	
Influencing the candidate's job choice (PR).	
Assisting the candidate in making an appropriate job choice (RJP).	
Total interview time devoted to activities other than accurately measuring whether the candidate can do the job.	

a typical sixty-minute interview, you have ten to thirty-five minutes left for measurement.

Now make another estimate in the assessment in Exhibit 9.2. How many different factors do you typically want to measure in the interview? Think about all of the different things that someone needs to know and be able to do if he or she is to do the job well. For example, technical knowledge and skill, attitudes, values, conflict resolution skills, leadership, decision-making skills, and team skills may be the factors you are measuring in candidates. Again, your answers will vary depending on the job, but make a quick estimate.

Your answer concerning the number of areas of measurement will most likely be anywhere from five to ten. Assuming

EXHIBIT 9.2. **Assessment: How Much Interviewing Time Do You Spend Measuring Whether the Candidate Can Do the Job?**

Activity	Time You Typically Devote to This Activity
How many factors do you attempt to measure in a typical interview?	
How much time is left in a sixty-minute interview to assess each of these factors? (Subtract the number in the last line of Exhibit 9.1 from 60.)	
On average, how much time can you spend per factor? (Divide the available interviewing time computed in the preceding row by the number of factors.)	

you are measuring at least five factors, you have approximately two to seven minutes to measure each one. With more areas of measurement, you have even less time to measure each one.

Many interviewers are shocked when they complete these assessments and realize how little time they actually devote to measurement during the interview process. Often when we add up the time that interviewers estimate they devote to introductions, conclusions, PR, and RJP, we find that there is literally no time left for measurement! Clearly, you will have difficulty hiring good employees if you don't take the time to measure their ability to do the job. Although this is the most glaring problem, other problems typically occur when interviewers do not manage the interviewing process effectively.

Problems of Interview Management

Besides failing to measure candidates' capacity for the job at hand, poorly managed interviews lead to inconsistent or contradictory messages to candidates, and subject candidates to redundant interviews that focus on gathering the same information over and over again.[5] These problems are discussed in upcoming paragraphs.

Insufficient Time Devoted to Measurement

Not spending the time to measure the candidate adequately is a serious problem for interviewers who want to hire good employees. This problem may be linked to the fact that in the typical interview, the interviewer often does most of the talking. Why does this occur? We think that one major reason is that interviewers like to talk about things with which they feel comfortable. Measuring the candidate's ability to perform the job requires the interviewer to know what to ask and what to look for in the answers. Since the typical interviewer has not prepared for the interview and isn't trained on how to measure performance, the interviewer talks about the things he or she knows—the organization (PR) or the job (RJP).

If the interviewer has done most of the talking during the interview and there has been little time devoted to measurement, the interviewer has to rely on general impressions for the decision. We can't expect interviewers to accurately assess candidates if they haven't devoted the necessary time to gather the data needed for the decision.

Failure to manage the interview process is the source of this problem. Interviewers are often given wide discretion in how they conduct their interviews. Without guidance, they are often unfocused within their individual interviews. Likewise, there often is very little coordination among interviewers in the process. As a result, a lot of time is spent on interviewing candidates, but the time is not focused on accurate measurement.

Inconsistent, Contradictory, or Misleading Messages

Failure to manage the interview process among multiple interviewers can also contribute to a negative image of your organization by sending an inconsistent or contradictory message. Most organizations haven't really thought through their PR objectives for interviewing and therefore don't manage the PR message. As a result, different interviewers may send different messages to a single applicant. One interviewer can lead a candidate to believe there are opportunities for advancement while another interviewer may leave the candidate with the impression that few higher-level positions are filled from within.

Organizations often assume that their interviewers are capable and skilled in providing the appropriate public relations information to candidates. As a result, interviewer training rarely, if ever, includes strategies for creating an accurate image of the organization.

Organizations do not expect everyone who must communicate with the media to be skilled in relating the corporate image without training or experience. For that, they hire trained PR experts. But they do not apply the same logic to interviews. They seem to accept the likelihood that different interviewers will convey different—and sometimes contradictory—messages about the organization.

Some interviewers send messages to candidates that they think the candidate wants to hear, without solid evidence that these messages interest the candidate. For example, in an effort to persuade the interviewee to accept a job offer, interviewers will attempt to sell the organization with exaggerated claims about the organization's culture or opportunities for advancement. A candidate who accepts a job offer after such a sales job is likely to find out very quickly that the image created by the interviewer does not match the organization's reality. When the new employee leaves shortly after starting the job, the organization has not only lost an employee, it has also created a negative image that may hurt future recruiting efforts.

Too much selling also leads recruits to second thoughts about the organization. Researchers have found that the more time the interviewer spent selling the job, the less attractive applicants perceived the job to be. Applicants became suspicious as to why the job had to be sold so extensively.[6]

Redundant Interviews

Interviewees often go through a series of back-to-back interviews, hearing similar comments and answering similar generic questions in each interview. This is a waste of everyone's time. Applicants may need to hear some PR, but they don't need to hear the same message from multiple sources. Applicants may need to receive the RJP, but they don't need to hear it several times, especially when that time could be used for other important purposes.

Redundant interviews send a negative message about your organization. Interviewees are also assessing the organization as they are being assessed.[7] Think for a moment about the impressions that you want to give top-quality candidates during the interview process. Then look at Exhibit 9.3, which outlines a candidate's day for a typical on-site interview.

What impression do you think the candidate forms after a full day of back-to back interviews if most of the interviews cover the same general topics? What impression would you form if you experienced this process? Do you get the message, "We are a high-quality organization where you will be accurately measured

EXHIBIT 9.3. **Typical Interviewee Day for On-Site Visit**

Time	Activity	Content
9 A.M.	Interview with human resource representative	Small amount of time devoted to outline of the day, most of the interview devoted to PR and the RJP. Little interview time devoted to competency assessment. This opening session may also include a brief tour of the facility and the department.
10 A.M.	Interview with hiring manager	Most of the interview devoted to PR and the RJP. Little interview time devoted to competency assessment.
11 A.M.	Interview with manager in related department	Most of the interview duplicates the earlier interviews.
Noon	Interview with peer	Most of the interview duplicates the earlier interviews.
1 P.M.	Lunch with hiring manager	Informal interview with more time devoted to candidate's own questions.
2 P.M.	Interview with peer	Most of the interview duplicates the earlier interviews.
3 P.M.	Interview with peer	Most of the interview duplicates the earlier interviews.
4 P.M.	Interview with human resource representative	Closing interview, devoted to answering candidate's questions.

and rewarded?" If you want to be able to attract and retain top applicants, you have to be able to generate this impression. Hiring bonuses and other incentives to work in an organization lose much of their effectiveness if candidates do not feel the organization can accurately measure their performance. Applicants who undergo a day of back-to-back interviews with interviewers asking the same generic questions are likely to form the impression that this is an organization where qualifications are unimportant. If qualifications were important, the organization would devote more time to measuring applicants in a more systematic, objective interviewing process.[8] The more the interview process focuses on measurement versus recruiting, the more likely highly qualified applicants are to pursue a job.

STRATEGIES FOR MANAGING THE INTERVIEW PROCESS

To address the problems of insufficient time devoted to measurement, inconsistent or contradictory messages, and redundant interviews, various strategies can be used at the individual and organizational levels to manage the interview process. At the same time, it is possible to maintain the interviewers' discretion in selecting candidates that meet their unique needs. For each strategy, we attempt to describe how it helps manage the interview process while allowing managers flexibility to address their particular concerns. As you read about each of the strategies, consider how you can use the strategies in your own interviewing process.

Strategy 1: Set Clear Goals for Each Interview

While we have noted that the goals of accurate measurement, influencing the candidate's job choice, and assisting the candidate in making an appropriate job choice are common to most interviews, the importance of these activities will vary based on the type of job and the situation of the organization. For example, for a job such as a high school or college internship, there may be little difference among the skill levels of the applicant pool. For this type of job, perhaps the interview should be primarily an RJP. For an organization with a poor reputation, PR may need to be a larger component of the interview. Interviewers should carefully consider what they are trying to accomplish within an individual interview and across the interview process.

Setting goals will provide a clear direction for interviewers as they develop and implement individual interviews. Setting goals can also help ensure that the desired objectives are obtained across the interview process. Perhaps the easiest way to manage the interview process is to have human resource or senior management within the area coordinate interviewers. Prior to a candidate's visit, HR or senior management could facilitate a discussion among interviewers on who will focus on which goals. Interviewers need to agree where in the interview process the candidate will be measured, and where PR and RJP will occur. Alternatively, hiring managers could develop an agenda for the candidate's on-site visit and specify the goals of each interview. Then the agenda could be reviewed by HR or senior management. These facilitated discussions and reviews are designed to clearly specify goals, to identify and eliminate redundancies, and to make interviewers aware of what is actually happening in their selection process.

Strategy 2: Train and Motivate Interviewers to Conduct Accurate Measurement

Training and motivating interviewers to accurately measure whether a candidate can do the job is another important strategy for managing the interview process. Without the tools and motivation needed to identify good employees, interviewers will not accurately measure whether the candidate meets the organization's needs. As we have noted, managers often fail to measure candidates simply because they don't know how to do it effectively.

Accurate measurement can also contribute to achieving the other two potential interview goals: influencing the candidate by selling the positive features of the job and the organization and providing the information needed to help the candidate make a good job choice. Accurate measurement creates a positive, professional image of the organization since it sends the message that the organization knows what it wants and how to measure it. Research suggests that applicants seek out organizations that match their values.[9] High-quality employees look for organizations that demonstrate commitment to high quality in the way they assess their applicants.

In addition, the types of questions that lead to accurate measurement simultaneously communicate the requirements for the job and help the candidate assess whether the job is a good fit. Giving interviewers the training and motivation to accurately measure candidates is a critical strategy for managing the interview process.

Strategy 3: Manage a Unified PR Message

Accurate measurement can contribute to an enhanced PR image within an individual interview. However, accurate measurement cannot ensure that key messages (other than quality standards) that the organization wants to send will get through to new hires. Also, accurate measurement cannot ensure that a consistent message is provided. For example, one of us recently met with the college recruiting team of a large organization. The organization is family friendly with an open and supportive culture. When asked how this culture is conveyed in the interview, the team replied, "We just hope it comes across." This very well-managed organization is very conscious of its external image—but it has no management processes in place to make sure its desired message is sent to candidates.

In addition, when ten interviewers from another organization were asked what they stressed about the benefits of the organization they worked for, seven different ideas were presented. All the interviewers agreed that the seven characteristics were reflective of their organization, but the interviewers each stressed what they valued the most and never addressed the others.

To present a unified PR message, the manager of the interviewing process needs to clearly define the image that the organization wants to create and the messages it intends to send—then clearly communicate the image and messages to all interviewers. Managing images and impressions with a unified approach will partially determine the kinds of candidates who are attracted to your organization as well as how the candidates will interact with you.

For a unified approach to PR:

1. Gather good data on the kind of information that candidates want before they accept an offer of employment. You can gather the information by anonymously surveying new hires shortly after their employment regarding what impressed them about the organization and led to their decision to join it. The survey must be clearly designed and grant anonymity for the respondents. New hires might be reluctant to openly express their views if they believe their responses will affect how others perceive them or their performance. (Exhibit 9.4 provides a sample recruiting assessment questionnaire.)

2. Use these data as part of interviewer training on PR. Once you understand what candidates typically want to know,

EXHIBIT 9.4. **Recruiting Assessment Questionnaire**

This questionnaire is sent to all new hires one month after starting with our organization. The purpose of the questionnaire is to help us evaluate our recruiting efforts. Please be assured that your responses are anonymous.

  Please do not identify yourself anywhere on the questionnaire. Return it by mail and it will be opened and analyzed by individuals who were not involved in hiring you. Your responses will be combined with the responses from others to ensure confidentiality.

1. Please briefly describe any images or impressions that you developed about our organization based on how we recruited you. Please be specific. If you feel you received unclear messages or you received different messages from different individuals, please describe.

2. What, if any, of these messages or impressions influenced your decision to join us? Why and how did it influence you?

(continued)

EXHIBIT 9.4. *(continued)*

3. Now that you have been employed, do you think we gave you an accurate picture of our organization?   '

☐ yes   ☐ no   ☐ somewhat

If you did not answer yes to this question, please indicate how we could have been clearer or what should have been added.

4. What, if anything, has surprised and delighted you about working in our organization?

5. What didn't we tell you that we should have told you that would have been helpful in your decision whether to join our organization and to help you get off to an effective start on your job?

6. The following information is designed to help us categorize your responses to improve the way we recruit people like you. Again, please be assured that your individual responses will not be shared with the people who recruited you or to whom you report.

_____ Department
_____ Grade level
_____ Functional area (Accounting, Human Resources, Sales, etc.)

you can design a message that will meet the information needs of your candidates. Target this message to the top-quality candidates you are attempting to attract and hire. Each interviewer needs to know the messages the organization wants to send and how to contribute to a unified, positive image of the organization and the job.

3. Evaluate whether the organization's messages are accurately communicated. To attract and retain top-quality employees, an organization needs not only to have the right message and image but also to convey it accurately. Evaluating the message that your new hires received during the interview process will help you determine whether your interviewers are really conveying the message you want them to convey.

These steps will not restrict management's ability to send the messages they believe should be sent about the job and the organization. Managers still have the discretion to provide specific information that is unique to their particular area. These steps will ensure, however, that applicants receive the desired common message that the organization wants to present.

Strategy 4: Evaluate Your RJPs

Providing truly realistic job previews should increase retention since candidates will self-select out of the hiring process if the organization does not meet their needs. In addition, new hires should hit the ground running and be effective sooner since they will be aware of key hurdles. This initial success should create a "success breeds success" cycle.

Research on RJPs has not uniformly documented the glowing outcomes that were anticipated for their use. But one reason for the gap between intentions and results is the fact that RJPs do not always accurately convey the reality of the job.[10]

As with PR, the judgment regarding what is realistic is often left to the interviewer. In addition, interviewers are typically not trained in effectively conveying the information, and rarely do interviewers get feedback about how well they conveyed the message. To make this process more effective, you must evaluate your realistic job previews to ensure that they are accurately reflecting the job and are clearly communicated. This information must be effectively summarized and fed back to interviewers to help them improve the effectiveness of their RJPs.

How can this be done? Organizations typically do exit interviews to determine why people leave. We are suggesting the addition of an "entrance assessment process" to improve the ability to attract and retain candidates. You can evaluate RJPs simply and inexpensively by sending anonymous questionnaires to new hires to assess whether the key realities have been described. Again, see Exhibit 9.4. You can modify the questions to suit your specific organizational needs. If your organization is large, you might reduce costs by distributing the questionnaire to just a sample of new recruits.

Strategy 5: Use Other Media for PR and RJP

One way to reduce some of the time devoted to PR and the RJP in the interviews is to use other media to communicate the information. This can be done by sending candidates information before the interview. Many organizations now have systems by which candidates can apply on-line. They provide PR information through their Web sites. Web sites also can be used to provide some preliminary RJP to allow candidates to do some initial screening of the organization. Certainly, the interviewer will still need to provide some PR and some RJP, but it will be more efficient to use the time primarily to clarify information that was sent via other sources.

Strategy 6: Evaluate the Effectiveness of Your Interviewing Process

One strategy to help the organization recognize the need for management of the interview process is to undertake a small pilot study to assess the extent to which the interview process is achieving its goals. At the end of the interview day, applicants can be asked to complete a short anonymous questionnaire about their opinions of the organization, their understanding of the job requirements, and their view of the interview process (for example, amount of redundancy and accuracy of measurement). They should be informed that their responses, which can be returned by mail, will be analyzed by someone not involved in the hiring decision and will be used only for measuring the effectiveness of the interview process. Exhibit 9.5 is an example of the type of questionnaire that could be used, although it should be adapted for the specific goals of the interview process.

The results from the questionnaires can create the baseline for assessing how your applicants perceive the strengths and weaknesses of your interviewing process. You can also determine the level of coordination that currently exists in the process. By monitoring these data over time, your organization can make adjustments to improve its effectiveness in selecting top-quality candidates. Many organizations will be surprised when they discover how they are perceived by the people they are trying to hire.[11]

EXHIBIT 9.5. **Interview Assessment Questionnaire**

We would like your feedback about your interview(s) with our organization.

We want your assessment of the day as a part of our continuing commitment to improve our selection process. Please do not identify yourself on this questionnaire. This questionnaire is anonymous and will have no impact on your hiring decision. No one involved in your hiring process will see your responses.

1. Overall, the interviews were an accurate assessment of my abilities to do the job that I was interviewed for.
   ☐ Strongly Agree ☐ Agree ☐ Neither Agree nor Disagree ☐ Disagree ☐ Strongly Disagree

   Please provide any information that would help us understand your answer.

2. Overall, I thought the organization showed me respect by making good use of my time.
   ☐ Strongly Agree ☐ Agree ☐ Neither Agree nor Disagree ☐ Disagree ☐ Strongly Disagree

   Please provide any information that would help us understand your answer.

3. I have a good understanding of the positive aspects of working for the organization.
   ☐ Strongly Agree ☐ Agree ☐ Neither Agree nor Disagree ☐ Disagree ☐ Strongly Disagree

   Please provide any information that would help us understand your answer.

4. I received a balanced view (the positive aspects and the challenges) of what it is like to work in the organization.
   ☐ Strongly Agree ☐ Agree ☐ Neither Agree nor Disagree ☐ Disagree ☐ Strongly Disagree

Please provide any information that would help us understand your answer.

Please provide any other information about any aspect of your interaction with our organization that would help us understand your views.

Thank you for completing this questionnaire. Please return the questionnaire in the attached envelope.

SUMMARY

In this chapter, we have described developing realistic goals to manage the interview process. We discussed the potential goals of interviewing and the problems that can occur when accurate measurement is squeezed out of the process, leaving managers to rely on general impressions for the hiring decision. We proposed a variety of strategies that manage the process while allowing managers the flexibility to address their needs. Strategies you can use for managing the interview process more effectively include setting clear goals for each interview, training and motivating managers to conduct accurate measurement, managing a unified PR message, evaluating your RJPs, and evaluating the effectiveness of your interviewing process.

o   o   o

Richaurd Camp is a professor of management at Eastern Michigan University. His primary research interest is staffing, with a specific focus on employment interviewing.

Mary E. Vielhaber teaches managerial communication, human resource development, organizational behavior, organization development, and leadership at Eastern Michigan University.

Jack L. Simonetti is adjunct professor of executive education at the University of Michigan Business School and professor emeritus at the University of Toledo.

Chapter Ten

Employment Law from a Manager's Perspective

Dana M. Muir

Put yourself in the shoes of Wendy's employer. When Wendy caught her husband looking at an adult Internet site, she convinced him that it would spice up their marriage if they set up a similar site. Wendy posed for provocative photographs, which her husband took and posted to their site. To access the site, a viewer had to claim to be an adult. Professionally, Wendy worked as a counselor to troubled youths. One of the youth's parents told Wendy's manager about the Web site and demanded that Wendy be fired.

As Wendy's manager, what would you do? More important, what factors would you consider in making your decision? Would it matter if Wendy had a long history of excellent performance appraisals? What if Wendy had done all the work for the Web site on her own time and with her own computer equipment?

Certainly, one of the factors in your thinking would need to be potential legal issues. As a manager, you don't want to cause your company or yourself unnecessary legal complications, such as lawsuits for wrongful termination. More positively, you need to know what latitude the law does and does not give you in your efforts to build and manage the best possible workforce.

All too often I have seen managers who are frustrated with the legal system. After frequent interactions with human resource professionals, management consultants, and attorneys, managers end up believing that the law requires them to hire a certain job candidate even though another candidate is far more qualified, that they cannot discipline the employee who spends more time out of work because of illness than at work, or that the law prevents them from firing an employee whose performance is lousy. All of these beliefs are fallacies. With a proper understanding of the law, managers can hire the most qualified workers. Managers can discipline employees for unreasonable absences. And managers can fire employees who cannot or will not perform the critical functions of their jobs.

As a manager, you can always get specific legal advice for some issue that confronts you, and often you should. On the other hand, you don't want to run up the cost, whether in time or money, of seeking professional counsel every time an employment question arises that might have legal implications. To manage efficiently, you need an internal compass that can guide much of your everyday decision making and let you know when you really need to get expert advice.

This chapter provides the basic road map for considering the legal implications of almost any employment-related decision you might make. In the pages that follow, I first explain the primary concept underlying U.S. employment law, employment-at-will. Next I summarize some key exceptions to the basic rule. To provide some perspective, I then briefly compare the U.S. system and the approach taken by many other developed countries.

The discussion of employment-at-will shows that as a manager, you have significant flexibility in dealing with workforce issues in the United States. However, the nature of our legal system has some implications that can be at least as important as the substantive legal rules when you are evaluating a potential employment decision. Therefore, I also address some unique features of the U.S. legal system.

Finally, it's important to understand that managing legal risk and opportunity in employment decisions is just a special case of what you already do as a manager. Accordingly, I end the chapter by integrating the discussion of U.S. employment law with the basic concepts of managerial risk taking.

EMPLOYMENT-AT-WILL

The underlying concept governing the legal relationship between employer and employee in the United States is known as employment-at-will. The concept itself is surprisingly simple to understand. It becomes complex only because of the exceptions that have developed over time. Before reading on, though, try your hand at the fact or fallacy questions in Exhibit 10.1.

The Basic Rule

At its most basic, the principle of employment-at-will permits you, as a manager, to fire an employee for any reason, whether it is a good reason, a bad reason, or even no reason at all, so long as any reason that you do have is not an illegal reason. Historically, the logic behind this rule was that employees and

EXHIBIT 10.1. **Fact or Fallacy? #1**

1. You don't need good cause to legally fire an employee.	☐ Fact	☐ Fallacy
2. Unless you put a promise to an employee in writing, the promise will not be enforceable.	☐ Fact	☐ Fallacy
3. You cannot make any decisions about an employee or potential employee based on the person's physical characteristics.	☐ Fact	☐ Fallacy
4. You can make decisions on who to send to training based on employees' gender because nondiscrimination laws do not apply to decisions such as training.	☐ Fact	☐ Fallacy
5. You would have more flexibility in firing employees if you managed a workforce in almost any developed economy other than the United States.	☐ Fact	☐ Fallacy

employers should both enjoy roughly the same amount of freedom in establishing the terms of their relationship. Since employees generally were free to change jobs at will, employers also had the right to terminate the employment relationship at will. Individuals typically are employees at will when they are hired without a contract that specifies the duration of the employment or that imposes other obligations on the employer.

The employment-at-will standard also recognizes that companies are in the best position to determine their own employment needs. The law acknowledges that you need flexibility in determining the size of your workforce and the skills you require to get the job done. As a result, it shouldn't surprise you that courts have upheld the right of managers to fire employees for poor performance, for misrepresenting their credentials, and for insubordination. It may come as more of a surprise that courts have permitted managers to fire employees for being suspected of having an affair with the boss's son or because the employee's spouse, a police officer, ticketed the manager's wife. Whatever the merits of these reasons, none of them is specifically prohibited by law.

The first item in Exhibit 10.1 is therefore true. As a manager, you may fire an employee for any reason, even a lousy, arbitrary, or unfair reason, so long as it is not an illegal reason. Practically speaking, though, few managers choose to fire employees for lousy, arbitrary, or unfair reasons. Managers who act so arbitrarily not only sometimes fire good employees, they also contribute to poor morale and can make it difficult to attract skilled workers. In addition, it is legitimate to ask whether judges and juries look askance at managers who appear to have treated a good employee unfairly. So the advice here is not that you should start treating your employees arbitrarily or fire them for writing with blue instead of black pens. But it is useful to understand that the foundational concept of U.S. employment law recognizes your rights as a manager, within the constraints believed by our society to be appropriate, to make decisions about your employees' employment.

Consider how the employment-at-will standard would apply to Wendy. The beginning premise is that you, as Wendy's manager, have the right to fire her at will, so long as your reason is not illegal. Consequently, you can begin with the premise that you may fire her for working with her husband to establish the Web site and for permitting provocative pictures of herself to appear on the site. The only remaining question is whether any exception exists that would make your reason for firing Wendy illegal.

Exceptions to the Basic Rule

If applied without limitation, the concept of employment-at-will would permit a manager to fire an employee at any time for any reason. But the courts and legislatures have developed limitations to prevent managers from making employment decisions based on criteria that our society defines as unacceptable, such as certain types of discrimination.

These limitations, which act as exceptions to the concept of employment-at-will, sometimes frustrate managers because they are not always well defined. Still, you can get a grasp of the main limitations by understanding three basic categories of exceptions to employment-at-will: contracts, nondiscrimination statutes, and policy-based and statutory provisions.

Contractual Exceptions Some of the contractual exceptions to employment-at-will are obvious. When an employer enters into a written contract to employ an individual for a specific time period and with specific terms, that contract typically is enforceable. For example, top executives, coaches of professional sports teams, and actors in television sit-coms frequently have written contracts of this type. In contrast to those individualized contracts, a written collective bargaining agreement typically covers groups of employees in a unionized workplace. If you do manage unionized employees, though, you should recognize that properly negotiated collective bargaining agreements are enforceable contracts. In addition, in a unionized workplace, a separate and distinct set of federal laws governs employee-management relations.

More subtle issues of a contractual nature arise when a manager makes a verbal promise to an employee or to a recruit. Those promises might be enforceable if they are clear enough that the terms of the promise can be understood and a reasonable person would think the manager had the authority to make such a promise. Another factor that might affect the legal analysis is whether the employee or job candidate relied on the verbal promise in taking some action, such as quitting an existing job or turning down another job offer.

Consider what happened to Philip McConkey, who went to work for Ross & Co. as an insurance broker after playing football for the New York Giants. Alexander & Alexander (A&A) made considerable efforts to recruit McConkey, even arranging a meeting between its CEO and McConkey. At the meeting the CEO addressed McConkey's worry that A&A was up for sale and "assured him there was no intention to sell."[1] The company's chairman allegedly gave McConkey similar assurances. McConkey eventually accepted a position with A&A, but the company was sold later the same year. Less than a year after employing him, the company stripped McConkey of all responsibilities and subsequently laid him off. When McConkey learned that A&A had been negotiating the sale of the company at the same time it was recruiting him, he sued. A jury awarded him more than $10 million.

Item 2 in Exhibit 10.1 is therefore a fallacy. In practice, it can be difficult for judges and juries to evaluate who is telling the truth when employees and managers tell different stories about verbal promises allegedly made to employees or recruits. Nevertheless, verbal commitments can be enforceable. Moreover, casual written assurances can be as legally binding as a long, formal document that has been evaluated by the company's lawyers. As a manager, you should be circumspect about the commitments you make to your employees, whether or not you put them in writing.

Not all verbal representations are enforceable, however. Giles Wanamaker, in-house counsel for a company, alleged that he was told by a vice president and director that the job was a "career" job. Others reportedly told him "that there was no need for concern in that the position would be a job for the balance of [his] career."[2] After he was fired, Giles sued for breach of contract. He lost because New York law requires that oral promises must be very clear in establishing a fixed period for employment; otherwise, the basic rule of employment-at-will governs.

Many companies have taken steps to ensure that their employees understand that they are at-will employees. Offer letters, employment manuals, and other official company communications often explicitly explain employment-at-will. In addition, a company can take two steps to reduce the chances that its managers will make promises that undercut its employment-at-will relationships. First, the company can train its managers so they understand that careless statements might become enforceable commitments. In a column on how to retain valuable employees during times of economic retrenchment, the *Wall Street Journal* advised, "Bosses should 'whisper in the ears of those who keep their companies afloat that they're wanted—and will be rewarded with salary increases and bonuses.'"[3] That is a fine tactic—so long as the bosses and their companies understand that those whispers may be legally enforceable contracts. As a second tactic, the company can include language in its statements of at-will status explaining that only very specific agreements can change that status. In its offer letters to new hires, one major high-tech company first states that the person will be an at-will employee and explains what that means. Then it includes language similar to the following: "Your status as an at-will employee can be modified only by an explicit written agreement signed by both you and [the name of the company president]." This helps to ensure that a manager cannot undercut the company's at-will policy in recruiting a new employee or trying to retain a current one. In the long run, that protection is good for the company and its managers.

The application of the implied contract exception to employment-at-will is fairly easy in Wendy's case. Typically, in evaluating the potential existence of an implied contract, you would consider a variety of possibilities, such as an individualized written contract with Wendy, an employee handbook that indicates the company will terminate employees only for good cause or that establishes a defined disciplinary procedure, or the existence of other verbal or written commitments. Since there is no indication in the facts that as Wendy's employer you have limited your ability to fire her, it appears that Wendy is an at-will employee and the implied contract exception will not limit your alternatives.

Nondiscrimination Statutory Exceptions Perhaps the best-known but least understood limitations on a manager's right to fire employees are those based in nondiscrimination law.

Federal law prohibits an employer from discriminating against an employee or job candidate based on race, color, gender, national origin, religion, pregnancy, age of forty or older, and disability. State nondiscrimination laws generally are similar to the federal laws, but many protect additional characteristics of employees and job applicants. For example, several states and over a hundred cities and counties have laws that protect against discrimination on the basis of sexual orientation.

Michigan protects people against differential treatment based on height and weight. Alaska forbids employers from acting on the basis of a change in marital status, and North Dakota does not permit receipt of public assistance to be a factor in employment-related decisions. Even localities sometimes impose specific prohibitions against discrimination in employment.

As stated, item 3 in Exhibit 10.1 is mostly fact, but it is difficult to evaluate because it is so inclusive. Federal nondiscrimination law makes it illegal to discriminate against someone with a disability who, with or without reasonable accommodation, can perform the essential functions of a job. That, on its own, means that the law restricts what physical characteristics you can consider when making employment-related decisions. Similarly, some state laws, such as Michigan's protection of height and weight, further restrict your ability to make determinations based on physical characteristics. More subtle legal problems also can arise from issues associated with physical characteristics. More and more employees or former employees are filing lawsuits claiming their employer discriminated against them because of their appearance. For example, a court permitted a former employee to sue a ski resort that fired the individual for not having any upper teeth and refusing to wear her dentures, which she said caused her pain. The resort said it was concerned with its public image and had a policy that "employees will be expected to have teeth and to wear them daily to work."[4] In the view of the court, however, the toothless chambermaid's claim could fall within the ambit of the law against disability discrimination.

The extent to which you may consider physical characteristics depends primarily on two variables. The first is the law of the relevant state. Second, the job may require a specific physical characteristic. For example, it could be impossible for someone who is very tall to perform a job in a confined space that cannot be expanded.

The prohibition on discrimination tends to cover all phases of employment, such as salary, benefits, access to training, promotion, and all other terms, conditions, or privileges of employment. Consequently, item 4 in Exhibit 10.1 is a fallacy. The federal laws against discrimination protect employees against a wide variety of discriminatory acts in the workplace, including any acts that affect the employee's "terms, conditions, and privileges" of employment. Access to training, which can qualify an employee for a promotion, raise, or even continued employment, certainly is a privilege of employment.

During recent years, one of the most quickly growing categories of employment lawsuits has been suits alleging retaliation for making a complaint of discrimination. Between 1992 and 2000, the number of retaliation lawsuits almost doubled. In addition to the raw numbers, there is some evidence that juries are particularly hostile to employers who retaliate against employees who complain of discrimination. For example, a manager in Iowa who claimed that her employer retaliated against her because she complained of gender discrimination won more than $80 million in a jury award.[5]

One concern with application of the nondiscrimination laws occurs because of the "he said–she said" nature of the claims that arise. If you fire Wendy because you believe that her involvement in the Web site undermines her ability to do her job, or even because you simply disapprove of her actions, then it does not appear you have violated any federal, state, or local nondiscrimination laws. No jurisdiction that I know of specifically protects individuals who establish and appear in provocative Web sites from being discriminated against on that basis. Suppose, however, that Wendy claims that the reason you have given for her firing is a pretext and that the real reason is that she is a woman. Given the number of cases in which the employee argues that the employer had a prohibited discriminatory reason for a particular action, even while stating a different reason entirely, the law has developed a specific approach for evaluating these contradictory claims. Consider whether Wendy has a stronger case if male employees have been permitted to establish and appear on similar Web sites. Or what if the employer has a pattern of firing women, but not men, for engaging in unsavory behavior outside the workplace? In such cases, the disparity of treatment may increase the likelihood that a judge or jury will find that the employer discriminated against Wendy because of her gender.

Policy-Based and Statutory Exceptions in Your Jurisdiction
The most unpredictable category of exceptions to the principle of employment-at-will is made up of policy-based exceptions established by the courts and miscellaneous statutory exceptions in various jurisdictions. Even here, however, there are some trends that are of general interest to managers.

The first trend concerns public policy exceptions to the basic at-will principle. An employer might find itself embroiled in a wrongful termination lawsuit when it fires an employee for a reason that on the surface does not violate any state law, but that in some way undercuts the policies being protected by state law. One recurring fact pattern involves employers who fire employees for refusing to do something illegal. A trucker might refuse to drive an overweight load. An inspector in a food processing plant might refuse to approve a product that does not meet minimum safety standards. A worker at a nuclear power plant might refuse to falsify operating documents. Perhaps not surprisingly, workers tend to win these types of cases. Courts reason that an employee should not be forced to choose between keeping a job and complying with the law. Furthermore, because public policy exceptions tend to be tort claims, they provide the opportunity for plaintiffs to receive high damage awards. Therefore, aside from the ethical implications, no manager should ever ask an employee to do something that is illegal.

But when the facts are different, many jurisdictions construe the public policy exception quite narrowly. In one case, Karen Bammert worked for Don Williams, who owned Don's SuperValu. Karen's husband, a police officer, arrested Don's wife for driving under the influence of alcohol. Don fired Karen in retaliation for the arrest. Karen then sued, alleging that her firing violated Wisconsin public policy because her husband had an affirmative legal obligation to assist in the arrest of Don's wife and because state policy discouraged drunken driving. The Wisconsin Supreme Court decided that it would be pushing public policy too far to consider the legal duties of an employee's spouse. So, the basic policy of employment-at-will applied, and Karen lost the case.[6]

A somewhat similar concept is known as the good faith and fair dealing exception. Courts interpret most contracts, such as a contract for the sale of goods, to require the parties to deal with one another fairly and in good faith, even if the contract does not explicitly address this point. Employees have argued that employers owe the same duty to their employees because even an at-will employment relationship is based on contract law principles. If generally accepted, this exception would substantially corrode the rule of employment-at-will. Remember, historically you could fire employees for an arbitrary reason, such as writing with a blue pen instead of a black one. But if the law requires you to deal fairly and in good faith with your employees, at minimum it seems you would have to give the blue pen users a warning before you fired them.

It makes sense, then, that only a relatively small number of employees have won cases based on an implied duty of good faith and fair dealing. If an employer takes an egregious action, such as firing a star employee the day before payment of a sales bonus in order to avoid paying the bonus, then the employee may have a reasonable chance of winning on this theory. However, one case decided by the California Supreme Court emphasized how infrequently this exception applies. Over twenty-two years of employment, John Guz had successfully worked his way up the ranks in Bechtel National Inc. When Bechtel eliminated a division, it fired Guz. He argued that Bechtel's restructuring decisions and his firing were arbitrary. Guz lost when the court determined that as an at-will employee, he was only entitled to the benefit of promises made by his employer, and Bechtel had never promised him continuing employment.[7] Because California often sets employment law trends, it appears that the implied duty of good faith and fair dealing will not be important in most employment law cases.

Another category of exceptions to the doctrine of employment-at-will exists because states and other jurisdictions sometimes choose to protect employees from specific actions that might be taken by employers. These are probably the most varied exceptions and tend to be limited in theory only by the imagination of state lawmakers, and in practice by the desire of most states to encourage employment in the state. A few examples provide a sense of the scope of these exceptions. Numerous states provide protection to whistle-blowers, people who serve as jurors, and even employees who engage in specified conduct on their own time.

New York goes further in its protection of employees outside the workplace and prohibits employers from firing someone for engaging in legal activities, including "recreational activities." That law has led to some interesting cases. For example, Wal-Mart had a nonfraternization policy that prohibited a "dating relationship" between a married employee and any employee other than the spouse. The company fired both Laurel, who was separated from her husband, and Samuel because the two were dating. The state sued to have the employees reinstated, arguing that the employees' right to date qualified for protection under the law protecting recreational activities. On appeal, a New York court decided in Wal-Mart's favor. According to the judges, "'dating' is entirely distinct from and, in fact, bears little resemblance to 'recreational activity.'"[8] Therefore, the basic employment-at-will standard applied, and Wal-Mart could legally fire the employees for dating. This type of interpretative question, however, is a difficult one for the courts, and other courts using the same statute have held differently.

Consider now whether any of these exceptions would protect Wendy. You have not ordered her to do anything illegal. Nor does it seem likely that any state has a strong public policy in favor of titillating Web sites. So Wendy is unlikely to have a valid claim based on a generalized public policy exception. Nor is your act in firing her the egregious kind of act that tends to run afoul of the good faith and fair dealing exception. You should, though, check to see whether your state protects employees against being fired for engaging in activities outside the workplace. It is possible that a state law covering a broad range of endeavors, such as recreational activities, would affect your decision to fire Wendy. Those laws are so new, and the situation is so unique, that the legal analysis may not be entirely clear. At the end of the chapter, I will return to the topic of evaluating and managing these types of risk.

INTERNATIONAL COMPARISONS

Employment law in the United States has developed a reputation for preventing managers from firing lousy employees, so much so that many managers, both here and abroad, subscribe to item 5 in Exhibit 10.1. By now, though, you know that you actually have considerable flexibility in making employment decisions. For additional perspective on this issue, it is worth comparing U.S. law to the law of other developed countries. To put this comparison in context, consider two separate situations.

First, you are a manager at a large company that has been affected by a slowing economy. You need to downsize. Would you rather be located in the United States or in Western Europe?

In the United States, the basic rules are the ones outlined so far in this chapter and the Worker Adjustment and Retraining Act (WARN). WARN requires large businesses to provide employees and the state with sixty days' written notice when laying off groups of employees. Otherwise, you may set any criteria you choose and lay off as many employees as you choose, so long as you do not use any illegal criteria.

In many other countries with developed economies, the law is more stringent and might significantly limit your options. Other countries would still permit you to fire an employee for cause, such as for stealing from the company. But in other situations, such as downsizing, employees are entitled to notice and compensation. The amount owed to an employee usually depends on the individual's length of employment. In Germany, that might mean up to seven months' notice or pay, if a layoff can be negotiated at all. And in Germany, in deciding which workers to lay off, you must choose those who will be least socially affected by the layoff. That means that older workers, disabled workers, and workers with families receive the most protection.

Second, imagine you have a key employee who has become pregnant. In the United States, the Pregnancy Discrimination Act requires you to treat pregnant women equivalently to other employees. They are therefore entitled to be covered by your regular sick leave policy. If you do not provide paid sick leave for other illnesses, then federal law does not require you to pay the pregnant employee for the time she is off work due to illness associated with the pregnancy or delivery of her child. In addition, the Family and Medical Leave Act (FMLA) guarantees up to twelve weeks of unpaid leave and typically requires you return the person to her job at the end of her leave. Even then, though, the FMLA excludes from its protections certain key employees.

Compare Hong Kong and Switzerland. In each of those countries, employers must provide eight weeks of full pay for maternity leave. In France, women are entitled to up to twenty-six weeks off work, with salary substitution paid by government programs. In Australia, women are entitled to a full year of maternity leave.

In short, workers in other industrialized countries often receive more protection than U.S. law provides. France has a

35-hour maximum workweek. Employees there receive a minimum of five weeks vacation a year and eleven paid holidays. Volkswagen in Germany has a 29.9-hour workweek. Unionization rates in Western Europe are higher than in the United States, and generous government-sponsored pension programs have supported retirement at relatively early ages. The European Union (EU) is also developing directives that ban discrimination based on age and sexual orientation. The United States does not have any federal law prohibiting discrimination based on sexual orientation. And whereas U.S. federal age discrimination law applies only to people who are at least age forty, the EU directive protects both younger and older workers from discrimination based on age.

Why, then, do so many people believe that the United States has such an unfavorable climate for employers? One answer is the amount of ambiguity in U.S. employment law. Much of the lack of clarity comes about because of flexible doctrines such as the public policy exception to employment-at-will and the variation in state law. At each end of the spectrum of reasons for firing an employee, U.S. law is actually similar to that of other industrialized nations. It is legal to fire an employee for cause, such as for embezzling from the employer. It is never legal to fire an employee for reasons that the law defines as illegal discrimination. Where the laws differ is in cases where you, as a manager, are exercising significant discretion.

Return once again to the situation with Wendy. In many developed countries, you either could not fire Wendy at all or you would need to give her significant notice and separation pay. In contrast, in the United States, the only significant concern for you as a manager is whether the applicable state law protects Wendy's behavior outside the workplace. The newness of those laws and the uniqueness of Wendy's situation may mean that the answer is somewhat uncertain. If you wish to fire Wendy, it will make sense for you to obtain the advice of legal counsel in your state. While this ambiguity may be troubling, once managers understand the flexibility that the U.S. concept of employment-at-will gives them, they realize the benefits of that concept as compared to the heavy strictures in the legal landscape of many other developed countries.

UNIQUE FEATURES OF THE U.S. LEGAL SYSTEM

Another reason that some people give for believing that the United States has an unfavorable employment law climate for employers is the nature of the U.S. legal system. It is true that the structure of the legal system adds increased risk to the ambiguity already imposed by laws that are unclear in their application and that vary from state to state. This section discusses some of the unique features of the legal system that you need to take into account as you make employment-related decisions. Now try to answer the next round of fact or fallacy questions in Exhibit 10.2.

Contingent Fees

The first threshold that a potential plaintiff needs to overcome is hiring a lawyer. From an economic perspective, it would make some sense if an employee who feels wronged had to weigh the strength of the claim and the size of the expected recovery against the cost of paying an attorney. Many plaintiffs' lawyers, however, accept employment law cases on what is known as a contingent fee basis. That means that if the lawyer is able to win a case or negotiate a settlement on behalf of the

EXHIBIT 10.2. **Fact or Fallacy?** #2

1. If an employee sues you and loses, the employee will have legal fees to pay.	☐ Fact	☐ Fallacy
2. The most you can lose in an employment lawsuit is the amount the company would have paid the employee in salary and benefits if the employee had not been illegally fired, denied promotion, or whatever.	☐ Fact	☐ Fallacy
3. Juries are overly sympathetic to plaintiff claims, and appealing a jury decision is unlikely to be of much help to a company.	☐ Fact	☐ Fallacy
4. Increasingly, employers are bypassing the U.S. court system when they face employment law claims.	☐ Fact	☐ Fallacy

plaintiff, the lawyer will get a percentage, typically about a third, of the award or settlement. If the lawyer is unsuccessful in representing the individual, the plaintiff has little or no obligation to pay the lawyer beyond relatively small costs such as court filing fees.

From your perspective as a manager, this system means that a disgruntled employee will not face the costs of paying a lawyer if a legal claim is unsuccessful. Monetarily, then, there is little to discourage one of your employees or former employees from pursuing a weak claim. Yet it is in the interest of plaintiffs' lawyers to evaluate the strength of potential cases. It would not make much sense for a lawyer to invest the significant amounts of time and resources necessary to see a case through trial, and potentially through the appeal process, only to lose the case and not receive any compensation.

Two real-world factors affect the analysis of plaintiffs' lawyers, though. First, even in a weak case, a lawyer may be able to negotiate a quick settlement. Second, lawyers who are just getting started in practice, or who are temporarily underemployed for some reason, may be willing to accept relatively weak cases because having even weak cases is better than having no cases at all.

While the availability of contingent fees increases the likelihood that you might be sued by a disgruntled employee with a tenuous legal case, public policy does support those fees. Certainly some employees are fired, discriminated against in salary, or otherwise mistreated at work in ways that we all agree are and should be illegal. No one in this country suggests that children should be chained to machines and forced to work. Few managers would argue that the minimum wage laws should not be enforced against a competing company. However, enforcement of employment laws largely relies on claims by employees. Many employees, particularly the low-paid employees who might be most vulnerable to mistreatment, would not be able to afford the up-front costs of hiring a lawyer. In the absence of a contingent fee system, then, many clearly illegal employer actions might go unchallenged.

As a result, item 1 in Exhibit 10.2 is a fallacy. The contingent fee system makes it relatively easy for a disgruntled worker or job applicant to sue without having the money in hand to pay a lawyer. Many managers object to this system because it means that individuals take very little risk in suing a company for an employment-related claim, particularly if they were not hired at that company or have been fired. Supporters of the contingent fee system argue that it plays an important role in ensuring that people in the United States have access to the legal system.

Punitive Damages

An important factor to consider in evaluating any potential legal claim is the scope of possible damages you would have to pay if you lost. In an employment law case, a court may award a whole variety of damages, including reinstatement to a job, back pay, front pay, the employee's costs of finding a substitute job, emotional damages, and punitive damages.

It is the potential availability of punitive damages that makes item 2 in Exhibit 10.2 a fallacy. Indeed, the size of some well-publicized punitive damage awards, which can run into tens and sometimes even hundreds of millions of dollars, is a major reason that this type of damages has received so much notoriety—and why it is of particular concern to corporate defendants.

While punitive damages often get bad press, it is important to realize why they exist: they are intended to punish defendants who have acted egregiously and to discourage them and others from engaging in the illegal conduct in the future. That said, many areas of the law put no caps on punitive damages and the amount of damages may be unrelated to the actual harm experienced by the plaintiff.

The law limits the availability of punitive damages to employment law plaintiffs in some circumstances. Under federal nondiscrimination law, a plaintiff can recover punitive damages only when the employer intentionally discriminates and does so either maliciously or with reckless indifference. Even when an employer's conduct is that wrongful, the law limits the punitive damages in many cases depending on the size of the employer. For small employers the cap is $50,000. Awards against employers with more than five hundred employees can total up to $300,000. Caps may not apply, however, in cases of race or national origin discrimination. Furthermore, some states permit either higher levels of punitive damages or uncapped damages. For example, the jury award of $10 million in favor of Phillip McConkey, discussed earlier in the chapter, was based on state law. So was the Iowa judgment of $80 million in the retaliation case I discussed.

Jury Decisions and Appellate Review

Many people in the United States believe that juries are likely to be sympathetic with individual plaintiffs when they sue large corporations. All of us are familiar with the notion that companies are viewed as having deep pockets and that those pockets are like piggy banks waiting to be smashed by successful plaintiffs. So it is not unusual for managers to believe that item 3 in Exhibit 10.2 is true. But cases show that juries do not always take the plaintiff's side, even when the plaintiff is sympathetic. Furthermore, one recent study indicates that juries may be even less likely than judges are to give large punitive damage awards. Finally, the statistics about appeals in some types of employment law cases tend to surprise people.

To show that juries do not always take the side of a sympathetic plaintiff, consider another case brought against Wal-Mart. Shirley Gasper worked at a Wal-Mart store in Nebraska developing customer photographs. When Gasper noticed a picture that seemed to show a bruised infant crawling in a pile of marijuana with $50 and $100 bills scattered around the edges of the photograph, she turned the photograph over to the police without obtaining permission from the customer or her supervisor, who was out of town and could not view the pictures. The police praised her decision, but Wal-Mart fired her because her actions violated the company's policy of confidentiality for customer photographs. Gasper sued Wal-Mart, alleging that her firing violated public policy.

At least superficially, Gasper would seem to be a sympathetic plaintiff. After all, she did not get any personal gain from turning the photo over to the police. She believed she had a duty to report what she viewed as possible evidence of child abuse. Furthermore, Wal-Mart certainly fits the profile of a deep-pocketed defendant. Nevertheless, the Nebraska jury decided in Wal-Mart's favor, and the appellate court also found for Wal-Mart. It seems likely that Wal-Mart persuaded the jury that Gasper should have discussed the pictures with a higher level of store management rather than taking it on herself to violate the company's confidentiality policy.

When an employer does lose an employment law case at trial, a recent study of cases of employment discrimination indicates it may be in the employer's best interest to appeal. The study determined that when employers lost at trial and appealed, they won their appeal almost 44 percent of the time. In contrast, when the employer won at trial and the employee appealed, less than 6 percent of those appeals resulted in reversals in the employee's favor. These statistics are in stark contrast to the averages for all categories of appeals in federal courts. On average, when defendants lose at trial, they succeed on appeal only about 33 percent of the time, significantly less than the rate for employers in employment discrimination cases. And when plaintiffs lose at trial, they succeed on appeal about 12 percent of the time, or about twice the rate of plaintiffs in employment discrimination cases.[9]

The study did not attempt to explain why the statistics in these employment law cases are so much more favorable for employers than the overall statistics are for other categories of defendants. Still, the results should be encouraging to managers who fear that the court system may look at companies as deep pockets.

In sum, neither the jury system nor the appellate process may be as weighted against employers as many managers fear. Nevertheless, the realistic manager will consider the nature of the system when making any employment-related decision. Even if you have complied with all the technical legal requirements, do you want to risk explaining your actions to a judge or a jury where those actions might appear harsh, unfair, or arbitrary? On the other hand, would you feel more comfortable explaining your decision to fire an incompetent employee after you have counseled and warned that employee?

Avoiding the Court System

Many managers view the U.S. court system's role in employment disputes as a necessary evil—something akin to an occupational hazard that cannot be avoided and must be dealt with. Thus, item 4 in Exhibit 10.2 is true because employers are using arbitration and other nonadjudicative approaches to resolve disputes. In March 2001 the U.S. Supreme Court ruled that employers can enforce arbitration agreements against their employees.

Why do managers view arbitration as being a better way than the court system to resolve employment law disputes? There are several reasons. To begin with, managers often want to get employment disputes behind them and not wait years and years for the case to work its way through the courts. Arbitration cases can be heard more quickly and less expensively than a case that goes to trial, let alone one that proceeds to appeal. Furthermore, almost all court proceedings and written decisions are available to the public. As a result, managers often fear, quite reasonably, that even an employment law claim that has no basis in fact can damage the manager's and the company's reputation. In contrast, arbitration proceedings can be kept confidential, as can any written decision rendered by the arbitrator. Finally, many arbitration policies specify that arbitration is binding. In the absence of very unusual circumstances, such as bribery of the arbitrator, a decision in a binding arbitration case is final and cannot be appealed, a fact that saves both time and money.

Because arbitration has numerous advantages, companies are showing interest in requiring employees to arbitrate employment law disputes. For example, Sears, Roebuck began a new method of resolving disputes for almost sixteen thousand employees at two of its businesses. That method encourages employees to start by attempting to settle their disputes at a local level. Ultimately, if nothing else is successful, the process culminates in binding arbitration. Historically Sears has spent more money on legal costs for employment-related disputes than on any other type of legal issues.[10] The company hopes that the use of this new process, including binding arbitration, will decrease those costs.

Some open questions on employer-mandated arbitration policies remain and some people believe that it is unfair to require employees to arbitrate their claims. For example, some employers require employees to share the costs of paying for the arbitration. Those costs can climb into the thousands of dollars. Some courts have refused to enforce those cost-sharing requirements on the grounds that they act to discourage employees from pursuing their rights. The employees would not face similar costs in courts. For example, after he had a seizure at work, Waffle House fired Eric Baker, a grill cook who made $5.50 an hour. Rather than file for arbitration, Baker took his complaint that Waffle House had illegally discriminated against him because of a disability to the federal Equal Employment Opportunity Commission (EEOC). The EEOC has the power to seek enforcement of the federal nondiscrimination laws. The EEOC took interest in his claim and sued Waffle House on Baker's behalf. The U.S. Supreme Court decided, in 2002, that even if Baker had signed an enforceable arbitration agreement with Waffle House, that agreement could not prevent the EEOC from suing on his behalf.

Arbitration is not yet a standard with U.S. employers. Other issues remain, in addition to the question of whether employers may require employees to share the costs of arbitration. How significantly can an employer limit an employee's right to discovery? Who should choose the arbitrators? May an employer's policy limit the damages that an arbitrator can award? In spite of the gray areas, though, arbitration and other methods of alternative dispute resolution offer employers some opportunity to avoid the costs of lengthy litigation.

Recognizing Employment Law Issues as a Business Risk

As a manager, you should analyze employment-related issues as you do any other business problem: as both posing risks and offering rewards. Too often I see managers who are paralyzed by the fear of an employment lawsuit even though the same managers recognize and accept that they cannot completely avoid the risk of other types of lawsuits. For example, any manager involved with product development, design, or manufacture knows that it is impossible to guarantee that no customer will ever file a product liability lawsuit. Some lawsuits may be brought by customers who unreasonably misused the product or who otherwise have a very weak legal case. In addition, some of those lawsuits, even the weak ones, may damage the company's reputation. But without products, the company would be out of business, so accepting some risk of a lawsuit is critical to the continuing success of the company. The best managers not only recognize this fact but bring all of their own professional expertise to bear on their jobs. They seek outside advice from lawyers and other experts on how to minimize risks within the design and manufacturing parameters they establish.

I encourage you to view employment-related issues similarly. No business can maximize its potential unless it can hire outstanding employees, motivate its workforce, and fire incompetent employees. As you pursue excellence in your workforce, though, no one can guarantee that you will not be sued by a disgruntled job candidate, employee, or ex-employee. Nor can anyone promise that a weak lawsuit will not impose costs on your company in terms of time, money, or reputation.

Avoiding all potential employment law cases, however, is as unrealistic as avoiding all product liability cases. There will be times when you decide that the risks involved in addressing problems are well worth the potential rewards of improving the quality and morale of your workforce.

In addition, I believe that legal standards very typically are consistent with good management. As you set your moral compass for interactions with your employees, using common sense, consideration, fairness, and thinking through the implications of your actions often will help ensure that you are in compliance with relevant laws. After all, laws tend to reflect societal values. So by connecting with those values, not only will you be complying with the law, you will be actively preventing legal issues from arising. It will also help avoid situations where you may be in legal compliance with the law, but your actions appear so unreasonable or harsh that you and your company face bad publicity or lose a jury verdict because of negative perceptions.

In closing this chapter, let me emphasize that this is not intended to be a substitute for the intense training involved in a legal education. It does not give legal advice, nor does it cover the myriad of state and federal laws that can affect a final employment-related decision. Instead, it gives you a basic understanding of the fundamental concepts of U.S. employment law, which are no less important to you as a manager than a base knowledge of accounting, finance, or marketing. From there, you will be better prepared to discuss with the relevant experts the specific issues you encounter with your workforce, and you'll have a better idea of when to seek expert help.

One last time, consider the opening situation with Wendy. Upon learning of Wendy's involvement in the Web site, as Wendy's manager you have three options. First, you can be so fearful of an employment lawsuit that you decide to take no action at all. Second, you can react immediately and fire Wendy. Each of these actions reflects an extreme position and poses risk for you as a manager. In the first instance, you may confront serious problems from concerned parents of other children counseled by Wendy, the possibility of negative publicity for the counseling program, and even potential harm to the children if the children's access to the Web site somehow undercuts Wendy's effectiveness as a counselor. In the second option, a hasty decision to fire Wendy may leave open the possibility of a lawsuit whose risks you have not fully evaluated. A third approach would be to consider the situation using the basic principles of employment-at-will, the exceptions to employment-at-will, and the termination of employees. This analysis would raise a variety of specific questions, which you could then pose, if needed, to the appropriate person in your human resource department or to a lawyer. This, of course, is a wiser approach.

SUMMARY

The most basic concept in U.S. employment law is employment-at-will, which permits you, as a manager, to fire (or not hire or not promote) someone for any reason, even a lousy or arbitrary reason, so long as it is not an illegal reason.

There are three basic categories of exceptions to employment-at-will: contractual, nondiscrimination, and public policy and local statutory exceptions. Even allowing for those exceptions, a comparison of the U.S. approach with that taken in other industrialized countries shows that managers in the United States have considerable ability to select and motivate an exceptional workforce.

The nature of the U.S. legal system poses some specific challenges for employers and managers, including the availability of contingent fees and punitive damages. Nevertheless, the U.S. legal system is less weighted against employers than many managers believe. In addition, some companies are attempting to avoid or decrease the costs associated with employment litigation by establishing alternative dispute resolution policies. Typically those policies culminate in binding arbitration, which can limit publicity, cost, time, and acrimony.

As a manager, you should approach the legal aspects of employment questions as you do other business problems, as posing both benefits and risk. The mere possibility of a lawsuit should not determine your decisions; instead, you should carefully weigh risks and rewards, just as you do when confronted with other issues. By setting your internal compass to treat employees fairly, thoughtfully, and with consideration, most of the time you will also place yourself in compliance with legal standards.

○ ○ ○

Dana M. Muir is an associate professor of business law at the University of Michigan Business School. She serves as a member of the Department of Labor's Advisory Council on Employee Welfare and Pension Plans.

Chapter Eleven

Pick Relevant Metrics

Douglas K. Smith

Choosing Metrics That Fit the Challenge

Sometimes metrics are obvious, although even then there are important nuances. Other times, the best measures seem elusive. Consider, for example, a fellow who is overweight and feeling tired and stressed out. One day, this friend tells you he is going on a diet. Knowing the importance of focusing on outcomes instead of activities, you point out that dieting is an activity and ask your friend, "How would you know your diet was successful?" The response is, "I'll lose weight and feel better."

"Terrific!" you say. Now you suggest to him the power of getting specific. He has no problem getting specific about the first outcome he seeks (lose weight). With some thought and determination, he tells you, "I'll take off fifteen pounds!" So far, so good.

Still, there are nuances. You can help your friend become even more specific by noting two points—one obvious, the other not. First, you ask, "By when?" He responds, "In two months." Second, you suggest that taking weight off is only the critical first step in a weight-loss program. "But," you query, "what about keeping it off?" So, with your help, your friend has a relatively straightforward and specific outcome: *"I'll lose fifteen pounds in two months and keep it off for at least three months."*

Your friend can now benefit from the well-known advantages of pursuing performance outcomes with relevant and specific metrics:

- *Tracking:* With the assistance of a weight scale, he can track progress against the goal of losing fifteen pounds in the first two months and keeping it off in the following three. Absent the metric of pounds and the specific goal of fifteen, he would have no idea what to track.

- *Learning:* He can lean which weight-loss activities make the biggest difference. Such learning is as simple as observing cause and effect. As he eats less, eats more wisely, and exercises more, he can observe the connections between such efforts and the weight loss being tracked. By doing so, he can emphasize the dieting and exercise activities that are most effective for him and discontinue those that don't work.

- *Motivation:* His specific goal can fuel his effort with will and determination. Armed with a specific objective, he can convert his anxieties ("I don't know if I can really do this") into the focus and discipline that motivates success ("I *will* take and keep this weight off!").

So far, you have helped your friend a lot. But what about his other desired outcome—to feel better? In contrast to the outcome "lose weight," "feel better" is not so easily measured. "Feel better" is certainly an outcome, not an activity. But how would your friend know if he succeeded? Unlike pounds for weight loss, no obvious and universally accepted yardstick suggests itself. Do not, however, let him give up.

Indeed, in only a short time of creative brainstorming, you and your friend can generate several effective ways to measure success at feeling better. Your friend might seek to lower his blood pressure or to achieve a certain heart rate following a stress test or some particular form of exercise. Your friend might set specific goals to eliminate or reduce consumption of items such as cigarettes, alcohol, or coffee with well-established links to stress. He might choose an exercise such as bicycling or running and set a related performance goal (*"I'll run five miles every day and reduce my time by 15 percent within six weeks"*). Your friend might seek to attain one or more moments of well-being on a daily basis and keep a diary as a means to monitor his performance against that goal. Or he might set a goal that requires a spouse or colleague at work to help him monitor (*"Within a month, I will reduce the number of times I am short-tempered at work from several times a day to no more than once a week, and within two months, I will reduce it to zero"*).

When it comes to picking relevant metrics, many of today's most pressing organization performance challenges are more like "feel better" than like "lose weight." Consider, for example, delivering total customer satisfaction, being customer driven, achieving total quality, having the most respected brand, partnering with others, being the fastest, being the preferred provider, being the most innovative, having the best place to work, having one or more world-class competencies, being truly global or transnational or transcultural or diverse, and building one firm. These challenges demand attention to more than the financial economic metrics with which we are so familiar. Yes, there certainly is a link between success with such challenges and profits, revenues, costs, and market share. But profit revenue, cost, and market share goals too often fail to effectively capture the full purpose of many of today's critical aspirations—just as weight loss is an incomplete way to help your friend feel better. Like the dieting friend who wants to feel better, you and your colleagues must contend with a series of difficulties in trying to pick relevant and specific metrics.

There Is No Metric Universally Recognized as Effective
Weight itself, as measured in pounds or kilos, is universally accepted as an effective measure of weight loss. Similarly, revenues, profits, and market share are universally recognized as effective metrics of competitive superiority and financial performance. But no universally recognized metrics have emerged for such challenges as customer satisfaction, quality, partnering with others, being the preferred provider, innovation, and being the best place to work. Just like your friend who wants to feel better, you and your colleagues must find and use performance metrics that make sense. You must avoid getting stuck as the result of the absence of a universally recognized yardstick.

Some Criteria Are Quantitative and Objective;
Others Are Qualitative and Subjective
If your friend sets a performance goal of eliminating cigarettes entirely, he can monitor progress easily because the metric is quantitative and objective. But what about the goal to have one or more moments of well-being on a daily basis? As you know, stress-free people regularly experience such moments. Thus, it

is a performance outcome that is both specific and assessable. Using a diary, your friend can track progress and learn from such a goal. Still, this kind of outcome is far more qualitative than quantitative, and more subjective than objective. Candor and honesty are required for your friend to effectively use this metric because, otherwise, progress toward his goal is too easily manipulated.

Now, consider a company's aspiration to build partnering relationships with key suppliers or customers. On the one hand, establishing certain threshold goals about the amount of business conducted with each potential partner can provide quantitative and objective performance outcomes. On the other hand, the company and the supplier or customer might meet such criteria and still not have a true partnering relationship. Typically, partnership implies a variety of subjective and qualitative characteristics. For example, partners trust one another, regularly consult with one another on critical matters, share highly confidential information with one another, and seek out each other before anyone else regarding new opportunities and challenges. Yet, as with moments of well-being, setting and achieving performance outcomes related to phenomena such as trust demand candor and honesty in order to benefit from tracking, learning, and motivation. It is perfectly okay to use such qualitative and subjective criteria; indeed, sometimes they are the best, most accurate reflection of the performance challenge at hand. But you must recognize and then surmount the difficulties in doing so.

Many Metrics Require Extra Work and Effort

Obviously, criteria that are subjective and qualitative (such as your friend's moments of well-being or your company's number of partnering relationships) demand more work and effort to monitor than familiar goals such as weight loss or revenues, profits, and market share. Quantitative and objective perform- ance outcomes that are new or novel also can demand extra work. For example, in your friend's case, the use of heart rate as a metric for feeling better is both objective and quantitative. But it also demands extra work and effort because your friend probably does not currently monitor his heart rate following exercise. Similarly, an organization's goal to be the fastest, say, at product delivery can be measured objectively in terms of speed or cycle time. But it demands extra work and effort. The orga- nization must pick a starting point (perhaps when the customer places the order), an ending point (perhaps when the cus- tomer takes delivery of the order), and put in place the processes and practices needed to regularly and effectively measure time or speed. Do not let the burden of extra work prevent you from using a new metric that best fits the challenge before you.

If You Have Never Used a Chosen Metric Before, There Will Be No Baseline

Once again, consider an organization's desire to be the fastest at product delivery. If the organization has never monitored the speed of the process from order generation through delivery, people in the organization will have no preexisting baseline against which to pick specific goals and outcomes for improve- ment. In situations like this, the parties involved might throw up their hands and ask, "How can we set a goal if we don't know how we're doing now?" It is an understandable question. Yet a moment's reflection indicates that people and organiza- tions would *never* move beyond yesterday's metrics if the absence of a baseline for a new metric were seen as fatal. Instead, you must rely on gut feeling and whatever indicators you have to pick an outcome-based goal and then use your performance against that outcome to drive improvement as well as to set the baseline for future goals and performance.

Some Criteria Demand Contributions from People Who May Not Be Subject to Your Control or Authority

When your friend seeks the specific performance outcome of increasing the moments of well-being at work, he depends on the participation of other people. For example, his boss might have certain habits or behaviors that trigger stress. Without obtaining a shift in behavior from his boss, your friend is less likely to achieve the performance outcome he seeks. He would do well, therefore, to share his goal with his boss and other colleagues at work, and to ask for their support and help. However, your friend cannot command that help.

The same principle applies to many of today's performance challenges that require contributions from different departments or functions or silos. For example, the performance outcome of building the most respected brand requires much more than effective advertising. Organizations such as Coca-Cola, McDonald's, Nike, and the American Red Cross have respected brands because those brands make explicit promises that the entire organization effectively and routinely fulfills. For example, the American Red Cross brand communicates a promise of quick, effective, and comprehensive disaster relief that people throughout the Red Cross, not just those in marketing, make a reality. Accordingly, while the marketing people in your organization might aspire to build the most respected brand, they cannot do it themselves. Instead, the specific goals associated with such an effort require contributions from people over whom those in marketing have no direct control or authority. Do not permit your lack of control over other people to prevent you from selecting the metric that best fits your challenge.

Some Metrics Are Leading Indicators of Success: Others Are Lagging Indicators

When your dieting friend sets a goal to exercise regularly, his success is a leading indicator of feeling better. In other words, his success at meeting outcome-based exercise goals *causes* his success at feeling better. Put in the reverse, moments of well-being are a lagging effect of exercise. The central importance of this lead-lag phenomenon is relatively new in the world of organization performance. When financial and market indicators such as profits, revenues, and market share were all that mattered to the bottom line, most people in most organizations had no reason to concern themselves with the lead-lag relationship among their goals.

Today, the performance landscape has shifted. Consider, for example, the aspiration of total customer satisfaction. If your organization delivers total customer satisfaction, can you expect gains in revenue, profit, and market share? Yes. Okay, should you use revenue, profit, and share gains as the goals of customer satisfaction? No.

Why not? Because while revenue, profit, and share gains are a lagging effect of customer satisfaction, they are also a lagging effect of other causes (number and strength of competitors, effective purchasing, distribution presence and economics, and so on). Using revenue, profit, market share, and similar metrics as the sole measure of everything an organization does may be theoretically possible, but it is pragmatically nonsensical and even nightmarish. No one would know for sure what difference he or she was making. No one would really know whether and to what extent changes in, say, market share were due to shifts in customer satisfaction versus introduction of new products versus distribution strategies versus . . . well, anything and everything the organization is doing. Indeed, this financial-only approach is what most organizations are struggling to shun rather than embrace. Consequently, you and your colleagues must spend time sorting out the lead-lag relationship among the possible metrics you will use.

Make a Choice and Stick with It Long Enough to Learn
Having too many goals is the same as having no goal at all. A wonderful aspect of your friend's weight-loss goal is that it provides laser-like focus that is quantitative, objective, and universally recognized as effective. In contrast, none of the "feel better" goals are nearly so tidy; each has one or more of the faults we have just reviewed. Still, your friend must make a choice. He must select one or two, or maybe three, of the metrics associated with the "feel better" performance outcome. Choosing all of them will not work. Indeed, the greater the number of metrics and goals he pursues, the more likely he is to fall into the trap of losing focus.

This commonsense rule also applies to organizational aspirations such as being the best place to work, being the preferred provider, or being customer driven. With a bit of effort and creativity, you and your colleagues can brainstorm a list of possible metrics for setting and evaluating progress toward such performance aspirations. But you must avoid pursuing the entire list or even a very large part of it. You must make a choice. You must focus. And you must stick with your choice long enough to gain the benefit of tracking, learning, and motivation. Think what would happen if your dieting friend chose to reduce alcohol consumption, then two weeks later abandoned that in favor of seeking a lower heart rate following exercise, then a week later shifted to increasing his moments of well-being. Such skittish inconsistency won't work for your friend, nor will it work for you and your colleagues to shift so easily and often from one set of metrics and goals to another. You must give yourself a chance to benefit from tracking, learning, and motivation. You must stick with your chosen metrics and goals long enough to learn and progress.

○   ○   ○

Each of these difficulties generates anxiety and reluctance. And, of course, they compound one another. It is tough enough for your friend to set and stick with a specific goal to lose and keep off fifteen pounds. But it is far more difficult for your friend to establish the resolve—the will—to stick with a choice among the many possible goals and metrics related to feeling better, none of which are universally recognized, and several of which are subjective or qualitative, require extra work to track, or perhaps require the contribution of other people to achieve. Yet your friend must overcome such obstacles if he is to succeed. Similarly, you and your colleagues must summon the determination to work through such worries if you are to learn how to select the metrics that best fit today's most urgent performance challenges. The next section introduces you to four sets of metrics (the four yardsticks) that can help you become increasingly comfortable in choosing and sticking with the best measures of progress.

The Four Yardsticks

All performance challenges are measurable by some combination of what I call the four yardsticks:

1. Speed/time
2. Cost
3. On-spec/expec quality
4. Positive yields

The first three of these are objective and quantitative; the fourth is a blend of objective and subjective, quantitative and qualitative. If you learn to use the four yardsticks, you can eliminate many of the difficulties and anxieties related to picking the metrics that make a difference in today's most pressing performance challenges.

Speed/Time

Use this yardstick whenever your performance challenge relates to the speed or time it takes for something—typically, a process—to happen. If you and your colleagues are trying to become faster at a process, or if you need to eliminate unnecessary steps, reduce costs, or coordinate the efforts of many people across multiple tasks, then speed and time are powerful metrics to choose. For example, speed and time are critical metrics for any performance challenges that cut across the silos or functions of an organization—challenges such as product or service innovation, time to market, reduction of cycle time, total customer service, and manufacturing and logistics effectiveness. If you have ever reengineered work, you have contended with the challenge of speed and time.

To use speed and time effectively, you and your colleagues must define the process or series of steps you are measuring.

For example, many of today's organizations work hard to reduce the time it takes from generating customer orders through satisfying those orders. Having named the process, you must then *pick the* starting and stopping steps of that process. As Figures 11.1 through 11.3 illustrate, the starting and stopping steps in this cycle or process can vary—and the difficulty and impact of your challenge can also vary depending on the choices you make. The speed of challenge in receipt of customer order through customer receipt of delivery (Figure 11.1) is less difficult than receipt of customer order through customer first use (Figure 11.2) And first customer contact through complete customer satisfaction (Figure 11.3) is the most difficult and comprehensive of all three.

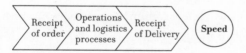

FIGURE 11.1. **Receipt of Customer Order Through Customer Receipt of Delivery**

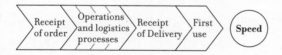

FIGURE 11.2. **Receipt of Customer Order Through Customer First Use**

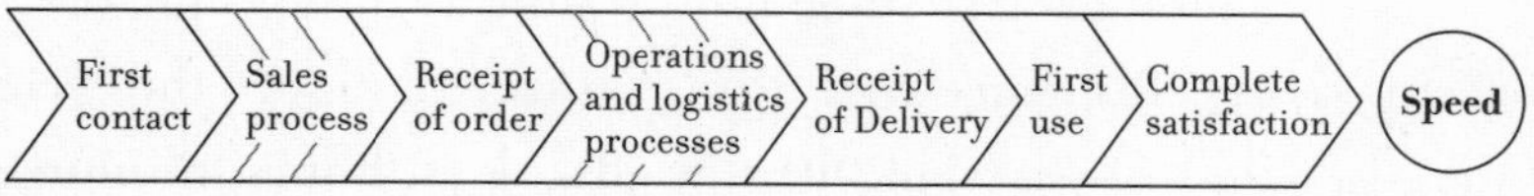

FIGURE 11.3. **First Customer Contact Through Complete Customer Satisfaction**

Why? Well, each of the starting and stopping points in Figure 11.1 is objectively identifiable. It is easy to identify the exact points in time when a customer order is received by your company and when the customer receives delivery of your goods. In contrast, the ending point in Figure 11.2 ("customer first use") demands much more work, requires the cooperation of the customer, and, in the case of software or complicated industrial products, calls for judgment about what constitutes first use. Figure 11.3 adds further complication. By designating "first customer contact" as the initial step, the entire sales process and all of the people included in it have been grafted onto the operations and logistics processes of Figure 11.1. Moreover, "complete customer satisfaction" involves even more steps (for example, customer service) and adds assessment difficulties (for example, qualitative, subjective metrics; extra work; customer cooperation; no universally recognized yardstick).

If your organization seeks to be totally customer driven as well as the fastest, Figure 11.3 portrays a far more comprehensive and customer-sensitive process than Figure 11.1. Figure 11.2 depicts a middle ground between the other two. None of these three is necessarily best. The point is that if you and your colleagues choose time and speed as your metrics, then you also must make choices about the starting and stopping points of the process you will measure—and you must do so in the light of the overall performance challenge you are trying to meet.

Next, you must *pick* some unit of time as the specific metric in your performance goal. Will you seek to reduce the cycle time in terms of years, months, weeks, days, hours, minutes, seconds, or fractions of seconds? Moreover, you must make a choice about number and frequency. Are you seeking to reduce the average time from receipt of order through receipt of delivery? Or are you seeking to ensure that 100 percent (or some other very high percentage) of orders fall below some cycle time threshold (for example, 100 percent of orders in less than twenty-four hours). Finally, you must make the effort required to measure speed and time. Having defined the starting and stopping points of what you'll measure as well as the time units, number, and frequency, you must actually do the work of measurement. As you know, this can have implications for information systems as well as people's roles in various parts of the organization.

Exhibit 11.1 summarizes the choices you must make to use speed and time effectively. By the way, the order-generation through fulfillment processes laid out in Figures 11.1 through 11.3 apply to services as well as products, and to individual consumers as well as commercial customers. For example, these figures pertain as easily to mortgages, haircuts, and lube and oil jobs as to cookies, vacuum cleaners, and automobiles. In business-to-business markets, they describe the order-generation through fulfillment process for maintenance, payroll, consulting, legal and other services, as well as the sale and delivery of industrial or other kinds of products.

The order-generation through fulfillment process is one of the most fundamental work processes in any organization. Other basic processes include new product–service introduction, customer service, integrated logistics, and hiring, development, and retention of people.

Cost

Of the four yardsticks, this is the most familiar. Most people in organizations have many years of experience attending to cost as well as setting and achieving cost goals. Still, there are nuances and choices. First, you must choose between focusing

EXHIBIT 11.1. **Speed/Time Choices**

1. What is the process or series of work steps you wish to measure?

2. What step starts the clock?

3. What step stops the clock?

4. What unit of time makes the most sense?

5. What number and frequency of items going through the process must meet your speed requirements?

6. What adjustments to roles and resources (such as systems) are needed to do the work of measurement and to achieve the goal?

on units of activity or materials and combinations of units of activities and/or materials. For most of the twentieth century, organizations focused more on unit costs than on combinations of activities, believing that if each person or department throughout the organization worried about reducing unit costs, then minimal total costs would follow. In this view, cost goals mimicked organization charges—individual unit costs rolled into departmental costs, then into functional costs, then into company costs. Many challenges still benefit from this view. For example, it is critical for organizations to work hard to reduce overall purchasing costs, and they can usefully focus on the unit costs of materials purchased to accomplish that.

In the past decade, however, this unit-by-unit view has fallen from favor out of preference for an activity, or process, view. Today, many of our most significant performance challenges require looking across a combination of different activities to reduce the total cost of that process. Thus, consider again the receipt of order through receipt of delivery process shown in Figure 11.1. It is important to recognize that just as in the case of speed and time, if you seek to reduce the cost of a combination or process, then you must define the starting point and stopping point of that combination or process.

In addition, for both traditional unit cost goals and activity or process cost goals, you must decide whether you will count indirect as well as direct costs and, if so, which indirect costs. Next, you must define an allocation method for the indirect costs you wish to count. Experience suggests that the more direct the relationship between any activity, unit, or material and the object of the costing effort, the easier it is to know what and how to count. For example, the salary, benefits, travel and entertainment, and office support costs associated with a purchasing officer are easily attributed to the materials or services purchased by that officer.

But the more indirect and abstract the relationship between a source of cost and the thing (activity, material, or combination) being costed, the more difficult it is to know what and how to count, the more likely it is that cost allocation schemes are arbitrary. Finally, the more arbitrary the cost allocation scheme, the less likely it is that the allocated costs will benefit from problem-solving techniques.

Let's explore this critical idea. Imagine for a moment that you and your colleagues seek to reduce total purchasing costs for hardware and software. You decide that you will count everything, even such overhead as the salaries and benefits of the CEO, the senior vice president of human resources, and other top executives. Here's what will happen. Because your company's top executives do not dedicate much, if any, time to hardware and software purchasing, you will inevitably pick some completely arbitrary method for assigning some of the top executives' salary and related costs to hardware and software purchasing. The same will happen with many other aspects of overhead. Nevertheless, say you move ahead and succeed in "totally" costing out the purchasing of hardware and software.

Now that you know "total" purchasing cost, you will turn your attention to problem solving in an effort to reduce purchasing costs. As you do, your group will soon discover that you cannot come up with any effective ideas for reducing the costs associated with the top executives and other arbitrarily allocated overhead. Consequently, you will focus your problem-solving efforts on those costs you *can* do something about. And these will largely be costs that are directly associated with purchasing. Put differently, you and your colleagues will treat the CEO-type, arbitrary allocations as a given that cannot be changed. The obvious question is, "Why did you include such allocated amounts in the first place?"

Note the important difference between the pure arbitrariness of allocating CEO time to purchasing hardware and software and the challenge of allocating and assigning total activity or process costs that, while perhaps new to you or others, are not arbitrary. Consider again the goal of reducing the total process cost of receipt of order through receipt of delivery, shown in Figure 11.1. You and your colleagues would be wise to form a team from operations, customer service, sales, logistics, and finance to tackle this challenge. Each function will contribute relevant knowledge and experience, but each will also bring areas of ignorance. For example, someone from a department that receives customer orders will know little about assigning costs from operations or sales and vice versa. Just because each person has an area of ignorance, however, does not mean that the team is ignorant. On the contrary, by working together, the team can figure out the best way to set, measure, problem-solve, and achieve a cost reduction goal for the whole process.

On-Spec/Expec Quality

This yardstick applies to any performance challenge that demands adherence to one or more specifications (*on spec*) or customer expectations (customer expectations, or "expec" for short). Product and service specifications generally derive from production and operational standards, legal and regulatory requirements, and customer and competitive demands. In this last sense, then, specifications overlap with customer expectations. But nearly always, there exist customer expectations that exceed the specifications any organization mandates for its products and services. Such expectations reflect an array of customer concerns as wide as human psychology itself, such as timeliness, availability, ease of use, friendly and helpful service at the time of sale and afterward, personalization, and customization.

A key point in using this family of metrics is to focus on specifications or expectations that are known and defined. Consider, for example, a direct mail computer company such as Dell or Gateway. Such organizations certainly have companywide aspirations regarding customer satisfaction. And many people at Dell or Gateway can use on-spec quality metrics to set and achieve goals that contribute to the whole company's customer satisfaction performance challenge. When a product is shipped, it should meet known specifications regarding the hardware and software to be included, as well as whether that hardware and software work as promised. Moreover, both Dell and Gateway know that customers have specific expectations about the ease and speed of setting up their new equipment.

Thus, goals regarding on-expec quality can also be set and monitored.

In contrast, customer expectations that are unknown cannot be intentionally achieved. You cannot set or achieve goals related to aspects of performance that you cannot even define. Should organizations ignore the unknown? Of course not. You can and should set goals to discover and meet new expectations that matter to customers. But these unknown aspects are better served through the family of metrics called positive yields (see below) than through on-spec/expec goals.

To succeed in the challenge of increasing the number of totally satisfied or delighted customers, organizations must deal with subjective issues such as feelings, attitudes, and emotions that cannot be fully captured through known specifications or expectations. Similarly, there are irreducible, abstract aspects to such overall aspirations as "most respected brand," "partnering relationships," and "total quality." Organizations should set and pursue such goals, using positive yields. But making unknown and elusive criteria the content of on-spec/expec goals only invites the same difficulty we saw with allocating CEO costs to purchasing. People will not have any useful way to problem-solve and seek improvements on that which remains unknown to them. By including only what is known in on-spec/expec quality goals, people can track and learn from failure. If, for example, Dell or Gateway finds that 40 percent of customer complaints concern the failure of a Microsoft program to boot up on the first try, a combined Dell or Gateway and Microsoft team can fix the problem. Of course, once the unknown becomes known, you can then easily include it in on-spec/expec goals.

In my experience, the most pragmatic on-spec/expec goals are expressed in terms of not falling short. That is, the goals seek to avoid the number and/or impact of defects, mistakes, or errors. For example, consider Motorola's Six Sigma aspiration. Six Sigma is a statistical measure that indicates fewer than four defects or errors per million opportunities for error. Motorola people enjoy telling audiences that, in comparison with Motorola's aspiration, most enterprises operate at between three and four sigma levels, that is, between six thousand and sixty-six thousand defects per million opportunities. By carefully and persistently setting Six Sigma goals, Motorola puts itself in a position to apply classic total quality tools to identify and overcome the root causes of defects.

Positive Yields

This last category is the catch-all yardstick. All the measures in this group reflect positive and constructive output or yield of organizational effort. These metrics answer the question, "What positive impacts are we trying to accomplish for our customers, for our shareholders, and for ourselves?" Many positive yields are familiar and objective: revenues, profits, number of customers, market share, new products, and the like. Others are not so familiar. The number of partnering, trust-based, or preferred relationships; the number of completely satisfied or delighted customers; the existence or strength of institutional skills or core competencies (such as flexibility or nimbleness); improvements in climate surrounding or morale among the people of the enterprise—these and other performance metrics provide ways to assess the positive yield of organizational effort.

Of the four yardsticks, positive yields are most prone to subjective and qualitative metrics, particularly for new kinds of performance challenges. When your performance challenge is to build partnering relationships, for example, then setting a goal to increase the number or percentage of such relationships makes sense. But evaluating relationships is a subjective, qualitative matter. It is hard to reduce this performance aspiration entirely to objective, quantitative criteria. Note, however, that subjective and qualitative goals are not bad or impermissible so long as they can be assessed and tracked with effective candor and honesty.

Notwithstanding such difficulties, positive yields often are the goals most directly related to the challenge at hand. Consider, for example, the aspiration to build the most respected brand. As shown in Figure 11.4, many criteria provide leading (e.g., percent of viewers who accurately recall television or other advertising) or lagging (e.g., market share) indicators of having the most respected brand. The positive yield of brand respect remains, however, the most direct measure of respect. The problem is that brand respect involves any number of subjective and qualitative aspects, such as customer testimonials or survey results regarding brand preferences. So be it. As the saying goes, "You get what you measure." If your organization is serious about having the most respected brand, then you must work hard to understand and measure respect itself.

Good performance goals nearly always reflect a combination of two or more of the four yardsticks. Moreover, the first two of the four yardsticks (speed/time and cost) measure the effort or investment *put into* organizational action, while the second two (on-spec/expec quality and positive yields) measure benefits you *get out of* that effort and investment. The best goals typically have at least one performance outcome related to the effort put in and at least one outcome related to the benefits produced by that effort.

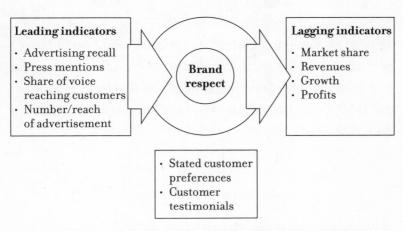

FIGURE 11.4. **Indicators of Having the Most Respected Brand**

For example, a consumer products company seeking to increase the pace and impact of innovation might set a goal to "reduce the time to market of new products by half while simultaneously doubling the hit rate of successful new products." This performance goal reflects two of the four yardsticks: the speed/time of the new product development process (the effort put in) and the positive yield of successful new products (the effect of that effort). Were the organization to concentrate its effort solely on reducing the input to innovation (in terms of cost or speed/time), it would risk lowering the number of commercial successes. If the focus were entirely on the positive yield of new product successes, those new products might take a very long time to appear and might carry uneconomically high costs. By choosing to deliver both faster innovation and more commercial successes, the people at the consumer products company are challenging themselves to work creatively to solve the inherent tension involved in introducing more new products at a faster pace.

o   o   o

Douglas K. Smith is a consultant specializing in organization performance, innovation, and change. He is author or coauthor of five books, and his work has been featured in *Business Week,* the *Wall Street Journal,* the *Harvard Business Review,* and the *New York Times.*

Chapter Twelve

How Change Really Comes About

Rosabeth Moss Kanter
Barry A. Stein
Todd D. Jick

Productive organizational changes, changes that increase a company's capacity to meet new challenges, tend to come about through a combination of five major building blocks, or events (see Figure 12.1). As identified in *The Change Masters* (Kanter, 1983), these patterns are often observed more after the fact than as a part of a formal planning process. However, whether recognized or not, it is these characteristics that enable change efforts to succeed. Thoughtful change managers, then, will benefit from looking for them and supporting their potential value:

○ *Event 1. Grassroots innovations.* Because of the constant motion in and around organizations, there are always activities that deviate from organizational expectations or formal intentions.

FIGURE 12.1. **Major Events in Change Histories:**
The Change Funnel

Some might be random or chance events reflecting coordination problems or "loose couplings" in the system; that is, no one does everything entirely according to plan even if he or she intends to, and slight local variations on procedures may result in new ideas. Some might be the result of "accidents," events for which there is no contingency plan, or the organization's traditional sources are exhausted, so the company innovates by default, turning to a new idea or a new person just to fill a gap. Others might deliberate innovations designed to solve a problem—the kind of constant experimentation found in Japanese consumer electronics companies or in GE's workout. Or a "hole" in the system may open up because another change is taking place: a changeover of bosses leaving a temporary gap, a new system being installed that does not yet work perfectly.

All these constitute "unplanned opportunities" for experiments or innovations that pave the way for further change. The ideas or experiences resulting from these unusual or new events then constitute "solutions looking for problems"—models that can be applied elsewhere.

Departures from tradition provide the organization with a portfolio of grassroots innovations—a foundation in experience that can be used to solve new problems as they arise or to replace existing methods with more productive ones. This foundation in experience also suggests the possibility of a new strategy, one that could not be developed as easily without the existence of those experiences. At the same time, they condition the direction of any new strategies. In effect, it is hard to see where you want to go until you have a few options, but those options do not limit later choices.

One lesson is straightforward: an organization that wants change should promote local experiments and variations on any plan. Those variations—sometimes more than the plan itself—may be the keys to future successes. And there need to be enough of these experiments to give organizational policymakers choices when they start reformulating strategies. This constitutes the internal equivalent of a diversified portfolio for turbulent times.

Successful experiments or small-scale innovations have another important value for the change process: they demonstrate the organization's capacity to take productive action. An unfortunate number of change efforts seem to begin with the negative rather than the positive—a catalogue of problems, a litany of woes. But identification of potential opportunities or descriptions of strengths seems to be a better and faster way to begin. In our own experience helping corporations develop new modes of operating, we have found it valuable to look for the already existing innovations that signal an ability to make the shift, and then to use these as the organization's own foundation for solving its problems and designing a better system. Exemplars—positive innovations—are better to highlight than trouble spots when one is trying to move a whole system. At

Xerox, for example, these exemplars were known as "proof sources"—unambiguous proof of possibility.

But unusual events do not by themselves produce major change. Large systems are capable of containing many contradictions and many departures from tradition that do not necessarily affect the organization's central tendency. What is more, innovations can easily disappear. Thus, deviant events result in overall change only under certain circumstances. Chief among them is a crisis or galvanizing event.

○ *Event 2. Crisis or galvanizing event.* The second cluster of forces causes the organization to pay attention to the need for change. Some crises are clearly external, such as a lawsuit, an abrupt market downturn, a critical raw material shortage, or a competitor's new-product introduction. Others occur within an organization's borders but outside current operating frameworks—for example, a new demand from a higher-level official, an alternative technology, or a growing staff turnover problem.

The event of crisis seems to require—even demand—a response. If the crisis is defined as insoluble by traditional means, if traditional solutions quickly exhaust their value, or if stakeholders indicate that they will not be satisfied by the same old response, then a nontraditional solution may be pushed forward. One of the grassroots experiments or local innovations may be grabbed, if only in desperation. In effect, variations from tradition create potential, but until the system has enough of a crack in its shell, they are not able to penetrate. Cultural differences play a role here. For example, some Japanese organizations are prone to identify crises with what seems to the Western observer to be almost hysterical rapidity, using them to startle people into innovation.

At the same time, effective response to a crisis may depend on the tradition departure factor. That is, if the organization already has in hand the possibility of a response with which it has experience, it can move much faster to make the changes the crisis seems to demand. Random departures from tradition that had occurred in a hit-or-miss fashion, it seemed, helped Procter & Gamble develop a new team-based work system in its factories that later became a full-blown model for the company.

But neither small-scale innovation nor crisis alone guarantees changes without two other conditions: explicit strategic decisions in favor of change and individuals with enough power to act as prime movers for its implementation.

○ *Event 3: Change strategists and strategic decisions.* Only now do we get to the point in the process identified in most of the change management or strategic planning literature as the beginning. Here strategies are developed that use the potential shown in event 1 to solve the problems inherent in event 2.

A new definition of the situation is formulated, along with a new set of plans that lifts the local innovations from the periphery to center stage and reconceptualizes them as the emergent tradition rather than as departures from it. While *strategic* is clearly an overused word, it does stress the deliberate and conscious articulation of a direction, saving the organization from change through drift. Absent that kind of strategy formulation to build on a set of innovations, the innovations will drift away, or so many innovations will pass by that none will gain the momentum to take hold. But the organization's readiness to engage in this formulation is the experience it has already had.

Not surprisingly, more flexible and innovative organizations have an advantage here. More people participating in the search for ideas creates pressure to do something with them. More overlap, communication channels, and team mechanisms keep more ideas circulating. And the existence of teams and teamwork at the top, drawing together many areas and exchanging ideas among them, increases the likelihood of tying together external circumstances and grassroots experience.

These new strategies build new methods, products, and structures into official plans, which in turn serve many purposes other than the obvious, as the organizational theorist Karl Weick (1979) has pointed out:

> Plans are important in organizations, but not for the reasons people think. . . . Plans are symbols, advertisements, games, and excuses for interactions. They are *symbols* in the sense that when an organization does not know how it is doing, or knows that it is failing, it can signal a different message to observers. . . . Plans are *advertisements* in the sense that they are often used to attract investors to the firm. . . . Plans are *games* because they often are used to test how serious people are about the programs they advocate. . . . Finally, plans become *excuses* for *interaction* in the sense that they induce conversations among diverse populations about projects that may have been low priority items.

In short, strategic decisions help set into motion the next two major clusters of events in change.

○ *Event 4: Individual implementers and change champions.* Any new strategy, no matter how brilliant or responsive, no matter how much agreed on and admired, will probably fail without someone with power pushing it. We have all had the experience of going to a meeting where, although many excellent ideas are developed and everyone agrees to a plan, nothing happens because no one takes any responsibility for doing anything about it. Even assigning accountabilities does not always guarantee implementation without a powerful figure pushing the accountable party to live up to it. Hence the importance of the corporate entrepreneur who remains steadfast in his or her vision and keeps up the momentum of the action team even when its effort wanes, or of a powerful sponsor or "idea champion" for innovations that require help beyond the actions of the innovating team. Empowering champions is one way managers solidify commitment to a new strategy.

Leaders push change in part by repetition, by mentioning the new idea or the new practice on every possible occasion, in every speech, at every meeting. There may be catch phrases that become slogans for the new efforts. Raymond Smith, the CEO of Bell Atlantic, developed and popularized the "Bell Atlantic Way." A major program at IBM was called "Just Say Yes" (to customers).

What is important about such communications is certainly not the pat phrases but that they remind people about the firm commitment of leaders and implementers to the changes. It is all too easy for people in a company to make fun of slogans if they are unrelated to specific actions or are not taken seriously by the managers themselves. Champions pushing a new strategy have to make absolutely clear that they believe in it and that it is oriented toward getting something that they want, because it is good for the organization. They might, for example—and should—visit local units, ask questions about implementation, and praise efforts consistent with the thrust. The personal tour by a top executive is an important tool of prime movers.

This is especially important for changes that begin with pressures in the environment and were not sought by the organization—changes in response to regulatory pressures or shifts to counter a competitor's strategy—because the drive for change must become internalized, especially if it originated externally. Otherwise, implementers cannot push with conviction, and the people around them will avoid wholehearted implementation.

People in organizations are constantly trying to figure out what their managers really want—which statements or plans can be easily ignored and which have command value—because there are too many things, suggesting too many courses of action, for people to act on. Leaders have to communicate strategic decisions forcefully enough, and often enough, to make their intentions clear. Otherwise nothing happens.

A chief executive of a major entertainment company—a man with a reputation for toughness and a knack for making people fall all over themselves to please him—was astonished to realize that his division managers had not acted on a certain business development request he had made. He badgered them to explain. Sheepishly, one manager confessed: "We didn't believe you meant it at first. You throw so many requests at us we can't possibly do all of them. We wait to see which ones you're committed to—the ones you remember to ask about next time."

Worse yet, overzealous subordinates, trying to interpret vague statements from the top, take strong action in the *wrong* direction. We call this the *"Murder in the Cathedral* problem," after T. S. Eliot's play. The drama, set in 1170, describes the events that followed when King Henry II of England said in frustration that he wished someone would get rid of that "troublesome priest" (the archbishop of Canterbury). His aides thereupon slaughtered Thomas à Becket in Canterbury Cathedral, and Henry spent the rest of his life doing penance. Many other unintended or even wrongful acts occur in organizations because leaders are often unclear about what they really want or don't want.

A few clear signals, consistently supported, can help steer an organization in a new direction; they are signposts in a morass of organizational messages. The job of prime movers is not only to "talk up" the new strategy but also to manipulate those symbols which indicate commitment to it. The devices that can be used to redirect that organizational attention range from the mundane (reports required, meeting agendas) to the spectacular.

At Raychem, then a small, rapidly growing high-tech company, the CEO, Paul Cook, shook his executives out of their customary thought patterns by staging an elaborate hoax. The annual executive conference began at the usual place with a rather long-winded recital of standard facts and figures by the CEO himself. His soporific speech was interrupted after an hour by the arrival of a fleet of helicopters, which flew the whole group to another, more remote place where the "real" meeting began—steadily punctuated by surprises like elephants on the beach—all stressing creativity, change, and stretch. A few such events can have importance far beyond their local effect.

Leaders can also demonstrate their belief in the new thrust the same way leaders do in the military—by being the first over the top. They are among the first to try out, to demonstrate, to go to the training program for it, or to model it in their own behavior. One senior vice president of a leading West Coast bank wanted to show his people that he really meant it when he exhorted them to take risks in selling the bank's lending services. He rode into the bank one morning on a horse, dressed as the "Loan Arranger," shooting water pistols at his staff and shouting: "Meet your lending goals or else!" Doing something this outrageous in a dignity-conscious bank was a clear signal that he would support risk taking in others.

Thus, leaders push, but for implementers to complete the process, they need ways to embody the change inaction.

○ *Event 5. Action vehicles.* The last critical cluster of events in productive change involves adding mechanisms that allow the new action possibilities to be realized in practice. The actions implied by a change remain ideas and abstractions until concretized in actual procedures, structures, or processes. Change recipients need to know what the change means for their activities.

Too many ideas are only partially implemented by organizations in the form of policy or mission statements while people scratch their heads wondering what this means they should actually do. Quality programs encouraging "customer focus" often suffer from this syndrome: lots of official endorsement and leaders pushing, but no new vehicles to support action. Sophisticated proponents of quality often decry the reduction of the concept to its manifestations in particular programs ("Quality is more than just a quality circle; it is a process. What counts is the journey.") But without some specific vehicles it may well be impossible to realize the principle.

This is a matter of balance. Organizations always have to steer a course between the need to express change in concrete actions and the danger of falling into faddism and action for its own sake—and too great emphasis on the big picture—with the danger that it becomes just another campaign that will pass in time. It helps to keep in mind that journeys are not simply *to* somewhere; they are also *from* somewhere—almost by definition, somewhere unsatisfactory.

Change from What? The Unsatisfactory Present

Change implementers must be concerned not only about changing *to* what: they must also be concerned with changing *from* what. The path of progress is not determined simply by the destination, a fact often overlooked by those who too glibly accept "benchmarking" results as a fixed road map for change. And even though every organization has its own uniqueness, some general principles can be discerned from observations of many organizations seeking change.

Most organizations, as it turns out, are riddled with problems, dysfunctional practices, and counterproductive arrangements. Though externally they may appear to be sophisticated and deliberate instruments of collective purpose, operationally they are often technologically bulls in society's china shop, with people lurching from one point to another, often seemingly out of control, and steered more by their sheer momentum and by change encounters than by design.

James Boswell, the biographer of the eighteenth-century scholar Samuel Johnson, once accompanied the ever-curious Dr. Johnson to the performance of a celebrated dog that walked on its hind legs. Boswell was disappointed; the dog, he said, didn't walk very well and did not always respond appropriately to its master's instructions, Johnson demurred, "It's not how well the thing is done," he said. "It's that the thing is done at all." Just so with most large organizations.

Larger corporations, more or less universally, are often not very effective. And the larger a company gets, the greater its potential for problems. Even the best—the so-called excellent organizations—are only moderately effective when judged by their capacity to use their resources well, especially their people. This standard, the utilization of organizational capacity, is just as important as the widely used measure of the utilization of manufacturing capacity, although the latter is much easier to measure. By this broader standard, large organizations, especially, are a rather poor lot.

In large organizations, people and systems operate much more effectively some of the time than they do most of the time. Therefore, there must exist a large reservoir of potential effectiveness that only occasionally gets tapped. This is such an elementary phenomenon of organizational life that it goes largely unremarked, and very few people ever ask the critical question: Can we operate in general the way we operate on occasion?

What accounts for the difference in levels of performance in the first place? Can it be people? Is it the quality of managers? Do some organizations have an extra allotment of bad apples in their barrel? No. We suggest that the quality of people is not the major issue at all. There are plenty of differences among organizations, and surely some have more incompetent or misguided people than others. But, in fact, the productivity of most people—as against organizations—is actually quite phenomenal, once we take into account the extraordinary effort and ingenuity with which they manage to do their work despite the apparently endless roadblocks, sources of resistance, and interference that are characteristic of large organizations. Daily, people are forced to violate formal policies, disobey instructions, and put themselves at risk to solve the problems they confront. Productivity is often measured as if people performed on a flat racetrack; in reality, it is an obstacle course.

The source of the problem is that some organizations in action are based on fundamentally inaccurate premises that produce inherently flawed structures and processes. Of course, these premises continue because they are so embodied in some national cultures and conventional practice that they are hardly ever questioned, never mind seriously confronted. This diagnosis is also confirmed by the fact that better organizational answers that are more accurate and powerful are well known but rarely used in practice.

○ *Wrong Premise One: All organizational outcomes can be traced to the specific contributions of individuals; rewards can and should be allocated accordingly.*

American, British, and some European companies remain devoted to the proposition that only individuals make a difference (Hofstede, 1991). Psychology thus becomes the quintessential American social science. This leads to the blaming of genuine victims, the canonization of accidental heroes, and a general incapacity to design more powerful social and organizational structures.

○ *Wrong Premise Two: People cannot be trusted; they work only as necessary, are interested mainly in money, and come equipped with fixed capacities, limits, and inclinations.*

Since the publication of *The Human Side of Enterprise* in 1960, Douglas McGregor's terms *Theory X* and *Theory Y* have been part of the linguistic armament of every manager. Yet it takes only the most cursory look to see that many present organizational arrangements are based largely on Theory X (although nearly everyone claims a commitment to Theory Y). For example, reward systems, especially in these "individualistic" countries, are based in practice on managerial "cream rises to the top" theory. If people "have it," they'll show it, and the best way to help is to let them fight it out. The unfortunate consequences include a staggering underuse of people's potential and capacity and a focus on selection and matching of people with jobs (both treated as fixed entities) rather than on development, growth, and change.

○ *Wrong Premise Three: Executives are largely responsible for their organizations' success (and failures): "If we're doing well (poorly), I must be making the right (wrong) decisions."*

In the French writer Antoine de St. Exupéry's classic fable, the Little Prince visits a small planet inhabited by the King of the Universe. The King tells his visitor that he makes everything happen. The Little Prince, duly impressed, asks him to make the sun go backward. *"You don't understand,"* says the

King. *"The secret to being King of the Universe is to know what to ask for."* Most executives are reluctant to accept this lesson.

Real managers, they think, make many orders. Frustrated CEOs then wonder why their explicit instructions often fail to be carried out. "Am I in charge here or not?" they ask. The answer, to a generally underrecognized degree, is, "No, you're not." In an important sense, no one is really in charge of an organization. Some things can be done by mandate, by bold strokes—for example, buying another company or closing a plant—in part because the tasks are simple to define and in part because one person in the right position can technically or legally bring it about. But such tasks as developing a high-productivity organization, responding fully to customers, or changing culture cannot be ordered. They require a long march. It is a matter, at root, of the limits of authority.

We are not arguing that these premises are the only important ones or that they are without validity. Clearly, people do count as individuals; they do have limits, and they differ in critical respects; and managers do need to make decisions, many of them authoritative. We are merely arguing that in the long run, and often in the short, replacing these wrong assumptions with three others will produce significantly better results. It is interesting to note that these "better premises" are often associated with Japanese culture and that of the rapidly growing "Little Tigers" in Southeast Asia (Hofstede, 1991):

○ *Better Premise One: Organizations are collective instruments whose outcomes mainly reflect joint effort.*

Individuals do make special contributions, to a great degree because the organization encourages and enables it. To borrow a line from the great scientist Sir Isaac Newton, if some people see further than others, it may be because they stand on the shoulders of a giant (organization). Correspondingly, when people fail, it may be because they are not allowed access to the organizational shoulder.

○ *Better Premise Two: People are interested in and capable of doing better rather than worse, being more rather than less effective, and increasing their skills, competence, and knowledge.*

Far from being fixed instruments, people share a remarkable facility for growth and development through their whole lives. Organizations have much to do with whether that potential is recognized, engaged, or realized. More effective businesses, and the more effective units in all organizations, are usually that way because they empower people broadly, maintain consistent standards, offer them rich and varied opportunities, provide appropriate rewards, and systematically coordinate their actions.

○ *Better Premise Three: The key task for managers, particularly senior ones, is to create a system that enables and helps others to act consistently in organizationally appropriate ways.*

This "enabling" function recognizes that executives ought to be primarily concerned not with solving specific operational problems but with increasing their organization's capacity to act appropriately, to respond to emerging contingencies, and to make good use—present and future—of potential resources. People throughout the organization need enough power—access to tools—to solve their own problems and contribute to larger objectives. In the short run, and close at hand, someone else can "do it" for them. But in the long run, and over time, no one can. This might be called the hook-and-ladder principle: the driver who controls the rear wheels of a fire engine is sooner or later going to be critically important; it can't all be done from up front.

This is true for several fundamental reasons. The greater the organizational distance and the more levels between "where the rubber meets the road" and those making decisions, the greater the distortion and the slower the response. In such a case, results tend to be too late or inadequate. Second, psychological ownership and commitment are lacking. People who watch others "do it" are part of the audience, not the show. Finally, it takes practice and opportunity to develop the necessary skills and to sharpen them over time. These improved premises are as critical to managing change as they are to other managerial tasks.

Implementing Change: A New Managerial Mind-Set

Getting ready for change implementation thus requires that managers think about organizations in some new ways. The first element of a change-friendly mind-set is simple to state, difficult to do: understand and accept reality. There is great reluctance to recognize just how fundamentally flawed many organizations are. This is a splendid example of what sociologists call pluralistic ignorance. Everyone is aware of the same thing, but because people think it true only for themselves, all pretend otherwise. Refusal to face the deep flaws at the core of organizations deflects attention from the real problems to the symptoms.

The second element of a change-friendly mind-set requires senior managers to accept a different orientation about their role and responsibility and to shift from simply blaming the individuals (including themselves) for problems or rewarding them for successes. Instead, they must recognize that results, for both better and worse, are often largely reflections of particular organizational structures and characteristics. Only with that perspective can executives address organizational problems as an exercise of leadership rather than an admission of personal failure.

The third element is an understanding that most of an organization's major problems are probably not unique errors or mistakes. Most problems recur. As managers know only too well, they "solve" problems only to have them pop up again and again. Problems mainly reflect existing underlying organizational patterns, reflecting the organization's character. Implementers can create the new patterns they want, but only by recognizing and facing up to one central fact: recurring problems are as much "products" of the organization as are the products the company markets. Both are predictable and logical consequences of the organization's design.

The fourth element is evidence and examples that demonstrate convincingly the shortfall between the organization's current reality and its future possibilities. One primary source of evidence is the high level of unusual internal performance. If an organization did it once, it ought to be able to do it again and again. Another is benchmarking results, examples of internal and external "best practices" or role models that can serve as both inspiration and demonstration.

The fifth and final element is a change execution plan that meets at least four criteria:

- It involves and empowers people throughout the organization.
- It reflects a valid conceptual framework.
- It is driven by and tied operationally to the organization's critical goals and objectives.
- It is based on a thorough understanding of the actual situation. Accurate diagnosis based on valid data is essential.

Given that understanding, how can the need for planning be balanced against the need to ensure continual adjustment? What does *helpful* planning look like, and what are its elements?

Making It Happen and Making It Stick

Effective implementation of change has eight important steps (Figure 12.2).

1. Coalition Building; Assembling Backers and Supporters

A critical first step is to involve those whose involvement really matters in getting the implementation process off the ground before proceeding with other actions and before going public with the change program. Share it first with potential allies and discuss it with key people. Feedback from these discussions (what one company calls a "sanity check") often improves the original idea. Specifically, seek support from two general groups: (1) power sources and (2) stakeholders.

Power sources are the holders of important supplies necessary to make the change work: information (expertise or data), resources (money or materials), and support (legitimacy, political backing). Getting them behind the change—willing to

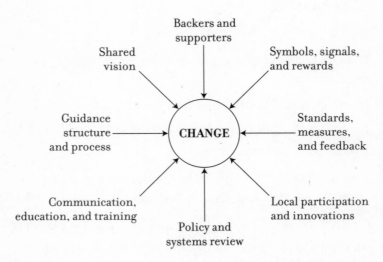

FIGURE 12.2. **Eight Elements in the Planning of Change**

invest their "power tools" in it—can be critical. Just as entre-preneurs need investors, so do leaders of change. Backers might also include key inside executives (or experts, opinion leaders respected by the staff, or an important board member), or use-ful outsiders such as consultants, financial backers, and gov-ernment officials.

Stakeholders include everyone who stands to gain or lose from the change. It is especially important to canvass the poten-tial losers early in the process, if they are remaining in the pic-ture, and to determine whether they can be given a piece of the action and converted into allies or else must be removed or neutralized before significant action begins. When stakehold-ers are organized (for example, in unions), it is even more crit-ical to consult with their leadership early or to define a strategy for dealing with them.

2. *Articulating a Shared Vision*

Once key supporters and investors have been assembled, it is important to articulate and spread the vision, the mission, goals, and desired results of the change.

A vision is a picture of a destination aspired to, an end state to be achieved through the change. It reflects the larger goal people need to keep in mind while concentrating on concrete daily activities. A vision is not necessarily a detailed and full-blown strategy; sometimes it is better seen as a general state-ment of purpose. One old lesson about organizations is that if goals are easily translated into actions, the actions become ends in themselves. Furthermore, without an articulated vision, changes launched by a manager can seem arbitrary or whimsi-cal and are therefore mistrusted or resisted. A vision shows that change efforts are guided by larger goals others can endorse, particularly if they've helped shape them.

What matters about a vision of the destination is both understanding and agreement. The details can (and often should) be worked out in the implementation process, but the general goals should be clear and reasonably stable from the start. First, sharing the vision ensures that the reason for making certain specific changes is understood, so that people do not confuse means with ends. For example, an effort to reposition the company for greater competitiveness that begins with cost cutting can be confused with "just another cost drive" if the vision does not show why it is more than that. Otherwise there is a risk that support will be lost and proactive contributions not made. Second, sharing the vision is critical in getting others to buy into it and make it theirs.

An inspiring vision can be highly motivating, helping overcome the reluctance to embrace change that comes from anxiety over uncertainty. All changes involve some risk and some discomfort: an exciting goal or a significant mission can make the risk worthwhile and the discomfort endurable.

3. Defining the Guidance Structure and Process

A major issue in effective implementation is to sort out and assign accountability and responsibility. It is important to identify who's in charge overall, as well as who is responsible for carrying out discrete tasks. Even though this may seem obvious, even highly sophisticated companies have been known to launch a whole series of actions and programs to refocus the business without giving much thought to either their coordination or the allocations of responsibilities and accountabilities for each activity. The same people who are managing ongoing operations may also be expected to implement change at the same time; moreover, there may be little guidance or oversight from anyone.

Clarity about who is guiding the change and where various activities "report" can help build commitment and avoid confusion and chaos. Possibilities for the change manager include:

- The manager himself or herself. (But this may be too time-consuming, given other responsibilities.)
- Another line manager. (same problem)
- A temporary "transition manager" reporting to the unit manager. (This provides a dedicated resource who can keep overall management involved and also work with a steering committee.)
- A "steering committee" composed of the unit manager and key others with a stake in the process. (This has the advantage of tapping multiple sources of knowledge and ensuring ownership of the change.)

In general, the more significant, complex, and time-consuming the change, the more important it is that time and people be dedicated to the change effort itself.

Similarly, depending on the nature of the activities involved in making the change, tasks may be identified in separate chunks and assigned to task forces or transition teams with either full-time or part-time responsibility. Task forces operating alongside the regular line organization for ongoing activities can be an effective way of generating widespread involvement in the change and widespread enthusiasm for it.

Regardless of the structure and reporting or oversight process chosen, it is important that they be clear to all participants. If new groups like task forces are formed, it is also important to clarify when they disband, how they are linked to the rest of the organization, and how their performance will be measured. Task forces have a tendency to take on a life of their own; they need to be reminded to communicate to the wider organization and reviewed periodically to ensure that they are on track. A schedule of meetings with the change manager or steering committee is also helpful.

4. Ensuring Communication, Education, and Training

Implementation of a change means that many people have to reorient, redirect, or engage in new activities—and they need the motivation, information, and skill to do so. Thus, managers need to plan for communication and education: when, how, and to whom information will be disseminated; when and how participants will be exposed to the new knowledge or skills necessary for carrying out their piece of the change process. Significant capital investments in major change efforts can fail to meet their targets because of a failure to invest in human capabilities, to use the system, to manage in new ways, or to understand fully the implications of the change.

Change managers also need to communicate with the whole organization either all at once or in steps; they can go out to various sites or bring key players to one location, communicate face to face or establish more impersonal media, do it once at the launch or on a continuing basis. Whatever strategy is chosen, two-way, face-to-face, continuing communication of the organization as a whole is especially important for changes that are:

- Of great strategic importance
- Of large scope
- With implications for many parts of the organization
- Involving many behavioral changes in day-to-day operations.

For this reason, managers leading a major cultural change should devote a significant part of their time to travel to major facilities for discussion sessions and to appearances at management education seminars. They may even launch changes with a "road show" in major locations. Executive conferences to introduce a change with fanfare and flair can create excitement, and the process can cascade down as participating managers get information and materials to carry back to their own communication sessions.

Similarly, the desirable formality of the education and training component depends on assessment of the new skills or procedures to be mastered. Big changes involving many new skills and a change in behavior patterns and work environment benefit from formal training programs to build skills and also from peer networks that can help support the change. It is unfortunate that many companies misdiagnose this, neglecting to invest sufficient time or resources in upgrading people's skills when changes are implemented. This omission can undercut or even destroy programs.

5. Undertaking Policy and Systems Review

In successful businesses, strategy, resource allocation, organization structure, daily operations and systems, the work environment, and people are all adequately aligned. In general, there should be a reasonable fit between policies and systems, which reinforces the organization's ability to carry out its strategic task. Changes in one major element may thus necessitate compensating or complementing changes in another.

Those implementing a major new course of action need to ensure that a continuous reassessment and readjustment process exists. Clearly, for example, changing organization structure without considering resource allocation, compensation policies, or communication systems might undermine or shift the goals of the change.

There are a number of ways to ensure this review. For example, a general manager can charge functional or product or market managers reporting to him or her to review their specific departments in the light of the desired change. For changes that have implications for relationships across areas, cross-functional teams may be established to review existing policies or systems and to develop new ones as needed. Or, for policies with broad organizational relevance, such as information systems or reward systems, special task forces might be convened, reporting to the overall manager or to the change management team.

6. Enabling Local Participation and Innovation

Although this is labeled step 6 in order of logic, it should be step 1 in the thinking of management. It is impossible to plan every step or every detail of an implementation effort from the top. Even if a leader could overcome the commitment problem, he or she would still be faced with the crystal ball problem— limited ability to anticipate every contingency surrounding a change or implementation effort. Even if this were possible, it would be extremely costly and thus wasteful. Furthermore, every change—no matter how well thought through in advance—is also a kind of experiment in which there is a chance to learn from the experience of doing it and thus even to improve on the initial plan.

The implementation process will benefit, then, from leaving some local options or local control over the details of the change. The extent to which different areas or different units can do it their own way depends on the kind of change. Of course, some may require more uniformity than others. (Note, however, that those at the top often tend to think more uniformity is necessary than those below.) Formal approaches for doing this range from explicit pilot tests, using different models, to greater local autonomy or options. In any case, it is important to build two things into the implementation plan:

1. Clarity about what is fixed or given versus what is open for local variation and positive encouragement of local innovation where it is allowable. (We suggest more of the latter except where it might compromise overall coherence.)

2. A communication and coordination process to get information about the variations, to spread useful ideas across areas, and to resolve any conflicts that might occur as a result of any differences. (Possibilities include reporting on local projects at quarterly conferences, charging a task force with monitoring and documenting projects, or using a corporate education program or video series to disseminate information.)

Periodically, the change guidance team or steering committee should review implementation projects and consider their implication: Where do we need to redirect our efforts? How is the change being implemented differently in different places, and what can we learn from that? What can be done to take greater advantage or opportunities?

7. Ensuring Standards, Measures, and Feedback Mechanisms

How do we know the change has happened? How do we know it has been successful? Along the way, how do we know it's on track and that events are likely to lead to the desired change? How can we get information to monitor the impact of the process of the change on the people carrying it out?

While planning for implementation, it is thus equally important to plan for measurement and evaluation. Two kinds of measures are helpful:

1. *Results measures*—how we will know that we're "there" and that we have "done it"

2. *Process measures*—how we will know we are doing the things all along that will get us to "it," or whether readjustments are in order

Routine data collection—either impersonal measures such as surveys or quantitative data, through managers checking in personally with people and operation, or through consultant interviews or focus groups—can allow the change management team to monitor progress and make midcourse adjustments. Process measures are particularly important. Often these can be developed by teams or special assignments, and of course can themselves be improved over time.

8. Providing Symbols, Signals, and Rewards

Sometimes managers announce a new emphasis or strategic direction, but skeptical employees and other managers (who may have been through this before or who may think this is just another impulse of their impulsive boss) withhold commitment or drag their feet on implementation actions. After all, even tangible actions (starting a new division, consolidating operations, or increasing financial investment in new products) take on meaning or importance only as part of a larger strategic thrust, and they can be more or less successful and more or less reversible, depending on the fervor with which they are pursued.

Organization members often wait for the signals that say "we mean it." (Or "we don't really mean it." For example, a decentralization campaign and a new formal organization chart doesn't help much if the general manager still insists on personally reviewing small decisions.) The leadership actions described earlier at Raychem (elephants on the beach) and Security Pacific (the manager as "Loan Arranger") provided important symbols and, despite the frivolity involved, important signs that the boss was serious about change.

New or special rewards are also an effective way to signal management's commitment to the change—finding new heroes, recognizing new achievements, offering special incentives. Rewards—or just sheer fun—are also important in motivating people to engage in the extra hard work that change requires. Conversely, maintaining a reward system that encourages business as usual does not help. It is particularly important to provide rewards for action on the change program itself, such as participation in a task force or time spent training others.

Tactical Choices

Often, change programs or methods associated with them are presented as if they were recipes: only this specific series of actions, carried out in exactly this way, will produce the results desired. Organizations that have been successful are only too quick to draw that conclusion and to market their recipe. Nothing could be further form the truth.

In fact, every change program or implementation plan, like every attempt to execute any decision, whether of purely local relevance or fundamental to the success of a giant organization, is full of opportunities for alternative courses of action. Not only is there not "one best way"; there are usually many paths for implementation of a given direction, change, or innovation, each of which might be useful and appropriate in some set of circumstances.

The issue, therefore, is for the change manager to consider the relationship between a set of options and the particular character of the situation within which those choices must be made. The determination is not precise, of course, but indicative. The more important some factors are, the more plausible or appropriate a certain choice may be. For example, here are some of the most critical choices facing the change manager, along with the central factors to be kept in mind:

Everywhere versus pilot sites? Should the change be introduced across the organization (rolled out) or step by step?

General factors to take into account:

- Degree of support for the change
- Extent to which change and its implications are well understood
- Sheer amount of change involved; change complexity
- Organization's experience with managing change
- Urgency of change
- Competitive environment and anticipated competitor response

BENEFITS OF PILOTS AND TESTS

- Examine alternative models
- Use extra time, plus pilot results, to sway opinion and build support
- Learn from experience, modify model
- Develop implementation expertise to make full implementation more efficient and effective

RISKS OF PILOTS AND TESTS

- Mobilize resistance
- Permit skepticism about leaders' commitment to the change (for example, withhold support because "this too will pass")

- Impede transfer due to NIH syndrome (others reject because of "not invented here")

- Prolong uncertainty anxiety

- Cost of running two systems

- Can't mount all the programs or projects needed to support the change (for example, because they are too costly just for a pilot site)

HOW BEST TO USE PILOTS AND TESTS

- Keep overall strategy clear (and role of pilot in the strategy)

- More than one site helpful—one sure to succeed, one problematic (if load for success, results can be written off as not applicable to "my" area)

- Build knowledge and involvement of rest of organization

- Document and learn; make experience transferable

Fast versus slow? How useful is it to attempt to move very quickly, for example, by devoting greater resources?

General factors to take into account:

- Cost: resource needs and availability

- Skills available: how much new capability required

- Urgency

- Competitive environment (how fast competition will exploit vulnerabilities or copy strategy)

- Degree of support for the change

- Complexity of the change

- Degree to which steps or areas are intertwined and interdependent, so that work can't be done on one without immediately affecting or being affected by the others

Is it better to *work through existing structures and roles,* or to create new roles, or groupings, or structures?

General factors to take into account:

○ Skills available: whether current people in current roles can manage the new state

○ Amount of time required for change and transition management tasks

○ Degree to which ongoing operations need to run at peak efficiency while the change is being implemented

Should the change be *mandatory* or *voluntary?*

General factors to take into account:

○ Power of leaders to compel compliance

○ Degree of support

○ Organizational norms and culture; degree to which autonomy valued

○ Motivational issues: volunteers tend to "believe," persuade others

○ Urgency of the situation

○ Risks of slippage or inefficiencies if not everyone complies

Should this be viewed as a *break with the past* or as continuity with tradition? If possible, should we start over or refurbish existing structures? This is one of the trickiest choice points in major change: balancing the revolutionary potential of a fresh start, as in a "greenfield" new site start-up in a new location with new people (for example, General Motors's Saturn Project), against the need for continuity, because organizations are, after all, managing ongoing operations that include valuable experiences as well as sunk costs. Financial cost is, of course, not the only consideration in deciding whether to break with the past; there is also a question about the signal sent to all the people currently in the organization. If all investment, energy, and excitement go to a start-up, it is highly demotivating to those responsible for current revenues and can lead to deterioration of current operations from lack of investment. One solution is to couple start-ups or greenfields with added opportunity to invest in changes and improvements in current operations.

GETTING STARTED

Before we address where a company begins, let's see where a company emphatically should *not* begin:

- Not with a master plan and a total program
- Not by trying to start at the *end* of the change process, when the shape of the new markets or the details of the new practices are well understood, can be readily communicated and institutionalized, and are able to be routinized
- Not by simply copying the current practices of companies that successfully transformed their businesses and ignoring all the false starts, messy mistakes, and controversial experiments that got them there

It is important to remember that change looks revolutionary only in retrospect. The connotation of "change" as an abrupt dysfunction, then a clean break, does not always match its reality.

Because early actions have consequences for one's ability to act later, they should be chosen with particular care. Later actions can be left more general and open-ended, since they will necessarily be shaped by the results of early actions. But early actions can carry particular weight. They should:

- Address an immediate, acute, potentially costly business problem (for example, a key executive threatening to leave, a critical customer defecting, a major machinery breakdown)
- Shape or reinforce a vision or strategy used to guide all future actions—that is, reinforce a direction or principle

○ Send a strong signal of commitment to the change

○ Demonstrate the nature of the effort required

Launching deliberate change is a matter of respecting three critical criteria that embody the lessons about organizational motion and organization potential:

1. *Begin with use-directed, action-oriented information from all stakeholders.* Improve the quality of information about the realities of customers' and employees' situations. Discover what people actually do, and assess how the organization's processes actually work. Diagnosis is essential—particularly from the point of view of the stakeholders. The best part of the Malcolm Baldrige National Quality Award in the United States, for example, may be that it gives companies a checklist of items to use for self-assessment; the worst part is that it encourages some companies to mount a Total Program to Fix Problems before they have even discovered a direction for change. Similarly, a real transformation does not begin with a glamorous new product or a program that capitalizes on a current bandwagon, such as quality or environmental concern (though that may be critical eventually), but simply by the provision of better information, such as how the business actually works today.

In addition to collecting concrete information about today's realities, consider unmet needs. Explore both customers' and employees' hopes and dreams. Examine the organization from the perspective of its owners; is "shareholder value" being realized? Take into account the views of other stakeholders, from suppliers to regulators. Then come back to customers. At the heart of market shifts in any industry is the changing nature of value as defined by customers. There are no products anymore, in the narrow sense; there are only services. Even manufacturing companies should be thinking about the services their products offer and what they permit people to do, not the products themselves. How customers can use what a company produces is what creates a market for it.

2. *Build on platforms already in place.* Begin by stepping back to define strengths and potentialities in existing resources, experiences, and bases. For example, Volkswagen may or may not be correct in some ultimate planning analytic sense in its belief that a strong European base is an excellent vehicle for global success, but that's what Volkswagen has, and it might as well make the most of it. VW cannot will itself into being another kind of company overnight; it must make changes out of its existing capabilities.

Every company, regardless of its difficulties, has some positive innovations to build on, some seeds of the future already blossoming. Even in troubled industries, some companies do well, for example, Dillard Department Stores in U.S. retailing. Even in troubled companies, some departments do well, providing a platform for growth, for example, the crafts department in another, more distressed retail chain.

Moreover, it is important not to insult people by assuming that the organization has no experience with the new phenomenon, as some companies do when they launch Total Quality Programs with the implicit message that no one has focused on quality until then.

3. *Encourage problem-solving and incremental experimentation that departs from tradition without destroying it.* Many companies begin major change programs with training when they should really begin with doing. Experimentation produces options, opportunities, and learning; training can then be provided to the innovating teams. A proliferation of such modest experiments adds to the organization's own experience with elements of many different business models. These elements also help

micro- and macro-changes to be joined, with major change often constructed out of the micro-actions of numerous entrepreneurs and innovators, as well as the larger actions of decision makers.

So-called breakthrough changes are actually related to the interplay of a number of smaller changes that together provide the building blocks for constructing the new organization. Even when attributed to a single dramatic event or a single sharp decision, major changes in large organizations are more likely in fact to represent the accumulation of accomplishments and tendencies built up slowly over time and implemented cautiously. "Logical incrementalism," to use James Brian Quinn's term, may be a better way to describe how major corporations change their strategy:

> The most effective strategies of major enterprises tend to emerge step by step from an interactive process in which the organization probes the future, experiments, and learns from a series of partial (incremental) commitments rather than through global formulations of total strategies. Good managers are aware of this process, and they consciously intervene in it. They use it to improve the information available for decisions and to build the psychological identification essential to successful strategies. Such logical incrementalism is not "muddling," as most understand that word. [It] honors and utilizes the global analyses inherent in formal strategy formulation models [and] embraces the central tenets of the political or power behavioral approaches to such decision making [Quinn, 1980].

The right kinds of integrative mechanisms, including communication between areas, can ensure coordination among the local strategies or substrategies and micro-innovations that ultimately result in a company's strategic posture. In short, effective organizations benefit from integrative structures and cultures that promote innovation below the top and learn from them.

Seen in this light, there is a link between microlevel and macrolevel change and innovation—the actions of numerous managerial entrepreneurs and problem-solving teams, on one hand, and the overall shift of a company's direction the better to meet current challenges on the other. The buildup of experiences from successful small-scale innovations or even the breakthrough idea that an innovator's work may eventually produce, in the case of new products or new technological processes, can then be embraced by those guiding the organization as part of an important new strategy.

In short, consider problem-solving action first, formal programs later. Get experience first; make a "strategy" out of it second. In many cases new structural possibilities from experiments by change implementers, and even recipients, make possible the formulation of a new strategy to meet a sudden external challenge of which even the implementers might have been unaware. The new strategy in effect elevates local experiments and experience to the level of policy. This is the ultimate form of change mastery for the new ideal of the flexible organization—change as an ongoing quest.

Major change built on a rapid succession of experiments from an existing platform resolves an important dilemma surrounding the very idea of corporate transformation. A company cannot neglect existing business while leaping into new ones. It cannot shut down one day and reopen as something totally different the next. Experimentation both requires and builds confidence. It permits a company to write its own case studies of successful change and to learn from its own experience. Large numbers of small experiments reduce risks while providing alternatives. The best can then be chosen for dissemination throughout the organization.

Where to begin the change process is clearly a complex determination, requiring organizational self-scrutiny. But *when* to begin is simple:

Now!

o   o   o

Rosabeth Moss Kanter is professor of business administration at Harvard Business School. She is former editor of the *Harvard Business Review* and a consultant to major corporations around the world.

Barry A. Stein is a consultant and president of Goodmeasure. He has advised executives and firms on productivity and innovation, organization design, and strategies for enhancing competitive strength and ensuring routine excellence.

Todd D. Jick is a managing partner of the Center for Executive Development. He was a professor at the Harvard Business School, London Business School, and Brandeis University's International School of Economics and Finance.

Chapter Thirteen

Learning to Lead Change

The New Principles
for CEOs and Companies

David A. Nadler, with Mark B. Nadler

No organization I've ever seen has started out, from day one, doing major change just right. It's impossible. There are too many variables, too many moving targets, too much information to collect and digest, too many techniques to try out and refine. There's just a lot to learn.

By the same token, no CEO, business unit president, division chief, department head—you name it—has ever moved up to a more responsible job and started work the first morning with a full understanding of the concepts and a total grasp of the techniques required to do the new job. There's a reason people always talk about the learning curve faced by someone in a new position.

Learning—both individual and organizational—is at the core of leading change. The champions of change are people who have opened their minds to learning from every new change experience. Beyond that, they understand the importance of helping the people around them—both individually and collectively—benefit from the same kind of learning. They also understand that learning doesn't just happen; there's nothing automatic about it. Learning, both on the individual and organizational scale, is a deliberate process.

Managerial Roles and Learning

If you're among those who entered the workforce more than ten years ago—indeed, even if you started working within the past decade—there's a good chance that your formative notions about work and careers were spawned by a world that no longer exists.

Those traditional expectations all rested on a presumption of stability. The classic career plan was to find a prosperous company with good prospects, one whose values and beliefs were consistent with your own, where the people and the atmosphere and the pace made you feel comfortable. Then, if you worked hard, performed well, mastered the essentials of office politics, and were loyal to your employer, you could reasonably expect to get your ticket punched in a clearly defined succession of jobs that would bring incremental increases in responsibility, status, and financial rewards.

Now consider that scenario in the light of the competitive environment. Maybe somewhere out there are isolated enclaves of stability, cut off from the flow of history like the marooned Japanese soldiers who hid in the jungles of the South Pacific long after the conclusion of World War II. Rest assured that if such places exist, it's only a matter of time before the inevitability of change catches up with them.

The only certainty now is uncertainty. Today's market leaders are tomorrow's also-rans. Cutting-edge technology becomes obsolete overnight. Companies are traded back and forth like baseball cards. Changes at the top produce disruption and instability. One restructuring follows another. Jobs are lost. Hierarchies are flattened. Strategies, objectives, and processes are tossed out the window and replaced. New owners and new management bring new values and beliefs, new people, new roles and requirements for managers.

All of us can and should count on all those things happening in our own working lives—and not just once, but two, three, or four times if we stay with the same organization. In the end, there is only one guarantee: nothing will stay the same.

For executives running the organization and driving change, the issues are challenging and complex. For managers at every level within organizations buffeted by change, the issues are intensely personal. In their minds the arrival of a new regime or the adoption of sweeping change, by definition, means someone upstairs is questioning the skill, judgment, and effectiveness of the stewards of the status quo. It's only human for managers to react to these upheavals with emotions ranging from anger, resentment, and betrayal to fear, insecurity, and a sense of self-doubt. Their deeply held assumptions of how careers should work has been shattered; their years of loyalty, hard work, and success suddenly count for nothing.

For managers, then, the issue of change involves profound choices. The first major decision is whether to stay or go. There are situations in which the manager finds the new direction, leadership, job requirements, and operating environment so much in conflict with his or her own beliefs that it's in everyone's best interests for that manager to leave, if that's an option. A Xerox executive, on hearing for the first time about the plan to massively restructure the company, said, "The only way I could do it [manage in that situation] is if you gave me a lobotomy." Even though the new structure apparently worked, given Xerox's impressive results since it was instituted, that doesn't mean it was the right situation for him to remain in as a senior manager, given his own deeply held ideas about how to manage. From that perspective, his personal decision to leave properly acknowledged the fundamental and irreconcilable clash between his beliefs and those of the company.

In the majority of cases, however, managers probably won't consider the impending changes abhorrent, repugnant, or disastrous—just different, unsettling, and perhaps a little scary. At that point managers must look within themselves and develop their own personal strategies. They must arrive at a firm conclusion about what kind of leadership role they intend to play. They must decide whether to think of themselves as authors, participants, or victims of change.

Obviously, the most effective managers are those who decide to take an active leadership role in implementing the new vision of change. In Richard Beckhard's terms, they are the ones who "make it happen" rather than those who passively "let it happen." And at the managerial level, leading change involves three basic requirements. It's no coincidence that all three match the requirements faced by the ultimate leaders of change, the CEO and the senior team.

First, the manager should constantly demonstrate behavior consistent with the change. It's not enough to tell other people to spend more time with customers, take risks, or improve their teamwork skills; the manager has to be seen and heard doing those exact same things. The manager, in short, has got to walk the talk.

Second, the manager has got to help other people understand the change. Periods of radical change are characterized
by message clutter, leaving everyone confused, anxious, and desperate to get answers to the question, What does this mean for
me? An important variant of that is, What do you want from
me? People eagerly look for signals telling them how they're
supposed to act, what they're supposed to do. It's the manager's
job to help them understand how they'll be affected and what
their new role should be.

The third element of leadership at the managerial level is
rewarding people for demonstrating the new behavior or performance the change requires. Indeed, reinforcing appropriate behavior is even more important than usual in change
situations. Not only does it support and energize the person
who's rewarded, but it's also one of the most effective ways to
send clear signals to others about how to succeed in the new
environment.

CHANGE MANAGEMENT PRACTICES

In more concrete terms, managers at all levels can solidify their
role as active supporters and drivers of change through a number of day-to-day leadership practices (see Figure 13.1).

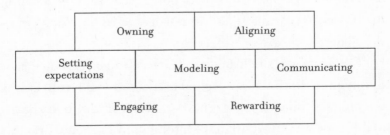

FIGURE 13.1. **Change Management Practices**

Owning

Successful managers do everything possible to publicly demonstrate their active personal involvement in the change process. At all costs, they want to avoid conveying the impression to their own people that the change is something "those guys upstairs" have imposed on the managers against their will. Managers who are perceived as grudgingly carrying out the will of others lose the confidence of their superiors, weaken their own stature among their subordinates, and put themselves in the counterproductive position of passively resisting inevitable change. Instead, they should do everything possible to identify themselves with the change and the executives who are pushing it. This period is crucial; this is when managers must seize the opportunity to become the owners of change rather than its potential victims. To succeed, they must go through several steps.

To begin, managers can't own the change if they don't really understand it. So they must first make an investment in learning, committing whatever time and intellectual energy are necessary to fully understand every aspect of the change. That means learning why the status quo was unacceptable, what strategic concepts are at the core of change, how the structure and culture of the organization will have to change. It means undergoing a personal version of guided discovery, replicating the process senior management pursued in its development of the change strategy.

Once managers fully understand the change, then they have to buy in on both an intellectual and emotional level. This is the point at which managers have to decide if they're on board and if they're willing to make a total commitment. I realize this advice may sound suspiciously like the slogans on those motivational posters sold in in-flight magazines, but take my word for it: there's no way successful managers can be disengaged or half-hearted about change. The moment managers demonstrate any hesitation or the slightest sign of skepticism, their ability to lead others is seriously impaired.

Managers have to articulate the essence of the change in a clear, concise, and consistent way. Years ago managers at Xerox used to practice what was then a fairly novel technique: the elevator speech. The premise was that if managers found themselves in an elevator with someone who asked, "So what's this quality thing all about, anyway?" they'd have thirty seconds between the lobby and the third floor to explain it in a nutshell. The managers—and top executives too—took this communication challenge seriously, videotaping their practice sessions and critiquing each other's delivery until they got it right. In recent years I've encountered more and more companies that use the term *elevator speech*, but unfortunately, not many of these speeches could be delivered in their entirety on an elevator ride.

Finally, effective managers concentrate on expressing and demonstrating personal ownership of the change. They make a point of using the word *we* rather than *they* in discussing the change, and they find appropriate opportunities to express their support for it.

Aligning

As strategic change at the executive level begins filtering down throughout the organization, effective managers make sure there is a clear alignment between their people's work and the new direction. This involves a concept sometimes described as the golden thread. In quality management, there's an explicit policy deployment process; at each level, managers take the set of general objectives developed at the level above them and then make them specific to their own unit's work. At each successive level, the objectives become narrower and more specific, but if they're done correctly, there's still a direct link to the companywide objectives. When you get down to the end of the process, every employee should still be able to identify the golden thread running directly from the CEO's change agenda to his or her individual objectives. It's the job of managers to direct and energize their own people's work by constantly reinforcing the direct connection between their own efforts and the organization's overall direction.

Setting Expectations

As the new organizational hardware and software take shape, it's up to managers to make them work—and work together. This is the time when managers must clearly articulate new goals for their people, being as explicit as possible. It's up to each manager to capture, focus, and boost the important signals coming down the line from the executive office. That means setting tough performance objectives that require people to stretch their skills, knowledge, and abilities. It means clarifying expectations of how people are expected to behave in the new operating environment. And in particular it means paying special attention to clarifying expectations for the next level of managers, who need to perform the same functions with their people.

Modeling

As people begin to better understand precisely what kind of behavior is expected of them in the changed organization, it becomes doubly important for managers to exhibit that behavior with absolute consistency. Most important, behavior has to be consistent with the values the organization has identified as the core of the new culture. A manager can't espouse "respect for the individual" as a lofty organizational value and then turn around and treat support staff as second-class citizens. Integrity, customer focus, teamwork—they're all values that managers can and should use as guides to their day-to-day behavior. Managers who do that not only contribute to further embedding those values in the culture of the organization, but they more closely link themselves to the new culture and its leadership. Inconsistency, in contrast, feeds both cultural confusion and cynicism among people, who begin to view managers as hypocrites.

Communicating

Effective managers, particularly during change periods, are effective communicators. They understand that during these turbulent change periods, people are desperate for information. Deprived of it, they will fill the void with rumors, gossip, and horror stories about impending changes that tend to be much worse than anything managers are really considering. Backstairs talk is always inevitable, but the best way to control it is by giving people as much information as possible. Effective managers also understand that what we often think of as communication is really a one-way flow of information, not a back-and-forth exchange that fully engages the interest and ideas of all concerned. Accordingly, they look for ways to develop genuine communication, in which information is traveling in both directions. Finally, managers should keep in mind that it's just as important to communicate up as down, making sure their supervisors are kept fully informed about staff's concerns, triumphs, and expectations.

Engaging

Communication is important but not sufficient. Effective managers look for ways to fully engage their people in shaping their own environment within the framework of the overall change agenda. These managers actively involve people in planning new directions and implementing change at their level. They give their people the freedom and resources to pursue the new objectives. They empower people to act, and give them support and encouragement as they work to develop new skills, acquire new knowledge, and exhibit new behavior.

Rewarding

Effective managers always make it a priority to reward people for demonstrating the desired performance and behavior. That's never more important than during a change situation when people tend to be frustrated, confused, and on the lookout for any positive sign that they're headed in the right direction. Rewards, particularly well-publicized ones, make it clear to people not only what the new requirements are but also that they are achievable and that managers understand and appreciate the effort people are putting forth. At the same time, it's also crucial to monitor activities more closely than usual and impose timely sanctions in cases where people are clearly ignoring or resisting the requirements of change.

THE IMPORTANCE OF MANAGERIAL LEARNING

Clearly, managers can't hope to direct, encourage, and sustain their people in all the ways I've just described unless they've personally undergone an individual transformation by learning, understanding, and internalizing what the change is all about. That kind of personal change is enormously difficult and generally involves overcoming some serious obstacles.

The first set of roadblocks can be categorized as external barriers to learning. Breaking these down is the responsibility of the more senior people in the organization. Inadequate training, inconsistent rewards, budgeting processes that undercut the new agenda, leadership models that reinforce old priorities—all these can critically impede a manager's ability to learn and digest new goals, objectives, and ways of behaving.

The second set of obstacles consists of internal barriers to learning—problems such as the following that are within each manager's power to control and overcome:

○ *Knowledge.* As I said earlier, it's the manager's responsibility to invest whatever time and effort are necessary to fully understand the change—the changing environment, the implications of not changing, the organizational and cultural characteristics that have to change—and how they must change.

○ *Skills.* New strategies, structures, work processes, and operating environments almost always require new managerial skills. In more and more organizations, the command-and-control drill sergeant style of management has been discredited and discarded. Now organizations need people who excel at thinking and acting strategically, leading teams, resolving conflicts, and empowering subordinates. Few of us are born knowing how to do those things well; successful managers have to make a conscious effort to learn them.

○ *Emotions.* Managers naturally have strong emotional ties to the vanishing organization. It's likely that they were initially attracted to and then nurtured by a set of organizational values and beliefs, which they probably internalized over time. The decision to become fully engaged in the changed organization involves an implicit decision to become emotionally detached from the old one.

○ *Inertia*. Management, like most other human behavior, becomes a matter of habit. With the passage of time, people simply get used to managing in certain ways. Consequently, managers mastering a dramatically different management style must not only learn new knowledge and skills and make emotional adjustments—they must break old habits. This fact was addressed in a particularly touching way in the film shown to all Xerox employees as the company launched its quality-based change in the mid-1980s. A service technician seen in the film was explaining how he wanted to do a good job for customers but his supervisor's priorities were getting in the way. Another scene then showed the service tech's supervisor at home over the weekend, tinkering with his motorcycle and talking about the changes going on at work. He says it's finally dawning on him that he's going to have to start doing some things differently, and he doesn't know if he can because he's managed people the same way throughout his entire career. "I'm going to try," he says, "but I don't know if I can do it." It's a particularly poignant scene, and one that struck a responsive chord among many of the managers who viewed it.

Consider Sydney Taurel, chief operating officer of Eli Lilly. A classic operational leader, Taurel came to understand that his penchant for what some considered micromanaging was inconsistent with changing management styles at the company. So he arose at a meeting of the company's managers to make it clear that he had gotten the message—that he had to change the way he did things. "I'm going to get less detail-oriented," he announced, prompting an outpouring of cheers and applause from the managers—extremely strong feedback, you could say.

All that's fine, but if you're Syd Taurel, how do you suddenly change after a lifetime of managing in one particular way? Change and learning are inseparable concepts. Change is impossible without learning; effective learning invariably results in change. To summarize, then, these are the steps managers need to go through in aggressively engaging themselves in the change process:

- Understand the change.
- Be open to change.
- Make both a personal and public commitment to the change.
- Observe others; learn from role models.
- Experiment with new behaviors.
- Gain feedback.
- Use that new learning to make continuous improvement.

Another way of describing that process is the learning cycle, a concept refined by David Kolb (1984) into these steps:

- *Active experimentation.* Based on available knowledge, skills, information, values, and beliefs, the individual attempts a new process or form of behavior.
- *Observation and feedback.* The individual actively seeks all available forms of assessment of the initial activity.
- *Reflection.* The individual analyzes the results of the experiment and the relative feedback, analyzing what went well and what didn't.
- *Insight and planning new actions.* In the light of feedback, analysis, and reflection, the individual plans how to incorporate what has been learned into the next experiment.
- *Experiment again.*

o   o   o

David A. Nadler is chairman of Mercer Delta Consulting. He has written extensively on organizational behavior, leadership, and organizational change.

Mark B. Nadler is a consultant at Mercer Delta. Previously he was a journalist and manager for several newspapers, including the *Wall Street Journal* and the *Chicago Sun-Times*.

Part Three

Communicating, Leading, and Motivating People

Chapter Fourteen

The Manager as Politician

Lee G. Bolman
Terrence E. Deal

Bill Gates was standing in the right place in the early 1980s when IBM's fledgling personal computer business came looking for an operating system. Gates didn't have one, but his partner, Paul Allen, knew someone who did. Gates paid $75,000 for QDOS (Quick and Dirty Operating System) in the deal—or steal—of the twentieth century. Gates changed the name to DOS and resold it to IBM, but he shrewdly retained the right to license it to anyone else. DOS quickly became the primary operating system for most of the world's personal computers. Gates himself was on the road to becoming one of the world's richest men (Manes and Andrews, 1994; Zachary, 1994).

Windows, a graphic interface riding atop DOS, fueled another great leap forward for Gates's Microsoft empire. But by the late 1980s, Gates had a problem. He and everyone else knew that DOS was obsolete, woefully deficient for existing personal computers, and even more inadequate for those to come. Millions of PC users were stuck in a high-tech version of *Waiting for Godot*.

The solution was supposed to be OS/2, an operating system developed jointly by Microsoft and IBM. It was a tense partnership. IBMers saw "Microsofties" as undisciplined adolescents. Microsoft folks moaned that "Big Blue" was a hopelessly bureaucratic producer of "poor code, poor design, poor process and other overhead" (Manes and Andrews, 1994, p. 425). Increasingly pessimistic about the viability of OS/2, Gates decided to hedge his bets by developing a new operating system to be called Windows NT. Gates recruited the brilliant but crotchety Dave Cutler from Digital Equipment to head the effort. Cutler had led the development of the VMS operating system that helped DEC dominate the minicomputer industry for many years. Zachary (1993) described Cutler as a rough-cut combination of Captain Bligh and Captain Ahab. Gates agreed that Cutler was known "more for his code than his charm" (p. A1).

Things started well, but Cutler insisted on keeping his team small and wanted no responsibility beyond the "kernel" of the operating system. He figured someone else could worry about such things as the user interface. Gates began to see a potential disaster looming, but issuing orders to the temperamental Cutler was as promising as telling Picasso to paint differently. Gates then brought in the calm, understated Paul Maritz. Born in South Africa, Maritz had studied mathematics and economics in Cape Town before deciding that software was his destiny. After five years with Intel, Maritz joined Microsoft in 1986 and became the leader of its OS/2 effort. When he was assigned informal oversight of Windows NT, no one told Cutler, who adamantly refused to work for Maritz. Twelve years Cutler's junior, Maritz got a frosty welcome:

> As he began meeting regularly with Cutler on NT matters, Maritz often found himself the victim of slights. Once Maritz innocently suggested to Cutler that "We should—" Cutler interrupted, "We! Who's we? You mean you and the mouse in your pocket?" Maritz brushed off such retorts, even finding humor in Cutler's apparently inexhaustible supply of epithets. He refused to allow Cutler to draw him into a brawl. Instead, he hoped Cutler would "volunteer" for greater responsibility as the shortcomings of the status quo became more apparent [Zachary, 1994, p. 76].

Maritz enticed Cutler with tempting challenges. In early 1990, he asked Cutler if it would be possible to put together a demonstration of NT in November for COMDEX, the industry's biggest convention. Cutler took the bait. Maritz knew that the effort would expose NT's weaknesses (Zachary, 1994). When Gates subsequently seethed that NT was too late, too big, and too slow, Maritz scrambled to "filter that stuff from Dave" (p. 208). Maritz's patience eventually paid off when he was promoted to head all operating systems development: "The promotion gave Maritz formal and actual authority over Cutler and the entire NT project. Still, he avoided confrontations, preferring to wait until Cutler came to see the benefits of Maritz's views. Increasingly Cutler and his inner circle viewed Maritz as a powerhouse and not an empty suit. 'He's critical to the project,' said [one of Cutler's most loyal lieutenants]. 'He got into it a little bit at a time. Slowly he blended his way in until it was obvious who was running the show. Him.'" (p. 204)

The *Challenger* case teaches a chilling lesson about how political pressures distort momentous decisions. Similarly, the implosion of firms such as Enron and WorldCom shows how the unfettered pursuit of self-interest by powerful executives can bring even a giant corporation to its knees. Many believe that the antidote is to free management from politics. But this is unrealistic so long as the political frame's basic conditions apply. Enduring differences lead to multiple interpretations of what is important, and even what is true. Scarce resources require tough decisions about who gets what. Interdependence means that people cannot ignore one another; they need each other's assistance, support, and resources. Under such conditions, efforts to eliminate politics drive differences under the rug or into the closet. There they fester into counterproductive, unmanageable forms. In our search for more positive images of the manager as constructive politician, Paul Maritz offers an example.

Kotter (1985) contends that too many managers are either naïve or cynical. Naïve managers view the world through rose-colored glasses, insisting that most people are good, kind, and trustworthy. Cynical managers believe the opposite: everyone is selfish, things are always political, and "get them before they get you" is the best survival tactic. Neither stance is effective: "Organizational excellence . . . demands a sophisticated type of social skill: a leadership skill that can mobilize people and accomplish important objectives despite dozens of obstacles; a skill that can pull people together for meaningful purposes despite the thousands of forces that push us apart; a skill that can keep our corporations and public institutions from descending into a mediocrity characterized by bureaucratic infighting, parochial politics, and vicious power struggles" (p. 11).

Organizations need "benevolent politicians" who steer a course between naïveté and cynicism: "Beyond the yellow brick road of naïveté and the mugger's lane of cynicism, there is a narrow path, poorly lighted, hard to find, and even harder to stay on once found. People who have the skill and the perseverance to take that path serve us in countless ways. We need more of these people. Many more" (Kotter, 1985, p. xi).

In a world of chronic scarcity, diversity, and conflict, the astute manager has to develop a direction, build a base of support, and learn how to manage relations with both allies and opponents. In this chapter, we start by laying out four basic skills for the manager as politician. Then we tackle ethical issues, the soft underbelly of organizational politics. Is it possible to be political and still do the right thing? We discuss four instrumental values to guide ethical choice: mutuality (is everyone playing by the same rules?), generality (would it be good if everyone did it?), openness (are we open to public scrutiny?), and caring (are we looking out for anyone beyond ourselves?).

POLITICAL SKILLS

The manager as politician exercises four key skills: agenda setting (Kanter, 1983; Kotter, 1988; Pfeffer, 1992; Smith, 1988), mapping the political terrain (Pfeffer, 1992; Pichault, 1993), networking and forming coalitions (Kanter, 1983; Kotter, 1982, 1985, 1988; Pfeffer, 1992; Smith, 1988), and bargaining and negotiating (Bellow and Moulton, 1978; Fisher and Ury, 1981; Lax and Sebenius, 1986).

Agenda Setting

Structurally, an agenda outlines a goal and a scheduled series of activities. Politically, agendas are statements of interests and scenarios. In reflecting on his experience as a university president, Warren Bennis (1989) arrived at a deceptively simple observation: "It struck me that I was most effective when I knew what I wanted" (p. 20). Kanter's study of internal entrepreneurs in American corporations (1983), Kotter's analysis of effective corporate leaders (1988), and Smith's examination of effective U.S. presidents (1988) all reached a similar conclusion: the first step in effective political leadership is setting an agenda.

The effective leader creates an "agenda for change" with two major elements: a vision balancing the long-term interests of key parties and a strategy for achieving the vision, recognizing competing internal and external forces (Kotter, 1988). The agenda must impart direction while addressing the concerns of major stakeholders. Kanter (1983) and Pfeffer (1992) underscore the close relationship between gathering information and developing a vision. Pfeffer's list of key political attributes includes "sensitivity"—knowing how others think and what they care about so that your agenda responds to their concerns: "Many people think of politicians as arm-twisters, and that is, in part, true. But in order to be a successful arm-twister, one needs to know which arm to twist, and how" (Pfeffer, 1992, p. 172).

Kanter (1983) adds: "While gathering information, entrepreneurs can also be 'planting seeds'—leaving the kernel of an idea behind and letting it germinate and blossom so that it begins to float around the system from many sources other than the innovator" (p. 218). This was exactly Paul Maritz's approach. Ignoring Dave Cutler's barbs and insults, he focused on getting information, building relationships, and formulating an agenda. He quickly concluded that the NT project was in disarray and that Cutler had to take on more responsibility. But Maritz's strategy was exquisitely attuned to his quarry: "Maritz protected Cutler from undue criticism and resisted the urge to reform him. [He] kept the peace by exacting from Cutler no ritual expressions of obedience" (Zachary, 1994, pp. 281–282).

A vision without a strategy remains an illusion. A strategy has to recognize major forces working for and against the agenda. Smith (1988, p. 333) makes this point about the American presidency:

> In the grand scheme of American government, the paramount task and power of the president is to articulate the national purpose: to fix the nation's agenda. Of all the big games at the summit of American politics, the agenda game must be won first. The effectiveness of the presidency and the capacity of any president to lead depend on focusing the nation's political attention and its energies on two or three top priorities. From the standpoint of history, the flow of events seems to have immutable logic, but political reality is inherently chaotic: it contains no automatic agenda. Order must be imposed.

Agendas never come neatly packaged. The bigger the job, the more difficult it is to wade through clamoring issues to find order amid chaos. Contrary to Woody Allen's dictum, success requires more than just showing up. High office, even if the incumbent enjoys great personal popularity, is no guarantee. Ronald Reagan was remarkably successful in his first year as president following a classic strategy for winning the agenda game: "First impressions are critical. In the agenda game, a swift beginning is crucial for a new president to establish himself as leader—to show the nation that he will make a difference in people's lives. The first one hundred days are the vital test; in those weeks, the political community and the public measure a new president—to see whether he is active, dominant, sure, purposeful" (Smith, 1988, p. 334).

Reagan began with a vision but without a strategy. He was not gifted as a manager or a strategist, despite extraordinary ability to portray complex issues in broad, symbolic brushstrokes. Reagan's staff painstakingly studied the first hundred days of four predecessors. They concluded that it was essential to move with speed and focus. Pushing competing issues aside, they focused on two: cutting taxes and reducing the federal budget. They also discovered a secret weapon in David Stockman, the only person in the Reagan White House who really understood the federal budget process. Stockman later admitted that he was astounded by the "low level of fiscal literacy" of Reagan and his key advisers (Smith, 1988, p. 354). According to Smith, "Stockman got a jump on everyone else for two reasons: he had an agenda and a legislative blueprint already prepared, and he understood the real levers of power. Two terms as a Michigan congressman plus a network of key Republican and Democratic connections had taught Stockman how to play the power game" (p. 351). Reagan and his advisers had the vision; Stockman brought strategic direction.

Mapping the Political Terrain

It seems foolhardy to plunge into a minefield without knowing where explosives are buried, yet managers unwittingly do it all the time. They launch a new initiative with little or no effort to scout the political turf. Pichault (1993) suggests four steps for developing a political map:

1. Determine channels of informal communication.
2. Identify principal agents of political influence.
3. Analyze possibilities for both internal and external mobilization.
4. Anticipate strategies that others are likely to employ.

Pichault offers an example of planned change in a large government agency in Belgium. The agency wanted to replace antiquated, manual records with a fully automated, paperless computer network. But proponents of the new system had virtually no understanding of how the status quo actually functioned.

Nor did they anticipate the interests and power of key middle managers and front-line bureaucrats. It seemed obvious to the techies that better access to data would dramatically improve efficiency. In reality, front-line bureaucrats made almost no use of the data. They applied standard procedures in 90 percent of the cases they encountered and asked their bosses what to do about the rest. Their queries were partly to get the "right" answer, but even more important they wanted to cover themselves politically. Even if the new technology were installed, front-line bureaucrats were likely to ignore or work around it. After a consultant clarified the political map, a new battle erupted between unrepentant techies, insisting their solution was correct, pitted against senior managers arguing for a less ambitious, more grounded approach. The two sides ultimately compromised.

A simple way to develop a political map for any situation is to create a two-dimensional diagram mapping players (who is in the game), power (how much clout each player is likely to exercise), and interests (what each player wants). Figures 14.1 and 14.2 present two hypothetical versions of the Belgian

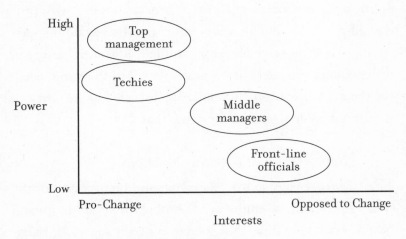

FIGURE 14.1. **The Map the Techies See**

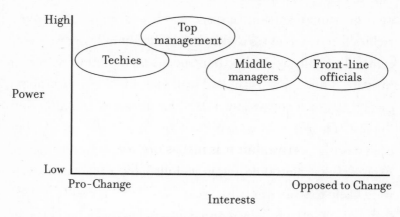

FIGURE 14.2. **The Real Political Map**

bureaucracy's political map. Figure 14.1 shows the map as seen by proponents of the new technology (the techies). Their view of the terrain shows little serious opposition to the new system, and they hold all the high cards; their map suggests a quick and easy win. Figure 14.2, the real map (as it might be seen by an objective analyst), paints a very different picture. Resistance is more intense and opponents more powerful. This view of the political terrain forecasts a stormy process imbued with protracted conflict. Though less comforting, the second map has an important message: success requires substantial effort to realign the existing field of political forces. The third and fourth key skills of the manager as politician, discussed in the next two sections, include strategies for doing that.

Networking and Building Coalitions

The *Challenger* disaster occurred despite recognition of the O-ring problem by engineers at both Morton Thiokol and NASA. For a long time, they tried to get their superiors' attention, mostly through memos. Six months before the accident,

Roger Boisjoly, an engineer at Morton Thiokol, wrote: "The result [of an O-ring failure] would be a catastrophe of the highest order—loss of human life" (Bell and Esch, 1987, p. 45). Two months later, another Thiokol engineer wrote a memo that opened, "HELP! The seal task force is constantly being delayed by every possible means" (p. 45). The memo detailed resistance from other departments in Thiokol. A memo to the boss is sometimes effective, but it is just as often a sign of political innocence. Kotter (1985) suggests four basic steps for exercising political influence:

1. Identify relevant relationships (figure out who needs to be led).
2. Assess who might resist, why, and how strongly (figure out where the leadership challenges will be).
3. Develop, wherever possible, relationships with potential opponents to facilitate communication, education, or negotiation.
4. If step three fails, carefully select and implement either more subtle or more forceful methods.

These steps underscore the importance of developing a sufficient power base. Moving up the ladder confers authority but also incurs increasing dependence because success depends on the cooperation of many others (Kotter, 1985, 1988). People rarely give their best efforts and fullest cooperation simply because they were ordered to do so. They accept directions when they perceive the people in authority as credible, competent, and sensible.

The first task in building networks and coalitions is to figure out whose help you need. The second is to develop relationships so people will be there when you need them. Middle managers seeking to promote change typically begin by getting their boss on board (Kanter, 1983). They then move to "preselling" or "making cheerleaders": "Peers, managers of related functions, stakeholders in the issue, potential collaborators, and sometimes even customers would be approached individually, in one-on-one meetings that gave people a chance to influence the project and [gave] the innovator the maximum opportunity to sell it. Seeing them alone and on their territory was important: the rule was to act as if each person were the most important one for the project's success" (p. 223).

Once you cultivate cheerleaders, you can move to "horse trading": promising rewards in exchange for resources and support. This builds a resource base that helps in getting the necessary approvals and mandates from higher management (Kanter, 1983). Kanter found that the usual route to success in "securing blessings" is to identify critical senior managers and to develop a polished, formal presentation to sway their support. The best presentations respond to both substantive and political concerns. Senior managers typically care about two questions: Is it a good idea? How will my constituents react? Once innovators obtain higher management's blessing, they can formalize the coalition with their boss and make specific plans for pursuing the project (Kanter, 1983).

The basic point is simple: as a manager, you need friends and allies to get things done. To get their support, you need to cultivate relationships. Hard-core rationalists and incurable romantics sometimes react with horror to such a scenario. Why should you have to play political games to get something accepted if it's the right thing to do? One of the great works in French drama, Molière's *The Misanthrope*, tells the story of a protagonist whose rigid rejection of all things political is destructive for him and everyone around him. The point that Molière made four centuries ago still has merit: it is hard to dislike politics without also disliking people. Like it or not, political dynamics are inevitable under conditions most managers face every day: ambiguity, diversity, and scarcity.

Ignoring or misreading those dynamics is costly. Smith (1988) reports a case in point. Thomas Wyman, board chairman of the CBS television network, went to Washington in 1983 to lobby U.S. Attorney General Edwin Meese. A White House emergency forced Meese to miss the meeting, and Wyman was sent to the office of Craig Fuller, one of Meese's top advisers:

> "I know something about this issue," Fuller suggested. "Perhaps you'd like to discuss it with me."
>
> Wyman waved him off, unaware of Fuller's actual role, and evidently regarding him as a mere staff man.
>
> "No, I'd rather wait and talk to Meese," Wyman said.
>
> For nearly an hour, Wyman sat leafing through magazines in Fuller's office, making no effort to talk to Fuller, who kept working at his desk just a few feet away.
>
> Finally, Meese burst into Fuller's office, full of apologies that he simply wouldn't have time for substantive talk. "Did you talk to Fuller?" he asked.
>
> Wyman shook his head.
>
> "You should have talked to Fuller," Meese said. "He's very important on this issue. He knows it better than any of the rest of us. He's writing a memo for the president on the pros and cons. You could have given him your side of the argument" [Smith, 1988, pp. xviii–xix].

Wyman missed an important opportunity because he failed to test his assumptions about who actually had power.

Bargaining and Negotiation

We often associate bargaining with commercial, legal, and labor relations settings. From a political perspective, though, bargaining is central to all decision making. The horse trading Kanter describes as part of coalition building is just one of many examples. Negotiation is needed whenever two or more parties with some interests in common and others in conflict need to reach agreement. Labor and management may agree that a firm should make money and offer good jobs to its employees but disagree on how to balance pay and profitability. Engineers and top managers at Morton Thiokol had a common interest in the success of the shuttle program. They differed sharply on how to balance technical and political trade-offs.

A fundamental dilemma in negotiations is choosing between "creating value" and "claiming value":

> Value creators tend to believe that, above all, successful nego-
> tiators must be inventive and cooperative enough to devise an
> agreement that yields considerable gain to each party, relative to
> no-agreement possibilities. Some speak about the need for
> replacing the win-lose image of negotiation with win-win nego-
> tiation. In addition to information sharing and honest commu-
> nication, the drive to create value can require ingenuity and may
> benefit from a variety of techniques and attitudes. The parties
> can treat the negotiation as solving a joint problem; they can
> organize brainstorming sessions to invent creative solutions to
> their problems.
>
> Value claimers, on the other hand, tend to see this drive for
> joint gain as naive and weak-minded. For them, negotiation is
> hard, tough bargaining. The object of negotiation is to convince
> the other guy that he wants what you have to offer much more
> than you want what he has; moreover, you have all the time in
> the world, while he is up against pressing deadlines. To "win" at
> negotiating—and thus make the other fellow "lose"—one must
> start high, concede slowly, exaggerate the value of concessions,
> minimize the benefits of the other's concessions, conceal infor-
> mation, argue forcibly on behalf of principles that imply favor-
> able settlements, make commitments to accept only highly
> favorable agreements, and be willing to out wait the other fel-
> low [Lax and Sebenius, 1986, pp. 30–32].

One of the best-known win-win approaches to negotiation was developed by Fisher and Ury (1981) in *Getting to Yes*. They argue that people too often engage in "positional bargaining": they stake out positions and then reluctantly make concessions to reach agreement. Fisher and Ury contend that positional bargaining is inefficient and misses opportunities to create an agreement beneficial to both parties. They propose an alternative: "principled bargaining," built around four strategies.

The first strategy is to separate the people from the problem. The stress and tension of negotiations can easily escalate into anger and personal attack. The result is that a negotiator sometimes wants to defeat or hurt the other person at almost any cost. Because every negotiation involves both substance and relationship, the wise negotiator will "deal with the people as human beings and with the problem on its merits." Maritz demonstrated this principle in dealing with the prickly Cutler. Even though Cutler continually baited and insulted him, Maritz refused to be distracted and persistently focused on getting the job done.

The second rule of thumb is to focus on interests, not positions. If you get locked into a particular position, you might overlook other ways to achieve the goal. An example is the 1978 Camp David treaty, resolving issues between Israel and Egypt. The sides were at an impasse over where to draw the boundary between the two countries. Israel wanted to keep part of the Sinai, while Egypt wanted all of it back. Resolution became possible only when they looked at each other's underlying interests. Israel was concerned about security: no Egyptian tanks on the border. Egypt was concerned about sovereignty: the Sinai had been part of Egypt from the time of the pharaohs. The parties agreed on a plan that gave all of the Sinai back to Egypt while demilitarizing large parts of it (Fisher and Ury, 1981). That solution led to a durable peace agreement.

Fisher and Ury's third recommendation is to invent options for mutual gain, looking for new possibilities that bring advantages to both sides. Parties often lock on to the first alternative that comes to mind and stop searching. Efforts to generate more options increase the chance of a better decision. Maritz recognized this in his dealings with Cutler. Instead of trying to bully Cutler, he asked innocently, "Could you do a demo at November COMDEX?" It was a new option that created gains for both parties.

Fisher and Ury's fourth strategy is to insist on objective criteria—standards of fairness for both substance and procedure. When a school board and a teachers' union are at loggerheads over the size of a pay increase, they can look for independent standards, such as the rate of inflation or the terms of settlement used in other districts. A classic example of fair procedure finds two sisters deadlocked over how to divide a pie between them. They agree that one will cut the pie into two pieces and the other will choose the piece that she wants.

Fisher and Ury devote most of their attention to creating value—finding better solutions for both parties. They downplay the question of claiming value. Yet there are many examples in which shrewd value claimers have done very well. In 1980, Bill Gates offered to license an operating system to IBM about forty-eight hours before he had actually obtained the rights. Meanwhile, Microsoft neglected to mention to QDOS's owner, Tim Paterson of Seattle Computer, that they were buying his operating system to resell it to IBM. Microsoft gave IBM a great price: only $30,000 more than the $50,000 they'd paid for it. But they were smart enough to retain the rights to license it to anyone else. At the time, IBM was an elephant and Microsoft was a flea. Almost no one except Gates saw the possibility that people would want an IBM computer made by anyone but IBM. But the new PC was so successful, IBM couldn't make enough of them. Within a year, Microsoft had licensed MS-DOS to fifty companies, and the number kept growing

(Mendelson and Korin, n.d.). Onlookers who wondered why Microsoft was so aggressive and unyielding in battling the Justice Department's antitrust suit twenty years later might not have known that Gates had been a dogged value claimer for a long time.

A classic treatment of value claiming is Schelling's 1960 essay, *The Strategy of Conflict*, which focuses on the problem of how to make a credible threat. Suppose, for example, that I want to buy your house and am willing to pay $250,000. How can I convince you that I'm willing to pay only $200,000? Contrary to a common assumption, I'm not always better off if I'm stronger and have more resources. If you believe that I'm very wealthy, you might take my threat less seriously than if I can get you to believe that $200,000 is the furthest I can go. Common sense also suggests that I should be better off if I have considerable freedom of action. Yet I may get a better price if I can convince you my hands are tied—for example, I'm negotiating for a very stubborn buyer who won't go above $200,000, even if the house is worth more. Such examples suggest that the ideal situation for a bargainer is to have substantial resources and freedom while convincing the other side of the opposite. Value claiming gives us a picture of the bargaining process:

1. Bargaining is a mixed-motive game. Both parties want an agreement but have differing interests and preferences. (IBM and Microsoft both wanted an operating system deal. But the IBM negotiators probably thought they were stealing candy from babies by buying it royalty free for a measly $80,000. Meanwhile, Gates was already dreaming about millions of computers running his code.)

2. Bargaining is a process of interdependent decisions. What each party does affects the other. Each player

wants to be able to predict what the other will do while limiting the other's ability to reciprocate. (IBM was racing to bring its PC to market; a key challenge was making sure they had an operating system to go with it.)

3. The more player A can control player B's level of uncertainty, the more powerful A is. (Microsoft was an intermediary between Seattle Computer and IBM but kept each in the dark about the other.)

4. Bargaining involves judicious use of threats rather than sanctions. Players may threaten to use force, go on strike, or break off negotiations. In most cases, they much prefer not to bear the costs of carrying out the threat.

5. Making a threat credible is crucial. It is effective only if your opponent believes it. A noncredible threat weakens your bargaining position and confuses the process.

6. Calculation of the appropriate level of threat is also critical. If I underthreaten, I may weaken my own position. If I overthreaten, you may not believe me, may break off the negotiations, or may escalate your own threats.

Creating value and claiming value are both intrinsic to the bargaining process. How does a manager decide how to balance the two? At least two questions are important: "How much opportunity is there for a win-win solution?" and "Will I have to work with these people again?" If an agreement can make everyone better off, it makes sense to emphasize creating value. If you expect to work with the same people in the future, it is risky to use value-claiming tactics that leave anger and mistrust in their wake. Managers who get a reputation for being manipulative and self-interested have a hard time building networks and coalitions they need for future success.

Axelrod (1980) found that a strategy of conditional open-ness works best when negotiators need to work together over time. This strategy starts with open and collaborative behavior and maintains the approach if the other responds in kind. If the other party becomes adversarial, however, the negotiator responds in kind and remains adversarial until the opponent makes a collaborative move. It is, in effect, a friendly and for-giving version of tit for tat—do unto others as they do unto you. Axelrod's research revealed that this conditional openness strategy worked better than even the most fiendishly diabolical adversarial strategy.

A final consideration in balancing collaborative and adver-sarial tactics is ethics. Bargainers often deliberately misrepre-sent their positions—even though lying is almost universally condemned as unethical (Bok, 1978). This leads to a profoundly difficult question for the manager as politician: What actions are ethical and just?

MORALITY AND POLITICS

Block (1987), Burns (1978), and Lax and Sebenius (1986) explore ethical issues in bargaining and organizational politics. Block's view assumes that individuals empower themselves through understanding: "The process of organizational politics as we know it works against people taking responsibility. We empower ourselves by discovering a positive way of being polit-ical. The line between positive and negative politics is a tightrope we have to walk" (Block, 1987, p. xiii).

Block argues that bureaucratic cycles often leave individuals feeling vulnerable, powerless, and helpless. If we confer too much power to the organization or others, we fear that the power will be used against us. Consequently, we develop manipulative strategies to protect ourselves. To escape the dilemma, managers need to support organizational structures, policies, and procedures that promote empowerment. They must also empower themselves.

Block urges managers to begin by building an "image of greatness"—a vision of what their department can contribute that is meaningful and worthwhile. Then they need to build support for their vision by negotiating agreement and trust. Block suggests dealing differently with friends than with opponents. Adversaries, he says, are simultaneously the most difficult and most interesting people to deal with. It is usually ineffective to pressure them; a better strategy is to "let go of them." He offers four steps for letting go: (1) tell them your vision, (2) state your best understanding of their position, (3) identify your contribution to the problem, and (4) tell them what you plan to do without making demands.

Such a strategy might work for conflict originating in a misunderstanding of one's self-interest. But in a situation of scarce resources and durable differences, bringing politics into the open may backfire. It can make conflict more obvious and overt but offer little hope of resolution. Block argues that "war games in organizations lose their power when brought into the light of day" (1987, p. 148), but the political frame questions that assumption.

Burns's conception of positive politics (1978) draws on examples as diverse and complex as Franklin Roosevelt and Adolf Hitler, Gandhi and Mao, Woodrow Wilson and Joan of Arc. He sees conflict and power as central to leadership. Searching for firm moral footing in a world of cultural and ethical diversity, Burns turned to the motivation theory of Maslow

(1954) and the ethical theory of Kohlberg (1973). From Maslow, he borrowed the idea of the hierarchy of motives. Moral leaders, he argued, appeal to a higher level on the needs hierarchy.

From Kohlberg he adopted the idea of stages of moral reasoning. At the lowest, "preconventional" level, moral judgment is based primarily on perceived consequences: an action is right if you are rewarded and wrong if you are punished. In the intermediate or "conventional" level, the emphasis is on conforming to authority and established rules. At the highest, "postconventional" level, ethical judgment rests on general principles: the greatest good for the greatest number, or universal and comprehensive moral principles.

Maslow and Kohlberg offered a foundation on which Burns (1978) constructed a positive view of politics:

> If leaders are to be effective in helping to mobilize and elevate their constituencies, leaders must be whole persons, persons with full functioning capacities for thinking and feeling. The problem for them as educators, as leaders, is not to promote narrow, egocentric self-actualization, but to extend awareness of human needs and the means of gratifying them, to improve the larger social situation for which educators or leaders have responsibility and over which they have power. What does all this mean for the teaching of leadership as opposed to manipulation? "Teachers"— in whatever guise—treat students neither coercively nor instrumentally but as joint seekers of truth and of mutual actualization. They help students define moral values not by imposing their own moralities on them but by positing situations that pose moral choices and then encouraging conflict and debate. They seek to help students rise to higher stages of moral reasoning and hence to higher levels of principled judgment [pp. 448–449].

In Burns's view, positive politics evolve when individuals choose actions appealing to higher motives and higher stages of moral judgment. Lax and Sebenius (1986), regarding ethical issues as inescapable, present a set of questions to help managers decide what is ethical:

1. Are you following rules that are mutually understood and accepted? (In poker, for example, everyone understands that bluffing is part of the game.)

2. Are you comfortable discussing and defending your action? (Would you want your colleagues and friends to be aware of it? Your spouse, children, or parents? Would you be comfortable if it were on the front page of your local newspaper?)

3. Would you want someone to do it to you? To a member of your family?

4. Would you want everyone to act that way? Would the resulting society be desirable? (If you were designing an organization, would you want people to act that way? Would you teach your children to do it?)

5. Are there alternatives that rest on firmer ethical ground?

Although these questions do not yield a comprehensive ethical framework, they embody four important principles of moral judgment. These are instrumental values—guidelines not about the right thing to do but about the right way of doing things. They do not guarantee right action, but they substantially reduce ethical risks. As evidence, we note that these values are regularly ignored wherever we find an organizational scandal:

1. Mutuality. Are all parties to a relationship operating under the same understanding about the rules of the game? Enron's Ken Lay was talking up the company's stock to analysts and employees even as he and others were selling shares. In the period when WorldCom illegitimately improved its profits by booking some of its operating expenses as capital investments,

it made major competitors look bad and generated considerable puzzlement. Top executives at both AT&T and Sprint felt the heat from analysts and shareholders and wondered, *What are we doing wrong? Why can't we get the results they're getting?*

2. Generality. Does a specific action follow a principle of moral conduct applicable to all comparable situations? When WorldCom violated a basic accounting principle to inflate its results, it was secretly breaking the rules, which does not amount to following a broadly applicable rule of conduct.

3. Openness. Are we willing to make our thinking and decisions public and confrontable? It was Justice Oliver Wendell Holmes who observed many years ago that "sunlight is the best disinfectant." Keeping others in the dark was a consistent theme in the corporate ethics scandals of 2001–2002. Enron's books were almost impenetrable, and the company was hostile to anyone who asked questions, such as *Fortune* reporter Bethany McLean. Enron's techniques for manipulating the California energy crisis had to be secret to work. One device involved creating the appearance of congestion in the California power grid and then getting paid by the state for "moving energy to relieve congestion without actually moving any energy or relieving any congestion" (Oppel, 2002, p. 1).

4. Caring. Does this action show care for the legitimate interests of others? Enron's effort to protect its share price by locking in employees so they couldn't sell Enron shares in retirement accounts as the market plunged is only one of many examples of putting the interests of senior executives ahead of everyone else's.

The scandals of the early 2000s were not unprecedented; such a wave is a predictable feature of the trough that follows every business boom. The 1990s, for example, gave us Ivan Boesky and the savings and loan crisis. There was another wave of corporate scandals back in the 1970s, and in the 1930s the president of the New York Stock Exchange literally went to jail in his three-piece suit (Labaton, 2002). There will always be temptation whenever gargantuan egos and large sums of money are at stake. Top managers too rarely think or talk about the moral dimension of management and leadership. Porter (1989) notes the dearth of such conversation: "In a seminar with seventeen executives from nine corporations, we learned how the privatization of moral discourse in our society has created a deep sense of moral loneliness and moral illiteracy; how the absence of a common language prevents people from talking about and reading the moral issues they face. We learned how the isolation of individuals—the taboo against talking about spiritual matters in the public sphere—robs people of courage, of the strength of heart to do what deep down they believe to be right" (p. 2).

If we choose to banish moral discourse and leave managers to face ethical issues alone, we invite dreary and brutish political dynamics. In a pluralistic secular world, an organization cannot impose a narrow ethical framework on employees. But it can and should take a moral stance. It can make its values clear, hold employees accountable, and validate the need for dialogue about ethical choices. Positive politics, absent an ethical framework and a moral dialogue, is no more likely to occur than farming without sunlight or water.

CONCLUSION

The question is not whether organizations are political but rather what kind of politics they will have. Political dynamics can be sordid and destructive. But politics can also be the vehicle for achieving noble purpose. Organizational change and effectiveness depend on managers' political skills. Constructive politicians recognize and understand political realities. They know how to fashion an agenda, map the political terrain, create a network of support, and negotiate with both allies and adversaries. In the process, they encounter a practical and ethical dilemma: when to adopt an open, collaborative strategy or when to choose a tougher, more adversarial approach. They have to consider the potential for collaboration, the importance of long-term relationships, and, most important, their own values and ethical principles.

o   o   o

Lee G. Bolman is chair in leadership at the Bloch School of Business and Public Administration, University of Missouri–Kansas City. He consults worldwide to corporations, public agencies, universities, and schools.

Terrence E. Deal is scholar in residence at the Rossier School, University of Southern California, and an international consultant to business, health care, military, educational, and religious organizations.

Chapter Fifteen

Artful Listening

Steven B. Sample

The average person suffers from three delusions: (1) that he is a good driver, (2) that he has a good sense of humor, and (3) that he is a good listener. Most people, however, including many leaders, are terrible listeners; they actually think talking is more important than listening. But contrarian leaders know it is better to listen first and talk later. And when they listen, they do so artfully.

A contrarian leader is an artful listener, not because it makes people feel good (which it does), but rather because artful listening is an excellent means of acquiring new ideas and gathering and assessing information.

If a leader can listen attentively without rushing to judgment, he will often get a fresh perspective that will help him think independently. This kind of leader listens carefully to his official advisers, especially those in his inner circle; he occasionally listens to self-appointed advisers—even the most obnoxious among them; and he continues to listen to his inner voice which reflects his own personal experience and creative impulses.

"Minds are of three kinds," Machiavelli wrote. "One is capable of thinking for itself; another is able to understand the thinking of others; and a third can neither think for itself nor understand the thinking of others. The first is of the highest excellence, the second is excellent, and the third is worthless." While Machiavelli makes great sense here, I would alter his words to say that the best mind of all for a leader is one that can both think for itself and understand the thinking of others. The latter ability depends on artful listening.

Artful listening is important for maintaining the contrarian leader's intellectual independence. It enables him to see things through the eyes of his followers while at the same time seeing things from his own unique perspective—a process which I like to call "seeing double." The contrarian leader prizes and cultivates his ability to simultaneously view things from two or more perspectives. He can listen to what others have to say about important issues without surrendering his principles or his creative judgment. He avoids becoming immobilized by conflicting points of view, and he never abdicates to others the responsibility for fashioning his own unique vision.

A leader's inner circle of advisers should be founded on mutual understanding and trust. It should be composed entirely of individuals who are committed to the institution's and the leader's best interests, and whose filters, prejudices, and attitudes are well understood by the leader. Toward that end it is usually best to keep one's inner circle of advisers relatively small—typically no more than eight.

At the University of Southern California (USC), the five senior vice presidents who report directly to me, along with my wife, comprise the core of my inner circle of advisers. Each of these persons is free to say, and willing to say, "Steve, your proposed approach to this situation is just plain wrong!" We frequently have no-holds-barred discussions among two or more of us. But all of the senior vice presidents understand that once a decision has been made, we will carry out that decision as a team.

My closest and longest-term adviser is my wife of forty years, Kathryn Sample. I trust her more than any other person, and I take harsher criticism from her than from anyone else, because I believe she always has my best interests at heart. Kathryn certainly knows my strengths and weaknesses more intimately than other people. Moreover, after four decades of our living together, her personal agenda is essentially congruent with mine (although our perspectives are radically different). Of course, I don't always follow my wife's advice, any more than I do that of any other adviser, but I always listen to her opinions with great care and interest. It's a plus in our relationship that Kathryn has no desire whatsoever to share in the authority of the presidency or be the de facto deputy president.

One should never underestimate the value of a stable long-term marriage to the success of a leader. In his classic book *On Becoming a Leader,* Warren Bennis notes that the overwhelming majority of successful corporate CEOs and other leaders whom he interviewed were involved in very stable long-term marriages and that these leaders felt their spouses were major factors in their success. Many people have the impression these days that a person can scarcely be a successful politician, military leader, corporate CEO, or university president unless he has been involved in myriad affairs and changed spouses at regular intervals. But the facts bespeak otherwise.

A leader's inner circle of advisers carries a special importance as the only group with whom he consults on the full, broad array of matters within his purview. Machiavelli argues in *The Prince* that the inner circle should consist of "the wise men of the state" who are instructed to speak honestly and candidly on any matters on which the prince seeks their counsel, and he goes on to say that the prince should seek their counsel on every matter of importance.

Harry Truman very deliberately sought out advisers, such as George C. Marshall and Dean Acheson, who knew more or were wiser than he. That takes considerable courage and humility on the part of the leader, more than most can summon.

Machiavelli saw the inner circle of advisers as a means whereby the prince could safeguard himself against flatterers, who prey on every leader's natural desire to think well of himself. Machiavelli's approach continues to have value. It's not easy to accept unpleasant advice and even personal criticism from one's closest advisers. Yet Machiavelli insisted that a leader should demand this degree of candor from his inner circle, and should show indignation if he senses he isn't getting it.

Granted, it is as difficult for an adviser to send harsh messages to his boss as it is to receive them. After all, advisers have their own personal agendas; they therefore have a natural tendency to choose their battles, especially if they function not only as sounding boards but also as line operating officers. "Does the president really want me to be candid here?" an adviser might wonder. "I'm going to need her support later on when we get to my item on the agenda, so why should I upset her now over this item in which I have no real stake?"

Many leaders reject the idea of using line officers as inner-circle advisers because such people inevitably have a narrower set of priorities and perspectives than the leader. "Charlie is responsible only for manufacturing, not for sales, engineering, marketing, or finance. How can he possibly advise me (the leader) on issues affecting the whole company?" Leaders who feel this way generally choose their inner circle of advisers from among staff, as opposed to line, personnel. But staff people bring with them their own special problems and limitations.

Personally, I prefer line officers as inner-circle advisers (my wife being the exception) because they know what it's like to take the heat for their decisions—how painful it is to be the person who has to let people go or close down a program or reallocate resources.

But whether staff or line, advisers are human beings, not machines. It is to be expected that they will have their own agendas. Every person, when he opines, has an agenda, perhaps so well hidden that he may not recognize it himself. That's why I expect my inner circle of advisers to have openly acknowledged agendas. It helps us work together to see whether and how their individual priorities can be integrated into an overall plan.

Far too often an ambitious adviser will prostitute his special access to the leader to get his own agenda implemented while hiding behind the leader's skirts. This is a great temptation for an adviser: to use the leader's power in order to hurt a rival or carry out a plan without reprisal or accountability if the tactic fails. Trust within the inner circle is the best antidote for this disease.

Leaders must remember that creating genuine trust is not like dumping instant coffee into hot water. A leader who seeks to operate effectively over the long term needs to minimize turnover among his senior advisers in order to allow trust and candor to develop on a solid foundation.

On the other hand, every organization, large or small, has a curia of sorts, a top level of bureaucracy analogous to those persons in the Vatican closest to the pope. A curia can easily become incestuous, with each person voicing and revoicing the perspective of his fellow curiales. An inner circle that becomes too narrow and ingrown is a significant stumbling block to effective leadership.

Boards of directors, trustees and regents, employee committees, unions, faculty senates, vestries, elders, presidential commissions, task forces, Boy Scout councils—all of these bodies fall into the category of elected and appointed advisers. In the case of boards of directors and boards of trustees, these "advisers" have in fact the authority to approve or reject the leader's plans and ultimately the power to hire and fire the leader himself. But unless there is a revolution afoot, even these governing bodies usually operate as advisers to the leader.

Several years ago I made a presentation to the Finance Committee of the USC board of trustees about a project in which I was particularly interested and for which I needed the committee's approval. At the end of my presentation, one of our smartest, toughest, and most influential trustees said, "You know, Steve, that has to be the dumbest plan I've ever heard of. It's inconceivable to me that your plan would work under any circumstances. But hey, Steve, you're the president, and if you want to give this plan a try, I'll back you 100 percent!" After thinking it over for a millisecond or two I had the good sense to say, "Thanks, Bill, for your support, but if you don't mind, I'd like to pull this plan from today's agenda and give it a little more thought." In this case, my governing board was serving as an official adviser to me, not as my boss, and I was artfully listening to their advice.

When it comes to elected and appointed advisory groups (and self-appointed advisers as well), the main challenge for the leader is figuring out whom they really represent and for whom they can credibly speak. We have twenty-five hundred full-time faculty members at USC, each of whom enjoys enormous professional independence. Does anyone really believe that on a given Wednesday afternoon, a faculty senate of forty-three members can discern and articulate the collective thinking of USC's faculty as a whole? Of course not. But because its members are elected by the faculty as a whole, the faculty senate can in fact represent the interests of their peers in important ways.

Perhaps we might usefully paraphrase the philosopher Eric Hoffer here, to the effect that a leader should listen very carefully to his elected and appointed advisers but never take them too seriously. In particular, the leader should never attach more importance to the words of an official adviser than the adviser's true status among his constituents would warrant.

Unsolicited advice confronts a leader at every turn—and this is especially true for a university president. Letters, faxes, e-mails, and phone calls come in to my office; an alumnus bumps into me at the grocery store; a professor corners me at the faculty club; a student organization sends me its latest manifesto for improving the university. Machiavelli suggests that it's a waste of time to listen to such advice at all. I disagree. Unsolicited advice often provides the leader with an opportunity to learn something he'd never learn from his official advisers. At the same time, however, such advice can be grossly misleading.

Often a leader will be approached by individuals purporting to represent others. In some cases, these people are legitimate representatives of a particular constituency; at other times, they are self-appointed. In either case, the leader must always keep in mind that the most dedicated and vocal members of any constituency may not represent the collective thinking of that group at all.

For example, if you hold an elective office, how might you discern on any given day what the voters in your district are thinking? How would you measure how firmly they hold their convictions? Would you weigh the letters or count the e-mails on one side or the other of an issue? Would you take a poll?

In physics there is a well-established law known as the Heisenberg Uncertainty Principle. It says, in essence, that under certain circumstances, the very process of measurement can affect the outcome of a measurement in unpredictable ways. We can see a similar uncertainty principle at work when it comes to judging the mood of voters or customers or faculty— the very act of asking the question can dramatically skew the answer.

The academic landscape is littered with the corpses of deposed deans whose faculties were reasonably content until some small group of professors decided to take a poll on the question: "Should Dean Higgens be asked to step down in view of the problems currently confronting our college?" And lo and behold, it turned out a majority of the faculty agreed it was time to cashier old Higgens, even though prior to the poll, most of them couldn't have cared less about Dean Higgens one way or the other.

Be wary when an adviser, be he official or self-appointed, tells you that "our customers want this" or "our employees want that" or "the faculty are upset about such and such." The contrarian leader never takes such counsel at face value; the first question she asks is, "Who is saying what to whom?" One needs to understand whether the person giving the advice is communicating opinions from two people or two hundred and whether he heard those opinions directly or indirectly.

Often an adviser hears a few people say things that comport with his own agenda. Then, subconsciously or otherwise, he exaggerates in his own mind the support for that agenda among the larger body politic. At other times, the reporting process is simply sloppy, with secondhand comments and rumors being passed along as hard facts. At such times, the leader must be extremely artful as she sorts through a mishmash of contradictory advice. Occasionally she must simply stop listening to anything other than her own inner voice.

The person who can turn listening into an art is one who goes beyond merely listening passively; he becomes intensely interested in what's being said and draws out the other person. In the process, he gains not only additional details, but also valuable information about the filters and biases of the person presenting the information. Active listening, with relevant and probing questions, can help the leader find out if the speaker is being slipshod or meticulous in his reporting, and can create an atmosphere of accountability in which the speaker realizes he is expected to offer defensible information rather than mere pontification.

There is much to be learned from listening to two different people separately recount the same event. No matter how hard he tries, a single human being can never give you a completely unbiased report on any event or issue; he will always give you a view that is filtered to some extent through his own prejudices. However, if you make it a point to get independent assessments of the same event from two or more people whose biases you know, you'll be in a better position to discern the truth of the matter. If I know that one of my senior vice presidents tends to take a cynical view of most events and another tends to take an overly optimistic view, it is often fruitful for me to sit down with each of them separately and carefully listen to their individual accounts of a particular situation.

The conventional rules of social discourse that most leaders learn on their way to the top do not generally equip them to be artful listeners. For one thing, leaders who listen attentively and carefully run the risk of being misunderstood. In particular, sympathetic listening by a leader can be misinterpreted by his followers as giving his assent. Franklin Roosevelt suffered especially from this problem. Almost everyone who had a private conversation with FDR left feeling the president agreed with him, while in fact Roosevelt might well have been in total disagreement with the person doing the speaking. This shortcoming on Roosevelt's part led to a lot of hard feelings and battles royal within his administration.

Thus, it is the leader's responsibility to ensure that the person who is speaking to him is not inadvertently misled by the leader's genuine efforts to understand and appreciate what's being said. Achieving this delicate balance is a fine art.

For a leader, an important part of thinking gray (taking in information and suspending judgment with respect to its truth or falsity as long as possible) is listening gray—absorbing stories, reports, complaints, posturings, accusations, extravagant claims, and prejudices without immediately offering a definitive response.

Moreover, the leader is in a position to hear things differently from how they're heard by followers closer to the front lines, who may feel compelled to protect their staff or their own policies. Because the leader is often more detached from a situation, he has a chance to rise above defensiveness and acknowledge concerns without making judgments.

Occasionally someone approaches me to complain—in person, or by letter, fax, or e-mail—about an experience or interaction he had with some of our staff or students that left him angry or dissatisfied. My first reaction is to acknowledge his concerns by offering what I call a "temporizing response." I might quickly send a letter saying, "Mr. Smith, the kind of behavior you described in your recent letter to me is totally unacceptable here at USC. I have asked Senior Vice President Jones to look into the matter; she will report her findings and actions directly to you and to me within ten days." What I don't say is, "Mr. Smith, what happened to you is terrible," because I do not in fact know what happened to him, and I won't be in a position to form a judgment on that question until the other side (or sides) of the story have been heard.

The discipline here is to not be dismissive or unresponsive on the one hand, or rush to judgment on the other. Mr. Smith complained to the president, and he received a prompt reply from the president. My reply was sympathetic and indicated that his values and mine were in close harmony. In this way, Mr. Smith knows that we're listening to him and that we are willing to change our ways in response to his complaint if changes are in order. But my response also made it clear that I was not necessarily accepting his rendition of what happened.

In fact, I may never have to reach a conclusion as to what actually happened—it's usually a matter for someone else to decide. After I assure the complaining party that I've taken notice of his concerns, I send a note to the appropriate senior officer asking her to look into it. I don't send her a searing message telling her to fix the problem; I simply say something like, "Mr. Smith claims to have been mistreated by some of our students. I have no idea if his claims are true, but if they are, please tell me what you are going to do about it."

A related point is that I always refer the matter to a senior vice president who reports directly to me—not to the manager who is closest to the problem. By holding the senior officer accountable for fixing the problem, all the staff under her are also accountable. If I were to directly charge a middle manager with correcting a problem, I would be undercutting the senior vice president's authority and responsibility for that problem. Moreover, in a short period of time, that middle manager would feel he was reporting to me, and not to the cognizant senior vice president.

There is one airline I use more than any other. Occasionally I'll write the CEO of that airline a letter complimenting one of his staff for exceptional service, and occasionally I send him a letter of complaint. I've always been amused by the fact that he responds personally to complimentary letters, but the responses I receive to complaints always come from a staff assistant. What a wimp! I should have thought he'd be man enough to respond to both compliments and complaints.

An important part of artful listening is to know when to stop listening. At some point, the leader must either make a decision himself or delegate it to someone else, and then move on. The good news is that listening carefully and intensively at the beginning can save the leader a lot of time at the end. Indeed, artful listening is a key element in stretching the leader's time and effectiveness.

Just as one can think gray without ever needing to reach a conclusion, one can listen gray without ever needing to deliver a response. Sometimes a response is not really necessary, and sometimes no response at all is the best response.

One final aspect of listening gray is that a leader shouldn't make up his mind about people's credibility unless and until he has to. Many failed leaders felt they had to decide right away whether someone was worth listening to. They tended to write off apparent fools, only to find that inarticulate people sometimes have the most valuable things to say. I'm often amazed at how easily some would-be leaders are taken in by glib, highly educated idiots, while dismissing out of hand deep thinkers who find it difficult to put their thoughts into words. The key is to not rush to a conclusion—either about what you hear or from whom you hear it.

Various observers have said that Eckhard Pfeiffer's tenure as CEO of Compaq ended abruptly in significant part because of his tendency to divide people into an A-list, to whom he listened, and a B-list, to whom he paid little or no attention. When he set the company on course to become a leader in e-business, his inability to hear the good ideas of B-list people resulted in a loss of direction and a loss of confidence that in turn resulted in Pfeiffer's startlingly swift fall from grace.

I'm an enthusiastic proponent of open communication in an organization as a means of cutting through the swampy bog of bureaucracy. I appreciate having the freedom to talk informally to employees and colleagues over a wide range of levels in the hierarchy—freely giving and receiving ideas and opinions about what we do at USC and the people we serve.

The danger here is one of undercutting the authority and responsibility of line administrators and managers. As I noted earlier, it's very easy for a leader to inadvertently change the de facto reporting relationship of a person several layers down in the organization simply by the leader's talking directly to that person.

In my experience, the best way to walk this tightrope is through something I call "open communication with structured decision making." Under this rubric, everyone in the organization is free to communicate directly with everyone else in the organization, with the explicit caveat that any and all commitments, allocations, and decisions will be made strictly through the hierarchy.

What does this mean in practice? It means that I can talk directly with any department chair or faculty member or nonacademic manager I please without going through the intervening layers of authority, and similarly anyone in the organization can communicate directly with me or with any senior vice president or dean. Sounds simple, doesn't it? It is in theory, but it works only if everyone understands and accepts the second half of the equation—structured decision making.

Let's take an example. Suppose a distinguished professor calls me to complain about the egregious sins of his department chair. I listen closely and ask questions until I fully understand the points he's trying to make. He then might ask me what changes I'm going to make or directives I'm going to issue in order to fix the problem, and I reply, "None." "What?" he asks, "you're not going to take things in hand yourself and address my grievances?" And I say, "Look, Professor, you've explained the problem to me in great detail, and I've listened carefully and fully understand your point of view. I will faithfully report what you've told me to the provost, who I'm sure will discuss it at great length with the dean, who in turn will undoubtedly discuss it with the chairman of your department. But I hire and fire the provost, not the department chairs. I could, if I chose, reach down through our bureaucracy and directly manipulate budgets and appointments in your department, but I strictly adhere to the rule of structured decision making. Indeed, if I were to do otherwise, your and my freedom to talk directly to each other without fear of reprisal or rebellion would almost certainly be curtailed."

A friend of mine, who is an extraordinarily successful business leader and entrepreneur, once took issue with me about the concept of open communication with structured decision making. He told me of an experience he had had in which he stopped by the laboratory of one of the engineers in his company to see what was going on and ask a few questions. A few days later, the manager of that division complained to my friend that he had redirected the work in that engineer's laboratory. My friend felt terrible about it. "All I did," he said, "was ask a few questions." But what he didn't realize was that he has a well-deserved reputation as a hands-on CEO. The engineer had misinterpreted my friend's innocent questions as a directive from the big boss to change direction. Once again, open communication works only if the other half of the bargain, structured decision making, is strictly and faithfully adhered to.

Artful listening can provide unexpected leverage, something that was demonstrated many times by an old friend of mine, Sam Regenstrief. Sam had retained me as an engineering consultant to his dishwasher manufacturing company, located in a small town in southern Indiana. At one time, this company was shipping six thousand dishwashers a day under thirteen different brand labels, which represented a 40 percent market share of all the dishwashers being built in the United States.

Sam was brilliant, but he certainly didn't come across that way on first meeting. He had poor vision, which was corrected with awkward-looking Coke-bottle eyeglasses, and he suffered from a kind of verbal dyslexia. These characteristics often led people we negotiated with (especially those in major cities) to think they were dealing with a naive bumpkin who was ripe for plucking.

During negotiations, Sam would bombard the other side with seemingly stupid questions and would often ask people to repeat things. He seemed to get things mixed up and often appeared befuddled. Frustrated by this time-consuming, round-about route to consensus, the other side would almost always revise the deal more and more to our liking.

Sam's power as a negotiator came not from an aggressive, take-charge approach, but rather from his ability to spend inordinate amounts of time asking for clarifications and listening to others' demands. He disarmed people with his confused and confusing approach. They thought he wasn't listening at all, while in fact he was always the most artful listener in the room.

Most university presidents, Fortune 500 CEOs, or heads of state can't afford to come across as bumpkins. Nonetheless, I learned a great deal from Sam that has proven useful to me over the years. When I'm involved in a tough negotiation, I often hold back, take what the other side says in bits, go off in a tangential direction when the pressure is on, and then circle back to the main topic from a fresh perspective. I never say, "No, absolutely not," or "This isn't negotiable." I stay flexible, ask people to tell me more, and listen carefully for a hint of softening or change in the other side.

Conventional wisdom tells us that once an outside person has been named to lead an organization, he should seize the reins of power as quickly as possible. This may be good advice if the organization is in crisis and about to go under, which is often the case when an outsider is named to head a profit-seeking corporation. But in other cases, the newly named leader from the outside would be wise to insist on a period of a few months between the announcement of his appointment and the time at which he actually takes office. During this interregnum, he can listen and question and listen some more without any responsibility for making any decisions whatsoever. Everyone within the organization will want to bare his soul to the CEO-elect during this period. And never again will the new leader have a better opportunity to understand the strengths and weaknesses of the organization, the talents of the people in it, and its prospects for the future.

I'm always amazed by the really egregious mistakes that new CEOs make when they come to an organization from the outside. It's not that they're stupid; it's just that they're ignorant. A few months spent in artful listening as the CEO-elect before actually donning the mantle of office would almost guarantee their getting off to a good start.

In my own case, I insisted that there be a period of four months between the date on which I was named president of the State University of New York, Buffalo, and the date on which I actually took office in 1982, and I negotiated a similar interregnum during my transition from Buffalo to USC in 1991. If in fact I have been successful in these two posts, I attribute much of that success in both cases to my having had the luxury of a long period of artful listening prior to my taking on the responsibilities of leadership.

There are many people in leadership positions who are poor listeners—who care little for what others have to say, or who lack the skills to listen artfully. A few of these people may appear to be very successful. But my guess is that the number of truly effective leaders who have not developed good listening skills is quite small. For the vast majority of us who aspire to excellence in leadership, artful listening isn't just an asset—it's a necessity.

o   o   o

Steven B. Sample is president of the University of Southern California. He is the university's first holder of the Robert C. Packard President's Chair.

Chapter Sixteen

Establish Competence and Build Trust

Terry Pearce

Three fundamental relationships underlie any leader-inspired change. One is that between you as the leader and the message. The relationship you are trying to affect is between other people and the message, so that people become committed to a cause voiced by you, the leader. Yet this commitment will happen only when the third and primary relationship, the one between you and those you hope to inspire, is based on competence and trust.

Trust is the fundamental requisite for people to listen to others without filters of fear or suspicion. Many who hold the position of leader, who sit in a corner office or have a title, make the mistake of thinking, "After all, I may be a bad communicator, but I am still the boss. They have to listen to me anyway." But people do not have to listen. Certain constituents may have to leave their backside in the seat while the boss talks, but real listening is not required. More important, people can never be required to act with any more conviction than it takes to go through the motions. Required action differs in both quantity and substance from inspired action.

Accordingly, communication about change starts with building credibility: a sense of your competence, and the feeling that you are trustworthy.

ESTABLISHING COMPETENCE

As you develop your message platform, there are questions that you have to ask yourself and answer to others. This platform stands on the elements that display competence: clear purpose and credentials.

Clarity of Purpose

What needs to change? What piece of compelling evidence do you have?

As a leader, you must have answers to these questions. To suggest the change, you have to consider it vital to progress. To support the change, you must have either objective evidence or observations that make it clear to you that there is a compelling need. To be authentic, you have to be able to state these elements strongly and explicitly at the beginning of the message and let others know that you are asking for change. Without being challenged to act, people will simply not engage. They may be entertained or bored, they might even be interested, but they will not engage. For this, you need a clear statement of purpose.

Franklin Raines, chairman and CEO of Fannie Mae, often carries the message that the African American effort for equality is not over. His purpose is, as he said in a speech to the

Howard University graduating class, to identify racial gaps and determine why they exist and how we can close them. What is the compelling need? According to Raines, "If America had racial equality in education, and jobs, African Americans would have . . . two million more high school degrees, two million more college degrees, . . . and nearly $200 billion more income." The disparity that exists, shown by the numbers, totals "over $1 trillion in wealth."[1] Clear purpose, clear need.

Gaining clarity of purpose focuses your attention on your strongest conviction, and clarity of purpose focuses others' attention in a single direction. As it does, it begins to establish your own confidence, and their perception of competence in you, the leader.

Rebekah Saul Butler, a candidate for master's degrees in business and in public health at the University of California, developed this statement of purpose to anchor her leadership effort in encouraging more conscious end-of-life decisions: "End-of-life care is central to our national concern over the budget and the aging population, since almost 30 percent of all Medicare funds are spent in the last year of life. [Accordingly] I am going to advocate that we all have frank, open discussions in our families about these issues . . . about aging, death and dying, what they mean, and how you will confront them."[2]

Death is not an easy issue to deal with; clarity at the outset serves notice to everyone that we are entering difficult territory with some courage behind our conviction. The more difficult the issue, the more clarity is needed.

An advertising executive, Jim Losi, felt strongly about the power of diversity in his work group. As he prepared to lead this issue, he wrote out his intention to himself, articulating the importance as he saw it: "It's not my purpose to make anyone uncomfortable, but it is my purpose to engage this group with frank and sometimes personal communication. I want them to have a crystal clear understanding of the importance of this issue and be ready to take some personal action to deal with it. For most of the group, that will mean a change in the way they operate; but for many of them, it will also mean a change in the way they think."

Authentic decisiveness creates respect. Others' disagreement with a leader on an issue can be countered by that leader's willingness to engage truthfully and boldly. Accordingly, the more difficult the issue, the more desirable it is to be candid and forthright in formulating and stating your purpose. As a result of your strength, others will perceive a new possibility being created, and you will be marked as a person of principle, a person of strong conviction and of competence.

Political leaders know this principle well, and generally get their point of view out very early in any communication. Consider the first sentence of the text of Senator Edward Kennedy's prepared speech on Iraq in late 2002: "I have come here today to express my view that America should not go to war against Iraq unless and until other reasonable alternatives are exhausted."[3]

Clear purpose and strength of purpose help establish competence, and compel others to engage.

Credentials for the Cause

What gives you the confidence that you are competent to lead this effort? Your competence to lead a given change with a given group is a function of your directly relevant work experience, life experience, and education, as well as additional credentials that might be important to the particular constituency. If you have the title of "leader," you might well have the authority to lead. But to follow your lead with commitment, people will need to know how you gained your competence in your chosen field.

Many of us are likely to underplay our credentials, either out of modesty or a belief that others should just know our background. But would you consider following anyone else's lead without knowing that individual's credentials? At the beginning of message development, you do have to consider your qualifications and be clear about them. You needn't highlight every bit of experience and education—just those that are especially meaningful to you and that would be meaningful to the group you are trying to lead. You then need to find a way to make the group aware of those qualifications to give them confidence in your ability.

Each culture recognizes certain general credentials that it considers fundamental to anyone's ability to lead. These may seem superficial, but in the early stages of a change effort, before others have had a chance to evaluate what you say or to hear your conviction on the subject, you need to establish a foothold of competence, just to open the group's collective mind to your leadership. In Europe, family history, social standing, and school ties are generally considered more important than in the United States, where life experience—what you've done on your own— might be considered more important than your alma mater. In the Far East, credentials are often established in some subtler way, to avoid the leader's being perceived as self-serving.

Groups of people engaged in specific professions will also demand different evidence to demonstrate competence. An academic group will indeed be interested in your academic credentials, even if they are not directly related to the topic. But if you are leading a business group to take more risk, then work or life experience is far more valuable in establishing credibility. Bill Gates's or Steve Jobs's work experience is certainly adequate to establish their credibility, despite the fact that neither graduated from college.

A few years ago, young environmentalist Rob Nicholsen was developing a message to lead his peers in conservation. In preparing the base message, he included this statement of credentials:

> I have been extremely fortunate to have spent most of my life educating myself for my work. I have spent almost twenty-five years in schools and over thirty years in the outdoors. I've traveled from the Arctic Ocean to the Equator, climbed some of the highest peaks in Europe and trekked through the jungles of Borneo. As an environmental consultant for six years, I've visited more garbage dumps than I care to remember. I've been involved with oil spills off the coast of Alaska and train wrecks in densely populated urban areas.

His conclusion from all these experiences was that we are not living a sustainable existence and have to change the way we relate to our environment.

Rob's notations of credentials were not arrogant or self-serving. By formulating them, he was able to feel more powerful about the topic, as well as to prepare to simply and colorfully let others know what life experience, education, and work experience was relevant to his committed course of change. He intentionally referred to himself as "extremely fortunate," because he really felt that way. In the process of relating his experience, he did not set himself above others. This statement rather showed his real humility, and began to move him toward a deeper connection with his work and with others he hoped would participate.

BUILDING TRUST

With competence established through clarity and credentials, you can move toward establishing your trustworthiness. People trust others whom they know authentically and who have their best interest at heart. The operative word is *authentically*.

If you really don't care about others, if you have no urge or instinct to acknowledge them as you encourage change, you will not be able to gain their trust, even if you follow verbal conventions. Without caring, these conventions are simply rituals that sound good but allow people to avoid connection rather than facilitate it. These conventions were at one time meaningful, but like most other formal expressions of a past experience, have since become only rules that we follow (usually unconsciously) to avoid real contact.

How many times have you heard or participated in this exchange?

"May I help you?"

"No thanks, I'm just looking."

Retail chains spend millions to get rid of this conventional conversation. In 2000, Safeway instituted a policy, openly mocked by many union members, that required check-out personnel to offer customers help to their cars and to call them by name. Rules such as these rarely help accomplish the objective. If the people staffing the check-out stands really want to serve, really want to connect, they will do so with no rules. Yet if retail salespeople aren't really interested in helping, it will come through without regard to what they say.

In many social situations, we use conventional words of acknowledgment to get us over the initial anxiety of meeting: a speaker saying, "It's wonderful to be here tonight"; an auditor saying, "We're here to help," and the person being audited replying with, "We're glad to see you." If you avoid using these conventions and instead enter into the relationship consciously, you can signal your intention to interact more authentically. I can illustrate.

In 1983, I was fortunate enough to meet with former president Jimmy Carter in Beverly Hills. My partner, Tom Green, and I were acting on behalf of some business and political leaders, promoting a very simple plan to relieve political tension between the United States and the Soviet Union. Carter had agreed to a short meeting to hear about it.

A Secret Service agent ushered us into the suite; Carter entered briskly shortly thereafter. Since Tom was standing closer to him, he shook Carter's hand first and said something like, "I am honored to meet you, Mr. President. You have been a real inspiration to me." Carter looked right at him and said, "Oh really, Tom, how's that?" I quickly ducked my head and waited for my partner to come up with something good, and in that painful ten seconds of silence that seemed like a day and a half, I learned a valuable lesson about appreciation. If it's real, it's written on your heart by experience, not on a piece of paper by convention. My partner's comment was real; he just had not reflected on why it was real.

Tom made a nice recovery, saying something about Carter's obvious deep partnership with Rosalyn and his courage in running for the presidency against heavy odds. When Carter shook my hand, I did not offer a gratuitous comment.

How many leaders could pass muster answering Carter's question? Imagine the host of a party stopping you after you have said, "What a lovely home," with the comment: "Oh really, Tom, how's that?"

By learning how to acknowledge others authentically rather than conventionally, a leader can establish uncommon intimacy very quickly. Affirmation of others is the first principle of trust building and includes the ability to authentically express gratitude and to acknowledge others' points of view. The second principle is being willing to be known and includes revealing your personal motivation and showing vulnerability.

Expressing Gratitude

Steve Farber, a fellow devotee of leadership and a superb public speaker, frequently asks his audience: "How many of you have ever received a note from someone expressing sincere appreciation?" Most in the audience will raise their hands. "How many of you still have that note?" Most will keep their hands up. He then asks how long the members of the audience have kept the notes. "Five years?" "Ten years?" Many hands remain up even as Steve asks, "Twenty-five years?" The record is forty years, and when Steve asked his respondent if he remembered what the note said, the person reached into his pocket and pulled the note from his wallet. After forty years, he still considered it one of his most prized possessions.

How many of us have kept a similar note? And for those of us who have, what is our opinion and feeling about the person who wrote it?

These are not rhetorical questions. The ability and willingness to express sincere appreciation is one of the most valuable skills of leadership communication. People will be inclined to follow others who make them feel good about themselves, who display an honest appreciation for who they are and what they do for the organization. As a leader, why not ask yourself what you are truly thankful for, with regard to this chance to communicate? Who—and what circumstance—can you authentically acknowledge as a gift?

It sounds simple, yet as the story of the notes indicates, the expression of sincere gratitude is rare and valuable. It is not easy to convey authentic appreciation; moreover, it is not considered important in a world where convention rather than authenticity rules most of our communication.

A few years ago, I was attending a program conducted by Brother David Steindl-Rast, a Benedictine monk and a prolific writer on gratefulness, a wonderful teacher, and a person I count as a rare, authentic human being. Brother David described an exercise that one of his teachers had prescribed for him as he was trying to understand gratitude. "For one year," said the teacher, "I want you to write two notes of gratitude before you leave your room in the morning."

"Easy enough," thought Brother David, until the teacher added, "and you have to experience the gratitude!"

We all know how to say "thank you," just as we know how to say, "May I help you?" yet few of us consider how to generate the experience of being grateful. Unfortunately, unless we do generate that experience in ourselves, the object of our thanks will experience only the conventional and obligatory communication—"Thanks"—hardly a note worth keeping.

Leaders have to develop the capability of generating the experience of gratitude in themselves in order to engender the kind of loyalty displayed by those who keep notes for forty years.

I've tried the "don't leave your room until you feel grateful" exercise myself. It is enlightening, and enheartening. Should you try it, you would find that real gratitude is accessed from experience, not from rhetoric. From experience comes specificity and feelings, both generators of an authentic response. A friend and client, the late Ned Dean, was chairman of the Pacific Bank in 1994. He wanted to acknowledge one of his board members at a stockholders' meeting after a difficult two years. After several false starts and some coaching, he wrote the following and later conveyed it to his stockholders:

I want to give special thanks to Mark Hubbard, who attended more than fifty board and committee meetings last year, strictly out of his dedication to helping us turn the situation around. I remember one such occasion, about seven o'clock at night in the dead of winter, when I was leaving my office as Mark was coming in. He had just finished a day at his own company, and it was raining, a cold rain that would turn to snow in any other city. He had forgotten his umbrella, so his head was soaked as he came into the lobby. I actually felt guilty leaving so early. Now it's not as though Mark doesn't have other interests. He came to that meeting because he is dedicated, more as a friend of the company than as a board member. And he did it more than fifty times when we needed him most. I feel very lucky to have such friends serving all of us.

By reflecting on his specific experience, Ned was able to access real gratitude, not merely talk about conceptual gratitude. His authenticity moved the audience, Hubbard, and Ned himself, with more than information.

Karen Chang had a similar experience in conveying gratitude for her group of senior vice presidents of Schwab. These were people who had traveled extensively in the previous year, moving from branch to branch in a major change effort. Karen could have merely said, "I want to particularly express my appreciation to the senior vice presidents for their tireless efforts and extensive travel this last year." By convention, that would be acceptable. But rather than staying with convention, Karen did a bit of research and conveyed her feelings this way: "I want to particularly thank the senior vice presidents who made this happen by being on the road. They were gone from their homes an average of fifteen nights a month last year. All of them have families; and believe me, I know that a hundred and eighty nights is a lot of nights to go to bed without a hug from someone you love. I deeply appreciate them and their families for that."

Magic. She included herself, was specific, and made it real. Her feelings were obvious, as were the feelings of everyone else in the room. By conveying feelings that came from a real experience, she made the entire episode reflect what she wanted to reflect. Learning to express authentic gratitude is central to leadership communication, and the assignment can be enriching to everyone, including you, the leader.

Acknowledging Resistance

Your expressions of authentic gratitude will help others recognize your humanity but might do little to give them an experience of your empathy with their own points of view. Resistance and disagreement are natural responses to a call for change. Before making the call, you need to consider what people are thinking and feeling about this issue. You need to consider what their natural mental and emotional resistance to this change might be.

When Alfred Sloan, head of General Motors, was in a board meeting and an important decision was about to be made, he said, "I take it that everyone is in basic agreement with this decision." Everyone nodded in agreement. Sloan looked at the group and said, "Then I suggest we postpone the decision. Until we have some disagreement, we don't understand the problem."[4]

As you build your message platform, considering other points of view or objections is important to your being able to think through the cogency of your own ideas. More important, it is central to being able to acknowledge others as a way of building trust.

Most of us fail to do this. We think through others' arguments, but we define them only as hurdles that we have to knock down to get our own way, rather than the reasonable points of view of others we hope to lead into a relationship of trust. Your strong statements of purpose will of course amplify feelings and ideas of resistance in others, and will probably provoke expressions of discontent. But these contrary ideas and feelings of discontent are present whether you acknowledge them or not. By bringing them to the surface, you establish your ability to be empathetic, and you demonstrate your willingness to become a partner rather than an adversary. By shining light on these thoughts and feelings early, you maintain and reinforce your motivation. In fact, recognizing resistance as normal gives you yet another chance to create real limbic resonance with others, to connect with their hearts and not just their minds.

Conversely, if you pretend that acceptance of your new proposal will come without uncertainty, you will lose your credibility and risk being undermined, and you will never gain the full commitment of others. They may comply, but their resistance will manifest itself in negativity and an absence of energy for the task at hand. Resistance not dealt with will continue to thrive, not only as others listen to your comments but also in the halls, bathrooms, highways, and homes where people say what has not been said in your presence.

Unfortunately, those with the most resistance to your ideas will frequently avoid expressing it. Few people are willing to risk the disapproval of a leader by actually voicing doubts about a new direction, and the stronger their objections, the more intense their fear. Instead, those reservations are expressed only to those the leader loves, respects, and trusts. Accordingly, it is your responsibility to create an atmosphere that will honor dissenting views and feelings. Only by doing so can you maintain the respect and positive engagement of those you lead. By acknowledging resistance, you are acknowledging reality and maintaining the aura of authenticity.

I first heard of this idea from Harvey Stone, an excellent speech coach and writer in Santa Fe, New Mexico. Harvey used the example of a domestic "discussion," in which a couple is in heated exchange, sometimes for days, until one of them (Harvey says that in his house, it is most often his wife) acknowledges the other's feelings and opinions. Imagine yourself in a combative mood, as your adversary stops, pauses, and says: "You know, I didn't realize that you felt so strongly about this issue. You sound as though you feel hurt, and I know that you honestly disagree with my point of view."

There is no agreement in this statement, only honest noticing and honoring of some strong feelings and a different opinion. While the discussion certainly isn't over, one can feel the adverse energy drain out of the situation, such that ears might be open to hear for the first time in the "discussion." This same release occurs whenever negative feelings and opinions are acknowledged. The respect voiced by the leader for other points of view can open the minds of dissenters as the leader's motivation becomes less suspect. Such acknowledgment does not guarantee agreement with your position, but it will dissipate the argumentative energy and open the possibility of honest dialogue.

Rational Resistance and Cynicism The easiest resistance to suspend is based on misunderstanding. The leader simply has information that others do not have. Others may be cynical about the proposed change because it (or perhaps something that sounds like it) has been tried before, or they may be fearful of change because of their lack of knowledge. Such resistance can be considered and acknowledged in the beginning of any message. It can be refuted later, but in the spirit of common understanding rather than argument.

What does this look like?

In developing his message platform for a change in supply chain management, John Ure of Agilent was suggesting a new focus on customers, a holistic approach that would create an integration of the supply chain. He made the following notes about resistance:

> When thinking about this new way, I can hear voices, my own included, that argue, from Marketing, "I already focus on the customer, although perhaps not to the point of actual intimacy, so why the need to change?" or from Purchasing, "I have already developed excellent partnerships with our suppliers, why do we need to change?" or from Design, "Don't come and tell me how to design a product, I am perfectly competent, just get on with getting the best price." Indeed we do all of those things, and I don't want to lose this focus, this partnership, or this competency in design.

These notes on resistance do not in themselves refute the resistance. They merely help John and others know that he was under no illusions about their points of view. In fact, he acknowledged his own resistance at the same time ("my own included"). When the other players realized that John knew about their doubts and was open to them, they were, in kind, open to hear what else he had to say, and they were willing to engage with him, knowing that he could acknowledge their point of view.

The same thinking can be applied to selling, to promoting a new product to a large audience of potential consumers.

David Craford, a sales executive with Affymetrix in California's Silicon Valley, was a leader in advocating acceptance and use of bioengineered food. He realized that many people were legitimately fearful of such food and acknowledged that resistance in his message development: "I know that a few people have doubts about this technology, they might well be afraid of putting 'bioengineered' foods into their body or having them grown in their fields. I understand these concerns. It's important for us to have a common understanding of how this technology works, and why we need it to work on a local and global level."

Again, David could not possibly eliminate all the fears surrounding bioengineered foods. What he could do, however, was to anticipate others' thoughts and feelings as preparation for letting them know early that he appreciated their point of view. This opened an opportunity for them to hear what he had to say with their strong feelings suspended, and to engage with him as a leader, not merely as a contrarian.

Resistance based on a different or inadequate understanding of the facts can be relieved with explanation. John Ure went on to address the resistance later in his message, by explaining the difference in his new plan and the status quo, and David Craford explained the methods of development for high-tech tomatoes, using common metaphors to educate others and assuage their fears.

Irrational Resistance Other resistance comes not from any lack of understanding but from incorrect and entrenched beliefs. Such resistance cannot be corrected logically. It's important that you, as leader, realize this and not yield to indignation. Although most people who hold onto such beliefs are not good candidates for partnership and may well leave the organization, if you understand and acknowledge their point of view, you may create an atmosphere in which some of them listen rather than withdraw.

Consider the following comments from Jim Losi's message platform on diversity, referred to earlier in this chapter. His company was launching an initiative on the need for more diversity in the workforce. This is a particularly emotional issue in Jim's industry, which has traditionally been dominated by white males. After introducing the subject, Jim made the following notes on resistance:

> Some people may still wonder why this topic is getting so much attention; they may still think that it is a response to government regulation or that it is only a moral issue that supports our values as a company. Frankly, a year ago, I might have held similar misconceptions. But after a year on the task force, reading demographic predictions, and thinking about the future of our company, I have a considerably different view.
>
> Some of them also might be threatened by the issue. Those in the majority might feel that it means less opportunity, or an institution of quotas. Some of them might still be under the illusion that increasing diversity will lower standards.
>
> Those who see themselves as not a member of the majority might feel that the issue puts unreasonable attention on them, that they might be viewed as needing special attention, or that it is their task to educate the majority.
>
> These are understandable fears, but they are only fears. Some of them might be justified by reality. None of them is a reason not to move forward.

Jim was able, in this statement, to acknowledge the fears, respect others' points of view, and challenge them to move forward anyway. Like all other leadership issues, Jim's topic dealt with a suggested course of action to change the status quo. He is calling on others in the company for trust, asking them to progress through their fears to a new future. Understanding and acknowledging their resistance is another step in establishing authentic conviction about change.

Gratitude and the acknowledgment of resistance lead others to gauge if the leader truly has their interest at heart. The motivation of the leader is still a critical element in developing trust.

Personal Motivation

To agree to action, people want to know why a change is important to the organization and how they will benefit from it. But to commit to follow a leader down an uncertain path, they have to know the leader's personal motivation. Personal motivation is central to trustworthiness. It doesn't have to do with material outcome; it has to do with meaning. "I have a dream," was Martin Luther King Jr.'s personal motivation. Examining your own and revealing it is part of building trust.

The best example I've ever heard of this aspect of earning trust was brought to my attention by Peter Alduino, a leadership consultant from Santa Cruz. He found a videotape, made in 1974, of the late Barbara Jordan. Jordan was then an African American member of the U.S. House of Representatives, from Texas, and on the tape was speaking to the committee hearing the evidence to impeach former President Nixon. As a junior member of the committee, she spoke for fifteen minutes, including this prologue:

> Earlier today, we heard the beginning to the preamble to the Constitution of the United States . . . "we the people," a very eloquent beginning. But when that document was completed on the 17th of September in 1787, I was not included in "we the people."
>
> I felt somehow for many years that George Washington and Alexander Hamilton just left me out by mistake. But through the process of amendment, interpretation and court decision, I have finally been included in "we the people."
>
> Today I am an inquisitor, and hyperbole would not be fictional and would not overstate the solemnness that I feel right now. My faith in the Constitution is whole, it is complete, it is total. And I am not going to sit here and be an idle spectator to the diminution, the subversion, the destruction of the Constitution.[5]

There is no question about Jordan's personal motivation, and any constituent who felt equally disenfranchised would be inspired by her statement. Notice that it is personal, not theoretical, not talking about people in general. Jordan did not say, "We should be diligent in protecting the Constitution, because it is the basis of our freedom as a nation." Although she certainly would agree with that statement, her personal motivation is what creates the platform for her very personal leadership on this issue.

Meaning is conveyed when we can connect our actions to our personal values. Sometimes that is done with a story, as when I realized the connection between delivering kids to college and delegation. While on a different scale, the experience made delegation meaningful for me, just as Barbara Jordan's very intense personal experience made the health of the Constitution meaningful for her.

Many might think that this connection can't be made in a business environment, but consider the story of Howard Schultz. Schultz was very clear about his personal motivation for building Starbucks into the kind of company it is, where everyone feels like a partner. His experience with his father drove his values to the surface, and he was able to express them later in his business. Schultz's revelation carried with it not only his personal motivation but the aura of vulnerability that brings others close.

Relevant Vulnerability

The final element of building trust is knowing and acknowledging what you don't bring to the table. An honest assessment of your capabilities and limitations reinforces the insight that others are interacting with a real human being, and brings an uncommon sense of trust to relationships. As you begin developing your message of change, reflect on your shortcomings. What are you trying to become better at? What will people assume about you that simply isn't true? Write it down, and reflect on how you can reveal it.

Mario Cuomo was a champion of abortion rights as a matter of public policy. But he was also a practicing Catholic. He was asked to address the combined faculty and administration of Notre Dame on the subject, and found it the perfect opportunity to think through and ferret out his own thinking and feeling on this subject in a way that he had not before. The address that he eventually gave formed the basis for his extemporaneous remarks on the subject of the relationship of his faith to his public policy for the rest of his career. Considering the audience for this speech, and his constituents in general, he felt the need to tell them directly who he was and who he was not. As he said:

> Let me begin this part of the effort by underscoring the obvious. I do not speak as a theologian, I do not have that competence. I do not speak as a philosopher; to suggest that I could would be to set a new record for false pride. I don't presume to speak as a "good" person except in the ontological sense of that word . . . [rather], I speak here as a politician. And also as a Catholic, a layperson baptized and raised in the pre–Vatican II church, educated in Catholic schools, attached to the church first by birth, then by choice, now by love. An old-fashioned Catholic who sins, regrets, struggles, worries, gets confused, and most of the time feels better after confession. The Catholic church is my spiritual home. My heart is there, and my hope.[6]

Aside from the beautiful words, the content of this supplementary self-introduction did far more for Cuomo's credibility with this audience than the fact that he was a governor who wrestled with public policy every day. He established his connection with this audience as a human being by including his personal motivation to speak and his personal vulnerabilities. Despite the fact that he was advocating a position very unpopular with this group, he was going to be trusted.

You cannot be the expert on all the mechanisms necessary to effect major change. You can, however, acknowledge those shortcomings without giving up your ability to lead. In fact, you will enhance your own credibility, giving others clear signals about their potential contribution.

Here is John Ure's commentary about his own supply chain expertise: "If any think I'm new to this field, they'd be right. I don't profess to be a purchasing expert. . . . I have zero time served in this discipline. I don't profess to be a supply chain guru, or a quality systems expert. Indeed my eyes start glazing over when I hear some of you talking about the areas in which you do have these skills."

As you may have surmised, vulnerability is the flip side of credentials. Clear purpose, credentials, vulnerability, personal motivation, expressing gratitude, and acknowledging others' points of view—these are all aspects of a leadership communication that you need to ponder and record before you move into the issue itself. And, of course, these are all aspects of emotional intelligence, and your willingness to consider them supports your decision to lead, not just dictate, change. Your relationship to those you hope to inspire and your relationship to the message you hope to deliver have to be clear and deep for you to be perceived as an authentic leader, both competent and personally trustworthy. Once you have completed this thinking, you have a chance of gaining real, committed support. The beginning of this message platform sets the tone and the limits for the leader and those the leader wishes to engage, inviting them to entertain change. The degree of both confidence and trust that develops between you and others will be determined by the authenticity you can transmit. The tone of your credentials, the way in which you show appreciation for your listeners, the strength of your purpose, the empathy you

portray for their resistance and the cost and benefit they perceive in your advocacy—each of these elements will affect their
willingness to engage.

o　　o　　o

After you have included these rudiments (Exhibit 16.1), you
need to record your perspective, the story that compels you to
seek change at all, this change in particular, and to do it now.

EXHIBIT 16.1. **Questions to Ask in Building Trust and
Establishing Competence**

Clarity of purpose
- What problem needs to be solved—specifically?
- What needs to change?
- What pieces of compelling evidence do I have? What is the
  overriding piece of compelling evidence that something needs
  to change?

Credentials
- What gives me confidence that I am competent to lead this
  effort?
- What life experience, work experience, or portion of my education is relevant?
- What will my constituents need to know about me to be confident in my leadership?

Gratitude
- What am I truly thankful for, with regard to this chance to
  communicate or those with whom I will interact?
- What circumstance, group, or individual can I authentically
  acknowledge as a gift?

Acknowledging resistance
- How can I demonstrate my interest in others?
- What are people thinking and feeling about this issue?
- What will be their natural mental and emotional resistance to
  this change?

(continued)

EXHIBIT 16.1. *(continued)*

- ○ What objective resistance do others have?
- ○ What emotions will likely be present in others?
- ○ What commonality do we share?
- ○ What aspirations do we share?

Personal motivation
- ○ Why does this issue matter to me personally?
- ○ What story could demonstrate my conviction?
- ○ What personal value is represented by this change?
- ○ Am I taking a stand about a principle that is important to me?
- ○ What core principles, values, or beliefs motivate me to want to resolve this fairly, with everyone's interest being served?

Relevant vulnerability
- ○ What is it that I don't know?
- ○ What are the areas in which I don't yet have expertise with regard to this issue?
- ○ What help will I need?
- ○ What mistakes might I have made with regard to this issue or with this group that I could acknowledge?
- ○ What obstacles are in this for me personally?
- ○ What are some personal qualities that I could convey to others that would allow them to connect with me as a human being?

○   ○   ○

Terry Pearce is a communication consultant, leadership and communication lecturer in the Haas School of Business, University of California, Berkeley, and a visiting lecturer at the London School of Business.

Chapter Seventeen

Read People

Identifying Emotions

David R. Caruso
Peter Salovey

What does it mean to be able to identify emotions accurately? Managers with this skill are described by the statements in column A of Table 17.1. Managers who struggle with this skill are often described by statements such as those listed in column B.

Let's take a look at two people, each of whom is better described by one of these lists of attributes than the other.

What Does It Mean to Identify Emotions?

Managers have to work with people. As simple and obvious as this sounds, it is not always easy to do well. Failures of interpersonal relationships at work can occur for many different reasons. In Bill's case, the reason seems to be his struggle in figuring out how people feel.

TABLE 17.1. **Identifying Emotions**

Column A: Skillful	Column B: Not Skillful
Knows what people feel	Misreads people's emotions
Will talk about feelings	Doesn't talk about feelings
Can show how they feel	Never shows feelings
Expresses feelings when upset	Does not know how to express feelings
Smiles when happy or pleased	Maintains neutral expression
Reads people accurately	Fails to identify how others feel
Good at recognizing own feelings	Misunderstands own feelings

Bill Just Doesn't Seem to Get It

Bill, age forty-five, was an outgoing and energetic person. He was considering a career change to consulting, as he had extensive experience in his industry and was well educated. However, Bill's colleagues reported that Bill wasn't always effective with them or with clients in general. In the words of one colleague, "Bill isn't always there. He seems a bit 'off' at times. He just doesn't seem to get it."

Bill didn't pick up on others' nonverbal signals. During a conversation, when it was clear to most people that the discussion wasn't going anywhere, Bill would obliviously continue to expound on his points and end up completely losing the audience.

He also didn't seem able to appreciate his own emotional state of mind. For instance, Bill had a mild temper problem. After an especially difficult week in the office, it appeared that Bill was quite angry. He would fling his briefcase around, speak gruffly to his secretary, and generally stomp around the office. Asked how he was feeling, he replied, "Fine, I'm fine." One colleague ventured to say to Bill, "It seems like you're really angry with the way that deal is going," only to have Bill almost yell at him, "I am not angry! Understand? I am not angry!" And he really meant it! He was oblivious to his own emotions and to those of others.

Bill's ability to identify emotions was modest at best.

Bob Gets It

Bill lacked basic emotional awareness, but many managers who are aware of emotions can't accurately identify them. Having emotional awareness and accurate emotional data is the basis for most effective relationships, as the case of Bob illustrates.

Bob was a hail-fellow-well-met sort of guy. A second-generation Italian American, Bob had risen from junior bookkeeper to managing partner at one of the biggest public accounting firms in the world. The first impression Bob usually gave people was that he was unsuited for a role as a managing partner. He was big and brash and loud. His speech and mannerisms reflected his blue-collar background rather than the upper-crust polish evident in his fellow partners.

It was surprising that not only had he survived but he had thrived in this staid, conservative environment. However, that surprise was based on externals. As we worked with Bob, we came to discover many qualities that were hidden below the surface—qualities that his colleagues knew about and had appreciated for more than two decades.

Bob had a great sense about people, and he could zero in on the mood of the room or, as he said it, "I feel the vibes in the organization." He was an astute observer of people, and even as he talked to you, you could feel that there was continuous thinking and processing going on in Bob's head.

At times, he surprised people with his insights on how a client felt about a proposal or how a meeting went. On one occasion, when everyone else agreed that the meeting had gone well and the client seemed pleased, Bob differed. He insisted that there was more to it than that and that there were still unresolved issues in the client's mind. It turned out that Bob was correct. Bob's ability to identify emotions accurately was strong.

How Do We Identify Emotions?

The ability to identify accurately how other people feel is critical not just to success and happiness but perhaps to our very survival. This point was dramatically illustrated (with examples from many different species) by Charles Darwin in his wonderful book *The Expression of the Emotions in Man and Animals*.[1] Recognizing the difference between a stranger who is friendly and ready to help you and a stranger who is unfriendly and ready to attack you can spell the difference between living another day and ending up dead.

The ability to identify emotions consists of a number of different skills, such as accurately identifying how you feel and how others feel, sensing emotion in art and music, expressing emotions, and reading between the lines. Perhaps most critical is the ability to detect real versus fake emotions.[2]

Accurate Awareness

Without emotional awareness, how can we distinguish whether we are feeling tired or sad, happy or nervous? Awareness is the essential building block for emotional intelligence.

The ability to introspect has been highly touted among self-help advocates as a critical component of personal growth and development. What most self-help gurus fail to understand is that introspection and reflection can lead to worsening mood and can result not in insight but in feelings of depression and shame.[3] Awareness is certainly an important component of emotional intelligence, but it must be accurate and not obsessive. We must know how we feel and be able to label our feelings appropriately if we wish to better understand ourselves and others. When we attempt to determine how we feel, we have to be fully aware of gradations and shifts of feeling. It's important to know whether we're frustrated during a sales presentation, or bored, or just tired. This information provides insights about the sales message itself.

Expression of Emotion

If emotions serve as a sophisticated but efficient signaling system, then we not only need to be able to decipher signals but send them as well. Expressing emotion is relatively easy, but doing so accurately is somewhat more difficult. Some people are hard to read, and the signals they send are either not clear or too subtle to be detected. Others are purposefully unexpressive. They may feel that it is inappropriate to express themselves, or they may be afraid of emotional expression for more personal reasons. In this case, they have the ability to express emotion, but they choose not to do so. Cultural and organizational display rules also come into play.

The inability to accurately express emotion means that we do not send signals about ourselves, and as a result, our needs may not be met. If I am sad regarding a lost computer document that I required for a major meeting later that day, I need support at that time. My expression of sadness is likely to increase the chances of being supported, which, in this case, means someone taking time to help me recover the lost file. In another situation, if I am calm and at ease but communicate a message that says something different about my emotional state, another person may incorrectly perceive me as a threat and take action against that perceived threat. "I didn't think he really cared" is something that many managers will say about an employee who masks his passion for the job.

The ability to communicate has survival value in other ways. Our interpersonal communications consist of both verbal and nonverbal cues. Our tone of voice, gestures, posture, and facial expressions are conduits for information. If the information enhances the verbal message, it is likely that the message will be communicated in a more accurate and meaningful way.

Paul Ekman, a psychologist in the field of emotional expression, has studied people's ability to express emotions. Even though emotional expression begins to develop in infancy,[4] Ekman finds that people differ greatly in their ability to express various emotions.[5]

Ability to Read People

Right now, you are feeling a certain way—perhaps content and satisfied. Then a colleague approaches you and asks why you look so unhappy; he asks what the problem is. In this case, your colleague's perceptions are not accurate. He may definitely feel that you are unhappy, but if you are not, then his perceptions are off base.

The ability to read facial expressions and identify the emotion expressed in that face accurately is a core skill. This ability is essential to our interpersonal survival and, perhaps, to our physical survival as well. Emotions are a signaling system, and emotions contain important data. If we are unable to read these signals, then our data and information about a situation is either incorrect or flawed.

Distinguishing between a person who is enraged and a person who is calm can make a critical difference in our own well-being. Determining friend from foe is only part of the importance of this ability. Perceiving emotion accurately allows us to approach a situation with some finesse.

By the way, it's not just people who display emotion. Our four-skill model of emotional intelligence also posits that this ability extends beyond emotional displays to the perception of emotion in art forms such as music and sculpture and paintings. Art makes us think and feel. Art moves us, not just intellectually but emotionally as well. The power of music to convey emotion is well understood, or rather, well "felt" by most of us. Think of the chill of suspense that certain musical scores provide or the happiness you feel listening to certain tunes. Also consider the billions of dollars that are spent on advertising, trade shows, logo design, and branding. These seek to influence how people feel about a product, as well as how they think about it.[6]

Ability to Read Between the Lines

Accurate emotional identification also means that you can't be easily fooled by people who are expressing an emotion they don't actually feel.[7] Although it is very easy to be able to smile on demand—witness many photographs with everyone smiling—it is harder to create a true smile if you are not feeling happy.

Sometimes people who are not emotionally aware pay a little bit of attention to facial and emotional expressions—just enough to see that there is an emotional display. What they miss, however, are the subtle cues that help to distinguish genuine from manipulated expressions of emotion. And sometimes you may be paying a great deal of attention to emotional displays but still misread the emotion.

Some managers who don't pick up on emotional cues at all, especially false cues, accept others at face value. They don't go beyond the surface expression of emotion because they don't see any need to do so. The result is that they see a smile, but it doesn't occur to them that it might be a forced smile—one in which the mouth is smiling but the eyes are not crinkling as they should. This leads them to an incorrect conclusion, wrong basic assumptions, and faulty emotional information.

Why Is Identifying Emotions Important?

The advice offered to Professor Harold Hill in *The Music Man* ("but you gotta know the territory") applies not just to sales but to all our interactions. That is, you need to have a basic understanding of a person or a sales territory in order to be effective.[8]

Data for Decisions

Accurate emotional identification results in core emotional data that are required for decisions and actions. Without this base of data, how can we hope to make good decisions and take appropriate action?

Even slight inaccuracies can have a major downstream impact on our lives. It's like what happens when we take a compass bearing and follow it to some distant point. If that point is not far away, a slightly inaccurate reading has little impact on us. But a compass reading that is off by just one or two degrees, over a journey of hundreds of miles, can lead us to a point very far distant from our intended destination.

Accurate emotional identification is important, even in seemingly routine managerial tasks such as budget planning. Consider a meeting in which you present your annual budget to your direct reports and seek their buy-in and agreement. Lots of things need to happen correctly for you to get the data you need. First, your direct reports have to feel that you want feedback. Whether that message gets communicated will depend on the way you express emotion. You may subtly invite comment, or you may send signals indicating that you really don't want any feedback. Second, your ability to read between the lines and pick out the accurate emotional signal in all of the noise of the team's moods requires a fair amount of skill. One of your managers says that the plan looks fine to him, but he sure does not seem fine to you, as he shifts nervously in his chair. Another direct report complains that not enough money was allocated for his people, but there doesn't seem to be much passion behind the complaint. Likely enough, he's just trying to pad his budget against possible cutbacks later in the fiscal year.

Opportunities to Explore

Recognizing negative emotions accurately is a key to our well-being and, in some cases, to our physical survival. Accurately reading positive emotions may not have immediate survival value (at least for humans; in animals it may be an important cue for a mating opportunity), but it does help us develop and grow. Opportunities to explore our environment, to experiment, and to invent arise from positive emotions. We approach situations and other people when we perceive positive emotions. Wouldn't it be useful if we could detect the subtle signs of interest during a sales presentation or when we are interviewing for a job? Would that be a hint that you could use? Perhaps the encouragement you also seek?

Your ability to be aware of positive emotions and to recognize them accurately can provide you with extremely important information about your world. It's easy to dismiss the hunches or the gut feelings we have, and perhaps some of us should if our emotional read is inaccurate. But if we are accurate, then attending to positive feelings means we are onto something good.

It's like the game kids play when they search for a hidden object, and the person who hid the object tells them whether they are getting colder (farther away) or warmer (closer). Positive—warm—feelings can signal that we are on the right track.

Social Interaction and Communication

Nonverbal information is often the basis for successful social interaction. This information consists of gestures, voice tone, and facial expressions. If we focus on a person's words alone, we are at serious risk of misunderstanding the underlying message.

Although the concept of body language received bad press some years ago, when it was exploited as a tool to pick up potential romantic partners, a great deal of research has been conducted in the area of nonverbal communication.[9] Estimates vary, but as little as 10 percent of the information in an interchange between two people comes from their actual words, and the rest from tone of voice, gestures, and facial expression.[10]

Accurately identifying facial expressions and accurately expressing emotions is therefore a key to appropriate and successful interpersonal interactions. The person who is not skilled in identifying his or her own or another person's emotions through subtle cues is likely to behave quite boorishly, whether intending to or not.

o   o   o

David R. Caruso is a research affiliate in the Department of Psychology at Yale University. He is also a management psychologist.

Peter Salovey is a professor and dean of the Graduate School of Arts and Sciences at Yale University. He published the first scientific articles on emotional intelligence (with John D. Mayer), introducing the concept to the field of psychology.

Chapter Eighteen

The Seven Essentials of Encouraging

James M. Kouzes
Barry Z. Posner

All the goodness, beauty, and perfection of a human being
belong to the one who knows how to recognize these qualities.
Georgette Leblanc, English actress and poet

While he was president of North American Tool and Die (NATD), Tom Melohn enjoyed giving out Super Person of the Month awards to employees who went the extra mile to help the company move toward its goal of high quality and no product rejects. Melohn made himself highly visible to everyone in the workplace. But more than this, he personally presented the Super Person awards with a gregarious style that was his trademark. Because of his high level of engagement with the people around him, people felt they knew him. He put himself out there fearlessly, giving his leadership a little extra pizzazz, which tended to be mirrored back to him in the enthusiasm people brought to the workplace. Through the strength of his presence, Melohn revealed that he knew what was going on and that he cared about people, got a great deal of pleasure from his work, and took pride in the accomplishments of others.

Over the years, we've used Melohn as our best-practices example of how a leader can encourage the heart. One specific incident in particular, in just two minutes, truly exemplifies all the essential principles and actions that form the foundation of this practice. In this description of a Super Person award ceremony, pay particular attention to how Melohn interacts with Kelly and "the gang," as Melohn affectionately calls them, who have gathered to witness the award presentation. Notice the level of delight Melohn expresses and how he engages everyone in the room through his questions and by adding dramatic elements to the celebration. As you read this case example, see what essentials you can tease from it.

This scene takes place on the shop floor of NATD. Employees are gathered in the employee break area near the boxes and machinery of the plant, for a Super Person of the Month award.[1]

"We've got a new award today," Melohn announces to the assembled group. "It's called the North American Tool and Die 'Freezer' Award. Now, who knows what that's for and who won it? Anybody? Anybody got an idea?"

Somebody shouts out: "Kelly!"

"There's something in the freezer," Melohn says. "Kelly . . . go on, Kelly, look in the freezer. Go on. Come on. Hurry up!"

Kelly opens the door of a freezer standing nearby and reaches inside. He finds a metal rod and cylinder. There's an envelope stuck to them.

Melohn laughs. "Come on up here."

Everyone joins in the joy and laughter as Kelly walks up and Melohn shakes his hand. Melohn laughs some more, obviously delighted with the fun the group is having at this ceremony. Melohn takes the envelope and metal rod out of Kelly's hand.

"Oh, that's cold!" Melohn exclaims. He hands the envelope back to Kelly and sets the metal part on a table.

Kelly opens the envelope and pulls out a check for fifty dollars.

"Okay?" Melohn asks Kelly.

"Yeah!" Kelly says, smiling shyly.

"Remember this job?" Melohn asks the group. "I went through the shop one day and I saw Kelly going in the freezer. I thought, 'What the hell is going on? Is he goofing off or making margaritas for Joe, or what?' You know what he did? He couldn't get this (Melohn points to the metal rod) into here (he points to the metal cylinder), so he said, 'Hey, I'm going to put this in the freezer. It'll shrink, and then I'll put the part together.' And it worked! And I said, 'Where in the hell did you get that idea?' He said, 'What? It's just part of the job, right?'" Melohn looks at Kelly.

"Yep," Kelly says.

Melohn turns to Kelly, puts his arm around his shoulder, and says, "What else can I say, gang? God love you, baby. God love you." Then he turns to the group, holds the part in the air, and says, with pride and caring in his voice: "And remember: no rejects, no rejects, no rejects! That's why we're here, gang."

If you'd like to watch this scene and an in-depth interview with Melohn about leadership and employee partnership, they're in the film *In Search of Excellence: The Video.*[2]

We've asked thousands of people in our classes and work-shops to watch the Melohn case on video and tell us what they observe. We tell them that if they can learn to incorporate what Melohn did into their daily leadership actions, they'll earn nearly perfect scores on encouraging the heart (that is, show-ing appreciation for people's contributions and creating a cul-ture of celebration—it's how leaders visibly and behaviorally link rewards with performance).

What precisely did Tom Melohn do? What actions did he take? What words did he use? What nonverbal behaviors did he exhibit? What values did he exemplify that encouraged the heart? Here are some of the viewers' representative responses:

> "He was genuine; he was a real person."

> "He saw Kelly do this; he was out on the shop floor, and he took note of it."

> "He showed that he believed in people."

> "He put his arm around Kelly."

> "He really loved his employees."

> "He made it fun."

> "He recognized Kelly in public, not behind a closed door in his office."

> "He told a story about Kelly."

> "He didn't just talk about recognition, he lived it."

> "He gave out the award himself; he didn't delegate it."

> "He was clear about the standards: total quality."

> "He repeated the statement 'no rejects' several times."

> "He gave Kelly a check, sharing some of the organization's benefit from Kelly's action."

> "He was laughing and having a good time. He really enjoyed recognizing Kelly."

As these observations testify, close analysis of the NATD "Freezer" Award ceremony (and others like it) teaches us that underlying the practice of encouraging the heart there is a set of recognizable, learnable, and repeatable actions leaders take that both make people feel special and reinforce the standards of the enterprise. From people's observations, we've identified seven essentials to encouraging the heart. When leaders do their best to encourage the heart, they:

1. Set clear standards.

2. Expect the best.

3. Pay attention.

4. Personalize recognition.

5. Tell the story.

6. Celebrate together.

7. Set the example.

Let's take a closer look at the Melohn case so that we can fully illuminate the essentials of encouraging the heart.

SET CLEAR STANDARDS

At the close of the Super Person of the Month ceremony, Tom Melohn said something that is crucial to understanding how to be most effective in encouraging the heart: "Remember: no rejects, no rejects, no rejects! That's why we're here, gang."

Melohn had a clear set of standards that he expected people in the organization to live up to. Whether he was walking the floor, making a presentation, talking to a customer, or holding a meeting, he and others knew what the expectations were. The most important for NATD was no rejects! None, zero, nada, not one. It was why they were in business. Anything less in the highly competitive market they served meant loss, and maybe the death, of business.

In recognizing individuals, we sometimes get lost in the ceremonial aspects. We think about form, but we forget substance. Recognitions are reminders; quite literally, the word *recognize* comes from the Latin to "know again." Recognitions are opportunities to say to everyone, "I'd like to remind you one more time what's important around here. Here's what we value. Now, let me give you one example of how someone in this organization demonstrated what it means to meet or exceed our standards."

The first prerequisite, then, to encouraging the heart is to set clear standards. The standards were as much the focus of the freezer award as was the action that won Kelly his reward. In this entertaining moment, Melohn linked the reward with the standards that had been set. The reward was for an action in service of a clear purpose.

To be successful in encouraging the heart, it's absolutely critical that everyone cherish a common set of standards. (We've chosen to use the word *standards* to mean goals as well as values or principles.) It's certainly not very encouraging to be in the dark about what we're expected to achieve or never to know where we stand relative to what's important. Only when we know the standards can we set our sights for success. By clearly defining the values and principles for which we're held accountable and by linking performance to those standards, leaders establish a benchmark for achievement.

However, not just any standards will do. They must be standards of excellence. They must be aspirational and bring out the best in us. They must make us feel like winners when we attain them. Certainly, "no rejects" is a lot more aspirational and inspirational than, say, "Five out of ten will do."

Melohn may have ended his presentation to Kelly with the statement about no rejects, but he also began with it—in his mind. Everyone knew what was expected. Repeating the standard at the end was just one more way of reinforcing the values that everyone, ahead of time, knew were important. Repetition is a powerful pedagogical device. By repeating the standard, Melohn reinforces a crucial principle for employees of North American Tool and Die. He links appropriate performance to the reward, signaling that if one follows this model of behavior, then other rewards follow.

Expect the Best

Every time we watch this video segment, several people invariably comment on how genuine Melohn is, how much he cares, how much he really believes that the people on the front line can achieve a standard of no rejects. Describing the practices of leadership, Melohn puts it this way: "In my judgment, the best leaders have two characteristics. The first is an unswerving, single-minded, utterly all-consuming set of values not unlike the NATD currencies. The second, shared trait of leaders is a similar perception of people. Over and over again, they express their belief in the innate goodness of human beings. All the energies of the best leaders—in fact, their entire lives—are dedicated to helping people achieve their full potential."[3]

Melohn is right. The best leaders believe that no matter what their role, people can achieve the high standards that have been set. It's called the Pygmalion effect, a belief so strong that even if others don't believe in themselves initially, the leader's belief—or the teacher's or parent's or colleague's—gives rise to self-confidence, to a belief that, "Yes, I can do it." It becomes a self-fulfilling prophecy.

Belief in others' abilities is fundamental to encouraging the heart. Like it or not, our beliefs about people are broadcast in ways we're not even aware of. We just give off certain cues that say to people either, "You can do it, I know you can do it," or, "There's no way you'll ever be able to do that." How can you expect someone to get extraordinary things done if she picks up the signal that you don't believe she can? Even if you said, "Thanks, great job," how genuine would it be perceived to be?

When leaders expect people to achieve, they do. When they label people underachievers, performance suffers. Passionately believing in people and expecting the best of them is another prerequisite to encouraging the heart.

PAY ATTENTION

"I went through the shop one day," Melohn told us. This gives us an immediate clue as to the kind of leader he is. He's a wanderer, a walk-arounder, a leader who is right there with you. He's a leader in the truest sense of the word—a venturer. We quickly learn from the little scene at NATD that Melohn is a leader who delights in "catching people doing things right."

But it's more than just catching people doing things right, it's also paying attention and understanding the significance of their actions. All too often, we notice something happening but we ignore it. We just pass on by or file it away, thinking to ourselves that we'll get to it later. Melohn's own description of this practice tells us the difference. You've probably heard of MBWA, managing by walking around. Melohn calls it CBWA: caring by walking around. A one-word difference, but what a word. *Caring* just feels different from *managing*, now, doesn't it?

As Melohn tells the story, on one of his CBWA tours he noticed Kelly doing something unusual. At that point, he could have ignored what was going on. But being curious and because he cared, he didn't. Instead, he went up to Kelly, started asking questions, and engaged him in conversation. Learning what Kelly was doing, Melohn understood that this man's actions were the very embodiment of the standards NATD wanted people to maintain. He was so impressed by Kelly's going the extra mile that he decided to make a positive example of him. By telling Kelly's story, he would encourage the heart of everyone there to hook up their work efforts to the value of no rejects.

We must add something. Even though he was owner and, as he referred to himself, "head sweeper," of NATD, Melohn wasn't the one to pick the Super Person winners. Supervisors and foremen nominated candidates once a week, and that same group chose the monthly winner. Melohn would occasionally make suggestions, but his wasn't the deciding vote. This is even more reason that paying attention is so important. Melohn could have passed the incident by because he wasn't the one who would pick the award winners. But he cared enough to notice, invest the attention, and persuade others of the merits.

Leaders are always on the lookout for exemplars of the values and standards. Wherever they are, whatever they're doing, the best leaders have a special radar that picks up positive signals.

PERSONALIZE RECOGNITION

Notice what Melohn did to make this award special for Kelly. While the Super Person of the Month was a regular feature at NATD when Melohn was there, this award was special. He gave it a unique, attention-getting name: the North American Tool and Die "Freezer" Award, tying it specifically to something that Kelly—and nobody else—had done. Melohn personalized it. He customized the award and the ceremony just for Kelly.

Melohn didn't stand up in front of the room and say, "Today I want to present Kelly with an award for working to achieve the company standard of no rejects. Here's a check, Kelly. Thanks." Instead, he choreographed the whole thing. He put the metal part in the freezer so that when the time came Kelly would go back to the freezer, open it, and take out the part. This is clearly not something that happens every day. The fact that it was unusual, fun, and dramatic all helps to imprint the event and the stated values in people's minds.

This emphasis on the individual uplifts Kelly and sends the message to others that singular efforts really can make a difference. We've learned time and time again that people have become cynical about perfunctory thank-yous and gold watches. We've collected cases where people even received something of great monetary value, but because the leader hadn't put any thought into it, hadn't considered the individual who was being recognized, the effect was the opposite of what was intended. It didn't inspire the person to do his best; rather, it convinced him that the leader really didn't know him and didn't really care about him. The leader was doing it because she learned somewhere that what leaders were supposed to do was encourage others.

Before recognizing someone, then, the best leaders get to know people personally. They learn about their likes and dislikes, their needs and interests. They observe them in their own settings. Then, when it comes time to recognize a particular person, they know a way to make it special, meaningful, and memorable.

Tell the Story

Storytelling is one of the oldest ways in the world to convey the values and ideals shared by a community. Before the written word, stories were the means for passing along the important lessons of life. We know how important they are in teaching children, but sometimes we forget how important they are to adults. In fact, research tells us that stories have more of an impact on whether businesspeople believe information than do straight data.[4] Venture capitalists (some of the most numbers-driven people on the planet) always talk about how important "the story" is when taking a company public and selling the initial public offering to Wall Street.

The story is just as crucial to encouraging the heart. But why tell the story? Why not just bring Kelly up, give him the check and public recognition, and then have him sit down? Why take the time to reenact what was done? What difference does it make?

Well, let's see. Here's how the ceremony might have gone without the story.

> "We've got another Super Person award today," Melohn announces. "Let's see, who won it? Uh, Kelly. Kelly won it. Come on up here, Kelly."
>
> Everyone watches passively as Kelly walks up to the front of the room. Melohn hands Kelly the monthly Super Person plaque and a check for fifty dollars.
>
> "Thank you, Kelly," Melohn says matter-of-factly. "You really showed us what it means to implement our policy of zero defects."
>
> "Remember," he continues, turning emotionlessly to the group, "no rejects, no rejects, no rejects! That's why we're here, gang."

Yawn. Not only is this boring, but everyone, including Kelly, will forget about it the instant it's over. There's absolutely nothing in this rendering that's memorable.

The intention of stories is not just to entertain. Oh, they're intended to do that for sure. But they're also intended to teach. The influential educator and philosopher Marshall McLuhan is reported to have said, "Those who think there's a difference between education and entertainment don't know the first thing about either one."

Good stories move us. They touch us, they teach us, and they cause us to remember. They enable the listener to put the behavior in a real context and understand what has to be done in that context to live up to expectations. By telling the story in detail, Melohn was illustrating what everyone, not just Kelly, could do to live by the standard of no rejects. In effect, he was saying, "Whenever you encounter a situation like this, do as Kelly did. Knowing that we value zero rejects around here, Kelly didn't want to waste even one part. So he thought about what he could do to live up to that standard. You can do the same in your job." Melohn wanted people who faced similar opportunities to say to themselves, "Well, when Kelly was faced with that problem, he took personal initiative to find a solution. Now, let me see what I can do."

Melohn could have said all that didactically, but he didn't. He just told the story. Not only did he tell the story, he actually got Kelly to reenact a portion of it, much like a skilled director on the set of a movie. The story captures our attention and excites and entertains us. Even while capturing our attention, the narration of what happened provides a behavioral map that people can easily store in their minds. We get the message, and we remember it far longer than if he gave us a lecture on total quality management.

Besides giving us context, good stories do another thing for us. They enable us to see ourselves. We learn best from those we can most relate to—people most like ourselves. CEO stories might be good examples for other CEOs or to those who aspire to that job, but they're not very good examples for people on the shop floor. It's not that CEOs can't be good examples, but people can't relate to someone who's not like them. Besides, there's only one CEO per organization, while there are a lot of folks in other roles. We need to hear stories about those other folks if we're going to learn how to behave.

Although the live example is the most powerful of ways to publicize what people do to exemplify values, there are other media available to leaders. Newsletters, annual reports, advertisements, even voice mail and e-mail can be used to encourage the heart and teach positive stories about what people do to exemplify our values. These media sure are a lot more powerful than posting our values on a wall somewhere.

CELEBRATE TOGETHER

Melohn could have called Kelly into his office and privately thanked him. However, far more is achieved by recognizing him in public. There's no point in simply telling the story in private; Kelly already knows what he did. The story is more for the benefit of others. It's how groups learn lessons. The public ceremony provides a setting for broadcasting the message to a much wider audience.

Many of us are reluctant to recognize people in public situations like this, perhaps fearing that it might cause jealousy or resentment. But if the leader is genuine, this doesn't happen. Teresa Bettencourt, a production worker at NATD, once remarked about the Super Person award: "You feel great. You really go home and say, 'Hey, I must be pretty good. I got to be Super Person this time.' You would think that there would be some people who would say, 'How come she got it and I didn't?' But no. Everybody is happy when somebody gets it."[5]

Most of us want others to know about our achievements, and the public ceremony does that, sparing us the need to go around bragging about ourselves. The experience of leaders who recognize others publicly is that it rarely causes hard feelings, and in most cases it helps bring people closer.

Imagine for a moment that Melohn does call Kelly into his office and gives the award privately. If Melohn believes that doing so publicly will create jealousy among the workers, the scene might go something like this:

> "Kelly, I heard that you did something to help our efforts to achieve our goal of no rejects. To thank you for your initiative, here's a check for fifty dollars."
>
> "Thanks," says Kelly. They shake hands, and as Kelly walks out the door, Melohn stops him and says, "One more thing. Please don't tell anyone else you got this. It might cause some friction on the floor, and we don't want that."

Kelly may have fifty extra bucks in his pocket, but he's also got a burden. He can't tell anyone. He can't be proud of himself and what he's done. He can't receive the high-fives and the "Way to go, Kelly!" congratulations because he can't say anything. The opportunity has also been lost to teach a valuable lesson by example. This is no way to create an atmosphere of encouragement. Just the opposite.

We see in Melohn and Kelly's story that ceremonies of this kind are hardly frills or luxuries that we can dispense with in the workaday world. Today's leaders are discovering that encouraging the heart through public events builds trust and strengthens relationships in the workplace. By lifting the spirits of people in this way, we heighten awareness of organization expectations and humanize the values and standards such that we motivate at a deep and enduring level. But even more, public recognition serves as a valuable educational mechanism demonstrating company values and encouraging others to duplicate the actions that they see rewarded.

Public ceremonies serve another powerful purpose. They bring people closer together. As we move to a more virtual world, where communication is by voice mail, e-mail, cell phone, videoconference, and pager, it's becoming ever more difficult for people to find opportunities to be together. We are

social animals, and we need each other. Those who are fortunate enough to have lots of social support are healthier human
beings than those who have little. Social support is absolutely
essential to our well-being and to our productivity. Celebrating
together is one way we can get this essential support.

Set the Example

You can't delegate encouraging the heart. Every leader in the
organization—every person, in fact—has to take the initiative
to recognize individual contributions, celebrate team accomplishments, and create an atmosphere of confidence and support. It's not something we should wait around for others to do.
"Do unto others as you would have them do unto you" clearly
applies here. The foundation of leadership, as we have already
said, is credibility. What is credibility behaviorally? Over and
over again, people tell us credibility is "doing what you say you
will do." Leaders set the example for others. They practice what
they preach. If you want others to encourage the heart, you
start by modeling it yourself.

That's certainly what Melohn did. He set high standards.
He believed in others. He invested his attention in others
through CBWA. He personalized the recognition. He told the
stories. He celebrated with others. He set the example. You
can't expect others in the organization to follow your lead if
you don't take the first step yourself.

Personal involvement is also a genuine expression of caring. It helps foster trust and partnership. Leadership cannot be
exercised from a distance. Leadership is a relationship, and relationships are formed only when people come into contact with
each other.

Melohn also put his money where his mouth is in other
ways. He made the recognition tangible by presenting Kelly

with a check for fifty dollars and putting Kelly's name on a plaque that went on public display. By themselves, the check and plaque didn't significantly contribute to sustaining the value of the action in people's minds. However, when combined with all the rest, these tangible rewards helped memorialize the event. The money, though certainly not a fortune, confirmed that the organization took the action seriously and was willing to share some of its gain with Kelly. The plaque offered a constant reminder to everyone that the organization values people who demonstrate the behaviors consistent with the values and standards.

o   o   o

P.S.: Let's not confuse Melohn's positive role modeling as an example of someone who's "soft." Zero defects is a very tough standard. CBWA is a demanding practice. Effective communication, if you're serious about it, requires dedication and self-control. Public displays of emotion are not for the fainthearted. It's become well known that people are more frightened of public speaking than they are of dying. Supporting others, particularly in times of great change, can be physically and emotionally draining.

It may seem easy, but we have learned that encouraging the heart is one of the two most difficult of the five practices of exemplary leadership. We've found that it's much easier for leaders to challenge the process, for example, than it is for them to encourage the heart. There's still a lot leaders have to learn.

We begin to see from all this that the seven essentials of encouraging the heart are core leadership skills. They are not just about showing people they can win for the sake of making them feel good. This is a curiously serious business. When striving to raise quality, recover from disaster, start up a new service, or make dramatic change of any kind, leaders must make sure that people experience in their hearts that what they do matters.

o   o   o

James M. Kouzes is chairman emeritus of the Tom Peters Company, executive fellow in the Center for Innovation and Entrepreneurship at the Leavey School of Business, Santa Clara University, and a leadership speaker.

Barry Z. Posner is dean and professor at the Leavey School of Business, Santa Clara University. He is also a speaker and executive development program leader.

Chapter Nineteen

Motivating and Satisfying Excellent Individuals

Edward E. Lawler III

The organizational behavior research on how reward systems affect individuals has focused on two topics: motivation and satisfaction. These two topics need to be well understood and effectively managed in order for a reward system to motivate excellent behavior and satisfy excellent employees. The literature is vast; thousands of studies have been done on employee motivation and employee satisfaction.[1] At the risk of oversimplifying the vast and complex literature on these topics, I will briefly review what is known about rewards as motivators and what is known about the causes and consequences of satisfaction with rewards.

PAY FOR PERFORMANCE

In an increasingly competitive and capitalistic world, few disagree that individuals who contribute more should receive greater rewards. There is also universal recognition that motivation is critical to organizational effectiveness and nearly universal recognition that an effective pay-for-performance system can increase motivation.

It is, of course, one thing to say that pay for performance is a great idea; it is another to develop an effective pay-for-performance system. The devil is in the details—the details of the design and management of the delivery system. It is probably an understatement to say that pay-for-performance systems are complex to design and that they often have difficulty living up to the hopes and expectations of the employees who are paid by them and the organizations that create them.

For the past century, work organizations have primarily used two approaches to paying for individual performance. The first is strongly associated with factory work and scientific management and flourished during the 1920s and 1930s. Often called *incentive pay* or *piecework pay*, it involves paying employees directly for the amount of work they produce. Engineers study jobs and determine what an employee should be paid for various steps in the manufacturing process. Employees are then told that they will be paid a fixed amount of money each time they complete a particular operation. Incentive pay is also a common way to pay salespeople. They are paid a predetermined amount of money for each product or service they sell.

The incentive-pay approach to paying for performance has produced an enormous research literature that details its advantages and disadvantages.[2] There is little question that it typically increases the amount of rewarded work that an employee does; there is also little question, however, that the systems are difficult to design, maintain, and manage. Over time, they often collapse from their own bureaucratic weight or are sabotaged by clever workers who figure out ways to beat the system.

The second major approach to paying for performance is merit pay—the "standard" approach to paying for performance in most of the developed world (Japan was one of the last hold-outs, but in the 1990s, many major Japanese firms, including Toyota and Honda, adopted it). Unlike incentive pay, which peaked in popularity in the first half of the twentieth century, merit pay continues to be popular.[3] Also unlike incentive pay, it typically covers most of the employees in an organization, except perhaps those in nonmanagement positions and those who are covered by incentive pay. It typically involves employees' getting an increase in their pay as a result of a subjective performance rating by their boss. The pay raises become an annuity for the employees who receive them because their regular pay is permanently increased.

Like incentive pay, merit pay has been the subject of a considerable amount of research.[4] The results suggest that merit pay does a poor job of relating pay to performance and, as a result, does a poor job of motivating employees. Its faults, which I will discuss in more detail later, typically include poor performance measures and relatively small rewards for performance.

At this point, it may seem appropriate to conclude that pay for performance is a great idea that cannot be effectively implemented and therefore cannot be an effective motivator of performance. This is just what has been concluded by some critics of the idea.

Perhaps the most visible and vocal critic for a number of years was W. Edwards Deming, the world-renowned expert on total quality management.[5] Deming spoke strongly against individual pay for performance and management by objectives. He correctly pointed out that they often produce dysfunctional competition among employees and are bureaucratic and administrative nightmares. He strongly emphasized the importance of eliminating merit ratings and the "evils" associated with them. Interestingly, my research shows that even companies that adopt total quality management on a wide scale still maintain pay-for-performance systems.[6] Apparently, either hope springs eternal when it comes to pay for performance, or managers simply don't believe their systems are as dysfunctional as Deming thinks they are.

A second group advocating the elimination of pay for performance focuses on the research literature concerned with motivation, in particular on findings concerned with intrinsic motivation—the type of motivation that comes from the pleasure of performing a task.[7] Research in this field suggests that pay for performance can cause people to stop finding intrinsic pleasure from doing work, and as a result, cause employees to do things only when they are paid for doing them.[8] Therefore, they suggest concentrating on creating work that is challenging and motivating and not worrying about using money as a motivator of performance. They are particularly critical of the types of piecework incentive plans that were popular in the 1930s and 1940s. They also reject the theorizing of behavioral psychologist B. F. Skinner, who emphasized reinforcing individual behaviors in order to get people to perform in a particular way.

Pay as a Motivator

I agree with many of the criticisms of merit pay that Deming makes. The problems with it are well documented, and he is not the first person to criticize merit-pay systems. I also agree with many of the intrinsic motivation theorists' arguments that intrinsic motivation can be an important driver of behavior and that extrinsic rewards such as pay should not interfere with it. But I do not agree that the best route to organizational effectiveness is through abandoning pay for performance. Rather, I believe the best route is through developing pay-for-performance systems that fit modern organization designs and business strategies. Given the potential power of pay to motivate performance, the best solution is not to eliminate pay as a motivator, thereby losing an important driver of performance, but to get it to motivate the right behavior.

Unfortunately, critics such as Deming and the advocates of intrinsic motivation do not provide viable alternatives to the traditional pay-for-performance approaches; they only provide compelling criticisms of them. Deming, for example, suggests "paying everyone fairly," instead of paying for performance. This is obviously not an adequate alternative to pay for performance because, among other things, in many societies pay is deemed fair only when different amounts are paid to workers who make different contributions. Deming also fails to acknowledge that motivation can be created by effective pay-for-performance systems. Ironically, evidence to support the argument that pay can be a motivator is embedded in his criticisms of existing pay-for-performance systems. If pay were not a motivator, it could never cause the many dysfunctional behaviors that he and others ascribe to it.

The intrinsic motivation advocates, for their part, also fail to provide an adequate alternative to pay for performance. They talk about the importance of intrinsic rewards and how they can be powerful drivers of performance. So far so good. The research evidence leaves little doubt that intrinsic rewards can be important motivators. What the advocates of intrinsic motivation do not recognize is that in most cases, intrinsic rewards are not sufficient in and of themselves to motivate all the behaviors that are needed to make most organizations successful. In the absence of pay-for-performance systems, it is hard to imagine, for example, how an organization can motivate people to work effectively on tasks such as chicken processing or making cold sales calls for telephone services and credit cards. Furthermore, they fail to recognize that intrinsic rewards sometimes motivate the wrong behaviors. Unfortunately, what is fun and interesting is not always what is best from an organizational effectiveness point of view.

Intrinsic motivation theorists also do not deal with the issue of fairly distributing the profits and value that corporations create as a result of the efforts of the individuals who have invested their human capital. In order to have a fair and just organization and a fair and just society, there needs to be a division of the profit that is made from the collective efforts of organization members.

Perhaps the most compelling argument for creating pay-for-performance systems rests on the fact that money is a unique commodity. It is relatively easily distributed, is valued by most individuals, can be given in a wide variety of forms, and exists in every organized society. Furthermore, it is something that everyone expects to get when they work for a business organization. Indeed, business organizations cannot operate without distributing money to their employees. This distribution does not have to be based completely or even partially on performance or, for that matter, on the value of human capital, but the research evidence suggests that distributing at least part of it based on performance contributes to organizational effectiveness. Specifically, when pay is based on performance, it is seen as fair and motivating.

Pay for performance is sometimes presented as a silver bullet that can be easily shot and can yield large improvements in performance. As my discussion so far clearly indicates, this is a naive view. Nevertheless, it is true that pay for performance can have a large, positive impact on organizational performance.

Creating an effective reward system takes a substantial understanding of the kind of impact that pay can have on employee behavior and on the business strategy of an organization, its structure, its information systems, and its performance. Thus, it is important to look at how rewards affect individual motivation and behavior.

MOTIVATION AND REWARDS

Reward Importance

Organizations can directly give a variety of rewards such as recognition, fringe benefits, cash, titles, and a host of other items. Indeed, a best-selling book in the 1990s was *A Thousand and One Ways to Reward Employees*. The rewards offered by corporations today are truly diverse. Private rodeos with mechanical bulls, fly fishing on western ranches, flying in a fighter plane, river rafting, and a lifetime supply of Ben and Jerry's ice cream are all rewards that have been given by corporations. The key questions about any of them are, How great is their appeal? and Are they valued more than their cost?

The starting point for most theories of motivation is the concept of reward importance. The argument is that to be a motivator, a reward needs to be important to the person receiving it. The importance of a specific reward, in turn, is said to depend on at least two major determinants: (1) how much the individual values the particular type of reward being offered and (2) how much of the reward is being offered. The more an individual values the type of reward and the more of it that is offered, the more motivation potential there is in the reward.

One behavioral example of the importance of reward size can be observed by anyone who lives in an area that has a lottery with varying sizes of payouts. As the size of the prize goes up, the number of participants playing the lottery increases dramatically. A $100 million payoff attracts many more players than a $1 million payoff. People will stand in line for hours to buy a ticket when the payoff is large. In the case of a lottery, the probability of winning is extremely low and gets even lower as more people play. Nevertheless, when the reward is big enough, individuals will endure quite a bit just to play.

A common question that managers ask me is, How much money has to be offered in order for it to be important enough to motivate behavior? Unfortunately, there is no precise research-based answer to this.[9] Generally, the amount needed to achieve a motivating level of importance is best thought of as a percentage of the amount somebody already has. Thus, in the case of salaries, in order to understand how important a $500 bonus will be to a group of employees, it is necessary to take their salaries into account. If $500 represents less than 1 percent of their annual salary, it will probably not be important enough to influence motivation. But if it is 5 percent or greater, it may well be important enough.

I feel some anxiety about mentioning the 5 percent figure, because it may be taken as a minimum amount that will automatically motivate people. Unfortunately, the situation is not that clear-cut. In most cases, 5 percent probably is enough to be an important reward to the typical individual, but, depending on how strongly an organization wants to influence motivation and on the needs of the individual, 10, 15, or 20 percent or more may be needed.

To make the importance of rewards a bit more complex, it is also true that small amounts of money can sometimes be important, particularly when the money is given in a way that involves recognition, goal achievement, and status. Just as small amounts of money can be a positive reward, and therefore a motivator, so can other forms of recognition. For example, employees can sometimes be motivated by the opportunity to become the employee of the month, to get a letter of commendation from their manager, or to receive a simple "thank you" from their supervisor.

Before it merged with BankAmerica to form the new Bank of America, NationsBank gave a reward that was highly prized by its employees. NationsBank's corporate culture dripped with military metaphors; thus, it was not too surprising that its major recognition reward was a crystal hand grenade modeled after a real one that the CEO kept on his desk. One of many cultural mismatches between NationsBank and BankAmerica involved this type of reward. The San Francisco–based BankAmerica executives saw the crystal grenade as a joke and characteristic of the overly autocratic, top-down culture of NationsBank. Nevertheless, it was an important reward in NationsBank and therefore worked as a motivator there.

The crystal hand grenade, like many other symbolically important rewards, had a series of identifiable characteristics associated with it. A brief review of those will highlight what must happen to make nonfinancially significant rewards important:

○ *The rewards are public.* Because symbolic rewards rely heavily on recognition for their value, it is particularly important that they be public. This can happen as a result of the way they are given and through publicity that is associated with their reception. Furthermore, they can be visibly in the possession of the recipient. In the case of the crystal hand grenade, for example, the winners proudly placed them on their desk.

○ *The rewards are given infrequently.* Symbolic rewards tend to lose their value if they are given too frequently; their recognition value and significance tend to decrease. Instead of being special rewards that denote status, they become entitlements and everyday occurrences.

○ *The reward process is credible.* The selection of recipients for symbolic rewards must be done by a highly credible process. It is particularly important that it be done by respected individuals who have good information about the performance and accomplishments of potential winners.

○ *The rewards are associated with winners.* Symbolic rewards gain their importance and their status in part by who has received them in the past. It is crucial that winners (particularly early winners) have high status and be well respected in the organization. Without this, symbolic rewards can become rewards that no one wants to be associated with.

○ *The rewards are meaningful in the culture.* The nature of the reward can sometimes make a difference. Picking the right artifact or symbol can provide a tremendous boost to the visibility and meaningfulness of the reward. The crystal hand grenade is a good example; it worked in the culture of NationsBank because it was tied to a respected CEO. As became clear when NationsBank merged with BankAmerica, it is not a reward that works everywhere. Other companies give similar types of idiosyncratic and symbolic rewards that work because they fit a particular historical event in the company or a characteristic of the company's leader.

The nature and amount of the reward are only part of the equation that determines how important a reward will be to a particular person. Also important are the person's needs and desires. Much of the early research on motivation focused on determining and influencing individuals' needs. This research establishes that most people have the same basic needs. Maslow did a reasonably good job of identifying them when he put forth his theory, arguing that people have certain physiological survival needs, as well as needs for social interaction, respect from others, self-esteem, and personal growth and development. He also made the point, as have many other need theorists, that there are tremendous individual differences in need strength. This, of course, is what leads individuals to attach different degrees of importance to rewards such as money and recognition from a supervisor.

A number of factors influence people's needs and desires. Maslow made the point that unless the basic physiological needs for security, food, and water are satisfied, the higher-order needs (growth, esteem, self-actualization) are not likely to come into play. This point has been generally accepted in the field of psychology as valid. Beyond this point, a number of factors seem to help determine the importance of needs. The cultural and environmental conditioning that individuals experience is clearly one important determinant; age and maturity also seem to be factors. Finally, as needs become satisfied, they tend to become less important. For example, people seem to need only so much food, water, and social interaction.

A whole industry has grown up around the study of the importance that people place on different kinds of rewards. Visible products of this industry include regular reports on how generations differ in what they value. It may well be that members of Generation X are somewhat different from those of other generations—they did grow up in a world very different from the one my generation experienced—but the differences are most likely small. Like any other generation, the most significant point about this one is likely to turn out to be the differences among the members of the generation rather than the differences between this and other generations.

There is also a constant stream of studies on what the latest research has shown about how important different rewards are to employees. Pay, career, family time, interesting work, and having a good boss are among the factors that researchers frequently argue are the most important. Most of this research is of poor methodological quality and shouldn't be taken seriously. Often the major reason that studies obtain different results is that the questions they ask are worded differently. For example, studies that ask about the importance of fair pay often find pay rated as one of the more important, if not the most important, feature of jobs. However, the results of studies that ask about the importance of getting rich or having high pay often show the importance of pay to be less than the importance of career opportunities and the challenge that a job offers. All I can do here is issue a blanket warning: be very suspicious of any study that claims to report on what "employees really want from their jobs," particularly those arguing that one thing is much more important than others.

Perhaps the best general conclusion that can be reached about the importance of needs is that the needs of individuals differ substantially—so much so that when it comes to rewards, an organization that wishes to motivate its members needs to proactively take individual differences into account, particularly when the workforce is diverse and global and when different kinds of employment relationships exist within the organization.

In many respects, it would be easier to deal with employees if they could say accurately what they value. Many attitude surveys that I have seen distributed in organizations try to tap into individual differences in need strength by asking employees what they value. Unfortunately, the accuracy of self-report data about reward importance is highly questionable. For a variety of reasons, it is difficult for most people to state what is most important to them. First, they may not know themselves well enough to respond to the question effectively. Second, in some cases, social desirability and what seems to be appropriate can prevent people from reporting their feelings accurately. This is particularly true in the case of money. In many societies, it simply isn't good impression management to say, "I work for money"; as a result, individuals sometimes understate its importance.

CEOs and other senior executives are often the most adamant about the fact that money is not a powerful motivator for them. They go on to add that they deserve to be paid a large amount because of their tremendous contributions but that the amount they earn is not that important to them. At first blush, this argument makes a lot of sense, particularly given how much they make. But something must account for the tremendous increase in CEO compensation over the past decades in the United States. Somebody seems to be working awfully hard on increasing the amount of CEO compensation. Pay levels don't just double or triple or quadruple without some effort being put into it.

Based on what I have seen in a number of corporations, CEOs share at least part of the blame (or credit) for the fact that their compensation has increased so dramatically. They are often very tough negotiators when it comes to dealing with corporate boards. Particularly when they are hired from the outside, they often make extremely high compensation demands and get boards to meet their demands. CEOs are also skillful at selecting compensation consulting firms that will support their claims for high pay by effectively lobbying boards. In short, CEOs seem to put a lot of effort into being sure they are well compensated. On the surface, this suggests that the amount of money they make is important to them, even though without any special effort, most could make more money in a year than most people make in a lifetime.

The effort that CEOs put into determining their compensation leads us to ask why they do it. Perhaps the best explanation concerns their need to achieve and to receive recognition for their achievements. CEOs are highly competitive, achievement-oriented individuals, and their compensation is a clear, objective, and highly visible measure of their level of achievement.

Given that people are not good reporters of the importance they give to money, how can reward preferences be determined? Often the best way is to offer individuals a choice and see what they choose. This should begin with the hiring process, when by offering a particular package of rewards to potential employees, organizations can help determine the kinds of needs their employees will have. People often choose to join an organization based on whether it offers the rewards they value. Once individuals join an organization, giving them opportunities to choose among rewards is another way to understand what they value most. Once this is established, the most valued rewards can be used to motivate their performance.

In several respects, the difficulty of knowing what individuals desire argues for using financial rewards as motivators.

Although money may not be the most important reward for some, it usually is important to most. Money has a certain universality about it because purchasing power and status are attached to it in every society. Money is also easily quantified into and allocated in varying amounts.

Money can be converted into other commodities such as the clocks, vacations, and the many other items that some companies give instead of money. However, before giving noncash rewards, companies should explore whether in fact they are good purchases, that is, whether their cost is more or less than the value that recipients attach to the dollars used to purchase them. Clearly, if an item is not more valued than the dollars, it doesn't make sense to convert the dollars into the item. The first key to a motivating reward system is to use only rewards that are valued.

Expectations and Motivation

Expectancy theory emphasizes that individuals act in ways they believe will lead to rewards they value.[10] Expectancy theory argues that individuals are mostly rational decision makers who think about the consequences of their actions and act in their own best interests. The theory doesn't deny that individuals sometimes have misperceptions about reality, make mistakes in their estimates of the likelihood that things will happen, or badly misread the realities of situations. It does argue that they try to deal rationally with the world as they see it and to direct their behavior in ways that will meet their needs. In that sense, it views people as proactive, future oriented, and motivated to behave in a particular way when they feel there is a good chance that the behavior will lead to valued rewards.

Part of the reason expectancy theory is so popular is that it is useful for understanding how to motivate individuals in most aspects of their lives. This is particularly true with respect to their work lives. Simply stated, expectancy theory suggests that the rewards organizations give out should be tied to individuals behaving in ways that support the organization's basic business strategy and performance needs. In essence, it says that pay for performance is a viable motivator if performance can be measured and if valued amounts of pay can be tied to performance.

The connection between performance and rewards is often called the line of sight. Perhaps a better term would be *line of influence* because it refers to the fact that, in order to be motivated in an organizational setting, people must see how their behavior influences a performance measure that, in turn, drives the allocation of a reward. Expectancy theory argues that if valued rewards are clearly seen as being tied to a particular performance behavior, the organization is likely to get more of that behavior. Unsaid but also important to remember is that if a particular behavior is not rewarded, the organization is likely to get less of that behavior.

Expectancy theory can also be used to explain people's job choices. It is particularly useful in this respect because it leads to a simple valid conclusion: people choose to join and remain members of organizations that offer them the best mix of the rewards they value. Thus, the issue of attracting and retaining employees becomes a relatively "simple" matter. Organizations need to offer a very attractive mix of rewards to people they particularly want to join their organization and to those they want to retain.

Expectancy theory clearly does not argue that individuals are motivated only by extrinsic rewards. To the contrary, it argues that individuals may reward themselves for certain kinds of performance because they feel they have accomplished something that is worthwhile, achieved a personal goal, learned a new skill, or were intellectually stimulated and excited. Thus, in the framework of expectancy theory, individuals can be motivated by both organizationally given rewards and intrinsic rewards they give to themselves. Furthermore, it does not see a cancellation or interference effect between the two kinds of rewards. Rather, it argues that the greatest amount of motivation is present when individuals are doing tasks that are intrinsically rewarding to them when they perform them well and that provide important financial and recognition rewards for performance.[11]

Expectancy theory places great emphasis on the importance of goals—an emphasis that is supported by the research on goal setting. Research evidence shows that when individuals commit themselves to a goal, they become highly motivated to achieve it because their self-esteem and sense of self-worth get tied to accomplishing that goal.[12] Of course, they may also be motivated to achieve a goal because a financial reward is tied to achieving it.

Goal difficulty is an issue that often comes up when goals are discussed; expectancy theory provides an interesting way of thinking about it. The theory argues that if goal difficulty gets too high, individuals may see a low probability of achieving the goal. This in turn will destroy the connection between their effort and the receipt of a reward. This doesn't necessarily mean that individuals will never try to achieve hard goals. It does suggest, however, that if they are going to be motivated to achieve hard goals, two conditions need to exist. First, the connection between achieving the goal and the reward needs to be clear. Second, the amount of reward, either intrinsic or extrinsic, that is associated with goal accomplishment needs to be large. When there is a low probability of achieving a goal or the rewards are small, it is almost certain that individuals will not put forth the effort to try to achieve the goal.

Goal difficulty is an interesting issue with respect to the combination of extrinsic and intrinsic rewards. Some evidence from the research on the desire to achieve suggests that as goal difficulty rises, people feel a greater sense of accomplishment and achievement when they actually reach a goal. Thus, under certain conditions, individuals may be more motivated to achieve difficult than easy goals, even though the line of sight between trying and achieving the goal is weak. In essence, what happens is that the intrinsic rewards associated with accomplishing something significant and difficult become so large that individuals are willing to try to achieve difficult goals, even though the probability of accomplishing them may be relatively low. This is like the lottery example, except that in this case, the rewards are intrinsic.

To summarize, motivation is a function of reward importance and the degree to which rewards are tied to a particular kind of performance or behavior. The implication of this is that organizations can motivate individuals to perform in particular ways if they develop a line of sight between important rewards and performing in that way. The kinds of performance that can be motivated this way include learning new skills and abilities, developing new competencies, dealing courteously with customers, producing a certain number of products per hour, increasing sales volume—in short, any behavior that is measurable and therefore can be related to organizationally given rewards.

There is no reason to make a trade-off between designing interesting work and motivating through extrinsic rewards. Nor is there a reason to debate the relative importance of recognition rewards versus financial rewards, and so on. Any reward can be a motivator if it is important. The key in any particular work situation is to identify what rewards are important to the employees involved and emphasize them in a reward-for-performance system.

Job Satisfaction

One of the long-standing myths in the field of management is that job satisfaction is an important determinant of motivation and performance. As expectancy theory points out, it is anticipated satisfaction rather than present satisfaction that drives motivation because anticipated satisfaction is what reward importance is all about. Satisfaction comes about as a result of individuals' receiving valued rewards and feeling good about it. Thus, satisfaction is best thought of as being determined by an individual's reward level. Indeed, performance may indirectly cause satisfaction if it causes rewards that, in turn, cause satisfaction.

Causes of Satisfaction

Satisfaction is strongly influenced by the amount of reward an individual receives but is determined by more than simply the quantity of the reward. Individuals compare the amount of reward they receive with a standard. When the reward level meets that standard, they are satisfied; when it falls short, they are dissatisfied. On those few occasions when it exceeds the standard, they feel guilty or overrewarded.

The research evidence suggests that feelings of being overrewarded tend not to last long.[13] Individuals usually quickly rationalize the situation they are in and decide that they are, in fact, fairly paid or even underpaid. On rare occasions, they actually reduce their reward level by declining rewards or giving them away. The same is not true when individuals feel under-rewarded. In this condition, they tend to try to obtain additional rewards in order to improve their situation, thus reducing their uncomfortable feelings of dissatisfaction.

The key to understanding how satisfied individuals will be with a particular reward level lies in understanding how they set the standard against which they compare reward amounts. The research literature on this topic suggests that they set their standard by looking at what others who are similar to them receive.[14] They then use what "similar others" receive as the basis for comparison.

What do individuals consider in choosing with whom to compare their rewards? The answer seems to be a variety of things, including performance, training, and background; in short, it can be any characteristic they think is important. They are particularly likely to think that those attributes of themselves that are particularly outstanding should be the basis on which they are rewarded. For example, if they are well educated, they think education should be very important in determining the amount of their rewards, and they compare themselves to individuals who are well educated. If they perceive themselves to be high performers, as most people do, they tend to compare their pay with the pay of "other" high performers.

Reward comparison choices are sometimes upsetting to those responsible for reward allocation, because individuals tend to pick reward comparisons that make their own reward levels look low. For example, if they are highly paid compared to others in their own organization, they may look at other organizations for their comparisons in order to find individuals who are paid more. They also tend to rate their own performance very highly and, as a result, to compare their rewards with those of the best performers in their organization and indeed in other organizations as well.

The tendency of individuals to make remote connections in establishing what their reward level should be is clearly exemplified by CEOs who sometimes compare their reward levels to those of star athletes and entertainers. Time and time again, I have heard CEOs and senior executives say, "Well, I'm worth at least as much as Michael Jordan or Michael Jackson." This is an apples and oranges comparison, to say the least. Interestingly enough, they don't compare their pay with that of Michael Jordan's coach or with that of the president of the Chicago Bulls. Similarly, they don't compare their pay with that of Michael Jackson's business manager. In many respects, these would be much better comparisons because these lower-paid individuals are doing administrative, leadership, and coaching activities that are more similar to what CEOs do than what Jordan and Jackson do. The reason they make their comparisons to Jordan and Jackson is, of course, not because of the similarity of their work or skills but because of their very high rates of compensation.

One final point: although the pay comparison processes that individuals go through are oriented toward producing a high standard, they typically are not completely irrational. Production workers typically do not compare themselves with CEOs, and sales representatives typically do not compare themselves with vice presidents of human resources. Thus, it is possible to find sales representatives and production workers who are just as satisfied with their rewards as are CEOs and vice presidents of human resources, even though they are paid much less.

In addition to focusing on the amount of reward, individuals also focus on how rewards are distributed. The perceived fairness of the method of distribution can influence satisfaction.[15] It is difficult to state exactly what will lead to a perception on the part of employees that "distributional or procedural justice" exists, but some factors usually contribute positively to perceptions of fairness and satisfaction.

Openness about the decision process is one way to build trust and a perception of a fair process. A second key is having the "right" individuals involved in the decision process—in this case, those who are trusted because they have integrity, as well as valid information on which to make reward distribution decisions. Third, reward distribution is likely to be seen as fair when clearly stated criteria are used for the distribution. Fourth, individuals are more likely to feel fairly treated when they have a chance to participate in the decision process. Finally, perceptions of fairness are more likely when an appeal process exists that allows individuals to safely challenge decision making that they feel is unfair, uninformed, or unreasonable.

It is precisely because individuals often choose very high comparisons when they set their reward standard, and because they expect procedural justice, that pay satisfaction is often low in organizations. In many attitude surveys that I have done and seen, pay is an area of great—indeed, often the greatest—employee dissatisfaction. The level of pay satisfaction typically does vary from company to company, and it is related to how well organizations pay relative to the external marker.

When interpreting pay dissatisfaction survey data, it is important and valid to focus on changes in pay satisfaction over time and to compare satisfaction scores for different parts of an organization and for different organizations. The time to be concerned is when my satisfaction drops and when it is low compared to other organizations. Comparing pay satisfaction with satisfaction in other work areas such as job security and supervision often leads to the false conclusion that pay is a more important problem in an organization than it actually is. This occurs because pay dissatisfaction is high even when the best pay practices are used and pay is high.

Typically, 50 percent or more of all employees in an organization report dissatisfaction with their pay. Given the types of comparisons they make, this is probably inevitable. Even when pay is high, employees can always find comparisons that make their pay look lower than it should be. If they can't find these comparisons within their organization, they can always look outside and find people who seem to be contributing less and have less value but are making more.

It is often useful to compare the pay satisfaction of high performers with that of low performers and to track the satisfaction of those who are key sources of the organization's core competencies and organizational capabilities. These comparisons are important in determining how well an organization is managing its key human capital and can give an organization an early warning that it is about to lose key human capital, since pay dissatisfaction is an important cause of turnover.

Most theoretical approaches to job satisfaction make no definitive predictions about which facets of the job (for example, pay, supervision, or work) are the most important in determining overall job satisfaction. Instead, as is true with motivation theory, they argue that large individual differences exist and that, as a result, what is a satisfying job situation for one person may not be so for another. What is true is that over time, individuals tend to gravitate to work situations that meet their needs; as a result, their satisfaction often goes up over time. This point argues that it is futile to debate whether, for example, money, recognition, interesting work, or promotion opportunities is the most important determinant of employee satisfaction. For some, there is little doubt that money is the most important; for others the work itself is key. For still others, it is the social relationships or maybe the opportunity to learn new skills.

The implication of individual differences in reward importance is relatively straightforward. It is imperative that an organization employ individuals who are satisfied by the rewards that the organization has to offer. In short, just as is true with motivation, organizations need to put hiring and development processes in place that do a good job of matching individuals to the reward and work systems that exist in the organization. For example, it can be very expensive and foolish to try to motivate and satisfy with money a scientist who is driven by making an important discovery. Similarly, it is foolish to try to motivate and satisfy with interesting and challenging work a production line worker who cares only about off-the-job activities.

Satisfaction and Performance

Simply increasing job satisfaction is unlikely to have a positive effect on performance; rather, it may have a negative effect because, at least temporarily, people will cease to seek additional rewards. It is the anticipation of rewards and satisfaction that motivates, not being satisfied. However, the fact that satisfaction does not drive motivation and performance does not mean that it is unimportant.

Study after study has shown that job satisfaction is strongly related to individuals' membership behavior and organizational commitment, that is, their willingness to continue to work in a particular setting and, indeed, their willingness to show up for work on a daily basis.[16] This finding is predictable from expectancy theory.

What employees are indicating when they say they are not satisfied with their job is that they do not see positive consequences associated with coming to work and remaining part of an organization. Satisfaction with the current situation is the major determinant of an individual's anticipation of how satisfied he or she will be in the future. Thus, it is hardly surprising that dissatisfied employees typically begin to look elsewhere for employment and ultimately leave if they find a situation that offers a better mix of rewards. If they don't leave, they become disgruntled employees who seek to change the current situation by organizing and voting for a union, becoming an activist within the organization, filing lawsuits, and engaging in other actions that they think will improve their situation.

Even though pay satisfaction does not have a direct impact on the job performance of most individuals, it can have an important impact on organizational performance because of its effect on turnover and absenteeism. Turnover can be a particularly costly item for organizations. It is relatively inexpensive to replace unskilled labor, but knowledge workers and highly skilled employees can be very costly to replace. Estimates vary considerably, but a reasonable estimate is that replacing skilled employees can cost anywhere from the equivalent of six to twenty times their monthly salary. Costs rise as the level of complexity of the work the individual does rises and as the scarcity of their skills increases.

Job satisfaction can be particularly important in service organizations. In addition to its impact on turnover, which can disrupt effective customer service routines and capabilities, it also may affect customer retention in a second way. A significant amount of research has shown that people prefer to do business with organizations that have satisfied employees because the experience is more enjoyable.[17] Thus, although satisfaction does not directly affect the performance of individual employees, it does affect customer retention and therefore the long-term profitability and viability of the business. Because of this, retailers such as Sears, Neiman Marcus, and Nordstrom focus on having satisfied employees. They regularly measure employee satisfaction and evaluate store managers on the basis of how satisfied their employees are.[18]

Research on service organizations suggests that job satisfaction is particularly important in organizations that wish to develop a relationship with customers, that is, organizations wanting customers to feel a sense of commitment to a particular service provider and a certain amount of confidence in that provider. In service situations that are primarily transaction oriented, job satisfaction is much less important and may not be important at all. Apparently, customers going into 7-Elevens do not particularly want to make friends with the cashier; they simply want to be served by a person who quickly completes their transaction. The same applies to many fast food restaurants, as well as to toll takers, parking lot attendants, and a host of other transaction-oriented sales situations.

The implications of the research on satisfaction for attracting and retaining human capital are straightforward. If organizations want to attract and retain the best human capital, they have to create work environments that are satisfying and attractive to the investors of that capital—the people who have those skills. This is more easily said than done because the rewards that need to be offered may be costly. Furthermore, because of individual differences, there are likely to be many variations in what individuals want. Nonetheless, in order to attract and retain excellent employees, organizations have to give rewards that are at least equal to what other organizations are giving to people with similar skills and knowledge. Organizations must also distribute rewards internally in a way that is generally seen as fair and just. If they fail to do these two things, they will have high levels of dissatisfaction and will fail to attract and retain the best human capital. Thus, satisfaction is important, even though it is not a direct determinant of job performance.

Concluding Thoughts on Motivation and Satisfaction

Motivation and satisfaction are at the same time complicated and simple topic areas—complicated because of the enormous individual differences that exist and the complexity of human beings; they are simple in that there are some key truths that can be used to guide the design of effective reward systems. These are worth repeating here because they are fundamental:

- Rewards must be important to be motivators.
- Individuals differ in the importance they attach to rewards.
- Individuals are motivated to perform when they believe they can obtain rewards they value by performing well.
- Individuals are attracted to jobs and organizations that offer the rewards they value.
- Job satisfaction is determined by how the rewards individuals receive compare to what they feel they should receive and how the rewards are distributed.
- Satisfied employees are unlikely to quit and be absent.

o   o   o

Edward E. Lawler III is a professor and director of the Center for Effective Organizations at the University of Southern California's Marshall School of Business. He is also a consultant.

Chapter Twenty

How to Give Feedback

Harvey Robbins
Michael Finley

I worked for the firm for nineteen months, and no one ever said boo to me. There were times I wasn't sure if I was doing a good job or a bad one, but no one ever complained or suggested a better way to me. Then one day, I got a pink slip—unsigned, in the mail. It was the most cowardly thing I ever saw in my life."

One of the hardest tasks for new leaders is giving people feedback. "Giving people feedback" is a neutral description for something decidedly unneutral—telling people how they could be doing their jobs better. And because it is a loaded area, with a high potential for ticking people off and alienating them just when you need them to be "on your side," lots of leaders get confused and inept.

Why is giving feedback hard for us? Probably because people think it has to be done very cleverly—delicately—so as not to offend anyone. And most of us are not clever, so we despair. And procrastinate. And when push finally comes to shove and we sit down with the person in question, we criticize crappily.

How do we do that? Let us list the ways:

○ *We do it too formally.* We invite the other person in to the boss's office. We sit on opposite sides of a desk. We refer to reports for information, sometimes hiding behind the pages. Six-month evaluations may be good for record keeping, but a better way to keep people on point is to evaluate them every single day, with attention, instruction, availability, and acknowledgment of a job well done. Fix a problem informally, and it need never appear in someone's file.

○ *We wait too long.* "Harold, it's come to our attention you've been taking two-hour naps every afternoon since 1994." The time to step in and advise is early, before something becomes a bad habit, and before you become irritated with the behavior's deep-seatedness. Also, workers have every right to protest. They would have been happy to make the change earlier—if someone had only asked. Delaying puts an unnecessary black mark on their record.

○ *We keep it one-way.* Feedback is properly described as a loop. You tell them something, they tell you something, and so on. The process belongs to both of you. If it's just you informing a worker—much less, a teammate—that they have failed, doesn't that tell you something about the team?

○ *We apologize.* We mince about. There is no way to tell someone an unpleasant truth and come out of it more popular than you went in. The proper and honest thing to do is say it directly: "Mary Ann, I'm concerned about the quality of your follow-up work. Several times I've had customers complain, and I want to fix the problem right now, before it becomes a real problem." They may not like you more. They may emerge from the talk bruised and a little scared. But they will know what is expected of them. Clarity will help them survive, whereas friendly gobbledygook could lead them to destruction.

○ *We beat around the bush.* We say nineteen positive nice things in order to soften the blow of the twentieth item, which is negative. In all things, strive for clarity. A good meeting has a single purpose. "Jack, I want to talk to you about your absence last week."

○ *We don't think it's feedback unless it's negative.* We're not saying to camouflage the one negative observation behind nineteen compliments. But why is it we call workers in to see us only when we have bad news? Invite them in when you notice something great. What a simple message to communicate: we value your positive contributions, and we want to encourage you to keep trying.

○ *We go in with too much certainty.* "Dave, you've not been attentive in your work." Instead, try: "Dave, I'm concerned that you aren't giving your work your full attention. You make a lot of funny remarks at team meetings, but I'm not sure you're kicking in with the right amount of effort. Do you agree with that assessment?"

○ *We put it all on the other person.* Maybe Esther isn't meeting quota for reasons that Esther has little control over. Maybe you think Esther has been properly trained, but she hasn't. Maybe there's something you can do that will help Esther perform.

○ *We criticize, but we are vague about future action.* Feedback must be action oriented, or it is just blather. State a desired outcome, and slap a schedule on it. Then, if the teammate misses the outcome by the date agreed on, who can complain about the consequences?

If it helps, don't think of evaluation as a dreaded task, like handing out report cards. See it as part of a logical continuum. A leader's job, after all, is to communicate the mission. Usually you do that with the whole group. With feedback, you're doing the same thing with people on a one-to-one basis. Communicating the mission, with specific reference to performance—that's all feedback is.

So don't fear it. It's not your enemy. In fact, it's your quality check, to make sure everyone is clear on the leadership you've been providing. (For some ways to give feedback, see Exhibit 20.1.)

But we've run into three special categories of people who may require special consideration. We're going to use shorthand to label them: brats, jerks, and demons. These categories may sound flippant, but you will be glad you have them when you have to assess people you just can't accommodate on your team:

○ *Brats are people who just don't seem able to carry a grown adult's load.* They can be young, or they can be old. But they have a defect in their nature. Mature people have what is called an internal locus of control—they see themselves as primary actors in their lives and careers. Immature people have an external locus of control—they see themselves as spinning in a blender, the victims of forces beyond their control.

In the workplace, brats may be fair workers, but they are awful team members because they are hard-pressed to step forward with ideas and disinclined to take the risks associated with innovation. Big corporations have a history of taking ordinarily capable people and turning them into brats through policies and procedures that strip them of accountability. We call this the environment of entitlement—where workers can perform or gather wool, and they get paid either way.

EXHIBIT 20.1. **How to Give Information to People**

There are three ways to give information to people so it is real to them:

1. Verbally. (Tell them face to face.)

2. In writing. (Tell them on paper or via e-mail.)

3. Kinesthetically. (Let them learn by doing, as they like to work through the process.)

Which way is best? Depends. Try being bimodal (provide information two ways at once). Say, call them on the phone and follow up with an e-mail note, or vice versa.

Remember to give feedback based on the receiver's personality:

○ Doers wish to be leaders, to be in charge of something. They need the least direction, because they are already motivated by nature and expend great effort to achieve things. If someone is a Doer, feedback needs to be direct, specific, brief, and with new outcomes and expectations. Bullet points are good.

○ Creatives easily generate new ideas and fresh perspectives. Their great need is to get stuff out of themselves. With a Creative, you need to support your target's ability to generate ideas and provide lots of options for future outcomes.

○ Socials like working with other people. They derive the greatest satisfaction from communicating and relating to others. For a Social, you must make sure not to bruise that fragile ego. Be gentle and kind—but hold firm to expected outcomes.

○ Thinkers are gifted in reason and able to achieve deep understanding of issues and facts. For these people, the most important thing is to be right. For a Thinker, you need to have specific behaviors listed as examples, with lots of documentation.

Brattism in the news: A state-run university in the southwestern United States discovered that for the past eleven years, more than forty workers in the plant services department were working four days a week for five days' pay. This unwritten and unmeasured practice continued under four consecutive administrators, each one afraid to withdraw a valued perk. The cost in squandered productivity was staggering: an estimated $18 million of taxpayers' money. When the university ordered the practice discontinued, workers sued the university for breach of contract!

The correct response to brattism, whether it is innate to the individual or created by a pampering corporate culture, is—you saw it coming—to lower the boom on the brat. If your organization does not have a riot act, now is the time to draft one, and to read it loud and clearly to these people: swim or sink.

But be forewarned: many of these people won't get it even when you write it in the snow for them. Their feelings of helplessness, of being on the receiving end of everything, are too deeply ingrained. Sadly for them, they will have to learn to change the hard way, by finding a new job.

○ *Jerks are people who are unable to see the effect they have on others.* A more clinical way to describe them is "socially impoverished." Ordinarily, we would not lose sleep over jerks. But many jerks are very talented. Indeed, it seems to be their curse to have an imbalance of gifts: to be very good at nonpeople matters but astonishingly inept with people. They can be cruel, callous, stupid, or just monumentally insensitive. Famous jerks include Steve Jobs, Miles Davis, and Sharon Stone. But many more are jerks in relative anonymity.

A celebrated New York magazine editor agreed to create a new magazine with a $40 million start-up bankroll. But the publisher learned to his dismay that turnover at the Fifth Avenue headquarters was running 25 percent per month. The editor was too demanding, too critical, and too crazy for even ambitious journalists to be around for very long. The publisher's solution: retain the woman's glamour assets by promoting her to executive editor and putting her in charge of media appearances—with only indirect management of the magazine's content.

So the leader with a jerk on the team has a big problem: how to capture the brilliance without inhaling the exhaust. Forget sensitivity training. Jerks don't take well to it.

First, acknowledge the truth: that this person can't help behaving in a beastly fashion. Perhaps you can sit your jerk down for a heart-to-heart talk and go over the most egregious behavior and the ways it screws things up. But you are not going to be able to tame this rude, snorting creature and get anything else done.

Second, create a playpen. Jerks who are geniuses need their own space and a special relationship to the rest of the team. Some leaders draw a dotted line and set the jerk up as a resource to the rest—but a resource like a fire-axe, one you don't turn to except in dire emergencies. Or you can name the jerk to a one-person team, or even let the jerk work from home, phone in the genius, and save a parking space for someone else.

○ *Demons are outright sociopaths.* Brats and jerks you can work around. Demons, you can't. A demon is constitutionally unable to work with other people and is quite likely to endanger team projects.

Demons include people who have been brutalized into pathology; people who have abused themselves with addictions and obsessions until they can no longer function healthily; angry people who have a score to settle and don't mind settling it with you; and sadists, who enjoy inflicting pain and causing trouble.

Anoushka was the only child of a financial services entrepreneur in New Delhi. Her father wanted to bring her up in his company and started her out as assistant director of marketing and communications. She knew nothing about the business and wasn't interested in learning about it. Her focus was on intimidating workers and vendors. She was just plain mean. A special triumph for her was to have work done, and then make the contractor eat the costs. She thrived on this kind of behavior for four years until her reputation reached the nostrils of her father, who, sensing her poisonous impact on his business network, granted her every ambitious executive's dream—early retirement.

It doesn't matter if a demon is a genius. It doesn't matter if the demon has the manners of an angel. It doesn't matter if a demon has a recipe for cold fusion in a desk drawer. Demons are fatal news to whatever organization will have them. And once you have identified a person as being this toxic, your only choice is to scrub them totally out of your organization.

o   o   o

Harvey Robbins is a licensed psychologist, business consultant, and trainer specializing in the tensions and problems of people in the workplace.

Michael Finley is a prolific author and journalist whose work has appeared in hundreds of publications including *Paris Review, Harvard Business Review,* and *Rolling Stone.*

Chapter Twenty-One

Developmental Relationships

Cynthia D. McCauley
Christina A. Douglas

THE ROLE OF OTHER PEOPLE IN THE LEADER DEVELOPMENT PROCESS

When asked to reflect on the most important learning experiences in their careers, about a third of managers and executives will describe how they learned from other people (Douglas, 2003; McCall and Hollenbeck, 2002; McCall, Lombardo, and Morrison, 1988; Morrison, White, and Van Velsor, 1992). The "other person" was most likely a boss; but mentors, peers, and short-term interactions with others are also mentioned. In the Corporate Leadership Council's 2001 Leadership Survey of over eight thousand managers, leader development activities that were grounded in feedback and relationships (mentoring, executive coaching, and interaction with peers, for example) were rated as more effective for development than job experiences and education. About two-thirds of executives report having had at least one mentoring relationship in their career (Roche, 1979). Nine out of ten employees who receive mentoring report that it is an effective developmental tool (McShulskis, 1996).

Why are relationships experienced as important for leader development? Relationships can contain each of the elements essential for leadership development—assessment, challenge, and support. To better understand how relationships serve these functions, let us examine the various developmental roles that people in relationships play for one another. These roles are grouped by the major elements of the assessment-challenge-support (ACS) model in Table 21.1. Note that although each role represents just one aspect of a relationship, most developmental relationships are made up of multiple roles. At the end of this discussion are illustrations of how roles are combined to form different types of developmental relationships.

Assessment

Assessment, the formal and informal processes for generating and delivering data about an individual, is an important element of an effective development process. One key developmental role in assessment is that of feedback provider: a source of day-to-day, ongoing feedback on how a person is doing in seeking to learn new skills or perspectives. An in-depth feedback-intensive program or data from a 360-degree feedback instrument might provide the impetus for taking on particular development goals, but it is the continuous feedback that people receive as they work to achieve those goals that becomes critical.

TABLE 21.1. **Roles Played by Others in Developmental Relationships**

Element	Role	Function
Assessment	Feedback provider	Ongoing feedback as person works to learn and improve
	Sounding board	Evaluation of strategies before they are implemented
	Comparison point	Standards for evaluating own level of skill or performance
	Feedback interpreter	Assistance in integrating or making sense of feedback from others
Challenge	Dialogue partner	Perspectives or points of view different from own
	Assignment broker	Access to challenging assignments (new jobs or additions to current one)
	Accountant	Pressure to fulfill commitment to development goals
	Role model	Examples of high (or low) competence in areas being developed
Support	Counselor	Examination of what is making learning and development difficult
	Cheerleader	Boost in own belief that success is possible
	Reinforcer	Formal rewards for progress toward goals
	Companion	Sense that you are not alone in your struggles and that if others can achieve their goals, you can too

Someone acting in the role of feedback provider observes a person who is working to improve and provides in-the-moment feedback. For example, after getting feedback that she dominated meetings, Melissa set a goal of giving others an opportunity to share their views and influence the group. She asked two coworkers who were often in meetings with her to give her feedback on how well she was achieving this goal. For the next six months, she checked in with them after each meeting to get feedback and any suggestions they had for improvement.

People also need feedback on strategies and ideas before they are implemented. In other words, they need sounding boards. People bring their ideas to a person acting as a sounding board for reactions and fine-tuning: What should I do in this situation? What would be the likely consequences if I took this action? Which of these three options is the best? George, a manager of a nonprofit organization, was about to lead his board in a strategic planning process for the first time. He contacted a manager in another organization who was considered an expert in strategic planning and asked for help; the two met regularly to debrief and plan next steps. For George, engaging in a new challenge while having access to a knowledgeable sounding board made the experience a particularly developmental one.

People also gain informal assessment data by comparing themselves to others. In this type of relationship, the other people take the role of comparison points. There are two types of comparison points: comparing oneself to someone who is seen as a model or expert (How do I compare to the best? How do I compare to someone who is doing what I want to be doing?) and comparing oneself to people in similar situations (Am I doing as well as others? Have I been able to achieve as much as others?).

Comparing themselves to a model helps people see how they measure up and where improvement is needed. After spending several days shadowing a top executive in a major organization, a younger executive running a smaller company noted that although her own work required tackling problems that were just as big, a major difference was the number of problems the other executive had to juggle at once. She realized that this skill of managing multiple problems and finding their interconnections was what she needed to develop if she ever hoped to occupy a similar position.

Comparing themselves to others in similar circumstances gives people insights about how well they are doing. A small group of employees who are going through a year-long leadership development program get together periodically to update each other on their progress toward development goals. These meetings serve as a sounding board for addressing the obstacles they are encountering, but they also serve as a context for judging how well each person is accomplishing his or her goals relative to the others.

Finally, other people serve in the role of feedback interpreter. As such, they usually do not provide assessment information directly but instead help people make sense of the feedback they receive. In one feedback-intensive program, all participants spend half a day with a feedback specialist who helps them (usually in a private meeting) discover themes in their data, connect those themes to their current context, and begin thinking about next steps. Many organizations that use 360-degree feedback provide recipients with access to a professional who can help them interpret the feedback. This role, however, does not have to be a formal one; people often turn to a trusted colleague to help make sense of feedback received informally from a boss or direct report.

Challenge

Challenge—pushing oneself or being pushed beyond the normal comfort zone—is another important element of a development process. One way other people push individuals beyond their comfort zone is by challenging their thinking. We refer to people in this role as dialogue partners. They expose people to different perspectives and help each other explore these differences by questioning, prodding, and reflecting on underlying assumptions. This exploration of different perspectives is often the first step in developing more complex and adaptive frameworks for understanding and acting in the world. For example, members of a cross-functional team addressing a major business issue discovered that in the process of digging beneath their differences and learning together, they shed some of their functional biases and developed more of an integrated perspective on the problem.

Other people also play important developmental roles when they provide individuals with assignments that stretch their capacities; we call this role assignment broker. These assignments can be new jobs, new responsibilities added to the current job, increased decision-making latitude in the current job, or temporary assignments outside a person's normal job responsibilities.

Another way that people motivate others to learn and grow is by holding them accountable for the development goals they have set; this is the role of accountant. Bosses are often expected to play the roles of assignment broker and accountant simultaneously. For example, as part of many performance management systems, employees decide with their bosses on development goals for the coming year. Part of the boss's responsibility is to find the challenging experiences that help move the employees toward those goals and then monitor their progress in the assignment.

Individuals are also challenged when they attempt to emulate role models. They step outside their comfort zones, trying new or more complex skills and behaviors. Rita, a high-potential manager who had been assigned a mentor as part of a leader development program, observed a style of supervision in her mentor that was different from her own. The mentor used a style Rita termed "hands-in" (auditing a subordinate's work), while Rita herself tended toward a hands-on approach (looking over subordinates' shoulders while they are doing the work). She was attracted to her mentor's style, but trying it out was a stretch for her.

Support

People need support to help them effectively deal with the struggles of a developmental experience. That support often comes from other people, who play a variety of support roles for one another.

One is the role of counselor, providing emotional support during the difficulties of the learning process. Counselors encourage people to explore the emotional aspects of the learning situation: fear of failing, anxiety about leaving the familiar behind, stress in trying to learn and change while carrying a heavy workload, frustration at not making progress, or anger with others who do not support development.

In a relationship with a strong counseling component, people can vent frustrations and negative emotions without feeling judged. They know that there is someone they can turn to if they need to, and this alone can give them the confidence to take risks or try new things. Michael had a tendency to redo the work of subordinates if the work did not meet his standards, rather than giving them feedback and coaching. He lived in a constant state of frustration and finally shared those feelings with a trusted and more experienced colleague. The colleague helped Michael see that he was contributing to his own frustration by his perfectionist tendencies and his fear of giving negative feedback. With a better understanding of his emotions and a colleague who cared enough to help him reach this understanding, Michael felt he could begin trying to change his behaviors.

Support is also provided by people who play the similar developmental roles of cheerleader and reinforcer. Cheerleaders are on the sidelines, encouraging learners, expressing confidence in them, and providing affirmation. Reinforcers reward people for making progress toward development goals. Julie, an R&D project leader, shared with her mentor her desire to become more assertive and forceful with her ideas. Knowing Julie's reserved nature, her mentor knew that the change would require a long and sometimes difficult learning process. So she became Julie's cheerleader, helping her celebrate small wins along the way and assuring her that the changes she was making in her attitude and behaviors were indeed valued by the organization. As Julie improved, her mentor reinforced the changes, giving her opportunities to represent the organization at several important external forums and writing a letter to her divisional vice president that praised Julie for the progress she had made and pointed out the resulting positive benefits for the company.

There is a final role that provides valuable support to the learner, albeit a more passive form of support. We refer to this role as companion. These are people who are struggling with the same challenges and thus can empathize with each other. People find great comfort in connecting with others facing similar challenges, realizing that they are not alone. Members of a network focused on managing innovation in organizations cited this type of support as a major reason for remaining in the network. Back in their companies, they often felt alone, struggling to make innovation a priority. However, connecting with like-minded people during network meetings left them reinvigorated to face their challenges again.

Companions can also provide people with the living proof that they can learn to master the challenges of the journey. Seeing others who are similar to themselves doing it, people believe they can do it too. Brad, a school superintendent who was working hard to be more delegating and to give his direct reports authority to make major decisions, got an unexpected boost from Jack, another superintendent he knew well. While they were both away at a national convention, a crisis arose back home in Jack's district. Assuming that Jack would rush back home to handle the crisis, Brad offered to take over his friend's remaining responsibilities at the convention. To his surprise, Jack replied that he had touched base with the key leaders back home and was confident they could handle it, so he would be staying at the convention. Brad suddenly felt renewed in his own development efforts: if Jack could delegate the responsibility for handling a crisis, surely he too could learn to delegate and trust the decision-making capacities of others. Not only did Jack serve as a role model, but because Brad saw Jack as someone in the same job experiencing the same types of demands as he did, Brad felt more strongly that he could succeed, too.

From Roles to Relationships

Each developmental relationship in a person's life provides a mixture of roles. A boss might be both accountant and assignment broker. A former colleague might act as both sounding board and companion. A spouse may play many roles at different times: role model, counselor, accountant, dialogue partner. Note that these kinds of relationships provide differing developmental roles. There is no prototypical developmental relationship, no one role or combination of roles that have to be present in order to make it developmental.

Some relationships, however, are more developmental than others. At least two factors seem to be at work here. First, some relationships are more developmental because they provide more such roles. Mentoring relationships, for example, are usually long term, and the two individuals develop a personal closeness. Over time, mentors are likely to play a number of roles: sounding board, counselor, feedback provider, assignment broker, cheerleader, reinforcer, role model. Bosses are also often in the position to play multiple developmental roles.

Second, a relationship can be especially developmental because it provides just the right role that the person needs at the time. Having someone in a counseling role may be particularly developmental during a hardship experience. Someone to provide feedback and encourage from the sidelines may be exactly what a person needs the most as he or she tries to change an ingrained habit. The lesson is that at various times, depending on the development need, different types of relationships are seen as the most essential.

Of the various relationships that contribute to leader development, mentoring relationships have been studied and written about the most. However, bosses and developmental networks have been emphasized in recent years. We shall briefly review some of the highlights from this literature.

Mentors A mentoring relationship is typically defined as a committed, long-term relationship in which a senior person (mentor) supports the personal and professional development of a junior person (protégé). In understanding how mentors influence the development of protégés, scholars distinguish between functions that facilitate and enhance career advancement (sponsorship, coaching, and providing challenging assignments, for example) and ones that support psychological and social development (such as counseling, acceptance and confirmation, and role modeling) (Kram, 1985; Noe, 1988). The benefits of having a mentor, particularly early in one's career, have long been espoused by adult development and career theorists (Hall, 1976; Kram, 1985; Levinson, 1978). Research indicates that receiving support from a mentor is associated with higher performance ratings, more recognition, greater compensation, more career opportunities, and more promotions (Burke and McKeen, 1997; Chao, 1997; Dreher and Ash, 1990; Fagenson, 1989; Orpen, 1995; Scandura, 1992; Turban and Dougherty, 1994; Whitely, Dougherty, and Dreher, 1991).

Mentoring continues to be a topic of high interest among scholars and practitioners. From 1986 to 1996, more than five hundred articles on mentoring were published in popular and academic publications in business and education (Allen and

Johnston, 1997). Research has focused on the phases of mentoring relationships; the roles served by mentors; the benefits for protégés, mentors, and the organization; mentoring issues and obstacles for diverse employees; and the individual and organizational factors that affect the cultivation of mentoring relationships (Hegestad, 1999; Russell and Adams, 1997). Recognizing the value of mentoring, organizations have increasingly experimented with formalizing these relationships as part of their management development strategy.

Bosses In the Center for Creative Leadership's original study of key events in executive careers (McCall, Lombardo, and Morrison, 1988), about 20 percent of the events featured another person. Most of these people (90 percent) were the manager's immediate boss or another superior that the manager was working closely with. This general pattern was found in extensions of the research to more diverse samples (McCall and Hollenbeck, 2002; Morrison, White, and Van Velsor, 1992), although white female executives reported a higher proportion of boss-relationship key events than white males or African American managers did (Douglas, 2003; Van Velsor and Hughes-James, 1990).

There is additional evidence that the boss-employee relationship is a central one for development. Managers report receiving more mentoring when their mentor is their direct supervisor than when he or she is not (Burke and McKeen, 1997; Fagenson-Eland, Marks, and Amendola, 1997). And supervisor support has consistently been linked to greater employee participation in development activities (Hazucha, Hezlett, and Schneider, 1993; Noe, 1996; Tharenou, 1997).

Bosses are in the unique position of working directly with a manager, having regular contact, feeling responsible for the manager's continued success, and having the power to access organizational resources for the manager. Thus, bosses have the opportunity to play many of the roles that provide assessment, challenge, and support. It is important to note, however, that not all of the relationships with bosses that were reported as key events were positive; about a third of the bosses were experienced as having few redeeming qualities. In these situations, rather than enjoying the benefits of a developmental relationship, managers learned what not to do and how to persevere in adverse conditions.

Developmental Networks There is a growing realization that individuals do not rely solely on single mentors or their current boss for development. Rather they have a network or "constellation" of relationships that they rely on for developmental assistance and support (Higgins, 2000; Higgins and Kram, 2001; Kram, 1985; McCauley and Young, 1993). These relationships can be lateral or hierarchical, within an organization or spanning organizations, ongoing or specific to a particular job transition, and job-related or career-related (Eby, 1997). Higgins and Kram (2001) suggest that the structure of the network will influence the developmental consequences for the protégé. Networks with stronger relationship ties spanning more diverse subgroups will have more developmental power.

"Build informal networks" has long been a staple of advice for managerial success. Yet the stated reasons for these networks has highlighted increased ability to access others for information and expertise, resources, and cooperative action—what might be regarded as the more instrumental functions of a network. Given the changing context of work (for example, increased mobility, flatter and more team-based structures, more diverse employees), long-term relationships for development are becoming more unattainable and connections with a wider array of colleagues more probable. This context creates the impetus to look beyond the instrumental value of networks and see them as sources of support and development (Eby, 1997; Higgins and Kram, 2001).

INDIVIDUAL STRATEGIES FOR USING DEVELOPMENTAL RELATIONSHIPS

To capitalize on the developmental power of relationships, how might people approach them? What steps should they take? If you are involved in helping people in your organization plan their development, here are some strategies you might suggest to them:

1. *Regard the boss as a partner in development.* As noted, bosses are in a unique position to provide various developmental roles or access to other development resources. Make development a topic of discussions with the boss. Bosses and employees should develop a mutual understanding of what each can expect from the other in terms of developmental effort and support. Often these expectations are tacit and not explicitly discussed, thus increasing the possibility for misunderstanding, misguided efforts, and missed opportunities.

2. *Seek out multiple relationships for development.* It is unlikely that one person can provide all of the roles needed in ongoing leader development. There are just too many diverse roles for one person to handle them all, and no one person should be burdened with all those expectations. Even if a person has a close relationship with a mentor, the mentor is unlikely to meet all the

development needs of the individual. Instead, people should cultivate a range of relationships across a variety of settings. Exposure to a breadth of viewpoints and experiences is important, and overdependence on one individual can actually limit a person's career progression (McCall and Lombardo, 1983).

3. *Figure out which roles are needed to help with current development goals, and find the right people for those roles.* What is actually needed, a role model who can demonstrate the skills and behaviors this person wants to develop? Encouragement, to stay motivated? Ongoing support to change an ingrained habit? A dialogue partner to move the individual beyond accustomed ways of looking at issues?

Once needs have been clarified, the question becomes, Who can best meet these needs? As with all other human capacities, people excel in different developmental roles, perhaps because of their innate gifts. For example, certain people seem naturally meant for a coaching relationship. They are motivated to teach others; they may be keen observers, enabling them to give clear and specific feedback; they know when to give stretch assignments and how to encourage without pressuring. Others are much better in the role of counselor. They are good listeners, sense the personal issues underlying development problems, and are comfortable with close relationships in the work setting.

Other differences are due to the nature of formal roles in organizations. For example, bosses are often in a better position to provide stretch assignments, hold individuals accountable for development, and reinforce learning through the formal reward system. Peers in a work group might be the best source of comparison points; people in other functions or even outside the organization might be the best source of fresh perspectives.

The point is to strive to understand which people—because of their personal strengths or the nature of their relationship—have high potential to fulfill particular developmental roles.

4. *Make full use of lateral, subordinate, and external relationships.* People often look upward in organizations for the developmental relationships they need. A more senior manager can provide important forms of assessment, challenge, and support, but the hierarchy gets narrower toward the top, and higher-level managers are often difficult to access. An experienced colleague, a peer in another division, or even the retired executive who lives down the street may serve your development needs just as well. Learning partnerships can also develop with subordinates (sometimes referred to as "reverse mentoring"); a supervisor coaching a direct report in one area could easily receive coaching in another area in return.

5. *Do not assume that relationships need to be long term or intense to be developmental.* As a result of the dominance of the mentoring concept, most people have a certain type of relationship in mind when they think of learning and development. They might miss or underestimate the opportunities to learn from relationships involving only modest contact. We have found that people can learn a great deal from shadowing a role model for several days, from working on a short-term project with a cross-functional team, from bosses that they were not particularly close to, or from colleagues they see a couple of times a year. Instead of focusing on the length or depth of the relationship, the real question is whether the experience with the person brings a different perspective, new knowledge, willingness to engage, belief in one's capabilities, insight, or talent for keeping people motivated.

6. *Be especially aware during times of transition.* It is particularly important for people to reassess their development needs

during times of transition; this includes reassessing the kinds of developmental relationships they need. Going through a transition is challenging in and of itself and may require special advice and support from others. Developmental relationships become more important during times of restructuring or downsizing, for example, because they act as an antidote to the stress (Kram and Hall, 1989). Also, being in a new situation puts new and different demands on people, which is likely to require development in new areas. This in turn calls for new role models, new sources of support, and people with expertise connected to the challenges in the new setting. For example, managers in expatriate assignments need role models for how to work in the new culture and advice to help them interpret and make sense of their new environment.

o   o   o

Cynthia D. McCauley is a senior fellow at the Center for Creative Leadership (CCL). She has held various research and management positions there and codeveloped two management feedback instruments.

Christina A. Douglas is a former faculty member of CCL and feedback specialist in CCL's Leadership Development Program. She has also worked in human resources for Xerox Corporation.

Part Four

Getting the Work Done

Chapter Twenty-Two

The Call for Results

Clinton O. Longenecker
Jack L. Simonetti

Several years ago, we conducted an executive education program with a group of senior managers in a growing service organization. In a serious discussion of what factors they considered to be most important to their career success, a heated debate broke out. Opinions were strong and varied about how to keep your job and get ahead. All the executives seemed to have their favorite three or four success factors that they championed during this discussion. Here are some of the typical opinions that emerged from this energized exchange:

"Be sure to take care of the bottom line."

"It all comes back to who you know and your connections."

"You've got to be willing to pay the price."

"Get as much cross-functional experience as you can."

"Find a mentor to help show you the way."

"Surround yourself with the best people possible."

"You've got to keep improving yourself."

"Get your systems and processes working in concert."

"Get involved in high-profile projects."

"Be willing and able to make the difficult decisions."

The passion, interest, and energy generated by this discussion encouraged us to explore this critically important career issue in greater depth since these views were only opinions at this point. To do this, we conducted a formal survey of more than five thousand managers all across the United States. Top, middle, and front-line managers were surveyed from nearly every major U.S. industry, including high tech, chemical, health care, automotive, banking, financial services, steel, retail, telecommunications, and transportation. In this study, managers were asked to identify and rank-order the factors they considered to be most important to their personal career survival and success. Stop right now and on a sheet of paper, list the top five most important factors that you feel are essential for your career survival and success in your current situation.

If you are like the managers in our study, getting better results is most likely on your list in some way, shape, or form.[1] Although some variance exists across organizations, industries, and management levels, people completing this survey made it very clear that getting results is almost always the most critical career survival and success factor and the name of the career game.

The CEO of a Fortune 500 manufacturing organization that we were recently working with made a telling comment in a management development strategy meeting: "What we need are more managers who know how to get the right results in the right way if we are going to be able to hit these aggressive numbers and take care of our customers and people." Although his organization was very successful financially, it was experiencing increasing competition, eroding profit margins, shortened life cycles on technologies, and rapid turnover of its product line. It became clear to all in this organization that managers had to become more results oriented if their organization was to endure.

How to Get Results: What Managers Think

If this tenet is indeed true, it begets the most important question, one that every manager must think about and explore: How do I go about getting better results in the ultracompetitive workplace of the twenty-first century? To explore this issue in greater depth, we surveyed over sixteen hundred high-performance managers on what they believe are the keys to getting results and learned a host of important lessons. Our sample of managers averaged forty-six years of age with seventeen years of management experience; 64 percent were men and 36 percent women. Participants in this study were all labeled "high performers" by their organization and collectively possessed over twenty-seven thousand years of management experience. Follow-up interviews were conducted with an additional four hundred high-performance managers to solicit further input, examples, cases, and personal anecdotes and quotes.

We analyzed the data generated from both the survey and interviews and ranked the results factors in their order of importance to the managers in this study. Exhibit 22.1 contains the top twenty management fundamentals that these managers deemed most important in their quest for results.

EXHIBIT 22.1. **Key Research Findings for Getting Results**

1. Use effective and dynamic communication practices.
2. Lead by example to demonstrate character and competence.
3. Establish and maintain a clear and meaningful vision and mission.
4. Provide motivation to create ownership and accountability for results.
5. Clarify performance expectations with all employees.
6. Foster teamwork and cooperation.
7. Develop clear and balanced performance goals and metrics.
8. Develop key working relationships.
9. Provide ongoing employee training and education.
10. Conduct appropriate and systematic planning activities.
11. Remove performance barriers quickly.
12. Keep yourself current, and practice personal development.
13. Provide ongoing performance feedback and coaching.
14. Demonstrate extreme care in staffing your operation.
15. Clarify your value-added role as manager.
16. Provide ongoing performance monitoring and measurement.
17. Equip people with resources they need to perform.
18. Proactively improve your processes.
19. Practice constructive employee appraisal and development.
20. Maintain balance in both your professional and personal life.

Note: These are the findings from more than two thousand managers.

The information in Exhibit 22.1 lets us dispel several myths. First, when managers are described as being results oriented, they are frequently viewed as being too task oriented, with little or no regard for people or the human side of organizations. On the contrary, these findings make it clear that getting results requires a balance between effective people-oriented practices and effective task-oriented practices, with the balance favoring the people side of the equation. High-performance managers make this point loud and clear: unless you engage people power, you cannot create great long-term performance.[2]

Second, although the words of the legendary football coach Woody Hayes—"You win with people!"—ring true, concern for people alone does not bring a manager desired results. An executive friend of ours is often heard saying, "Even the best people can only get so far without effective systems, processes, support, and resources." This is a view shared by managers in this study: managers must be task oriented in very specific ways to create an overall process and workplace system that is set up to get desired results. Yet we know from previous research that many managers tend to gravitate toward task-oriented practices at the expense of people-oriented issues and that people-oriented issues are frequently lost or tossed aside in the heat of battle.[3] Thus, although most managers truly want better performance and the results that follow, they frequently lack the focus, skills, passion, knowledge, and balance necessary to create an effective personal management system that addresses both the people issues and the systems issues in concert.

THE RULES OF THE GAME: FIVE ABSOLUTES FOR GETTING RESULTS

The ability of managers to get results and improve their performance is driven to a great extent by their ability to address what we have come to call the Five Absolutes for Getting Results. "There are no absolutes anymore" is a well-worn axiom of modern business—but it's simply not true. The intent of this oft-repeated saying is probably to remind us that the rules of business and the marketplace are constantly in a state of change (so don't look for pat answers or standardized solutions to fix complex problems or deficiencies). Yet this line of thinking can lead managers to look for a quick fix or ignore tried-and-true practices that can help make the complex issue of improving performance much easier to understand and address.

Based on our findings, it is our position that when it comes to getting results, there are a few critical results-oriented practices. We have carefully selected the word *absolute* as a moniker for each set of results-oriented practices that emerged from this research. An *absolute* is defined as something that possesses the characteristic of being complete in nature. We found that the twenty results-oriented practices identified by the managers in this study can be categorized into Five Absolutes for high performance. Furthermore, for a manager to create and sustain a level of complete performance that will produce desired results in these pressure-packed times, all of the following Five Absolutes must be present:

Absolute 1. Get everyone on the same page: Focus on the purpose of your organization. Create and maintain a clear and unambiguous focus on desired results for yourself, your people, and your operation as a whole—and create a means to measure performance.

Absolute 2. Prepare for battle: Equip your operation with tools, talent, and technology. Progressively staff your operation with high-quality people, develop effective planning practices, provide ongoing training and education for your people, and ensure people have the tools they need to get the job done.

Absolute 3. Stoke the fire of performance: Create a climate for results. Create an operational climate that measures performance, provides ongoing performance measurement and feedback, motivates people, and removes barriers to performance in an ongoing and systematic fashion.

Absolute 4. Build bridges on the road to results: Nurture relationships with people. Identify, foster, nurture, and sustain relationships, practice effective communication, and foster cooperation through the practice of trustworthy leadership with the people you need to get results.

Absolute 5. Keep the piano in tune: Practice continuous renewal. Continuously improve and renew yourself, your processes, and your people, and maintain balance in all facets of your life for long-term success.

Together, these Five Absolutes represent the pieces of a puzzle, all of which managers must put together to create a complete high-performance system that is capable of getting and sustaining results. If one of the pieces of the puzzle is missing (or any piece is only partially in place), the performance puzzle is incomplete and performance will suffer. All the pieces must be brought together in unison, and dynamic and trustworthy leadership that creates real change and desired results must be provided by the manager. Figure 22.1 illustrates this concept, showing how each of the Five Absolutes represents a critical component that is needed to improve performance and get better results.

If a manager lacks skill in (or ignores) a particular area, results will not be optimal. In this context, it is easy to see why getting better results can be a daunting challenge—because it requires focus, skill, discipline, and passion in a host of different or even competing arenas. But herein is also the reason for hope, enthusiasm, and encouragement. Almost all managers have specific areas of performance that already work well and others that can be identified, targeted, and improved on to increase overall effectiveness.

Mastering the Five Managerial Absolutes

To identify areas of your performance that are currently effective and areas that need work to make you a more complete and effective manager, stop right now and complete the Getting Results Assessment in Exhibit 22.2.

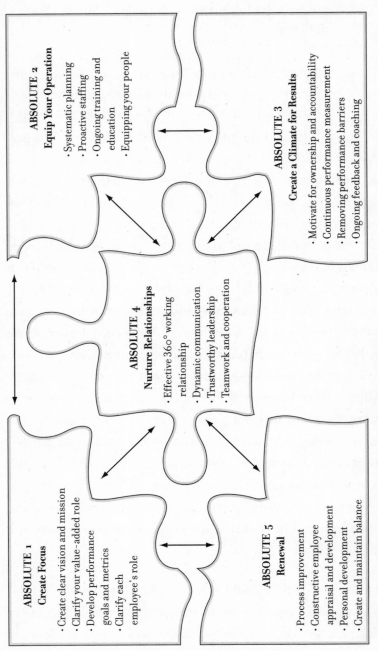

ABSOLUTE 2
Equip Your Operation

· Systematic planning
· Proactive staffing
· Ongoing training and
  education
· Equipping your people

ABSOLUTE 3
Create a Climate for Results

· Motivate for ownership and accountability
· Continuous performance measurement
· Removing performance barriers
· Ongoing feedback and coaching

ABSOLUTE 4
Nurture Relationships

· Effective 360° working
  relationship
· Dynamic communication
· Trustworthy leadership
· Teamwork and cooperation

ABSOLUTE 1
Create Focus

· Create clear vision and mission
· Clarify your value-added role
· Develop performance
  goals and metrics
· Clarify each
  employee's role

ABSOLUTE 5
Renewal

· Process improvement
· Constructive employee
  appraisal and development
· Personal development
· Create and maintain balance

FIGURE 22.1. **The Five Absolutes for Getting Results**

EXHIBIT 22.2. **Getting Results Assessment**

Instructions: Answer each of the following questions in an honest and open fashion to assess the extent to which you are effectively engaged in the practices that lead to improving performance and results. Use the following rating scale:

1 = Never 2 = Rarely 3 = Sometimes   4 = To a Great Extent 5 = Always

To What Extent Do I . . .

1. Practice effective communications to understand others and to be understood? _____

2. Lead by example and demonstrate competency and character in the workplace? _____

3. Have a clear vision and mission for where I am leading my people? _____

4. Hold people accountable and motivate them to increase their performance? _____

5. Clarify performance expectations with all my employees? _____

6. Foster cooperation and teamwork with the people who need each other to get results? _____

7. Use clearly defined and balanced performance metrics to measure performance? _____

8. Work at continually developing and nurturing key working relationships? _____

9. Ensure that my people are properly trained and educated to get results? _____

10. Employ appropriate and systematic planning practices? _____

11. Work to rapidly remove performance barriers that get in the way of getting results? _____

12. Keep myself up-to-date with the skills necessary to be effective in my job? _____

13. Provide ongoing performance feedback and coaching to my people? _____

14. Take extreme care in staffing the operation? _____

15. Proactively clarify my value-added organizational role? _____

(continued)

EXHIBIT 22.2. *(continued)*

16. Regularly monitor and measure the operation's performance? _____

17. Work to make sure that people are properly equipped to perform their jobs? _____

18. Have mechanisms in place to improve processes on an ongoing basis? _____

19. Constructively appraise my employees' performance and establish plans for their development? _____

20. Work to maintain balance in all facets of my life? _____

Interpretation: Any practice that receives less than a score of 4 is a potential target behavior for improving your personal performance and propensity for getting better results.

So what is it that you need to be working on to complete your performance puzzle? Do you have a clear sense of purpose for your operation? Do you have a meaningful set of goals and metrics that you and your people are pursuing? Are all of your people clearly focused on performing the duties that are most critical to the success of your operation? Do people in your operation cooperate with each other in serving your internal and external customers? Is effective staffing and training of personnel a priority? Do you move to remove performance barriers in a timely fashion? Do you have a plan to improve your personal performance? Is developing your people an activity that you take seriously?

These are just a few of the critical questions to address as you lay the foundation for developing a system for improving your ability to get results and your long-term career survival and success. In the end, your ability to improve your performance and corresponding results will be dictated to the greatest extent by your ability to develop and master the Five Absolutes.

In these dynamic and competitive times, it is easy for managers to feel overwhelmed and perhaps even to begin to despair, because the organizational demands for improvement are never ending. Managers are being paid to get results for their organizations and their approach to leading people, and creating effective business processes is critical in any effort to improve performance. But it is our purpose here to provide all our readers with a sense of hope and optimism about their future. Our core belief is a simple one: as things get more complex, complicated, dynamic, and fast-paced, managers at all levels must get back to mastering the managerial absolutes that drive improvement, because it is here that the seeds of success or failure are found.

o   o   o

Clinton O. Longenecker is professor at the University of Toldeo's College of Business Administration and a speaker and consultant. *Jack L. Simonetti* is adjunct professor of executive education at the University of Michigan Business School and professor emeritus at the University of Toledo.

Chapter Twenty-Three

Operating Within the Realities of Organizational Life

J. Davidson Frame

Several years ago, I was sitting in a hotel lobby with four experienced project managers, idling away the time by swapping stories about project management experiences. One manager made a remark that clearly struck a responsive chord in the others: "I spend a lot of time fantasizing about how much I could get done on my projects if one day my company and its budget officers and upper-level managers and purchasing agents and lawyers all went poof!—evaporated into the stratosphere." His three colleagues vigorously nodded their heads in approval. If this comment were made before an audience of one thousand project managers, I think that you would find most of them nodding their heads in approval also. There is a strong consensus among project managers that projects would be better undertaken outside the usual organizational environments.

It is easy to sympathize with this view. However, it is unrealistic. Projects occur in organizations. To design and manage projects out of their organizational context is similar to designing machinery for a frictionless world. In both cases, we have something that looks good on paper but will not work very well in the real world.

To study projects out of the context of their organizational setting is a fruitless undertaking. In this chapter, we focus on organizational realities and how to work effectively with them, as opposed to struggling against them. As an introduction to these realities, consider the hypothetical case of Jerry Wallenstein and his first hands-on encounter with project management and organizational realities. The experiences Jerry faces are common to inexperienced project professionals. This case, which follows Jerry from the first to the last day of his project, shows that things can easily get out of hand even when project staff do their best.

The Education of Jerry

Jerry was delighted when he was made manager of a project to explore the possibility of integrating his company's purchase order processes into the supply chain management (SCM) system his company, Globus Enterprises, was developing. The SCM project was the largest that Globus had ever implemented. The order processing subproject was one component of the larger SCM project.

Once developed, the SCM system would enable Globus to establish seamless connections with its vendors. Although Globus already incorporated computers in its order processing system, the bulk of transactions entailed manual interventions. This caused the order fulfillment function to operate slowly and led to errors because the manual interventions were error prone.

With the new SCM system, customers would enter orders using the Internet. Once captured by the SCM system, the orders would be processed entirely by the computer.

This project provided Jerry with his first real management experience. He had received his M.B.A. degree directly after finishing college and then was hired right out of business school by Globus Enterprises, where he spent two years as special assistant to Max Weiner, vice president of operations. The job gave him plenty of exposure to high-level decision making, but was somewhat frustrating because he was a spectator in the decision-making process, not a performer. Now, with the order processing subproject, he could do something tangible and have real responsibilities.

Jerry put together a list titled "Things to Do." At the very top of the list was the item "Assemble Project Staff." He approached his boss, Max, and asked how big a staff he would have and who would be on it. "Use anyone you need," Max responded. "The important thing is to give me a report on your findings within a month. Your preliminary investigation will give us an idea of how we should go about computerizing the order processing function at Globus, and we need that information in time for our next quarterly executive meeting."

Jerry determined that to do a good job on his project, he needed the following people: a secretary, an assistant, a logistics expert, an Internet expert, an accountant, and a representative from each of the company's five divisions. He reckoned that he, the secretary, and an assistant would be the only full-time workers on the project. Nonetheless, the other members of the project team would have to make a fairly substantial commitment to the project if it was to be completed in a month; each would have to dedicate about 25 percent of his or her time to the project.

According to Jerry's plan, the five divisional representatives would each write a section of the study, detailing the impacts of the order processing system on their operations and defining whatever order processing needs they have. His assistant would write the technical portions of the report. Jerry's chief function would be to coordinate the efforts of the others and to integrate all the pieces into a cohesive whole.

As Jerry started to put his team together, he immediately ran into trouble: he was unable to get a secretary assigned full time to the project. Because his division was in the midst of a reorganization, all secretarial staff were already overcommitted. When Jerry went to Max with his problem, Max nodded sympathetically and told him that he would just have to make do with whomever was available on a given day.

Jerry's luck in obtaining a full-time assistant was a little better—or so it seemed at first. After spending half a day trying to find someone who was free to work on the project, he came across the name of Bob Roulette, who worked in the contracts and procurement department. Bob, it was reported, was two months from retirement, so his workload was being reduced. A one-month assignment would dovetail nicely with the plans to ease him into retirement.

The easiest team member to recruit was the Internet specialist. Jerry approached the information resource management chief (IRM is located in the information technology division) and told him of his need for an Internet expert. The IRM chief immediately assigned Margaret Block to help Jerry with Internet matters. Unfortunately, the company had little practical experience with e-commerce systems, so Jerry was told that he would have to go to an outside consultant for the e-commerce expertise he might need.

Jerry met with varying degrees of success in recruiting representatives from the different divisions. He had a good reception from the finance division; the vice president of finance, Mary Garrett, announced that it was about time Globus Enterprises entered into the twenty-first century and said she would be glad to assign someone from her office to help Jerry on the project. In contrast, his reception at the information technology (IT) division could not have been cooler. His request for assistance from the division's vice president, Sam Ruff, was met with an uncomfortably long silence. Finally, Sam said, "I don't fully understand why you and Max are playing the lead role on something like this. Building an order processing system is basically an information technology chore and should be left to the IT experts. As it turns out, I've had a couple of our people looking into the matter of automating the order processing system for several months." He dismissed Jerry without promising cooperation and said something vague about having to "look into things personally."

Jerry was unnerved by his encounter with the IT vice president. Until now, all of his experiences at Globus had been quite friendly. He was still brooding about his meeting with Sam when he was accosted outside his office by Bob Roulette, his new assistant on the project.

"Listen, Jerry," Bob said. "As you know, I'll be retiring in just under two months. I'd like to help you on this project of yours, but let me say that I really don't know anything about computers or order processing. To tell you the truth, I hate computers and think order processing is horridly dull. Frankly, I think somebody did both of us a dirty trick putting me on this project. I'll gladly work with you, but don't expect too much from me."

All these things happened by the third day of the project, a Thursday. To get the project moving quickly, Jerry tried to arrange a kickoff meeting of all project staff for nine o'clock the following Monday morning. Sam Ruff's office (IT) still had not assigned a representative, so it would not be represented at the meeting. The finance division representative said he thought it was a great idea to get moving so quickly, but unfortunately he would be out of town throughout the week. The other project staff members said that they would attend the meeting, but they sounded less than eager. The only individual who sounded interested in the meeting was Margaret Block, the Internet expert. Jerry wasn't sure what he would do about getting an e-commerce expert. He would talk to Max Weiner about it next week.

Jerry spent all day Friday, Saturday, and Sunday preparing for the meeting. He put together a five-page preliminary position paper, identified milestones the team members would have to meet, created guidelines for the activities to be undertaken, and read several journal articles on Internet technology. On Monday, at nine o'clock, Jerry arrived at the conference room and found it empty. By nine-thirty, only two other project team members had shown up. Conspicuously absent were his assistant, Bob Roulette, and Margaret Block.

When a much-discouraged Jerry returned to his office, he found a message asking him to call Margaret. He called her. She apologized for missing the meeting and explained that her boss in the information resource management department (part of the IT division) had told her that he was pulling her off the project. She wasn't sure why.

At one-thirty, Max Weiner called Jerry into his office to tell him that he was putting the order processing automation project on hold. "All hell's broken loose," he explained. "Sam went to the big guy and complained that you and I, a couple of amateurs, were running amok, doing things we had no business doing. Sorry, Jerry. You win some and lose some. Next time we'll do better, right?"

"Sure," said Jerry in a daze. He didn't really understand what all this meant. All he could think of was that someone had told the company CEO that he, Jerry, was some kind of amateur. Jerry wondered about his future at Globus.

ORGANIZATIONAL REALITY: THE DIVORCE OF RESPONSIBILITY AND AUTHORITY

Although most of our first experiences with project management are—I hope—not as traumatic as Jerry's, his experiences at Globus illustrate a number of traits common to the great majority of projects. One of the most obvious is that Jerry was given responsibility for getting the job done, but he had very little authority to see to it that his decisions were implemented. This was reflected in his problems in recruiting project team members and evidenced in the fact that he could exercise only marginal control over Bob Roulette, his assistant and the only other full-time team member.

This feature of Jerry's story—the divorce of responsibility and authority—is the rule in project management. Project professionals have little authority to carry out their work. They have little or no direct control over the people and things that make the difference between project success and failure. Their staff generally are on temporary loan to them. The people who make decisions on whether these staff members get promoted, get a pay raise, or get tuition paid for graduate course work—that is, their true bosses, and thus the people who really count—work elsewhere. Similarly, the material resources they need on their projects—work stations, mass spectrometers, bulldozers—are usually controlled by others and must be borrowed.

"Well, then," an observer of this plight might say, "it seems that this problem can be easily addressed. Let's give the project professional authority over all resources—material and human—employed on the project." This is easier said than done and, in most cases, bad management. It is not an accident that project professionals have so little direct control over anything. It stems from the very nature of projects, as well as organizational requirements that resources not be squandered but used efficiently. To see this, we need merely reflect on several features of the basic definition of projects that was posited in the Introduction. Consider the following:

○ *Projects are temporary.* Projects occur in a finite period of time: minutes, hours, days, weeks, months, or years. Jerry's project was supposed to last one month. Generally, the organization in which they are carried out existed before their beginning and endures after their end. For that reason, it is often difficult on economic grounds to justify assigning staff and material resources to the project on a full-time basis.

○ *Projects are unique.* Projects are one-of-a-kind undertakings. At Globus Enterprises, feasibility studies of order processing systems are not a daily occurrence. Projects are structured to address momentary needs.

○ *Projects are systems.* Projects are composed of different pieces linked together in intricate ways. People with specialized skills often work on the individual pieces. On the order process-ing automation project, the team was structured in such a way that most of the members would bring their own specialized skills to the project (for example, knowledge of the Internet, knowl-edge of the workings of the finance division, typing skills). Often, though, the skills are so specialized that they are employed only briefly. It is not at all uncommon to have the composition of the project team continually changing as the project progresses through its life cycle. The person who can be usefully employed full time on a project is the exception rather than the rule.

The very nature of projects requires that human and mate-rial resources be borrowed rather than permanently assigned to the undertaking. As long as project professionals are dealing with borrowed resources, they have limited control over them. This reality overwhelmed Jerry in the one week that he was "managing" his project. The narrative is full of instances in which he is incapable of getting people to do what he needs to have done. He cannot get a secretary assigned full time to his project. His full-time assistant makes it clear that he is just treading water until his retirement, and he doesn't even show up for the important kickoff meeting. Jerry finds a cooperative and competent colleague in Margaret Block, the Internet expert, but owing to the political dynamics of the situation, she is pulled off the project by her boss. Because Globus does not have an e-commerce expert, Jerry will have to obtain the necessary expertise from an outside consultant, over whom he may or may not be able to exercise some degree of control.

From Jerry's perspective, the problem is that he is not the boss, although he is project manager of the order processing automation feasibility study. It would be understandable if, after spending hours mulling over his first project debacle, he had concluded that he could have been successful on the project if only Max Weiner had made him a boss—someone who could exercise clear and unambiguous authority over the resources he needed to employ in his work. While understandable, this would be a naive conclusion. It would suggest that Jerry did not learn much from his unpleasant project experience. To be boss, he would have to possess control over the career development of all the personnel working on the project—in view of the nature of his small project, highly impractical.

One final word on Jerry's unfortunate adventure: a substantial share of his problems is rooted in his inexperience. For example, he does nothing to strengthen his authority. Rather than go out on his own in dealing with people in other departments at Globus, he should have worked through his vice president, Max Weiner. He could have drafted a memo, signed by Max, that explained the purpose of his inquiries. In this way, he would not look like a loose cannon. It is particularly bothersome that Jerry dealt directly with vice presidents in the company. For all the talk we hear of flattened organizations, business entities remain hierarchical and do not countenance junior employees' initiating important meetings with senior managers in other departments. It really is not surprising that the information technology vice president saw Jerry's actions as an infringement on his territory.

NURTURING AUTHORITY

If project professionals lack authority and this presents a problem for them, why don't they create and nurture it? Successful project professionals do exactly that. They emphasize their strengths and use these strengths to build a base of authority.

Authority is the capacity to get people to take us seriously and to do our bidding. In the old days, kings had authority based on their power, which was embodied in their troops. When the powerful king issued a command, wise citizens listened and obeyed. A doctor's authority lies in a knowledge of medicine that allows him or her to heal patients. People certainly take their doctors seriously; they generally follow the regime suggested and swallow the pills prescribed without questioning the wisdom of such behavior.

One of the most common authoritarian characters in our everyday lives is the police officer, an individual whose very survival in some communities depends on the ability to project an image of authority. In fact, when a community is in the throes of lawlessness and rioting, we often ascribe this situation to "a breakdown of authority."

Advertising specialists recognize that an important consequence of authority is that people do the bidding of those who possess it. Thus, we find sober men and women in medical garb—looking every bit like everyone's image of the family physician—hawking all manner of medication on television, from allergy medicine to analgesics.

If project professionals want people to take them seriously and to do their bidding, they have to create and nurture a base of authority. Here we look at five kinds of authority that they can focus on. The first three are all derived from the specific organizational circumstances in which they arise: formal, purse string, and bureaucratic. They are rooted in the specific organizational setting in which project professionals find themselves. The two other kinds of authority, technical and charismatic, are personal. They are intrinsically tied to the project professional's personality and achievements.

Formal Authority

All project professionals possess some degree of formal authority to carry out their work. This formal authority is automatically conferred on them as soon as they are appointed to the project. The appointment itself suggests that an organization's leaders have confidence that a particular individual can carry out a project, and this further suggests that he or she has backing from above, no matter how tenuous.

If the formal authority that project professionals possess is no more than a vague sense that someone has confidence in their abilities, that authority will not be very helpful in getting others to do their bidding. If, in contrast, the corporate CEO makes a big show of appointing the project professional and makes it clear to everyone that the new appointee has the CEO's fullest backing, people in the organization will be readier to take note of the project professional's wishes. In this instance, the formal authority can be translated into real operational authority. The project professional has acquired borrowed authority.

Most project professionals do not receive the kind of clear-cut upper management backing that will make whatever formal authority they have very meaningful. Usually the little formal authority they have is not enough to offset other forces that keep them from exercising direct control over people and material resources.

Preferences for and dependence on formal authority are common among inexperienced, insecure, and unimaginative project professionals. What they find most appealing about it is that authority is conferred on them; they don't have to work at developing it. Unfortunately for them, the authority they derive in this way is often more apparent than real.

Purse-String Authority

If project professionals have some budgetary discretion and use it effectively, they can exercise authority of the purse strings. Clearly, this kind of authority is effective only in dealing with individuals who are affected by a project professional's budgetary actions. It is particularly useful in dealing with outside vendors and contractors, whose livelihood depends on payment for goods and services delivered.

The power of purse-string authority can lie in both the offering of a carrot and the wielding of a stick. Promises of future business or the payment of an incentive bonus for work done ahead of schedule may encourage outside vendors and contractors to do a good job. Threats of withholding payment for poor work may stimulate lackadaisical vendors to improve their performance; however, by the time it becomes obvious that a stick is necessary, poor schedule, cost, or quality performance may have already seriously jeopardized the project.

A problem that project professionals face is that typically they do not have much control over budgets. However, if they use their imagination, they may still be able to employ purse-string authority through their control of nonmonetary resources. For example, they have some measure of control over people's time: they can determine who gets the good assignments and who gets the dog work. They may also determine who gets the new equipment or occupies the most desirable office space.

Bureaucratic Authority

History is filled with examples of individuals who attained power in their organizations through the quiet mastery of bureaucratic skills. This is summarized in a comment made by

Lyndon Johnson, one of the most effective American politicians of the twentieth century: "Learn how the system works so that you can work the system." The colorless Joseph Stalin is a case in point. In vivid contrast to Lenin's charisma-based authority, Stalin's authority lay in his capacity to manipulate the Communist party and government bureaucracies to do his bidding. He focused on the smallest details of personnel assignments and was a master of organization charts.

To project professionals with good bureaucratic skills, the organization is not an obstacle. In fact, knowledge of the organization and the rules that make it tick is a positive blessing. Bureaucratic managers do not struggle against the organizational current; rather, they go with the flow. Their authority is based precisely on an understanding of the importance of filling out the paperwork properly, meeting seemingly arbitrary due dates for project status reports, and knowing the details of the organization's procurement procedures.

Technical Authority

Technical workers typically have a high degree of respect for technical competence. Often they judge the value of other workers according to their technical capabilities. In a laboratory environment, for example, a researcher may hold a fellow scientist in low esteem because he or she "hasn't published anything worth a damn in five years."

The emphasis that technical workers place on technical capabilities often causes them to resent management's authority over them. I have heard many researchers in laboratories complain about working for bosses who "aren't all that sharp technically." One scientist I know quit his job on this account and set up his own company, vowing that he'd never again work for someone who wasn't smarter than he. For an employee who measures a person's worth according to whether he or she understands quantum mechanics, working for a boss who never went beyond first-year calculus may be a bitter pill to swallow.

In our society, we tend to have a high regard for people of technical or intellectual accomplishment. Consider the public's adoration of past men and women of great intellectual accomplishment, such as Thomas Edison, Marie Curie, and Albert Einstein. On a more mundane level, we are in awe of the wizards of our own organizations: the people who can program computer code ten times faster than the norm, or who are masters of the intricacies of the tax code, or who have managed to secure two patents annually over the past fifteen years. When these people speak, we listen. If they make a request of us, it is an honor to oblige them.

Project professionals who possess technical authority can use this authority to great effect. They can get people to do their bidding not because they control salaries or prospects for promotion but simply because people respect their technical competence.

Lack of technical competence may preclude an individual from managing technical projects. On projects that require the project professional to carry out technical tasks—a common arrangement in, for example, small software development projects—this is understandable. But frequently a technical background is required of project professionals even when they do not carry out technical duties. In part, the rationale here is that only a technically trained individual can appreciate the technical nature of the problems faced by the project staff. Perhaps more significant is the feeling that nontechnical managers lack credibility with the project staff and will not be taken seriously by them. That is, nontechnical managers lack the technical authority to manage the project.

Charismatic Authority

Project professionals who possess charismatic authority are able to get others to listen to them and do their bidding through the force of their personality. The principal appeal of such authority is that it is "portable"; it can be carried from project to project and from organization to organization. If properly developed, it can be employed by the project professional to gain some influence over the many actors in the project environment who can make the difference between project success and failure.

Charismatic authority is rooted in a number of different traits. The charismatic manager often possesses a sense of mission, has a good sense of humor, is empathetic to staff needs, is enthusiastic, and is self-confident. The charismatic manager is a leader.

The Importance of Multiple Forms of Authority

It should be clear by now that project professionals who do not possess formal or purse-string or bureaucratic or technical or charismatic authority are in trouble. Actually, if they possess only one of these forms of authority, they probably are still in trouble. For example, if a project professional has only charismatic authority, staff may initially enjoy his management style but ultimately may perceive him as all form and no substance. If his bureaucratic skills are not well honed, he may miss crucial deadlines for filling out nuisance forms. And so on.

In general, project professionals should develop and nurture at least two forms of authority; three is even better. The importance of authority is that it gives project professionals some leverage over the many other actors in the project environment. Without such leverage, project professionals are not really in control of their project.

THE FULL PROJECT ENVIRONMENT

Jerry's dismal experience has given us only a small glimpse of the project environment. It is something like looking through a keyhole into a room. With some effort, we are able to discern a chair here and a lamp there, but at best we have only a vague idea of the full layout of the room.

A view of the full project environment reveals a situation that, from a management point of view, is extremely complex. Figure 23.1 portrays the full project environment from a Ptolemaic point of view: the project manager stands at the center of things. Of course, this is a distorted view. In truth, project managers must cope with a Copernican reality: like the earth, they are but a small speck off in a corner of their galaxy.

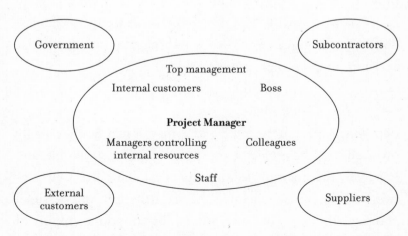

FIGURE 23.1. **The Project Manager's Operating Environment**

A survey of this figure confronts us with a couple of interesting facts. First, the sheer number of actors that project managers must deal with ensures that they will have a complex job guiding their project through its life cycle; problems with any of these actors can derail the project. For example, suppliers who are late in delivering crucial parts may blow the project schedule. To compound the problem, project managers generally have little or no direct control over any of these actors.

The figure also shows that project managers often have to deal with the environment external to the organization, as well as with the internal environment. What we have here is a complex management milieu—certainly more complex than what a manager in a retail store or a manufacturing environment faces.

In dealing with human relations on projects, books and courses usually focus on project managers' relationships with their staff. These relationships certainly are important and warrant close scrutiny. It should be noted, however, that relations with the other actors identified in Figure 23.1 are also important, because problems with any one of them can jeopardize the project. On a more positive note, it might be added that good relations with any of them can aid project managers tremendously. Let us look in some depth at these actors and their relationships to the project professional.

Top Management

Top management in the organization may or may not be directly involved with the project. Large projects are highly visible, and it is likely that their project managers will have direct interaction with top management. IBM's launching of the personal computer in the 1980s and Steve Jobs's ongoing support of new-generation computers at Apple are well-known examples of projects that receive constant top management scrutiny.

Obviously, managing a high-visibility project has both advantages and drawbacks. On the plus side, the highly visible project is more likely to have top management support, which means that it will be easier to recruit the best staff to carry out the project and acquire needed material resources. This visibility can also significantly boost the project manager's professional standing within the organization.

On the minus side, any failure will be quite dramatic and visible to all. Furthermore, if the project is a large and expensive one (and highly visible projects usually are), the cost of failure will be more substantial than for a smaller, less visible project.

Another negative feature of highly visible projects is that top management may find the temptation to meddle in them irresistible, leading to micromanagement. Micromanagement by top management puts project managers in an awkward position. It takes strong, self-confident, and brave project managers to resist the intense second-guessing of their efforts by the organization's top brass.

With low-visibility projects, direct top management involvement is unlikely. Nevertheless, top management can still have a major impact on how the project is carried out, because it sets the tone for the whole organization. For example, if top management establishes an atmosphere of free and open communication in the organization, project managers and their staff are more likely to be honest in reporting successes and failures. If top management creates an atmosphere in which failure is not tolerated, it is likely that project managers and their staff will be less than honest in reporting progress (or lack of it).

Boss

Today, the concept of "boss" is being reassessed. As modern organizations move away from traditional chain-of-command structures and drift toward team-focused structures, the issue of who reports to whom becomes quite clouded. Although we have clearly moved away from autocratic models of supervisors who possess absolute authority over their workers, bosses have not become extinct. They still exist and still must be dealt with. The importance of the boss to project professionals is obvious, since the boss plays a significant role in creating the daily working environment and is instrumental in determining the project manager's career prospects within the organization.

Our boss can make life in the organization reasonably comfortable or painful. Typically, the boss decides what our assignment is and who can work with us on our project. If things go wrong on our project (and they probably will), it is nice to have an understanding and supportive boss who will go to bat for us if necessary. If, on the contrary, the boss pounces on us at the first sign of trouble or disowns us, our lives can be very uncomfortable.

Colleagues

Fellow project managers and other peers in the organization can be friends or foes, or—quite commonly—a little bit of both. They can be friends in at least two senses. First, they can be useful resources, providing a project manager with important information or human or material assistance. Second, they can serve as helpful allies in getting things done within the organization. For example, whereas individual project managers may not have enough clout to get their company to purchase what they perceive to be a necessary piece of equipment, in concert with their colleagues they may possess sufficient collective influence to release funds for the purchase.

Colleagues can also be foes. An obvious source of conflict between colleagues is resource scarcity. It is not uncommon for project managers to find themselves competing against their fellows to get good staff or necessary equipment. If this competition is undertaken in a friendly spirit, it need not get out of hand. Colleagues may also be foes in the sense that they are competitors for career advancement. This last point can be particularly poignant in this era of downsized and flattened organizations.

Staff

I have noted that the staff whom project managers have available to them are usually borrowed rather than assigned to the project on a permanent, full-time basis. Recognizing this fact, project-oriented organizations occasionally organize themselves into a matrix structure.

A pure matrix structure is pictured in Figure 23.2. Running along the horizontal axis are the functional groups that serve as resource repositories. The engineering department is filled with a wide assortment of engineers, the data processing department is peopled with programmers and analysts, the finance department is filled with accountants and financial experts, and so on. On the left side of the matrix, along the vertical axis, are the individual projects that present specific resource needs. Project A, for example, has a need for engineers and data processors. When this need ends, they return to their respective functional groups, where they are available for work on other projects.

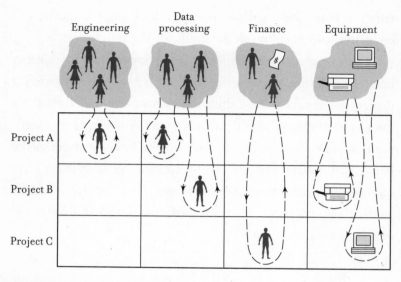

FIGURE 23.2. **Matrix Structure**

The matrix structure formally incorporates what I have noted several times: because of the temporary, unique, and complex character of projects, it makes more sense to have a project borrow resources on an as-needed basis than to assign resources full time to the project throughout its duration.

Today, there are two driving forces behind matrix management. One is that when it functions properly, it leads to the efficient employment of resources. If I need editors for only two days on a three-week project, why should I hire them for three weeks? With the matrix, we use resources as we need them, and when we are done with them, we send them home to their functional areas.

A second force behind matrix management is that it allows for cross-functional solutions to problems. Today's complex problems require inputs from a broad range of players. For example, to increase the likelihood of customer satisfaction, a software development team should contain members who are aware of business concerns as well as technical issues.

Although the matrix approach may reduce resource inefficiencies and encourage cross-functional problem solving, it also is the primary source of the project managers' chief complaint: that they have little control over the resources they need, since these resources are only on loan to them and owe allegiance elsewhere—usually to their functional groups and their functional group manager.

Managers Controlling Internal Resources

One special category of colleague that is particularly important to a project professional is other managers who control needed resources. Because project managers are typically in a position of borrowing resources, their relations with the people controlling these resources are especially important. If their relations are good, they may be able consistently to acquire the best staff and the best equipment for their projects. If relations are not so good, they may find themselves unable to get the people and material resources necessary to get the job done properly.

Internal Customers

Projects may be undertaken to satisfy the needs of internal or external customers. Internal customers are individuals within the organization who have particular needs that will be addressed with an internally executed project. Data processing department projects, for example, are usually carried out to meet internal demands. Perhaps the data processing department wants to upgrade the corporate accounts receivable system or help an office in its automation effort.

External Customers

External customers are individuals and organizations in the external environment. Projects can address their needs in two ways. In the first, a project may focus on developing a product or process that will eventually be marketed to outside consumers. In this case, there is no guarantee that the consumer will want to buy the product or process, so the project faces the serious risk that it might fail in the marketplace. Project managers may be ever conscious of producing something that will succeed in the market. If they are developing an important new product, it may be especially crucial that they complete their project in a timely fashion; if they do not, the product may lose its competitive edge. The business press is filled with stories of companies announcing the forthcoming introduction of a new product and then being embarrassed when the product hits the market several months behind schedule.

Projects also address external customer needs through contracts. The government, for example, commonly funds contractors to carry out desired projects. Here project managers have a clear idea of who the customers are; given this knowledge, they are obliged to maintain good communications with customers, to make sure that they are indeed meeting the customer needs.

This is easier said than done. Customers often do not have a precise idea of what they want. Consequently, their needs tend to change as the project evolves and they gain a better appreciation of precisely what the project is developing. In such circumstances, project managers must balance their desire to satisfy customers with knowledge that constant changes to the project will lead to time and cost overruns.

Government

Most project managers do not have to deal with government in their projects unless they are government contractors, in which case the government is their customer. However, those working in certain heavily regulated environments—for example, in the pharmaceutical, pesticide, or banking industries—must be fully conversant with government regulations that bear on their projects. Not only do they face the problems common to all other project managers, but they must work under additional stringent regulatory constraints as well.

Subcontractors

There are times when organizations do not have sufficient skills or capabilities to undertake all project tasks themselves. This is often true of large, complex projects and of construction projects in general. Under these circumstances, work is farmed out to subcontractors. Project managers working with subcontractors must keep close tabs on their performance, since the success of the project will depend in part on their work.

Any number of problems can arise with subcontractors. The quality of their work may be substandard, or they may run into cost overruns, or they may face schedule slippages. Keeping tabs on them is not easy, since they operate outside the project professional's immediate organizational environment. It is hard enough trying to keep tabs on individuals one encounters on a daily basis within the organization; keeping tabs on outsiders is even more difficult.

In working with subcontractors, the project manager should have substantial knowledge of the provisions in the contract with the subcontractor, as well as a rudimentary knowledge of contract law.

Suppliers

Many projects are heavily dependent on goods provided by outside suppliers. This is true, for example, of construction projects, where lumber, nails, brick, and mortar come from outside suppliers. If the supplied goods are delivered late or are in short supply or are of poor quality, or if the price at delivery is higher than the quoted price, the project may suffer seriously. Many construction projects are thrown off schedule because required materials do not arrive on time, or because the delivered goods are of such poor quality that the delivery has to be rejected.

Reliable suppliers are important to successful project management. The Japanese have long recognized this in the manufacturing sector. Major Japanese corporations dedicate a good deal of attention to their relationships with suppliers, and the famed just-in-time system, in which supplies arrive at the plant the day they are to be used, has been an important factor in Japan's phenomenal success at producing high-quality goods at a low price.

Project managers have so many balls to juggle that they are often tempted to downplay potential supplier problems in order to focus their attention on other crucial actors. "These suppliers are professionals, and I will assume that they will behave in a professional manner," they say to themselves. The project manager who operates on this assumption, and consequently pays little attention to possible supplier problems, may be in for a number of nasty surprises.

THE POLITICS OF PROJECTS

Politics is the art of influence. The fundamental job of candidates running for public office is to influence a majority of the electorate to vote for them. This is what the speeches, the kissing of babies, and the paid political advertisements are all about. Once in office, the politicians are busy influencing other politicians to back them on legislative proposals, position themselves to be appointed the chair of important committees, and release funds for projects that will enrich their constituencies. The purpose of all this effort is to influence the electorate to vote for them again in the next election. This ability to influence others to do one's bidding is a politician's most important asset.

With rare exceptions, politicians are not inherently powerful people. Generally, they do not have large sums of money that they can use as an instrument of power. They do not flex large biceps to intimidate people into doing what they want. They do not possess invaluable knowledge of the secrets of nature that gives them a hold over others. The power they possess is rooted in their ability to influence others. When they lose this ability, they no longer function effectively as politicians. Even the seemingly omnipotent—such as Winston Churchill during World War II—fall quickly when they can no longer exert sufficient influence over their fellows.

Project managers are something like politicians. Typically, they are not inherently powerful, capable of imposing their will directly on coworkers, subcontractors, and suppliers. Like politicians, if they are to get their way, they have to exercise influence effectively over others. We saw previously in this chapter that one way to get others to do one's bidding is to create and nurture authority. But politicians need more than the simple possession of authority; they also need to possess a keen understanding of the overall environment in which this authority is to be exercised. They need to be realists.

Block defines a process that good project politicians follow.[1] It is reduced here to six steps:

1. Assess the environment.
2. Identify the goals of the principal actors.
3. Assess your own capabilities.
4. Define the problem.
5. Develop solutions.
6. Test and refine the solutions.

The first four steps are designed to help the project professional acquire a realistic view of what is happening. Most project professionals, when tackling a project, skip over those steps and immediately begin offering solutions to problems. They are not good project politicians.

Because all projects involve politics and these politics often have an important bearing on whether projects proceed smoothly or roughly, it is worthwhile to examine these six steps in some detail.

Step 1: Assess the Environment

The most important elements in the environment are the other actors involved either directly or indirectly with a project. In assessing the environment, the project professional should try to identify all the relevant actors. This is harder to do than it may seem at first blush.

Consider, for example, a project to introduce a new accounting system into an office. Good project management practice suggests beginning with an analysis of the needs of the users of the accounting system. Who are the users? An obvious set of users are accountants who maintain the company's books and the finance experts who use the accounting data to carry out financial analyses of the company's business performance. Another important set of users are all managers who engage in any sort of financial transactions. Their principal need is for an accounting system that generates reports with the information they require to do their job. For example, department heads need data on expenditures incurred by their departments, and the payments office requires information on accounts receivable. Clerical personnel who input data into the accounting system are a type of user as well. Their principal need is for a system that accepts data readily and is easy to use.

Beyond these obvious users are additional stakeholders that need to be considered. Because implementing an accounting system requires substantial cooperation from the IT department, the views of IT personnel about approaches to implementing the accounting system should be solicited. Their chief concern is that the system that is implemented make technical sense. The executive committee of senior managers comprises important stakeholders. They want to be sure that the accounting system that is adopted will serve the organization's overall needs. A stakeholder we often overlook that has a role to play on many projects is the purchasing department. If we plan to purchase goods and services in the course of the project, we better consult with the folks in the purchasing department, because they have a set of procedures that we need to follow; if we ignore them, we may not get the goods and services we need in a timely fashion.

Once the relevant actors have been identified, we try to determine where the power lies. In the vast cast of characters we confront, who counts most? Whose actions will have the greatest impact?

Step 2: Identify Goals

After determining who the actors are, we should identify their goals. What is it that drives them? What is each after? In examining their goals, we should not shy away from speculating about psychological motivations, since these may be more powerful than purely work-related motivations.

We should, of course, pay attention to stated goals. However, we should also be aware of the hidden agenda, that is, goals that are not openly articulated. In the example of updating the computerized accounting system, one overt goal of the project sponsor might be to increase productivity and accuracy of financial data; a hidden goal might be to be recognized as the foremost guru who promotes best practices in the organization. To satisfy both the overt and hidden goals, the project professional should consider purchasing high-quality accounting software that also has a nifty look to it.

In dealing with both overt and hidden goals, we should focus special attention on the goals of the actors who hold the power. By knowing who holds the power and recognizing their overt and hidden goals, we reduce the likelihood of making gaffes that upset those people whose actions have great impact. Furthermore, we can use our knowledge in a positive way to determine how we can influence these people to help us achieve our project goals.

Step 3: Assess Your Own Capabilities

Know thyself. Project professionals should have a good idea of their strengths and weaknesses and should be able to determine how those traits bear on the project. Self-assessment is a crucial step in developing a realistic outlook on the project and its environment. If project managers have a distorted view of their own capabilities, the project is likely to run into trouble.

Particularly important capabilities are the abilities to work well with others and to communicate well. Project professionals who are basically inarticulate should not offer to make weekly progress presentations to higher management, since these presentations will only highlight their poor ability to communicate. If weekly management reviews are necessary, inarticulate managers should rely heavily on articulate staff members.

In assessing their own capabilities, project professionals should also be sensitive to their personal values. To a large extent, our own value systems define who we are. They are the perceptual filters that determine how we view the world and offer us guidance on how to behave.

Project professionals are not automatons emerging from a common template. Their decisions are governed by their value systems. Some project professionals may see their project as one small element in their broader life, whereas others may subordinate everything to the project. Operationally, the first will be less willing to put in overtime on weekends, while the second may eat, sleep, and drink project efforts round the clock. Project professionals who are sensitive to their personal values will avoid situations that generate value conflicts, or, if these conflicts are unavoidable, they will at least understand the sources of the conflicts.

Step 4: Define the Problem

Only now, after project professionals are thoroughly familiar with their project environments and their own capabilities, are they ready to intelligently define the problems facing them. The problem definition effort should be systematic and analytical. The facts that constitute the problem should be isolated and closely examined. The basic assumptions underlying the approach to defining the problem should be understood.

Over and over again, the following question should be raised: "What is the real situation?" Project professionals who take this approach are unlikely to define the problem according to superficial realities.

Step 5: Develop Solutions

Too often, project staff begin the whole process at this step. They start offering solutions before they fully understand the problem. With such an approach, the solutions they offer are not very useful.

If instead they can exercise self-control and refrain from offering premature solutions while they carry out the first four steps, the ultimate solutions they develop will have the important advantage of being realistic and relevant to the real problem that must be addressed. Consequently, they diminish the likelihood of project failure—that is, of producing deliverables that are rejected, underused, or misused by customers.

Step 6: Test and Refine the Solutions

The solutions devised in step 6 will be rough, requiring further refinement. Solutions must be continuously tested and refined. If project staff have done the proper spadework with the first five steps, this last step should involve no major rework effort, but rather should focus on putting the finishing touches on intelligently developed, realistic solutions.

Using the Steps to Develop Superior Solutions

There is nothing novel about these six steps. They incorporate a good commonsense outlook. The most remarkable thing about them is that they are rarely followed, even after project management staff have acknowledged their importance.

I have conducted about fifty nonscientific experiments on my project management students to see how they tackle problem solving. I give a group of students a case study that describes a typical situation and requires them to offer management advice on how the organization should proceed. I have never had a group that systematically attempted to identify the full roster of actors affected by the project, or a group that consciously took account of the actors' motivations, or a group that spent any time trying to uncover the hidden agenda implicit in the project situation. Rather, what they typically do is to immediately begin offering solutions to the problem as stated in its most superficial form. It is usually apparent that these early solutions are woefully inadequate, so the groups spend most of their time refining and reworking their original efforts. Generally, the problem they are working on remains superficially articulated, a one-dimensional solution in a three-dimensional world.

After the students have finished with their exercise, I point out that they have ignored the fundamental precepts of developing deep, rich, and realistic solutions to problems. I give them a new case study and explicitly ask them to employ the six-step methodology discussed here. The resulting solutions are vastly superior to the earlier ones. The solutions now take into account a broader array of actors, hidden agendas, and personal values; consequently, they are more viable than their one-dimensional counterparts.

Conclusion

Projects are carried out in organizations, and a thorough understanding of their organizational context is necessary for project success. This obvious point is easy to lose sight of as project managers wrestle with the intricacies of PERT/CPM charts, resource loading charts, and budgets. Too often, we confuse the management of projects with mastery of the well-known budgeting and scheduling techniques that have been developed as project management tools. The tools are easy to learn. An understanding of organizational intricacies is not. The most effective project managers are those who are as skilled at understanding the organization in which they work as they are proficient in using the basic scheduling and budgeting tools.

o   o   o

J. Davidson Frame is dean of academic affairs at the University of Management and Technology in Arlington, Virginia. Previously, he established the project management program at George Washington University.

Chapter Twenty-Four

Solving the Problem of Bad Meetings

Patrick Lencioni

Meetings are a puzzling paradox.

On one hand, they are critical. Meetings are the activity at the center of every organization.

On the other hand, they are painful. Frustratingly long and seemingly pointless.

The good news is that there is nothing inherent about meetings that makes them bad, and so it is entirely possible to transform them into compelling, productive, and fun activities. The bad news is that in order to do this, we will have to fundamentally rethink much of the way we perceive and manage meetings.

That means we cannot keep hating them. And we must abandon our search for technological solutions that will somehow free us from having to sit down face to face. And we have to stop focusing on agendas and minutes and rules, and accept the fact that bad meetings start with the attitudes and approaches of the people who lead and take part in them.

The best news of all: for those organizations that can make the leap from painful meetings to productive ones, the rewards are enormous. Higher morale, faster and better decisions, and inevitably, greater results.

The purpose of this chapter is to provide a brief summary of my meeting theory so you can implement all or part of it within your organization, and reap some of those rewards.

The first question that needs to be asked and answered about meetings is this: What is the real problem? Actually, there are two.

First, meetings are boring. They are tedious, unengaging, and dry. Even if people had nothing else to do with their time, the monotony of sitting through an uninspired staff meeting, conference call, or two-day off-site would have to rank right up there with the most painful activities of modern business culture. And when we consider that most of the people struggling through those meetings do indeed have other things to do, that pain is only amplified.

Second, and even more important, meetings are ineffective. The most justifiable reason to loathe meetings is that they don't contribute to the success of our organizations. With so many demands on people's time, it is especially frustrating to have to invest energy and hours in any activity that doesn't yield a commensurate return.

So the big question is why? Why are meetings boring and ineffective?

Meetings are boring because they lack drama. Or conflict. This is a shame because most meetings have plenty of potential for drama, which is essential for keeping human beings engaged. Unfortunately, rather than mining for that golden conflict, most leaders of meetings seem to be focused on avoiding tension and ending their meetings on time. And while these may seem like noble pursuits, they lie at the heart of bad meetings.

To make meetings less boring, leaders must look for legitimate reasons to provoke and uncover relevant, constructive ideological conflict. By doing so, they'll keep people engaged, which leads to more passionate discussions, and ultimately to better decisions.

Meetings are ineffective because they lack contextual structure. Too many organizations have only one kind of regular meeting, often called a staff meeting. Either once a week or twice a month, people get together for two or three hours of randomly focused discussion about everything from strategy to tactics, from administrivia to culture. Because there is no clarity around what topics are appropriate, there is no clear context for the various discussions that take place. In the end, little is decided because the participants have a hard time figuring out whether they're supposed to be debating, voting, brainstorming, weighing in, or just listening.

To make our meetings more effective, we need to have multiple types of meetings, and clearly distinguish between the various purposes, formats, and timing of those meetings.

The remainder of this chapter provides a more complete discussion of the two underlying problems with meetings: lack of drama and lack of structure. It also includes tangible solutions for addressing them, as well as warnings about the challenges that can often get in the way.

Problem 1: Lack of Drama

Meetings are not inherently boring. By definition, they are dynamic interactions involving groups of people discussing topics that are relevant to their livelihoods. So why are they so often dull? Because we eliminate the one element that is required to make any human activity interesting: conflict.

I took a screenwriting class in college and, as a hobby, have written a few screenplays myself. In the process of my study and practice of the craft, I learned something about drama that I believe is completely relevant to meetings.

You see, conflict is at the center of every great movie. It is the essence of drama, and it is the reason audiences become and remain engaged in a story. And whatever type of conflict it is—man versus man (Luke Skywalker and Darth Vader in *Star Wars*), man versus nature (Chief Brody and the shark in *Jaws*), man versus himself (John Nash struggling with his mental illness in *A Beautiful Mind*)—without it we lose interest.

But what do movies and meetings have to do with one another? Think about it this way. Most movies are written to be approximately two hours in length, give or take twenty minutes or so. Many of our meetings go for about two hours, give or take twenty minutes.

Now imagine if I were to ask a room full of executives which they enjoy more: meetings or movies? They would probably think I was joking. And yet, meetings should be more interesting than movies because they have more inherent potential for passion and engagement than movies do.

Meetings Versus Movies

First, meetings are interactive; movies are not. You can interrupt someone during a meeting and say, "I think you should reconsider your decision. . . ." But you can't interrupt an actor on the screen and say, "Don't go into the house, you knucklehead. You're going to get your head lopped off!" When you go to a movie, you are a passive observer, not a participant.

Second, meetings are directly relevant to our lives; movies are not. Decisions made during a meeting have an impact on how we will spend our time and energy in the immediate future. At the end of the movie, nothing tangible has changed in our lives. We are not required to alter the course of our actions in any way as a result of how the story was resolved.

And so how is it that we can enjoy one activity that is inherently passive and irrelevant and loathe another that is interactive and relevant? Because screenwriters and directors figured out long ago that if you avoid nurturing conflict in your story, no one will want to watch your movie. And they also figured out that it is during the first ten minutes that they must use drama to hook their viewers, so that they are willing to stay engaged for another two hours.

The Hook

The key to injecting drama into a meeting lies in setting up the plot from the outset. Participants need to be jolted a little during the first ten minutes of a meeting, so that they understand and appreciate what is at stake.

This might call for the leader to illustrate the dangers of making a bad decision or highlight a competitive threat that is looming. It can also be accomplished by appealing to participants' commitment to the larger mission of the organization, and its impact on clients, employees, or society at large. If this sounds far-fetched or contrived, consider the following example: a leader kicking off a meeting about controlling expenses:

> *Typical opening scene:* "All right, people, we are 12 percent over budget, and from what I can tell, we're spending way too much money on travel. Going forward, we need to have better controls and

monitoring so we can meet the corporate guidelines laid out in the budget . . ."

More dramatic opening scene: "Okay, everyone, we're here to talk about cutting expenses, which doesn't sound like much fun. But consider that there are plenty of people out there who have a vested interest in the way we spend our money. Our competitors are hoping we throw our money around carelessly. And they're certainly looking for ways to reduce their own unnecessary expenses. Our customers don't want to have to pay higher prices for our products to cover our lack of discipline. Our families would rather see more money in our paychecks than in our travel and entertainment budget. So let's dive into this issue with a sense of urgency and focus, because I certainly want to make sure that we're using the resources in the way our investors and shareholders intended."

Employees aren't expecting Hamlet, but they're certainly looking for a reason to care. And that's what the leader of a meeting should be giving them.

Ironically, most leaders of meetings go out of their way to eliminate or minimize drama and avoid the healthy conflict that results from it, which only drains the interest of employees.

So, am I advocating the provocation of drama and confrontation among team members to create interest during meetings? Actually, yes. And I'm encouraging leaders of meetings, as well as participants, to be miners of conflict.

Mining for Conflict

When a group of intelligent people come together to talk about issues that matter, it is both natural and productive for disagreement to occur. Resolving those issues is what makes a meeting productive, engaging, even fun.

Avoiding the issues that merit debate and disagreement not only makes the meeting boring, it guarantees that the issues won't be resolved. And this is a recipe for frustration. Ironically, that frustration often manifests itself later in the form of unproductive personal conflict, or politics.

And so a leader of a meeting must make it a priority to seek out and uncover any important issues about which team members do not agree. And when team members don't want to engage in those discussions, the leader must force them to do so, even when it makes him or her temporarily unpopular.

When I am working with executives and their teams, I force myself to mine for conflict whenever I can. When I do, it is almost a certainty that many of the executives will come to me afterward and say something to the effect of, "Thank you for making us confront that issue. Our meetings were getting so uncomfortable because we were avoiding it, and everyone knew it was a problem."

The truth is, the only thing more painful than confronting an uncomfortable topic is pretending it doesn't exist. And I believe far more suffering is caused by failing to deal with an issue directly—and whispering about it in the hallways—than by putting it on the table and wrestling with it head on.

Of course, getting people to engage in conflict when they aren't accustomed to it is a challenge. I have found one simple method to be particularly helpful in making this easier.

Real-Time Permission

After a leader announces to a team that more conflict will be expected from them—and it is critical that this is made clear— there will be a key moment when team members take their first risks in engaging one another in active debate. And no matter how much we prepare them for this, it is going to feel uncomfortable.

When this happens, a leader can minimize the discomfort and maximize the likelihood that conflict will continue by interrupting the participants and reminding them that what they are doing is good. As simple, even paternal, as this may seem, it is remarkably effective.

It is probably worth presenting a glimpse of how this might work, using an example:

> Connor presents his advertising plans for the coming year.
>
> Afterward, Sophia takes a risk and announces to Connor, "I'm not sure I'm on board with your new advertising proposal." Immediately, she is a little tense.
>
> As is Connor. "Okay. What are your concerns?"
>
> "Well, I don't think it fits with the branding we discussed last month, and I'm afraid it's going to confuse customers."
>
> Connor is now a little frustrated. "Well, the firm that handled our branding reviewed the ads last week, and they didn't seem to have a problem with them."
>
> Sophia turns just a little red. "Well, maybe they didn't pay close enough attention. Or maybe they're not very familiar with our customers."
>
> Connor sighs. Before he responds, Casey [their boss] interrupts. "Before you continue, and I definitely want you to continue, I just want to say that this is exactly the kind of thing I was talking about when I said we need to start engaging in more conflict. And even though it can be frustrating for you, Connor, to have to rethink the work you've been doing, it's Sophia's job, and all of ours, to question you if we think it can make the final outcome better."

Based on my experience, the impact of Casey's remarks would be the following: Connor and Sophia would let go of a considerable amount of the unnecessary interpersonal tension they had been feeling. This would allow them to retain their ideological passion around the issue and continue to advocate their positions without being distracted or discouraged by their fears of personal rejection.

Unfortunately, even if leaders of meetings learned to master the art of producing and directing terrifically dramatic meetings filled with compelling and engaging conflict, they would still fail if that's all they did. That's because there is another big problem with meetings.

PROBLEM 2: LACK OF CONTEXTUAL STRUCTURE

No matter what kind of organizations I work with—regardless of size, industry, or geography—the same general experience drives people crazy when it comes to meetings. Here is a typical example:

Let's say the meeting in question is a standard Monday morning staff meeting, scheduled to go from 9:00 A.M. to 11:00 A.M. The leader prepares an agenda, which is basically a list of five or six items that he sends to everyone, asking for their reactions, comments, or additions. Of course, he receives none.

The meeting begins at approximately 9:00 A.M., with the first item on the agenda (but not necessarily the most important one). This topic occupies the first long hour of the meeting because people know that they're going to be there for the whole time, so they find something to say.

The second topic (again, not necessarily the second most important one) then soaks up another forty-five minutes. This leaves fifteen minutes for the final three topics (which may or may not be the most important ones), not to mention any other administrative, tactical, or strategic issues that someone inevitably decides needs to be discussed.

The meeting adjourns at 11:20, with everyone frustrated for different reasons.

One team member is peeved that the meeting went over-time, again, because it means she is now late for her next meeting, and that's going to set her entire day back.

Another is upset that his issue didn't get put on the table until the end of the meeting, when there was little time and even less interest remaining.

Still another believes that the meeting was too administrative, with no focus on the important strategic issues like competitive positioning and branding, while the one sitting across from her actually thought that there was too much brainstorming and not enough time focused on solving immediate, tactical problems like expense controls and vacation policies.

Finally, one member of the team is upset because, once again, they failed to set a final date for the company picnic.

And the leader walks away bloodied by the dissatisfaction of the team and dumbfounded that so many people could be so unhappy about so many different things. He vows that the next meeting will be more practical, more strategic, shorter, and yes, a date will be set for the picnic.

This may not be exactly like meetings in your organization. But it represents many of the problems that I encounter time and time again in the companies that I observe. All of these problems amount to one big mess that I call "meeting stew."

Meeting Stew

The single biggest structural problem facing leaders of meetings is the tendency to throw every type of issue that needs to be discussed into the same meeting, like a bad stew with too many random ingredients. Desperate to minimize wasted time, leaders decide that they will have one big staff meeting either once a week or every other week. They sit down in a room for two or three or four hours and hash everything out—sales strategies, expense policies, potential mergers, employee recognition programs, budgets, and branding—so that everyone can get back to their "real work."

Unfortunately, this only ensures that the meeting will be ineffective and unsatisfying for everyone. Why? Because some people want the meeting to be informative and quick, an efficient exchange of data and tactical information. Others think it should be interactive and strategic, providing key analysis and data to make critical decisions. Others would like to step back, take a breath, and talk meaningfully about company culture and people. Others just want to make clear decisions and move on. Who's right? Everyone. And that's the point.

The Four Meetings

There should be different meetings for different purposes, and each of them serves a valid and important function. I propose that every organization consider adopting something like the structure in Table 24.1, which involves four basic types of meetings.

Meeting 1: The Daily Check-In I hesitate to start with this one, because it is not necessarily practical for every organization. But for those that can make it work, the daily check-in is powerful. And even for those that can't, it is helpful to understand its rationale.

The daily check-in is something that I adopted and adapted from a friend of mine, Verne Harnish, who wrote a great book called *Mastering the Rockefeller Habits* in which he refers to a similar type of meeting as a "huddle." The daily check-in requires that team members get together, standing up, for about five minutes every morning to report on their activities that day. Five minutes. Standing up. That's it.

TABLE 24.1. The Four Meetings

Meeting Type	Time Required	Purpose and Format	Keys to Success
Daily check-in	5 minutes	Share daily schedules and activities.	○ Don't sit down. ○ Keep it administrative. ○ Don't cancel even when some can't be there.
Weekly tactical	45–90 minutes	Review weekly activities and metrics, and resolve tactical obstacles and issues.	○ Don't set agenda until after initial reporting. ○ Postpone strategic discussions.
Monthly strategic (or ad hoc strategic)	2–4 hours	Discuss, analyze, brainstorm, and decide on critical issues affecting long-term success.	○ Limit to one or two topics. ○ Prepare and do research. ○ Engage in good conflict.
Quarterly off-site review	1–2 days	Review strategy, industry trends, competitive landscape, key personnel, team development.	○ Get out of the office. ○ Focus on work; limit social activities. ○ Don't overstructure or overburden the schedule.

The purpose of the daily check-in is to help team members avoid confusion about how priorities are translated into action on a regular basis. It provides a quick forum for ensuring that nothing falls through the cracks on a given day and that no one steps on anyone else's toes. Just as important, it helps eliminate the need for unnecessary and time-consuming e-mail chains about schedule coordination.

The daily check-in can be impractical for many organizations where team members work in different locations and time zones. And while a check-in can be done by phone, it isn't always wise to go to great lengths to make them happen in an organization where it is just not feasible. Still, though not indispensable for every team, the daily check-in can be a valuable tool for many organizations who want to better align their activities.

Inevitable Challenges. One of the certain challenges in making the daily check-in work will be getting team members to stick with it initially, long enough to make it part of their routine. It will be all too easy for busy team members to lobby for abandoning the daily check-in before they have given it a chance.

The key to overcoming this is to keep these meetings consistent in terms of where and when they occur. In addition, it will be extremely important not to cancel any, even if only two members of the team are in the office on a given day.

A more common challenge with the daily check-in will be keeping it to five minutes. If the meetings exceed their time limit slightly because team members are socializing a little, that's actually okay. But if they're going long because team members are trying to address issues every morning that should be discussed at the weekly tactical meeting, this is a problem.

What will ultimately happen is that people will get tired of having what feels like a daily staff meeting.

One way to avoid this is to prohibit people from sitting down during daily check-ins. More important, the team must be disciplined, even unreasonably so, about ending the sessions after no more than ten minutes.

Finally, to avoid both of these likely obstacles, teams should commit to doing daily check-ins for a set period of time—perhaps two months—before evaluating whether they are working.

Meeting 2: The Weekly Tactical Every team needs to have regular meetings focused exclusively on tactical issues of immediate concern. Whether it takes place weekly or every other week doesn't really matter. What does matter is that everyone always attends and that it is run with a sense of discipline and structural consistency.

A weekly tactical meeting should last between forty-five and ninety minutes, depending on its frequency, and should include a few critical elements, including the following.

The Lightning Round. This is a quick, around-the-table reporting session in which everyone indicates his or her two or three priorities for the week. It should take each team member no more than one minute to quickly describe what is on their respective plates. Even a large team should be able to accomplish this in ten minutes or so.

The lightning round is critical because it sets the tone for the rest of the meeting. By giving all participants a real sense of the actual activities taking place in the organization, it makes it easy for the team to identify potential redundancies, gaps, or other issues that require immediate attention.

Progress Review. The next key ingredient for the weekly tactical meeting is the routine reporting of critical information or metrics: revenue, expenses, customer satisfaction, inventory, and the like. What is reported depends on the particular industry and organizational situation. The point here is to get into the habit of reviewing progress relating to key metrics for success, but not every metric available—maybe four or six. This should take no more than five minutes, even when allowing for quick questions for clarification of numbers. Lengthy discussion of underlying issues should be avoided here.

Real-Time Agenda. Once the lightning round and progress review are complete (usually no more than fifteen minutes into the meeting), now it is time to talk about the agenda. Counter to conventional wisdom about meetings, the agenda for a weekly tactical should not be set before the meeting, but only after the lightning round and regular reporting activities have taken place.

This makes sense because the agenda should be based on what everyone is actually working on and how the company is performing against its goals, not based on the leader's best guess forty-eight hours prior to the meeting. Trying to predict the right priorities before these critical pieces of information are reviewed is unwise.

Leaders of meetings must therefore have something I call disciplined spontaneity, which means they must avoid the temptation to prepare an agenda ahead of time, and instead allow it to take shape during the meeting itself. While this might mean sacrificing some control, it ensures that the meeting will be relevant and effective.

Settling on the real-time agenda isn't terribly hard because the important topics will be easy to identify by that point.

Inevitably, a few issues that need to be discussed will jump out: "Should we increase advertising this month to jump-start sales?" "Should marketing or business development talk to analysts about our product issues?" "Should we freeze hiring or accelerate it?" "What are we going to do about the spending overruns?" Tactical issues that must be addressed to ensure that short-term objectives are not in jeopardy.

During the weekly tactical meeting, there are two overriding goals: resolution of issues and reinforcement of clarity. Obstacles need to be identified and removed, and everyone needs to be on the same page.

Inevitable Challenges. A number of likely obstacles can prevent the proper implementation of weekly tactical meetings.

One of them is the temptation to set an agenda ahead of time, either formally or informally. While this is understandable given conventional wisdom, it is not wise. That's because it is critical for team members to come to the weekly tactical with an open mind, and to let the real activities and progress against objectives determine what needs to be discussed.

Another common problem is the tendency of team members to go into too much detail during the lightning round. This causes others to lose interest, which clouds the ability of the team to identify the right issues for discussion and resolution. The key to avoiding this challenge is to hold team members to sixty seconds during the lightning round, which is plenty of time to provide a quick summary of key activities and even answer a question or two for clarification. If this is difficult to believe, stare at a clock for sixty seconds. You'll realize that it is a lot longer period of time than it seems and that a lot of information can be relayed during it.

While these are both important problems to be aware of, by far the most common and dangerous challenge in making weekly tacticals work is the temptation to get into discussions about long-term strategic issues. Why is this such an important problem to avoid?

First, there isn't enough time during a weekly tactical meeting to properly discuss major issues. Important, complex topics deserve enough time for brainstorming, analysis, even preparation. Moreover, even the best executives don't easily shift back and forth between topics of different magnitude, like deciding whether to change the policy on business-class air travel and whether to merge with a competitor. It is the equivalent of a husband and wife trying to discuss what to do about their child's discipline problem in the same breath as deciding what to have for dinner.

A final problem with mixing strategic and tactical topics during meetings has to do with the tendency of leaders to inappropriately reconsider strategic decisions when faced with inevitable tactical obstacles. Limiting weekly tactical meetings to specific, short-term topics requires people to focus on solving problems, rather than backing off of long-term decisions that have already been made.

The key to overcoming this challenge is discipline. When strategic issues are raised—and they will inevitably be raised—it is critical for the leader to take them off the table and put them on a list of possible topics to be discussed during a different meeting: the monthly strategic.

Meeting 3: The Monthly Strategic This is the most interesting and in many ways the most important type of meeting any team has. It is also the most fun. It is where executives wrestle with, analyze, debate, and decide on critical issues (but only a few) that will affect the business in fundamental ways. Monthly strategic meetings allow executives to dive into a given topic or two without the distractions of deadlines and tactical concerns.

The length of a monthly strategic will vary depending on the topic or topics being considered. However, it is advisable to schedule at least two hours per topic so that participants feel comfortable engaging in open-ended conversation and debate.

Whether teams decide to have these meetings once a month or every two weeks is not really important. What is important is that these strategic meetings occur regularly so that they can serve as a timely "parking lot" for critical strategic issues that come up during the weekly tactical meetings. This gives executives the confidence to table critical issues, knowing they will eventually be addressed.

Ad Hoc Strategic Meetings. In some cases, a strategic or critical issue that gets raised in a weekly tactical meeting cannot wait for the next monthly strategic meeting on the schedule. Still, that doesn't mean it should be taken up during that weekly tactical.

Instead, executives should create an ad hoc meeting specifically for the purpose of taking on that issue. It should be clearly separated from the weekly tactical so that executives can reset their minds to the nature of the meeting, and so enough time can be allotted for appropriate analysis and discussion. If all this requires that executives clear their schedules later that day or stay into the evening, then so be it. If the issue is truly critical, then it is worth such a sacrifice.

In many ways, this ad hoc strategic meeting is the most important one that occurs in an organization. It demonstrates that an executive team knows how to identify those rare strategic issues that deserve immediate attention even at the expense of the urgent but less important tactical concerns that surface every day. Great organizations rally around these issues with the kind of focus and urgency that allow them to outmaneuver competitors who are too mired in the monotony of their meetings or who wait for a full-blown crisis before rallying around an important topic.

If these strategic meetings can take place whenever an issue warrants them, then why did I call them monthly strategics? Because if we do not schedule regular meetings to talk about important topics, we will find ourselves looking back after four months and wondering why we haven't had any strategic conversations at all. Choosing a regular interval is an important step to ensuring that strategic meetings don't fall by the wayside.

Inevitable Challenges. The most obvious challenge in implementing monthly strategic meetings (or the ad hoc variety) is the failure to schedule enough time for them. In the heat of daily schedules and demands on executives' time, the idea of carving out three or four hours for one or two issues is harder than it seems in theory. But it is critical. Sometimes it takes forty-five minutes of discussion at the beginning of a monthly strategic just to unearth the real underlying issue at the heart of a problem.

A related challenge has to do with putting too many items on the agenda. This is an understandable temptation for executives who want to discuss every important issue. Unfortunately, it only dilutes the quality of the debate around the most critical ones.

The key to avoiding both of these challenges is to ensure that more than enough time is scheduled for each issue. That means if there are three issues to resolve, the meeting needs to be much longer than if there is only one. Again, if that means clearing everyone's calendars for an entire day, so be it.

In my work, I have found that most executives have far too many tactical and administrative items on their schedules, which is often the result of an adrenaline addiction—the need to stay occupied with moment-to-moment activities. And so they initially resist taking an entire day for meetings to discuss strategy, because they fear falling behind in their daily adrenal activities. However, once they force themselves to carve out time for strategic conversations, they almost always are glad they did, and they are surprised that they didn't really miss anything critical by being away from their desks for the afternoon.

Another challenge in making strategic meetings work is the failure to do research and preparation ahead of time. The quality of a strategic discussion, and the decision that results from it, are improved greatly by a little preliminary work. This eliminates the all-too-common reliance on anecdotal decision making. The key to ensuring that preparation occurs is to let team members know as far in advance as possible what issues will be discussed during the monthly or ad hoc strategic meeting. Of course, the leader must also hold team members accountable for coming to the meetings prepared.

Finally, I would be remiss if I didn't mention a final challenge: the fear of conflict. Monthly and ad hoc strategic meetings cannot be effective unless there is a willingness on the part of team members to engage in unfiltered, productive ideological debate. This also applies to the final type of meeting: the quarterly off-site review.

Meeting 4: The Quarterly Off-Site Review The executive off-site has earned a reputation as a time-wasting, touchy-feely boondoggle, and in many cases, rightly so. Whether executives are golfing, catching each other falling out of trees, or exploring their collective inner child, many off-site meetings contribute little lasting benefit to an organization.

This is a shame, not only because of the time, money, and credibility that are sacrificed, but because of the critical role that off-site meetings should play in the context of all the other meetings that serve the organization.

Topics to Cover. Effective off-sites provide executives an opportunity to regularly step away from the daily, weekly, even monthly issues that occupy their attention, so they can review the business in a more holistic, long-term manner. Topics for reflection and discussion at a productive quarterly off-site review might include the following:

- *Comprehensive strategy review:* Executives should reassess their strategic direction—not every day, as so many do, but three or four times a year. Industries change and new competitive threats emerge that call for different approaches. Reviewing strategies annually or semiannually is usually not often enough to stay current.

- *Team review:* Executives should regularly assess themselves and their behaviors as a team, identifying trends or tendencies that may not be serving the organization. This often requires a change of scenery so that executives can interact with one another on a more personal level and remind themselves of their collective commitments to the team.

○ *Personnel review:* Three or four times a year, executives should talk, across departments, about the key employees within the organization. Every member of an executive team should know whom their peers view as their stars, as well as their poor performers. This allows executives to provide perspectives that might actually alter those perceptions based on different experiences and points of view. More important, it allows them to jointly manage and retain top performers and work with poor performers similarly.

○ *Competitive and industry review:* Information about competitors and industry trends bleeds into an organization little by little over time. It is useful for executives to step back and look at what is happening around them in a more comprehensive way so they can spot trends that individual nuggets of information might not make clear. Even the best executives can lose site of the forest for the trees when inundated with daily responsibilities.

Inevitable Challenges. A variety of challenges can prevent a team from correctly establishing effective quarterly off-site reviews. None are particularly dangerous by themselves, but together they can hinder the effectiveness of these important meetings, and ultimately lead to their demise.

One of the challenges is the tendency to overburden and overstructure the meetings, which usually takes the form of tightly scheduled slide presentations and lengthy informational sermons. The purpose of a quarterly off-site review is to reflect on and discuss the state of the organization, not to provide executives with presentations and white papers.

Another challenge is the temptation to make these meetings too much of a boondoggle by having them at exotic locations that require extensive travel and by including too many social activities. The purpose of getting out of the office is not to entertain the attendees, but rather to allow them to step back from daily distractions and interruptions. As a result, driving an hour away to a comfortable hotel or conference center is usually enough to do the trick. Flying to Aruba or Hawaii does not eliminate distractions; it merely substitutes one type (say, snorkeling and golf) for another (work interruptions).

Another interesting problem is inviting outsiders to attend the meeting, in the spirit of inclusivity. While this may be tempting for a variety of reasons (for example, more input, or involvement and exposure for employees), it is a very bad idea for exactly one: it changes the team dynamic. Adding even one employee who is not a member of the team, no matter how well liked or well informed that person is, can negate one of the most important reasons for having off-sites: improving team unity.

The only exception to this rule might be the use of an outside facilitator, someone who is trusted by the team, understands the organization's business, and is driven to help the team accomplish its objectives, not his or her own objectives. The greatest benefit of using such a facilitator is that it allows the leader of the team to participate fully in the discussions without having to worry about playing a more objective, supporting role.

The Biggest Challenge of All: The Myth of Too Many Meetings

Most of my friends reacted the same way when they heard that I was writing a book called *Death by Meeting*. As you may have done, they assumed I was going to make a case for having fewer meetings.

And so, on hearing about daily check-ins, weekly tacticals, monthly strategics, and quarterly off-site reviews, you might be thinking, "This is crazy. Where am I going to find the time to do all this? I'm already going to too many meetings."

While it is true that much of the time we currently spend in meetings is largely wasted, the solution is not to stop having meetings, but rather to make them better. When properly used, meetings are actually time savers.

Good meetings provide opportunities to improve execution by accelerating decision making and eliminating the need to revisit issues again and again. They also produce a subtle but enormous benefit by reducing unnecessarily repetitive motion and communication in the organization. The reason that we don't see this at first glance is that we fail to account for something that I like to call "sneaker time."

Sneaker Time

Most executives I know spend hours sending e-mail, leaving voice mail, and roaming the halls to clarify issues that should have been made clear during a meeting in the first place. But no one accounts for this the way they do when they add up time spent in meetings.

I have no doubt that sneaker time is the most subtle, dangerous, and underestimated black hole in corporate America. To understand it, it is helpful to take a quick look at the basic geometry of an executive team within the context of an organization.

Consider that an executive team with just seven people has twenty-one combinations of one-to-one relationships that have to be maintained in order to keep people on the same page. That alone is next to impossible for a human being to track.

But when you consider the dozens of employees down throughout the organization who report to those seven and who need to be on the same page with one another, the communication challenge increases dramatically, as does the potential for wasting time and energy. And so when we fail to get clarity and alignment during meetings, we set in motion a colossal wave of human activity as executives and their direct reports scramble to figure out what everyone else is doing and why.

Remarkably, because sneaker time is mixed in with everything else we do during the day, we fail to see it as a single category of wasted time. It never ceases to amaze me when I see executives checking their watches at the end of a meeting and lobbying the CEO for it to end so they can "go do some real work." In so many cases, the "real work" they're referring to is going back to their offices to respond to e-mail and voice mail that they've received only because so many people are confused about what needs to be done.

It's as if the executives are saying, "Can we wrap this up so I can run around and explain to people what I never explained to them after the last meeting?" It is at once shocking and understandable that intelligent people cannot see the correlation between failing to take the time to get clarity, closure, and buy-in during a meeting, and the time required to clean up after themselves as a result.

o　　o　　o

Patrick Lencioni is president of the Table Group, a management consulting firm and a highly sought-after speaker.

Chapter Twenty-Five

Politically Astute Negotiating

Kathleen Kelley Reardon

No one gets to the top without skillful negotiation. When told something can't be done, truly effective negotiators think about how they can get it done. When told they must do something, they begin to think of how they might do it to their advantage, or not do it at all. Telling them "no" or "this is not negotiable" is equivalent to issuing them a challenge. Their brains shift into a negotiation gear at the merest hint of being blocked.

I've spent a good part of my career studying what separates those who get a good deal from those who settle prematurely or don't bother to negotiate at all. Insights gleaned from that study, in addition to the experiences of dozens of people I've interviewed, form the core of this chapter. It takes considerable study and practice to become an expert negotiator, and some very good books have been published on the subject. But

what it takes to be a politically astute or street-smart negotiator is somewhat different. That's our focus here.

PREPARING FOR STREET-SMART NEGOTIATION

"When I'm negotiating an important deal," a New York
City–based negotiation expert with an impressive clientele told
me, "I listen for quite a while. As I present a proposal, I watch
to see if several people seem opposed to it. In that case, I do a
little constructive deception. If one of them expresses some
agreement with me, I might use him to divide the group. After
coaxing him to my side, I'll gradually turn against him myself.
The others, who are by then angry with him, become more
open to my proposal, especially if I throw in some things they
want. Essentially, the person who initially agreed with me
becomes the common enemy. And nothing brings people
together so well as that."

This is hardball negotiation. In fact, in this type of scenario,
most people don't even see the ball coming. It's a counterintuitive strategy because negotiators usually try to locate someone
who agrees with them, then look for a way to create a win-win
outcome. Instead, the above negotiation expert engages in
"constructive deception," outwitting a cohesive group by locat-
ing its most cooperative member and alienating him.

This example alone shows how important it is to develop
street-smart negotiation skills. You have to distrust the obvious,
and recognize hardball tactics when you see them.

IMPRESSION TRAPS

Faulty impressions are the number one enemy of negotiation
effectiveness, especially in politicized organizations. "They'll
never fire us" are the famous last words of many people who

find themselves invited to leave organizations. It's always better to enter any situation with healthy skepticism about your assumptions and some acquired insights into what the assumptions are of the other negotiators.

Consider the assumptions of the following three people about to enter into an important business negotiation. They've come together to negotiate a product production and distribution deal between two companies: Customware (Mike and Ellen's company) and Blueprint (Gene's company). The deal could strengthen Blueprint's presence in Europe and give Customware an entrée into the European market. Having met briefly earlier in the evening, they're in their hotel rooms preparing for the next day's negotiation. Here are their thoughts:

> Gene had Mike figured. He'd seen the type before—aloof, arrogant even—the kind who looks right through you, doesn't give an inch until you've given away the farm, and then makes you think he's done you a favor. The thing to do was wait him out, feign indifference, stare him down if necessary, and make him sweat. Treat any gesture of accommodation with skepticism. Gene prided himself on being able to tell a tiger by its stripes. This one didn't know who he was dealing with. The woman, thought Gene, was more difficult to read. She had depth—you could see that in her eyes. But what difference did it make? Ellen is just along for the experience. Maybe they planned to play "good cop, bad cop" with him. For their own sake, Gene thought, they'd better have a backup plan.
>
> Reading his own bio on the plane had bolstered Mike's confidence, not that much bolstering was necessary. His M.B.A. said all that needed to be said. Gene didn't have one. It wasn't snobbery, Mike assured himself. He had met some crafty negotiators in his time who hadn't had fancy degrees, but Gene didn't strike him as particularly savvy. This observation, coupled with his own superior intellect, was enough to make Mike feel pretty sure of

who'd walk away with the best deal. Their brief meeting earlier in the evening had only confirmed these impressions. Mike's biggest challenge was on his own team. Why had his boss sent Ellen? Sure she was smart—had an M.B.A. and her record in sales and marketing had made her his equal in status. But this would be a crucial negotiation. Her credentials would do her little good when the heat was on Hopefully, she would follow his lead, maintain a low profile, and keep her input to a minimum. He'd tell her his expectations in the morning. The most important thing was the negotiation's outcome, not whose ego got strokes. It was time to stop thinking. He'd need his rest after such a long trip—even to take on a lightweight thinker like Gene.

Before turning off the lights in strange hotel rooms, Ellen always arranged her clothes and her ideas for the next day, made a few notes about people to call, and eased herself into sleep with a novel. Tonight, though, she couldn't get her mind off the few minutes she'd spent earlier in the evening with Gene and Mike. The body language of the two men had told her neither of them saw her as a player—even Mike, who was on her team. This was nothing new to her—part of the territory as the younger partner and a woman to boot. She'd have to set Mike straight early on. She was confident, having learned from some well-placed snitches at the home office that he'd lost some ground of late. People weren't impressed any longer with such hard chargers, especially in international circles where this project could take them. The John Wayne days were ending, but Mike was obviously stuck in a style rut. He was the take-control, take-no-prisoners type. As she dozed off, she practiced how she'd manage Mike the next day. She didn't come thousands of miles just to cheer him on.

Gene, Mike, and Ellen are three people on the path to negotiation failure. Gene believes he has Mike figured out because he's seen his type before. He decides he won't be fooled this time. There's no indication that he intends to check any of his assumptions or seek more details. Why bother? He read a few road signs and decided he has all the facts he needs.

Mike is no different in this regard. He has himself convinced that his M.B.A. is the ticket to success with the supposedly less accomplished Gene. He has already decided that Ellen is a liability despite her track record. Ellen has concluded that both Gene and Mike have excluded any possibility that she might be important to this negotiation. She decides to make setting them straight her first priority. In only a few minutes' time, each of these people has charted a course for the next day—the wrong course.

In most negotiations, instincts overtake reason. When negotiating, our mouths can start running before our minds have a chance to filter. We react and we blow the deal before it's even off the ground. Truly effective negotiators monitor their reactions and think ahead to how their choice of responses might shape those of the other person. They avoid the tendency to react without checking assumptions and confirming the other person's meaning.

Most important, effective negotiators prioritize well. They steer around issues that might take them down a path away from important goals. They bypass or minimize small annoyances and occasional petty comments to ensure their primary goals will be attained.

Let's take Gene as a case in point. He is about to approach Mike with a wait-him-out, feign-indifference, stare-him-down-if-necessary, and make-him-sweat series of strategies. He'll treat any gesture of accommodation with skepticism.

There's nothing wrong with Gene's formulating a first impression, but that's all it is—a first impression. It's like the first draft of a paper. Rely on it, and you blow the deal. Do you hand it in just because you've written a hundred papers before, or do you reread, revise, and spell-check it? Gene is about to hand in his first draft, a terrible error in judgment.

ARE YOU THE RIGHT PERSON TO NEGOTIATE?

There's the possibility that Gene, Mike, and Ellen aren't the best threesome to negotiate this deal. The likelihood of their recognizing this is low, given their focus on personalities more than on the deal itself. That's where a politically astute negotiator differs from the average one.

There are different styles of negotiation. Sometimes different styles don't mesh. University of Southern California (USC) professor emeritus Alan Rowe and I have developed an assessment tool for identifying negotiation style predilections. This tool (Exhibit 25.1) identifies preferences among four negotiation styles: Achiever, Analytical, Motivator, and Mediator.

Achievers (highest score in column 1) usually go right to the heart of an issue, moving things along quickly. They have little patience for long-winded logic, and they want to win. Analytical negotiators (highest score in column 2) provide a good deal of data and are inclined to walk people through their reasoning step by step. They speak in terms of priorities, and if they make concessions, they tend to make them along these lines. Motivators (highest score in column 3) pride themselves on finding clever, novel ways of reaching solutions. They also express enthusiasm in contagious fashion. Finally, Mediators (highest score in column 4) like to help people find ways to agree. They are inclined to seek compromise or to accommodate so that things work out well for everyone.

As you can see, each style type is potentially in conflict with the other types. The Achiever, for example, could become very

EXHIBIT 25.1. Instrument for Assessing Negotiation Style

To score the instrument, put an 8 next to the response most like you, a 4 for the response moderately like you, a 2 for the response a little like you, and a 1 for the response least like you. Then add down each column. The four numbers should equal 300. *You must answer all the questions. There are no right or wrong answers.* The answers reflect how you see yourself so respond with what comes first to your mind.

	1		2		3		4	
1. When I negotiate, I	Focus on my objectives		Explore workable solutions		Try to understand their thinking		Try to avoid arguments	
2. I explain my ideas best by	Being forceful		Presenting my ideas logically		Explaining the implication		Relating my points to theirs	
3. When I am confronted, I	React strongly to what is said		Explain my position with facts		Look for a common ground		Give in reluctantly	
4. I describe my expectations	Objectively		In complete detail		Enthusiastically		Amicably	
5. I get my best deals when I	Don't make any concessions		Use my leverage		Find creative solutions		Am willing to meet them halfway	
6. My objective in negotiation is to	Achieve my goal		Convince others to accept my position		Find the best solution for all		Look for an acceptable solution	
7. The way to win an argument is to	Be self-confident		Be logical		Have novel ideas		Look for consensus	
8. I prefer information that	Is specific and understandable		Is complete and persuasive		Shows a number of options		Helps to achieve rapport	
9. When I'm not sure what to do, I	Take direct action		Search for possible solutions		Rely on my intuition		Seek advice from others	
10. I dislike	Long debates		Incomplete information		Highly technical material		Having arguments	
11. If I've been rejected, I	Persist in my point of view		Rethink my position		Relate my ideas to theirs		Try to salvage the relationship	
12. If timing is important, I	Press for a quick decision		Rely on critical facts		Propose a compromise		Hope to postpone the inevitable	
13. When I am questioned, I	Answer emphatically		Rely on data for my position		Respond with a broad question		Look at how it affects me	
14. I prefer situations where	I am in control		I can use my logical ability		I can explore new opportunities		People are considerate	

	1	2	3	4	
15. I negotiate best when	I use my experience	A technical analysis is critical	I can explore many alternatives	I am in a win-win situation	
16. When I am the underdog, I	Do not show any weakness	Prepare carefully	Try to change the situation	Match my needs with theirs	
17. When one is antagonistic, I	Stand my ground	Reason things out carefully	Attempt to rise above the situation	Look for ways to reduce the tension	
18. If I'm in a losing situation, I	Become more determined	Consider all my options	Look for ways to turn it around	Appeals to their sense of fairness	
19. To achieve mutual gain, I	Show a workable solution	Clarify everyone's priorities	Suggest a mutually beneficial plan	Consider both sides of the issue	
20. In negotiating, it is important to	Know what each party wants	Clearly identify the agenda	Start by making a positive impression	Recognize that each party has needs	

Source: Alan J. Rowe and Kathleen K. Reardon, Dec. 29, 1997; revised March 27, 1998. This form may not be reproduced without written permission.

annoyed with an Analytical, who provides too much data; with a Motivator, who is a dreamer rather than a doer; or with a Mediator, who seems to be looking for happy endings.

Often backup styles (second- and sometimes third-highest scores on the inventory) prove helpful in bridging communication gaps. An Achiever with a backup Analytical style could be patient with a strong Analytical type because he or she is familiar with that style.

When the styles are at odds, though, and backup styles don't mesh either, the mix isn't conducive to successful negotiation. To be an effective negotiator, you need to pick up on when you're unable to stretch to accommodate the style preferences of the other party. That's when you may need to fold up your tent and let someone else take over or give you a hand.

Elizabeth Daley, dean of the Cinema School and head of the Annenberg Center at USC, told me that she learned long ago that relying solely on your own skill is a good way to dead-end your career. "I learned from a friend that there is an important difference between people who do really well and those who only do moderately well in their careers. When confronted with a challenge, the ones who do really well ask themselves, 'Who can help me with this?' Those who do only moderately well ask themselves, 'What can I do about this?'" It's a subtle but important distinction.

Returning to the earlier scenario, Mike has already made some serious mistakes, which his home office has noticed. That's why Ellen was sent along. But rather than focusing on the goal of the negotiation, she is focused on how each man is responding to her. And Gene is focused on what he sees as Mike's arrogance. They're all out to prove themselves. In approaching the negotiation, none of them is questioning whether his or her primary style is suited to the negotiation at hand. They aren't wondering, based on first impressions, whether their backup styles might help them stretch to communicate more effectively with the others. They're not demonstrating the kind of sensitivity to differences that it takes to negotiate effectively.

They should be asking themselves how their style strengths might prove useful at anticipated junctures in the upcoming negotiation. If Ellen knows, for example, that she is more Analytical than Mike and that he is more of an Achiever, then she may be better positioned than Mike to provide data to support their claims. Mike is better suited to creating a sense of urgency and ushering the negotiation away from excessive discussions that could take them away from reaching a workable solution.

Savvy negotiation requires this kind of questioning. Gene should be assessing how he might have to stretch his style to

get and keep Mike and Ellen's interest and attention. In negotiation, the goal is to achieve the best outcome under the circumstances. If you don't assess the circumstances, including
style differences, your outcome is likely to be compromised.

Organize Your Thoughts into Primary Issues, Secondary Issues, and Clutter Issues

Colin Powell uses the KISS principle to guide his communication: Keep it simple, stupid.[1] Too often people go into negotiation
without knowing which goals are most important to them. Politically savvy negotiators are organized: they keep things as simple
as possible (unless ambiguity actually helps them reach their
goals—even then the ambiguity is contrived, not accidental).

It never pays to go into negotiations with just one plan. You
need contingency plans too.[2] It's critical to establish and to
organize strategies and options in terms of preference. Most
important, you can't allow the discussion to get lost in minor
issues if you're going to make a good impression and get what
you're after. The best negotiators are very good at candidly
answering this question: Am I getting bogged down in details
that are taking me away from my main goal? In advance of
negotiations, they ask themselves, "What issues do I want to
avoid?" Then they apply the KISS principle, because they know
that too much complexity leaves open many avenues down
which the negation might meander to its demise.

Get Yourself a Good Opener

Since people often rush to judgment about each other and make
quick, negative assumptions, it's important to get negotiations
off to a strong start. In negotiation parlance, this is called a
strong opening stance. Sometimes this means beginning with

an apology, to decrease expected animosity. At other times, it means making a firm statement about expectations so the other side knows you're serious.

More often than not, a good opening stance is a well-planned one. Richard Lewis, CEO of Accountants Overload, has a good saying that applies here: "It's better to be silent and be thought a fool than to speak and remove all doubt." In negotiation, it's always better to think before you speak. Take the time to consider how what you say will influence the other party's reply and how that reply might limit your options.

Rather than starting by telling the other side your strongest argument or revealing your position, it's often a good idea to start with a question, although not just any question. The choice of question type should be strategic. Open-ended questions, for example, are ones that require more than a simple yes or no answer. "What would you like to achieve at this meeting?" and "What do you think of our plan?" are examples of open-ended questions. The best time to use these kinds of questions is when you need more information about how the other side is approaching the issue at hand. Another time might be when there's a good chance that they're angry with you and so you want to give them the opportunity to vent early in the negotiation.

To make the venting of anger work, you need to be careful not to react to any emotional outbursts or criticisms. Your response to such an occurrence might be: "I don't blame you for feeling as you do. There's been a considerable amount of misinformation prior to this meeting and some incidents that shouldn't have occurred. And that's why we're here today, to turn that situation around. Maybe you have some thoughts on how we might do that."

Openers set the stage. When the curtain goes up, a theater audience formulates an impression within seconds. Get it wrong, and the performers spend the next few hours making up for a poor start. What separates the politically astute negotiator from the less advanced is sensitivity to those first few seconds and minutes. Assess early on what matters to the other party, demonstrate that you are also concerned about these matters and that you're there to work with him or her, and you'll be off on the right track in 95 percent of negotiations.

Become a Multitracker

The ability to observe on many levels is one of the least discussed yet most important negotiation skills. One reason that so few people do this well is that there's a tendency to think that negotiation is mostly about words. Even the most popular negotiation books focus on what you should say to get the upper hand or achieve accord where there's been dissension. The truth, however, is that a considerable amount of success in negotiation comes from reading cues that others miss, calculating their importance, and sometimes giving them greater credence than the spoken word.

There are few people who've achieved the secret handshake without honing the skill of seeing what others disregard, whether it's a slight tilt of the CEO's head at a meeting, a senior vice president's glance at her watch, a rapid change of topic, or a momentary grimace. Whatever the subtle signal, the most savvy don't miss it. They think over their observations of subtle signals and decide whether they're meaningful. If the boss looks bored, they'll speak in a louder tone of voice, use direct eye contact, and perhaps use humor to shake him out of his malaise into interest and curiosity.

Should they notice a slight shake of their opponent's head, their response might be, "When I first heard this idea, I was skeptical, but another way to look at it is . . ." By recognizing the other person's skepticism, framing it as natural and even expected, and then leading him or her to another vantage point from which to view the questionable idea, a skillful negotiator can dispose of opposition before it has even been stated.

FIND THE CONNECTIONS

The key to negotiation, like the key to persuading, is to understand where the other person is coming from. Ask yourself: "What's most important to my boss or client?" "What are his greatest concerns?" "How do they connect to mine?" Go forward only after you've answered these questions.

One of the more sage pieces of advice given by the people I interviewed came from a foundation director speaking about difficult bosses: "One day you just have to face the fact that you work for these people. Once you do that, a lot of other things fall into place. You let them know if you disagree, you might even occasionally argue your position, but once they make up their minds, that's it. You find a way to do it." Of course, there are exceptions to this rule. If you're asked to do something against your moral principles, for example, you might not do their bidding. With that exception, what most politically sophisticated people do is find a way to do what their bosses want while also advancing one or more of their own goals. This means that it's your job to find a way to connect what you want to what they want. Those who go off mumbling to themselves about doing what they don't want to do usually haven't thought beyond the immediate request. They haven't stopped to consider how what is being asked of them might in some way, if handled right, be a positive step to advancement rather than an annoying diversion.

Perhaps this section should be called "How to Please the Boss and Yourself As Well" because that's what we're talking about here. Linking goals, whether to your boss or to a client, affords the negotiation of differences. It involves identifying how doing what he or she wants might give you what you want as well. Ellen Nichols, a Hartford-based insurance executive, does this all the time. "I go in prepared to compromise and then to compromise some more, but I also know what I really want to achieve in the transaction. At impasses, I'm ready to say, 'How should we work this out?' I always go in with alternatives and I try to get them to join in with a 'How about if we try this?' approach."

This is the preliminary step to effective linking. The more prepared you are in terms of having alternatives ready that keep your interests in mind while serving theirs, the more effective you'll be. Too often people go into negotiations wanting an outcome they're unlikely to get, and then they keep pushing for it long after it is futile. Nichols warns, "It's critical to remember that there is always a bigger picture out there and something you may not have understood in your preparations. You have to keep your eyes open for it. You don't want to be like an angry child. You have to know when to stop fighting for something."

Does this mean you allow yourself to lose occasionally? It does if you aren't able to find links between what you want and what the other party wants. Coy Baugh, vice president and treasurer of PacifiCare Health Systems, remembers almost losing an important deal over the placement of a comma in the contract. The discussion became very heated, to the point where Baugh suggested the general counsel take a walk around the block. Realizing that the comma debate could ruin every-thing, Baugh adhered to one of his own axioms: being right is only marginally helpful. He cooled things down and let the other side have their say. They worked out an addendum explaining how to move the "blasted comma," and everyone agreed to sign the documents. By hearing the other side out, controlling his temper, and finding a way to link their mutual concerns, he succeeded in the negotiation.

MAKE YOURSELF AND YOUR IDEAS MEMORABLE

We've established that the human brain declines to be overtaxed. But what we haven't discussed is how to get and keep attention. Astute negotiators know how to grab attention and focus it on themselves and their ideas. Since negotiation is what most of us do much of the day at work, this is a crucial skill. You're more likely to get noticed and considered for advancement if you make a positive, memorable impact when you speak.

Nancy Hayes, a former IBM executive and now CEO of the Starbright Foundation, believes men and women create ver-bal impact differently. "Every one of the guys wants to be the guy who says the thing that turns the meeting around." This is how men often make themselves memorable. "Women, on the other hand, wait and listen. They try to determine the position of each person because they want to achieve consensus."

Whichever approach you choose, don't overdo it. Done sparingly, both the turn-the-meeting-around and the integra-tor approaches can make an impact and also make headway in a negotiation. The choice depends to a large extent on the cul-ture of the company or companies. Watch carefully to see what gets people noticed where you work. If it's within your style reach, give it a try.

Politically astute negotiators also know the importance of making a nonverbal impact. James Farley was one of the pillars of the Democratic Party in the days of FDR. He was elected a member of the New York State Assembly in the early 1920s, and over the next twenty years his stature in the Democratic Party increased. He organized Roosevelt's successful campaign for governor of New York and, as chairman of the Democratic National Committee, led FDR's campaign for president. Had Farley not been Irish Catholic at a time when the United States wasn't ready to elect one, he might have taken the nomination he received to run for president in 1940. With all this success, it might seem frivolous to think that Farley bothered himself about being remembered in a unique nonverbal way. But he did. He started using green ink. And since no one else did, it made him memorable. He once said, "It occurred to me that it would be wise to have some little distinguishing mark that would induce the receiver to remember me as an individual. . . . Green ink did the trick so well that it was given the job permanently."[3]

It seems odd to think that some distinguishing trait or feature could turn the tide of your career, and maybe it can't. But it might help. There are so many people who daily cross the paths of those with the power to promote you that it's difficult to be on their radar screen if you don't have something that makes you stand out. Don Butler, president emeritus and board member of the Employers Group, told me that one of his identifying features is cufflinks. They're from all over the world. Each set is unique. At the time we spoke, he was wearing twenty-two-karat gold tigers with diamond eyes. "No one fails to notice them," he said. "Each set is a memorable conversation piece."

Congresswoman Bella Abzug made her mark as a feminist because of her ideas, but it was her hats that made her recognizable and memorable to the general public. When I rode around Dublin with her after attending the Global Forum for Women, she had on a large-brimmed, beige hat. No one could miss her. During our cab ride to see the scenery, the hat stayed on, and when she emerged from the cab, there was no doubt who she was.

After you've considered ways to make yourself visibly memorable, it's important to consider how to do the same for your ideas. Once again, in the morass of chatter that we experience each day, it's difficult to have your ideas reach front-and-center if you don't know how to get them noticed.

One way to make an idea memorable is to tell a short story about an instance when a similar idea worked effectively. You might also draw an image on the board, or conjure up an analogy that helps demonstrate how your idea fits with the discussion at hand. These memory-jogging, idea-clarifying techniques can be very powerful. Imagine, for example, that a joint venture is in trouble. You want to save it. The other side is dubious. You rise from your chair and draw a tree leaning precariously over a precipice. You turn to the group and say, "Our joint venture is like this tree. Its future seems in jeopardy. A strong wind could send it over the cliff. But let's look closer." You approach the board and draw several squiggles under the tree. "Beneath the surface, where we haven't been looking today, our tree has strong roots. It has weathered a number of storms, and if we feed it today with what it needs to survive, those strong roots will keep us secure."

An image can indeed be worth a thousand words, and an astute negotiator knows this. To the extent that you present yourself and your ideas in memorable ways, you create conditions for effective negotiation and advance your chances of being remembered when the time comes to select someone for a high-level position.

And if this ability isn't important enough already, there is good reason to believe it will be even more important in the future. Rolf Jensen, futurist and director of the Copenhagen Institute for Futures Studies, says, "We are in the twilight of a society based on data. As information and intelligence become the domain of computers, society will place new value on the one human ability that can't be automated: emotion, imagination, myth, ritual . . ." He predicts that in the future, products, and that means people too, will sell on the art of storytelling and that companies will recruit and retain people "based on how they express their spirit."[4]

If Jensen is right, and I believe he is, it isn't going to be enough to provide dry data to support the promotion of an idea or the promotion of people. If there aren't stories, images, and even myths as part of the package, then they'll be overlooked for something more tantalizing, something far more memorable. You'll want that something to be in you.

o   o   o

Kathleen Kelley Reardon is professor of management and organization at the University of Southern California's Marshall School of Business and a consultant and speaker.

Chapter Twenty-Six

Deal with Your Crises

Patrick J. McKenna
David H. Maister

W ill you be prepared when that major-panic, drop every-thing, what-are-we-going-to-do disaster occurs? Not likely. After all, it wouldn't be a crisis if you were prepared, would it? But it *will* occur. Something always does.

Crises can be precipitated by events such as the following:

○ A significant person decides to leave the firm.

○ Someone in your group behaves in an inappropriate manner or is perceived to be unethical.

○ The group loses a major client.

○ Economic conditions necessitate the release of some people.

○ A valued member of the group dies.

SOME KEY PRINCIPLES TO KEEP IN MIND

Managing a crisis is a finely tuned blend of art and science. We recommend the following steps:

1. Calmly attempt to get at the facts.
2. Identify the real problem.
3. Decide who should handle the crisis.
4. Involve everyone where possible.
5. Remember that in a crisis, everything (for example, emotions, results) is magnified.

Calmly Attempt to Get at the Facts

The inevitable challenge with any crisis is to avoid making a bad situation even worse. Your biggest dilemma may be determining whether you have the right information. Often you don't know what you don't know. There may be too little information with a lot of conjecture and rumor, or there may be too much information with no way to sift out what is factually relevant and what is not.

It's easy to overreact when you see your colleagues getting concerned about what they perceive the situation to be, but a measured, thoughtful approach to getting at the facts during any crisis is the best strategy.

Identify the Real Problem

The most pressing task in a crisis is identifying the real problem. When your practice team loses a major client, you might think the problem would be blatantly obvious—a loss of a significant chunk of revenues and perhaps a blow to your group's morale. However, these may not be the real problems.

The actual disaster may lie more in the effects of the incident:

- A distinct possibility exists that some senior professional may abandon your group to join the competitor now getting the work.

- Other clients may learn of this client's defecting, and it may have an impact on their ongoing confidence.
- This client loss may be an indication of much deeper quality or service problems that have remained hidden.
- Some of the junior group members, who were dependent on this client's work, may have to be let go.

If you don't take the time to identify the real issues, you are vulnerable to putting your energies and resources into addressing the wrong crisis.

Decide Who Should Handle the Crisis

Sometimes you are not the best person to be in charge of dealing with the crisis. Consider the situation where your group learns that a major client has decided to move all or a major potion of its work to a competitor. An internal marketing professional (or your firm's leader) may be better suited to visit with the client to ascertain what the central problem is (and whether anything can be done to appease this client). Or perhaps one of your senior professionals has been accused of an action that borders on sexual harassment. Perhaps an experienced external professional would have a better grasp of what steps should be taken to correct and contain the damage.

Your most important job may very well be to decide who is best equipped to handle the particular crisis. That doesn't mean you should abdicate your leadership responsibility. You need to remain on top of the situation.

Involve Everyone Where Possible

Sometimes your crisis needs only the attention of a few key professionals and it is quickly resolved. In other instances, it may take some concerted effort on the part of a much larger group of people. There may be times when you need to ask your entire team to stay late or work through an entire weekend. A crisis is an opportunity to bring out the hidden talents in members of your group. Find ways to make everyone feel that they played some role in helping save the day.

Remember That in a Crisis, Everything Is Magnified

Regardless of what kind of loss or crisis you face, you need to understand how the others in your group are going to perceive the situation. Often it isn't the precipitating event itself, but rather the perception of the other members of the group and their subsequent actions that can really cause a crisis. As Daniel J. Fensin commented:

> I don't want to say mine is the kind of position where you can't ever let them see you sweat, but if I worry a lot about something and really get concerned about it, it's like chaos in the corridors. It's, like, "Oh, my God, if he's worried about this, it's got to be really, really bad." To a certain extent, you have to maintain a level of calmness to allow the team to really do what they do best.[1]

A FEW RULES OF CRISIS COMMUNICATION

Handled badly, any crisis can harm the respect and loyalty you enjoy with your group. Handled well, it can boost your team's enthusiasm. Here are some basic guidelines for effectively handling your communication with the group.

- Keep every member of your group fully informed.
- Involve your group members in key decisions.
- Be accessible to your people.
- Don't lose your sense of humor.

Keep Every Member of Your Group Fully Informed

No one wants to have a negative situation exposed publicly. But during a crisis, trying to keep whatever details might be available hidden from your fellow group members is usually fruitless. If it's really a crisis that affects your group or people's careers or client retention, the story will eventually get out, no matter what you do. And the story that gets out will be rife with misinformation and probably far more damaging than the facts and the story you would have wanted to communicate.

Involve Your Group Members in Key Decisions

Obviously, when you are responsible for a large group of professionals in geographically dispersed offices, you can't start organizing group meetings to gain consensus on the best solution to take. But you do need to go as far as you can to involve your group. It is important to remember that to the extent that people are involved, they will feel far more committed to the ultimate decision and responsible for making it work.

Be Accessible to Your People

To the extent that any crisis becomes emotionally charged, it is a safe bet that many of your people will be anxious, aggravated, frustrated, or even enraged. Should people feel that you are too busy for them, they are likely to feel alienated and demoralized.

Make time for them to express their concerns, share their feelings, seek your advice, or offer their views. Make sure your colleagues feel that your highest priority is attending to their best interest.

Most real crises have an important and central communications challenge, whether dealing with external audiences or internal. But a crisis is not likely to be solely a communications challenge. Communications professionals often wind up managing a crisis because no one else wants to do it. In fact, communications is only one aspect of true crisis management.

Don't Lose Your Sense of Humor

It is an old cliché, but laughter really is the best medicine, especially when you need to take the pressure off or need to reduce people's stress. Strategy consultant Cliff Farrah told us that he purchased fireman helmets for his key team members and handed them out at a crisis meeting, telling everyone to keep them mounted on the wall. When he needed to rally the troops around a problem, he called them and said, "Better put on your helmet."

ADVICE ON SPECIFIC TYPES OF CRISES

Let's look at the common crises to examine what action you might want to take next.

A Key Player Is Defecting

You have just received word that one of the key players in your group is leaving and, even worse, leaving to join a competitor. Your own most natural reaction would be a sense of extreme disappointment, anger, even a feeling of betrayal. But you must also think of others. How is this going to affect the morale of the group? Are others also likely to defect? What void will this person's going leave in the group's client service capability?

You will probably be tempted to speculate about why this person has chosen to leave, what his motivations and future plans are, and whether it is likely to be a friendly departure. You may even react in anger, giving others in the group either a verbal or nonverbal indication that you knew the departure was imminent and are happy to see this individual go.

Whether or not there is any validity to your feelings, such a communication will run the danger of having others in your group begin to question their own value and what might be said about them if they ever decide to leave.

Your first step should be to have a talk with this person. Perhaps his decision isn't irrevocable. Maybe he doesn't truly want to leave but is looking for an indication that your group and the firm really value his contribution. He may be upset about something that was really a misunderstanding or miscommunication that can be resolved. Perhaps it's as simple as the person defecting because he has been offered a more lucrative compensation package. You need to discover firsthand what is motivating his move.

There is an inherent danger in trying to appease an individual who doesn't feel valued. This person may discern that your eagerness to keep him gives him the power to influence future situations to his personal best interest. So it is important that you do not overreact or make promises that will come back to haunt you. But you certainly have everything to gain and little to lose by speaking with this person face to face—and doing so before the word gets out that he is leaving and before you have to address the reality with your team members.

Ask what his intentions are. Ascertain what each of you should do to make that departure come about in the most amicable manner. Discuss how the internal and external communications should be handled so as to pose the least amount of disruption to the group. Collaborate on drafting a memo to all members of the group explaining what is happening and wishing him the best in his new undertaking. Develop a joint communication to clients.

Breaking the news to your group won't be a pleasant task, so you need to be as positive as possible. Tell them the reasons that the decision has been made. Follow the bad news by presenting them with a challenge that they can get their energy into, preferably something you are confident will work out well. Drive out suspicion and build trust. Remove as much uncertainty as possible by being clear and positive about how the group will go forward.

Somebody Made a Mistake

You find out that two married members of your group are having an affair. One of your colleagues has just discovered that she is being sued for professional malpractice. One of your people made an inappropriate gesture to someone in the firm of the opposite sex. Perhaps you have just been confronted with the evidence of poor judgment. How do you respond, and what do you do about it?

Your best response, in some cases, is to do absolutely nothing! You must distinguish between what may be immoral and what is a crisis. Something should be viewed as a crisis only if it interferes with the other members of your group or affects their work on behalf of clients.

If you are caught having erred, show that you are repentant. Don't try to hide it or cover it up. Most people are willing to forget and forgive if there are sincere expressions of error and repentance. During and after a crisis, leaders are judged not so much by the original negative actions, but by how they handle them. Nixon's crime was not the burglary at Watergate; it was the cover-up. The public can forgive a politician's infidelity, but not the act of lying outright.

People are capable of forgiving those who make mistakes, even fairly major blunders, if they are honest about the mistake, indicate that they have learned from it and will not repeat the error, and are truly concerned for how it may reflect on the group and on the firm.

If the behavior in question was something unlawful or contravened the code of ethics of your profession, then your situation is far more critical. Your course of action is usually apparent and spelled out clearly by that body governing your profession. In those instances, decisiveness is critical, and tough decisions have to be made fast. Your problem will never improve with age. Speed is of the essence. This crisis will not wait.

We Lost a Client

It is always preferable to err on the side of disclosure. Often you have to face your people with less than full information as to why the client was lost, because in many cases we may never really know. In those instances, it is best to state clearly that you don't know all the facts. Then promptly share the facts that you do know.

The bottom line is to tell the truth and tell it fast. Your established level of trust with the group is at stake. Whether your people will believe you when you badly need them to do so will depend on how much confidence you have established with them before the crisis occurs. If after the crisis, you try to snow them in any way or not disclose all of the facts, your trust will be irreparably harmed:

1. Face the reality of the lost client instead of denying it.

2. Do what you can do; do something instead of being fatalistic.

3. Hold a session with the group to analyze the mistakes or weaknesses. But avoid the blame-throwing syndrome. Instead, look at the problem, and search for answers.

4. Count your blessings, your other clients, and resolve to serve them even better.

5. Remember the old army maxim: "There are no bad soldiers, only bad officers." Your group needs to know that you are with them and that you aren't putting the blame on them when you talk to others outside the group.

We Have to Let Some People Go

We all know that at times, economic conditions can make it necessary for a firm to downsize. Perhaps some senior people are not performing up to standard. Perhaps some staff have become redundant.

When this crisis strikes, keep everyone in your group informed from the earliest possible stage. People always get wind of these things through the office grapevine, and when they do, their imaginations are likely to create a situation far more grave than it actually is.

Here's how to deal with cutbacks:

1. Don't give your group your best guess, and don't speculate. Find out the facts, and communicate whatever the group wants to know.

2. Don't stay quiet. That will not protect them.

3. After a downsizing, talk collectively to the members of your group who remain. Tell them that you regret what has happened and help them face the reality of the economic facts.

4. Recognize that many of your team may feel threatened, expecting the other shoe to drop—and the next time it could be them. Assure all of the remaining group members of how valuable they are and how each has an important contribution to make in helping the group get through the economic storm.

5. Get up and move on again. Fight self-pity.

6. Ask for help from a professional. You don't have to face it alone.

7. As you sense the crisis is passing, be sure to give the members of your group credit for handling the unpleasant situation well.

A Valued Colleague Dies

The worst possible thing has just occurred: a member of your group, your "family," has passed away. Some members of your group will feel this loss far more personally and far more deeply then you might ever imagine. These situations always have us reflect on our own mortality.

A person who comforts can be a tremendous help to those who are left grieving—either fellow team members or direct family members. Your support as the practice leader will help those grieving heal a little faster. However, there are some do's and don'ts to remember.

DO'S

- When you hear the news of a death, call the whole group together and tell them all at once.

- Be prepared for some colleagues to be extremely upset. Prearrange to have a professional counselor available.

- Cancel any scheduled meetings or presentations. Don't allow any of your group to think that you put work before people.

- Give your fellow team members time to go to the funeral.

- Make sure to send flowers on behalf of the group, independent from anything individual members decide to do on their own.

- Give individual members of your team plenty of time to get back to normal.

- Let people feel that they can talk about their loss. Speak naturally of the person who has died. Be empathetic. Don't allow it to be a taboo subject.

- Make a phone call or send a card to the surviving spouse or family, especially on anniversaries, because anniversaries can be the hardest.

- Tell the surviving spouse or family member to feel free to phone or visit you at any time (and mean it).

DON'TS

- Don't assume you know it all or that you have all the answers, and don't use textbook advice that is formal and rigid.

- Don't rush a grieving person through the need to talk about it. Give the person the gift of listening.

- Don't use anyone's grief to express your own grief. Avoid the temptation to talk about yourself, thereby stealing the conversation.

- Don't use clichés like, "I know how you are feeling."

- Don't compare the person's grief to someone else's experience. No two experiences are the same.

- Don't impose if your attention is not welcome.

- Don't intrude in the person's life. Give the person space and permission to be himself or herself.

- Don't break confidences.

- Don't expect too much, too soon, from any of the closest members on your team. Be prepared for mood swings.

CONCLUSION

No one wants to be involved in a crisis. Crises can cost money to resolve. They require time spent in remedial action. They keep you from your client work. A big one can undermine your group's morale.

But crises can also be exhilarating. They require an intensity of effort and a focus that is not normally needed. They create strong relationships among group members. Tempers may flare, but if the crisis is handled well, your group's commitment and focus can emerge even stronger. Helen Ostrowski, managing partner of U.S. Public Relations operations at Porter Novelli, tells the following story:

> Along with everyone else in our industry, we have had to deal with the issue of layoffs. We planned the process down to the last detail. We carefully figured out who would be spoken to, and by whom, covering those who had to be asked to leave and those remaining. We brought in an outplacement firm to train our top executive team in how to deliver the message, and I wrote the key messages myself, crafting every word. It was a tense day, but it all went off as planned, with good feedback about how compassionate and respectful we'd been.
>
> At the end of the day, the executive team all got together to discuss how the day went, and at that moment, I just lost it. I poured out my emotions in front of my top team, breaking every rule I had ever heard about maintaining an even keel. To my astonishment, rather than destroying my credibility, I received e-mails the next day from virtually everyone thanking me for my guidance through the process and asking if there was anything they could do to help me. It actually bonded us together. In retrospect, it was critical that I was cool, calm and collected while we dealt with the crisis, but it was also, to my surprise, probably a good thing that I allowed myself (and everyone else) the emotional release when it was over.

o   o   o

Patrick J. McKenna is a speaker and consultant on professional service firm management.

David H. Maister is a consultant on professional service firm management. Previously he was on the faculty at Harvard Business School.

Part Five

Leading Complex Organizational Processes

Chapter Twenty-Seven

Dealing with Conflict

Marick F. Masters
Robert R. Albright

At work as in life, you handle conflicts with people differently. Some you want to avoid. Others you try to accommodate. Occasionally you may get angry and aggressive. Alternatively, you may try to cooperate with people to find a mutually agreeable solution. Sometimes you may simply split the difference or find a happy medium.

How you respond depends partly on your natural style. It also depends on learned behavior—you learn what works best for you. In addition, your response varies with the situation and context. Who is involved? What are the consequences of confliction exchange? What does your organizational culture condone? Does it promote competition or cooperation?

In this chapter, we address the issue of what effective conflict management means and other related questions. More specifically, this chapter:

○ Identifies the goals you should seek when handling conflict

○ Presents you with strategic choices on how to deal with conflict

○ Unfolds a nine-step guide to collaborative conflict resolution

○ Maps the logical extensions of collaboration at work

○ Gives you options if collaboration "fails"

○ Shows you how to select and sequence alternative conflict resolution methods consistent with the goals of effective conflict management

○ Identifies the core competencies that you and your colleagues at work will need to deal with conflict better.

WHAT DO WE MEAN BY DEALING WITH CONFLICT EFFECTIVELY?

You might think that dealing with conflict effectively means reaching an agreement. But this is far too simplistic. Agreements can be meaningful or not. They can be enforceable or not. They can actually solve underlying problems or not. They can build or damage relationships. They can prevent or invite future conflict.

You should think of effective conflict management as consisting of several related goals:

○ Preventing escalation

○ Solving the real problem

○ Depersonalizing the disagreement

○ Inventing solutions

○ Building relationships

○ Achieving workplace goals

First, you know that escalated conflicts will often result in disruptive behaviors. You may become involved in a pointless shouting match. You might sulk. You might harbor anger and resentment that clouds your thinking and judgment. All of this because you allowed the situation to spin out of control. Dealing with conflict effectively means avoiding those actions that fuel the fire. Think before you act. Thomas Jefferson said that when he was angry, he counted to ten before he responded. When he was really angry, he counted to one hundred. Do not respond in anger, for that will likely set off a chain of reactions that make you even angrier.

Second, you want to solve the real problem. Think about how many disagreements you have had that have been wallpapered or disguised as something else. Visualize a subordinate who habitually shows up late to meetings. You extract a promise that this tardiness will not happen again. Problem solved? No! The real problem is that the subordinate disrespects you, lacks confidence in you. Showing up late merely manifests this disdain. Unless you deal with this problem, you will not avert future conflicts, though they may masquerade in different costumes, such as undermining you in the eyes of other colleagues.

Third, you must avoid personalizing the situation. Admittedly, this is easier said than done. When anger is being tossed at you, when criticism is being leveled against you, when a person is being obstinate and contrary, do not take it personally. Do not respond tit for tat. Count to ten or one hundred. Think empathetically. Remember you do not have to deny your interests, reach an unwise agreement, or tolerate abuse. Stay in control of yourself. If you think in terms of the situation rather than how hurt your feelings are, your response will be more effective. You must apply the breaks on conflict escalation to create an opportunity for meaningful dialogue.

Fourth, to manage conflict well, you must often invent where invention seems impossible. You need to think outside the box. What are the possible options? Imagine facing an employee disgruntled because he or she was denied a desirable assignment. You value the employee, but had to choose a more deserving candidate. You can understand the employee's anger and frustration. To deal with this, you could say that you will make the employee "happy" in the future. A better approach, however, is for you to deal promptly and openly with the underlying interest, which is recognition and opportunity for the employee. Do not let the discontent fester; neglect is the parent of outburst. Brainstorm possible approaches to give recognition and create opportunity. By approaching the matter inventively, you can defuse the anger, involve the employee, and show your respect.

Fifth, in dealing with conflict, you absolutely do not want to miss opportunities to build relationships. Sometimes you may not be able to satisfy everyone's needs or allay all relevant concerns. But you can make a good-faith effort that inspires trust, belief in your sincerity, and appreciation of the realities you confront. You create mutual understanding and respect—the building blocks of sound relationships.

Sixth, in a workplace context, effective conflict management requires you to keep an eye on the broader mission. Conflict resolution is a process—a means to an end. You are at work to perform, to help the company achieve its mission, to help others serve the mission. You cannot "solve" conflict by taking actions that are contrary to the goals and interest of the organization. You should not set harmful precedents, create inequities, falsely raise expectations, or squander resources in order to fix a problem. You may be tempted to appease a malcontent with a favor. But favoritism breeds envy and anger. Simply put, you should not deal with one conflict in such a way that invites many others that are even more serious. Table 27.1 summarizes the goals of effective conflict management. To a large extent, you will find them mutually supportive.

TABLE 27.1. Goals of Effective Conflict Management

○ Prevent escalation.	Avoid actions that escalate the conflict, forcing a response—counterresponse chain reaction of negative behaviors.
○ Focus on the real problem.	Get to the bottom of the situation. Do not mistake symptoms for causes. Probe the underlying issues.
○ Avoid personalization.	Try not to take things personally. Think empathetically and sympathetically. Speak in objective, situational terms.
○ Invent solutions.	There is more than one road to Rome or path to success. Think broadly and creatively. Do so even when you think it might not be absolutely necessary.
○ Build relationships.	Never miss a chance to build a relationship. Share interests, concerns. Inspire trust.
○ Achieve workplace goals.	Managing conflict does not occur in a personal vacuum. How you deal with it has broader professional and organizational implications. Never lose sight of the fact that how you deal with something today can come back to haunt you tomorrow.

Strategic Approaches to Dealing with Conflict at Work

You are an HR professional assigned to the organizational effectiveness staff at the research and development site of a global food manufacturer. One of your responsibilities is to work with newly created cross-discipline product development teams consisting of scientists, engineers, market researchers, and information systems analysts. Nominally, the scientists head the teams, but the groups are expected to function collaboratively. Your job is to see to it that they have the support from organizational effectiveness to work collaboratively.

One team in particular is encountering problems that are affecting harmony in the ranks. The head scientist is a bit authoritarian and elitist. Interpersonal relations are not his strong point. You have been asked to "coach" the team and the scientist. You have had one preliminary telephone conversation with the scientist, who said that "his team" did not need your interference and that it was doing just fine without "organizational effectiveness." It is now two days later, and you are on your way to your first in-person meeting with the scientist. What approach should you take?

In theory and reality, you do have options, but they are not likely to be equally effective. You have five choices on the menu: accommodation, avoidance, collaboration, competition, and compromise (see Table 27.2). You should view these as strategic choices. That is, you decide which one to use. You should bear in mind that you can switch choices as circumstances dictate. In addition, you may choose to act mildly or strongly one way or another. You do not have to be purely competitive or compromising. Also, none of these approaches requires you to be adversarial, disrespectful, hostile, or inciting, although competition is often associated with these behaviors.

TABLE 27.2. **Alternative Strategic Approaches to Conflict**

Strategy	Behavior
Accommodation	A party concedes to the other's position. Is not assertive of own interest or needs or positions.
Avoidance	A party ignores, denies, escapes. Is proactive in avoiding confronting the other party or issue.
Collaboration	A party seeks a win-win outcome that is naturally satisfactory. Is assertive of own interests and empathizes with the other party's.
Competition	A party is selfishly motivated and behaving. Is interested in winning, pure and simple.
Compromise	A party is willing to settle for half a loaf. Is inclined to split the difference to get the matter settled if not resolved.

Thus, as the HR professional, you may choose to accommodate, avoid, collaborate, compete, or compromise. Let's see how you would exercise your options. If you were to *accommodate*, then you would defer to the scientist. You would not challenge him to take a different tack. By no means would you be confrontational. In so doing, you would not deal with the problem, which is the scientist's unwillingness to be a team player. Most likely, you would only postpone a more difficult encounter by being an accommodator.

Alternatively, you could behave as the HR professional escapist—the consummate *avoider*. In this role, you would try to avoid the in-person encounter. Assuming, however, that the encounter occurred, you would try to avoid the subject. You might concoct an artificial agenda to deflect attention from the real issue. Most likely, you might find neutral territory to occupy, discussing innocuous topics. Once again, you have not addressed the problem. More disturbing, you have given your approval, however tacitly, to the scientist's conduct. Consequently, you will find it more difficult to correct in the future if compelled to do so.

Using your third option, you could approach the scientist *collaboratively*. You would attempt to identify the underlying interests and needs of the scientist. You would not deny or fail to assert the organizational interest in product development teamwork. But you would look for ways to serve that purpose while simultaneously satisfying the scientist's needs. Simply put, you look for ways to make his teamwork useful to him. You might appeal to his position as a role model and the critical leadership he provides because of his professional stature.

If you were to *compete* or try to dominate—your fourth option—you would be interested in controlling the exchange. You want to win an argument. You're interested in convincing the scientist he must change. It's "my-way-or-the-highway." No need to explore options, identify needs, or achieve mutual satisfaction. In the short term, you may get what you want: submission. But you will probably provoke resentment and invite vengeance.

Your fifth choice is *compromise*. In this case, you might attempt logrolling, giving one thing in exchange for another. You seek a temporary truce. You could, for example, ask the scientist to temper his style in exchange for a plum future assignment or a new team complement. In so doing, however, you have not solved the problem. Instead, you may have created a monster by setting a dangerous precedent.

WHICH STRATEGY SHOULD YOU USE?

We advocate collaborating. We also advocate acting collaboratively when you might be thinking competitively. In the case above, the HR professional should try to collaborate with the head scientist, no matter how difficult the process or the person.

Collaboration fits nicely with the goals of effective conflict resolution. It emphasizes getting to the real problem, exploring options, meeting interests, and building relationships. In other words, collaboration is outcome and relationship focused.

Figure 27.1 presents the "dual-concerns" model of conflict resolution. It suggests that the preferred strategy depends on two concerns: one, the degree to which the relationship is valued, and two, the degree to which the outcome is valued. When the outcome and relationship are highly valued, collaboration emerges as the preferred choice.

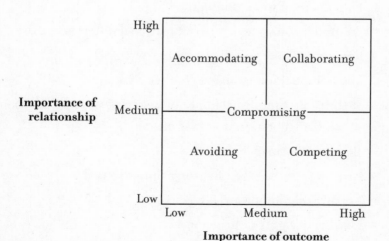

FIGURE 27.1. **Conflict Resolution Strategy Outcome-Relationship Graph**

At work, your willingness to collaborate is important because relationships are often long term and unavoidably proximate. The corporate push for teamwork reinforces this tendency. Also, you should not underestimate the importance of workplace outcomes to employees, no matter how minor or trivial they may appear at first glance. Sometimes the smallest recognitions, rewards, or opportunities can be valued quite highly, because they affect relative status or one's sense of fair treatment.

More specifically, collaboration is preferable when:

○ Relationships are important.

○ Relationships are interdependent.

○ Mutual interests exist.

○ Outcomes are important.

○ Maintaining teams is important.

○ Creating a team-based working environment is important.

○ The nature of work is integrated.

○ Cultural, professional, and occupational differences exist.

○ The parties want to achieve better outcomes.

○ The potential for escalated conflict is high.

At the same time, you should be aware of what collaboration is *not*. Collaboration does not mean:

○ Being overly nice.

○ Agreeing for the sake of getting things settled.

○ Jeopardizing important interests.

○ Sacrificing rights or principles.

○ Tolerating unacceptable or inappropriate behavior.

○ Avoiding difficult topics or people.

The Nine Steps of Collaboration

Exhibit 27.1 illustrates the nine steps of collaboration. Before diving in, you should know that this is not a lockstep procedure. Collaboration should be dynamic, fluid, and flexible rather than rigid, mechanical, or linear.

Feel free to move forward or backward as needed. Just keep your eye on the goal: effective conflict management. And remember the person with whom you are dealing may see the world, at work and elsewhere, quite differently from you. That is one reason that opening a dialogue and listening are so essential to making the process work.

EXHIBIT 27.1. **The Collaborative Approach: A Nine-Step Guide**

1. Take a step back.

2. Confront the situation.

3. Sit back and listen.

4. Capture the situation.

5. Invite exploration.

6. Assess and analyze.

7. Propose possibility.

8. Reach outcome.

9. Build relationship.

Step 1: Take a Step Back

The first thing you want to do wherever you can is to take a step back—give yourself some time to think. In the scenario involving the HR professional and the head scientist, you would want to spend some time diagnosing the situation, analyzing the problem, and preparing some solutions for discussion. What interests are involved from each party's and the organization's perspectives? Is the head scientist in over his head? Is the team poorly composed or equipped? Are there personality clashes at play? Is the concept of the team threatening to professional independence and stature? Has the organization done the necessary groundwork to prepare people for teams? Is the HR system—in terms of selection, compensation, and performance management—aligned with teamwork?

You also want to assess the nature of the issue: Are there principles or rights involved? Are the stakes high?

Step 2: Confront the Situation

You want to arrange a meeting. By going to the head scientist's office, you are signaling your respect. Find a mutually comfortable time. Break the issue situationally, asking if there is anything that organizational effectiveness can do. Give the head scientist an opportunity to explain the situation. Do not present the issue in a threatening, accusatory manner by saying something like: "You have presented me with quite a problem. What are you going to do to get yourself and me out of this predicament?" You may choose to say something more like: "Teams are challenging, and we are interested in making certain that they can benefit from your talents. How might we help you?"

Step 3: Sit Back and Listen

This is the golden opportunity you want to make happen. You must listen actively and empathetically. By listening actively, you hear not only the words but also the feelings, emotions, and thinking process behind what is being said. By listening empathetically, you put yourself in the other person's shoes. You comprehend what he is saying from his perspective. In other words, you are no longer filtering what he is saying through your own perspective of the world. Instead, you see it from his viewpoint. This is an important distinction because much of conflict is about perception. What makes no sense to you makes a lot of sense from another perspective because that person perceives the world differently.

Going back to the HR professional and head scientist, they undoubtedly have different personal, professional, and organizational perspectives. The HR professional has a responsibility to help teams work collaboratively. The scientist sees his contribution more in terms of applying scientific knowledge to inventing new products. When both parties realize that they are personally and professionally served by supporting an organizational climate conducive to teamwork that still respects everyone's contribution, you have the basis for making distinct progress.

Step 4: Capture the Situation

Once you have listened intently, you want to capture the situation. Think in terms of taking a moving picture and a snapshot. What has been said? What are the core issues (for example, professional integrity versus forced conformity)? What interests and needs are being raised? What are the facts surrounding the situation? Is the team actually performing as badly as portrayed? Is the team really an outlier, or is the problem more systemwide? Is the head scientist as authoritarian and elitist as described? Sometimes we enter meetings like this one between the HR professional and head scientist misinformed about the real situation. Be open to changing your perception of the situation if contravening data are presented.

Step 5: Invite Exploration

You need to create an environment in which the parties to a conflict (at whatever stage it might be) are open to exploring options to address the issues raised. You should, however, avoid the mistake of proposing the solution early in the session or meeting. Coming to the meeting with a preordained conclusion or solution closes your mind to better options. Also, you tell the other person that his or her thoughts really do not matter. You know what is right. When this happens, you may find the person disagreeing simply because of having been excluded.

What you want to do is discuss possible options and possible solutions. Brainstorm. Encourage creative ideas. And listen. Do not reject ideas just because they do not square with your thinking. You will be surprised at how inventive people can be if given the freedom to let their intellectual juices flow.

Step 6: Assess and Analyze

Once you have generated a list of options to meet the underlying interests, you need to assess them. This requires that you come up with some reasonable analytical criteria. Reasonable means in the eyes of both parties, not just one side's. Feasibility is a possible criterion. Another is whether the solution proposed is really a mutually agreeable one. Relative costs and benefits can also be explored more or less precisely. In short, you want to come up with a set of standards by which to assess the options.

For example, it might have been proposed that the head scientist's team invite a facilitator to help things work more smoothly. Is there precedent for that within the company? Are facilitators available? How much does a facilitator cost, and is that cost affordable? Is the head scientist comfortable with that option? Is he willing to let it work?

Step 7: Propose Possibilities

In this step, you want to steer the meeting toward a set of possible solutions. The analysis conducted in the preceding step should have weeded out some of the options. Now you can focus on the possible solutions in more depth. But these are possibilities, not decrees. Respond empathetically to possibilities offered by the other side. Identify their possible benefits before laundering the costs. Test reactions to your suggestions. This is an opportunity for trial balloons. You are fine-tuning the collaborative process.

Step 8: Reach Outcome

After you have proposed possibilities and explored their benefits and costs against various decision-making standards, reach a consensus. Reach a settlement or, ideally, a resolution. If facilitation is the basis for an agreement, discuss how it will work, how the facilitator will be selected, and what you expect to achieve. If you are uncertain that the proposed settlement or resolution will work, then propose revisiting the matter to assess progress in a timely manner.

Step 9: Build Relationship

To a certain extent, you have been trying to do this throughout the process. Too often, however, exchanges like these end with the settlement (outcome) highlighted and the relationship undernourished. After reaching an agreement, spend some time on relationship building. Stress the benefits of the exchange: getting an opportunity to see different perspectives, to generate new ideas, to understand the situation better, and to build a strong professional relationship. Open the door for future discussions on this and other matters. Invite continuing participation in the teamwork development process. This, as previously said, is an opportunity you do not want to miss.

COLLABORATIVE APPLICATIONS

The collaborative approach can be applied widely in the workplace. As we said earlier, it can be applied in conflicts involving interests, rights, and power, although it may need to be combined with other dispute resolution methodologies when issues involving rights or power struggles exist. (It becomes more difficult as a resolution technique standing alone when the conflict involves a contest of will or a fundamental right or principle.) In this vein, you can view workplace collaboration as the hub of the wheel. It can be used to address a myriad of workplace issues that may cause disagreement between those with a workplace nexus.

From this hub, you can draw several spokes to explain the business-related applicability of collaboration. As you can see in Figure 27.2, the spokes lead you in several important directions, which are central to work. These applications become increasingly more important as the nature of work and the workplace itself become more seamless. They become more relevant as the whole value chain of production becomes more integrated. And

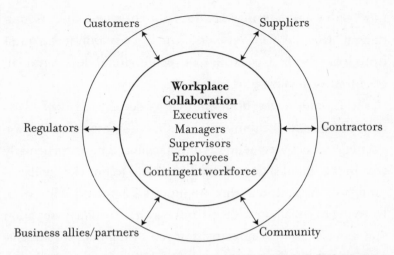

FIGURE 27.2. **The Hub and Spoke of Workplace Collaboration**

they become more important as the nature of the employment relationship becomes more varied, less permanent, and more flexible.

In short, you can avail yourself on the collaborative approach in a host of business interactions. Build an encompassing corporate capability in this regard with extensive internal and external applications. Think of collaboration as a way of building relationships between yourself, your team, your unit, and your company, on the one hand, and, on the other hand, your customers, your suppliers, your contractors, your regulators, and your community.

WHAT IF COLLABORATION "FAILS?"

In collaboration, the principal parties to a disagreement remain in control over the process, outcome, and their relationship, to the extent the context allows. But you know that collaboration, however desirable it may be, does not always succeed. Sometimes it "fails." What do you do then? You can look at this question from both a personal or professional level and an organizational viewpoint.

You should know, however, that we use the term *fail* advisedly. You should not think that collaboration has failed because a settlement or agreement was unobtainable. This is particularly true in the initial stages of collaboration. Do not view collaborating as a discrete, one-shot attempt. It is a process. Moreover, by trying to collaborate, the parties may have avoided escalation and moved closer to agreement or resolution than would have otherwise been the case. And their relationship may be better off for having made the effort, even though settlement proved elusive. The situation is not hopeless and the parties are not hapless when collaboration falls short of agreement.

You should view collaboration between the principals as the first step of what is sometimes a long journey. A good conflict resolution system opens the door for other alternative dispute resolution procedures (see Figure 27.3).

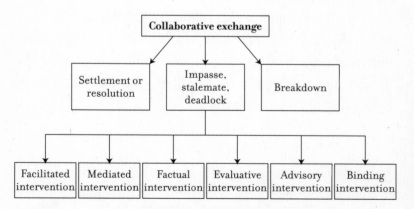

FIGURE 27.3. **Alternative Dispute Resolution Procedures If Collaboration "Fails"**

If you do not achieve a settlement or resolution (one that you hope addresses the real problem in a mutually satisfactory way), you may have entered a phase in the conflict resolution process where you are at an impasse, stalemate, or deadlock. For whatever reason, be it interpersonal conflict or division over fundamental principals, you cannot resolve matters in disagreement. But you are still interested in pursuing agreement without resorting to arbitration, litigation, or something even worse, such as sabotage, public embarrassment, or exodus. You need assistance. You want to salvage the effort and relationship before things break down to the point where litigation, striking, or quitting the organization are the only options the parties can see.

When the principals struggle with seeming futility, inviting further decay in the relationship, they need to think about third-party intervention. These interventions can be distinguished by the nature and extent of the third party involved. Figure 27.3 presents these interventions in what you may view as a progression in decision-making involvement.

Facilitated Intervention

In this case, a facilitator or conciliator becomes involved in trying to improve the flow of information between the disputing parties. The facilitator focuses on process, not outcome. The rationale is that by improving information exchange, you will be better able to find your way to agreement.

Mediator Intervention

To some, this is a notch above facilitation. In traditional mediation, the neutral mediator works with the parties to fashion an agreement. The mediator, like the facilitator, does not have authority to impose an agreement. But the mediator's involvement may be more substantive than that associated with the facilitator.

Factual Intervention

In this arena, you may call on varyingly neutral and impartial fact finders, investigators, or ombuds to conduct an investigation to gather the relevant facts in a workplace dispute. These investigators do not have the power to impose settlements, though they may be empowered to recommend solutions and work toward a facilitated or mediated resolution. The principal expectation is that gathering the facts and portraying them in an objective light will motivate the parties to resolve the conflict themselves.

Evaluative Intervention

In this methodology, you are moving closer to decision making. This approach is sometimes referred to as neutral evaluation or early neutral evaluation. Essentially, before you go to a decision-making venue (such as litigation or arbitration), you ask the neutral to opine about how such a decision might come out if pushed to a higher level, so to speak. Presenting the neutral with the facts and arguments behind a dispute, you invite his or her informed evaluation or forecast. This is another way of trying to get the parties to assess realistically the risks and costs of going to court. Again, bear in mind you are pursuing means of alternative dispute resolution.

Advisory Intervention

Advisory intervention moves you another step closer to decision making. You empower a neutral or panel of neutrals to issue an advisory judgment. The neutral hears the evidence, then presents a recommended settlement. The disputing parties are not bound by the advice, but they are expected to give it serious consideration. Otherwise, a lot of time and effort have simply gone down the drain. Advisory arbitration fits this bill of particulars.

Binding Intervention

At this stage, you invite a binding decision. The process is typically structured to be adversarial, though not as formalized or costly as litigation. Once again, a neutral or panel of neutrals is commissioned to hear a dispute and then render a judgment. Unlike advisory judgments, these judgments are binding on the parties. Binding arbitration is an increasingly prevalent alternative to litigation in the arena of employment or workplace disputes.

THE BUILDING BLOCKS OF CONFLICT RESOLUTION

You now have the basic items on the conflict resolution menu. First, you may work with the disputing party through one or more of the conflict resolution strategies. Second, if you, as one the principals, cannot resolve the matter in conflict, you may avail yourself of a host of third-party interventions shy of litigation or some other extreme measure. Now the question you face is how to organize these options in a sequence or order that makes sense.

Table 27.3 diagrams a few alternative ways to sequence the building blocks of conflict resolution. As you can see, the alternatives vary according to the basic nature of the dispute. We advise that this is only one approach. You want to build a model that serves your organizational needs consistent with certain legal and moral principles.

TABLE 27.3. **The Building Blocks of Conflict Resolution**

Conflict Type	Nonintervening	Nondecisional Involvement	Decisional Intervention
Interest based Physiological Psychological	Collaboration	Facilitation, investigation, or mediation	Advisory
Emotional			
Professional			
Occupational			
Social			
Spiritual			
Economic			
Rights based Equity Justice	Collaboration	Facilitation, investigation, or mediation	Binding
Procedural			
Power based Abuse Dereliction	Collaboration	Facilitation, investigation, or mediation	Advisory or binding
Inappropriate use			

To refer to the conflict-type classification we presented earlier, you can group most conflicts as those involving interests, rights, and power. (You realize, however, that conflicts may fall into more than one category and evolve into multifaceted disputes over time.) *Interest-based conflicts*, which cover a wide spectrum of workplace disputes, can arise over anything from the need to satisfy certain psychological needs and the adequacy of basic workplace safety and health conditions to the need for appropriate recognition and reward. Involving basic interests, these types of conflicts are often viewed as quite amenable to collaborative resolution if the parties are willing to make the effort. In any event, noninterventionist strategies to resolve these conflicts—collaboration, bargaining, and so forth—are preferred as a first step to give the parties control over the processed outcome.

If that fails, then a nondecisional intervention may be employed. In this vein, facilitation or mediation become viable steps. These conflict resolution alternative procedures do not impose settlements, but they should improve the process of interaction to make settlement or resolution possible.

Last, if this intermediate stage fails, the parties may resort to an advisory decisional mechanism, such as advisory arbitration. Here, they are given the benefit of a neutral's advice in the form of a formal recommendation. But they are free to reject it. Thus, they still retain ultimate control over the outcome.

Rights-based controversies arise over matters involving equitable treatment, justice, and procedural fairness. For example, employees may feel that they were denied promotions because of their age, race, gender, or disability, all situations protected by law. These conflicts can often be very contentious, emotional, and wrought with core principles. They can lend themselves to adversarial confrontations. To the extent, however, that they involve misunderstandings or underpinning interests, then it makes sense to try to resolve them collaboratively or, if that does not work, through nondecisional interventions such as mediation. However, because rights are involved, it is important that the parties know that the ultimate settlement will not depend on a contest of power or the whim of the organization. That is why a binding, neutral decision is often desirable as a last step. This binding process can be structured so that it is much less expensive and time-consuming than litigation. But the opportunity for finality through a balanced, neutral process is critical when one party, for example, a disgruntled low-ranking clerical worker, might feel either overpowered or oppressively disadvantaged.

Power-based struggles are more difficult to get a handle on because the term is so nebulous. But power conflicts can range from a pure contest of will (where collaboration can seem hopeless or pointless) to questions about whether power has been abused or inappropriately used. Very often these questions will also involve rights or interests. For instance, a supervisor who fails to promote an employee may be charged with discrimination or the inappropriate use of power if the seemingly objective criteria used to make the decision were improperly applied.

Accordingly, there are circumstances in which the parties may be encouraged to resolve the disagreement collaboratively and nonbinding third-party interventions may be made available to clear the air and get to the bottom of the situation. If that fails, then you may want to consider advisory or binding arbitration of the dispute. Sometimes power-based controversies can boil down to managerial or organizational discretion. If the goal is to preserve such discretion while offering the aggrieved some recourse, then the advisory option gains favor.

In sum, you can arrange conflict resolution options, from collaboration to binding arbitration, to give your organization multiple venues in which to resolve disputes. The availability of a sequence of options can permit the early resolution of conflict while avoiding litigation should the principals' efforts fail to yield a settlement. The sequencing can also be used to reinforce the basic rights of employees and to arrest the abuse or misuse of power.

Core Competencies

To manage conflict effectively, you need more than awareness of the menu of options and knowledge about the technique of collaboration. You need to develop certain core competencies that will improve your overall conflict resolution capability. Such development benefits you personally and professionally, increasing your satisfaction at work and your value to the organization.

As a key organization player, you can help build an organizational capability to handle conflict constructively. You may help design a training program to develop employees' core competencies in this area. You can also serve as a role model for others at various organizational levels to emulate. By broadening the capability of others to manage conflict, you benefit in two specific ways. First, you reduce the number of conflicts into which people will drag you because they cannot deal with them by themselves. People will manage their own conflicts better, freeing you to do other things of more strategic value. Second, your company's environment as a whole should improve. It will reflect a greater capacity to manage relationships internally and externally. The costs of doing business should go down, releasing resources that can be more productively spent. If your company is saddled with huge conflict-related costs (for example, litigation fees, turnover, workers' compensation, formal complaints), it has less to devote to other things, from hiring needed personnel to rewarding current employees adequately. Conflict resolution affects the bottom line.

Figure 27.4 identifies five sets of core competencies associated with conflict resolution. You first need a good set of interpersonal skills, which include being able to communicate verbally and in writing, to listen actively and empathetically, to work as a member of a team playing various team roles, and to exercise discretion in dealing with others.

You also need to be developed managerially. To the extent that you can coach others, delegate tasks, manage time, and manage meetings, you can be instrumental in handling conflict.

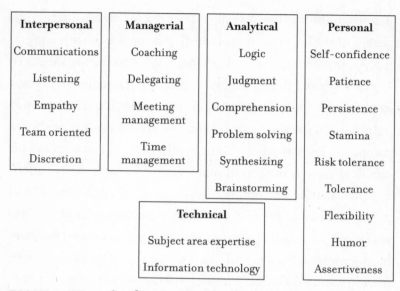

FIGURE 27.4. **Conflict Resolution Core Competencies**

Think of the number of meetings in which conflict has arisen because the sessions have been poorly managed. Think about the number of tight spots you have gotten into because you have not managed your time well or ignored matters that would eventually come back to haunt you.

Third, your ability to handle conflict is enhanced to the extent that your analytical skills are developed. How good are you at problem solving, synthesizing information, brainstorming, thinking things through logically to reach viable decisions? How well do you comprehend the contexts, subtleties, and nuances of conflict? These are important elements to possess to deal with conflict at work.

Fourth, as a person, you are helped if you possess certain traits. Are you self-confident and assured? Are you patient, persistent, tolerant, and flexible? Are you assertive? Do you have a sense of humor to help deflect anger and defuse hostility? These qualities can contribute to effective conflict management.

Finally, in some instances, you may be aided by possessing relevant technical knowledge or expertise. This is particularly important when the source of conflict is over technical problems or a debate as to which technical approach is best. Are you capable of speaking the language of people with technical specialties? Can you relate realistically to what they are saying? Furthermore, do you have ability to use information technology to reduce and manage conflict? Can you use information technology to present data in a way that clarifies issues rather than crating confusion that spawns more disagreement? As misinformation is often the cause of conflict, effective use of information technology can help you address this difficulty.

o   o   o

Marick F. Masters is a professor of business administration and of public and international affairs at the University of Pittsburgh, where he is the executive director of the Center on Conflict Resolution and Negotiation.

Robert R. Albright is head of the Department of Management at the United States Coast Guard Academy.

Chapter Twenty-Eight

Overcoming the Five Dysfunctions of a Team

Patrick Lencioni

In the course of my experience working with CEOs and their teams, two critical truths have become clear to me. First, genuine teamwork in most organizations remains as elusive as it has ever been. Second, organizations fail to achieve teamwork because they unknowingly fall prey to five natural but dangerous pitfalls, which I call the five dysfunctions of a team.

These dysfunctions can be mistakenly interpreted as five distinct issues that can be addressed in isolation from the others. But in reality, they form an interrelated model, making susceptibility to even one of them potentially lethal for the success of a team. A cursory overview of each dysfunction, and the model they comprise, should make this clearer (Figure 28.1).

The first dysfunction is an *absence of trust* among team members. Essentially, this stems from their unwillingness to be

FIGURE 28.1. **The Five Dysfunctions of Teams**

vulnerable within the group. Team members who are not genuinely open with one another about their mistakes and weaknesses make it impossible to build a foundation for trust.

This failure to build trust is damaging because it sets the tone for the second dysfunction: *fear of conflict*. Teams that lack trust are incapable of engaging in unfiltered and passionate debate of ideas. Instead, they resort to veiled discussions and guarded comments.

A lack of healthy conflict is a problem because it ensures the third dysfunction of a team: *lack of commitment*. Without having aired their opinions in the course of passionate and open debate, team members rarely, if ever, buy in and commit to decisions, though they may feign agreement during meetings.

Because of this lack of real commitment and buy-in, team members develop an *avoidance of accountability*, the fourth dysfunction. Without committing to a clear plan of action, even the most focused and driven people often hesitate to call their peers on actions and behaviors that seem counterproductive to the good of the team.

Failure to hold one another accountable creates an environment where the fifth dysfunction can thrive. *Inattention to results* occurs when team members put their individual needs (such as ego, career development, or recognition) or even the needs of their divisions above the collective goals of the team.

And so, like a chain with just one link broken, teamwork deteriorates if even a single dysfunction is allowed to flourish.

Another way to understand this model is to take the opposite approach—a positive one—and imagine how members of truly cohesive teams behave:

1. They trust one another.
2. They engage in unfiltered conflict around ideas.
3. They commit to decisions and plans of action.
4. They hold one another accountable for delivering against those plans.
5. They focus on the achievement of collective results.

If this sounds simple, it's because it is simple, at least in theory. In practice, however, it is extremely difficult because it requires levels of discipline and persistence that few teams can muster.

It might be helpful to assess your team and identify where the opportunities for improvement lie in your organization.

DYSFUNCTION 1: ABSENCE OF TRUST

Trust lies at the heart of a functioning, cohesive team. Without it, teamwork is all but impossible (Exhibits 28.1 and 28.2).

Unfortunately, the word *trust* is used—and misused—so often that it has lost some of its impact and begins to sound like

EXHIBIT 28.1. Characteristics of Teams Without Trust

Members of teams with an absence of trust . . .

- Conceal their weaknesses and mistakes from one another
- Hesitate to ask for help or provide constructive feedback
- Hesitate to offer help outside their own areas of responsibility
- Jump to conclusions about the intentions and aptitudes of others without attempting to clarify them
- Fail to recognize and tap into one another's skills and experiences
- Waste time and energy managing their behaviors for effect
- Hold grudges
- Dread meetings and find reasons to avoid spending time together

motherhood and apple pie. That is why it is important to be very specific about what is meant by trust.

In the context of building a team, trust is the confidence among team members that their peers' intentions are good and that there is no reason to be protective or careful around the group. In essence, teammates must get comfortable being vulnerable with one another.

This description stands in contrast to a more standard definition of trust, one that centers on the ability to predict a person's behavior based on past experience. For instance, one might "trust" that a given teammate will produce high-quality work because he has always done so in the past.

As desirable as this may be, it is not enough to represent the kind of trust that is characteristic of a great team. It requires team members to make themselves vulnerable to one another and be confident that their respective vulnerabilities will not be used against them. The vulnerabilities I'm referring to include weaknesses, skill deficiencies, interpersonal shortcomings, mistakes, and requests for help.

EXHIBIT 28.2. **Characteristics of Trusting Teams**

Members of trusting teams . . .

- Admit weaknesses and mistakes
- Ask for help
- Accept questions and input about their areas of responsibility
- Give one another the benefit of the doubt before arriving at a negative conclusion
- Take risks in offering feedback and assistance
- Appreciate and tap into one another's skills and experiences
- Focus time and energy on important issues, not politics
- Offer and accept apologies without hesitation
- Look forward to meetings and other opportunities to work as a group

As "soft" as all of this might sound, it is only when team members are truly comfortable being exposed to one another that they begin to act without concern for protecting themselves. As a result, they can focus their energy and attention completely on the job at hand rather than on being strategically disingenuous or political with one another.

Achieving vulnerability-based trust is difficult because in the course of career advancement and education, most successful people learn to be competitive with their peers and protective of their reputations. It is a challenge for them to turn those instincts off for the good of a team, but that is exactly what is required.

The costs of failing to do this are great. Teams that lack trust waste inordinate amounts of time and energy managing their behaviors and interactions within the group. They tend to dread team meetings and are reluctant to take risks in asking for or offering assistance to others. As a result, morale on distrusting teams is usually quite low, and unwanted turnover is high.

Suggestions for Overcoming Dysfunction 1

How does a team go about building trust? Unfortunately, vulnerability-based trust cannot be achieved overnight. It requires shared experiences over time, multiple instances of follow-through and credibility, and an in-depth understanding of the unique attributes of team members. However, by taking a focused approach, a team can dramatically accelerate the process and achieve trust in relatively short order. Here are a few tools that can bring this about.

Personal Histories Exercise In less than an hour, a team can take the first steps toward developing trust. This low-risk exercise requires nothing more than going around the table during a meeting and having team members answer a short list of questions about themselves. Questions need not be overly sensitive in nature and might include the following: number of siblings, home town, unique challenges of childhood, favorite hobbies, first job, and worst job. Simply by describing these relatively innocuous attributes or experiences, team members begin to relate to one another on a more personal basis and see one another as human beings with life stories and interesting backgrounds. This encourages greater empathy and understanding, and discourages unfair and inaccurate behavioral attributions. It is amazing how little some team members know about one another and how just a small amount of information begins to break down barriers. (Minimum time required: 30 minutes.)

Team Effectiveness Exercise This exercise is more rigorous and relevant than the previous one but may involve more risk. It requires team members to identify the single most important contribution that each of their peers makes to the team, as well as the one area that they must either improve on or eliminate for the good of the team. All members then report their responses, focusing on one person at a time, usually beginning with the team leader.

While this exercise may seem somewhat intrusive and dangerous at first glance, it is remarkable how manageable it can be and how much useful information, both constructive and positive, can be extracted in about an hour. And though the team effectiveness exercise certainly requires some degree of trust in order to be useful, even a relatively dysfunctional team can often make it work with surprisingly little tension. (Minimum time required: 60 minutes.)

Personality and Behavioral Preference Profiles Some of the most effective and lasting tools for building trust on a team are profiles of team members' behavioral preferences and personality styles. These help break down barriers by allowing people to better understand and empathize with one another.

The best profiling tool, in my opinion, is the Myers-Briggs Type Indicator (MBTI). However, a number of others are popular among different audiences. The purpose of most of these tools is to provide practical and scientifically valid behavioral descriptions of various team members according to the diverse ways that they think, speak, and act. Some of the best characteristics of tools like the MBTI are their nonjudgmental nature (no type is better than another, although they differ substantially), their basis in research (they are not founded on astrology or new age science), and the extent to which participants take an active role in identifying their own types (they don't simply receive a computer printout or test score that alone dictates their type). Many of these tools do require the participation of a licensed consultant, which is important to avoid the misuse of their powerful implications and applications. (Minimum time required: 4 hours.)

360-Degree Feedback These tools have become popular over the past twenty years and can produce powerful results for a team. They are riskier than any of the tools or exercises described so far because they call for peers to make specific judgments and provide one another with constructive criticism. The key to making a 360-degree program work, in my opinion, is divorcing it entirely from compensation and formal performance evaluation. Rather, it should be used as a developmental tool, one that allows employees to identify strengths and weaknesses without any repercussions. By being even slightly connected to formal performance evaluation or compensation, 360-degree programs can take on dangerous political undertones.

Experiential Team Exercises Ropes courses and other experiential team activities seem to have lost some of their luster over the course of the past ten years, and deservedly so. Still, many teams do them with the hope of building trust. And while there are certainly some benefits derived from rigorous and creative outdoor activities involving collective support and cooperation, those benefits do not always translate directly to the working world. That being said, experiential team exercises can be valuable tools for enhancing teamwork as long as they are layered on more fundamental and relevant processes.

o o o

While each of these tools and exercises can have a significant short-term impact on a team's ability to build trust, they must be accompanied by regular follow-up in the course of daily work. Individual developmental areas must be revisited to ensure that progress does not lose momentum. Even on a strong team—and perhaps especially so—atrophy can lead to the erosion of trust.

The Role of the Leader

The most important action that a leader must take to encourage the building of trust on a team is to demonstrate vulnerability first. This requires that a leader risk losing face in front of the team, so that subordinates will take the same risk themselves. What is more, team leaders must create an environment that does not punish vulnerability. Even well-intentioned teams can subtly discourage trust by chastising one another for admissions of weakness or failure. Finally, displays of vulnerability on the part of a team leader must be genuine; they cannot be staged. One of the best ways to lose the trust of a team is to feign vulnerability in order to manipulate the emotions of others.

Connection to Dysfunction 2

How does all of this relate to the next dysfunction, the fear of conflict? By building trust, a team makes conflict possible because team members do not hesitate to engage in passionate and sometimes emotional debate, knowing that they will not be punished for saying something that might otherwise be interpreted as destructive or critical.

DYSFUNCTION 2: FEAR OF CONFLICT

All great relationships, the ones that last over time, require productive conflict in order to grow. This is true in marriage, parenthood, friendship, and certainly business. Unfortunately, conflict is considered taboo in many situations, especially at work. And the higher you go up the management chain, the more you find people spending inordinate amounts of time and energy trying to avoid the kind of passionate debates that are essential to any great team (Exhibits 28.3 and 28.4).

It is important to distinguish productive ideological conflict from destructive fighting and interpersonal politics. Ideological conflict is limited to concepts and ideas and avoids personality-focused, mean-spirited attacks. However, it can have many of the same external qualities of interpersonal conflict—passion, emotion, and frustration—so much so that an outside observer might easily mistake it for unproductive discord.

But teams that engage in productive conflict know that the only purpose is to produce the best possible solution in the shortest period of time. They discuss and resolve issues more quickly and completely than others, and they emerge from heated debates with no residual feelings or collateral damage, but with an eagerness and readiness to take on the next important issue.

Ironically, teams that avoid ideological conflict often do so in order to avoid hurting team members' feelings, and then end

EXHIBIT 28.3. **Characteristics of Teams That Fear Conflict**

Teams that fear conflict . . .

- Have boring meetings
- Create environments where back-channel politics and personal attacks thrive
- Ignore controversial topics that are critical to team success
- Fail to tap into all the opinions and perspectives of team members
- Waste time and energy with posturing and interpersonal risk management

EXHIBIT 28.4. **Characteristics of Teams That Engage in Conflict**

Teams that engage in conflict . . .

○ Have lively, interesting meetings
○ Extract and exploit the ideas of all team members
○ Solve real problems quickly
○ Minimize politics
○ Put critical topics on the table for discussion

up encouraging dangerous tension. When team members do not openly debate and disagree about important ideas, they often turn to back-channel personal attacks, which are far nastier and more harmful than any heated argument over issues.

It is also ironic that so many people avoid conflict in the name of efficiency, because healthy conflict is actually a time saver. Contrary to the notion that teams waste time and energy arguing, those that avoid conflict actually doom themselves to revisiting issues again and again without resolution. They often ask team members to take their issues "off-line," which seems to be a euphemism for avoiding dealing with an important topic, only to have it raised again at the next meeting.

Suggestions for Overcoming Dysfunction 2

How does a team go about developing the ability and willingness to engage in healthy conflict? The first step is acknowledging that conflict is productive and that many teams have a tendency to avoid it. As long as some team members believe that conflict is unnecessary, there is little chance that it will occur. But beyond mere recognition, there are a few simple methods for making conflict more common and productive.

Mining Members of teams that tend to avoid conflict must occasionally assume the role of a "miner of conflict"—someone who extracts buried disagreements within the team and sheds the light of day on them. They must have the courage and confidence to call out sensitive issues and force team members to work through them. This requires a degree of objectivity during meetings and a commitment to staying with the conflict until it is resolved. Some teams may want to assign a member of the team to take on this responsibility during a given meeting or discussion.

Real-Time Permission In the process of mining for conflict, team members need to coach one another not to retreat from healthy debate. One simple but effective way to do this is to recognize when the people engaged in conflict are becoming uncomfortable with the level of discord, and then interrupt to remind them that what they are doing is necessary. As simple and paternal as this may sound, it is a remarkably effective tool for draining tension from a productive but difficult interchange, giving the participants the confidence to continue. And once the discussion or meeting has ended, it is helpful to remind participants that the conflict they just engaged in is good for the team and not something to avoid in the future.

Other Tools There are a variety of personality style and behavioral preference tools that allow team members to understand one another better. Because most of these include descriptions of how different types deal with conflict, they can be useful for helping people anticipate their approach or resistance to it. Another tool that specifically relates to conflict is the

Thomas-Kilmann Conflict Mode Instrument, commonly referred to as the TKI. It allows team members to understand natural inclinations around conflict so they can make more strategic choices about which approaches are most appropriate in different situations.

The Role of the Leader

One of the most difficult challenges that a leader faces in promoting healthy conflict is the desire to protect members from harm. This leads to premature interruption of disagreements and prevents team members from developing coping skills for dealing with conflict themselves. This is not unlike parents who overprotect their children from quarrels or altercations with siblings. In many cases, it serves only to strain the relationships by depriving the participants of an opportunity to develop conflict management skills. It also leaves them hungry for resolution that never occurs.

Therefore, it is key that leaders demonstrate restraint when their people engage in conflict and allow resolution to occur naturally, as messy as it can sometimes be. This can be a challenge because many leaders feel that they are somehow failing in their jobs by losing control of their teams during conflict.

Finally, as trite as it may sound, a leader's ability to personally model appropriate conflict behavior is essential. By avoiding conflict when it is necessary and productive—something many executives do—a team leader will encourage this dysfunction to thrive.

Connection to Dysfunction 3

How does all of this relate to the next dysfunction, the lack of commitment? By engaging in productive conflict and tapping into team members' perspectives and opinions, a team can confidently commit and buy in to a decision knowing that they have benefited from everyone's ideas.

DYSFUNCTION 3: LACK OF COMMITMENT

In the context of a team, commitment is a function of two things: clarity and buy-in. Great teams make clear and timely decisions and move forward with complete buy-in from every member of the team, even those who voted against the decision. They leave meetings confident that no one on the team is quietly harboring doubts about whether to support the actions agreed on (Exhibits 28.5 and 28.6).

The two greatest causes of the lack of commitment are the desire for consensus and the need for certainty:

- Consensus. Great teams understand the danger of seeking consensus and find ways to achieve buy-in even when complete agreement is impossible. They understand that reasonable human beings do not need to get their way in order to support a decision, but only need to know that their opinions have been heard and considered. Great teams ensure that everyone's ideas are genuinely considered, which then creates a willingness to rally around whatever decision is ultimately made by the group. And when that is not possible due to an impasse, the leader of the team is allowed to make the call.

- Certainty. Great teams also pride themselves on being able to unite behind decisions and commit to clear courses of action even when there is little assurance about whether the decision is correct. That's because they understand the old military axiom that a decision is better than no decision. They also realize that it is better to make a decision boldly and be wrong—and then change direction with equal boldness—than it is to waffle.

EXHIBIT 28.5. Characteristics of Teams That Fail to Commit

A team that fails to commit . . .

- Creates ambiguity among the team about direction and priorities
- Watches windows of opportunity close due to excessive analysis and unnecessary delay
- Breeds lack of confidence and fear of failure
- Revisits discussions and decisions again and again
- Encourages second-guessing among team members

Contrast this with the behavior of dysfunctional teams that try to hedge their bets and delay important decisions until they have enough data to feel certain that they are making the right decision. As prudent as this might seem, it is dangerous because of the paralysis and lack of confidence it breeds within a team.

It is important to remember that conflict underlies the willingness to commit without perfect information. In many cases, teams have all the information they need, but it resides within the hearts and minds of the team itself and must be extracted through unfiltered debate. Only when everyone has put their opinions and perspectives on the table can the team confidently commit to a decision knowing that it has tapped into the collective wisdom of the entire group.

Regardless of whether it is caused by the need for consensus or certainty, it is important to understand that one of the greatest consequences for an executive team that does not commit to clear decisions is unresolvable discord deeper in the organization. More than any of the dysfunctions, this one creates dangerous ripple effects for subordinates. When an executive team fails to achieve buy-in from all team members, even if the disparities that exist seem relatively small, employees who report to those executives will inevitably clash when they try to interpret marching orders that are not clearly aligned with

---

EXHIBIT 28.6. Characteristics of Teams That Commit

A team that commits . . .

- Creates clarity around direction and priorities
- Aligns the entire team around common objectives
- Develops an ability to learn from mistakes
- Takes advantage of opportunities before competitors do
- Moves forward without hesitation
- Changes direction without hesitation or guilt

---

those of colleagues in other departments. Like a vortex, small gaps between executives high up in an organization become major discrepancies by the time they reach employees below.

Suggestions for Overcoming Dysfunction 3

How does a team go about ensuring commitment? By taking specific steps to maximize clarity and achieve buy-in, and resisting the lure of consensus or certainty. Here are a few simple but effective tools and principles.

Cascading Messaging One of the most valuable disciplines that any team can adopt takes just a few minutes and is absolutely free. At the end of a staff meeting or off-site, a team should explicitly review the key decisions made during the meeting and agree on what needs to be communicated to employees or other constituencies about those decisions. What often happens during this exercise is that members of the team learn that they are not all on the same page about what has been agreed on and that they need to clarify specific outcomes before putting them into action. Moreover, they become clear on which of the decisions should remain confidential and which must be communicated quickly and comprehensively. Finally, by leaving meetings clearly aligned with one another, leaders send a powerful and welcomed message to employees who have grown accustomed to receiving inconsistent and even contradictory statements from managers who attended the same meeting. (Minimum time required: 10 minutes.)

Deadlines As simple as it seems, one of the best tools for ensuring commitment is the use of clear deadlines for when decisions will be made, and honoring those dates with discipline and rigidity. The worst enemy of a team that is susceptible to this dysfunction is ambiguity, and timing is one of the most critical factors that must be made clear. What is more, committing to deadlines for intermediate decisions and milestones is just as important as final deadlines, because it ensures that misalignment among team members is identified and addressed before the costs are too great.

Contingency and Worst-Case Scenario Analysis A team that struggles with commitment can begin overcoming this tendency by briefly discussing contingency plans up front or, better yet, clarifying the worst-case scenario for a decision they are struggling to make. This usually allows them to reduce their fears by helping them realize that the costs of an incorrect decision are survivable and far less damaging than they had imagined.

Low-Risk Exposure Therapy Another relevant exercise for a commitment-phobic team is the demonstration of decisiveness in relatively low-risk situations. When teams force themselves to make decisions after substantial discussion but little analysis or research, they usually come to realize that the quality of the decision they made was better than they had expected. What is more, they learn that the decision would not have been much different had the team engaged in lengthy, time-consuming study. This is not to say that research and analysis are not necessary or important, but rather that teams with this dysfunction tend to overvalue them.

The Role of the Leader

More than any other member of the team, the leader must be comfortable with the prospect of making a decision that ultimately turns out to be wrong. And the leader must be constantly pushing the group for closure around issues, as well as adherence to schedules that the team has set. What the leader cannot do is place too high a premium on certainty or consensus.

Connection to Dysfunction 4

How does all of this relate to the next dysfunction, the avoidance of accountability? In order for teammates to call each other on their behaviors and actions, they must have a clear sense of what is expected. Even the most ardent believers in accountability usually balk at having to hold someone accountable for something that was never bought into or made clear in the first place.

DYSFUNCTION 4: AVOIDANCE OF ACCOUNTABILITY

Accountability is a buzzword that has lost much of its meaning as it has become as overused as terms like *empowerment* and *quality*. In the context of teamwork, however, it refers specifically to the willingness of team members to call their peers on performance or behaviors that might hurt the team.

The essence of this dysfunction is the unwillingness of team members to tolerate the interpersonal discomfort that accompanies calling a peer on his or her behavior and the more general tendency to avoid difficult conversations (Exhibits 28.7 and 28.8). Members of great teams overcome these natural inclinations, opting instead to "enter the danger" with one another.

EXHIBIT 28.7. **Characteristics of Teams That Avoid Accountability**

A team that avoids accountability . . .

- ○ Creates resentment among team members who have different standards of performance
- ○ Encourages mediocrity
- ○ Misses deadlines and key deliverables
- ○ Places an undue burden on the team leader as the sole source of discipline

EXHIBIT 28.8. **Characteristics of Teams That Hold One Another Accountable**

A team that holds one another accountable . . .

- ○ Ensures that poor performers feel pressure to improve
- ○ Identifies potential problems quickly by questioning one another's approaches without hesitation
- ○ Establishes respect among team members who are held to the same high standards
- ○ Avoids excessive bureaucracy around performance management and corrective action

Of course, this is easier said than done, even among cohesive teams with strong personal relationships. In fact, team members who are particularly close to one another sometimes hesitate to hold one another accountable precisely because they fear jeopardizing a valuable personal relationship. Ironically, this only causes the relationship to deteriorate as team members begin to resent one another for not living up to expectations and for allowing the standards of the group to erode. Members of great teams improve their relationships by holding one another accountable, thus demonstrating that they respect each other and have high expectations for one another's performance.

As politically incorrect as it sounds, the most effective and efficient means of maintaining high standards of performance on a team is peer pressure. One of the benefits is the reduction of the need for excessive bureaucracy around performance management and corrective action. More than any policy or system, there is nothing like the fear of letting down respected teammates that motivates people to improve their performance.

Suggestions for Overcoming Dysfunction 4

How does a team go about ensuring accountability? The key to overcoming this dysfunction is adhering to a few classic management tools that are as effective as they are simple.

Publication of Goals and Standards A good way to make it easier for team members to hold one another accountable is to clarify publicly exactly what the team needs to achieve, who needs to deliver what, and how everyone must behave in order to succeed. The enemy of accountability is ambiguity, and even when a team has initially committed to a plan or a set of behavioral standards, it is important to keep those agreements in the open so that no one can easily ignore them.

Simple and Regular Progress Reviews A little structure goes a long way toward helping people take action that they might not otherwise be inclined to do. This is especially true when it comes to giving people feedback on their behavior or performance. Team members should regularly communicate with one another, either verbally or in written form, about how they feel their teammates are doing against stated objectives and standards. Relying on them to do so on their own, with no clear expectations or structure, is inviting the potential for the avoidance of accountability.

Team Rewards By shifting rewards away from individual performance to team achievement, the team can create a culture of accountability. This occurs because a team is unlikely to stand by quietly and fail because a peer is not pulling his or her weight.

The Role of the Leader

One of the most difficult challenges for a leader who wants to instill accountability on a team is to encourage and allow the team to serve as the first and primary accountability mechanism. Sometimes strong leaders naturally create an accountability vacuum within the team, leaving themselves as the only source of discipline. This creates an environment where team members assume that the leader is holding others accountable, and so they hold back even when they see something that isn't right.

Once a leader has created a culture of accountability on a team, however, he or she must be willing to serve as the ultimate arbiter of discipline when the team itself fails. This should be a rare occurrence. Nevertheless, it must be clear to all team members that accountability has not been relegated to a consensus approach, but merely to a shared team responsibility, and that the leader of the team will not hesitate to step in when it is necessary.

Connection to Dysfunction 5

How does all of this relate to the next dysfunction, the inattention to results? If teammates are not being held accountable for their contributions, they will be more likely to turn their attention to their own needs and to the advancement of themselves or their departments. An absence of accountability is an invitation to team members to shift their attention to areas other than collective results.

DYSFUNCTION 5: INATTENTION TO RESULTS

The ultimate dysfunction of a team is the tendency of members to care about something other than the collective goals of the group. An unrelenting focus on specific objectives and clearly defined outcomes is a requirement for any team that judges itself on performance (Exhibits 28.9 and 28.10).

It should be noted here that results are not limited to financial measures like profit, revenue, or shareholder returns. Although it is true that many organizations in a capitalist economic environment ultimately measure their success in these terms, this dysfunction refers to a far broader definition of results, one that is related to outcome-based performance.

Every good organization specifies what it plans to achieve in a given period, and these goals, more than the financial metrics that they drive, make up the majority of near-term, controllable results. So while profit may be the ultimate measure of results for a corporation, the goals and objectives that executives set for themselves along the way constitute a more representative example of the results it strives for as a team. Ultimately, these goals drive profit.

EXHIBIT 28.9. **Characteristics of Teams That Are Not Focused on Results**

A team that is not focused on results . . .

- Stagnates/fails to grow
- Rarely defeats competitors
- Loses achievement-oriented employees
- Encourages team members to focus on their own careers and individual goals
- Is easily distracted

EXHIBIT 28.10. **Characteristics of Teams That Are Focused on Results**

A team that focuses on collective results . . .

- Retains achievement-oriented employees
- Minimizes individualistic behavior
- Enjoys success and suffers failure acutely
- Benefits from individuals who subjugate their own goals/interests for the good of the team
- Avoids distractions

But what would a team be focused on other than results? Team status and individual status are the prime candidates:

- Team status. For members of some teams, merely being part of the group is enough to keep them satisfied. For them, the achievement of specific results might be desirable, but not necessarily worthy of great sacrifice or inconvenience. As ridiculous and dangerous as this might seem, plenty of teams fall prey to the lure of status. These often include altruistic nonprofit organizations that come to believe that the nobility of their mission is enough to justify their satisfaction. Political groups, academic departments, and prestigious companies are also susceptible to this dysfunction, as they often see success in merely being associated with their special organizations.

- Individual status. This refers to the familiar tendency of people to focus on enhancing their own positions or career prospects at the expense of their team. Although all human beings have an innate tendency toward self-preservation, a functional team must make the collective results of the group more important to each individual than individual members' goals.

As obvious as this dysfunction might seem at first glance, and as clear as it is that it must be avoided, it is important to note that many teams are simply not results focused. They do not live and breathe in order to achieve meaningful objectives, but rather merely to exist or survive. Unfortunately for these groups, no amount of trust, conflict, commitment, or accountability can compensate for a lack of desire to win.

Suggestions for Overcoming Dysfunction 5

How does a team go about ensuring that its attention is focused on results? By making results clear and rewarding only those behaviors and actions that contribute to those results.

Public Declaration of Results In the mind of a football or basketball coach, one of the worst things a team member can do is publicly guarantee that his or her team will win an upcoming game. In the case of an athletic team, this is a problem because it can unnecessarily provoke an opponent. For most teams, however, it can be helpful to make public proclamations about intended success.

Teams that are willing to commit publicly to specific results are more likely to work with a passionate, even desperate desire to achieve those results. Teams that say, "We'll do our best," are subtly, if not purposefully, preparing themselves for failure.

Results-Based Rewards An effective way to ensure that team members focus their attention on results is to tie their rewards, especially compensation, to the achievement of specific outcomes. Relying on this alone can be problematic because it assumes that financial motivation is the sole driver of behavior. Still, letting someone take home a bonus merely for "trying hard," even in the absence of results, sends a message that achieving the outcome may not be terribly important after all.

The Role of the Leader

Perhaps more than with any of the other dysfunctions, the leader must set the tone for a focus on results. If team members sense that the leader values anything other than results, they will take that as permission to do the same for themselves. Team leaders must be selfless and objective, and reserve rewards and recognition for those who make real contributions to the achievement of group goals.

SUMMARY

As much information as is contained here, the reality remains that teamwork ultimately comes down to practicing a small set of principles over a long period of time. Success is not a matter of mastering subtle, sophisticated theory, but rather of embracing common sense with uncommon levels of discipline and persistence.

Ironically, teams succeed because they are exceedingly human. By acknowledging the imperfections of their humanity, members of functional teams overcome the natural tendencies that make trust, conflict, commitment, accountability, and a focus on results so elusive.

o   o   o

Patrick Lencioni is president of the Table Group, a management consulting firm, and a highly sought-after speaker.

Chapter Twenty-Nine

Myths and Realities of Leading Virtual Teams

Deborah L. Duarte
Nancy Tennant Snyder

This is the age of the "accidental" virtual team leader, a person who is asked to lead a virtual network, parallel, project or product-development, or action team. Sometimes a reorganization propels someone into the leadership of a virtual work team, service, or production team. Also, when organizations merge or form joint ventures, especially internationally, it is not uncommon for people who have been leading functional areas to find that they are virtual team leaders or on virtual management teams.

Very quickly, most "accidental" virtual team leaders discover that leading a virtual team is not like leading a co-located team. Although many traditional leadership principles apply to virtual teams, virtual team leaders experience unique challenges.

First, they have to rely on electronic communication technology to send and receive information. As a result, they need to modify the ways in which they provide feedback and gather data. In most instances, the team leader cannot walk down the hall to ask a question, work out an issue over lunch, or call his or her team together for a meeting in the conference room. Some virtual teams struggle to find a common language. If the team is located throughout the world, the team leader must be available in all time zones, while balancing heavy work demands with home life. An audio conference at 6:30 A.M. in the United States or 8:30 P.M. in Asia may be the only way to talk through a problem. When virtual team leaders are asked about the biggest challenge in leading a virtual team, they usually mention the increased sense of burden and responsibility it places on them. Perhaps because of geographical dispersion and the potential for team member isolation as a result of cultural and language differences or functional specialty, the team leader usually feels as if he or she is the glue that holds the team together.

More often than not, organizations and team leaders pay little systematic attention, beyond cross-cultural awareness training, to developing the competencies that team leaders need in a virtual environment. This is a mistake. Virtual team leaders need to find ways to develop competencies that are specific to virtual teams, even if the organization does not formally support their development.

The first step in developing competencies is to understand (1) what it is really like to lead a virtual team and (2) the competencies needed for success. Once people have experienced leading virtual teams, they quickly identify mistaken ideas that they held prior to their virtual team experiences and they begin to realize the competencies they need to develop.

Myths Regarding Virtual Teams

There are several common myths about virtual team leadership. Competencies necessary for leading a virtual team effectively can be aligned to the myths, and developmental activities can be recommended for each area of competence.

Myth 1: Virtual Team Members Can Be Left Alone

The knowledge that this is a myth distinguishes successful virtual team leaders from unsuccessful ones. Successful virtual team leaders understand the fundamental principles of team output and accountability and do not let time and space alter these precepts. The team leader, whether virtual or co-located, is accountable for the team's output. Top management and customers hold the virtual team leader accountable for the performance of the team. Even when the team's task calls for a high level of team member autonomy, the leader still is accountable for the final output of the team.

Some virtual team leaders believe that because they are spread out and under time pressures, each member can produce output without coordinating with the leader and other team members. It seems awkward for a team member in Bangkok to have to check with the team leader in London on key decisions. For this reason, successful virtual team leaders are very explicit with their team members concerning the issues about which they have to be informed, when they need to be involved, and on what level decisions will be made. Virtual leaders need to work with team members to develop a shared understanding of the level of detail the leader needs to know before and after a decision is made. Virtual team leaders also need to be effective in coaching and in managing performance in virtual environments.

Competence 1: Performance Management and Coaching

Effective virtual team leaders actively balance the tension between business and people.[1] Although team member autonomy, empowerment, and participation are important concepts in making a virtual team successful, there is a task that needs to be completed. An effective virtual team leader is the team's leader, performance manager, and coach. Effective team leaders understand that they can provide some autonomy within a structure that facilitates results. Managing performance occurs at the team level and at the individual level.

Managing Team Performance At the team level, the leader is accountable for completing the task within certain technical requirements. Activities at the team level that can make this happen include the following:

- Developing the team's vision, mission, and strategy with input from team members and stakeholders. In a virtual setting, clarity and shared understanding of vision, mission, and strategy direct the actions of team members in ambiguous situations.

- Negotiating the accountabilities of the team members in relation to one another. In a virtual setting, because team members cannot see one another's work, it is very important that there is shared understanding about roles and accountabilities. This leverages expertise, facilitates coordination, and avoids redundancy and duplication of work.

- Identifying results-oriented performance measures for the team and for each team member.[2] Although all team leaders should identify performance measures, performance measures for virtual teams may have to be more concrete and results oriented than they do for co-located teams. Because there is no day-to-day feedback about the efforts of individual team members, results-oriented measures provide an objective and reliable way to determine whether action is needed to get the team back on track.

○ Developing methods to review progress and results. Working virtually does not allow the give-and-take of normal, day-to-day feedback on progress and problems. As a result, successful virtual team members don't take anything for granted and create formal mechanisms to accomplish this. Weekly audioconference updates and templates for reporting remotely often are critical parts of a strategy to provide visibility in team performance.

○ Sharing best practices with other teams in the organization. Virtual team leaders often develop or provide input into "lessons learned" databases, electronic bulletin boards, and other mechanisms by which to share intellectual capital. Most large consulting firms have "sharing knowledge and best practices" as a job requirement for their team leaders.[3]

Effective virtual team leaders, even if they are not leading project teams, often borrow practices from the discipline of project management to help them accomplish team-level performance-management activities. Some of the first virtual teams were project teams, and many of their management methods can be used with most virtual teams, especially in the areas of team start-up and chartering and in the development of ongoing status and review mechanisms.

Managing Individual Performance and Coaching There are a myriad of activities in the area of managing performance and coaching that virtual team leaders need to undertake with individual team members. Leaders must provide members with timely feedback about their performance. In virtual teams, this often requires soliciting informal input from various people, such as customers and remote stakeholders, who interact with team members. It also can include formal communication with invested parties about the performance of team members. Often—especially in parallel, project, or product teams—negotiating a performance rating for a team member includes gathering input from functional leads, customers, matrix managers, and/or the team's sponsor.

A successful virtual team leader uses this input and acts as a performance coach for team members. It is dangerous to assume that anyone can perform effectively without timely feedback. Virtual team leaders need to interact with team members on a regular basis regarding their performance. Virtual team leaders in cross-cultural environments also must adapt their coaching styles to accommodate team members from different cultures. For example, team members from high-power-distance cultures may expect more direct coaching than members from low-power-distance cultures may expect.

Managing Compensation A virtual team leader may have accountability for the compensation of team members. Most organizations use the same compensation and benefits system for virtual teams as they use for the rest of the organization. A virtual team leader should determine whether special circumstances must be acknowledged for the virtual team's unique nature. For example, some virtual teams count vacation accrual in terms of hours rather than days. This is to account for the unusual work schedule that some virtual teams have.

The real difficulty, especially with ongoing work, service, and production teams, arises when compensation systems do not flow across boundaries and the organization does not have one compensation structure for all businesses. If virtual team members are pulled out of disparate places, with different compensation structures, the compensation and benefits schedule for virtual team members is impossible for the team leader to manage. When this is the case, the team leader must address the issue with top management and push for an organization-wide solution.

Development Actions

Development activities in this area of competence include:

1. Participating in organization-sponsored courses in performance management and coaching

2. Developing a performance plan for the team and a performance and coaching plan for each individual team member

3. Participating in organization-sponsored or external courses in project management or reading about project management and applying its principles to the virtual team

4. Meeting with compensation specialists within the organization to understand what is possible and what is not

5. Leading or working in as many virtual teams as possible

Myth 2: The Added Complexity of Using Technology to Mediate Communication and Collaboration over Time, Distance, and Organizations Is Greatly Exaggerated

The complexity of communicating over time, distance, and organizations causes unique problems that are not easy to solve. Practical experience and research show that, when not managed properly, virtual teams can be less effective than traditional teams. For example, virtual teams often take longer to get started in meetings and to produce results than many traditional teams do.[4] Even the use of very advanced technology, such as groupware, is no guarantee of success.

One virtual team that was tasked with developing recommendations to increase customer satisfaction for a lagging product line used a distributed electronic meeting system to help generate ideas to increase sales. Although the system was well suited to assist in the task, hardware- and software-compatibility issues made it difficult for people in Europe to participate. As a result, their input was not well represented in the final product, although it should have been, because the product was lagging in sales more in Eastern Europe than in any other part of the world. The team no longer uses the system, but the European team members still have negative feelings about the team.

Competence 2: Appropriate Use of Information Technology

Virtual team leaders must select and use appropriate methods of communication and collaboration. A leader cannot rely exclusively on technology to satisfy all of a team's communication, information-sharing, and productivity needs, but technology provides the critical link. A team leader must be able to match the appropriate technology to the team's task, the current stage of the project, the type of team, and the level of technological sophistication of the team members. The leader also needs to keep up with new technology to evaluate its usefulness for the team.

Matching Technology to the Task and the Type of Team

Effective virtual team leaders have a number of technology-based strategies for communication and collaboration. They understand that the nature of a team's task will, to some extent, dictate which technology is selected. Tasks that are ambiguous often require a communication and collaboration technology that is media rich and provides a wide bandwidth that mimics the give-and-take of normal conversation. For example, using audioconferences and e-mail to design a complex technical system may not be as effective as using a combination of video, audio, whiteboard, data conferencing, and face-to-face interaction.

The team leader also needs to match the use of technology to the type of team. Work and production teams, for example, are more likely to need work flow software than are parallel or action teams. A parallel team that is working on a complex organizational problem is more likely to have an ongoing need for groupware that can import project management software than is a virtual management team.

Virtual team leaders also must consider whether to use synchronous or asynchronous methods. Synchronous methods are better for complex and ambiguous subjects, for brainstorming and reaching consensus, and for collaborative writing and authoring sessions. Asynchronous methods, such as scheduling software, e-mail, and voice mail, can be used for updates and information exchanges and for collaborating on schedules. They are very appropriate for work flow processes. Team leaders need to be competent in developing agendas for and facilitating both synchronous and asynchronous meetings.

Matching Technology to the Team's Life Cycle Another critical skill is aligning the use of technology and face-to-face interaction to the team's life cycle. Typically—and especially with a team whose members have not worked together virtually—information-rich technologies, such as videoconferencing, desktop videoconferencing, and face-to-face interaction, are necessary at the beginning of the team's life so that the team members can get to know one another.[5] Leaders of project and parallel teams may select these types of technologies and face-to-face interaction at the beginning of the project and in the middle, in order to maximize team dynamics.

Matching Technology to the Team Members' Backgrounds
In many large and complex organizations that operate on a global basis, there are wide discrepancies between the levels of technological sophistication of employees. People who work in information systems or engineering functions may be very comfortable working with groupware, whiteboards, and e-mail as their primary means of communication. People in other functions, however, may not have much skill in using these technologies.

Discrepancies also can exist between a team and its external partner organizations. The virtual team leader needs to select a set of technologies that matches the skill levels of all team members or provide training and backup resources in the technologies selected. The team leader also needs to address hardware- and software-compatibility issues and ensure that all team members' systems work well. If necessary, the team leader should provide technical support at each team member's location.

Humility and Skepticism   Finally, virtual team leaders must know what they don't know about technology. Virtual team leaders who are not technical experts need to seek help in evaluating the use of technology and in facilitating distributed meetings using technology that they are not familiar with. They must be aware of new systems and technologies that might be of use to their teams, and they should remain skeptical enough not to use an untested system without trying it out first. Team leaders also can attend conferences on and demonstrations of new technologies and ask to pilot-test technologies that might help their teams.

Development Actions

Development activities in this area of competence include:

1. Developing a technology-utilization plan that takes into account the appropriateness of the technology to the team's task, the type of team, and how the selection of technology may change over the team's life cycle

2. Participating in organization-sponsored or external courses in selecting and using information technology

3. Attending technology conferences and demonstrations and asking to have one's team serve as a pilot team for new technology

4. Keeping a log of and noting which technologies work well and which do not in different situations

Myth 3: The Leader of a Cross-Cultural Virtual Team Needs to Speak Several Languages and Have Lived in Other Countries

People who are new to working virtually or globally often over-rate the need to speak several languages or to have lived in different cultures in order to be effective in a cross-cultural environment. Conversely, team leaders often underrate these attributes, believing that the language of the headquarters country is what is widely accepted. Speaking multiple languages or having lived in other countries is not a requirement for a virtual team leader. What is required is a sensitivity to other cultures and an attempt to learn how to communicate on more than a "menu" level with team members.

Competence 3: Managing Across Cultures

Managing across cultures entails understanding more than the obvious differences in backgrounds and languages. There are what O'Hara-Devereaux and Johansen call a multitude of subtle and less obvious ways in which culture affects the ways in which people work.[6] The challenge for the virtual team leader is to understand the differences among team members and to leverage them to create an advantage. Virtual team leaders need to develop multicultural as well as multidisciplined perspectives. In doing this, they need to become aware of their own cultural biases and how those affect personal assumptions and behaviors toward team members. Furthermore, they need to understand the many ways in which each team member's culture affects his or her biases and his or her expectations of other team members and the team leader.

Team leader competence goes beyond knowledge of surface similarities and differences; the leader must proactively create what O'Hara-Devereaux and Johansen call "third ways" of working.[7] Third ways of working are techniques for working or interaction that do not elevate one cultural bias over another. For example, one team leader from North America made the mistake of taking a typically North American management custom—publicly recognizing an individual on a team for his work—and applying it to a multicultural setting. To make matters worse, he singled out, complimented, and gave a generous individual performance reward to a team member from Japan in front of the entire team (most were from Japan and China). For a North American, this may have been slightly embarrassing. For this Japanese team member, who was from a collective culture, to be singled out for high performance in front of other team members who had also contributed to the team's performance was not a rewarding experience. After discussing the matter with more experienced team leaders, the leader in question said that the next time he led a multicultural team, he would ask the team members individually how they would like to be recognized before planning to do so.

Development Actions

Development activities in this area of competence include:

1. Participating in organization-sponsored courses on working cross-culturally

2. Aligning with another team leader or mentor who has worked cross-culturally

3. Keeping a log or journal of actions and biases and tracking what works and what doesn't

4. Asking people from other cultures how they prefer to work

5. Visiting as many countries as possible and observing cultural mores

6. Working in a number of cross-cultural teams

Myth 4: When You Can't See People on a Regular Basis, It Is Difficult to Help Them with Current Assignments and Career Progression

Most of us are not used to working with people whom we don't see frequently. Some virtual team leaders think that if they can't see a team member, they can't assist in the person's career development. However, the virtual environment does not change the fact that the leader is still a primary force in planning for the team members' next assignments and career progressions. Because it is easy for virtual team members to feel isolated and unnoticed, it is even more important for the virtual team leader to actively assist them with their career planning and development. If members of virtual teams feel that they have been shortchanged in this important area, their motivation to work on such teams will diminish rapidly.

Competence 4: Aiding in Team Members' Career Development and Transition

When virtual team members are asked about the negative aspects of working in virtual teams, they almost always say that they are afraid that their careers will suffer. Their fear is that no one will keep track of their contributions and professional growth. Many high-performing professionals have been passed over for good assignments in favor of someone who has more visibility with management.

Virtual team leaders must anticipate this concern and develop specific strategies to deal with it. This is especially true for parallel, project, and product development teams during the closeout phases of the team's work. Even if a team member is assigned formally to a local or functional manager, the team leader needs to act as an advocate for that person and provide the manager with a solid understanding of the team member's accomplishments, experiences, abilities, and interests.

In a work, production, service, or management team, the team leader is responsible for the virtual team members' careers and must fulfill the role of mentor and career coach. Care must be taken not to give preference to people who are closer geographically. The team leader also needs to be diligent about being cognizant of the team members' accomplishments, goals, and objectives by actively seeking this information.

The virtual team leader is in a position to help team members to obtain good assignments after a project has been completed. Team leaders can serve as advocates for team members with the team members' managers, stakeholders, and other virtual team leaders. Team members' reassignments should be planned in advance in order to minimize downtime and to optimize the utilization of newly acquired expertise. Virtual team leaders who show concern for the welfare of their team members after the end of their projects provide a valuable service to the organization and gain reputations as good people to work for.

Another frequently mentioned problem with virtual teams is the transition period required for new members to get up to speed on the project and the technology used. A virtual team leader needs to have competence in training and coaching new team members. The quality and timeliness of the orientation new members receive can affect the entire team's productivity. An inadequate or untimely orientation of a single member can result in wasteful downtime for the entire team. Good team leaders develop novel ways to orient members, such as using a partner system for the first few weeks of participation. Some create partners for the entire project.

Development Actions

Development activities in this area of competence include:

1. Participating in organization-sponsored courses on career development

2. Creating and using a process for career planning and next-assignment planning for team members

3. Holding career development discussions with team members

4. Attending to personal career needs

5. Asking team members about their next-assignment preferences and coordinating this information with other team leaders, stakeholders, and customers

Myth 5: Building Trust and Networking Are Relatively Unimportant in Virtual Teamwork

One of the biggest mistakes a virtual team leader can make is to underestimate the power of trust. Charles Handy points out that trust is one of the foundations for performance in a virtual setting.[8] He suggests that if we do not find ways to build trust and understand how technology affects it, people will feel as if they are always in a very precarious state. The fact that virtual team members might be outside what we consider to be our normal radius of trust, the immediate work group, makes the task of developing and maintaining trust even more critical for performance. Trust requires leadership to set and maintain values, boundaries, and consistency.

In addition, even though the use of technology is omnipresent in virtual teamwork, the team leaders should never forget that work is accomplished through people. Networking, keeping people informed, and soliciting input from team members, stakeholders, partners, and customers will always be an integral part of a team leader's job. Because virtual teams are more dispersed than traditional teams, team leaders may find themselves spending even more time networking across boundaries.

Competence 5a: Building and Maintaining Trust

Although trust usually is thought of in the context of a long-term relationship, when people join teams for a short period of time, building and maintaining trust is more difficult, and therefore more important.

In face-to-face settings, we perceive a number of familiar clues that help us to determine whom we should trust and whom we should not. Direct exposure to people provides us with the history and context necessary to understand their motivations and therefore to make judgments about their trustworthiness. We are able to evaluate people's nonverbal communication and observe their interactions with other team members. Part of the way in which we judge trustworthiness is through our perceptions, over time, of the other person's reliability and consistency.

In a virtual team, team members may never have the opportunity for face-to-face contact or to use other traditional sources of information that form the basis for developing trust. In a virtual team, creating trust requires a more conscious and planned effort on the part of the team leader. For example, when one of us assumed leadership of a virtual project team and took a tour to meet the team members, people in three locations voiced serious concerns about what would happen to them after the team had finished its work. These individuals had known other people who had worked on a similar project. When the project failed nine months into the work, none of the team members was able to find new work on interesting assignments. It seems that the team leader not only did not help them find new assignments but allegedly criticized the team to upper management. It was clear that these individuals would have a difficult time focusing on the new team's work until the issue of trust was addressed.

Development Actions

Development activities in this area of competence include:

1. Developing an explicit trust plan for the team
2. Examining the behaviors of someone you trust, noting what the person has done to build this trust, and modeling your actions after that person's
3. Asking team members what you can do to build trust and asking team members to state how they will evaluate whether they trust you

Competence 5b: Networking

If we analyze how effective virtual team leaders spend their time for the first few weeks of the project, we notice that often no "real work" is completed. Activities are focused on establishing links across boundaries and networking. These boundaries and networks are numerous. Networks include team members, managers from local and remote functional areas, customers, and people who are external to the organization, such as partners, customers, vendors, and suppliers. A large portion of the team leader's time needs to be spent finding ways to create shared perceptions among outsiders about the project and its goals. The network has to be broad and strong enough to withstand competing priorities and changing requirements, to obtain needed resources, and to instill a sense of trust in the team and its work.

By way of example, NORTEL has identified crossing boundaries and networking as key competencies for its virtual project managers. When NORTEL explored the key competencies for project managers in the twenty-first century, the ability to understand and work across boundaries and to develop a strong network emerged as critical for success. A team leader's credibility often is perceived to be directly related to the extensiveness of his or her network and his or her ability to obtain resources across traditional organizational lines.

The irony of crossing boundaries and networking in a virtual environment is that in the early stages, much of it takes place face-to-face. Attending planning meetings with senior management, conducting team-initiation sessions with team members, and visiting customers to establish expectations are all expected of the team leader. After solid relationships have been established, some of the face-to-face interaction can be replaced with technology.

Development Actions

Development activities in this area of competence include:

1. Analyzing relationships with important people across different boundaries, noting patterns of good and poor relationships and what may cause them, and noting what you can do to address the poor patterns

2. Examining the behaviors of someone you respect as a good networker, noting what the person has done and modeling your actions after that person's

3. Asking team members in what areas they believe the team is effectively networked and in what areas it is not, and then working with them to develop a plan to network more effectively and to reach new and important stakeholders

Myth 6: Every Aspect of Virtual Teams Should Be Planned, Organized, and Controlled So That There Are No Surprises

Virtual teams exist in adaptive, changing environments. These environments can turn chaotic and can menace or destroy a team's progress. Team leaders should lead in an adaptive way, helping the team members to understand the uncertainty and nonroutine nature of their work. Managing a virtual team with rigid controls and plans will destroy the team's ability to experience breakthrough performance. Balancing structure with adaptability is a constant tension that virtual team leaders face.

Competence 6: Developing and Adapting Standard Team Processes

At Anderson Consulting, software development team processes are standardized around the world. As a result, newly formed teams require little time to establish processes, such as how they will develop their software, plan their work, and document their results. Team members and team leaders understand the processes. Anderson has a strong corporate culture that enhances the probability that teams will adopt standard approaches. To provide the optimum degree of flexibility, however, teams are free to adapt processes if the customer or project demands it. No two customers have exactly the same requirements.

In some organizations, although standard processes are available, there may be significant functional or regional differences. The team leader must be adaptable enough to adjust these for the team's task and situation. For example, Whirlpool Corporation uses a standard product development process. Although the process is used globally, there are distinct differences between regions in how it is implemented. The research and development organization in North America requires more detailed technical documentation at the first review point than other functional areas in North America do. North American functions in general require more detailed documentation (engineering, financial, marketing, and so on) than European functions do. An experienced virtual team leader at Whirlpool understands that there is a need for subtle differences in implementing the process and can lead a team in doing it.

A leader who has detailed process knowledge and a practical understanding of process exceptions is able to address such issues early and provide the team with needed adaptability.

Development Actions

Development activities in this area of competence include:

1. Speaking with other virtual team leaders to discover if there are common processes that are relevant to all teams

2. At the team-initiation session, developing a list of standard and agreed-on practices and noting the processes that can be adapted

Using the Competencies in Selection and Development

Exhibit 29.1 is a diagnostic instrument that can be used to determine the readiness of virtual team leaders through self- or peer assessment. The instrument evaluates the seven areas of competence. The resulting scores can be used to help identify and develop virtual team leaders. To improve the accuracy of this instrument, it is recommended that other team leaders, team members, partners, and/or customers also complete the assessment with respect to the individual.

The results of the assessment will help to identify areas for developmental action.

Developing Expertise

Development efforts should be focused on areas of strategic importance to the organization and the team and on areas that are critical to the leader's career. Virtual team leaders can identify their needs for competence development by taking the following assessment and then asking these four questions:

1. Given the goals of the organization and of the team, what are the important requirements for succeeding as a virtual team leader?

2. Given my results on the competence audit, what are the areas in which I need development? What are my strengths?

EXHIBIT 29.1. Competence Audit

Instructions: Select the level in each area of competence that best characterizes the current skills and experience of the individual being assessed (your own skills and experience if this is a self-assessment).

Competence Area	Skills	Skill Level Rating (1 = low, 2 = medium, 3 = high)	Experience	Experience Level Rating (1 = low, 2 = medium, 3 = high)
Performance management and coaching	○ Is able to develop strategy and set performance objectives ○ Can establish measures for team effectiveness ○ Is able to give and receive informal and formal performance feedback ○ Is able to implement strategies that make the contributions of team members visible to the organization		○ Has led and managed a number of virtual teams ○ Has been accountable for a team output	
Appropriate use of technology	○ Can plan for the use of technology, given the team's task and type, the backgrounds of team members, and the sophistication of the organization ○ Is skilled in planning agendas and facilitating virtual work meetings ○ Is aware of general technology options to support virtual work		○ Has experience using a number of different electronic communication and collaboration technologies ○ Has planned and facilitated a number of virtual team meetings	

Competence Area	Skills	Skill Level Rating (1 = low, 2 = medium, 3 = high)	Experience	Experience Level Rating (1 = low, 2 = medium, 3 = high)
Cross-cultural management	○ Is able to constructively discuss dimensions of cultural differences ○ Is able to create ways of working that not only accommodate but optimize cultural differences ○ Is able to plan major team activities, such as planning, communicating, reviews, and team meetings while taking into account how these activities interact with the cultures of team members		○ Has worked in teams with cross-cultural membership	
Career development and transition of team members	○ Is able to work with team members to plan careers and transition processes ○ Is able to act as an advocate for team members' careers and transitions to new assignments		○ Has acted as a career and transition coach for team members	
Building trust	○ Keeps commitments ○ Can state personal values ○ Can portray the team's work to management ○ Is able to build personal relationships in short periods of time		○ Has worked in a virtual team or in a virtual environment	

(continued)

EXHIBIT 29.1. (continued)

Competence Area	Skills	Skill Level Rating (1 = low, 2 = medium, 3 = high)	Experience	Experience Level Rating (1 = low, 2 = medium, 3 = high)
Networking	○ Can identify important stakeholders ○ Is able to plan and implement networking activities ○ Is able to exert influence over time and distance		○ Has worked in a number of different locations and functions within the organization ○ Has worked with external partners, such as vendors and suppliers	
Developing and adapting team processes	○ Is able to identify the types of standard team processes appropriate for the team's task ○ Is able to identify standard processes that link to team performance ○ Is able to adapt team process to the task, the culture of team members, and functional differences		○ Has worked with major organizational processes ○ Has created and/or adapted team processes for other virtual teams	

Total number of 3s: ＿＿＿   Total number of 3s: ＿＿＿

Total number of 2s: ＿＿＿   Total number of 2s: ＿＿＿

Total number of 1s: ＿＿＿   Total number of 1s: ＿＿＿

Total: ＿＿＿   Total: ＿＿＿

Scoring

Instructions: Total the numbers in the skills and experience boxes for each competence (for example, circling 3 in all skill areas would give you a total score of 21 for skills). Interpret the numbers as follows:

Skill

7 or less: You are probably just getting started in leading a team in a virtual setting. Your challenge is to gain skill in the areas of competence in which you scored 2 or less. This can be accomplished through training, reading, working with a mentor, and working in multiple virtual teams with experienced leadership.

8 to 15: You have a solid understanding of the requirements of virtual team leadership. Your main challenge is to refine your skills for application in a number of different situations. This can best be accomplished through leading multiple virtual teams under the mentorship of experienced managers.

15 and above: You have excellent virtual team leadership skills. You may want to work on skill areas in which you scored 2 or less and to help others acquire knowledge in this area. This can best be accomplished through working as a mentor or coach or by leading multiple virtual teams.

Experience

7 or less: You probably have not had the chance to practice team leadership in a virtual setting. Your main challenge is to gain experience. This can be accomplished through working with a mentor or by beginning to lead virtual teams under the guidance of experienced management.

8 to 15: You have solid experience in leading in a virtual team setting. Your main challenge is to broaden your experience in a number of different situations. This can be best accomplished through working with a mentor or by leading multiple virtual teams.

15 and above: You have exceptional experience in leading virtual teams. You may want to expand your experience in any areas in which you scored 2 or less and to help others to acquire skills and experience. This can be accomplished through working as a mentor or coach and through leading multiple virtual teams.

3. Where do gaps exist between what the organization and the team require and my personal career plans, skills, and experience?

4. What developmental actions (such as training, special assignments, reading, sharing lessons learned and best practices, mentoring, on-the-job experiences) can I take to fill the gaps?

Exhibits 29.2 and 29.3 together provide a framework for analyzing competence gaps and a format for constructing an action plan for improving skills and experience in target areas.

Points to Remember

1. There are many "accidental" virtual team leaders.

2. Experienced virtual team leaders recognize the myths associated with leading virtual teams.

3. Leading a virtual team requires the development of additional competencies that go beyond the traditional ones.

4. A virtual team leader needs to have a personal development plan that is based on the seven competencies.

o   o   o

Deborah L. Duarte is a consultant on innovation, knowledge management, and leadership to companies, nonprofits, and government agencies.

Nancy Tennant Snyder is corporate vice president of core competencies and leadership development for Whirlpool Corporation and a consultant.

EXHIBIT 29.2. Rating of Individual Competence

Instructions: Locate the rating of each area of competence as a high, medium, or low priority for your virtual team. Note areas in which there is a mismatch between the priority for the team and your level of competence. Developmental priorities are areas in which a high team priority exists and your competence rating is medium or low.

Type of Team	Performance Management and Coaching	Appropriate Use of Technology	Cross-Cultural Management	Career Development and Transition of Team Members	Building Trust	Networking	Developing and Adapting Team Processes
Network	Medium	High	Depends on team composition	Low	High	High	High
Parallel	Medium	High	Depends on team composition	Medium	High	Medium	High
Project or Product	High	High	Depends on team composition	Medium to high	High	Medium	High
Work or Production	High	Medium to high	Depends on team composition	Medium to high	High	Medium to high	Medium to high
Action	Medium to high	Medium to high	Depends on team composition	Low to medium	High	Medium to high	Medium to high
Service	High	Medium to high	Depends on team composition	Medium to high	High	Low to medium	Medium to high
Management	Medium	Medium	Depends on team composition	Medium	High	High	Medium
Priority for development? (Yes/No)							

EXHIBIT 29.3. **Worksheet for Planning Developmental Actions**

Instructions: Use the following worksheet to plan training, on-the-job-assignments, and other activities that can develop your skills and/or experience.

Area of Competence	*Developmental Plans*	*Estimated Time Frame*
Performance management and coaching		
Appropriate use of technology		
Cross-cultural management		
Career development and transition of team members		
Building trust		
Networking		
Developing and adapting team processes		

Chapter Thirty

Building Companies Where Innovation Is a Way of Life

Robert I. Sutton

I admit it. I call the novel ideas in this chapter "weird" to get your attention. After all, unexpected, even strange, management practices are more fun and memorable than bland old ideas. But there is another reason these ideas may seem counterintuitive: To innovate, companies must do things that clash with accepted management practices, with common but misguided beliefs about the right way to manage any kind of work.

Most managers are quick to say that drastically different practices are needed for innovation, as opposed to routine work. Yet many managers don't act as if they mean it. They see practices that spark innovation as strange, even downright wrong. And they act as if practices suited only for routine work are generically good for running all businesses all the time. So they end up stifling innovation instinctively.

This happens to the best managers and companies. Start-ups are as vulnerable as established companies. A typical scenario is that a young company generates some great ideas. Once successful, the company reaches a point where it needs "discipline," or as some venture capitalists say, "It's time for some adult supervision." This means that part of the company—sometimes most of it—is organized for routine work. Tasks like accounting, sales, and human resource management can be done in innovative ways. But when "professional management" is brought into a start-up, routinization takes hold. After all, experimenting with unproven accounting practices can increase the chances a young company will stumble. The trouble starts, however, when the "adult" practices spread to innovative work. Although these managers have the best of intentions, they may unwittingly destroy what made the company vibrant in the first place.

Consider what happened at the Lotus Development Corporation in the mid-1980s. Lotus (which is now part of IBM) was founded in 1982 by Mitchell Kapor and Jonathan Sachs. The company's first product was Kapor and Sach's Lotus 1-2-3, a business productivity tool. Industry observers give this "killer app" much credit for the success of the IBM personal computer in the mid-1980s. Lotus 1-2-3 sales grew from 53 million in 1982 to 156 million in 1984, which led to an urgent need for experienced professional managers. McKinsey consultant James Manzi was brought in as president in 1984 and became CEO in 1985. Manzi built enormously profitable marketing and sales operations, focusing on building operations modeled after Fortune 500 companies. The head of sales was from IBM, as was most of his sales force. Many early employees were resentful of the compensation and other perks granted to the sales force.

They saw these salespeople as merely order takers, because Lotus 1-2-3 was flying off the shelves.

Revenues continued to grow. But Lotus started having trouble developing successful new products. Part of the problem was that techniques suitable only for managing routine work were being used throughout the company. By 1985 or so, around the time the company had grown to over three thousand employees, many original members felt they no longer fit in at Lotus. Some were simply not competent, but most were creative people who couldn't find a place in the company and found that their skills were no longer valued. Most of the new hires were cut out of the "big company mold," having worked for such firms as Coca-Cola and Procter & Gamble and then going on to get M.B.A. degrees. One disenchanted early hire described them as "boring people who had never created a product or a company spirit."

In 1985, Mitchell Kapor (then chairman of the board) and Freada Klein (then head of organizational development and training) tried an experiment. With Kapor's approval, Klein pulled together the résumés of the first forty people to join the company. She changed each résumé slightly, usually just disguising the employee's name. Kapor's was changed a bit more because he was known for working as a disk jockey and teaching transcendental meditation. Some of these people had the right technical and managerial skills for the jobs they applied for, but they also had done a lot of "wacko and risky things." They had been community organizers, clinical psychologists, and transcendental mediation teachers (not just Kapor), and several had lived at an ashram.

Not one of the forty applicants was called back for an interview. Kapor and Klein viewed this as a sign that Lotus was unwittingly screening out innovative people. All signs are that they were correct. The only hit product invented by the company after Lotus 1-2-3, Lotus Notes, was developed twenty miles from headquarters, as Klein put it, "so the team could work unfettered by the narrow Lotus culture." Lotus did need great marketing and sales organizations to cash in on its innovative ideas. The narrowness that came along with these changes, however, was a double-edged sword. It is hard to generate new ideas when practices are used that screen out (and drive out) people with varied ideas and who see things in disparate ways. Kapor and Klein's experiment shows that every company, even a great one like Lotus, needs to be mindful about what it takes to spark innovation. Otherwise, it will be filled with replicants who think alike and act as if the future will be a perfect imitation of the past.[1]

In this chapter, I provide guidelines that can help you apply the weird ideas or, better yet, provoke you to invent your own weird—and not so weird—ideas for sustaining innovation. You can use them to build a team or company that keeps developing new ideas and cashing in on its creativity. Or if your team is charged with doing routine work, you can use them every now and then to shake things up, to get people to imagine and try new ways of thinking and acting.

THE BEST MANAGEMENT IS SOMETIMES NO MANAGEMENT

Leading innovation can require a soft touch, or getting out of the way completely. Leaders of some of the most innovative companies expect and encourage their so-called subordinates to ignore and defy them. They institute policies to make sure that employees can follow their hunches, even when their bosses believe those hunches are wrong.[2] Yet some managers still have a hard time bringing themselves to "manage by getting out of the way." After all, everything from Hollywood movies to an M.B.A. education teaches us that management is about overseeing people, giving them orders, goading them on, and inspiring them to perform. As we have also seen, managers can have huge positive effects by creating self-fulfilling prophecies or allocating critical resources to a project. But managers can be oblivious to the harm they cause. Rather than following Pfeffer's advice that, like physicians, managers should "first, do no harm," they take ignorant actions that make things worse. William Coyne, former head of research and development at 3M, tells how a human resource manager once threatened to fire a scientist who was asleep under his bench. Coyne took the HR manager to 3M's "Wall of Patents" to show him that the sleeping scientist had developed some of 3M's most profitable products. Coyne advised, "Next time you see him asleep, get him a pillow."[3] Unfortunately, not all executives are so wise.

Why do so many managers delude themselves into believing they are helping their companies even though they have no effect or are even hampering innovation? One reason is that managers overestimate their value. Gordon MacKenzie, the former "Creative Paradox" from Hallmark, shows how this happens in a fantasy about how Hallmark's "Prince of Profit" would manage a herd of cows: "Outside the zigzag of the fence stands a rotund gentleman in a $700 powder-blue pinstripe suit . . . shaking a stern finger at the cows." As the cows peacefully chewed their cud, the "Prince" would holler, "*You slackers, get to work or I will have you butchered.*"[4] The "Prince" could not understand "that his shouting will not cause cows to produce more milk."[5]

Mackenzie's fantasy is backed by an experiment at Stanford. M.B.A.s in the "experimental group" were duped into believing they were supervising a subordinate who was sketching a wristwatch advertisement in the next room. "Supervision" ranged from low (only seeing the work at the end), to medium (seeing it once in the middle but giving no feedback), to high (seeing it once in the middle and giving feedback). When the drawing was allegedly completed, the "supervisor" rated its quality and the worker's ability. These evaluations were compared to ratings by M.B.A.s in the control group who were not duped into believing that they had supervised the work. The same drawing was shown to all subjects, so it was impossible for the "supervisors" to influence it. Yet the students who believed they were "supervisors" rated the drawing far more favorably than the ones in the control group. And those who believed that they had engaged in closer supervision rated the drawing and worker more favorably than those who believed they had used lighter supervision.[6] As in Gordon MacKenzie's fantasy about the "Prince of Profit" hollering at the cows, these "supervisors" believed they had enhanced the output even though it was impossible for them to have done so.

This delusion, called the self-enhancement bias, helps explain why so many companies hesitate to delegate authority despite strong evidence that it enhances productivity and employee commitment. Yet when managers can bring themselves to get out of the way, good things can happen. Basketball coach Phil Jackson, who won numerous championships with the Chicago Bulls during the Michael Jordan era, and more recently with the Los Angeles Lakers, is a great example. Jackson is renowned for his light touch, for sitting quietly and not calling time-outs during slumps and crucial junctures in the game.[7] Most coaches shout out numerous plays during a game, but "Jackson almost never calls plays; he thinks play calling makes players feel as if they are on a string of (his)."[8] The key to Jackson's success, like David Kelley at IDEO and managers at Corning's lab, is that he has the humility to lead skilled people by giving them what they need to do their jobs and then to leave them alone. When Jackson arrived in Los Angeles, he was ballyhooed as the team's savior, the one person who could lead the underachieving Lakers to a championship. He responded, "I'm no savior. . . . They have to be the savior of themselves."[9] Ironically, he *was* the Lakers' savior because he made it clear that winning was up to the players, not him.

INNOVATION MEANS SELLING, NOT JUST INVENTING, NEW IDEAS

Creativity is in the eye of the beholder. As cases from the Beatles' music to Ballard's fuel cell show, no matter how wonderful something new is, it will be accepted only if the right people can be persuaded of its value. Ralph Waldo Emerson was wrong when he said, "If you build a better mouse trap, the world will beat a path to your door." Too many innovations succeed because they are sold better, not because they are objectively superior to those of competitions.

The competition between gas and electric lighting in the 1880s is a good illustration.[10] Researchers Andrew Hargadon and Yellowlees Douglas show how there was little difference in the illumination provided by gas lamps and the twelve-watt light bulbs Thomas Edison sold at the time. Early electric lighting was plagued by blackouts, unreliable lamps and light bulbs, and fires from short circuits and poor wiring. It was more expensive than gas, and "the Welsbach mantle, introduced in 1885 as a response to the incandescent bulb, provided a sixfold increase in the candlepower of gas lamps, changing the flickering of the faint, yellow glow into a clean white light."[11] Even though electric lighting was not clearly superior, gas lighting was nearly extinct in the United States by 1903. Hargadon and

Douglas show how this innovation triumphed largely through Edison's marketing skill and design decisions that, rather than making it as technologically advanced and inexpensive as possible, made electric lighting systems, lamps, and the language used to describe them as similar to gas lighting as possible. Remember, familiarity is comforting.

Selling a completed new product or service is crucial for cashing in on any idea. That is why Bob Metcalfe, who invented the Ethernet and founded 3Com, said, "Most engineers don't understand that selling matters. They think that on the food chain of life, salespeople are below green slime. They don't understand that nothing happens until *something gets sold.*"[12] As we have seen, selling starts inside companies long before an innovation is brought to market. Disney employees are invited to pitch ideas for new "attractions" at monthly open forums. At 3M, inventors write proposals for $50,000 "Genesis Grants" to develop prototypes and market tests. The innovation process in every big organization—from Ford, to the National Aeronautics and Space Administration, to McDonald's, to Virgin Airlines, to Siemens—is punctuated with formal and informal gatherings where innovators try to sell their ideas to peers and bosses. A hallmark of successful innovations in big companies is that they are promoted by persistent and politically skilled champions.[13]

Similarly, all but the wealthiest entrepreneurs must convince investors to support their start-ups. Experienced entrepreneurs and investors Audrey MacLean and Mike Lyons teach Stanford students how to do so with an "elevator pitch" exercise. Class that day is conducted inside two elevators in a five-story building. Aspiring entrepreneurs are graded on how well they sell their product, market opportunity, and management team to McLean and Lyons during a two-minute elevator ride. McLean and Lyons believe that if you can't create investor excitement in two minutes, you won't get funding for your company. Indeed, a small industry of "venture packagers" has emerged to help entrepreneurs sell their ideas. Carryer Consulting in Pittsburgh, for example, writes convincing business plans, develops PowerPoint presentations, and critiques pitches for entrepreneurs. Babs Carryer (who runs the firm with her husband, Tim) also uses her theatrical background to teach entrepreneurs how to tell stories that excite investors.[14]

This is about innovation, not persuasion. But if an innovator can't sell an idea or find a representative to do it, then it rarely travels beyond the inventor's mind. This is why so many people practice selling their ideas, study how others do it, seek coaching, and read books such as Robert Cialdini's *Influence*.[15] Innovators especially need to know that judgments of them and their ideas are intertwined, perhaps inseparable. As Arthur Rock, the pioneer venture capitalist who funded Intel and Apple Computer, emphasizes, "I generally pay more attention to the people who prepare a business plan than to the proposal itself." When Rock meets entrepreneurs, he looks for those who "believe so firmly in the ideas that everything else pales in comparison," and he claims, "I can usually tell the difference between people who have that fire in their stomachs and those who see their ideas primarily as a way to get rich."[16]

Similarly, Kimberly Elsbach and Roderick Kramer's research on how scripts are pitched to Hollywood producers suggests that if you want people to believe your ideas are creative, persuading them that *you* are imaginative is more important than the ideas themselves.[17] Being slick isn't always important, and it can backfire if one is boring, stiff, recites a list of facts, or comes across as "just a guy in a suit." Such "pitchers" are seen as insincere and passionless, as dull people who lack imagination. Conversely, being naive or quirky can convince others that a "pitcher" has fresh ideas and rejects conventional thinking. People also shouldn't pitch a laundry list of ideas. One producer noted, "There's not a buyer in the world you can convince that you have the same passion for five different projects. What you're selling is your passion. You're rarely selling your idea. You are selling *you*. You're selling your commitment, your point of view." The best pitchers spark creative thoughts in "catchers," who join them as "creative collaborators" rather than passive listeners. The filmmaker Oliver Stone told Elsbach: "I think that magic is perhaps the most important part of the pitch. And in a sense . . . it's a seduction, a promise of what lies ahead. At a certain point the writer needs to pull back and let the producer project himself as the creator of the story. And let him project what he needs onto your idea that makes the story whole for him."

Oliver Stone's point is crucial for selling any idea. Once buyers become excited enough to add their own creative touches, it means they are infected by the pitcher's passion and commitment. Elsbach and Kramer emphasize that people who make *others* feel more creative will be seen as people with more imaginative ideas. It is important to remember, however, that it is easier to sell good ideas. As Babs Carryer puts it, "A great idea with a crappy business plan will still get funded, but a crappy idea with a great business plan won't," which is why her ideal client is an "inarticulate engineer with a great idea."[18]

INNOVATION REQUIRES BOTH FLEXIBILITY AND RIGIDITY

Innovation requires flexibility. Generating different ideas and seeing old things in new ways can be accomplished only by people who can revise their beliefs easily. But recall how much rigidity, how much downright stubbornness, was required for

Geoffrey Ballard to develop those fuel cells and for the team at Sun to develop the Java language. Some rigidity is necessary for developing successful innovations. It helps to define problems narrowly enough so they can be talked about in a constructive way, so people know what to focus attention on and what to ignore, and so ideas can be developed and tested in sufficient depth to see if they are any good.

A useful guideline for striking a healthy balance between rigidity and flexibility is to hold either the solution or the problem constant and to let the other vary. The most common strategy is to find a problem and then to search for and evaluate alternative solutions, to keep the problem rigid and the possible solutions flexible. Efforts in the eighteenth century to develop an accurate method for calculating longitude illustrate such a "problem-driven search." Dava Sobel writes in *Longitude* that so many ships and people were lost from navigational errors that "the governments of the great maritime nations—including Spain, the Netherlands, and certain city-states of Italy—periodically roiled the fervor by offering jackpot purses for a workable method. The British Parliament, in its famed Longitude Act of 1714, set the highest bounty of all, naming a prize equal to a king's ransom (several million dollars in today's currency) for a 'Practicable and useful' means of determining longitude."[19] The prize required a navigational tool that could provide longitude to within half a degree (two minutes of time), which would be tested on a ship that sailed "over the ocean, from Great Britain to any such Port in the West Indies as those Commissioners Choose . . . without losing their Longitude beyond the limits before mentioned."[20] Hundreds of ways to calculate longitude were tried until the English clockmaker John Harrison came up with an ingenious mechanical solution.

Much innovation in modern times is also problem driven. McDonald's has tried thousands of solutions to the problem of getting more people to visit their restaurants. Disney's Imaginers constantly tinker with solutions to the intertwined problems of making the long lines of "guests" in their parks *actually* move quickly and *seem* to move quickly. Gillette's research and development laboratory in Reading, England, will test virtually any material or design if it might lead to a fashionable product that works. The lab's ultimate goal is crystal clear: a closer and more comfortable shave, "The Holy Grail as far as shaving techies are concerned."[21]

The other way to balance rigidity and flexibility is to hold the solution constant and let the problems vary, or a "solution-driven search." This is what a two-year-old does with a hammer: hit everything in sight to see what happens. It happens when some new or old technology, product, theory, or service is treated as the possible solution to many as-yet unknown problems. 3M's Microreplication Technology Center used a three-dimensional surface composed of tiny pyramids to develop a display for laptop computers that used less power than conventional displays. Microreplication was developed in the 1950s to increase the brightness of overhead projectors. 3M managers believed that the microscopic pyramids could be used in many other applications, but did not know exactly how or where. They opened the center to find ways to put Microreplication in as many products as possible. It is now used in dozens of 3M products, including recording tape, sandpaper, traffic lights, grinders, and mouse pads.

The Freeplay Group in Cape Town, South Africa, also innovates via a solution-driven search. They invent and sell "self-powered" devices that generate electricity when the user cranks the handle on a two-inch wide, twenty-foot-long ribbon of carbonized steel. As the spring unwinds, it produces enough electricity to power a radio (the firm's first product) for thirty minutes. This radio is not just a cool gadget that attracted computer geeks at the Consumer Electronics Show in Las Vegas. It is changing the lives of the world's poorest people, who can now have working radios without using (unattainable) electricity or expensive batteries. Co-CEO Rory Stear says, "We are not just in the radio business. We are in the energy business. We always ask ourselves, What else can we do with this technology?" This solution-driven thinking has led them to develop, or start developing, self-powered products including a flashlight, global-positioning system, land-mine detector, water purifier, and a mechanism for a toy monster truck.[22]

INCITE AND UNCOVER DISCOMFORT

Discomfort is an inevitable and desirable part of innovation. The weird idea to hire people who make you uncomfortable makes this point directly. Discomfort can also be generated by hiring people you don't need, when employees defy bosses, when people imagine dumb things and try to do them, and when people argue over their precious ideas. Discomfort isn't much fun, but it helps people to avoid and break out of mindless action.

Unfamiliar ideas and things generate negative feelings like irritation, anxiety, and disapproval, as do interruptions of routine action and challenges to taken-for-granted assumptions. If everyone always likes your ideas, it probably means that you are not doing many original things. When Howard Schultz, founder of Starbucks, wanted to partner with former basketball star Magic Johnson to build seven coffee houses in low-income

African American neighborhoods in Los Angeles, other Starbucks executives objected because it was risky. They had built many Starbucks overseas but never in an inner-city neighborhood. These executives also reacted with discomfort when, to appeal to African American tastes, Johnson wanted to sell food like sweet potato pie and play music like Miles Davis and Stevie Wonder. Schultz and other Starbucks executives ultimately decided to build these stores and to tailor them to the inner city. This decision to overcome their discomfort proved to be wise: the initial agreement with Johnson was expanded after the first stores posted spectacular sales and profits and executives' fears that crime would be rampant in and around the stores proved unfounded.[23]

The belief that new ideas provoke discomfort helped Herman Miller develop Resolve, a furniture system that "re-solves" the uniform "squaresville" of the traditional office cubicle environment.[24] "Instead of muted-gray walls and severe right angles, it features lightweight, translucent screens and generous 120-degree angles." Resolve also is said to revel "in bright colors and personal touchers."[25] Lead designer Jim Long says, "My metaphor is a screen door. . . . It offers openness but not complete openness, not total visibility." During the early phases of development, Long showed a prototype to two hundred information technology managers, designers, and facility managers. He was pleased that most didn't like it because if the reaction had been more positive, it "would have meant that the ideas were too ordinary."[26] At Sempra Energy Information Solutions, a test site, the first reaction was "culture shock." As employees became accustomed to Resolve, their enthusiasm grew; they found that communication improved and the office was quieter. Herman Miller isn't ready to pronounce that

Resolve is the office of the future. But whatever the office of the future is, their designers anticipate that the first reactions to it will be negative.

Discomfort plays another role. Many successful ideas were invented because someone got upset about something and then did something about it. Inventor David Levy uses "The Curse Method."[27] Levy says, "Whenever I hear someone curse, it's a sign to invent something."[28] Levy designed the Wedgie lock after he heard a coworker cursing because a thief had stolen his bicycle seat. Levy noticed that the streets near his lab in Cambridge, Massachusetts, were filled with abandoned bikes without seats, suggesting there was a market for a good bicycle seat lock. Being uncomfortable or downright unhappy isn't much fun, but it can be an innovator's inspiration. Says Levy, "When I lie in bed, I try to think of things that suck."[29]

Treat Everything Like a Temporary Condition

The organizing principles for routine work reflect the assumption that everything is a permanent condition; the organizing principles for innovative work reflect the opposite assumption. Both are useful fictions. After all, exploiting existing knowledge is wise only if what worked in the past will keep working. And bringing in varied ideas—seeing things in new ways and, of course, breaking from the past—makes sense only when, even if old ways still work, they will soon be obsolete. Leaders of innovative companies constantly create alarm and warn that just because things are working well now does not mean that they will work later. Andrew Grove of Intel is famous for being paranoid that a "disruptive" change—a new technology that makes their technology or business model obsolete—will appear. John

Chambers of Cisco does pretty much the same thing, as does Jorma Ollila, CEO of the Finnish telephone giant Nokia:

> The chairman and chief executive of Nokia Corp. said Monday that one of his biggest concerns is that "we are not as quick as we were six years ago," when the company had half the 56,000 employees it has today. "You start to believe that what you created three years ago is so good, because it was good two years ago and 18 months ago, and you continue to make money. . . . And then there's someone in Israel and Silicon Valley just loving to kill you with a totally new technology."[30]

Sustaining innovation requires treating everything from procedures and product lines to teams and organizations as things that might be useful now but will need to be discontinued. It can also mean forming temporary companies, not just temporary projects and teams like AES and Lend Lease. The goal at birth would be planned and graceful death, with disbanding done once the company had completed a project or intertwined set of projects. The argument for temporary organizations is that constant disbanding and re-forming keeps variance and *vu ja de* (seeing old things in new ways) high in a company, and makes it difficult for people to engage in mindless action.

This is why some traditional companies, including a team at General Motors Research and Development Center in Warren, Michigan, have examined the film industry to get ideas about sparking innovation. The "Hollywood model" is intriguing because these days, a temporary production company is formed to make most films. After the film is completed, any money made by these single-project organizations is distributed, the team is disbanded, and the life-of-project workers go on to their next job. Hollywood was once dominated by large studios like MGM, Warner Brothers, and Paramount, which employed all workers, including directors, writers, and actors.

In contrast, contemporary Hollywood producers rely on brokers to supply "packages" of people and to help build the temporary companies that make films. Talent agencies like William Morris and the Creative Artists Agency are among the enduring hubs in a complex network of formal and informal relationships, which explains why, although film production companies are temporary, there is much stability and predictability in the industry.

There are intriguing parallels between Hollywood and new-economy industries. There has been a great rise in contract work—especially by skilled professionals with technical skills—and an associated set of agencies to supply companies with temporary help to meet short-term demands in high-tech industries. Although there is much rhetoric about forming "built-to-last" companies in Silicon Valley, most start-ups in this region are temporary. Those that endure as freestanding firms are rare; far more are acquired by large firms, and demise is even more likely. Regardless of whether employees are classified as temporary or permanent, there is enormous turnover in Silicon Valley. This didn't start in the Internet age: turnover has averaged over 20 percent per year in high-technology companies since the early 1980s. In both Hollywood and Silicon Valley, people constantly take new roles, work with an ever-changing case of characters, and new companies are constantly formed with new combinations of existing talent.

I don't mean to imply that temporary organizations are the only path to sustained innovation; enduring companies like 3M, Motorola, Hewlett-Packard, Home Depot, and Virgin suggest that other paths are possible. But if you think about the three principles for organizing innovation, building and constantly disbanding temporary organizations helps ensure that variance, *vu ja de*, and breaking from the past are ways of life. Big companies that treat products and projects as temporary conditions can accomplish the same thing, as when CEO Bob Galvin decided to market Motorola's color televisions under the Quasar brand in 1967. He did so because, looking ahead, he realized it would be easier to sell their television business if its brand name was distinct from the Motorola brand. This move set the stage for Motorola to sell the Quasar television trademark and production facilities to Matsushita in 1974, when televisions had become inexpensive commodities with slim profit margins, just as Galvin had predicted a decade earlier.

Make the Process as Simple as Possible

A hallmark of innovative companies and teams is that they follow the law of parsimony: make everything as simple as possible (but no simpler). They use work practices that help people focus on what matters and ignore the rest. Needless complexity arises when companies consider every contingency and involve anyone who could possibly improve, support, or be opposed to an idea. These misguided efforts to inject order and control, and to achieve perfection, can tangle aspiring innovators in red tape and condemn them to meeting after meeting with people who barely understand their work (but don't hesitate to give them advice about how to do it). These complex and dysfunctional processes can also require innovators to devote too much time to selling ideas and playing organizational politics, and not enough to developing ideas.

Consider a consumer products firm I studied a few years ago. Senior executives believed that nearly every step in the development process could be specified and applied to every product. I can't name the company, but I can tell you that executives insisted that ideas for new products travel through an eight-step process comprising over thirty more specific milestones. There were eight formal reviews along the way, each with more than one hundred time-consuming tasks (for example, "financial plan" and "trademarks") that had to be completed before it could pass to the next stage. The process specified when each of twenty-five groups should and should not be involved (from senior management to marketing) and when each of thirty-five or so questions should be asked (for example, What are the features? Are all plans complete?). The designers of the process had great faith in it, boasting it would speed innovation, increase consensus, and reduce mistakes. Although it was at least five years old at the time, not one of the managers I interviewed at this company could recall a single product that actually made it through this gauntlet, even through all the managers had devoted many hours to trying to push products through it. This does not mean that this company failed to develop new products. Quite a few successful products had been developed, but all by teams that had enough power or political skill to work outside the official process.[31]

Innovation is easier to sustain in companies that follow the law of parsimony. General Electric's Jack Welch says, "Bureaucracy hates simplicity. . . . Simple messages travel faster, simpler designs reach market faster, and the elimination of clutter allows faster decision making."[32] A simpler structure and incentive system helped one of Guidant's biggest businesses, the Vascular Intervention Group, push Johnson & Johnson aside to become the market leader in coronary stents (tiny metal tubes that prop open blocked arteries). Conflict and communication problems between R&D and manufacturing were hampering the group's ability to bring new stents to market. President Ginger Graham and her team simplified the structure by making the same executive head of both R&D and manufacturing. They also simplified the incentive system so that people in both

R&D and manufacturing had the same large stake in the success of development efforts. This shift to a simple, fast-moving development process has been crucial to maintaining Guidant's market dominance, since a new stent is rarely sold more than a year before it is replaced with a superior design.[33]

Innovation can be simplified by reducing the number of products or services developed and sold. When Steve Jobs returned to Apple in July 1997, the company was selling so many computer models that, as he put it, "we couldn't even tell our friends which ones to buy." These included the 1400, 2400, 3400, 4400, 5400, 5500, 650, 7300, 7600, 8600, 9600, the Twentieth Anniversary Mac, e-Mate, Newton, and Pippin. This long list not only confused Apple customers, it confused Apple developers, who wanted to know which products to work on and which to ignore.[34] By 1998, Apple was selling none of these products, and by 1999, Apple had only four computer models: a laptop and desktop for home and educational markets and a laptop and desktop for business markets. This simplification was crucial to Apple's return to profitability.

Finally, a simple philosophy about what an innovation will be—and will not be—reduces unnecessary distraction and effort. If everyone follows a simple vision, it speeds development, focuses effort, and results in simpler products or services (which will be easier to build or implement). Jeff Hawkins, inventor of the Palm Pilot, also led the development of the hugely successful Palm V, telling the design team, "This product is all about style, it's all about elegance." He said, "I gave examples of products. I said—when the first [StarTac] phone came out, it sold for $1,600, and people were lining up to buy it. Why? Because it was new and it was elegant. So I said—I want to do the StarTac of PDAs." The team pressed Hawkins to add features like more software and a microphone. But he said, "No, no. Palm V is all about elegance and style and I won't entertain anything else." This simple vision, and Hawkins's persistence in putting it into action, made crystal clear to the team where to focus their creative efforts.[35]

LEARN TO FAIL FASTER, NOT LESS OFTEN

If you believe this chapter, you will cringe when people talk about making innovation more efficient. It usually means they want to use the logic of routine work to manage innovative work. Once companies try to "reduce the number of screwups," innovation usually grinds to a halt. The key to more efficient innovation is failing faster, not less often. Consider what Audrey MacLean told me about failure. MacLean was CEO of Adaptive and is now a successful "angel" investor (she calls herself a "mentor capitalist") who has been featured in *Forbes* and *Red Herring* cover stories in recent years. She argues that one unrecognized reason people made so much money investing in Internet firms during the late 1990s was that failure was inexpensive. MacLean notes that it costs far less to try a new Web site than to develop computer hardware or a medical device or to write a complex software program. The feedback from the market was so fast that "you could fail faster and cheaper than anything we had ever seen before. Most people focus on how much money was made on the upside, but don't talk about the fact that it was—and still is—so much cheaper than most businesses on the downside." MacLean warns, "None of this applies if you waste millions promoting a consumer Web site with no clue of how you are going to become profitable." But she adds, "Since it didn't take much time or money to put up a Web site, you could find out pretty quickly if it was going to fly or not. A lot of money was made very quickly when something worked, and not much money was lost on failed experiments."

It isn't easy to set things up so the plug can be pulled at the right time. The same confidence and persistence that increases the chances a risky idea will succeed is a double-edged sword. It can result in massive resistance to disbanding a company or project, even long after there is objective evidence it is time to quit. We have seen how stubborn innovators refuse to quit against long odds. There also may be historical or structural factors that make it hard to pull the plug. One of the most dramatic cases of commitment to a failing course of action was the decision to design and build the Shoreham Nuclear Power Plant by the Long Island Lighting Company. When this plant was first proposed in 1966, officials estimated it would cost about $75 million. Financial and safety concerns were raised at virtually every turn, and the plant was not completed until 1985. Shoreham was shut down in 1988 because of concerns about design and construction defects and ever-escalating costs, as well as a finding by a federal jury that company officials had deceived the State of New York in obtaining rate increases to build the plant. By the time the decision was made to shut the plant (which was never fully operational), over $5 billion had been spent.

Barry Staw and Jerry Ross have studied the problem of throwing good money after bad for over twenty-five years. Their study of the Shoreham case identifies forces that led to an "escalation syndrome."[36] This included public statements from top managers that the project would never be stopped and powerful coalitions inside and outside the company that stood to gain from building the plant. The rationalization that "too much had been invested to quit" led to decisions to waste even more money. Staw and Ross have developed guidelines for avoiding such situations. The most important one is that people who are responsible for starting some project or company, and who have made public statements saying they are committed to it and it is destined to succeed, should not be involved in deciding its fate. Projects need to be structured so that separate groups make decisions about starting and stopping. This is why most banks use one group to sell loans and a different group to decide whether to pull the plug on troubled loans.

Irrational persistence can also be reduced by eliminating or softening the costs of failure. If people believe that their reputations will be ruined by failure, they may rightly believe that pulling the plug means certain ruin and that—no matter how slim the chances—their only hope is to find some way to succeed. AES, Hewlett-Packard, and SAS Institute are well known for such "soft landings." Staw and Ross also advise that "just knowing that one is under the sway of escalation can help." They suggest looking at situations from an outsider's perspective, routinely stopping and asking: "If I took the job for the first time today and found this project going on, would I support it or get rid of it?" This sort of question prompted Intel executives Gordon Moore and Andy Grove to get out of the unprofitable memory chip business in 1985 and focus on microprocessors, a decision that made Intel billions. An even more aggressive way to avoid escalation situations is to sow the seeds for pulling the plug while a company, project, or product is still a success. Smart executives keep their people vigilant about ways that a current success can turn bad or be eclipsed by competitors. Cisco CEO John Chambers warns his people, "The companies that get into trouble are those that fall in love with 'religious technologies.' . . . The key to success is having a culture with the discipline to accept change and not fight the religious wars."[37]

OPEN IS GOOD, CLOSED IS BAD

Being open to ideas from other people and places brings in variance and different perspectives, which can help your company avoid getting stuck in the past. And by being open to outsiders, ideas that are old to them, but new to you, can be borrowed or blended with what you already know to invent new management practices, services, and products. The value of openness is perhaps the main lesson from AnnaLee Saxenian's book *Regional Advantage*, which shows why Silicon Valley companies like Hewlett-Packard, Intel, Sun Microsystems, and Cisco have been so innovative, while once-great companies on Boston's Route 128 like DEC, Want, and Data General declined and died. She shows how Silicon Valley thrives because engineers share ideas so openly, both to get help with technical problems and to show off how much they know.[38] This doesn't happen just inside companies; it happens between engineers from different companies. Not only do engineers routinely violate their intellectual property agreements, several CEOs have admitted to me that being a bit "leaky" in the right conversations is expected and desirable, because everyone understands that it makes innovation happen.

There are, of course, limits to how open a company can and should be about ideas. Concerns about protecting intellectual property are legitimate, and companies that are careful to guard their ideas can make a fortune, at least for a while. Kevin Rivette and David Kline show, for example, that many companies are sitting on unused patents that are worth millions.[39] IBM licensed its unused patents in 1990 and saw its royalties jump from $30 million a year to more than $1 billion in 1999, providing over one-ninth of its annual profits. Intellectual property constraints can also lead to innovation because if one company owns a solution to some problem, it can spur people in other companies to invent an alternative solution.

Nonetheless, companies that are paranoid about their precious ideas being stolen can kill innovation because when people from the company get a reputation for listening to other companies' ideas but not talking about their own, the lack of reciprocity may lead others to clam up. Or if people from such companies realize they can't engage in two-way exchanges, they may avoid talking with outsiders who can give them useful advice. Excessive secrecy appears to have played a role in the demise of Interval Research, a think tank started by Paul Allen, Microsoft cofounder and billionaire. As the *New Yorker* put it, "In March of 1992, Interval opened its doors, then promptly slammed them shut."[40] The dream behind Interval was that it would have the virtues of Xerox PARC, especially brilliant technologists who developed ideas that formed entire industries, and none of the drawbacks, such as developing great ideas that others profit from. Allen hired former Xerox PARC superstar David Liddle to run Interval. Liddle brought in a mix of well-known technologists, including the inventors of the laptop computer and inkjet printer, as well as behavioral scientists, artists and musicians, and brilliant young researchers from prestigious universities.[41] The problem, according to Paul Saffo, director of the Institute for the Future, was that "they were plopped down in the middle of the greatest technology minds on the planet, in the middle of the biggest revolution of the century, and they never came out from behind their sandbags. . . . They hermetically sealed the place from Day One."[42] Interval was closed on April 21, 2000, and even Bill Savoy, the executive who announced the closing to Interval's staff, admitted, "We probably should have brought in more outsiders earlier so we weren't breathing our own air."[43]

Among the most extreme and impressive illustrations of openness is the development of open source or free software. This includes Linux, currently the only serious challenge to Microsoft Windows. The main benefit of open source development is what is called Linus's Law: that "with more eyes, all bugs are shallow."[44] As the development community grows, each new release grows more resilient and bug free because more people find and fix bugs. The open source community has developed a method of licensing that protects their openness. Open source software is protected by what they call "copylefting" work—not copyrighting it. Open source licenses that follow the copyleft principle add "distribution terms, which are a legal instrument that gives everyone the rights to use, modify, and redistribute the program's code or any program derived from it but only if the distribution terms are unchanged. Thus, the code and the freedoms become legally inseparable."[45]

These restrictions allow the code to stay open. Anyone has access to the source code and is free to modify it, but modifications must be returned to the code base. This causes odd situations in companies and other organizations like universities where a programmer improves some code that his or her employer wants to copyright and profit from, but the copyleft agreement makes that leverage impossible. An open source Web site points out: "When we explain to the employer that it is illegal to distribute the improved version except as free software, the employer usually decides to release it as free software rather than throw it away."[46] There are philosophical reasons for developing free software, but much of the recent enthusiasm for the open source principle is pragmatic: by being open to diverse people and their ideas, the product keeps getting better and better.

o   o   o

Robert I. Sutton is professor of management science and engineering at the Stanford Engineering School, codirector of the Center for Work, Technology, and Organization, and cofounder of the Stanford Technology Ventures Program.

Part Six

Sustaining the Great Manager

Chapter Thirty-One

Leading from Within

Parker J. Palmer

"Leadership" is a concept we often resist. It seems immodest, even self-aggrandizing, to think of ourselves as leaders. But if it is true that we are made for community, then leadership is everyone's vocation, and it can be an evasion to insist that it is not. When we live in the close-knit ecosystem called community, everyone follows and everyone leads.

Even I—a person who is unfit to be president of anything, who once galloped away from institutions on a high horse—have come to understand that for better or for worse, I lead by word and deed simply because I am here doing what I do. If you are also here, doing what you do, then you also exercise leadership of some sort.

But modesty is only one reason we resist the idea of leadership; cynicism about our most visible leaders is another. In America, at least, our declining public life has bred too many self-serving leaders who seem lacking in ethics, compassion, and vision. But if we look again at the headlines, we will find leaders worthy of respect in places we often ignore: in South Africa, Latin America, and eastern Europe, for example, places where people who have known great darkness have emerged to lead others toward the light.

The words of one of those people—Václav Havel, playwright, dissident, prisoner, and now president of the Czech Republic—take us to the heart of what leadership means in settings both large and small. In 1990, a few months after Czechoslovakia freed itself from communist rule, Havel addressed a joint session of the U.S. Congress: "The communist type of totalitarian system has left both our nations, Czechs and Slovaks, . . . a legacy of countless dead, an infinite spectrum of human suffering, profound economic decline, and, above all, enormous human humiliation. It has brought us horrors that fortunately you have never known." (I think we Americans should confess that some in our country have known such horrors.)

> It has [also] given us something positive: a special capacity to look, from time to time, somewhat further than those who have not undergone this bitter experience. Someone who cannot move and live a normal life because he is pinned under a boulder has more time to think about his hopes than someone who is not trapped in this way.
>
> What I am trying to say is this: we must all learn many things from you, from how to educate our offspring and how to elect our representatives to how to organize our economic life so that it will lead to prosperity and not poverty. But this doesn't have to be merely assistance from the well-educated, the powerful, and the wealthy to those who have nothing to offer in return.
>
> We too can offer something to you: our experience and the knowledge that has come from it. . . . The specific experience I'm talking about has given me one certainty: Consciousness precedes Being, and not the other way around, as Marxists claim. For this reason, the salvation of this human world lies nowhere else than in the human heart, in the human power to reflect, in human modesty, and in human responsibility. Without a global

revolution in the sphere of human consciousness, nothing will change for the better . . . and the catastrophe toward which this world is headed, whether it be ecological, social, demographic or a general breakdown of civilization, will be unavoidable.[1]

The power for authentic leadership, Havel tells us, is found not in external arrangements but in the human heart. Authentic leaders in every setting—from families to nation-states—aim at liberating the heart, their own and others', so that its powers can liberate the world.

I cannot imagine a stronger affirmation from a more credible source of the significance of the inner life in the external affairs of our time: "Consciousness precedes Being" and "the salvation of this human world lies nowhere else than in the human heart." Material reality, Havel claims, is not the fundamental factor in the movement of human history. Consciousness is. Awareness is. Thought is. Spirit is. These are not the ephemera of dreams. They are the inner Archimedean points from which oppressed people have gained the leverage to lift immense boulders and release transformative change.

But there is another truth that Havel, a guest in our country, was too polite to tell. It is not only the Marxists who have believed that matter is more powerful than consciousness, that economics is more fundamental than spirit, that the flow of cash creates more reality than the flow of visions and ideas. Capitalists have believed these things too—and though Havel was too polite to say this to us, honesty obliges us to say it to ourselves.

We capitalists have a long and crippling legacy of believing in the power of external realities much more deeply than we believe in the power of the inner life. How many times have you heard or said, "Those are inspiring notions, but the hard reality is . . . "? How many times have you worked in systems based on the belief that the only changes that matter are the ones you can measure or count? How many times have you watched people kill off creativity by treating traditional policies and practices as absolute constraints on what we can do?

This is not just a Marxist problem; it is a human problem. But the great insight of our spiritual traditions is that we—especially those of us who enjoy political freedom and relative affluence—are not victims of that society: we are its co-creators. We live in and through a complex interaction of spirit and matter, of the powers inside of us and the stuff "out there" in the world. External reality does not impinge on us as an ultimate constraint: if we who are privileged find ourselves confined, it is only because we have conspired in our own imprisonment.

The spiritual traditions do not deny the reality of the outer world. They simply claim that we help make that world by projecting our spirit on it, for better or for worse. If our institutions are rigid, it is because our hearts fear change; if they set us in mindless competition with each other, it is because we value victory over all else; if they are heedless of human well-being, it is because something in us is heartless as well.

We can make choices about what we are going to project, and with those choices we help grow the world that is. Consciousness precedes being: consciousness, yours and mine, can form, deform, or reform our world. Our complicity in world making is a source of awesome and sometimes painful responsibility—and a source of profound hope for change. It is the ground of our common call to leadership, the truth that makes leaders of us all.

SHADOWS AND SPIRITUALITY

A leader is someone with the power to project either shadow or light onto some part of the world and onto the lives of the people who dwell there. A leader shapes the ethos in which others must live, an ethos as light-filled as heaven or as shadowy as hell. A good leader is intensely aware of the interplay of inner shadow and light, lest the act of leadership do more harm than good.

I think, for example, of teachers who create the conditions under which young people must spend so many hours: some shine a light that allows new growth to flourish, while others cast a shadow under which seedlings die. I think of parents who generate similar effects in the lives of their families or of clergy who do the same to entire congregations. I think of corporate CEOs whose daily decisions are driven by inner dynamics but who rarely reflect on those motives or even believe they are real.

We have a long tradition of approaching leadership via the "power of positive thinking." I want to counterbalance that approach by paying special attention to the tendency we have as leaders to project more shadow than light. Leadership is hard work for which one is regularly criticized and rarely rewarded, so it is understandable that we need to bolster ourselves with positive thoughts. But by failing to look at our shadows, we feed a dangerous delusion that leaders too often indulge: that our efforts are always well intended, our power is always benign, and the problem is always in those difficult people whom we are trying to lead!

Those of us who readily embrace leadership, especially public leadership, tend toward extroversion, which often means ignoring what is happening inside ourselves. If we have any sort of inner life, we "compartmentalize" it, walling it off from our public work. This, of course, allows the shadow to grow unchecked until it emerges, larger than life, in the public realm, a problem we are well acquainted with in our own domestic politics. Leaders need not only the technical skills to manage the external world but also the spiritual skills to journey inward toward the source of both shadow and light.

Spirituality, like leadership, is a hard thing to define. But Annie Dillard has given us a vivid image of what authentic spirituality is about: "In the deeps are the violence and terror of which psychology has warned us. But if you ride these monsters down, if you drop with them farther over the world's rim, you find what our sciences cannot locate or name, the substrate, the ocean or matrix or ether which buoys the rest, which gives goodness its power for good, and evil its power for evil, the unified field: our complex and inexplicable caring for each other, and for our life together here. This is given. It is not learned."[2]

Here Dillard names two crucial features of any spiritual journey. One is that it will take us inward and downward, toward the hardest realities of our lives, rather than outward and upward toward abstraction, idealization, and exhortation. The spiritual journey runs counter to the power of positive thinking.

Why must we go in and down? Because as we do so, we will meet the darkness that we carry within ourselves—the ultimate source of the shadows that we project onto other people. If we do not understand that the enemy is within, we will find a thousand ways of making someone "out there" into the enemy, becoming leaders who oppress rather than liberate others.

But, says Annie Dillard, if we ride those monsters all the way down, we break through to something precious—to "the unified field, our complex and inexplicable caring for each other," to the community we share beneath the broken surface of our lives. Good leadership comes from people who have penetrated their own inner darkness and arrived at the place where we are at one with one another, people who can lead the rest of us to a place of "hidden wholeness" because they have been there and know the way.

Václav Havel would be familiar with the journey Annie Dillard describes, because downward is where you go when you spend years "pinned under a boulder." That image suggests not only the political oppression under which all Czechs were forced to live but also the psychological depression Havel fell into as he struggled to survive under the communist regime.

In 1975, that depression compelled Havel to write an open letter of protest to Gustav Husak, head of the Czechoslovakian Communist party. His letter—which got Havel thrown in jail and became the text of an underground movement that fomented the "Velvet Revolution" of 1989—was, in Havel's own words, an act of "autotherapy," an alternative to suicide, his expression of the decision to live divided no more. As Vincent and Jane Kavaloski have written, Havel "felt that he could remain silent only at the risk of 'living a lie,' and destroying himself from within."[3]

That is the choice before us when we are "pinned under a boulder" of any sort, the same choice Nelson Mandela made by using twenty-eight years in prison to prepare inwardly for leadership instead of drowning in despair. Under the most oppressive circumstances, people like Mandela, Havel, and uncounted others go all the way down, travel through their inner darkness—and emerge with the capacity to lead the rest of us toward community, toward "our complex and inexplicable caring for each other."

Annie Dillard offers a powerful image of the inner journey and tells us what might happen if we were to take it. But why would anybody want to take a journey of that sort, with its multiple difficulties and dangers? Everything in us cries out against it—which is why we externalize everything. It is so much easier to deal with the external world, to spend our lives manipulating material and institutions and other people instead of dealing with our own souls. We like to talk about the outer world as if it were infinitely complex and demanding, but it is a cakewalk compared to the labyrinth of our inner lives!

Here is a small story from my life about why one might want to take the inner journey. In my early forties, I decided to go on the program called Outward Bound. I was on the edge of my first depression, a fact I knew only dimly at the time, and I thought Outward Bound might be a place to shake up my life and learn some things I needed to know.

I chose the week-long course at Hurricane Island, off the coast of Maine. I should have known from that name what was in store for me; next time I will sign up for the course at Happy Gardens or Pleasant Valley! Though it was a week of great teaching, deep community, and genuine growth, it was also a week of fear and loathing.

In the middle of that week, I faced the challenge I feared most. One of our instructors backed me up to the edge of a cliff 110 feet above solid ground. He tied a very thin rope to my waist—a rope that looked ill-kempt to me and seemed to be starting to unravel—and told me to start "rappeling" down that cliff.

"Do what?" I said.

"Just go!" the instructor explained, in typical Outward Bound fashion.

So I went—and immediately slammed into a ledge, some four feet down from the edge of the cliff, with bone-jarring, brain-jarring force.

The instructor looked down at me: "I don't think you've quite got it."

"Right," said I, being in no position to disagree. "So what am I supposed to do?"

"The only way to do this," he said, "is to lean back as far as you can. You have to get your body at right angles to the cliff so that your weight will be on your feet. It's counterintuitive, but it's the only way that works."

I knew that he was wrong, of course. I knew that the trick was to hug the mountain, to stay as close to the rock face as I could. So I tried it again, my way—and slammed into the next ledge, another four feet down.

"You still don't have it," the instructor said helpfully.

"Okay," I said, "tell me again what I am supposed to do."

"Lean way back," said he, "and take the next step."

The next step was a very big one, but I took it—and, wonder of wonders, it worked. I leaned back into empty space, eyes fixed on the heavens in prayer, made tiny, tiny moves with my feet, and started descending down the rock face, gaining confidence with every step.

I was about halfway down when the second instructor called up from below: "Parker, I think you'd better stop and see what's just below your feet." I lowered my eyes very slowly—so as not to shift my weight—and saw that I was approaching a deep hole in the face of the rock.

To get down, I would have to get around that hole, which meant I could not maintain the straight line of descent I had started to get comfortable with. I would need to change course and swing myself around that hole, to the left or to the right. I knew for a certainty that attempting to do so would lead directly to my death—so I froze, paralyzed with fear.

The second instructor let me hang there, trembling, in silence, for what seemed like a very long time. Finally, she shouted up these helpful words: "Parker, is anything wrong?"

To this day, I do not know where my words came from, though I have twelve witnesses to the fact that I spoke them. In a high, squeaky voice, I said, "I don't want to talk about it."

"Then," said the second instructor, "it's time that you learned the Outward Bound motto."

"Oh, keen," I thought. "I'm about to die, and she's going to give me a motto!"

But then she shouted ten words I hope never to forget, words whose impact and meaning I can still feel: "If you can't get out of it, get into it!"

I had long believed in the concept of "the word become flesh," but until that moment, I had not experienced it. My teacher spoke words so compelling that they bypassed my mind, went into my flesh, and animated my legs and feet. No helicopter would come to rescue me; the instructor on the cliff would not pull me up with the rope; there was no parachute in my backpack to float me to the ground. There was no way out of my dilemma except to get into it—so my feet started to move, and in a few minutes I made it safely down.

Why would anyone want to embark on the daunting inner journey about which Annie Dillard writes? Because there is no way out of one's inner life, so one had better get into it. On the inward and downward spiritual journey, the only way out is in and through.

Out of the Shadow and into the Light

If we, as leaders, are to cast less shadow and more light, we need to ride certain monsters all the way down, explore the shadows they create, and experience the transformation that can come as we "get into" our own spiritual lives. Here is a bestiary of five such monsters. The five are not theoretical for me; I became personally acquainted with each of them during my descent into depression. They are also the monsters I work with when I lead retreats where leaders of many sorts—CEOs, clergy, parents, teachers, citizens, and seekers—take an inward journey toward common ground.

The first shadow-casting monster is insecurity about identity and worth. Many leaders have an extroverted personality that makes this shadow hard to see. But extroversion sometimes develops as a way to cope with self-doubt: we plunge into external activity to prove that we are worthy—or simply to evade the question. There is a well-known form of this syndrome, especially among men, in which our identity becomes so dependent on performing some external role that we become depressed, and even die, when that role is taken away.

When we are insecure about our own identities, we create settings that deprive other people of their identities as a way of buttressing our own. This happens all the time in families, where parents who do not like themselves give their children low self-esteem. It happens at work as well: how often I phone a business or professional office and hear, "Dr. Jones's office—this is Nancy speaking." The boss has a title and a last name but the person (usually a woman) who answers the phone has neither, because the boss has decreed that it will be that way.

There are dynamics in all kinds of institutions that deprive the many of their identity so the few can enhance their own, as if identity were a zero-sum game, a win-lose situation. Look into a classroom, for example, where an insecure teacher is forcing students to be passive stenographers of the teacher's store of knowledge, leaving the teacher with more sense of selfhood and the vulnerable students with less. Or look in on a hospital where the doctors turn patients into objects—"the kidney in Room 410"—as a way of claiming superiority at the very time when vulnerable patients desperately need a sense of self.

Things are not always this way, of course. There are settings and institutions led by people whose identities do not
depend on depriving others of theirs. If you are in that kind of
family or office or school or hospital, your sense of self is
enhanced by leaders who know who they are.

These leaders possess a gift available to all who take an
inner journey: the knowledge that identity does not depend on
the role we play or the power it gives us over others. It depends
only on the simple fact that we are children of God, valued in
and for ourselves. When a leader is grounded in that knowledge, what happens in the family, the office, the classroom, the
hospital can be life-giving for all concerned.

A second shadow inside many of us is the belief that the
universe is a battleground, hostile to human interests. Notice
how often we use images of warfare as we go about our work,
especially in organizations. We talk about tactics and strategies,
allies and enemies, wins and losses, "do or die." If we fail to be
fiercely competitive, the imagery suggests, we will surely lose,
because the world we live in is essentially a vast combat zone.

Unfortunately, life is full of self-fulfilling prophecies. The
tragedy of this inner shadow, our fear of losing a fight, is that it
helps create conditions where people feel compelled to live as
if they were at war. Yes, the world is competitive, but largely
because we make it so. Some of our best institutions, from corporations to change agencies to schools, are learning that there
is another way of doing business, a way that is consensual, cooperative, communal: they are fulfilling a different prophecy and
creating a different reality.

The gift we receive on the inner journey is the insight that
the universe is working together for good. The structure of

reality is not the structure of a battle. Reality is not out to get anybody. Yes, there is death, but it is part of the cycle of life, and when we learn to move gracefully with that cycle, a great harmony comes into our lives. The spiritual truth that harmony is more fundamental than warfare in the nature of reality itself could transform this leadership shadow—and transform our institutions as well.

A third shadow common among leaders is "functional atheism," the belief that ultimate responsibility for everything rests with us. This is the unconscious, unexamined conviction that if anything decent is going to happen here, we are the ones who must make it happen—a conviction held even by people who talk a good game about God.

This shadow causes pathology on every level of our lives. It leads us to impose our will on others, stressing our relationships, sometimes to the point of breaking. It often eventuates in burnout, depression, and despair, as we learn that the world will not bend to our will and we become embittered about that fact. Functional atheism is the shadow that drives collective frenzy as well. It explains why the average group can tolerate no more than fifteen seconds of silence: if we are not making noise, we believe, nothing good is happening and something must be dying.

The gift we receive on the inner journey is the knowledge that ours is not the only act in town. Not only are there other acts out there, but some of them are even better than ours, at least occasionally! We learn that we need not carry the whole load but can share it with others, liberating us and empowering them. We learn that sometimes we are free to lay the load down altogether. The great community asks us to do only what we are able and trust the rest to other hands.

A fourth shadow within and among us is fear, especially our fear of the natural chaos of life. Many of us—parents and teachers and CEOs—are deeply devoted to eliminating all remnants of chaos from the world. We want to organize and orchestrate things so thoroughly that messiness will never bubble up around us and threaten to overwhelm us (for "messiness" read dissent, innovation, challenge, and change). In families and churches and corporations, this shadow is projected as rigidity of rules and procedures, creating an ethos that is imprisoning rather than empowering. (Then, of course, the mess we must deal with is the prisoners trying to break out!)

The insight we receive on the inner journey is that chaos is the precondition to creativity: as every creation myth has it, life itself emerged from the void. Even what has been created needs to be returned to chaos from time to time so that it can be regenerated in more vital form. When a leader fears chaos so deeply as to try to eliminate it, the shadow of death will fall across everything that leader approaches—for the ultimate answer to all of life's messiness is death.

My final example of the shadows that leaders project is, paradoxically, the denial of death itself. Though we sometimes kill things off well before their time, we also live in denial of the fact that all things must die in due course. Leaders who participate in this denial often demand that the people around them keep resuscitating things that are no longer alive. Projects and programs that should have been unplugged long ago are kept on life support to accommodate the insecurities of a leader who does not want anything to die on his or her watch.

Within our denial of death lurks fear of another sort: the fear of failure. In most organizations, failure means a pink slip in your box, even if that failure, that "little death," was suffered in the service of high purpose. It is interesting that science, so honored in our culture, seems to have transcended this particular fear. A good scientist does not fear the death of a hypothesis, because that "failure" clarifies the steps that need to be taken toward truth, sometimes more than a hypothesis that succeeds. The best leaders in every setting reward people for taking worthwhile risks even if they are likely to fail. These leaders know that the death of an initiative—if it was tested for good reasons—is always a source of new learning.

The gift we receive on the inner journey is the knowledge that death finally comes to everything—and yet death does not have the final word. By allowing something to die when its time is due, we create the conditions under which new life can emerge.

INNER WORK IN COMMUNITY

Can we help each other deal with the inner issues inherent in leadership? We can, and I believe we must. Our frequent failure as leaders to deal with our inner lives leaves too many individuals and institutions in the dark. From the family to the corporation to the body politic, we are in trouble partly because of the shadows I have named. Since we can't get out of it, we must get into it—by helping each other explore our inner lives. What might that help look like?

First, we could lift up the value of "inner work." That phrase should become commonplace in families, schools, and religious institutions, at least, helping us understand that inner work is as real as outer work and involves skills one can develop, skills like journaling, reflective reading, spiritual friendship, meditation, and prayer. We can teach our children something that their parents did not always know: if people skimp on their inner work, their outer work will suffer as well.

Second, we could spread the word that inner work, though it is a deeply personal matter, is not necessarily a private matter: inner work can be helped along in community. Indeed, doing inner work together is a vital counterpoint to doing it alone. Left to our own devices, we may delude ourselves in ways that others can help us correct.

But how a community offers such help is a critical question. We are surrounded by communities based on the practice of "setting each other straight"—an ultimately totalitarian practice bound to drive the shy soul into hiding. Fortunately, there are other models of corporate discernment and support.

For example, there is the Quaker clearness committee. You take a personal issue to this small group of people who are prohibited from suggesting "fixes" or giving you advice but who for three hours pose honest, open questions to help you discover your inner truth. Communal processes of this sort are supportive but not invasive. They help us probe questions and possibilities but forbid us from rendering judgment, allowing us to serve as midwives to a birth of consciousness that can only come from within.[4]

The key to this form of community involves holding a paradox—the paradox of having relationships in which we protect each other's aloneness. We must come together in ways that respect the solitude of the soul, that avoid the unconscious violence we do when we try to save each other, that evoke our capacity to hold another life without dishonoring its mystery, never trying to coerce the other into meeting our own needs.

It is possible for people to be together that way, though it may be hard to see evidence of that fact in everyday life. My evidence comes in part from my journey through clinical depression, from the healing I experienced as a few people found ways to be present to me without violating my soul's integrity. Because they were not driven by their own fears, the fears that lead us either to "fix" or abandon each other, they provided me with a lifeline to the human race. That lifeline constituted the most profound form of leadership I can imagine—leading a suffering person back to life from a living death.

Third, we can remind each other of the dominant role that fear plays in our lives, of all the ways that fear forecloses the potentials I have explored in this chapter. It is no accident that all of the world's wisdom traditions address the fact of fear, for all of them originated in the human struggle to overcome this ancient enemy. And all of these traditions, despite their great diversity, unite in one exhortation to those who walk in their ways: "Be not afraid."

As one who is no stranger to fear, I have had to read those words with care so as not to twist them into a discouraging counsel of perfection. "Be not afraid" does not mean we cannot have fear. Everyone has fear, and people who embrace the call to leadership often find fear abounding. Instead, the words say we do not need to be the fear we have. We do not have to lead from a place of fear, thereby engendering a world in which fear is multiplied.

We have places of fear inside of us, but we have other places as well—places with names like trust and hope and faith. We can choose to lead from one of those places, to stand on ground that is not riddled with the fault lines of fear, to move toward others from a place of promise instead of anxiety. As we stand in one of those places, fear may remain close at hand and our spirits may still tremble. But now we stand on ground that will support us, ground from which we can lead others toward a more trustworthy, more hopeful, more faithful way of being in the world.

o   o   o

Parker J. Palmer is an educational activist. He is a senior associate of the American Association for Higher Education and a senior adviser to the Fetzer Institute.

Chapter Thirty-Two

Reflective Action

Robert E. Quinn

I t was Plato who once argued that the unexamined life is not worth living. To this someone once responded, "Yes, and the unlived life is not worth examining." Reflective action is a concept that combines both arguments. It is not easy to integrate both reflection and action. In the world of business, for example, there is a tremendous imperative toward action. If we err between action and taking the time to reflect, we err on the side of action.

Given the bias toward action in modern life, let us begin our examination of the practice of reflective action from the other direction—from the viewpoint of a man who had chosen a life of reflection and contemplation.

A MONK'S TALE

Thomas Merton was one of the most influential religious writers of the last century. A convert to Catholicism, he became a Trappist monk. In 1948 he published a best-selling book, *Seven*

Storey Mountain. It was the first of many successful books and the beginning of a life of high visibility in which he continued to write beautifully of the value of solitude, reflection, and contemplation.

Ten years later, on March 18, 1958, Merton had an epiphany. It occurred while he was standing on the corner of Fourth and Walnut Streets, in the middle of the shopping district in Louisville, Kentucky:

> I was suddenly overwhelmed with the realization that I loved all those people, that they were mine and I was theirs, that we could not be alien to one another even though we were total strangers. It was like walking from a dream of separateness, of spurious self-isolation in a special world, the world of renunciation and supposed holiness. The whole illusion of a separate holy existence is a dream. Not that I question the reality of my vocation, or the monastic life; but the conception of a "separation from the world" that we have in the monastery too easily presents itself as a complete illusion: the illusion that by making vows we become a different species of being, pseudo angels, "spiritual men," men of interior life, what have you [Merton, 1966, p. 156].

After this event, Merton changed. He could no longer go on just writing about meditation, even though it was of great value. He could not bury himself in typical monastic concerns. He had to begin to face what he called the big issues of life and death in the world. From that point on, he became much more involved in the social issues of his day. He did not give up reflection and meditation. Rather, he brought about an integration of reflection and action.

Most of us in the organizational world have the opposite challenge. We are engulfed in action, at the expense of contemplation and reflection. This extreme is just as isolating as the extreme of contemplation divorced from action. With a deep apology to Merton, let me rewrite his vision as it might be reported by a suddenly enlightened executive standing in the foyer of a monastery:

> I was suddenly overwhelmed with the realization that I loved all those people, they were mine and I was theirs, that we could not be alien to one another, even though we were total strangers. It was like walking from a dream of separateness, of spurious self-isolation in a special world, the world of corporate involvement and endless work. The whole illusion of a separate powerful existence is a dream. Not that I question the reality of my vocation, of the corporate life, but the conception of being in the material world that we have in the corporation too easily presents itself as a complete illusion: the illusion that by making money we become a different species of being, pseudo power figures, wealthy people of analytic genius, people of power, what have you.

In the corporate world, we often become addicted to action. We develop organizational cultures that carry the expectations that people will come in early and leave late. We reinforce the compulsive patterns of type A personalities. We complain endlessly about the loss of balance in our lives and the pain of burnout. We assume that there is no place for reflection. We dare not speak of the need for spiritual awareness and personal integration. In this distorted world where we have institutionalized the split of action and reflection, we are trapped in the vortex of slow death. People often recognize the problem but lack the courage to anything about it. They choose slow death over deep change.

Mark Silverberg was a frantic company president. He felt that he was trapped in the requirement for perpetual action and that there was no way out. If he stopped "jumping from crisis to crisis," the organization would surely collapse. Yet Mark made the courageous decision to change. He learned to listen to his inner voice, made time for the things that mattered to him, and he became a centered human being. Once he did this, his world changed. It reorganized to support the new Mark.

My experience suggests that nearly all of us can benefit by carefully considering Mark's story, yet most of us will not. Instead we will find a way to dissociate ourselves. We will tell ourselves that Mark must have been some kind of anomaly, that we cannot do what he did. Most of us "know" that there is no way out. We "know" this because doing what Mark did requires more faith and courage than we think we can muster. In this sense, we are like Merton before his epiphany, except that we are at the other end of the reflection/action polarity. Like Merton, we are living half a life. We need to move from constant action to an appreciation of the power of reflection. Then, like Merton, we need to integrate the two. When we take the time to integrate action and reflection, we begin to behave differently. In reflecting deeply on our behavior, we travel to "the center of our existence." There we find our best self. We also find the courage to enter the fundamental state of leadership. We then change our patterns of behavior. As we become more purpose centered, internally driven, other focused, and externally open, we more fully integrate who we are with what we are doing. At this point, what we are doing enlarges our best self, and our best self enlarges what we are doing.

REFLECTIVE ACTION

The positive tension of the state of reflective action can be seen in Table 32.1. We can be so mindful and reflective that we become stagnant and inactive. On the other hand, and much more commonly in organizational life, we can be so active and energetic that we become mindless and unreflective.

TABLE 32.1. **Reflective Action**

Negative	Positive	Integrative	Positive	Negative
This person is so mindful and reflective as to be stagnant or inactive.	This person is mindful and reflective	This person practices reflective action.	This person is active and energetic.	This person is so active and energetic as to be mindless or unreflective.
Stagnant; inactive	Mindful; reflective	Reflective and active	Active; energetic	Mindless; unreflective

Reflective action: This person is active and energetic while also being mindful and reflective. While deeply engaged in the world, the person also spends time in reflective contemplation. Contemplation when away from a task increases the capacity for mindfulness during the task. The person acts and learns simultaneously and is both mindful and energized while actively creating.

Personal orientation: I continually renew my understanding of who I am and why and how I am doing the things I do by learning from action and acting from an ever-expanding consciousness. I live in a reciprocal relationship between action and reflection. I practice reflective action.

The challenge is to be both reflective and active. We can do this by making a practice of regularly reflecting on what is happening in our lives. At first, we make time for contemplation when we are away from our usual tasks so as to increase our capacity for mindfulness during the tasks. Eventually we act and learn simultaneously. We are both mindful and energized while creating the life we want to live.

Practicing Reflective Action

We begin by examining the group approach and then move on to the discipline of writing.

The Group Approach

The culture of the corporate world tends to drive out the possibility for deep reflection. To counteract this pattern, we often need support.

I think, for example, of a young man I have worked with for some years. During those years, he has become president of a midsized corporation. Like most other people in that role, he feels constant pressure to be in the action mode. We were discussing this when he told me how much he has come to value his membership in the Young Presidents' Organization (YPO). I asked him why. He described the typical agenda for their regular meetings. There is no content agenda. Instead, these young executives take time to identify the issues that are most on their minds, from complicated business problems to serious personal dilemmas. Each person shares an issue, and then the group spends time sharing ways to think about the issues.

My friend told me that these meetings have become the most valuable time he spends each month. He said confidentiality breeds trust, and people stretch in their efforts to be helpful. In those conversations, he can get clear about who he is and what he needs to do next. The process allows him to reflect in ways he normally does not.

After listening to his story about the structure of these meetings, I developed the following exercise. In my next weeklong executive education class, I asked the participants to engage in the exercise.

REFLECTING ON CORE ISSUES

1. Record brief answers to the following. Then prepare a three-minute report conveying your most important present concern.

   During the past month:

   What was the best thing to happen to you?

   What is the most challenging thing to happen to you?

In the next month:

What professional situation will be most demanding?

What personal situation will be most demanding?

2. Each person should give his or her report in three minutes or less. Be disciplined about time. As each report is given, group members should take notes on what is said.

3. The group should identify the key themes in the pre-sentations. The issues may include such things as marriage, divorce, taking a small company public, problems with children, how to cope with a pressing organizational issue, or a wide range of other topics. During the week, the group will have one hour each day to address the five most important topics.

4. During that hour, one person will be assigned to make a short (five-minute) presentation on the topic, and one person will be assigned as a coach to the pre-senter. At the conclusion of the presentation, the coach acts as the facilitator of the discussion.

5. The facilitator invites people to give advice. The facilitator is responsible to see that participants do not make "You should do" statements but rather "It has been my experience . . ." kinds of statements.

In my next week-long executive education class, I asked the participants to engage in the exercise. Afterward, they reported the very same reaction as my friend did to his experience in YPO. They were amazed that as strangers, they could achieve such intimacy. They were amazed that they could walk away from their discussions with such a sense of insight. I pointed out to them that the exercise can be executed by any group.

Indeed, people in many companies have created such groups and used my book *Deep Change* as a tool for reflecting on daily patterns of action. One way to gain support for integrating action and reflection is through such a group approach.

The Discipline of Writing

Perhaps the most common way to integrate action and reflection is through the habit of journal writing. This entails a commitment to set aside some time each day to reflect and write about the patterns currently unfolding in your life. Some people turn activity into a process of diary writing, simply recording what happened during the day. Reflective action requires more that just recording events. It requires careful examination of who we are and how that matches with what we are doing. It often requires an exploration of the link between our present and our past. Consider an example.

I once had an opportunity to write a chapter with my son Shawn (Quinn and Quinn, forthcoming). He had just received his master's degree in organizational psychology at Columbia University, and he intended to become a consultant. The chapter was about the process of becoming a transformational change agent. It consisted of two letters. In the first letter, I wrote to Shawn explaining some of the basic concepts of transformation. The concepts, like the ones here, suggested high personal accountability and would lead almost anyone to conclude that they could not be expected to live in a transformational way, especially when just starting a career. However, I asked Shawn to do an unusual thing. I asked him to reflect deeply on action. In particular, I asked him to reflect on action that had already taken place in his life.

The key thought here is that Shawn and the rest of us carry a treasure. When most of us survey our current situation, we are sure that there is no way we can be transformational. We suspect that we never will be. Yet in our treasure trove, there often are data that contradict our tightly held position. Often there are patterns of action in our past that were in fact patterns of deep change. Reflecting on these patterns can have a great impact on how we see ourselves and how we see our situations.

In responding to my request, Shawn expressed some deeply held fears. Then he wrote insightfully about his basketball career in high school, his experiences as a missionary, and his first managerial job. Here I will quote the last of these reflections as an illustration of how reflecting on the past can lead to new learning.

> My first job out of college was working for one of the country's fastest growing trucking companies. I was the assistant to the president of the Western Division and thus had frequent opportunities to work with the CEO. After a short period the CEO and I developed a trusting relationship. I think that relationship was a function of what I learned in [my previous experiences].
>
> At one point he decided to invest in a company offering a new information technology. They had an innovative information system that would allow for the tracking and managing of our trucks and trailers. We believed that implementing the system would greatly improve our bottom line. Yet the implementation process did not go well. There were many problems and much resistance. The utilization rate was 5%. At that point I was asked to take charge of the project.
>
> After a couple of weeks of analysis, I decided to do two things. First, each time a driver was sent to me with questions about the system, I sent the driver back to get his manager. I would then teach the manager how to use the system. When the managers first came in, they were usually resistant, but as they gained a sense of control, they got excited about what they could

do. They then went back and coached their other drivers. Second, I spent a lot of time talking to people at higher levels. I continually pushed the need for them to include competency with the system as part of their job evaluations. Gradually, this came to pass, and it helped a great deal.

Despite measurable progress, there were still a number of drivers and driver managers who were not using the technology. At first, I was tempted to blame them, but instead I decided to own the problem. If they were not using the system, I had to bear some responsibility. So this realization forced me to develop new strategies. I committed to continuously talk to everyone, at every level, about the bigger picture. I explained that if we could make the technology work, it would help the technology company go public and, since we owned part of the company, it would help our bottom line. I did this relentlessly. I also continually shared data showing the improvements in time utilization. I did interviews and distributed questionnaires seeking to learn every problem they were encountering. I made sure we took action to remedy each one. I identified the non-users and started spending my time with them. I did whatever was necessary to free them up to learn and teach the system.

Utilization rates started to climb. In four months we went from 5% to 60% utilization. As this happened, we discovered some of the real problems with the technology. Here my integrity failed. I worried a lot about pleasing the CEO. He wanted the new technology company to be successful. So I had a tendency to soften my accounts of the problems in the new technology. I also failed to confront the people in the technology company. I should have challenged them to be more honest with themselves, to embrace and deal with their real problems. They did not want to face the pain of reality, and I did not have the courage to impose the pain. In the long run, they had to drop a part of their product line. They suffered and we suffered.

In this account, Shawn works hard to be very honest with himself. He not only tells of his success, but lays bare his failure, his lack of integrity. As opposed to keeping a diary, this kind of writing leads to deep personal learning. The author begins to learn things about the author. Here are the lessons that Shawn identifies:

Lessons: In the first phase I did a lot of rational explanation, telling people why they should change. I also used political leverage by getting management to evaluate people. I used a number of participative techniques, involving people in the learning process. Yet, even after all that effort, we were still only partially successful. At that point, I very much wanted to blame others. Instead, I tried to change myself, trying to take more accountability for the results and increasing my integrity. That led to greater commitment, effort, and change from myself and from others. It brought a lot of success.

Yet in perhaps the most key area, I had a failure of integrity. I was more concerned with impressing the CEO than I was with the good of the enterprise. As I tried to move forward at the edge of chaos, my fears triumphed. I now see things in that episode that I could not see then. I see things I was denying. Being transformational is a function of our ability to constantly engage that which we least want to engage, our own hypocrisy. I think it will help me to approach such situations differently in the future.

Shawn's comments point to a future of continued effort to engage in reflective action. He concludes his letter with further reflections on all he has learned and what these lessons mean for him as he moves forward:

In trying to become a professional change agent, I have had the experience of negotiating and designing some interventions. In these initial interventions, I have felt very much like a novice. I found myself saying and doing things that a novice would do. I have been too worried about what authority figures think. I have tried to say what I think they want to hear. Other times I have tried to do what I thought was right but made statements that only led to discomfort. I was challenging but not supportive. . . . I need to stop describing and trying to sell the process model. Instead I need to live it.

When I consider the insights derived here, I see myself behaving differently in the future. I know that by being more

internally driven and other focused I will begin to make decisions that can benefit more people than myself. I will try to
look past my deceptions and the deceptions of others. I will
constantly need to ask myself, what can I change to improve a
relationship or situation? I will seek to free myself of the rules
and scripts so that I can learn to live in a state of co-creation. I
know these things are far easier to say than to do. However, recognizing that I have taken these steps in a few cases in the past
should help me move forward.

Last week I watched a movie. The movie is about a woman
living a superficial life, and denying the pain associated with such
a life. She finds out she is going to die and begins to clarify what
matters. She begins to make choices at work that most people
are afraid to make. She immediately becomes more authentic.
She takes risks and creates relationships. She ends up getting
great new offers.

My challenge is to do what she did, without death to motivate me. I need to live authentically because I choose to do so.
I hope to move closer to becoming a transformational change
agent, because, if I am growing, it may also help others to
grow.

Entering the Fundamental State of Leadership

As Thomas Merton discovered, we must integrate reflection
and contemplation with engagement in the realities of life. My
friend found that joining with others in a group process helped
him to do this. Shawn found that analyzing his present in the
light of his past helped him to do it. Here you might reflect on
what technique might best help you.

Preparation for Entering the Fundamental State of Leadership

Choose a quiet time when you can reflect on the meaning this
chapter has for you. Begin by assessing where you are today, as
honestly as you can.

Questions for Reflection

1. Check each item that describes you as you are today.

   ❏ I take the time to meditate.

   ❏ I learn from every experience.

   ❏ I carefully evaluate each victory and failure.

   ❏ I have identified the transformational moments in my past.

   ❏ I have articulated the lessons of my transformational moments.

   ❏ I have a personal, experience-based theory of change.

   ❏ I continually clarify my values.

   ❏ I know who I am.

   ❏ I recognize the greatness in me.

   ❏ I recognize the greatness in others.

   ❏ I am centered and productive.

   ❏ I am peaceful and focused.

   ❏ I am very active.

   ❏ I am full of energy.

   ❏ I get lots of things done.

   ❏ I see the potential in every situation.

   ❏ I am shaping the unfolding future.

   ❏ I choose my own emotional state.

   ❏ I am living with deep conviction.

   ❏ I love what I am doing.

2. Now assess yourself on the following scale by circling the number under the characteristics that currently describe you. Note that the "negative" areas of the scale represent the overemphasis of a positive characteristic so that it becomes a negative. The "integrative" part of the scale represents the integration of opposing positives. If you feel you model the integration of mindful reflection and energetic action, circle

one of the numbers under "Integrative." Otherwise circle two numbers, one on each side of the scale.

Negative	Positive	Integrative	Positive	Negative
Stagnant; inactive	Mindful; reflective	Reflective and active	Active; energetic	Mindless; unreflective
-3 -2 -1	1 2 3	4 5 4	3 2 1	-1 -2 -3

Self-Improvement

1. Based on the assessments you have completed, write a one-paragraph self-description on the theme of reflective action. In your own words, describe where you are today with respect to this aspect of the fundamental state of leadership.

2. Write a strategy for self-improvement in the area of reflective action. Try to be as concrete as possible in describing steps you are willing to take beginning today.

Helpful Hints for Practicing Reflective Action

Treat time as a precious resource.

Maximize the time you spend doing what only you can do.

Minimize the time you spend doing what others can do.

Have a daily, weekly, monthly, and yearly plan for accomplishing your goals.

Analyze your past daily, weekly, monthly, and yearly plans, and learn from them.

Design every action to a clear objective.

Leave no action open-ended. Connect every action to a next step.

When you begin to feel intuitive unease, seek to understand why. Do a root cause analysis of your misgivings.

Take time every day to ask who you are and who you are becoming.

Continually clarify your values.

Examine the link between your values and your current behavior.

Do not give in to taking the easiest way out.

Demand productive action from yourself.

Analyze the relationships in your life.

Establish a group for discussing key life issues.

Have a sacred time devoted to reflection.

Develop spiritual disciplines.

Have a regular physical workout.

Do something every day that gives you joy.

Schedule play into your life.

Understand your weaknesses, and work to improve them.

Understand your strengths, and work to build on them.

Challenge yourself to consider alternative routes.

Constantly monitor your level of vitality.

See that your values and behavior are always aligned.

Sharing Insights

If in responding to the questions above, you have an important insight or a meaningful story that you would like to share, visit www.deepchange.com and look for the links to submit stories for possible posting on the Deep Change Web site. You may thus help many people. If you would like to review such insights and stories, go to the same Web site.

○   ○   ○

Robert E. Quinn is a professor at the University of Michigan Business School and a consultant and speaker.

Chapter Thirty-Three

From Success to Significance

David Batstone

So many of my friends and colleagues who work in corporations tell me they feel trapped. Although the corporation may offer them the best platform and set of rewards to develop their career, they wonder whether they are selling out—selling out their life priorities, selling out their integrity, selling out the promises they make to themselves and to other people.

Lots of us are too cynical to believe it can be otherwise. Isn't that simply the price you pay to join the corporation?

Case studies show that it can be otherwise. In fact, the evidence indicates that a business will thrive once it aligns the ethos of the company with the values that drive its customers and its own workers. To get there, the people inside a company need to ask themselves, again and again, one question: What are we in business for?

I keep coming back to the message that Russell Ackoff gave to his students at the Wharton School: "Profit is a means, not an end." That wisdom hit home for me most powerfully when I was CEO of a start-up company in the late 1990s. At the time, new technologies were forcing corporations to rethink the way they ran their business operations. The blur of innovation made it difficult for senior managers to separate the real from the hype. My company saw an opportunity amid that confusion; we aimed to become the trusted adviser matching real business needs with real working technology. I'll spare you the rest of the pitch.

Back then, I spared no words or effort on behalf of my company. No one who has passed through fire and storm to launch a business will ever forget the experience. I worked with my executive team eighty or ninety hours a week to write a business plan (and thereafter rewrite it daily, or so it seemed) and to develop financial projections, sales strategies, technology platforms, and operational protocols. All the while, we were out courting potential customers and investors, making the rounds to blue-chip venture capitalists and corporate fund managers looking for the best partners to fuel our enterprise.

After nine months and few victories, it looked as if our ship finally was coming in. We were introduced to Michael Milken, who was busy stitching together a group of companies under one canopy named Knowledge Universe (KU). Our company fit well into KU's strategic plan, and our services were quite complementary to some of the assets Michael already had acquired. Over a series of meetings with him and his chief advisers, we negotiated the details of our business relationship. Michael wanted KU to be the sole investor in our company, and he pledged tens of millions of dollars of financing as long as we met a schedule of performance benchmarks. In exchange, KU would acquire a huge slice of our company.

Although Michael's legacy will be forever linked to junk bonds, corporate raiders, and a prison sentence, he dealt with our team in complete good faith and earned my respect. He is a tough-as-nails negotiator, mind you, and possesses the most brilliant financial mind I have ever encountered.

As we were closing in on a deal with KU, I decided to jump off the spinning carousel to clear my head. I took my family to Lake Tahoe for a few days of hiking and boating. Midway through the holiday, Michael gave me a call. We went over a few final details to our mutual satisfaction, and then he put to me his final test: "David, I trust you realize that once we make this deal, this company will be your life."

I swallowed hard, told him I completely understood, and the call ended with the exchange of a few pleasantries. In fact, his words thudded on top of me like a ton of bricks. The impact was immediate and served as a catalyst for a kind of spiritual awakening.

It was not as if I was doing anything that violated my moral compass. I can imagine any number of people who, being in the same position, could accept the investment, and it would be the best possible decision for them to make. But I was forced to confront my motivation, that is, my purpose for being in this business. Down deep I knew the reason: I was hawking widgets, pieces of technology. I had no passion, none at all, to help corporations solve their operational dilemmas and become more efficient. To be completely honest, I was in it for the money.

This will be your life. Once off the telephone and returning to my family in the cabin, I put together a mental inventory of the things that I deeply valued. I saw four small children who had not seen much of their dad for the previous year. I thought of my love for teaching at the university, my passion for writing, and the profound meaning I gained promoting human development in poverty-stricken countries. What was the price tag I could put on all that? *Priceless*, my inner voice replied.

I returned home several days later with the clarity I went looking for. I would resign. Most difficult of all was sharing the decision with my executive team, with whom I had labored and made considerable financial sacrifice. Meeting with them was the second test of my conviction, because I knew they would try to talk me out of it. I certainly don't blame them for trying. We were finally on the cusp of receiving our reward. My pulling out of the company meant disaster. Michael was investing in our management team, a remarkably talented group of professionals, as much as our business. Although I felt terrible for letting them down, I knew that I could not go forward. We floated the option of accepting KU's investment and then six to twelve months down the road finding a new CEO. But I rejected that idea out of hand. I was sure of Michael's intention, and playing that game would be nothing short of betrayal.

The next day, I contacted Michael and explained my decision to step down as CEO. He was surprised at first, but our conversation soon turned philosophical. He shared that he too believed in using one's talents to make a meaningful contribution to the world and made note of his own impressive philanthropic work. Creating financial wealth enabled him to do those things, he added, implying I was making a false choice between significance and financial success.

What I said in reply to Michael—and believe firmly to this day—is that living with soul transcends the matter of money. One cannot give enough money away to heal a broken spirit. Nor, for that matter, does turning one's back on money ensure the slightest degree of enlightenment. The person who lives his or her life in pursuit of success—be that measured by wealth, fame, or social status—will be sorely disenchanted with the pot at the end of the rainbow. Success alone cannot satisfy our deepest longings for significance.

Each individual holds within a passion for significance that awaits discovery. The actual makeup of that dream is not the same for each person and is a blend of innate skills and personality, social circumstance, and lived experience. Figuring out the origin of the dream is wasted speculation. Realizing our passion and pursuing it is our life's work. When we follow that path, we are never disappointed by the results, whatever they may turn out to be.

I was never a big fan of the television series *Ally McBeal,* to be honest, but I must admit that I was touched by the final episode. Ally told her colleagues that she was moving to New York from Boston after five years with her firm (exactly the duration of the series). "You're the soul of this place," sighed one of her colleagues lamenting her departure. "In some way, you've become the soul of all of us."

At this moment, the corporation sorely needs leaders—not people with titles, but true leaders at every level of the corporate ladder—to live with soul. In my case, I had to leave the helm of a company to pursue my path toward significance. That may be the risk other corporate workers may have to take as well. I am inclined to believe, however, that for most people, it is not a new path but a truth about themselves that awaits discovery. Once they start living out of that discovery, they inspire everyone who surrounds them.

No greater tribute could we receive from a coworker: *You, my friend, are the soul of this place.*

o   o   o

David Batstone is a professor at the University of San Francisco, journalist, and entrepreneur. He was a founding editor of *Business 2.0* magazine and is executive editor of *Sojourners* magazine.

Chapter Thirty-Four

If Not Me, Then Who?
If Not Now, When?

Bill George

We shall not cease from exploration,
And the end of all our exploring,
Will be to arrive where we started,
And know the place for the first time.
T. S. Eliot, "Four Quartets"

In May 1992 my father died in peace at the age of ninety-three and my older son graduated from high school, all in the same week. For me it was the passing of a generation. As a close friend told me, "Bill, you just moved up to the front pew."

It won't be long until you are asked to move to the front pew and take charge—or perhaps you already have been. My advice is, don't wait to be asked. Don't wait until you get the top job.

In thinking about whether to step up and lead, ask yourself these two simple questions:

If not me, then who? If not now, when?

The world needs your leadership today.

My generation was inspired and motivated by a young president, John F. Kennedy, who said in his inaugural address, "The torch has now been passed to a new generation of Americans." Many responded to his call to serve their country in small ways and large. Just as it was forty years ago, the torch is again being passed to a new generation. To your generation of leaders the trumpet has sounded. If you listen carefully, you will hear the clarion call to lead in a different way than many in my generation have:

To be motivated by your mission, not your money.

To tap into your values, not your ego.

To connect with others through your heart, not your persona.

To live your life with such discipline that you would be proud to read about your behavior on the front page of the *New York Times*.

As a leader, you have the task of engaging the hearts of those you serve and aligning their interests with the interests of the organization you lead. Engaging the hearts of others requires a sense of purpose and an understanding of where you're going. When you find that special alignment, you and your team will have the power to move mountains. Nothing will be able to stand in your way.

What Is Your Unique Calling?

Recently, a young leader complained that his generation seemed to lack any causes to be passionate about. I suggested that he open his eyes and observe the world around him. Seeing the human needs out there doesn't take a magnifying glass. You don't have to look far to see:

> The pain and suffering caused by poverty, abuse, and discrimination
>
> The need for healing, in body and in spirit
>
> The desire for healthy families
>
> The decline in our environment and our natural resources
>
> The hunger for security and a sense of well-being

Do any of these challenges strike a resonance deep within you? Can you find your passion and couple it with your ability to make a difference in the world?

> Reducing poverty . . .
>
> Eliminating abuse . . .
>
> Stopping discrimination . . .
>
> Helping others heal . . .
>
> Restoring our environment . . .
>
> Building organizations dedicated to service . . .
>
> Feeling safe and secure . . .
>
> Helping people develop themselves . . .
>
> Improving quality of life for others . . .
>
> Bringing joy to the world?

What will be your legacy? At the end of your days, what will you tell your grandchild you did to better humankind? No matter how large or small a difference you make, it will become the legacy that you leave the world.

Consider these challenges society faces as you think about where to devote your passions:

We live in a world of enormous wealth, yet three-quarters of the world's population have barely enough to survive.

With our greater affluence has come increased mental and physical abuse of the helpless and vulnerable.

Forty years after the civil rights movement began, discrimination is still rampant at all levels of our society.

We have the greatest medical technology in history, yet the rate of disease continues to grow.

We abuse our natural resources and ignore the growing contamination of our rivers, our open spaces, our cities, and our environment.

We no longer feel safe or secure in our cities after dark.

We stand idly by as our leaders focus more on serving themselves than their customers.

We merge companies to create ever-larger organizations and then treat the people who made them successful like robots.

We treat quality of life as if it were a distraction from the real work of people.

We ignore the deeper meanings of life and the source of all joy.

As an authentic leader, you can change these things. You only need to be your own person, lead in your own style with purpose and passion, be true to your values, build your relationships, practice self-discipline, and lead with your heart.

As much as we want to ensure a happy, secure future for our families and ourselves, we have learned the hard way that money alone is insufficient to provide either security or happiness. But making a difference in the lives of others can bring unlimited joy. Leading a life of significant service can bring unlimited ful-fillment. Sharing yourself with others authentically can bring unlimited love.

At the end of the day, what is more important than joy, ful-fillment, and love? When we experience them, we will arrive where we started and know the place for the first time.

○   ○   ○

Bill George was the CEO and chairman of the board of Medtronic. He is an executive-in-residence at Yale University School of Management and professor of leadership and gover-nance at IMD in Lausanne, Switzerland.

Notes and References

CHAPTER TWO

1. For more information about the original studies, see B. Z. Posner and W. H. Schmidt, "Values and the American Manager: An Update," *California Management Review*, 1984, *26*, 202–216; and B. Z. Posner and W. H. Schmidt, "Values and Expectations of Federal Service Executives," *Public Administration Review*, 1986, *46*, 447–454.

2. We analyze these findings and discuss their implications in detail in J. M. Kouzes and B. Z. Posner, *Credibility: How Leaders Gain and Lose It, Why People Demand It* (San Francisco: Jossey-Bass, 1993).

3. Our own research is supported by a recent study by the Corporate Leadership Council, an organization that provides best practices to human resource executives in leading global corporations. They found exactly what we did: honesty is at the top of the list of what people look for in their leaders. Sixty-one percent of their respondents said this was an important leadership attribute. See *Voice of the Leader* (Washington, D.C.: Corporate Leadership Council, 2001).

4. J. M. Kouzes, B. Z. Posner, and M. Krause, *Summary of the Executive Challenges Survey* (Santa Clara, Calif.: Executive Development Center, Leavey School of Business and Administration, Santa Clara University, 1986). Our own research is confirmed by a joint Korn/ Ferry–Columbia University study. Seventy-five percent of respondents in that assessment ranked "conveys a strong vision of the future" as a very important quality for CEOs today; it was so ranked by an almost unanimous 98 percent for the year 2000. The desirability of this ability didn't vary by more than three percentage points across the regions studied (Japan, western Europe, Latin America, and the United States). Korn/Ferry International and Columbia University Graduate School of Business, *Reinventing the CEO* (New York: Korn/Ferry International and Columbia University Graduate School of Business, 1989), p. 90.

5. For more on the role of positive emotions and leadership, see D. Goleman, R. Boyatzis, and A. McKee, *Primal Leadership: Realizing the Power of Emotional Intelligence* (Boston: Harvard Business School Press, 2002); and B. L. Fredrickson, "The Role of Positive Emotions in Positive Psychology: The Broaden-and-Build Theory of Emotions," *American Psychologist*, 2001, *56*, 218–226.

6. F. F. Reichheld with T. Teal, *The Loyalty Effect: The Hidden Force Behind Growth, Profits, and Lasting Value* (Boston: Harvard Business School Press, 1996), p. 1.

7. F. F. Reichheld, *Loyalty Rules: How Today's Leaders Build Lasting Relationships* (Boston: Harvard Business School Press, 2001), p. 6.

8. F. F. Reichheld and P. Schefter, "E-Loyalty: Your Secret Weapon on the Web," *Harvard Business Review*, July-Aug. 2000, p. 107. See also Bain & Company and Mainspring, "Bain/Mainspring Online Retailing Survey" (Boston: Bain & Company, Dec. 1999), a joint survey of 2,116 on-line shoppers in the categories of apparel, groceries, and consumer electronics; and Reichheld, *Loyalty Rules*, p. 8. For additional information on Web credibility, see B. J. Fogg and others, "What Makes Web Sites Credible? A Report on a Large Quantitative Study," Stanford University, 2001 [http://www.webcredibility.org].

9. For a study of the believability of politicians and journalists, and the difference in their roles, see Times Mirror Company, *The People and the Press* (Los Angeles: Times Mirror, 1986). For a more recent analysis of trust in major political institutions and prospective presidential candidates, see Times Mirror Center for the People and the Press, *The New Political Landscape* (Washington, D.C.: Times Mirror, 1994).

10. In a national study of the credibility of leaders and other public figures from a variety of settings, the Public Relations Society of America Foundation found that "the amount of credibility the public grants any particular information source . . . is an amalgam of specific issues, interwoven with demographics, attitudes, peer influence, experiences, ideology, and the level of the individual's participation in the working of society." See "National Credibility Index," Public Relations Society of America Foundation, 1999. [http://www.prsa.org/nci].

11. P. H. Mirvis, personal correspondence, Jan. 1992. See D. L. Kanter and P. H. Mirvis, *The Cynical Americans: Living and Working in an Age of Discontent and Disillusion* (San Francisco: Jossey-Bass, 1989).

12. See F. Newport, "Military Retains Top Position in Americans' Confidence Ratings," Gallup Organization, June 25, 2001. [http://www.gallup.com/poll/releases/pr010625.asp].

CHAPTER THREE

1. J. W. Gardner, "The Antileadership Vaccine," *Annual Report of the Carnegie Corporation* (New York: Carnegie Corporation, 1965), p. 12.

2. The phrases *transformative leadership* and *transactional leadership* come from J. M. Burns's seminal book *Leadership* (New York: Harper & Row, 1978), chaps. 3, 4.

CHAPTER FOUR

1. H. Mintzberg, *The Nature of Managerial Work* (New York: HarperCollins, 1973); H. Mintzberg, "The Manager's Job: Folklore and Fact," *Harvard Business Review*, July-Aug. 1975, pp. 49–61.

2. P. F. Drucker, *Management: Tasks, Responsibilities, Practices* (New York: HarperCollins, 1973).

3. M. E. Porter, *Competitive Strategy* (New York: Free Press, 1980). For a comparison of strategy as perspective and position, see H. Mintzberg, "Five P's for Strategy," *California Management Review*, Fall 1987, pp. 11–24.

4. A. Noël, "Strategic Cores and Magnificent Obsessions: Discovering Strategy Formation Through Daily Activities of CEOs," *Strategic Management Journal*, 1989, *10*, pp. 33–49.

5. J. P. Kotter, *The General Manager* (New York: Free Press, 1982).

6. Noël, *Strategic Cores*.

7. See R. Simons, "Strategic Orientation and Top Management Attention to Control Systems," *Strategic Management Journal*, 1991, *12*, 49–62; R. Simons, "The Role of Management Control Systems in Creating Competitive Advantage: New Perspectives," *Accounting, Organizations and Society*, 1990, *15*, 127–143.

8. See H. Simon's discussion of intelligence, design, and choice in *The New Science of Management Decision* (Upper Saddle River, N.J.: Prentice Hall, 1960).

9. H. Gulick and L. F. Urwick, *Paper on the Science of Administration* (New York: Columbia University, 1937); see also H. Fayol, *Administration industrielle et générale* (Paris: Dunod, 1916), English translation, *General and Industrial Administration* (London: Pelman, 1949).

10. See F. W. Roethlisberger and W. J. Dickson, *Management and the Worker* (Cambridge, Mass.: Harvard University Press, 1939).

11. See Karl Weick's criticism of my inclusion of leading as a role in my 1973 book in K. Weick, "Review Essay of *The Nature of Managerial Work*," *Administrative Science Quarterly*, 1974, *19*, 111–118.

12. M. Maeterlinck, *The Life of the Bee* (New York: Dodd, Mead, 1918).

13. L. R. Sayles, *Managerial Behavior: Administration in Complex Organizations* (New York: McGraw-Hill, 1964); Mintzberg, *The Nature of Managerial Work*; Kotter, *The General Manager.*

14. L. R. Sayles, *The Working Leader* (New York: Free Press, 1993).

15. T. Peters, *The Case for Experimentation: or, You Can't Plan Your Way to Unplanning a Formerly Planned Economy* (Palo Alto, Calif.: Tom Peters Group, 1990).

16. A. Grove, *High Output Management* (New York: Random House, 1983).

17. K. E. Weick, *The Social Psychology of Organizing* (Reading, Mass.: Addison-Wesley, 1979). See also H. Mintzberg, "Crafting Strategy," *Harvard Business Review*, July-Aug. 1987, pp. 66–75.

18. See H. Mintzberg, "Managing as Blended Care," *Journal of Nursing Administration*, 1994, *9*, 29–36.

CHAPTER SEVEN

1. This list is somewhat shorter than my earlier list of sixteen practices describing "what effective firms do with people." See J. Pfeffer, *Competitive Advantage Through People: Unleashing the Power of the Work Force* (Boston: Harvard Business School Press, 1994), chap. 2.

2. R. M. Locke, "The Transformation of Industrial Relations? A Cross National Review," in K. S. Wever and L. Turner (eds.), *The Comparative Political Economy of Industrial Relations* (Madison, Wis.: Industrial Relations Research Association, 1995), pp. 18–19.

3. H. Kelleher, "A Culture of Commitment," *Leader to Leader*, 1997, *1*, 23.

4. J. E. Delery and D. H. Doty, "Modes of Theorizing in Strategic Human Resource Management: Test of Universalistic, Contingency, and Configurational Performance Predictions," *Academy of Management Journal*, 1966, *39*, 820.

5. L. S. Chee, "Singapore Airlines: Strategic Human Resource Initiatives," in D. Torrington (ed.), *International Human Resource Management: Think Globally, Act Locally* (Upper Saddle River, N.J.: Prentice Hall, 1994), p. 152.

6. "Southwest Airlines," Case S-OB-28 (Palo Alto, Calif.: Graduate School of Business, Stanford University, 1994), p. 29.

7. B. O'Reilly, "The Rent-a-Car Jocks Who Made Enterprise #1," *Fortune*, Oct. 28, 1996, p. 128.

8. L. Graham, *On the Line at Subaru-Isuzu* (Ithaca, N.Y.: ILR Press, 1995), p. 18.

9. See, for instance, C. A. O'Reilly, J. A. Chatman, and D. F. Caldwell, "People and Organizational Culture: A Profile Comparison Approach to Assessing Person-Organization Fit," *Academy of Management Journal*, 1991, *34*, 487–516; and J. A. Chatman, "Managing People and Organizations: Selection and Socialization in Public Accounting Firms," *Administrative Science Quarterly*, 1991, *36*, 459–484

10. Graham, *On the Line at Subaru-Isuzu*, p. 31.

11. Graham, *On the Line at Subaru-Isuzu*, p. 31.

12. Graham, *On the Line at Subaru-Isuzu*, p. 33.

13. R. Batt, "Outcomes of Self-Directed Work Groups in Telecommunications Services," in P. B. Voos (ed.), *Proceedings of the Forty-Eighth Annual Meeting of the Industrial Relations Research Association* (Madison, Wis.: Industrial Relations Research Association, 1996), p. 340.

14. R. D. Banker, J. M. Field, R. G. Schroeder, and K. K. Sinha, "Impact of Work Teams on Manufacturing Performance: A Longitudinal Field Study," *Academy of Management Journal*, 1996, *39*, 867–890.

15. "Work Week," *Wall Street Journal*, May 28, 1996, p. A1.

16. Batt, "Outcomes of Self-Directed Work Groups," p. 344.

17. Batt, "Outcomes of Self-Directed Work Groups," p. 344.

18. Batt, "Outcomes of Self-Directed Work Groups," p. 346.

19. Graham, *On the Line at Subaru-Isuzu*, p. 97.

20. M. Parker and J. Slaughter, "Management by Stress," *Technology Review*, 1988, *91*, 43.

21. Whole Foods Market, *1995 Annual Report* (Austin Tex.: Whole Foods, 1995), pp. 3, 17.

22. C. Fishman, "Whole Foods Teams," *Fast Company*, Apr.-May 1996, p. 104.

23. Fishman, "Whole Foods Teams," p. 107.

24. H. Shaiken, S. Lopez, and I. Mankita, "Two Routes to Team Production: Saturn and Chrysler Compared," *Industrial Relations*, 1997, *36*, 31.

25. A. Markels, "Team Approach: A Power Producer Is Intent on Giving Power to Its People," *Wall Street Journal*, July 3, 1995, p. A1.

26. K. D. Grimsley, "The Power of a Team," *Washington Post*, Feb. 12, 1996, p. F12.

27. M. van Beusekom, *Participation Pays! Cases of Successful Companies with Employee Participation* (The Hague: Netherlands Participation Institute, 1996), p. 7.

28. R. Thompson, "An Employee's View of Empowerment," *HR Focus*, July 1993, p. 14.

29. Thompson, "An Employee's View of Empowerment," p. 14.

30. T. R. Bailey and A. D. Bernhardt, "In Search of the High Road in a Low-Wage Industry," *Politics and Society*, 1997, *25*, 179–201.

31. G. Collins, "In Grocery War, the South Rises," *New York Times*, Apr. 25, 1995, p. C5.

32. V. C. Harnish, "Company of Owners," *Executive Excellence*, May 1995, p. 7.

33. M. Rowland, "Rare Bird: Stock Options for Many," *New York Times*, Aug. 1, 1993, p. F14.

34. D. Jacobson, "Employee Ownership and the High-Performance Work-place," working paper no. 13, National Center for the Work-place, Berkeley, Calif., 1996.

35. B. Gurley, "Revenge of the Nerds: The Stock Option Square Dance," Mar. 14, 1997. [www.upside.com/texis/archive/search/article.html?UID=970314003].

36. Fishman, "Whole Foods Teams," p. 105.

37. Fishman, "Whole Foods Teams," p. 104.

38. J. P. MacDuffie and T. A. Kochan, "Do U.S. Firms Invest Less in Human Resources? Training in the World Auto Industry," *Industrial Relations*, 1994, *34*, 153.

39. MacDuffie and Kochan, "Do U.S. Firms Invest Less in Human Resources?" p. 163.

40. Shaiken, Lopez, and Mankita, "Two Routes to Team Production," p. 25.

41. C. Truss and others, "Soft and Hard Models of Human Resource Management: A Reappraisal," *Journal of Management Studies* 1997, *34*, 60.

42. Truss and others, "Soft and Hard Models of Human Resource Management," pp. 60–61.

43. Bailey and Bernhardt, "In Search of the High Road in a Low-Wage Industry," p. 5.

44. Men's Wearhouse, *1994 Annual Report* (Fremont, Calif.: Men's Wearhouse, 1994), p. 3.

45. M. Hartnett, "Men's Wearhouse Tailors Employee Support Programs," *Stores*, Aug. 1996, p. 47.

46. Hartnett, "Men's Wearhouse Tailors Employee Support Programs," p. 48.

47. T. A. Stewart, "How a Little Company Won Big by Betting on Brainpower," *Fortune*, Sept. 4, 1998, p. 121.

48. Stewart, "How a Little Company Won Big by Betting on Brain-power," p. 122.

49. Graham, *On the Line at Subaru-Isuzu*, pp. 107–108.

50. S. Schlosberg, "Big Titles for Little Positions," *San Francisco Chronicle*, Apr. 29, 1991, p. C3.

51. "Doing the Right Thing," *Economist*, May 20, 1995, p. 64.

52. Whole Foods Market, *Proxy Statement*, Jan. 29, 1996, p. 15.

53. S. McCartney, "Salary for Chief of Southwest Air Rises After Four Years," *Wall Street Journal*, Apr. 29, 1996, p. C16.

54. Fishman, "Whole Foods Teams," p. 106.

55. Fishman, "Whole Foods Teams," p. 104.

56. Fishman, "Whole Foods Teams," p. 105.

57. "Jack Stack (A)," Case 9–993–009 (Stanford, Calif.: Business Enterprise Trust, 1993), pp. 2–4.

58. "Jack Stack (A)."

59. "Jack Stack (A)," p. 5.

60. T.R.V. Davis, "Open-Book Management: Its Promise and Pit-falls," *Organizational Dynamics*, 1997, *25*, 7–20.

61. "Jack Stack (A)," p. 3.

62. B. Becker and B. Gerhart, "The Impact of Human Resource Management on Organizational performance: Progress and Prospects," *Academy of Management Journal*, 1996, *39*, 786.

CHAPTER NINE

1. C. K. Stevens, "Antecedents of Interview Interactions, Interviewers' Ratings, and Applicants' Reactions," *Personnel Psychology*, 1998, *51*, 55–85.

2. J. P. Wanous, *Organizational Entry*, 2nd ed. (Reading, Mass.: Addison-Wesley, 1992).

3. M. Richtel, "Online Revolution's Latest Twist: Computers Screening Job Seekers," *New York Times*, Feb. 6, 2000, pp. 1, 19.

4. A. E. Barber, *Recruiting Employees: Individual and Organizational Perspectives* (Thousand Oaks, Calif.: Sage, 1998).

5. G. N. Powell and L. R. Goulet, "Recruiters and Applicant Reactions to Campus Interviews and Employment Decisions," *Academy of Management Journal*, 1996, *39*, 1619–1640.

6. D. B. Turban and T. W. Dougherty, "Influence of Campus Recruiting on Applicant Attraction to Firms," *Academy of Management Journal*, 1992, *35*, 739–765.

7. D. B. Turban, J. E. Campion, and A. R. Eyring, "Factors Related to Job Acceptance Decisions of College Recruits," *Journal of Vocational Behavior*, 1995, *47*, 193–213.

8. A. E. Barber, J. R. Hollenbeck, S. L. Tower, and J. M. Phillips, "The Effect of Interview Focus on Recruitment Effectiveness," *Journal of Applied Psychology*, 1994, *78*, 845–856.

9. D. M. Cable and T. A. Judge, "Interviewer's Perceptions of Person-Organization Fit and Organizational Selection Decisions," *Journal of Applied Psychology*, 1997, *82*, 546–561. See also B. Schneider, D. B. Smith, S. Taylor, and J. Fleenor, "Personality and Organizations: A Test of the Homogeneity of Personality Hypothesis," *Journal of Applied Psychology*, 1998, *83*, 462–470, and B. Schneider, H. W. Goldstein, and D. B. Smith, "The ASA Framework: An Update," *Personnel Psychology*, 1995, *48*, 747–773.

10. J. P. Wanous and A. Colella, "Organizational Entry Research: Current Status and Future Directions," in K. Rowland and G. Ferris (eds.), *Research in Personnel and Human Resource Management*, 7 (Greenwich, Conn.: JAI Press, 1989).

11. S. L. Rynes, R. D. Bretz Jr., and B. Gerhart, "The Importance of Recruitment in Job Choice: A Different Way of Looking," *Personnel Psychology*, 1991, *44*, 487–521.

CHAPTER TEN

1. "Retired Wide Receiver Catches $10M Jury Award," *National Law Journal*, Feb. 7, 2000, p. A15. A court later reduced the award to $6.1 million. M. Fisk, "Creative Plaintiffs' Counsel Target Employers, Ballparks and Laser-Eye Surgeons, A Survey on Emerging Causes of Action Shows," *New Jersey Law Journal*, Dec. 18, 2000.

2. Wanamaker v. Columbian Rope Co., 907 F. Supp. 522, 538 (N.D.N.Y. 1995).

3. C. Hymowitz, "Using Layoffs to Battle Downturns Often Costs More Than It Saves," *Wall Street Journal*, July 24, 2001, p. B1.

4. L. Pechman, "Appearance-Based Discrimination," *New York Law Journal*, Sept. 25, 1996.

5. S. Baderian and J. Kozak, "Claims of Retaliation Continue to Increase," *National Law Journal*, Nov. 20, 2000, p. B13.

6. Bammert v. Don's SuperValu, Inc., 632 N.W.2d 124 (Wis. 2001).

7. Guz v. Bechtel, 8 P.3d 1089 (Cal. 2001).

8. New York v. Wal-Mart, 207 A.D.2d 150 (N.Y. Sup. Ct. 1995).

9. J. Bravin, "U.S. Courts Are Tough on Job-Bias Suits," *Wall Street Journal*, July 16, 2001, p. A2.

10. A. Longstreth, "Sears Starts an ADR Program for Its Retailers," *National Law Journal*, Jan. 7, 2002, p. A21.

CHAPTER TWELVE

Hofstede, G. *Cultures and Organizations: Software of the Mind.* New York: McGraw-Hill, 1991.

Kanter, R. M. *The Change Masters: Innovation for Productivity in the American Corporation.* New York: Simon & Schuster, 1983.

McGregor, D. M. *The Human Side of Enterprise.* New York: McGraw-Hill, 1960.

Quinn, J. B. *Strategies for Change: Logical Incrementalism.* Burr Ridge, Ill.: Darwin, 1980.

Weick, K. *The Social Psychology of Organization.* (2nd ed.) Reading, Mass.: Addison-Wesley, 1979.

CHAPTER THIRTEEN

Beckhard, R. *Organizational Development: Strategies and Models.* Reading, Mass.: Addison Wesley Longman, 1969.

Kolb, D. A. *Experiential Learning: Experience as the Source of Learning and Development.* Upper Saddle River, N.J.: Prentice Hall, 1984.

CHAPTER FOURTEEN

Axelrod, R. "More Effective Choice in the Prisoner's Dilemma." *Journal of Conflict Resolution,* 1980, *24,* 379–403.

Bell, T. E., and Esch, K. "The Fatal Flaw in Flight 51-L." *IEEE Spectrum,* Feb. 1987, pp. 36–51.

Bellow, G., and Moulton, B. *The Lawyering Process: Cases and Materials.* Mineola, N.Y.: Foundation Press, 1978.

Bennis, W. G. *Why Leaders Can't Lead: The Unconscious Conspiracy Continues.* San Francisco: Jossey-Bass, 1989.

Block, P. *The Empowered Manager: Positive Political Skills at Work.* San Francisco: Jossey-Bass, 1987.

Bok, S. *Lying: Moral Choice in Public and Private Life.* New York: Vintage Books, 1978.

Burns, J. M. *Leadership.* New York: HarperCollins, 1978.

Fisher, R., and Ury, W. *Getting to Yes.* Boston: Houghton Mifflin, 1981.

Kanter, R. M. *The Change Masters: Innovations for Productivity in the American Corporation.* New York: Simon & Schuster, 1983.

Kohlberg, L. "The Claim to Moral Adequacy of a Highest Stage of Moral Judgment." *Journal of Philosophy,* 1973, *70,* 630–646.

Kotter, J. P. *The General Managers.* New York: Free Press, 1982.

Kotter, J. P. *Power and Influence: Beyond Formal Authority.* New York: Free Press, 1985.

Kotter, J. P. The *Leadership Factor.* New York: Free Press, 1988.

Labaton, S. "Downturn and Shift in the Population Feed Boom in White Collar Crime." *New York Times,* June 2, 2002. [www.nytimes.com/2002/06/02/business/02CRIM.html?].

Lax, D. A., and Sebenius, J. K. *The Manager as Negotiator.* New York: Free Press, 1986.

Manes, S., and Andrews, P. *Gates.* New York: Touchstone, 1994.

Maslow, A. H. *Motivation and Personality.* New York: HarperCollins, 1954.

Mendelson, H., and Korin, A. "The Computer Industry: A Brief History." Palo Alto, Calif.: Stanford Business School, n.d. [http://wesley.stanford.edu/computer_history/].

Oppel, R. A. "How Enron Got California to Buy Power It Didn't Need." *New York Times,* May 8, 2002, p. A1.

Pfeffer, J. *Managing with Power: Politics and Influence in Organizations.* Boston: Harvard Business School Press, 1992.

Pichault, F. *Resources humaines et changement stratégique: Vers un management politique* [Human resources and strategic change: Toward a political approach to management]. Brussels, Belgium: DeBoeck, 1993.

Porter, E. "Notes for the Looking for Leadership Conference." Paper presented at the Looking for Leadership Conference, Graduate School of Education, Harvard University, Cambridge, Mass., Dec. 1989.

Schelling, T. *The Strategy of Conflict.* Cambridge, Mass.: Harvard University Press, 1960.

Smith, H. *The Power Game.* New York: Random House, 1988.

Zachary, G. P. "Climbing the Peak: Agony and Ecstasy of 200 Code Writers Beget Windows NT." *Wall Street Journal,* May 26, 1993, pp. A1, A6.

Zachary, G. P. *Showstopper! The Breakneck Race to Create Windows NT and the Next Generation at Microsoft.* New York: Free Press, 1994.

CHAPTER SIXTEEN

1. F. D. Raines, "Racial Inequality in America," *Vital Speeches of the Day,* 2002, *68,* 400.

2. R. S. Butler, "Planning for Death in a Century of Cure," speech presented at the Haas School of Business, Berkeley, Calif., Mar. 22, 2002.

3. E. Kennedy, "Eliminating the Threat: The Right Course of Action for Disarming Iraq, Combating Terrorism, Protecting the Homeland, and Stabilizing the Middle East," Sept. 27, 2002 [http://Kennedy.senate.gov/kennedy/statements/02/09/2002927718.html].

4. R. K. Cooper and A. Sawaf, *Executive EQ* (New York: Grosset, 1996), p. 100.

5. B. Jordan, videotaped speech, National Broadcasting Company, 1974.

6. M. Cuomo, *More Than Words: The Speeches of Mario Cuomo* (New York: St. Martin's Press, 1993), p. 35.

CHAPTER SEVENTEEN

1. C. Darwin, *The Expression of the Emotions in Man and Animals* (definitive edition with introduction, afterword, and commentaries by Paul Ekman) (New York: Oxford University Press, 1998). (Originally published 1872.)

2. For a more thorough discussion of identifying emotions, see P. Ekman, *Emotions Revealed* (New York: Times Books, 2003).

3. See, for example, S. Nolen-Hoeksema, *Women Who Think Too Much* (New York: Holt, 2003).

4. D. Rosenstein and H. Oster, "Differential Facial Response to Four Basic Tastes in Newborns," *Child Development*, 1988, *59*, 1555–1568.

5. Ekman, *Emotions Revealed.*

6. See, for example, M. Gobe, *Emotional Branding* (Oxford, England: Windsor, 2001); J. S. Martins, *The Emotional Nature of a Brand* (São Paulo, Brazil: Marts Plan Imagen, 2000).

7. P. Ekman, *Telling Lies: Clues to Deceit in the Marketplace, Marriage, and Politics* (New York: Norton, 1985).

8. M. Wilson, *The Music Man* (Milwaukee, Wis.: Hal Leonard Corporation, 1957).

9. N. M. Henley, *Body Politics: Power, Sex, and Nonverbal Communication* (Upper Saddle River, N.J.: Prentice Hall, 1977).

10. H. A. Elfenbein, A. A. Marsh, and N. Ambady, "Emotional Intelligence and the Recognition of Emotion from Facial Expression," in L. F. Barrett and P. Salovey (eds.), *The Wisdom in Feeling: Psychological Processes in Emotional Intelligence* (New York: Guilford Press, 2002).

CHAPTER EIGHTEEN

1. To learn more about the Super Person of the Month award, see T. Melohn, *The New Partnership: Profit by Bringing Out the Best in Your People, Customers, and Yourself* (Essex Junction, Vt.: Oliver Wright, 1994), pp. 127–138.

2. *In Search of Excellence: The Video* (Chicago: Video Arts, and Nathan Tyler, 1987). Videotape.

3. Melohn, *The New Partnership*, p. 225.

4. J. Martin and M. Powers, "Organizational Stories: More Vivid and Persuasive Than Quantitative Data," in B. M. Staw (ed.), *Psychological Foundations of Organizational Behavior*, 2nd ed. (Glenview, Ill.: Scott, Foresman, 1983), pp. 161–168.

5. Melohn, *The New Partnership*, p. 127.

CHAPTER NINETEEN

1. C. C. Pinder, *Work Motivation in Organizational Behavior* (Upper Saddle River, N.J.: Prentice Hall, 1998); G. D. Jenkins Jr., A. Mitra, N. Gupta, and J. D. Shaw, "Are Financial Incentives Related to Performance? A Meta-Analytic Review of Empirical Research," *Journal of Applied Research*, 1998, *83*, 777–787.

2. W. F. Whyte (ed.), *Money and Motivation: An Analysis of Incentives in Industry* (New York: HarperCollins, 1955); E. E. Lawler III, *Pay and Organizational Effectiveness: A Psychological View* (New York: McGraw-Hill, 1971); R. B. McKenzie and D. R. Lee, *Managing Through Incentives* (New York: Oxford University Press, 1998).

3. R. L. Heneman, *Merit Pay* (Reading, Mass.: Addison-Wesley, 1992).

4. Heneman, *Merit Pay*.

5. W. E. Deming, *Out of the Crisis* (Cambridge, Mass.: MIT Press, 1986).

6. E. E. Lawler III, with S. A. Mohrman and G. E. Ledford Jr., *Strategies for High Performance Organizations: The CEO Report* (San Francisco: Jossey-Bass, 1998).

7. A. Kohn, *Punished by Rewards* (Boston: Houghton Mifflin, 1993); F. Herzberg, *Work and the Nature of Man* (Orlando, Fla.: Harcourt Brace, 1966).

8. Kohn, *Punished by Rewards;* Herzberg, *Work and the Nature of Man*; E. L. Deci, *Intrinsic Motivation* (New York: Plenum Press, 1975).

9. C. G. Worley, D. E. Bowen, and E. E. Lawler III, "On the Relationship Between Objective Increase in Pay and Employees' Subjective Reactions," *Journal of Organizational Behavior*, 1992, *13*, 559–571; A. Mitra, N. Gupta, and G. D. Jenkins Jr., "A Drop in the Bucket: When Is a Pay Raise a Pay Raise?" *Journal of Organizational Behavior*, 1997, *18*, 117–137.

10. V. H. Vroom, *Work and Motivation* (New York: Wiley, 1964); L. W. Porter and E. E. Lawler III, *Managerial Attitudes and Performance* (Homewood, Ill.: Irwin, 1968).

11. E. E. Lawler III, *Motivation in Work Organizations* (Pacific Grove, Calif.: Brooks/Cole, 1973).

12. E. Locke and G. P. Latham, *A Theory of Goal Setting and Task Performance* (Upper Saddle River, N.J.: Prentice Hall, 1990).

13. Lawler, *Motivation in Work Organizations;* Pinder, *Work Motivation in Organizational Behavior.*

14. J. S. Adams, "Toward an Understanding of Inequity," *Journal of Abnormal Psychology,* 1963, *67,* 422–436; J. S. Adams, "Injustice in Social Exchange," in L. Berkowitz (ed.), *Advances in Experimental Social Psychology* (Orlando, Fla.: Academic Press, 1965).

15. R. Folger and M. Konovsky, "Effects of Procedural and Disruptive Justice on Reactions to Pay Raise Decisions," *Academy of Management Journal,* 1989, *32,* 115–130; J. Greenberg, "Looking Fair vs. Being Fair: Managing Impressions of Organizational Justice," in B. M. Staw and L. L. Cumming (eds.), *Research in Organizational Behavior, 12* (Greenwich, Conn.: JAI Press, 1990).

16. Pinder, *Work Motivation in Organizational Behavior.*

17. B. Schneider and D. E. Bowen, *Winning the Service Game* (Boston: Harvard Business School Press, 1995).

18. A. J. Rucci, S. P. Kirn, and R. T. Quinn, "The Employee-Customer-Profit Chain at Sears," *Harvard Business Review,* 1998, *76*(1), 83–97.

CHAPTER TWENTY-ONE

Allen, J., and Johnston, K. "Mentoring." *Context,* 1997, *14*(7), 15.

Burke, R. J., and McKeen, C. A. "Benefits of Mentoring Relationships Among Managerial and Professional Women: A Cautionary Tale." *Journal of Vocational Behavior,* 1997, *51*(1), 43–57.

Chao, G. T. "Mentoring Phases and Outcomes." *Journal of Vocational Behavior,* 1997, *51*(1), 15–28.

Douglas, C. A. *Key Events and Lessons for Managers in a Diverse Workforce: A Report on Research and Findings* Greensboro, N.C.: Center for Creative Leadership, 2003.

Dreher, G. F., and Ash, R. A. "A Comparative Study of Mentoring Among Men and Women in Managerial, Professional, and Technical Positions." *Journal of Applied Psychology,* 1990, *75,* 539–546.

Eby, L. T. "Alternative Forms of Mentoring in Changing Organizational Environments: A Conceptual Extension of the Mentoring Literature." *Journal of Vocational Behavior,* 1997, *51*(1), 125–144.

Fagenson, E. A. "The Mentor Advantage: Perceived Career/Job Experiences of Protégés Versus Non-Protégés." *Journal of Organizational Behavior,* 1989, *10,* 309–320.

Fagenson-Eland, E. A., Marks, M. A., and Amendola, K. L. "Perceptions of Mentoring Relationships." *Journal of Vocational Behavior,* 1997, *51*(1), 29–42.

Hall, D. T. *Careers in Organizations*. Pacific Palisades, Calif.: Goodyear, 1976.

Hazucha, J. F., Hezlett, S. A., and Schneider, R. J. "The Impact of 360-Degree Feedback on Management Skills Development." *Human Resource Management*, 1993, *32*, 325–351.

Hegestad, C. D. "Formal Mentoring as a Strategy for Human Resource Development: A Review of Research." *Human Resource Development Quarterly*, 1999, *10*, 383–390.

Higgins, M. C. "The More the Merrier? Multiple Developmental Relationships and Work Satisfaction." *Journal of Management Development*, 2000, *19*, 277–296.

Higgins, M. C., and Kram, K. E. "Reconceptualizing Mentoring at Work: A Developmental Network Perspective." *Academy of Management Review*, 2001, *26*, 264–288.

Kram, K. E. *Mentoring at Work*. Glenview, Ill.: Scott, Foresman, 1985.

Kram, K. E., and Hall, D. T. "Mentoring as an Antidote to Stress During Corporate Trauma." *Human Resource Management*, 1989, *28*(4), 493–510.

Levinson, D. J. *The Seasons of a Man's Life*. New York: Knopf, 1978.

McCall, M. W., Jr., and Hollenbeck, G. P. *Developing Global Executives: The Lessons of International Experience*. Boston: Harvard Business School Press, 2002.

McCall, M. W., Jr., and Lombardo, M. M. *Off the Track: Why and How Successful Executives Get Derailed*. Greensboro, N.C.: Center for Creative Leadership, 1983.

McCall, M. W., Jr., Lombardo, M. M., and Morrison, A. M. *The Lessons of Experience: How Successful Executives Develop on the Job*. San Francisco: New Lexington Press, 1988.

McCauley, C. D., and Young, D. P. "Creating Developmental Relationships: Roles and Strategies." *Human Resource Management Review*, 1993, *3*, 219–230.

McShulskis, E. "Coaching Helps But Is Not Often Used." *HR Magazine*, 1996, *41*(3), 15–16.

Morrison, A. M., White, R. P., and Van Velsor, E. *Breaking the Glass Ceiling: Can Women Reach the Top of America's Largest Corporations?* (updated ed.) New York: Perseus Books, 1992.

Noe, R. A. "An Investigation of the Determinants of Successful Assigned Mentoring Relationships." *Personnel Psychology*, 1988, *41*(3), 457–479.

Noe, R. A. "Is Career Management Related to Employee Development and Performance?" *Journal of Organizational Behavior*, 1996, *17*(2), 119–133.

Orpen, C. "The Effects of Mentoring on Employees' Career Success." *Journal of Social Psychology*, 1995, *135*, 667–680.

Roche, G. "Much Ado About Mentors." *Harvard Business Review*, 1979, *57*(1), 14–28.

Russell, J.E.A., and Adams, D. M. "The Changing Nature of Mentoring in Organizations." *Journal of Vocational Behavior*, 1997, *51*(1), 1–14.

Scandura, T. A. "Mentorship and Career Mobility: An Empirical Investigation." *Journal of Organizational Behavior*, 1992, *13*, 169–174.

Tharenou, P. "Organisational, Job, and Personal Predictors of Employee Participation in Training and Development." *Applied Psychology*, 1997, *46*(2), 111–134.

Turban, D. B., and Dougherty, T. W. "Role of Protégé Personality in Receipt of Mentoring and Career Success." *Academy of Management Journal*, 1994, *37*(3), 688–702.

Van Velsor, E., and Hughes-James, M. W. *Gender Differences in the Development of Managers: How Women Managers Learn from Experience*. Greensboro, N.C.: Center for Creative Leadership, 1990.

Whitely, W., Dougherty, T. W., and Dreher, G. F. "Relationship of Career Mentoring and Socioeconomic Origin to Managers' and Professionals' Early Career Progress." *Academy of Management Journal*, 1991, *34*(2), 331–351.

CHAPTER TWENTY-TWO

1. J. L. Simonetti, "Key Pieces of the Career Survival and Success Puzzle," *Career Development International*, 1999, *4*, 312–317.

2. C. O. Longenecker and T. C. Stansfield, "Why Plant Managers Fail: Causes and Consequences," *Industrial Management*, Jan.-Feb. 2000, 24–32.

3. R. A. Portnoy, *Leadership: Four Competencies for Success* (Upper Saddle River, N.J.: Prentice Hall, 1999).

CHAPTER TWENTY-THREE

1. R. Block, *The Politics of Projects* (Englewood Cliffs, N.J.: Yourdon Press, 1983).

CHAPTER TWENTY-FIVE

1. C. Powell, speech for Outreach America Program at Sears Headquarters, Chicago, Feb. 9, 1999.

2. R. Fisher and W. Ury, *Getting to Yes* (New York: Penguin Books, 1991).

3. "The Greatest Irish Americans," *Irish America*, Nov. 1999, p. 57.

4. C. Olofson, "Dream Society," *Fast Company*, Oct. 1999, p. 84.

CHAPTER TWENTY-SIX

1. D. Fensin, interview with Patrick McKenna, n.d.

CHAPTER TWENTY-NINE

1. W. W. Burke, personal communication, 1998.

2. M. Apgar IV, "The Alternative Workplace: Changing Where and How People Work," *Harvard Business Review*, May-June 1998, pp. 121–139.

3. A. Clark, C. Downing, and D. Coleman, "GroupWare at the Big Six Firms: How Successful Was It?" in D. Coleman (ed.), *GroupWare: Collaborative Strategies for LANs and Intranets* (Upper Saddle River, N.J.: Prentice Hall, 1997).

4. R. T. Hightower, L. Sayeed, M. Warkentin, and R. McHaney, "Information Exchange in Virtual Work Teams," in M. Igbaria and M. Tan (eds.), *The Virtual Workplace* (Hershey, Pa.: Idea Group Publishing, 1998).

5. J. F. Nunamaker and others, "Lessons from a Dozen Years of Group Support System Research: A Discussion of Lab and Field Findings," *Journal of Management Information Systems*, Winter 1996–1997, pp. 163–207.

6. M. O'Hara-Devereaux and R. Johansen, *Globalwork: Bridging Distance, Culture, and Time* (San Francisco: Jossey-Bass, 1994).

7. O'Hara-Devereaux and Johansen, *Globalwork*.

8. C. Handy, "Trust and the Virtual Organization," *Harvard Business Review*, 1994, *73*(3).

CHAPTER THIRTY

1. This experiment was described to me in a telephone interview I conducted with F. Klein on Oct. 12, 2000.

2. C. Fishman, "Creative Tension," *Fast Company*, Nov. 2000, pp. 358–388.

3. From a speech that W. E. Coyne gave at Motorola University, Schaumburg, Ill., July 11, 2000.

4. G. MacKenzie, *Orbiting the Giant Hairball* (New York: Viking, 1998), p. 63.

5. MacKenzie, *Orbiting the Giant Hairball*, p. 64.

6. J. Pfeffer, R. B. Cialdini, B. Hanna, and K. Knopoff, "Faith in Supervision and Self Enhancement Bias: Two Psychological Reasons Why Managers Don't Empower Workers, *Basic and Applied Psychology*, 1988, *20*, 313–321.

7. D. Shields, "The Good Father," *New York Times Magazine*, Apr. 23, 2000, pp. 58–61.

8. Shields, "The Good Father," p. 60.

9. Shields, "The Good Father," p. 60.

10. A. Hargadon and Y. Douglas, "When Innovations Meet Innovations Meet Institutions: Edison and the Design of the Electric Light," working paper, Warrington College of Business Administration, University of Florida, Gainesville, Sept. 2000.

11. Hargadon and Douglas, "When Innovations Meet Innovations Meet Institutions," p. 19.

12. B. Metcalfe, "Invention Is a Flower, Innovation Is a Weed," *MIT Technology Review*, Nov.-Dec. 1999, p. 56.

13. See, for example, B. A. Burgelman, "A Process Model of Internal Corporate Venturing in the Diversified Firm," *Administrative Science Quarterly*, 1983, *28,* 223–244.

14. P. D. Nguyen, "A Faster Plan," *Red Herring*, May 2000, pp. 138–146.

15. R. B. Cialdini, *Influence: The New Psychology of Modern Persuasion* (New York: Quill, 1984).

16. A. Rock, "Strategy vs. Tactics from a Venture Capitalist," *Harvard Business Review*, Nov.-Dec. 1987.

17. K. D. Elsbach and R. M. Kramer, "Assessing Images of Others' Creativity: Impression Formation in the Hollywood Pitch," working paper, Graduate School of Business, Stanford University, Palo Alto, Calif., 1999.

18. Nguyen, "A Faster Plan," p. 144.

19. D. Sobel, *Longitude: The True Story of a Lone Genius Who Solved the Greatest Scientific Problem of His Time* (New York: Penguin, 1996), p. 8.

20. www.rog.nmm.ac.uk/museum/harrison/longprob.html, Royal Observatory, Greenwich, England, downloaded Dec. 21, 2000.

21. J. Surowiecki, "The Billion-Dollar Blade," *New Yorker,* June 15, 1998, pp. 43–49.

22. C. Dahle, "The Agenda-Social Justice," *Fast Company*, Apr. 1999, pp. 166–182.

23. L. Platt, "Magic Johnson Builds an Empire," *New York Times Magazine*, Dec. 10, 2000, pp. 118–121.

24. C. Chapman, "Designed to Work," *Fast Company*, Apr. 2000, pp. 259–268.

25. Chapman, "Designed to Work," p. 256.

26. Chapman, "Designed to Work," p. 268.

27. L. MacFarquhar, "Looking for Trouble," *New Yorker*, Dec. 6, 1999.

28. MacFarquhar, "Looking for Trouble," p. 80.

29. MacFarquhar, "Looking for Trouble," p. 78.

30. *Dow Jones Online News*, June 26, 2000.

31. Some identifying features of this firm and process are changed to protect their anonymity, but the crucial facts—that the process contained multiple stages and was too complex and that no product had ever made it through this gauntlet—are true.

32. R. Slater, *Jack Welch and the GE Way* (New York: McGraw-Hill, 1999), p. 135.

33. From an interview by J. Pfeffer and R. Sutton with P. McInnes and V. Nayak in Santa Clara, Calif., Dec. 9, 1999, and an e-mail message from G. Graham, Dec. 29, 2000.

34. S. Jobs, speech given at DeAnza College Flint Center, Cupertino, Calif., May 6, 1998.

35. From an interview R. Sutton conducted with J. Hawkins, Aug. 2, 2000.

36. J. Ross and B. M. Staw, "Organizational Escalation and Exit: Lessons from the Shoreham Nuclear Power Plant," *Academy of Management Journal*, 1993, *36*, 701–732.

37. D. Bunnel, *Making the Cisco Connection* (New York: Wiley, 2000), p. 75.

38. A. Saxenian, *Regional Advantage; Culture and Competition in Silicon Valley and Route 128* (Cambridge, Mass.: Harvard University Press, 1996).

39. K. Rivette and D. Kline, *Rembrandts in the Attic* (Boston: Harvard Business School Press, 1999).

40. J. Heilman, "The Next Big Idea," *New Yorker*, Feb. 23, Mar. 2, 1998.

41. T. O'Brien, "The Think Tank That Tanked," *Silicon Valley Magazine*, Sept. 2000, p. 3.

42. O'Brien, "The Think Tank That Tanked," p. 3.

43. O'Brien, "The Think Tank That Tanked," p. 3.

44. E. D. Raymond, *The Cathedral and the Bazaar: Musings on Linux and Open Source by an Accidental Revolutionary* (Sebastopol, Calif.: O'Reilly, 1999), p. 27.

45. www.gnu.org/copyleft/copyleft.html.

46. Ibid.

CHAPTER THIRTY-ONE

1. V. V. Havel, speech delivered to joint meeting of the U.S. Congress, from *The Art of the Impossible* by V. Havel, trans. Paul W. and others (New York: Knopf, 1997), pp. 17–18.

2. A. A. Dillard, *Teaching a Stone to Talk* (New York: HarperCollins, 1982), pp. 94–95.

3. V. V. Kavaloski and J. Kavaloski, "Moral Power and the Czech Revolution," *Fellowship*, Jan.-Feb. 1992, p. 9.

4. See R. Livsey and P. J. Palmer, *The Courage to Teach: A Guide for Reflection and Renewal* (San Francisco: Jossey-Bass, 1999), pp. 43–48.

CHAPTER THIRTY-TWO

Merton, T. *Conjectures of a Guilty Bystander.* New York: Doubleday, 1966.

Quinn, R. E., and Quinn, S. E. "Becoming a Transformational Change Agent." In L. Greiner and F. Ponfett (eds.), *Handbook of Management Consulting: The Contemporary Consultant.* Cincinnati, Ohio: Southwestern, forthcoming.

Name Index

Subject Index

(Continued)